2.

Time Out

California

timeout.com/california

D0048290

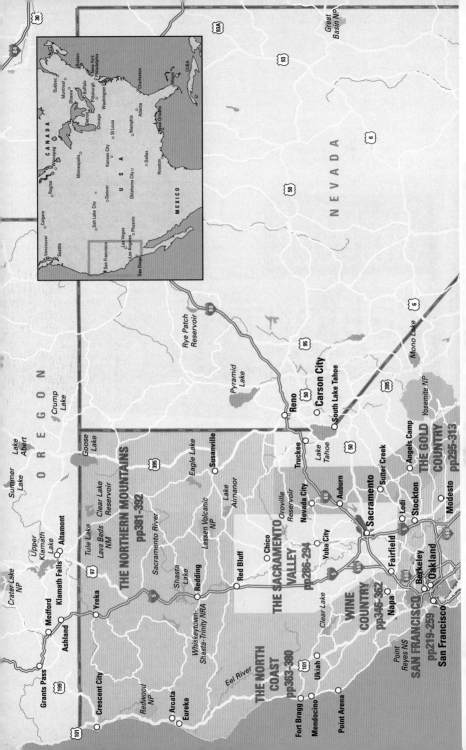

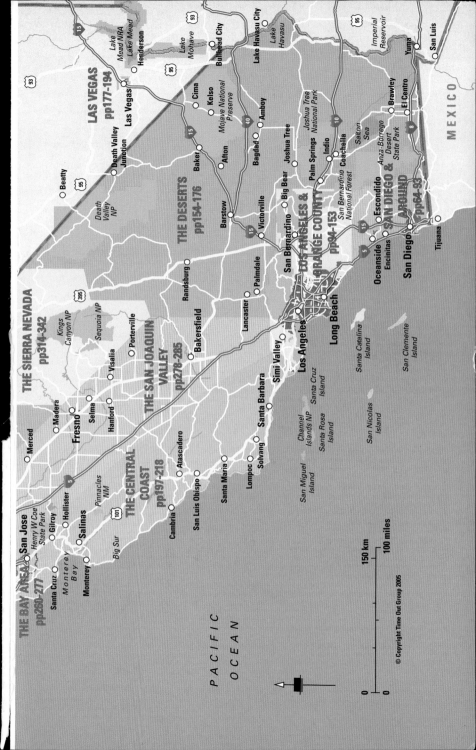

Published by Time Out Guides Ltd, a wholly owned subsidiary of Time Out Group Ltd.
Time Out and the Time Out logo are trademarks of Time Out Group Ltd.

© Time Out Group Ltd 2005

10 9 8 7 6 5 4 3 2 1

This edition first published in Great Britain in 2005 by Ebury
Ebury is a division of The Random House Group Ltd,
20 Vauxhall Bridge Road, London SW1V 2SA

Random House Australia Pty Limited, 20 Alfred Street, Milsons Point, Sydney, New South Wales 2061, Australia
Random House New Zealand Limited, 18 Poland Road, Glenfield, Auckland 10, New Zealand
Random House South Africa (Pty) Limited, Endulini, 5A Jubilee Road, Parktown 2193, South Africa

Random House UK Limited Reg. No. 954009

Distributed in USA by Publishers Group West
1700 Fourth Street, Berkeley, California 94710

Distributed in Canada by Penguin Canada Ltd
10 Alcorn Avenue, Toronto, Ontario, Canada M4V 3B2

For further distribution details, see www.timeout.com

ISBN 1-904978-24-X

A CIP catalogue record for this book is available from the British Library

Colour reprographics by Icon, Crowne House, 56-58 Southwark Street, London SE1 1UN

Printed and bound by Cayfosa-Quebecor, Ctra. De Caldes, KM 3 08 130 Sta, Perpètua de Mogoda, Barcelona, Spain

Time Out Guides Limited
Universal House
251 Tottenham Court Road
London W1T 7AB
Tel + 44 (0)20 7813 3000
Fax + 44 (0)20 7813 6001
Email guides@timeout.com
www.timeout.com

Editorial

Editor Will Fulford-Jones
Deputy Editor Simon Coppock
Listings Editor Elise Proulx
Proofreader Tamsin Shelton
Indexer Jonathan Cox

Editorial/Managing Director Peter Fiennes
Series Editor Ruth Jarvis
Deputy Series Editor Lesley McCave
Business Manager Gareth Garner
Guides Co-ordinator Holly Pick
Accountant Sarah Bostock

Design

Art Director Mandy Martin
Deputy Art Director Scott Moore
Senior Designer Tracey Ridgewell
Designer Oliver Knight
Junior Designer Chrissy Mouncey
Digital Imaging Dan Conway
Ad Make-up Charlotte Blythe

Picture Desk

Picture Editor Jael Marschner
Deputy Picture Editor Tracey Kerrigan
Picture Researcher Ivy Lahon

Advertising

Sales Director Mark Phillips
International Sales Manager Ross Canadé
Advertising Sales (California) Susan M Werner
Advertising Assistant Lucy Butler

Marketing

Marketing Director, Guides Mandy Martinez
US Publicity & Marketing Associate Rosella Albanese

Production

Production Director Mark Lamond
Production Controller Samantha Furniss

Time Out Group

Chairman Tony Elliott
Managing Director Mike Hardwick
Group Financial Director Richard Waterlow
Group Commercial Director Lesley Gill
Group General Manager Nichola Coulthard
Group Circulation Director Jim Heinemann
Group Art Director John Oakey
Online Managing Director David Pepper
Group Production Director Steve Proctor
Group IT Director Simon Chappell

Contributors

Introduction Will Fulford-Jones. **History** Hugh Graham. **California Today** Matthew Duersten. **On the Road** Will Fulford-Jones. **The Great Outdoors** Biking, Camping, Hiking Ann Marie Brown; Golf Shaw Kobre; Hot springs Marjorie Gersh-Young; Kayaking, rafting & canoeing Bill Tuthill; Skiing Martha Perantoni; Surfing Juan Gonzalez-Vega. **Food & Drink** Doreen Schmid. **Where to Stay** Will Fulford-Jones. **Festivals & Events** Alexis Raymond. **San Diego & Around** Bart Mendoza. **Los Angeles & Orange County** adapted by Will Fulford-Jones from Time Out Los Angeles, with additional material by Geoff Carter, Matthew Duersten and Katy Harris; Santa Catalina Island James P Reza; Lake Arrowhead, Big Bear Lake Alissa Anderson. **The Deserts** Introduction Ruth Jarvis; The Anza-Borrego Desert Ruth Jarvis, with additional material by Will Fulford-Jones; The Coachella Valley Dan Epstein; Joshua Tree Laurie Berger; Mojave National Preserve Ruth Jarvis; North to Death Valley Will Fulford-Jones. **Las Vegas** adapted by Will Fulford-Jones from Time Out Las Vegas, with additional material by James P Reza. **The Central Coast** Will Fulford-Jones; Santa Barbara Matt Kettmann. **San Francisco** adapted by Simon Coppock from Time Out San Francisco, with additional material by Bonnie Wach. **The Bay Area** The North Bay, The East Bay Elise Proulx; The South Bay Grace Krilanovich. Additional material by Bonnie Wach. **The San Joaquin Valley** Will Fulford-Jones. **The Sacramento Valley** Alexis Raymond; Davis Will Fulford-Jones. **The Gold Country** Will Fulford-Jones. **The Sierra Nevada** Ann Marie Brown. **Wine Country** Doreen Schmid; Calistoga Will Fulford-Jones. **The North Coast** Jackie Bennion; Arcata & Trinidad, North to Oregon Will Fulford-Jones. **The Northern Mountains** Jackie Bennion, with additional material by Simon Coppock. **Directory** Ruth Jarvis.

Maps JS Graphics (john@jsgraphics.co.uk).

Photography Heloise Bergman, except: pages 7, 13, 38, 51, 98, 157, 173, 174, 204, 207, 209, 280, 283, 285, 301, 302, 305, 307, 309, 312 Will Fulford-Jones; page 14 AKG; page 15 Getty Images; pages 15, 16, 20, 59, 60 Corbis; page 24 Rex Features; pages 31, 45, 94, 105, 108, 111, 112, 115, 117, 123, 127, 130, 134, 138, 143, 144, 149, 150 Amanda C Edwards; pages 47, 223, 231, 232, 235, 236, 240, 243, 245, 247, 252, 253, 255, 256, 262, 264, 266 Jonathan Perugia; page 48 Barry J Holmes; page 55 Mission San Juan Capistrano; pages 176, 177, 181, 185, 186, 189, 191 Elan Fleisher; page 182 Paul Avis; page 192 Jerry Metellus Costumes: Thierry Mugler © 2003 Cirque du Soleil Inc; page 295 Ruth Jarvis.

The Editor would like to thank Nyx Bradley, Jessica Eveleigh, Sam Le Quesne, Anna Norman and all contributors to Time Out Los Angeles, Time Out San Francisco and Time Out Las Vegas, whose work forms the basis for parts of this book.

The Editor's car in California was provided by Alamo (UK: 0870 400 4562, www.alamo.co.uk; US: 1-800 462 5266, www.alamo.com).

Contents

For a full list of the maps in this book, see p10.

Introduction

The contradictions, paradoxes and ironies are immense, almost as immense as the place itself. It's a state more blessed than any other with immaculately preserved natural landmarks, but one that also contains some of the ugliest urban sprawl in the country. It's a progressive, free-thinking and Democratic region that nonetheless gave Ronald Reagan his political break by electing him Governor in 1966, and recently turfed out its Democrat Governor in favour of a Hollywood superstar running on the Republican ticket. It's rich in history, and yet among the most forward-looking states of the union. At certain times of the year, you can – with binoculars, granted – see people skiing atop snowy mountains while driving through the arid desert. It is home to the highest point in the contiguous United States, the 14,495-foot peak of Mount Whitney, and the lowest point in the Western Hemisphere: Badwater, which sits 282 feet below sea level in Death Valley National Park. The two are a mere 136 miles apart.

Still, should we be surprised? Surely any place as vast as California is bound to throw up all kinds of contradictions. The state covers a mind-boggling 158,693 square miles, more than three times the size of England and bigger than any US state except Alaska and Texas. And what's more, it's growing: not in land mass, but in simple population terms. The US Census Bureau estimated that in 2003, some 35,484,453 citizens called the state home, a rise of 4.8 per cent in the three years since the 2000 Census.

So, no, California's diversity isn't as much of a shock as it first appears, but that doesn't make it any less overwhelming, or any less engrossing, or any less unknowable. All human life is here, but a good deal of wildlife also calls the place home. There are desolate deserts and rainy cities, winding coast roads and ten-lane urban freeways, the glamorous movie business and the scruffy agricultural industry. In short, California has it all, and it's all covered within these 416 pages. Have a great trip.

The best Golden State attractions

Big ones that deliver

Disneyland (*p118*), **Death Valley** (*p174*), **Hearst Castle** (*p207*), the **Monterey Bay Aquarium** (*p216*), **Alcatraz** (*p232*) and **Yosemite** (*p324*) live up to all expectations.

Big ones that don't

Hollywood (*p106*) and **SeaWorld** (*p76*) fail to impress, as do **Cannery Row** (*p215*) and San Francisco's **Fisherman's Wharf** (*p233*).

Big ones on the borderline

Big Sur (*pictured; p209*) is magical, unless your windshield view is of the back end of an crawling RV, as it may well be in summer. Gorgeous **Wine Country** (*pp347-362*) suffers similar visitor overload during summer: if you can't visit out of season, consider smaller, lesser known and less expensive wine regions such as **Amador County** (*p305*), **Pasa Robles** (*p219*) and the **Santa Ynez Valley** (*p203*).

Blink and you might miss them

Lost in the glut of visitables but well worth a stop, if just to cure attraction fatigue, are the locals' towns of **Davis** (*p291*), **Downieville** (*p300*), **Guerneville** (*p363*), **Bishop** (*p336*) and **San Luis Obispo** (*p204*). Natural highlights unfairly overshadowed by the monolithic must-sees include **Mono Lake**

(*p333*), **Ancient Bristlecone Pine Forest** (*p337*), **Rainbow Basin Natural Area** (*p174*) and **Anza-Borrego Desert State Park** (*p156*).

Blink and you should miss them

Parts of the **San Joaquin Valley** (*pp278-285*) is often left out of guidebooks for good reason. The snooty town of **Carmel** (*p212*) is nowhere near as cute as its residents think.

Cultural attractions

LA's new **Getty Center** (*p102*) and **Walt Disney Hall** (*p108*) and refreshed **Norton Simon Museum** (p115), along with San Francisco's **California Palace** (*p237*) and **SFMoMA** (*p229*) and San Jose's **Rosicrucian Egyptian Museum** (*p274*). **Palm Springs'** modernist architecture (*p162*) is now getting the level of recognition it deserves.

Roadside attractions

Many and varied: Fresno's **Forestiere Underground Gardens** (*p283*); Cambria's **Nitt Witt Ridge** (*p206*); the world's tallest thermometer, in sunny **Baker** (*p171*); Piercy's **Confusion Hill** (*p380*); the **Calico Ghost Town** near Barstow (*p173*); the **James Dean Memorial** (*p208*) west of Paso Robles; the abandoned crank resort of **Zzyzx** (see *p170*); and LA's Jetsonian googie coffeeshops.

ABOUT TIME OUT CITY GUIDES

Time Out California is one of an expanding series of travel guides produced by the people behind London and New York's successful listings magazines. Our writers, a mix of expert locals and experienced travel writers, have striven to provide the most up-to-date information you'll need to explore the region, whether you're a local or first-time visitor.

THE LOWDOWN ON THE LISTINGS

Above all, we've tried to make this book as useful as possible. Throughout the guide, we've included telephone numbers, open or closed times and admission prices (where no price is given for a museum or other attraction, assume admission is free). For attractions, national and state parks, hotels, visitor centres and selected other businesses, we've added websites. And in the chapters on San Francisco

and LA, listings incorporate travel directions: respectively, public transport information and details of a convenient freeway exit.

As far as possible, we've given details of facilities, services and events, all checked and correct at the time we went to press. However, owners and managers can change their arrangements at any time. Before you go out of your way, call and check opening times, dates of events and other particulars. While every effort has been made to ensure the accuracy of the information contained in this guide, the publishers cannot accept responsibility for any errors it may contain.

PRICES AND PAYMENT

We have noted whether venues such as shops, hotels and restaurants in major cities accept the following major credit cards: American Express (AmEx), Diners Club (DC), Discover (Disc),

Maps

Place of interest and/or entertainment	▨
Railway station	▨
Park	☐
Hospital/university	☐
Military area	▨
Beach	☐
Neighbourhood	BEL AIR
Interstate highway	🛡15
US highway	95
State or county highway	75
Ski resort	⛷
Golf course	⛳
Winery	🍾

MasterCard (MC) and Visa (V). Some businesses will also accept other cards, such as Carte Blanche. Many businesses will also accept US dollar travellers' cheques issued by a major financial institution such as American Express.

The prices we've supplied should be treated as guidelines, not gospel. Fluctuating exchange rates and inflation can cause charges to change rapidly. If prices vary wildly from those we've quoted, ask whether there's a good reason. If not, go elsewhere, and then please let us know.

THE LIE OF THE LAND

Time Out California is split into three sections, which have then been further subdivided into 13 chapters. The **Southern California** section includes chapters on LA and San Diego, plus a guide to the Californian deserts and a bonus chapter on the nearby Nevadan city of Las Vegas. **Central California** takes in the area from just north of LA to the San Francisco Bay Area, and all points directly east (including the Gold Country, the Sierra Nevada and Yosemite). And the **Northern California** section covers chichi Wine Country, the rugged North Coast and the lonesome Northern Mountains.

Each chapter begins with a map of the region; more detailed maps of major towns and attractions are included within the chapters. A map of California, showing how we've divided up the state, is at the front of this guide. For a full index of maps in the book, *see p10*.

TELEPHONE NUMBERS

All telephone numbers in this guide are prefaced with 1 and a three-digit area code: for example, 1-310 123 4567. If you're calling locally, you can drop the 1 and the area code and just dial the seven-digit number. Numbers preceded by 1-800, 1-866, 1-877 or 1-888 are freephone numbers: most can be dialled for free for anywhere in the US, but a few are free only from within California. The vast majority can also be dialled (though seldom free of charge) from the UK. For more on telephones, *see p402*.

ESSENTIAL INFORMATION

For all the practical information you might need for visiting the city – including customs and visa information, disabled access, emergency telephone numbers, a list of useful websites and so on – turn to the Directory chapter at the back of this guide. It starts on p394.

LET US KNOW WHAT YOU THINK

We hope you enjoy *Time Out California*, and we'd like to know what you think of it. We welcome tips for places that you consider we should include in future editions and take notice of your criticism of our choices. You can email us at guides@timeout.com.

Hotels & restaurants

HOTELS

Throughout this guide, the rates given for all lodgings are the rack rates for a double room, as quoted directly by the hotel, motel, resort or B&B in question. However, please note that other types of rooms may be available at some establishments: suites, cottages and, in a couple of extravagant cases, individual two-storey houses. In addition, be aware that prices vary wildly from season to season and even from day to day.

These price variations cut both ways. On holiday weekends, rates can rise dramatically in some regions. But conversely, outside peak season and especially midweek, prices can plummet far below advertised rates. Call ahead, check online and always ask about discounts and/or special package deals.

RESTAURANTS

Within this guide, we have denoted the price range of each restaurant listed with between one and five dollar symbols. These correspond approximately to the following price brackets, for a two-course meal with drinks per person (excluding gratuity).

$	under $15
$$	between $15 and $25
$$$	between $25 and $40
$$$$	between $40 and $55
$$$$$	over $55

Where more than one price range is given for a restaurant – for example, $$–$$$$ – it usually indicates the price differential between the lunch and dinner menus.

Advertisers

We would like to stress that no establishment has been included in this guide because it has advertised in any of our publications and no payment of any kind has influenced any review. The opinions given in this book are those of Time Out writers and entirely independent.

In Context

Features

Charlie Chaplin sets the reels in action in early Hollywood. *See p18.*

History

Building the dream.

The popular perception of California is of a land without history. The architecture is largely modern, the residents are mostly from somewhere else, and the search for eternal youth reigns supreme.

But that perception is wrong: California has been inhabited for at least 12,000 years. The first immigrants were nomadic hunters from Asia who arrived in California during the last Ice Age. Crossing a land bridge between what is now Russia and Alaska, the Indians followed herds of game south. Once in California, they continued their nomadic ways, migrating between California's valleys, coast and mountains according to the seasons.

By the 16th century the Indians had formed a complex society. The total population was around 300,000, divided into 100 tribes speaking 20 languages. Scattered throughout the state, the tribes subsisted on hunting – rabbit, deer, fish – and light agriculture, eating acorn meal, squash, beans, corn and pumpkins. With no intertribal warfare, and a rich landscape of oak woods, rolling hills and pristine beaches, it was a relatively idyllic existence. Until the Europeans arrived.

PALEFACE COME

Two years after Christopher Columbus first laid eyes on America, the Spanish claimed a huge chunk of the New World. The 1494 Treaty of Tordesillas, signed with the Portuguese, entitled Spain to all American lands west of Brazil. In 1519, determined to enlarge their colony of New Spain, they conquered Mexico. Then they looked north.

But it was a Portuguese explorer, Juan Cabrillo, who first visited California. The Spanish hired him to find the fabled land described in a popular novel – in *The Adventures of Esplandián*, Garcia Ordóñez de Montalvo had depicted California, a fantasy island dripping in gold and populated by Amazonian women. The Spanish also instructed Cabrillo to find another mythical place: the Strait of Anian, a waterway between the Pacific and Atlantic. Cabrillo failed on both counts, but in 1542 landed in San Diego, which he duly claimed for the King of Spain. Though he died soon after, his crew returned to Mexico with news of their discovery. The Spanish called the new territory California – and ignored it for the next 50 years.

The Spanish concentrated instead on sailing to the Philippines, where they traded Mexican silver for exotic Asian goods. But these Spanish galleons were routinely targeted by British privateers. The British explorer Sir Francis Drake was one of the most voracious plunderers. On one 1579 expedition, he got too greedy: before long his ship, the *Golden Hinde*, was almost sinking under the weight of Spanish silver. Forced to make landfall just north of present-day San Francisco (the area reputed to have been his landing spot is now called Drake's Bay), Drake claimed California for Elizabeth I. Long before the Pilgrims landed at Plymouth Rock, Drake named his discovery 'Nova Albion', Latin for 'New England'. Six weeks later, he set sail once more.

In 1595 Portuguese explorer Sebastian Rodriguez Cermeno, sailing under the Spanish flag, was shipwrecked in a nearby bay. In his gratitude to St Francis at being saved, he christened it Bahia de San Francisco. The saint was perhaps gratified when, in 1769, Spanish explorers erroneously identified the much bigger bay to the south as Cermeno's cove: the future San Francisco had received its name.

MISSION ACCOMPLISHED

California remained largely undeveloped until the 1760s, but then the Spanish started getting nervous. Russian ships had been making increasingly regular forays into Californian waters in search of seal and otter pelts, and it was feared Russia would extend its colony of Alaska southwards. At the same time, Spanish Catholic missionaries resolved to take their civilising mission north. They embarked on a major colonising expedition in 1769. Led by Franciscan priest Junipero Serra, they first founded a mission and *presidio* (military fort) at San Diego. The next year, another mission was established in Monterey. The dirt trail between them became known as El Camino Real; US 101 roughly follows its path today.

From his base in Monterey, Father Serra walked barefoot along El Camino Real establishing more missions: each was spaced apart from the other by the distance of one day's journey. By 1804 there were 21 of them, each following the same formula: a church and a cloistered residential building were surrounded by irrigated fields, vineyards and ranchlands. And who worked the land? The Native Americans, of course, kidnapped from their villages and forced to toil in the fields. Many fought back: the trademark red tiles that roof the missions were a replacement for thatch that was too easily burnt in arson attacks.

In addition to the missions, the Spanish also established *pueblos*, which were small towns designed to attract settlers. Los Angeles

Father Junípero Serra, who founded...

... **San Diego Mission.**

was founded in this way in 1781, although it initially attracted only a paltry hundred or so migrants.

A NEW STATE OF AFFAIRS

During the early 18th century Spain became embroiled in the Napoleonic Wars and neglected its colonies. When Mexico gained its independence in 1821, California became one of the new nation's territories. Determined to reduce the power of the Church, the new Mexican government secularised the Spanish missions and seized huge portions of mission land, which it redistributed to wealthy Mexican families in 16,000-acre *ranchos*.

> ### 'A wild, free, disorderly, grotesque society.'
> Mark Twain on Gold Rush-era San Francisco

Yet Mexico failed to establish any real kind of authority over the area. The Mexican government was particularly alarmed by the slow trickle of American explorers into California. In 1827 fur trapper Jedediah Smith made an overland journey to San Diego, proving the eastern mountain range could be crossed. Kit Carson, another frontiersman, carved the Santa Fe trail to Los Angeles in 1832. That same year a New England merchant named Thomas Larkin opened a shop in Monterey; he brought with him

his wife Rachel, making her the first American woman on the West Coast. And in 1835 William Richardson, captain of an English whaling ship, built the first private dwelling in San Francisco.

The newcomers were spurred on by the US government's policy of Manifest Destiny, a quasi-religious belief that America was destined to cover the continent from coast to coast. In 1846, worried that Britain might have designs on the West Coast, President James Polk offered Mexico $40 million to buy California. But his timing was bad: the US had just annexed Texas – which had seceded from Mexico in 1836 – and the Mexicans were furious. Not only did the Mexican government reject the offer, but it set about deporting Americans from its colony.

In response, American settlers in northern California staged a revolt. They raised a new flag – the Bear Flag – over Sonoma and declared California an independent republic. Meanwhile, back in Texas, the Americans went to war against the Mexicans. US troops prevailed in 1847; the next year, Mexico ceded California, Arizona and New Mexico to the US under the terms of the Treaty of Guadalupe Hidalgo. As for the Bear Flag Republic, it lasted less than a month. At least it had an enduring legacy: the California flag still sports a grizzly.

GOING FOR GOLD

It was just the Mexicans' luck. Within days of relinquishing California, gold was discovered west of Sacramento by carpenter

There's gold in them there hills...

Shake, rattle and roll

California's early settlers thought they'd found paradise: a mild climate, cheap land and dazzling scenery. But there's always a catch. Sure enough, on the morning of 18 April 1906, trouble came to paradise.

Shortly before 5am, dogs began howling, horses started to whinny, glasses tinkled and windows rattled across San Francisco. These eerie sounds preceded what was then the world's most notorious earthquake. Measuring 7.8 on the Richter scale, the quake killed at least 700 people, destroyed 500 city blocks, toppled 25,000 buildings and left 250,000 people homeless, more than half the city's population. Lasting a mere 48 seconds, the quake was felt as far afield as Los Angeles, Oregon and Nevada. Cliffs appeared out of nowhere, yawning chasms swallowed ancient redwoods and the new City Hall crumbled. Any building that wasn't destroyed by the tremors struggled to survive the 74-hour inferno that followed. The city was even bereft of its capable fire chief, Dennis Sullivan, who had been killed when the fire station collapsed on him.

'The sickening swaying of the earth threw us flat on our faces,' said one witness. 'Big buildings were crumbling as one might crush a biscuit in one's hand.' Author Jack London described the aftermath: 'Not in history has a modern imperial city been so completely destroyed. San Francisco is gone. Nothing remains of it but memories... It is like the crater of a volcano, around which are camped thousands of refugees.'

As the world later discovered, California lies on top of the San Andreas Fault, a boundary between two shifting tectonic plates. Some 800 miles in length and ten miles deep, it starts in the Mojave Desert and ends on the seabed off Mendocino.

The grinding plates move in opposite directions at 1.5 inches a year – at the present rate, LA and San Francisco will be next-door neighbours in a mere 15 million years – and produce 10,000 earthquakes annually in California. The 1989 quake in Loma Prieta, just outside Santa Cruz, measured 7.1 on the Richter scale; at least 63 people died, most of them perishing in their cars when a double-decker section of the Nimitz Highway (I-880) collapsed. A 6.6-quake hit Northridge, Los Angeles, in 1994, killing 57 people and proving to be the most expensive natural disaster in US history. But these are small fry compared to the Big One, a vast quake predicted by experts to occur in California within the next 50 years.

This might sound like bad news for the travel industry, but the rise of weather porn and the appearance of storm-seekers have brought a lucrative new market: earthquake tourism. To get yourself in the mood, stop off at **Universal Studios** (*see p115*) to experience an 8.3 simulation. Then, for the real deal, head to the town of Parkfield. This dusty ranch hamlet, midway between San Francisco and Los Angeles, lies smack dab on top of the San Andreas Fault. Dubbed the earthquake capital of the world, Parkfield experiences 500 small quakes a year and endures a magnitude-6 earthquake on average every 22 years; the most recent hit the town on 28 September 2004. One local businessman is cashing in on the town's notoriety: the slogan at the **Parkfield Inn** (1-805 463 2421, www.parkfield.com/inn.htm) is 'sleep here when it happens'. The restaurant serves steaks called 'the Big One'; desserts are called 'aftershocks'.

James W Marshall. Marshall was building a sawmill on the American River when he spotted a shiny nugget. Marshall and his landlord, the Swiss rancher John Sutter, tried to keep their discovery a secret, but rumours attracted a flurry of prospectors to the foothills around Sutter's Fort. By 1849, when newspaper publisher Sam Brannan dramatically waved a bottle of gold dust in San Francisco's main square, gold fever had already spread around the world. Fortune-seekers sailed around Cape Horn, while others trekked across Panama. Still more hopefuls crossed prairies

from the east in covered wagons, braving blizzards, treacherous mountain passes and hostile Indians.

With this influx of dreamers, California developed at a furious pace. In 1846 the state had a population of 14,000; by 1854 more than 300,000 had arrived, one of every 90 people then living in the US. Towns sprang up along what is now Highway 49, the heart of Gold Country, and San Francisco's population exploded. The latter was no place for the faint-hearted: it looked like a giant squatters' town; guns, lawlessness and frontier justice were the order of the day; and fortunes were squandered in brothels, gambling dens and bars. Mark Twain called it 'a wild, free, disorderly, grotesque society'. It's unclear whether he meant this as a compliment.

The Gold Rush began to wind down in 1853, but Henry Comstock's discovery of a rich blue vein of silver in western Nevada triggered a second invasion of fortune-seekers, the 1859 Silver Rush. Since the ore required more elaborate methods of extraction, the main beneficiaries were a small number of companies and tycoons. These silver barons built elaborate mansions in San Francisco, atop what became known as Nob Hill (adapted from 'nabob').

In 1850 California had become the 31st State of the Union. Even back then it was politically progressive: to attract the ladies, it became the first state to legally recognise the separate property of a married woman, and it was declared a 'free state' as opposed to a slave one, an event that fuelled tension between North and South on the eve of the American Civil War. During the war, the Union side (the Yankees) established forts in California to imprison Confederate soldiers and sympathisers. One of these forts, on a rocky island in the San Francisco Bay, later became the notorious prison Alcatraz. As the Civil War raged in the Eastern US, Californians were busy waging war of their own – against the Indians. By 1870 90 per cent of the Native American population had been wiped out by violence or disease.

In an irony lost on them, the settlers were busy killing Indians at the same time as they became obsessed with preserving California's natural heritage. Alarmed by the widespread logging of giant sequoia trees, citizens kicked up a fuss. In 1864 President Abraham Lincoln signed a bill that set Yosemite Valley aside as the first state park. It became a national park in 1890, along with nearby Sequoia.

If the Gold Rush put California on the map, the arrival of the transcontinental railroad in 1869 coloured it in. Previously, a trip across America in a stagecoach had taken at least a month; by train, the journey to the West Coast – Sacramento, initially – was a mere five days. In 1886 the transcontinental railway between St Louis and Los Angeles was completed. The next year, a price war broke out between train companies. Fares dropped, spurring a real-estate boom. Land speculators embarked on a campaign to attract settlers, placing ads in East Coast newspapers; it was during this phase that press baron Horace Greeley coined the famous phrase, 'Go west, young man'. The launch in 1902 of the Rose Bowl college football game and the parade that precedes it were also craven attempts to promote LA's benevolent climate.

MOVING TO THE MOVIES

California's 20th century started with a bang. The 1906 earthquake killed at least 700 people in San Francisco; the ensuing fire destroyed at least 1,000 buildings. Measuring 7.8 on the Richter scale, it remains one of the deadliest earthquakes in American history (*see p17* **Shake, rattle & roll**), yet it failed to stop California's rapid growth. San Francisco rose from the ashes and, in the first decade of the new century, the state's population increased by 60 per cent to 2,378,000. Then came the Mexicans: fleeing the revolution at home, they arrived in droves between 1910 and 1921, re-establishing a strong Latin presence in California. The economy also continued to flourish. The Panama Canal, which opened in 1915, proved a great boon, facilitating trade between East Coast and West.

Only one thing could stop California's furious growth: water. Or, more precisely, the lack of it. With this in mind, William Mulholland, an Irish immigrant, accomplished one of the great engineering feats in American history. In 1913 he built the Los Angeles Aqueduct. Stretching 230 miles, the aqueduct diverted creeks from the Sierra Nevada mountain range to Los Angeles, irrigating parched land such as the San Fernando Valley. (For more details of this extraordinary accomplishment, *see p94*.)

With a secure water supply, Los Angeles boomed; especially so after 1920, when oil was discovered in Huntington Beach, Santa Fe Springs and Long Beach. Not only did the oil fields put a stop to LA's regular fuel crises: they also encouraged the city's love affair with the automobile. Soon Southern California had thriving oil, automobile and tyre industries. Not even World War I could sap the state's commercial energy. The aeroplane industry, in particular, was a huge new growth area: California's sunny climate and cheap land, with plenty of wide open spaces, provided ideal conditions for flying, and it was here that companies such as McDonnell Douglas and Lockheed planted the roots of America's aviation industry.

California's natural attributes also attracted its most famous industry: the movies. The studios were established by industrious European Jews seeking a new life in the sun. Its founding fathers included Louis B Mayer and Samuel Goldwyn of MGM; Harry, Sam, Jack and Albert, the four Warner Brothers; and Carl Laemmle, who set up Universal. The moguls acquired land in a small subdivision outside LA called Hollywoodland, whose mild climate meant directors could shoot outdoors all year round. The state's varied landscape also helped. Westerns were shot in the Sierra

Land of fruits and nuts

'Turn on, tune in, drop out.' 'Make love not war.' 'Give peace a chance.' Back in 1967, during San Francisco's Summer of Love, such phrases were hippie mantras on the tip of each flowerchild's acid-stained tongue, usually in close proximity to 'far out', 'groovy', 'do your own thing' and 'flower power'. That such expressions are still so familiar three decades later speaks volumes about the cultural significance of that psychedelic summer.

Bizarrely, the CIA must accept some of the thanks for this hedonistic drug fest. Back in the 1960s the organisation was interested in the possibility of using psychotropic drugs as a truth serum during interrogations. In a series of experiments at Stanford University, it gave a number of students LSD. One of them, writer Ken Kesey – who had just achieved fame with his novel *One Flew Over the Cuckoo's Nest* – was so taken with the drug he decided to promote its virtues across California.

In his Magic Bus, Kesey tore around the state, staging Electric Kool-Aid Acid Tests for curious crowds. At parties, bowls of the popular children's soft drink were laced with acid. The Grateful Dead played their psychedelic blues as a soundtrack and, along with the surreal, swirly light shows, trippers were kept occupied for hours. The psychedelic gospel soon spread across the US. Thousands of young believers flocked to San Francisco, settling in the Haight-Ashbury ('Hashbury') district, which offered cheap rooms, bohemian coffeeshops and proximity to the concerts, love-ins and anti-war demonstrations. The media quickly dubbed California 'the land of fruits and nuts'.

The party reached its peak in January 1967 with the Human Be-In, held in Golden Gate Park. Attendees heard poetry by Allen Ginsberg, a speech from acid guru Timothy Leary, and music courtesy of the Grateful Dead and Jefferson Airplane. The latter were riding high in the charts with 'White Rabbit', which sagely reminds listeners to 'Remember what the dormouse said/"Feed your head, feed your head".' That spring Scott McKenzie released a single that predicted the legendary summer ahead. 'If you're going to San Francisco,' he sang, 'be sure to wear some flowers in your hair/If you come to San Francisco/Summer time will be a love-in there.' Thousands of young Americans converged on the city. The period reached its pinnacle with July's Monterey Pop Festival, which featured Janis Joplin, the Byrds, Jefferson Airplane and an incendiary performance from Jimi Hendrix.

The good times didn't last. Haight-Ashbury grew overcrowded and overpriced. Heroin and speed replaced cannabis and acid as the drugs of choice. Too much free love spawned an epidemic of STDs and rapes. Symbolic of how far astray the gentle people's message of peace and love had gone were a piece of thuggery at Altamont, where Hell's Angels murdered a black man at a 1968 Rolling Stones concert, and the psychotic violence of one-time flower-child Charles Manson. By the end of the '60s most of the original Haight-Ashbury crowd, including Kesey, had obeyed their own mantra and dropped out to more remote places – Arizona, New Mexico, Oregon – where pressure from the man was not as great. As the hippies were fond of saying, nothing good lasts forever.

foothills, desert movies were filmed in the Mojave or Death Valley, pirate movies went on location to Carmel, and the San Bernardino mountains stood in for Alpine scenes.

WORKING ON IT

During the Great Depression, the California dream proved irresistible to thousands of Americans. Scores of families from the prairie dust bowls headed west: John Steinbeck's epic novel *The Grapes of Wrath* depicts the plight of the Okies, unskilled labourers who tried to find work as farmhands. But the Depression wasn't entirely bleak. Los Angeles hosted the Olympic Games in 1932; to celebrate, 10th Street was

spruced up, renamed Olympic Boulevard and lined with majestic palms. To create employment, the government funded a number of major public works projects, among them the San Francisco Bay Bridge, the Golden Gate Bridge and the Hoover Dam (then called the Boulder Dam).

The 1930s and 1940s were also an important time for the farmers in California's Central Valley. By the 1920s California had grown into the most agriculturally productive state in the union, but at a sizeable cost. The Central Valley's groundwater supplies were vanishing and, despite the influx of Okies to labour on the farms, the industry looked doomed. Enter the Bureau of Reclamation, which set in motion

Cashing in their chips: computer companies dominate **Silicon Valley**. *See p21.*

an extraordinary and controversial series of measures to divert water to farmland. The Central Valley Project, approved in 1933 by the state legislature, took 18 years to complete but succeeded in securing the agriculture industry.

During World War II California became an industrial powerhouse. Major shipyards were established along the coast and aeroplane factories multiplied; following the bombing of Pearl Harbor, the US military moved its entire fleet to San Diego. Not only did this period lay the foundations for America's military-industrial complex, which would flourish until the end of the Cold War, but it also influenced urban planning: to supply manufacturing plants with workers, dormitory towns sprang up around the cities, a precursor to urban sprawl.

The war also accelerated California's growth. The population doubled in the 1940s, reaching ten million in 1950. Some of the newcomers were servicemen who fell in love with the place and stayed, but African-Americans and Mexicans also flocked to California to take advantage of the job opportunities. Their presence laid the groundwork for the state's ethnic diversity, but it also created tensions. In the 1943 Zoot Suit Riots, for example, white sailors pummelled Mexicans and African-Americans. The whites had needed new minorities to hate, what with all the Japanese-Americans already confined to internment camps in the wake of Pearl Harbor.

Yet there were positives. Fifty nations met in San Francisco, with the signing of the United Nations Charter on 26 June 1945 the excellent result. Had the Europeans not insisted the UN headquarters be moved closer to them, San Francisco rather than New York would have been the organisation's home.

'The "peace and love" movement soon morphed into something more radical.'

HAIGHT AND HATE

The 1950s were synonymous with the rise of suburbia. Developers bought land, subdivided it and sold it back to America as a fantasy of self-realisation. This was the era of the baby boom and every family seemed to want a white picket fence and two-car garage. The government covered the state with freeways and, in Southern California, two suburbs in particular began to spread like weeds: the San Fernando Valley and Orange County. The latter came into its own in 1955, when Disneyland opened in Anaheim. Real estate became California's number one industry.

The flipside to this suburban dream was the new counterculture. California attracted a growing number of disaffected youths, their initial template the writers of the Beat Generation. This bohemian movement, with novelist Jack Kerouac its reluctant figurehead, protested against the rampant consumerism and conformism of '50s America. Kerouac's *On the Road*, the story of a hedonistic coast-to-coast road trip, and Allen Ginsberg's lacerating and sexually explicit long poem *Howl* were the seminal works. Poets, artists and intellectuals congregated in San Francisco, their anti-establishment views prefiguring the New Left politics that swept America a decade later.

California became the global centre of flower power during the 1960s (*see p19* **Land of fruits and nuts**). The often unfocused anti-authoritanism of the Beats soon morphing into something altogether more radical. Berkeley University became a hotbed of student protests against the Vietnam War and calls for Civil Rights and freedom of speech; the 1965 Watts Riots, which spread from a black ghetto in LA, shook the white residents from their complacency; and the Black Panthers, a group of militant black activists, formed in Oakland the following year.

Amid the turmoil, Californians elected B-movie actor Ronald Reagan governor in 1966. He promised to restore order, but the chaos continued: in 1968 Robert Kennedy was assassinated in LA; in 1969 the Charles Manson cult murdered actress Sharon Tate in a Beverly Hills mansion. Then came the emergence of the Symbionese Liberation Army, an armed revolutionary group that gained notoriety after kidnapping heiress Patti Hearst. Magazine articles pronounced the end of the Californian dream, but people kept on coming, with California soon surpassing New York as America's most populous state.

The radical '60s spirit manifested itself in the 1970s with the rise of the gay liberation movement, with San Francisco its natural heartland. (Some social historians trace the city's queer roots back to the Gold Rush, when women were so massively outnumbered by men that same-sex relationships were inevitable.) Other progressive developments in the state included the 1973 election of LA's first African-American mayor, Tom Bradley, and the election of leftie Jerry 'Moonbeam' Brown as governor in 1975. In stark contrast to Reagan, Brown introduced radical anti-pollution laws and sweeping environmental protection schemes, though many people remember him solely for his dalliance with pop singer Linda Ronstadt.

WATER ON THE BRAIN

California became an economic behemoth in the 1970s , with technology playing a huge part in the transformation. Back in the 1950s, Stanford University had leased buildings to technological companies such as Hewlett-Packard, forging a partnership between academia and commerce. Before long, a host of other high-tech companies had set up shop along the highway between Palo Alto and San Jose. Then, in 1969, a UCLA computer-science professor sent the world's first email to a colleague at Stanford, ushering in the information age. Two years later, a journalist coined the phrase 'Silicon Valley' to describe the area south of San Francisco where the industry was centred. Finally, in 1976, Apple built the world's first personal computer.

The Californian economy also benefited from the state's burgeoning population: the war in South-east Asia brought in many Vietnamese people; Latin Americans fled here from the poverty and strife in their own countries; and the city's position on the Pacific Rim made it attractive to people (and capital) from Korea, the Philippines, Taiwan and Hong Kong.

Farming remained a constant, despite the state's hopeless lack of water. The benefits conferred by the Central Valley Project hadn't lasted and, by the late 1950s, California was once again running low on water. The State Water Project (SWP), approved in 1960, aimed further to boost water supplies in California.

The 770-foot Oroville Dam, the tallest earthfill dam in the United States, was completed in 1967, but the initial SWP facilities were not finished for another six years. California's residents benefited from the scheme, especially those in the south, but the real winners were California's agriculturalists. Already rich, they couldn't believe their luck: not only did the plan provide them with obvious direct benefits, but they were offered irrigation water at huge discounts, subsidised by the taxpayers who had paid for the construction of the SWP in the first place.

During the 1980s California became synonymous with healthy living and luxurious lifestyles, but the trickle-down effect of Reaganomics failed to trickle down to the state's impoverished minorities. As the influx of Latin Americans increased, so did hostility between them and California's African-Americans, particularly in LA's overcrowded South Central district. High unemployment didn't help; as the Cold War wound down, thousands of blue-collar jobs in defence and manufacturing simply disappeared.

> ## 'Though the smogs of LA have abated somewhat, respiratory allergies have reached epidemic level.'

Another sizeable California minority – the gay community – also endured a horrendous decade, with the AIDS epidemic arriving in 1981. Since the identification of the disease, 18,000 people have died of it in San Francisco alone. Other black marks of the decade include the 1984 McDonald's massacre just outside San Diego, in which a psychopath shot and killed 21 people. The social tension of the era was compounded by a series of natural disasters, including a huge drought between 1987 and 1992 and the terrifying Loma Prieta earthquake that rocked San Francisco in 1989.

ARNIE TO THE RESCUE

The 1990s got off to a pretty grim start. In 1991 a deadly fire in the Oakland Hills killed 25 people and destroyed 3,000 homes, while the same year saw the LAPD caught on video brutally beating a black man, Rodney King. When a jury acquitted the officers of assault in 1992, the worst riot in US history broke out. In three days in South Central LA, 50 people died and over 1,000 buildings were destroyed.

The racial dramas were only just beginning for Los Angeles. The arrest and trial in 1995 of OJ Simpson, gridiron hero and B-movie star, gripped the city and the nation. Simpson, an African-American, was accused of killing his white ex-wife and another man. His acquittal stunned many whites, but reassured blacks that the legal system could be on their side.

Despite continuing racial problems, California enjoyed an economic recovery in the late 1990s. As the aerospace industry declined, the entertainment industry exploded: there was the rise of the multichannel universe, the booming porn industry (based in the San Fernando Valley), and new forms of animation and digital special effects. Northern California experienced a 20th-century gold rush in the form of the dot-com boom, with techie geeks as modern prospectors, seeking their fortune in internet start-up companies. But the bubble burst in 2001 and jobs disappeared overnight. For once, California had spearheaded an unwelcome global trend: recession.

Other problems continue to plague California. Though the notorious smogs of LA have abated somewhat, respiratory allergies have reached epidemic proportions due to high ozone levels. The state also suffers from major power-supply problems: in the noughties, Californians endured repeated blackouts as the rickety electricity grid failed to meet rising demand.

Governor Gray Davis received much of the blame for California's woes. In an unprecedented display of voter power (and not a little commercial muscle in promoting the recall election), Californians turfed Davis out of office in the middle of his elected term. Proving that American politics is another branch of showbiz, Arnold Schwarzenegger – tough-guy actor turned Republican crusader – was voted in as his replacement. Ironically, California chose the same year to rediscover its 1960s radical spirit: on the eve of the Iraq war, San Francisco hosted some of the largest anti-war protests since the days of Vietnam, resulting in thousands of arrests.

Through all this commotion, California did what it always does: continued to grow. After all, the history of California – from the Native Americans through gold-seekers to the Hollywood starlets – is also the story of modern California, namely an energetic pursuit of the good life. It seems that nothing, not even the prospect of the next devastating earthquake – referred to by residents, almost fondly, as 'the Big One' – will stop locals from indulging in a little California dreaming.

▶ For more on **William Mulholland and LA's water supply**, see p94.
▶ For more on the **Gold Rush**, see p295.
▶ For more on the **missions**, see p214.

Key events

c10,000 BC Indians from Asia arrive
in California.
1519 Spain conquers Mexico.
1542 Portuguese explorer Juan Cabrillo
sails up the California coastline.
1579 Francis Drake lands north of San
Francisco Bay, claims the land for
Elizabeth I and christens it Nova Albion.
1769 Father Junípero Serra leads an
overland expedition to establish
a mission and fort at San Diego.
1775 Mission de San Francisco de Asis
is founded.
1781 A pueblo is established in Los Angeles.
1821 Mexico declares its independence from
Spain and annexes California.
1828 Fur trapper Jedediah Smith becomes
the first white man to reach California
across the Sierra Nevada mountains.
1835 English-born sailor William
Richardson sets up a trading post
in San Francisco.
1846 The Bear Flag Revolt takes place
against Mexican rule in California;
the US-Mexican War begins.
1848 Mexico relinquishes California to
the US.
1849 The Gold Rush swells San Francisco's
population from 800 to 25,000.
1850 California becomes the 31st State
of the Union.
1853 The Comstock Lode is discovered
in western Nevada, triggering the
Silver Rush.
1861 Civil War breaks out between the
Union and the Confederacy.
California remains largely untouched
by hostilities.
1869 The transcontinental railroad connects
Oakland with the rest of the US.
1886 The transcontinental railroad reaches
Los Angeles.
1890 Yosemite and Sequoia National Parks
are established.
1902 The Rose Bowl and Parade founded
in Los Angeles.
1906 The Great Earthquake strikes
San Francisco.
1910 Ten-year Mexican Revolution begins.
1912 Universal Studios founded in
Los Angeles.
1913 Los Angeles Aqueduct completed.
1915 Panama Canal is opened, facilitating
trade between East and West Coast.

1923 Warner Brothers founded.
1924 Universal Studios founded.
1929 Stock market crash;
Depression begins.
1932 Los Angeles hosts the Olympics.
1933 Death Valley National Park established.
1934 The General Strike brings San
Francisco to a standstill.
1936 Joshua Tree National Monument
established.
1937 Golden Gate Bridge completed.
1939 Pasadena Freeway opens.
1941 The Japanese attack Pearl Harbor
and the US enters World War II.
1943 Zoot Suit Riots.
1945 Fifty nations meet at the San Francisco
Opera House to sign the UN Charter.
1955 Disneyland opens in Anaheim.
1964 Student sit-ins and mass arrests at
Berkeley become more frequent as
the Civil Rights and anti-Vietnam War
movements gain momentum.
1965 The Watts Riots erupt.
1966 Ronald Reagan elected governor
of California.
1967 San Francisco's Summer of Love.
1968 Robert Kennedy assassinated at
the Ambassador Hotel in LA.
1969 The Charles Manson cult murder
Sharon Tate.
1973 Tom Bradley elected mayor of LA.
1978 Gay city councillor Harvey Milk and
Mayor George Moscone are shot and
killed by former supervisor Dan White.
His light sentence sparks riots in
San Francisco.
1981 The first cases of AIDS are recorded.
1984 LA hosts summer Olympics.
1989 The Loma Prieta earthquake strikes
(6.9 on the Richter scale).
1992 Fires in the Oakland Hills kill 25 and
destroy 3,000 homes.
1991 Rodney King arrested in LA.
1992 The King verdict sparks riots in South
Central LA.
1994 Earthquake in Northridge (6.6 on the
Richter scale).
1998 California state deregulates its
energy utilities.
2001 Californians endure rolling blackouts as
demand for electricity outstrips supply.
2003 Democratic Governor Gray Davis
defeated in a mid-term recall election
by Republican Arnold Schwarzenegger.

California Today

Enter the Governator. Roll credits?

In the wild, carnivalesque days of California's 2003 gubernatorial recall election, when porn stars and ex-child actors threw their hats into the Big Top and the rest of the world looked on in worried fascination, a certain lantern-jawed ex-Mr Universe banked on his Hollywood past by morphing his film lines into campaign slogans. In becalmed retrospect, Gray Davis's public ousting was blowback from voter anger after his perceived mishandling of the 2001 state energy crisis and the price-fixing scandal that followed.

But Arnold Schwarzenegger has turned out to be a more effective governor than anyone could have imagined: easing the political logjam in Sacramento, ably navigating through the biggest state deficit in history and leaning on California's powerful prison guards' union to accept a delay in Davis-era raises. He girded up for what was somewhat tastelessly referred to in the national press as an 'Indian fight' with the state's powerful $5-billion a year tribal gaming industry. ('Their casinos make billions, yet they pay no taxes and virtually nothing to the state,' pronounced Arnold in one of his campaign ads, before staring into the camera and squinting. 'I don't play that game.') He's even harnessed his Hollywood insider past to stem the loss of an estimated $10 billion per year from California production companies taking their business to New York, Louisiana, Canada and Australia.

Arnold's socially liberal, economically conservative views position him to the left of Republicans and to the right of Democrats. His popularity rating hovers in the 60s, near the all-time highs for a Golden State governor and more than 40 points above the end-of-term numbers for the man he 'terminated'. The Governator has arrived.

Less than a year after Schwarzenegger took office came the passing on 4 June 2004 of another controversial and beloved political colossus who also traded off an all-American image created by Hollywood: ex-screen actor, ex-governor of California and ex-President of the United States, Ronald Reagan. Like Richard Nixon before him, Reagan never fully abandoned California after he left the Presidency. Although he had been ailing for years, the death of the towering, athletic ex-lifeguard with the laminated Superman coiffure caught most Californians unprepared. Their outpouring of affection and emotion following the news was moving and genuine, no matter if people disagreed with his policies or the press was slow to recall his follies and failures. The public reaction, in fact, was the flipside, in every way, of the OJ Simpson freeway chase ten years earlier: the state seemed to halt in homage as TV relayed images of the motorcade bearing the President's body from LA to his gravesite in Simi Valley.

Reagan's passing seemed to draw a line under a turn-of-the-millennium shift in the landscape that had defined California in the previous decades. Political grandees Gray Davis, Richard Riordan, Gil Garcetti and Bernard Parks were all voted out of office. San Francisco's unsinkable political rascal Willie 'Boom Boom' Brown was replaced as mayor by the youthful Gavin Newsom, with his willowy model/prosecutor/TV host trophy wife Kimberly Guillfoyle. The couple acted as a quasi-Camelot reflection of Arnold and Maria and certainly took the spotlight from the relatively colorless James K Hahn and Dick Murphy, the current mayors of LA and San Diego respectively. The old power brokers of Hollywood are either dead (MCA's Lew Wasserman), missing in action (CAA's Michael Ovitz) or on their way down the staircase (Disney's Michael Eisner).

'It is time we terminate Gray Davis.' Arnold Schwarzenegger, campaigning for Governor, 2003

The new blood seems to be working in the short term: according to the insider political monthly *National Journal*, California's congressmen and women are the most powerful group of legislators in the nation's capital. So as long as Unka Arnie is in office, Californians will have to contend with Hummers, *sauerbraten*, cigar fetishism and jockish jibes about 'girlie men'. At least, of course, until Brad Pitt announces his candidacy.

AMERICA, ONLY MORE SO

The Golden State at the dawn of the 21st century remains an epic land of contrasting tastes, landscapes and egos so large that it doesn't compete with other states so much as with other nations. Its population of around 35 million, legal and otherwise, is greater than the whole of Canada's. It is the richest state in the nation, with a gross domestic product of around $1 trillion. If it were a sovereign nation, its economy would rank as the fifth largest in the world. In terms of agriculture, those vintage sun-splashed images of bounteous citrus groves pasted on to orange and lemon boxes were not just fabulist folk art: not only does California produce nearly 90 per cent of the nation's raisins and 94 per cent of its almonds, it's number one in crop production (topping Iowa) and number two in livestock, second to Texas.

All civic pride aside, the state contains everything that can be found in America: not just every imaginable climate and topography but unfathomable wealth and shocking degradation, unbridled hope and crushing alienation, ethnically diverse communities and profound racial ignorance. At the time of the prison abuses in Iraq and Afghanistan, California was confronting the demons of its penal system – again. California has the third largest prison system in the world, surpassed only by China and the rest of the US. The experiment in which the state has been engaged over the last three decades – the incarceration of unprecedented numbers of people for unprecedented lengths of time, partly due to the idiotic mandatory 'three strikes' sentencing laws that were the vogue in the 1990s – has come at enormous social and economic cost, with very debatable long-term benefits. While the number of inmates has increased seven-fold in the last 20 years, violent crime is no lower today than it was three decades ago.

There's a flip side to all that agricultural abundance, too. The buzzword in the 'burbs might be organic, but the Central Valley is cruelly chemical and cruel, period, to both intensively reared livestock and often illegal (and therefore powerless) workers, whose exploitation is getting increasingly systematic. And the water it uses – in what would largely be a desert, left to its own devices – is likely to be a dominant political issue in the coming decades, with supplies under increasing pressure here and in neighbouring states.

Not a new story, but one that's going to run and run, is the ever-evolving urban scourge that is traffic congestion, particularly in the City of Angels. A 2004 survey found an average Los Angeles commuter spent 93 hours stuck in traffic during 2002, nearly double the national average. Add to this gas prices that have been hitting record highs due to global turmoil, along with concerns registering even in Car City about pollution and global warming, and the gas-powered future doesn't look good for California's 20 million vehicle owners.

LA VS SF

Although the US lost a lot of foreign tourist trade after 9/11, the tide is turning. California, which attracts more foreign visitors than any other state save Florida, is reaping the benefits of a recent turnabout. The number of overseas visitors increased by 21 per cent during the first half of 2004, led by a surge of tourists from Australia and Japan.

Los Angeles remains the number one domestic flight destination in the US; San Francisco is number three. Yes, there is needle between the two cities – best exemplified in artist Sandow Birk's hilarious mockumentary *In Smog and Thunder* (2003), in which they attack each other with armies in 'the Great War

of the Californias' – but it's largely just that: a comical fantasy of imagined slights. Los Angeles even caught a bit of trickle-down bounty from Frisco's dotcom boom of the 1990s, particularly when design and new media firms moved into the industrial part of Santa Monica.

> **'I'm going to see the folks I dig / I'll even kiss a Sunset pig.'** Joni Mitchell, 'California', 1971

The odd thing was that when the bust arrived, the bottom never dropped out in LA in the way that it did in the Bay Area, much to everyone's surprise and the glee of some embittered Angelenos. Cutting-edge digital animation companies continue to arrive in the city, joining the already mythical Pixar. Even the once moribund aerospace industry and its floundering companies like Boeing saw a dramatic increase in jobs in 2004 alone. Ah yes, war does help, doesn't it?

Artistically, Angelenos have started to turn their eyes away from the East as a cultural mecca, particularly within the worlds of publishing and art. LA is now a place where young, serious writers come to live a literary life, quite a change for a city accused of killing off literature by choking the world with bloated action films and lowest-common-denominator TV shows. (Admittedly, many of them are from New York, whose TV industry has virtually laid down and died.)

Up north in San Francisco, the echo from the biggest boom and bust since the Gold Rush of 1849 is still receding over the bay. The lunatic pace of the dotcom age has eased, and among the survivors who stayed after the bottom fell

out there's a new kind of energy flowing through the city. Areas such as Dogpatch and the Mission/SoMa corridor have metamorphosed into bona fide neighbourhoods. Judging by the well-heeled crowds shopping for morel mushrooms and baby fennel at the new Ferry Plaza Farmers' Market, investors have every reason to be optimistic. The gorgeous new market, a one-stop shop for locally grown gourmet goodies, is perhaps San Francisco's first post-bust success story.

AND FINALLY, A WORD ON THE WHOLE FALLING-INTO-THE-SEA THING...

In his book *The Ecology of Fear*, urban historian Mike Davis reports that since 1909, around 140 novels and films have dealt with the apocalyptic destruction of California, and particularly LA, by natural disaster. Such overheated metaphor-wielding started to wane in the mid-1990s, particularly after the 6.6-magnitude Northridge Earthquake of January 1994: LA and its outlying areas didn't, as had been predicted, fall apart and eat their young, but instead toughed it out and helped each other cope. After the devastating fires of October 2003, the Governor impressed even his critics by greasing the State Capitol machinery to respond quickly to humanitarian needs in the wake of the destruction of over 300,000 acres and 1,000 homes. In its pure flinty survivalism, California has won points for rendering itself retrofitted for disaster.

This mettle may be tested soon. In September 2004, geologists measured a magnitude-6 earthquake in Parkfield, California, a small town that has the misfortune to be located right over the San Andreas Fault. Preliminary evidence told them the fault may have been giving off hints that it was about to rupture.

Welcome to California. Have a nice day!

On the Road

You may find yourself behind the wheel of a large automobile.

There are other ways to travel in California. Greyhound runs numerous bus services; Amtrak trains take in several key routes. But if you're coming to California for any kind of a holiday, you're most likely going to want a car. Actually, scratch that: you're going to *need* one.

California grew up through car travel; its infrastructure now depends on it. Indeed, the car, and how it came to be used in Southern California, changed the nature of commercial culture in the US. Where once businesses gathered on Main Street, in the '20s they saw the potential of simply setting up by the side of the road: any road, just so long as people used it. The drive-in restaurant wasn't born here (the first one actually opened in Texas in 1921), but in Southern California entrepreneurs picked up the drive-in ball and ran with it, creating eye-catching businesses that stood roadside and lured in passing trade. Route 66 was once packed with them; a few remain.

With the car came the commute. People no longer needed to ensure their home was near their place of work; they could easily live in pleasant isolation away from the action and distraction. LA grew up this way; other cities in the West followed suit. In the late 1940s LA constructed the epic freeway network that now defines the city; other road-building projects followed, in California and across the US.

However, history and urban sprawl are not the only reasons the car is such a central part of Californian life. For the holidaymaker aiming to travel beyond the three big cities, it's more or less essential – the sheer size of the place dictates that. But, more than a pragmatic exercise, choosing to drive is all about the surprises that the road reveals: the small towns, the tiny diners, the isolated parks and forests. And, of course, it's about the basic, liberating pleasure of an open road. Happy trails.

RULES OF THE ROAD

First things first, Brits: in the US, you drive on the right. Californian law requires drivers and passengers to wear seatbelts. Drink-driving rules are strict here, and penalties can be heavy.

Aside from a few roads that allow speeds of 70mph, the speed limit in California on interstates and other major freeways is 65mph. The limit on smaller highways outside urban areas is usually 55mph; in built-up areas, the speed limit is generally 35 or 25mph, occasionally lower (near schools, for example). Keep an eye out for signs posting speed limits: Californian police are quick to enforce the law. However, while we don't want to encourage law-breaking, anecdotal evidence suggests that polite and well mannered foreigners caught speeding are often treated more leniently than those with US licences.

Parking can be problematic in large cities. However, it's also awkward in the likes of Carmel and Sutter Creek, small towns popular with tourists but with narrow roads and few places to park. If you see a space close to where you're planning to park, take it; otherwise you risk driving around for another hour or being forced into using an expensive parking lot.

A system of colour-coding is in operation on curbs throughout California. If a curb is painted white or yellow, you're only allowed to stop in order to pick someone up or drop them off; a green curb means parking is permitted only for a limited time (20-30 minutes); blue curbs allow parking for disabled drivers only; and a red curb means no parking at all. However, always take care to read the posted signs before parking, unless you'd like your car to be ticketed, clamped or even towed. Parking is always forbidden in front of ramps and driveways, in tunnels and on bridges, and within 15 feet of a fire hydrant. You must also park in the direction of the traffic, so always park on the left-hand side of the road.

Renting a car

To rent a car in the United States, you'll need a credit card and a driver's licence (British photo licences are valid). Most companies refuse to rent cars to anyone under 25; those that do often add a hefty surcharge.

There are dozens of rental companies, and it pays to shop around. The national firms, which tend to offer the best deals, all have free 1-800 numbers; most rental firms require you to book on these numbers or online, rather than at the local office. Major US firms usually also have offices in the UK and elsewhere.

The basic price quoted in the US will not include sales tax or insurance. If you're not covered for insurance on your own policy at home (some US residents will be; check before you leave), you'll be offered liability insurance, for damage you cause to other cars and their occupants, and collision damage waiver (CDW), each around $10-$20 a day. We recommend you take out both. British readers should note that if you book via the British websites or numbers listed below, your quote will include full insurance. However, the vagaries of exchange rates and package deals often mean that UK residents can get a better all-inclusive price by booking from the relevant US site and taking the insurance option offered.

If you want to drop your car at a different location to that from which you collected it – for example, if you're on a one-way road trip, flying in to LA and leaving from San Fran – you'll also be charged a drop-off charge or have a premium added to the basic rental price. However, you may also qualify for a discount on your car rental: AAA members (and members of affiliated foreign clubs, such as the AA in Britain) usually are, as are some business customers. Don't be afraid to ask if you're eligible for a discount.

Rates see-saw wildly; it may be worth booking way ahead. You can put a hold on a car without committing yourself (and if it runs out of a car in that class, the hire company will upgrade you). The key is to shop around: you'd be amazed at the price differences between firms that are offering what basically amounts to the same product.

In addition to the major firms listed below (all of which, incidentally, rent four-wheel drive (4WD) vehicles for those planning on going off-road), three other options are worth considering. Despite the company's name, the vehicles offered by **Rent-a-Wreck** (1-800 944 7501, www.rent-a-wreck.com) are in good nick, nearly new vehicles offered at prices sometimes quite a bit below those of the major firms. For a hulking RV, **El Monte** (1-888 337 2214, www.elmonte.com) is the largest of several companies that rent them. For two-wheel rentals, contact **Eagle Rider Motorcycle Rental** (1-888 900 9901, www.eaglerider.com), which rents Harleys and other bikes from seven California locations.

Alamo US: 1-800 462 5266/www.alamo. com. UK: 0870 400 4562/www.alamo.co.uk.
Avis US: 1-800 230 4898/www.avis.com. UK: 0870 606 0100/www.avis.co.uk.
Budget US: 1-800 527 0700/www.budget. com. UK: 0870 153 9170/www.budget.co.uk.
Dollar US: 1-800 800 3665/www.dollar.com. UK: 0800 085 4578/www.dollar.co.uk.
Enterprise US: 1-800 261 7331/www. enterprise.com. UK: 0870 350 3000/ www.enterprise.com/uk.
Hertz US: 1-800 654 3131/www.hertz.com. UK: 0870 844 8844/www.hertz.co.uk.
National US: 1-800 227 7368. UK: 0116 217 3884. Both: www.nationalcar.com.
Thrifty US: 1-800 847 4389/www.thrifty. com. UK: 01494 751600/www.thrifty.co.uk.

ENJOY LIFE

Rent a Motorhome in the U.S.A.

EL MONTE RV

MOTORHOME VACATIONS™

www.elmonterv.com

HINTS AND TIPS

Running out of gas is everyone's idea of a nightmare, as much for the embarrassment as any inconvenience. However, it's easily done here, especially in the desert. Roads such as US 395 contain few gas stations; more than a few drivers have also been caught short while driving in and around Death Valley. If you think you'll be driving in an isolated area, fill up the tank whenever you get the chance.

Another difficulty with rural driving is the expense, though this can be trimmed with forethought. If you're driving down the Pacific Coast Highway between San Francisco and LA, for example, fill your tank before you leave either city: gas prices at stations on Route 1 can be up to 30¢ a gallon higher than in the city. Check **www.californiagasprices.com** and its various affiliated sites for details on the cheapest and priciest gas in the state.

When driving in the desert, especially in the sweltering summer, several precautions need to be observed. The main one, not just for your comfort but also for that of your car radiator, is always to carry a good deal of water. If your car does overheat, turn the air-conditioning off and open the windows. It sounds perverse, but having the air-conditioning cranked to max is actually a surefire way to heat up your engine. Conversely, if you're in an area where it's liable to snow heavily, be sure to carry snow chains.

While this guide contains maps to all the areas covered, you may need a dedicated road atlas. The two **DeLorme** atlases (both $19.95), one on Northern California and one on Southern California, are good; also worth considering is the atlas and recreation guide published by **Benchmark** ($24.95), which includes a full index of campgrounds, as well as maps pinpointing wineries in the Wine Country. But the winner for us is the spiral-bound road atlas published by **Thomas Brothers** ($24.95). The fabulous **AAA** (www.aaa.com) also provide maps, guides and other information, and it won't cost you a cent if you're a member of an affiliated organisation (such as the British AA). There are offices all over the state.

Great Californian drives

Coastal California

Cambria to Carmel, along Route 1.
In an ideal world, every traveller would have enough time to drive all the way up the Californian coast, from San Diego and the sun-bleached Southern Californian beaches, up the rugged north coast to no-nonsense Crescent City. But since that's not the case, the stretch everyone ought to drive at least once runs a smidgeon over 100 miles up Route 1, between Cambria and Carmel, taking in some of the

Hit the **Pacific Coast Highway**.

most awe-inspiring scenery in the United States. Eight miles north of Cambria, you'll reach San Simeon, where you can turn off for a tour at Hearst Castle. Yet even William Randolph Hearst's grandiose monument is overshadowed by the wondrous curves and swoops of Big Sur further up the coast. This is Californian driving at its most iconic, and American driving at its most spectacular.
● For more on the Central Coast, *see pp197-218.*

Escape to LA

Mulholland Drive in Los Angeles.
A dramatic confluence of Hollywood-style spectacle and wild Southern California bramble, the memorable Mulholland Drive springs to life by Leo Carillo State Beach in Malibu (where it's known as the Mulholland Highway) and dies out close to the Hollywood Bowl. The views along LA's spine encompass the dichotomies for which the city is known, from the broad views of the ocean and scalloped edges of the Santa Monica Mountains on the road's western extent to the softly blinking grid of the Valley and the puncturing tops of Downtown buildings out east. Note that seven miles of the road, between Canoga Avenue and Encino Hills Place, is closed to cars, a small but pointy thorn in the inflated expression that the City of Angels is only auto-accessible.

For an alternative view of LA, drive the length of mythic Sunset Boulevard, which runs through many of the city's smartest and most appealing neighbourhoods. Starting slightly north of Santa Monica, the road ebbs up around Brentwood and Bel Air, into Beverly Hills, along into West Hollywood (where it's known as the Sunset Strip) and Hollywood, before looping down through Silver Lake and Echo Park and coming to an end just north of Downtown.

● For more on Los Angeles, *see pp94-153.*

Flowers in your hair
The 49-Mile Scenic Drive around San Francisco.
Ironic, perhaps, that we should recommend driving in the only one of the three major Californian cities for which you don't need a car. But the 49-Mile Scenic Drive around San Francisco offers an excellent and frequently surprising idiot's guide to the city that any visitor with a few hours on their hands would do well to use as an introduction. The drive is too complicated to detail in full here, but begins Downtown and heads to Fisherman's Wharf, then edges across to Golden Gate Bridge, down along Ocean Beach and up again through Golden Gate Park, before winding its way through the Castro and the Mission. Lunatics with recently tested brakes will get ample opportunities to enjoy the city's trademark precipitous slopes. The route is signed throughout the city, but the San Francisco CVB publishes a map: you can buy it from its tourist office (*see p258*) or download it from its website (www.sfvisitor.org).

● For more on San Francisco, *see pp219-259.*

Get your kicks
Route 66, between Pasadena and San Bernardino.
The original Mother Road, an near-legendary 2,448-mile jog linking Chicago and LA, enters California at Needles and comes to its inevitable end on the coast at Santa Monica. Parts of it are now buried beneath interstates, or under Angeleno thoroughfares such as Santa Monica Boulevard and Sunset Boulevard. However, plenty remains. One stretch runs south of I-40 south of the Mojave National Preserve; another runs south of Barstow, through barely-there towns such as Hodge and Helendale.

But the most immediately diverting stretch of Route 66 in California links San Bernardino with Pasadena. The 50-mile road, known mostly as Foothill Boulevard (but also, as it approaches Pasadena, Colorado Boulevard), can be slow going as it traverses the suburbs, but a number of icons remain: in San Bernardino, the first ever McDonald's (now a museum); in Rialto, the Wigwam Motel (19 stucco teepees that, together, make the state's most eye-catching lodgings); and, in Fontana, the now-closed Bono's Historic Orange Stand (a huge, hollowed-out orange with a service counter).

● For more on Route 66, *see p171.*

Golden delicious
Highway 49 between Nevada City and Sierraville.
Named after the Gold Rush hopefuls (the '49ers through whose former dreamland it chiefly navigates, the gently undulating Highway 49 runs 350 miles between Vinton, directly north of Lake Tahoe, and Oakhurst, notable solely for its status as a gate-

way town to Yosemite. In between these two forgettable places, the road is rarely less than lovely, wending its way through a variety of historic Gold Country towns.

It's north of one of them, Nevada City, that Highway 49 is at its finest. Edging gently north into Sierra Nevada and the Tahoe National Forest, occasionally running alongside the North Yuba River, skipping through the picture-postcard town of Downieville, you'll reach the Yuba Pass, which climbs to an altitude of 6,708 feet before winding comfortably and confidently back down again. The drive from Nevada City to Sierraville is 90 miles and should take about three hours; it's also, though, only the first half of the Yuba Donner Scenic Byway, which continues for another 70 miles from Sierraville: south on Highway 89 to Truckee, then west on I-80 and Highway 20 back to Nevada City.

● For more on the Gold Country, *see pp295-313.*

Higher than the sun
Tioga Road, in Yosemite National Park.
There are two main problems with the 50-mile Tioga Road (aka Highway 120) through Yosemite National Park. The first is that it's closed for roughly half the year (October/November to May/June), when at least 20 feet of snow make it impassable. The second is that, when it's open, crowds descend in their thousands. However, if you time your visit carefully and don't mind rising with the sun, your passage through the High Country of Yosemite should be quiet and unimpeded. At its peak, the Tioga Pass on the park's eastern edge, it rises to an elevation of 9,945 feet; 1,000 feet below and a 20-minute drive west is Tuolumne Meadows, which affords fine views and some of the area's finest hiking trails.

● For more on Yosemite, *see pp324-331.*

Just deserts
Mojave to the Furnace Creek Visitor Center at Death Valley National Park, along Route 14, US 395 and Route 190.
Not every driver 'gets' the desert. Some claim, with reasoning that makes sense at least on the surface, that there's nothing much there. And there isn't: on this drive, which runs a little over 200 miles, the combined population of all the towns you pass is under 1,000, and natural sights run to some extraordinary rock formations at Red Rock Canyon State Park and, a little over two hours later, the roadside highlights of Death Valley.

But, well, the isolation is the point. To those drivers (and passengers) who understand that the beauty of the desert lies in its vastness and its isolation, in its immense skies and distant horizons, in the subtly changing reds, oranges, yellows and browns that colour its landscape, in its sheer *otherworldliness*, this drive is one of the most stunning in California. Footnote: the relative absence of police and other traffic means it's the perfect drive on which to see just how fast your rental car will go…

● For more on the desert and Death Valley, *see pp154-176.*

The Great Outdoors

Let California's outdoors experts show you around.

Biking

Whether your tastes run to fat or skinny tyres, Campagnolo or Rockshox, California is an mecca for two-wheeled explorers. The Golden State has all the right ingredients for bicycling nirvana: rolling backroads, vineyard-covered hills and valleys, long stretches of road and trail that parallel the windswept coast, and the dramatic undulations of the Sierra Nevada, Cascade and Coast mountain ranges. Indeed, biking history was made here. It was on the steep slopes of Mount Tamalpais, just north of San Francisco, that Gary Fisher, Joe Breeze and others held the first formal off-road bike races in the late 1970s. Their handmade bikes were heavy, clunky and downright dangerous, but a few years and modifications later, mountain bike fever caught on and an industry was born.

Those planning to pedal should note that some park agencies are friendlier than others to bicyclists. Although road biking is permitted on almost all public roads in California (excepting major multi-lane highways), mountain bikes are not allowed on every public trail. Riding is forbidden on almost all the famous national park trails, but permitted in national recreation areas such as Whiskeytown, Golden Gate and the Santa Monica Mountains. California state parks are similarly biased against mountain bikers. With a few exceptions (such as Montaña de Oro, Malibu Creek and Crystal Cove; see p35), mountain bikes are generally not permitted on state park trails. National forest lands, on the other hand, are open to mountain bikers, except on land designated as federal wilderness areas. Smaller county and regional parks abide by their own individual rules. To be on the safe side, check with the managing agency before riding.

About the authors

BIKING, CAMPING & HIKING

The author of 12 guidebooks to California recreation (*see p404*), **Ann Marie Brown** is a dedicated outdoorswoman, hiking, biking and camping more than 150 days each year in an effort to avoid routine, complacency and getting a real job. When she isn't traipsing along a California trail, Ann Marie makes her home a few miles from Yosemite.

GOLF

Santa Rosa resident **Shaw Kobre** is the co-author of *Golf California Universitee* (In the Loop Golf, $24.95) and four other books on golf in California. Once a nine-handicapper, Shaw quit hitting right-handed and began swinging from his natural side. Today, he can play poorly from either side of the tee.

HOT SPRINGS

Doing what she loves has gotten **Marjorie Gersh-Young** into hot water... literally. For two decades, she has explored the natural and developed hot springs of the US, and is the author of two guides, including *Hot Springs and Hot Pools of the Southwest* (Aqua Thermal Access, $19.95).

KAYAKING, RAFTING & CANOEING

Bill Tuthill is the main author of the *California Creekin'* website (http://creekin.net), a whitewater touring guide for the lower left coast of the US. To the chagrin of his wife and kids, Bill enjoys camping without amenities and boating over waterfalls.

SKIING & SNOWBOARDING

Martha Perantoni is the author of *Ski and Snowboard California's Sierra Nevada* (Falcon, $17.95). She lives in the mountains with her three cats and works for a ski resort, and when the snow is on, she's gone.

SURFING

Juan Gonzalez-Vega is the director of Quiksilver's Tech Division. Based in the surf capital of Huntington Beach, he surfs regularly up and down the Pacific Coast.

Many of California's ski resorts convert into mountain bike parks during summer. Bikers pay a fee to pedal all day on the resort's trails; this fee usually includes one or more rides uphill on a chairlift or gondola (with bike in tow!). Some of California's very best ski-resorts-cum-bike-parks are **Mammoth Mountain**, **Squaw Valley USA** (for both, *see p43*) and **Northstar-at-Tahoe**.

The state is also nationally recognised for its wealth of paved recreation trails, most of which had their beginnings as railroad rights-of-way. When the trains ceased, the track lines were removed and the land was converted to multi-use trails. More than 200 of these 'rail trails' exist, some in places as scenic as Yosemite Valley. Because of the popularity of these paths, bike shops are often found near them; travellers can easily rent a set of wheels and go for a spin.

Every California town of decent size has a bike shop. Although mom-and-pop bike shops still exist, they're being rapidly replaced by chains; two of the best are **Performance Bike** (www.performancebike.com), with 18 stores in California, and **Supergo** (www.supergo.com), found mostly in Southern California. Outdoor retailer **Recreational Equipment Inc**, aka REI (www.rei.com), is also a reliable source for anything bike-related. Below are ten of the state's best biking spots, listed north to south.

Whiskeytown Downhill

West of Redding (Whiskeytown National Recreation Area 1-530 241 6584/www.nps.gov). **Location** p383. This arduous 43-mile one-way ride follows the route of the '80s Whiskeytown Downhill, one of the state's earliest mountain bike races. Despite the name, the route is not all downhill, but a protracted series of climbs and descents. Campsites are found along the route for those who choose to break it into two days.

Downieville Downhill

Downieville (Tahoe National Forest 1-530 288 3231/www.fs.fed.us/r5/tahoe). **Location** p300. Possibly the most famous mountain biking trail in the state, the Downieville Downhill is a one-way, 13-mile ride from Packer Saddle in the Gold Lakes Basin, elevation 7,100ft (2,164m), to Downieville, elevation 2,800ft (853m). Shuttle vans are available in Downieville to return you to your starting point.

Flume Trail

Lake Tahoe, Nevada (Lake Tahoe-Nevada State Park 1-775 831 0494/www.state.nv.us). OK, so it's just across the border in Nevada, but this is a quintessential Sierra Nevada ride. The trail starts at Spooner Lake in Lake Tahoe-Nevada State Park and skirts the cliffs high above the eastern edge of Lake Tahoe, providing unforgettable views.

Markleeville Death Ride

Markleeville (1-530 694 2475/www.deathride.com). **Location** p322.

The ultimate challenge for skinny and fat tires alike, this annual cycling event brings even expert riders to their knees with its staggering 16,000ft (4,877m) of elevation change over 129 miles.

American River Parkway

Sacramento (American River Parkway Foundation 1-916 456 7423/www.arpf.org/www.bikewaymap. com). **Location** p287.

One of the oldest and longest paved bike paths in the United States, this 32.8-mile trail runs from Discovery Park in Sacramento to Folsom Lake. More than 500,000 people ride the trail each year.

Golden Gate Bridge & Marin Headlands

San Francisco (Golden Gate National Recreation Area 1-415 331 1540/www.nps.gov/goga). **Location** p236.

Locals and tourists both love to pedal across the Golden Gate Bridge, visit the Point Bonita Lighthouse and stop at Black Sand and Rodeo Beaches on this landmark coastal loop route.

Monterey Recreation Trail

Around the Monterey area (Pacific Grove Recreation Department 1-831 648 5730/www.monterey.org). **Location** p215.

This 18-mile paved trail runs from Castroville to Pacific Grove, passing by Cannery Row and the Monterey Bay Aquarium, plus miles of sand and sea.

Montaña de Oro State Park

San Luis Obispo (1-805 772 7434/www.parks.ca.gov). **Location** p205.

Lots of technical single-track for advanced mountain bikers, plus the novice-friendly Bluffs Trail. Lots of variety, spectacular spring wildflowers (hence the name, 'mountains of gold') and 6.5 miles of coastline.

Malibu Creek State Park

Los Angeles (1-818 880 0367/www.parks.ca.gov). **Location** p98.

Best known as the set for *M*A*S*H*, this state park in the Santa Monica Mountains has several great mountain biking routes, including the Crags and Bulldog Loop, which offers a rewarding 360-degree view from the summit of Castro Peak.

Crystal Cove State Park

Laguna Beach (1-949 494 3539/www.parks.ca.gov). **Location** p121.

Some of Orange County's best single-track cycling, as well as awesome views of the Pacific Coast. Trails cater to riders of all abilities; check with the park office to find a route suitable for your level.

Two wheels good: hitting the road in **Joshua Tree National Park**.

Camping

California camping runs the gamut. Would you like to pitch your tent at a backcountry site miles from the nearest trailhead? Or would you prefer to park your RV in a developed campground complete with electric hookups, hot showers and an internet connection? Somewhere in between the two extremes lie what most of us seek in a camping experience: a beautiful setting where we can drive up, set up our tent and enjoy the nature around us in relative isolation.

A host of regional agencies, such as county or regional parks, offer camping facilities, as do private companies, such as **Kampgrounds of America** (www.koa.com) and **Thousand Trails** (www.1000trails.com). However, the majority of campgrounds are run by one of three agencies, detailed below. For the most sought-after locations, such as anywhere along the coast or in world-famous parks such as Yosemite, advance reservations are a necessity.

● **California State Parks**, which controls state park lands. For information, see www.parks.ca.gov; for reservations, call 1-800 444 7275 or see www.reserveamerica.com.

● **National Park Service**, which controls national park lands. For information, see www.nps.gov; for reservations, call 1-800 365 2267 or see http://reservations.nps.gov.

● **US Forest Service**, which controls national forest lands. For information, see www.fs.fed.us; for reservations, call 1-877 444 6777 or see www.reserveusa.com.

At most campgrounds, you can expect a modicum of facilities for a nightly fee ranging from $10 to $20. Typically, campsites will have a picnic table with benches, a fire grill for cooking and a flat spot on which to pitch your tent. In areas where bears or other animals may attempt to raid your food stores, a 'bear box' or some other type of storage container may be at your site. Restrooms and water spigots, if they exist, are usually located in a common area.

You can anticipate a few generalities about a campground depending on who manages it. Private companies such as KOA usually offer the most amenities (fancy showers, for instance), but they also charge the highest prices. State park campgrounds are frequently good value, with well-lit, clean restrooms that have flush toilets and coin-operated showers, and a park ranger or other staff member on site. National park and national forest campgrounds are often the most rustic, with pit or chemical toilets and usually no shower facilities. Many national forest campgrounds do not even have

a water spigot; you must bring your own bottled water with you. These camps are usually the lowest priced; some are even free.

California is blessed with a Mediterranean climate, with winter rainfall and summer drought. With the exception of its higher mountain ranges, most of the state experiences mild winters. This means that during any month, camping opportunities abound. Desert and coast camping are often at their best during autumn, winter and spring, whereas mountain camping is usually reserved for summer, when the winter snows are a distant memory.

The hardest part is choosing where to go. Yosemite alone contains more than 1,400 campsites, most bookable in advance. The state park system contains nearly 18,000 campsites, many good or better than what you'll find at the national parks. But to get you started, here are ten favourites, listed roughly north to south.

Jedediah Smith Redwoods State Park

Crescent City (1-707 464 6101/www.parks.ca.gov). **Location** p379.
This rainforest-like park is lush with ferns, lichens and towering old-growth redwoods. Its cool, shaded camp is set beside the emerald-coloured Smith River, the longest free-flowing river in California.

Gerstle Cove Campground, Salt Point State Park

20 miles north of Jenner on the Sonoma Coast (1-707 847 3221/www.parks.ca.gov). **Location** p366.
Gerstle Cove Campground is one of the few places north of San Francisco where you can car-camp with an ocean view. Spend your days exploring tidepools, hiking the trails or diving for abalone.

White Wolf, Yosemite National Park

Off Tioga Road (1-209 372 0200/www.nps.gov/yose). **Location** p331.
Forgo the crowds in Yosemite Valley and Tuolumne Meadows and camp at this High Sierra favourite. Set at 8,000ft (2,438m) in elevation amid a forest of lodgepole pines, White Wolf is perfectly situated for day-hiking in the Tioga Pass Road area.

Saddlebag Lake

Lee Vining (1-760 647 3044/www.fs.fed.us/r5/inyo). **Location** p333.
At 10,087ft (3,075m), the highest car-accessible lake in California. Set in a stark landscape high above tree-line, the lake and its campground are only five miles from the Tioga Pass entrance to Yosemite. A boat taxi shuttles hikers and anglers across Saddlebag Lake to the 20 Lakes Basin in the Hoover Wilderness.

Minaret Falls Campground, Mammoth Lakes

Just outside Devils Postpile National Monument in Inyo National Forest (1-760 924 5500/www.fs.fed.us/r5/inyo). **Location** p335.

Not only a lovely view of Minaret Falls, but also easy access to fishing in the San Joaquin River, hiking trails to lakes and waterfalls and all the amenities in the nearby town of Mammoth Lakes.

Kirk Creek Campground, Big Sur
Highway 1 (1-831 385 5434/www.fs.fed.us/r5/lospadres). **Location** p211.
Located on a lonely stretch of road halfway between Cambria and Monterey, Kirk Creek Campground is set on a bluff overlooking the Pacific. Steep trails lead to the beach below, popular with surfers. Pay a visit to Jade Cove, a few miles to the south.

Cold Springs Campground, Sequoia National Park
At Mineral King (1-559 565 3134/www.nps.gov/seki). **Location** p342.
A glacial-cut valley, Mineral King is surrounded by 12,000-ft (3,658-m) granite and shale peaks and home to the headwaters of the East Fork Kaweah River. Trails ascend to high alpine lakes, giant sequoia groves, and awe-inspiring views of the jagged Sawtooth Ridge. Pick a site along the riverbanks or in the shade of quaking aspens.

Ricardo Campground, Red Rock Canyon State Park
25 miles north of Mojave (1-661 942 0662/www.parks.ca.gov). **Location** p174.
Ricardo Campground is set at the base of White House Cliffs, a colourful backdrop of eroded sandstone walls. Stargazing is so popular here that rangers post constellation charts by the restrooms.

Little Harbor, Santa Catalina Island
16 miles from Avalon (1-310 510 2000/www.scico.com/camping). **Location** p150.
If you're looking for a spot to indulge your Robinson Crusoe fantasies, head here. Palm trees grace a sandy beach cove; orange garibaldis swim in turquoise waters; a herd of bison graze on the coastal bluffs.

White Tank, Joshua Tree National Park
South of Twentynine Palms on Pinto Basin Road (1-760 367 5500/www.nps.gov/jotr). **Location** p167.
Cosy, private campsites among jumbles of boulders. Confine your camping to spring and fall: Joshua Tree is blistering in summer and blustery in winter.

Golf

When travellers think of Californian golf, the first image that springs to mind is Pebble Beach and the rugged Pacific coastline. While this area is the heart of oceanside golf, there are many other amazing coastal layouts, from San Diego to the Oregon border. The peak season for coastal golf in the north is April to October; in the south, it's year-round. The weather can be warm in summer, but it can also be foggy and windy. Ocean views don't come cheap,

especially at Pebble Beach and in Orange County. However, north of San Francisco, the **Links at Bodega Harbour** (1-707 875 3538, www.bodegaharbourgolf.com) and the **Sea Ranch Golf Links** (1-707 785 2468, www.searanchvillage.com) provide amazing ocean views for a fraction of the cost ($35-$90).

Less publicised, but no less entertaining, are the mountain courses. Lake Tahoe, Shasta and the Eastern Sierra possess scenic, rolling, tree-lined layouts at high elevations that create havoc with club selection (golf balls fly about ten per cent further in thin mountain air). Golf season here runs May to September, warm and with little rain. With the exception of the Tahoe region, green fees are reasonable ($40-$90).

If you're planning a winter vacation, head to the desert: there are over 100 courses within an hour's drive of Palm Springs. Peak season here is November through April, when the days are mild; during summer, the heat is extreme. If you're driving here from LA, there are some good courses en route, on or near I-10: try **Oak Quarry Golf Club** (1-909-685-1440, www.oakquarry.com), which may be the most visually stunning course in the state. And don't forget San Francisco, within whose city limits are **Harding Park Golf Course** (1-415 661 1865) and the **Presidio Golf Course** (1-415 561 4661). These two demanding, historic courses have recently been renovated, but don't expect world-class conditioning: they're still municipal courses, inhabited by old-timers and locals.

No matter where you play, book your tee times in advance. Some courses charge a premium for reservations more than one or two weeks ahead; it's worth paying the extra $10-$20 to ensure you get your preferred time. Handicap cards are not required. Online, California Tourism's www.californiagolf.com website contains a database of every public course in the state. But to get you started, here are ten top courses across California.

The Club at Wente Vineyards
Livermore (1-925 456 2475/www.wentegolf.com).
Rates *Summer: Mon-Thur* $60-$80; $45 twilight. *Fri-Sun* $85-$105; $55 twilight. *Winter: Mon-Thur* $65; twilight $40. *Fri-Sun* $90; $50 twilight.
Roughly an hour east of San Francisco along I-580, this Greg Norman-designed course is set on family vineyards. Dramatic elevation changes, marvellous views and superb conditioning make this the toast of the Bay Area.

Coyote Moon Golf Club
Truckee (1-530 587 0886/www.coyotemoongolf.com).
Rates $140-$155; $95 twilight. **Location** p317.
Situated 6,800ft (2,073m) above sea level near Tahoe, surrounded by majestic pines with granite outcropping, Coyote Moon is one of the West's best mountain layouts. Not suited for beginners; closed in winter.

Desert Willow Golf Resort: Firecliff Course

Palm Desert (1-800 320 3323/www.desertwillow. com). **Rates** *Jan-Mar* $125-$165; $65-$95 twilight. *Apr, May, Oct-Dec* $90-$130; $45-$75 twilight. *June-Sept* $55-$75; $25-$35 twilight. **Location** p166.
This spectacular desert golf course in the heart of the Coachella Valley, known for its immaculate conditioning, will challenge the low handicapper but will not abuse the better player.

Lost Canyons

Simi Valley (1-805 522 4653/www.lostcanyons.com). **Rates** *Shadow Course: Mon-Thur* $79; $49 twilight. *Fri-Sun* $89-$109; $75 twilight. *Sky Course: Mon-Thur* $95; $75 twilight. *Fri-Sun* $120; $75 twilight. **Location** p115.
Built on the original set of *Little House on the Prairie*, these two courses comprise 36 holes carved out of the canyons. Each hole is separated by rock and clay, giving you the feeling that you're the only ones on the course. Pick your tees carefully: long hitters may find the course more difficult at closer range.

PGA West: TPC Stadium Course

La Quinta (1-800 742 9378/www.pgawest.com). **Rates** *Jan-May* $170-$235; *May-Dec* $150-$175. **Location** p166.
It's rated as one of the hardest courses in California, but the TPC at PGA West, about a half-hour's drive south-east of Palm Springs, is more playable than its reputation. Ample bailout areas provide some safety from the deep bunkers and the water.

Pasatiempo Golf Course

Santa Cruz (1-831 459 9193/www.pasatiempo.com). **Rates** *Mon-Thur* $135-$155. *Fri-Sun* $155-$175. **Location** p375.
An Alister Mackenzie masterpiece in Santa Cruz, with narrow, rolling fairways and small, sloping greens that can drive a golfer to tennis. Mackenzie loved the course so much that he retired and lived here until his death.

Pebble Beach Golf Links

Pebble Beach (1-800 654 9300/www.pebblebeach.com). **Rates** *Non-resort guests* $395; lodge reservation necessary to secure advance tee time. **Location** p213.
Stepping on to the first tee here will give every golf nut the chills. Of course, some get them simply because they've just paid green fees of $400, safe in the knowledge that to secure a tee time, they've had to shell out another $500 to stay at the Lodge.

La Purisima

Lompoc (1-805 735 8395/www.lapurisimagolf.com). **Rates** *Mon-Thur* $43-$53; twilight $33. *Fri-Sun* $53-$63; $43 twilight. **Location** p204.
Factoring in the quality, the ambience and the cost, this may be the best course in California. The course is built into a hillside halfway between Santa Barbara and San Luis Obispo. There are hazards aplenty, mind: trees, brush, creeks, ponds and well-placed traps.

Driving, **Death Valley** style.

Pelican Hill: Ocean South Course

Newport Coast (1-949 760 0707/www.pelicanhill. com). **Rates** *Mon-Thur* $175-$195; $99 twilight. *Fri-Sun* $250-$270; $135 twilight. **Location** p121.
At this course, located on a hillside above the Pacific, you'll encounter canyon crossings, wind and unforgettable views of the Pacific.

Spyglass Hill Golf Course

Pebble Beach (1-800 654 9300/www.pebblebeach. com). **Rates** *Non-resort guests* $275; $160 twilight. **Location** p213.
Many locals and PGA Tour professionals believe that Spyglass, a three-minute ride from the Pebble Beach Golf Links and owned by the same company, is a better and more difficult course than its cousin.

Hiking

For many, hiking is the ideal outdoor activity: with a minimum of equipment, the whole of the outdoors is at your feet. Day-hikers can enjoy a long day on the trail while having the comfort of a car and a cosy bed; backpackers can pack a heavier load and disappear for days.

Most experienced hikers wouldn't dream of travelling without their own boots and other equipment, but if you need to stock up, try one of the **Recreational Equipment Inc** (REI;

www.rei.com) stores found in 16 cities in the state. Many Southern Californians are fans of **Adventure 16** (www.adventure16.com), which has six stores in LA and San Diego. If money isn't an issue, **Patagonia** (www.patagonia.com) has stores in Los Angeles and San Francisco; but if funds are tight, try the Patagonia outlet stores in Santa Cruz (415 River Street, 1-831 423 1776) or Reno, Nevada (8550 White Fir Street, 1-775 746 6878), just across the border and within easy reach of Lake Tahoe.

One of the most critical pieces of equipment every hiker should carry costs only a few bucks: a trail map of the park or region you are visiting. Many private sources publish excellent hiking maps: the best is **Tom Harrison** (1-415 456 7940, www.tomharrisonmaps.com). **National Geographic** (www.trailsillustrated.com) also publishes maps of California's national parks; the **United States Geological Survey** (USGS; http://store.usgs.gov) has topographical maps for every inch of the state. Most California public parklands also sell maps at entrance stations and/or visitor centres.

Whether you go for an afternoon meander or a ten-day wilderness backpacking trip, remember one rule above all others: never drink from natural water sources without filtering or boiling it first. The micro-organisms giardia lamblia and cryptosporidium are present in almost all Californian lakes, streams and rivers; drinking this water without treating it first is like playing Russian roulette with your digestive system. Staying both hydrated and healthy is a simple task: carry either bottled water or some type of water filtering system, available at all outdoor stores.

California's landscape is famous for its diversity: it contains both the highest and lowest points in the 48 contiguous United States (respectively, Mount Whitney and Badwater in Death Valley); the tallest, largest and oldest trees on earth (coast redwoods, giant sequoias and ancient bristlecone pines); and the tallest waterfall in North America (Yosemite Falls). And despite being one of the most populous states in the US, California contains an amazing amount of protected wildlands. The Golden State boasts nearly two dozen national parks, sure, but there are also 270 state parks, 19 national forests, over a dozen major mountain ranges and 14 million acres of federal wilderness area; 1,200 miles of coastline, 32 million acres of forest and 21 million acres of desert. If you'd rather walk in group company, check in with the local chapter of the **Sierra Club**: there are 13 in California (details at www.sierraclub.org/ca), and all organise regular walks and tours around their territories, as well as talks and other events.

National parks and some state parks also run guided walks. But if you'd rather hike alone, here are eight trails to get you started.

Bay Area Ridge Trail
www.ridgetrail.org.
A proposed 400-mile trail that will eventually connect public parklands in a ring around the San Francisco Bay. Many sections are already completed, allowing hikers access to an urban wildland like no other.

California Coastal Trail (CCT)
www.californiacoastaltrail.org.
Running for 1,200 miles from Mexico to Oregon, the California Coastal Trail hugs the edge of the Golden State's coastline almost every step of the way.

Half Dome
www.nps.gov/yose.
Everyone who comes to Yosemite is awed by Half Dome, a rounded block of granite that appears to have been sliced in half by some unseen hand. One look and you'll have the urge to get on top. The hike is a 17-mile round-trip with 4,800ft (1,463m) of elevation gain. Most hikers do it in a (tiring) day, although you can get a permit and make it a backpacking trip.

John Muir Trail (JMT)
www.pcta.org.
This 211-mile trail, which partially overlaps the PCT, starts near Mount Whitney, then travels north across a landscape of 13,000-ft (4,000-m) granite spires, deep sapphire lakes and Ansel Adams-esque vistas, before descending into Yosemite Valley. The trail is named for one of the state's great conservationists.

Mount Shasta
www.shastaavalanche.org.
Not much shorter than Whitney, 14,162-ft (4,317-m) Mount Shasta is a dormant volcano that blew its top aeons ago. Reaching the summit is more physically strenuous and challenging than Whitney; ice axes and crampons are almost always needed, and the elevation gain is more than 7,000ft (2,134m). Still, it's on almost every California hiker's itinerary.

Mount Whitney
www.fs.fed.us/r5/inyo.
Hard to believe, but most people climb to the summit of 14,495-foot (4,418-m) Mount Whitney by dayhiking. The 22-mile round-trip is a butt-kicker, with 6,000ft (2,134m) of elevation gain from the trailhead to the top. Most start walking around 4am with flashlights. The trip can be done as an overnight trip, but you're then stuck carrying a heavy pack.

Pacific Crest Trail (PCT)
www.pcta.org.
This long-distance trail extends all the way from the Mexican border to the Canadian border, sticking close to the crest of the highest mountains; it totals 2,650 miles, 1,700 of which are in California. Many people hike the entire thing, but if you just want to get a taste of the PCT, shorter hikes are possible.

Tahoe Rim Trail (TRT)

www.tahoerimtrail.org.
Completed in 2002, the TRT follows the crest of the Lake Tahoe Basin in a 165-mile loop around Tahoe, passing through two states and several counties.

Hot springs

California's regular earthquakes do have one enjoyable by-product: hot springs. The cataclysmic folding and faulting of the earth's crust over millions of years, combined with just the right amount of underground water and earth core magma, produces a hot surface geothermal flow that goes on for centuries. As volcanic activity dies down, fissures are formed in the solid rock layer above the porous layer and steam and hot water escape, producing hot springs, geysers and fumaroles.

As the water travels up through the earth, it accumulates different chemical properties. At least as far back as the time of the Greeks and the Romans, medicinal cures were attributed to the chemicals; waters were administered in a combination of drinking and soaking. But while many people still support the idea of mineral water cures, most people simply enjoy the feeling of a good hot soak.

California has a wide variety of places to put your body in hot water. Some are in relative luxury just steps from a main road; others are a lengthy hike into peaceful isolation. Most natural springs are in state or national parks, where camping is also available. If you're heading into the backcountry, check with the nearest ranger station for weather conditions, permits and maps. Be aware that nudity is often the mutually agreed-upon status at natural hot springs, even in areas where it's not legal. However, carry a bathing suit in case a ranger passes by and requests that you put one on.

Commercial hot springs vary widely from places where you can pitch a tent, rent a cabin, or go upscale all the way to fancy, high-end resorts. Many of the commercial springs are required by law to add minimal amounts of chemicals to the water; a good number are clothing-optional. A couple of towns have tourist industries that depend, to a large part, on their hot springs. For **Calistoga**, *see p354*; for **Desert Hot Springs**, *see p166*. Otherwise, though, read on for a selection of the best hot springs in all of California.

Buckeye Hot Springs

Nr Bridgeport. Directions: at north end of Bridgeport, take Twin Lakes Road west. Make a right at Doc & Al's Resort, then follow signs to Buckeye Campground. Take right fork up a short hill on the north branch of FS 017 to a parking lot. The main pools by the river are downhill from the lot. **Location** p333.

Buckeye, in the Sierra Nevada east of Yosemite, is set at the bottom of a large natural tufa mound where minerals have built up over the years. A small cave has been formed under the mound and candles often glow there at night. It's not unusual to find a family sitting in the hot springs with a fishing pole out in the river. Early morning is particularly beautiful, with the steam coming off the rocks.

Hot Creek

East of Mammoth. Directions: take US 395 south from Mammoth to Long Valley Airport Road. Turn east at the sign for the Hot Creek area. Look for the parking lot about 3 miles up on the left. **Location** p335.

This geological observation and interpretive site has a huge pond that's open during daylight hours. Hot water boils up from the bottom of a creek, creating eddies of hot water that you must carefully avoid in order not to get burned. The trail from the main pool goes upstream, where cold water is diverted around other hot spots. There are changing rooms, pit toilets and paved paths; bathing suits are required.

Located on the same plateau and off the main gravel roads are seven other sets of pools, built and maintained by volunteers. Many are close enough to the road to hike in during the winter; almost all the pools have views of white-capped mountains. One of the easiest to reach is **Hot Tub**: from Benton Crossing Road, drive 1.1 miles on 3S50 (the main gravel road) to the second one-lane dirt road on the right. Turn right and go for 150yds to a clearing, then bear left for another 150yds.

Sierra Hot Springs

Nr Sierraville (1-530 994 3773/www.sierrahot springs.org). Directions: From Highway 49, turn right on Lemon Canyon Road, then take the next right on to Campbell Hot Springs Road. **Location** p301.

A 600-acre resort surrounded by forests, meadows and streams. Hot mineral water flows into several terraced pools and waterfalls, a sandy-bottom pool at the edge of a meadow, a large swimming pool and hot pool, and private tubs. Because of the large flow of water, no chemicals are needed. Clothing is optional in all pool areas. Lodgings are available.

Tecopa region

Around Tecopa, off Highway 127 north of Baker. **Location** p171.

Hundreds of warm mineral springs supply water to the alkali desert east of Death Valley. Several small, funky resorts provide a variety of accommodation. Among them are **Delight's Hot Springs Resort** (1-800 928 8808, www.delightshotspringsresort.com), where chemical-free water feeds a variety of soaking pools and facilities include cottages; and **Tecopa Hot Springs Resort** (1-760 852 4335, www.tecopa hotsprings.com), which has two hot mineral water baths in private rooms and welcomes families.

If you prefer to soak in natural surroundings, head instead to the **Tecopa Desert Pond**, accessed by driving past the Tecopa Hot Springs bathhouse. The tub is at the foot of the small palm tree, just under a mile from Hot Springs Road. There are also some warm, smooth, clay-bottom ponds, a mile from the bathhouse. A clear but unmarked trail leads off to the right past the bathhouse; the ladder down into the pools is about 100 yards from a small rise on the left. Be sure to bring drinking water.

Travertine Hot Springs

Nr Bridgeport. Directions: south of Bridgeport, turn right on Jack Sawyer Road, staying straight on the unpaved road for around a mile. **Location** p333.
This group of volunteer-built soaking pools on large travertine ridges offer commanding views of the High Sierra Mountains. Locals maintain the pools in pristine condition. Very hot water can be controlled by temporarily diverting the inflow as needed. The pools are lovely and the views are magnificent. Go during the week, as weekends get very crowded.

White Sulphur Springs Inn & Spa

3100 White Sulphur Springs Road, St Helena (1-800 593 8873/www.whitesulphursprings.com). Directions: from Highway 29/Main Street in St Helena, turn on to Spring Street and continue for around two miles. **Location** p353.
This recently restored retreat is nestled in a tranquil wooded canyon in the heart of the Napa Valley, and boasts its own redwood grove and waterfall.

Perfectly charming lodgings complement the outdoor rock-lined soaking pool, outdoor jet tub and lovely swimming pool.

Kayaking, rafting & canoeing

California offers the highest concentration of exciting, diverse and accessible whitewater in the world. Visitors can expect a huge selection of enjoyable white and not-so-white water with excellent scenery and near-pristine water quality. Whether your preference is calm, scenic waters or the glorious rush of snowmelt – in spring and summer, snowmelt feeds a myriad of rivers tumbling from the **Trinity Alps**, the southern **Cascades** and the **Sierra Nevada** – you won't be stuck for places to paddle.

Along the coast, rivers often take a north–south course, following earthquake faults. Flows are highest (sometimes too high) after winter rains, when moderate coastal temperatures permit boating on hundreds of smaller streams. The Trinity Alps are drained by various forks of the Trinity River. Rivers originating in the Sierra Nevada, meanwhile, reach their highest flows from April to June, depending on headwater elevation. In late

Hiking in the **Sierra Nevada.**

Lake Tahoe.

summer and fall, dam releases provide adequate recreational flows on about a dozen Sierra rivers, and on the Trinity River.

Due to California's mountainous terrain, there are few rivers suitable for normal open canoeing. The most scenic river sections are too difficult for open canoes, and the easier sections often travel through less appealing agricultural areas. However, canoeists do frequent the easy sections of rivers, especially the **Russian River** near Healdsburg (*see p367*), where visitors can rent canoes for self-guided trips. The **American River** from Lake Natoma to Sacramento (*see p287*) is almost as easy, but outfitters there rent rafts and inner tubes, not canoes. In the southland, canoeists head east to the **Colorado River**, where there are several scenic canyons below Hoover Dam.

Flatwater enthusiasts may be drawn by California's thousands of reservoirs, but on summer weekends, you'll encounter a flotilla of motorboats and jet skis. Fortunately, there are many small alpine lakes at high elevations where motors are either forbidden or impractical. One fine example is **Cherry Lake**, accessible from Highway 120 west of Yosemite, where canoeists can find wonderful camping among granite outcroppings.

California's most popular rivers support a multi-million-dollar commercial rafting industry, especially active in spring and summer. In some spots (**Cache Creek**, for example), you can rent rafting equipment for self-guided tours. Among your many choices

for commercially guided trips is the South Fork of the **American River** (*see p303*), the most heavily used commercial whitewater river in the USA. Commercial trips are also readily available on the **Tuolumne River** (longer and tougher), and in spring and early summer on the **Merced River** (*see p281*), downhill from Yosemite. South of here, the lower **Kern River** is rafted for most of the summer; upstream, Forks of the Kern is one of the most outstanding raft expeditions in the world.

Because California's largest cities are near the ocean, sea kayaking has become very popular, despite the difficulties of wind, cold water and seasickness. In the south, the **Channel Islands** (*see p199*) are popular; further north, **Monterey Bay** (*see p212*) and **Tomales Bay** (*see p264*) offer semi-sheltered paddling locales with plenty of wildlife viewing opportunities. Good places to rent a sea kayak and spend part of the day touring are from **Point Arena** near Tomales Bay, **Moss Landing** into Elkhorn Slough (tide-assisted), or along the waterfront in the city of **Monterey** out into the bay (*see p215*). Sea kayakers also enjoy the salt waters of inland seas such as **Mono Lake** (*see p333*); more adventurous sea kayakers buy their own boats and spend time exploring **San Francisco Bay** (*see p260*) or the southern coast.

There are a number of good guides to paddlesports in California; *see p404*. Online, head for www.c-w-r.com and www.creekin.net.

Skiing & snowboarding

The dominant outdoor image in California is of surfers catching waves in the Pacific. However, thanks to the configuration of the Sierra Nevada, the moisture surging in from the South Pacific and the cold fronts bearing down from Alaska, the region is prime for water of a very different kind. Often called Sierra Cement, for its high moisture content and heavy texture, surprisingly large caches of powder show up in California, especially in February.

The state sports over 40 bona fide resorts; some huge, some one-chair wonders. But snow is snow, and if you live for winter, it won't matter much where it's found, as long as it's fresh and there's plenty of it. If you're planning to shred the SoCal resorts, LAX is the airport of choice. Rent a car and wonder at the landscape as you climb from temperate through arid and into sub-alpine terrain, especially up the US 395 corridor through the Owens River Valley. Northern resorts are best reached via Sacramento, Reno, San Jose or San Francisco, in that order. Below are the state's best resorts.

Mammoth Mountain

Mammoth Lakes (1-800 626 6684/www.mammoth mountain.com). **Location** p335.
Highest summit elevation, greatest amount of ski-able acreage, driest powder, finest steeps, best string of peaks, most impressive mountain management: this is, simply, California's premier resort.

Alpine Meadows

North Shore, Lake Tahoe (1-800 949 3296/www. alpinemeadows.com). **Location** p318.
Thanks to its open-boundary policy, Alpine Meadows is known both for the accessibility of its backcountry skiing and its out-of-bounds feel to the resort acreage. Ride the back bowls and traverse to Squaw, being mindful of avalanche hazard. Springtime lift management follows the sun for maximum goods.

Kirkwood

Off Highway 88, south-west of Lake Tahoe (1-209 258 6000/www.kirkwood.com). **Location** p322.
A destination resort for the mighty. In spite of its middling size, the best chutes, cornices and glades are here at the resort with the highest base elevation outside of the Tahoe Basin. Because of its location, orientation and high winds, the annual snowfall stays in long past the spring conditions of other resorts.

Sugar Bowl

I-80, at Donner Pass (1-530 426 9000/www. sugarbowl.com). **Location** p317.
A Donner Summit favourite: popular with Walt Disney, home of the state's first chairlift and the nation's first gondola, and holder of the overall 100-year record for snowfall. Sugar Bowl has an open-boundary Tahoe backcountry access policy, and, with the Palisades, the steepest chutes in California.

Yosemite

Yosemite National Park (1-209 372 0200/ www.nps.gov/yose). **Location** p325.
Badger Pass may be the easiest downhill terrain you'll ever ride: it's ideal for beginners. Alternatively, slap on some Nordic gear and tour the valley, or skin up to Glacier Point for the view of the Half Dome.

Royal Gorge

I-80, at Donner Pass (1-800 500 3871/www. royalgorge.com). **Location** p317.
This cross-country ski resort is North America's largest Nordic ski centre, with more skiable acres than most alpine resorts, over 200 miles of groomed trails, four surface lifts and two trailside lodges.

Squaw Valley USA

North Shore, Lake Tahoe (1-530 583 6985/ www.squaw.com). **Location** p319.
Challenging terrain off the backside and down KT22, as well as the chutes and cornices of Granite Chief. A pity that Squaw Valley's reputation keeps slopes crowded, lift lines long and staff unfriendly.

Mount Shasta

Off I-5 (www.shastahome.com). **Location** p386.
The alpine resort isn't bad, but Shasta's forte is in its backcountry skiing. Skin up and schuss down in some of California's best virgin powder, or pick a mountaineering route to the summit of this 14er. For safety's sake, be aware of avalanches.

Sierra-at-Tahoe

South Shore, Lake Tahoe (1-530 659 7453/ www.sierratahoe.com). **Location** p320.
Off the beaten track, fewer crowds, long groomers, and given most of the resort is below the treeline, the glade skiing is superb. Watch for launching pads off snow-covered boulders the size of VWs.

Surfing

The 1,500 miles of Californian coastline offer a terrific variety of surfing, from heavy reef to quality beach breaks, but it can be broken down into two areas. Southern California has a mild climate, and while the quality of the surf isn't always consistent, the coastline here is exposed to south/south-west swells. Another point in its favour is the friendliness of the locals. The Northern California coast, meanwhile, is colder, but does get pounded by bigger north-west swells (the same ones that hit Hawaii in winter).

The first place to head is Huntington Beach, aka Surf City USA. The town is a surfers' mecca: surf shops, surf-themed restaurants and bars, a surf museum (*see p121*), even a Surfing Walk of Fame. Make the world-famous **Jack's Surf Shop** (101 Main Street, 1-714 536 4516) your first port of call if you want to get the lowdown on the scene, though there are many shops that sell or rent boards and other gear.

Get dinner at **Duke's** (317 PCH, 1-7145 374 6446), a surf-slanted joint named for the founder of modern surfing, Duke Kahanamotu. Once you're through surfing here, just follow the Pacific Coast Highway in either direction.

Attire-wise, if you're visiting Southern California in summer, some board shorts or a spring suit will do; in winter, you'll need a 3/2mm full suit. There are plenty of shops where you can buy or rent boards and clothing: running south to north, they include **Emerald City** in Pacific Beach (3126 Mission Boulevard, 1-858 488 9224), **Killer Dana** in Dana Point (24621 Del Prado Avenue, 1-949 489 8380), the four **Val Surf** shops in the LA area (the largest at 4810 Whitsett Avenue, Valley Village, 1-818 769 6977), **ZJ's Boardinghouse** in Santa Monica (2619 Main Street, 1-310 392 5646), the **Channel Islands Surf Shop** in Santa Barbara (29 State Street, 1-805 966 7213) and the **O'Neill Surf Shop** in Santa Cruz (110 Cooper Street, Santa Cruz, 1-831 469 4377). The assorted **Quiksilver Boardriders Clubs** (not clubs, but stores; see www.quiksilver.com for locations) are also useful. Many shops, along with specialised surf schools such as the **Newport Surf Camp** (1-866 787 3226, www.newportsurfcamp.com), also offer surf lessons, though you'll need to book in advance.

For more information, pick up a copy of *Surfer* and *Surfing* magazines, or check online at www.surfdiva.com, www.surfersvillage.com and, especially, www.surfline.com. Below are the best surfing spots on the Pacific Coast, listed from south to north.

Windansea

La Jolla, San Diego. From La Jolla, take Nautilus Street off La Jolla Boulevard. **Location** p77.
Home to one of the first surf clubs in the country, beautiful Windansea always captures some kind of swell. Expect to find lots of longboards, big crowds and not-always-friendly locals. Suitable for intermediate to good surfers.

Trestles

San Onofre State Park, off I-5 about 5 miles south of San Clemente. **Location** p121.
One of the most photographed waves in the world, Trestles is often described as a surf/skate park. The gentle reef break works best on south swells, and while it gets very crowded, the rights and lefts are world class. Different breaks are available: uppers, lowers and middles. The beach is a 20-minute walk from the car park. Suitable for good to expert surfers.

The Wedge

Newport Beach, off US 1. **Location** p121.
This famous shore break gets very scary during the big south summer swells. It's typically a break dominated by bodyboarders and skimboarders, but the occasional suicidal surfer will give it a go. Hundreds of people stand on the beach enjoying the show as boards and bodies get broken on a regular basis. Needless to say, it's for experienced surfers only.

Huntington Beach

Huntington Beach, off US 1. **Location** p121.
Good surf on both sides of the pier catches any swell direction. There are usually crowds around the pier, but there's plenty of beach on which to find a quieter break. Suitable for all levels.

Malibu

Malibu, off US 1. **Location** p98.
Malibu's famous point break is on the north side of Malibu Pier: when you see the Jack in the Box fast-food chain, you're there. It gets crowded with longboarders, but it's still a nice place to stop and get wet. The level of surfing is intermediate to advanced.

Rincon Beach Park

About 3 miles east of Carpinteria, off US 101. **Location** p203.
This terrific right-hand point break breaks on a cobblestone-covered reef. Three-time world champ Tom Curren perfected his style on these world-class waves. It works mostly on north swells and can get epic; you'll likely have to share the water. Suitable for surfers of an intermediate to good standard.

The Ranch

Between Gaviota and Jalama Beach State Park. **Location** p203.
The Ranch is accessible only by boat from Gaviota; its shores are part of some multi-million-dollar properties, and inaccessible by land. However, the breaks here are world class, and devoid of big crowds.

Steamer Lane

Santa Cruz, south of the Boardwalk. **Location** p275.
This right-hand reef break, with sections that break along a big cliff, is a Northern California benchmark. The waters are cold and the surfers are serious; suitable for intermediate to experienced surfers.

Mavericks

A half-mile off the coast of Pillar Point in Half Moon Bay, off US 1. **Location** p273.
The state's biggest wave has claimed many lives, most famously Mark Fox. Jeff Clark rode it alone for years; now, the place is surfed by hardcore locals. The cold, sharky waters are not for the inexperienced.

Bodega Bay Area

Off US 1. **Location** p365.
Many surf spots here, mixed between beach and reef breaks such as Point Reyes. The surf is excellent, but it's crowded in summer, the locals are not always friendly, and there's a higher-than-average risk of meeting a shark. Intermediate to advanced surfers.

▶ For a list of the best guidebooks to California outdoor pursuits, *see p405*.

Food & Drink

Great wine and fine food are the Californian essence.

Californian food

How can dining in the Golden State best be characterised? Two words: simple, inventive. Easy words, but richly significant in the state that exports trends in food, fashion and lifestyle to all points east.

The term 'Californian cuisine' is bandied about so easily these days that it can seem meaningless. Worse, some practitioners are hidebound to particular styles of cooking, even though its inspiration was as much a philosophy as a method. The original meaning of the term referred to a new way of thinking about food from field to table, one that considered food sourcing and presentation to be key. This process-oriented approach was reflective of its birthplace, the radical think-tank town of Berkeley. It was here, 30 years ago, that Alice Waters of Chez Panisse fame spawned the concept of Californian cuisine: meals that were thoughtfully composed and prepared with the freshest and best-quality local ingredients. Simplicity and elegance in composition was

a hallmark of the movement, with a nod toward Asian, Italian and Mediterranean sensibilities. The prevailing attitude towards food was respectful but not reverential.

Today the phrase 'Californian cuisine' still signifies fresh ingredients and simple presentation. Unless, that is, it's being used to justify over-the-top presentation and prices, fawning and prostration over a lettuce leaf, or even the use of ingredients from far beyond any California zip code. At least the trend towards deconstruction, unbridled experimentation and bizarre combinations of sweet and savoury, often looking and tasting like nothing you've ever eaten (or ever wanted to eat), have settled down to a more sensible level of innovation than was the case a few years ago.

If ingredients from artisan farmers and fishermen continue to drive Californian cooking, menus could often be better described as 'global' or 'fusion'. The steak craze that hit Los Angeles in 2003 is reflective of the low-carb phase still ruling many American diets; this high-protein craze is also fuelling the use of such non-native ingredients as Peruvian fluke,

Places to eat

Ten varied Californian eating experiences not to be missed.

Big Kitchen, San Diego

There are many smarter and many fancier restaurants in San Diego, but there are none better than this delightfully relaxed neighbourhood diner. It's not hard to make the argument that the huge, no-nonsense breakfasts and brunches dished up here are the best in California. *See p78.*

Café Beaujolais, Mendocino

Some Californian coastal restaurants are content to coast on their reputation. Not this cosy, enormously popular little place, whose Californian cuisine (especially the seafood) never fails to please. *See p372.*

Chez Panisse, Berkeley

The exquisite sensibility of visionary chef Alice Waters, who thought up Californian cuisine, and superbly fresh Californian produce continue to delight diners at this culinary landmark. *See p271.*

Far Western Tavern, Guadalupe

It's hard to pick between Casmalia's lively Hitching Post and the nearby, slightly mellower Far Western Tavern, a pair of magnificent Californian oakwood barbecue eateries. We've plumped for the latter, purely on the basis that it serves breakfast (from 11am) and lunch, as well as spectacular steak dinners. *See p205.*

French Laundry, Yountville

Thomas Keller's imaginatively inventive and slyly humorous French-Californian cuisine is a perfectly divine dining experience. Voted the world's best restaurant in 2004 by *Restaurant* magazine. *See p351.*

Patina, Los Angeles

Restyled in a dreamily romantic mode in Downtown LA's spectacular new Frank Gehry-designed Walt Disney Concert Hall, Patina lives up to its promise and the stakes set by the original establishment. Masterly execution of modern American cuisine. *See p129.*

Sage & Onion, Santa Barbara

Californian cuisine cooked by a Brit really does add up to the best of both worlds at Steven Giles' splendid eatery, merely one of several in Santa Barbara. *See p201.*

Slanted Door, San Francisco

An original, exciting and fresh interpretation of authentic Vietnamese cooking, occasionally applied to Western ingredients with a sophisticated aesthetic. Another bonus: it's right at the amazing Ferry Plaza Farmers' Market. *See p244.*

Taqueria la Cumbre, San Francisco

The Mission District is famed across the country for its Mexican food, and this magnificent little eatery will explain way. If the lines are too long at Taqueria la Cumbre, and they often are, try nearby, late-opening Taqueria Cancun. *See p242.*

Valentino, Santa Monica

Seriously swoonsome food in a traditional Italian vein: impeccably prepared and served with suave Italian panache. Your best option may be abandoning the menu altogether and leaving yourself in the hands of chef Piero Selvaggio. *See p122.*

Ecuadorian shrimp and Thai tuna by ceviche bars, sushi houses and raw bars. Saké tastings are sprouting up at upscale Japanese restaurants and those with Asian-inspired fare.

Indeed, notwithstanding the frequent use of indigenous ingredients, food in California could be described as an anything-goes enterprise, its restaurant scene essentially an exaggerated, all-encompassing version of those in other major US states. California has attracted immigrants from countless different cultures, so it follows that any and every kind of ethnic cuisine can be enjoyed here. Los Angeles, in particular, boasts as many varieties of ethnic restaurant as it does

immigrant communities: Korean food in Koreatown, Taiwanese in San Gabriel and South American in East LA, to name but three.

Yet there are even distinctions to be made here. The tapas concept has lately moved far beyond its Spanish origins. The term now operates as a general term for small dishes of any cuisine, and the notion of a common table is increasingly prevalent in all manner of restaurants. By contrast, there are loads of wonderful Asian eateries in California, both North and South, but few have crossed the ethnic barrier to become fully fledged Western-style restaurants. The same can be said for

Mexican cuisine, a distinctly non-oxymoronic category that shines in Chicago and New York more than it does in California. Those Mexican eateries that do succeed, such as the taquerias of San Francisco's Mission district, tend to be fast-food places; California's countless low-budget eateries specialising in other ethnic cuisines, the food at which can be deeply satisfying, are usually in a similar vein.

That these many types of food and kinds of presentation succeed together is due to the simple fact that Californians are foodies, with an inquisitive eagerness about global foods and a fervour for new eating experiences. San Francisco, for example, was chock-full of cafés before New York (outside Little Italy, at least) was dialled into espresso culture. This is a Mediterranean culture – a culture of suntans in cafés – but reconfigured by the state that invented the idea of casual chic.

Despite the arrival of ultra-luxe eateries, an informal attitude, in itself archetypically Californian, runs throughout the state. The fabled fine French restaurants of the past have faded (as they have in many places, including France) to be replaced by more casual food and attitudes. Classic American comfort food is on the rise, expressing the healthy, clean-cooking characteristics of Californian cuisine – albeit a straight-edged, less ethnic version of the cuisine. The food served at many basic California cafés can be stunningly simple but utterly delicious, composed of ingredients grown, harvested or caught no more than a couple of hours from the table.

Hitting its stride after some gimmicky gastronomic episodes in the 1990s, Los Angeles has seen its position at the centre of the state's culinary scene suffer through a rash of upsets in 2004: chefs at promising spots jumping ship or being pushed, owners decamping. But California is the capital of self-reinvention and the food that bears its name will surely continue to thrive, not least because its population is always demanding the next new trend – now.

Californian wine

In May 1976 an expatriate Englishman named Steven Spurrier organised a wine tasting at the Intercontinental Hotel in Paris. The event was scheduled to coincide with the bicentennial of America's Declaration of Independence, but was widely expected to turn into a celebration of French wine. Nine Parisian judges, some of the pre-eminent wine authorities of the time, were to undertake a blind tasting and judge a number of new American wines against some perennially esteemed French varieties. The French wines would, of course, come out on top.

What happened next has gone down in wine folklore. The Californian wines took three of the top four spots in the white wine test, and a cabernet sauvignon from Stag's Leap Wine Cellars in the Napa Valley beat an assortment of French wines to take top spot in the reds category. The event, written up in *Time* magazine, sent shock waves through the international wine world. This small tasting, reported by a single journalist, single-handedly put Californian wine on the map.

THE PAST

At the time of the Paris test, Californians were widely seen as newcomers to the wine industry, despite wine having been produced in America since the 18th century. Early Spanish settlers, led by missionaries, planted grapes as they built the chain of missions that runs like rosary beads up what is now the state's coastal highway. The earliest vineyard was planted in 1779 at Mission San Juan Capistrano, about halfway between San Diego and Los Angeles.

The primary use for the wine was to meet the liturgical needs of the Catholic Church, though the wine was also enjoyed by secular explorers and pioneers. Until the Spanish missionary period ended in the mid 1830s, Mission San Gabriel near Los Angeles was the biggest winemaking area. Southern California

Pie in the sky, Californian style.

continued to lead production for the next 50 years, even though George Yount had planted the first grapevines in Northern California's Napa Valley way back in 1831.

At around this time, European immigrants arriving in California started producing their own wines for the family table. A Frenchman, the rather improbably named Jean Louis Vignes, even began importing cabernet sauvignon vines from his native Bordeaux to produce a first vintage in 1837. Ten years later a vineyard was planted in the Bay Area and, with the rush of immigrants during the 1849 Gold Rush, vineyards began to be planted with gusto in Northern California. Still thriving today, Buena Vista in Sonoma was founded by a dashing Hungarian count, Agoston Haraszthy, in 1857; Charles Krug introduced grapes to Napa in 1861. The Schramsberg champagne house began in 1862, Beringer followed in St Helena 14 years later, and newly minted Finnish millionaire Captain Gustav Niebaum founded what is now the Niebaum-Coppola estate in 1879.

Phylloxera, a louse that attacks the root system of a vineyard, devastated the budding Californian wine-growing industry between 1889 and 1900; then Prohibition (1920-33) closed nearly all the state's several hundred wineries. A handful stayed open to supply religious wines, but by the time the blight of Prohibition had ended, Californian wineries were 50 years behind the times. Supply dawdled along for another few decades, until a few pioneers in the 1960s, among them Robert Mondavi, laid the groundwork for the explosion of the 1970s and '80s.

The majority of the Napa Valley's 260-plus commercial vineyards were founded after the Paris test of 1976; virtually none of the tasting rooms and salons, restaurants, shops, spas and hotels that service the hordes trawling up and down Highway 29 in search of epiphanic wine experiences existed 30 years ago. Wine is now California's number one 'finished' agricultural product; after France, Italy and Spain, the state ranks as the fourth largest wine producer in the world.

A wine taster's primer

At times, when cruising and carousing around California's wineries, it's advisable to look as if you do actually know something about this tasting lark: to look like you're an aficionado, in other words, rather than a freeloading swiller. So, to help you out, here's our guide to the four S's of tasting wine.

First, approach the tasting table, looking confident. The general order of tasting is to drink white wines before reds, newer wines before older vintages. Sparkling wines serve as bookends during tastings, and are often referred to as 'palate refreshers'. Once you've decided on a wine...

Swirl. The pourer will deposit an ounce or two in your glass. They're not slighting you: this is a 'tasting' quantity. Swirl it around in the glass.

Smell. Release the wine's aromas and contain them in the glass by rotating it with your hand over the top (if you can do two things at once). Raise the glass to your nose and bury your nose in it, inhaling deeply. What are you looking for? Something to remember when you taste, first of all. Younger wines will smell grapier, older wines more complex. Whether you detect

pineapples or lychee fruit (white wines) or leather and violets (reds), make a mental note as to how it carries through into the tasting.

Sip. Take a good-sized mouthful of wine. Pucker up and suck some oxygen into your oral cavity; making a gurgling sound is perfectly acceptable (though you might still want to practise this part before trotting out to the tasting room). Swish the wine around your mouth vigorously. Irrigate the back of your palate. Think about the taste: is it earthy, mineral, flowery, fruity, spicy?

Spit. Then, just when you're really starting to savour the flavour, shimmy to the tasting spittoon, incline your head towards its bowl and, yes, spit. Even though you haven't swallowed, you'll have some sense of the wine's 'finish', whether short or lingering.

Now, having completed the process, you can consider yourself qualified to offer an opinion. But do stick to traditional wine parlance: 'Hmm. Cheeky, buxom and Mediterranean, I think; rather young, but with legs...'

THE PRESENT

The cooling effect of the Pacific Ocean on the coastal valleys makes California's climate ideal for wine production. Coastal mountain ranges dictate the best growing areas for cooler-weather grapes (such as pinot noir) and warmer ones (such as cabernet). Mountains also prohibit the flow of sea air to the interior in most areas, so coastal, mountain and interior areas each have very different soils and climates. Consequently, the state is able to produce many different types of grape.

Given this perfect climate, soil is the other major factor influencing how well vines grow. An amazing 33 different soil types have been identified in the Napa Valley alone, and soil differentiation within appellation areas is increasing. These days there's a lot of fine-tuning going on in vineyards. Moves towards better definition of growing sites and of which grapes excel in different areas have led to the creation of smaller, better differentiated appellation areas.

However, despite this emphasis on area appellation, the US was the world's first wine-growing country to simplify wine by labelling it varietally. Wines known by their grape varietals (chardonnay, merlot), instead of the traditional area names used in Europe (Bordeaux, Sancerre), began appearing in the 1970s, when wineries like Mondavi and Beringer starting making cabernet and chenin blanc instead of Burgundy and Chablis.

The two top-scoring wines in that legendary 1976 French tasting were a cabernet and a chardonnay, the two varietals that, despite interest in many new grapes, still fuel the Napa wine industry. California continues to make more chardonnay than anything else; cabernet is the second most popular wine, but in 2003 zinfandel nearly matched it for quantity of production. Rhône varieties, such as syrah and grenache, increase in popularity every year; the fickle pinot noir, whose fans tend to be a tad romantic about their infatuation with the grape, is made in much smaller quantities, little more than a tenth of cabernet's production. In the Italian varietals, barbera is inching its way up and there are some promising sangioveses.

THE FUTURE

In the last three years, the number of regular American wine drinkers has increased enormously. But while more consumers are buying wine, the real rise in market value comes from a smaller pool of consumers purchasing more expensive wines.

The stampede to become part of the burgeoning wine industry in the 1980s led to a rush on the part of those who had something to protect to embrace a European-style appellation system, called American Viticultural Areas (AVAs). Unlike the European appellation laws, however, which address viticultural issues such as where, what and how grapes could be grown, the American rules are more concerned with specifying that grapes from a particular designated area are what's in the bottle. Since the first set of these rules (established in 1978) outlived their usefulness, stricter denominations and sub-districts have been created.

'Napa Valley' still carries the most clout. While only accounting for four per cent of the state's production, its wines have the highest wine grape value; a bottle of wine legally labelled 'Napa Valley' costs an average of $6 more than one labelled only 'California'. Napa's fame was made with cabernet, still the most popular and most expensive Napa red. Varietals of meritage blends go for upwards of $50 and more; at the 2004 Napa Valley Wine Auction, an annual charity event, the gavel went down at $220,000 for three bottles of Screaming Eagle cabernet from 1995, 1996 and 1997.

There are over 1,000 active California wineries today. Around half of them in the Napa and Sonoma Valleys, areas dominated by wine tourism; a vacation here can get expensive in a hurry. The balance of California's wineries is divided between Mendocino and Lake Counties, the Sierra Foothills, the Livermore Valley, Santa Cruz, the Monterey Bay area, the Central Valley, and the counties of San Luis Obispo and Santa Barbara. Whether a cluster of wineries creates tourism or vice versa, the wine regions of California are an increasingly popular tourist destination. It's estimated that almost 15 million people visit California's wine-producing areas annually, spending $1.3 billion while they're in the area at hotels, restaurants, shops and, of course, wineries. Napa alone gets 5.5 million visitors a year.

The emphasis on tasting rooms as revenue generators for the wineries has changed too. In Napa Valley, it's not about attracting visitors, but the kind of visitors you attract. As the spittoon circuit evolves, tastes become more sophisticated, thus the one-on-one tasting experience becomes more marketable and lucrative. Today you can fork over upwards of $50 for some of these small, customised, sexy saloon tastings. You pays your money, as the saying goes, and you takes your chance.

► For more on **food in LA**, see pp122-132.
► For more on the wineries of the **Paso Robles** region, see p208.
► For more on the wineries of **Wine Country**, see pp345-361.

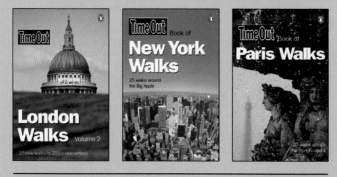

Where to Stay

Wherever you lay your hat...

Nowhere in the US offers as great a variety of lodgings as California, and it's not even close. Beverly Hills and West Hollywood has some of the plushest urban hotels in the world; a couple of the resorts in Orange County are even more extravagant. At the opposite end of the spectrum are the myriad campgrounds (*see p36*), many set amid stunning scenery. In between these two extremes lie all manner of alternatives: chic inner-city towers, twee B&Bs, austere hostels, luxuriant golfing resorts and historic roadside curiosities. The choice is vast.

Or, at least, the choice is vast if you book ahead. Despite the quantity, quality and variety of lodging options, it's often necessary to make reservations well ahead of time. Peak season runs from Memorial Day (late May) to Labor Day (early September) throughout the state, with two exceptions: the deserts, which are too hot for most during the scorching summer, and the ski resorts of the Sierra Nevada, also busiest in winter. During these peak seasons, hotels, motels and B&Bs habitually book up well in advance, and often charge premium rates.

Conversely, outside busy periods, there are plenty of bargains, as hotels cut prices in order to keep occupancy at respectable levels. Always check hotel websites, which often list special deals. You can also net discounts at some places

with AAA (*see p31*) or AARP (American Association of Retired People) membership; with US student or military ID; or by booking an extended stay. It all adds up to one golden rule: when booking, ask about discounts.

California has taken to the bed-and-breakfast trend with wild enthusiasm. Aside from the differences in size (most have six rooms or fewer), style (countryfied and cute) and service (you'll likely be looked after by the owners), B&Bs differ from hotels in practical regards. For one thing, bookings are often essential. For another, TVs and phones, standard in every hotel and motel guestroom, are found in only a handful of B&Bs. (Many B&B owners will allow you to make free local calls from their own phones.) And for a third, the breakfasts are often magnificent, miles better than the granite-hard croissants offered in many motels and hotels.

Major hotel & motel chains

The majority of lodgings listed in this guide are independent establishments, from huge resorts to tiny B&Bs and even campgrounds. However, there are also many chain hotels and motels across the state: in some cases, they supplement the independent operations, while in others, they provide the only lodging options.

Don't miss

Places to stay

Ten varied but exceptional Californian lodgings.

Chateau Marmont, West Hollywood

John Belushi died in Bungalow 3, but that hasn't put off the LA elite from frequenting this stylish, exclusive hotel. *See p145.*

Clift Hotel, San Francisco

How can something so ostentatious be so calm and classy? Feel the luxury at Ian Schrager and Philippe Starck's finest effort. *See p255.*

Hotel del Coronado, San Diego

The landmark building in all of San Diego, the beachside Del has a history (*Some Like it Hot* was filmed here) but also an impressive, luxurious present. *See p87.*

Madonna Inn, San Luis Obispo

Some rooms are fairly plain, but in others, pinks and reds blind the unprepared at what is surely the kitschest hotel in the US. *See p206.*

Meadowood Napa Valley, St Helena

Plush, becalmed, tasteful, expensive… Napa's desirable Meadowood is simply a classic Wine Country resort. *See p354.*

Nipton Hotel, Nipton

Location, location, location: like, right in the middle of the desert. This 1904-built adobe is entirely charming, even if you only have the railroad whistles for company. *See p172.*

Post Ranch Inn, Big Sur

No hotel in California boasts views as breathtaking as those from Post Ranch Inn's beautiful cottages, 1,200 feet (366 metres) above the Pacific on Big Sur. *See p211.*

Red Castle Inn, Nevada City

Quiet, friendly, immaculately maintained and deliverers of a knockout breakfast: the Red Castle is what a B&B should be. *See p299.*

Red Victorian, San Francisco

Hippie paradise on the Haight. Sami Sunchild's themed rooms are raucously decorated, but the meditation room ensures a bit of peace with your psychedelia. *See p257.*

Route 66 Motel, Barstow

Nothing luxurious, but this is a piece of living history: built in 1922, it's the oldest motel in a classic Route 66 town. *See p171.*

Hotel del Coronado.

Facilities vary between hotels in the same chain; this is especially true of motels at the lower end of the price range, which are run not by a central office but as individual franchises. However, a certain level of service and maintenance is fairly constant throughout all chains, as are their pricing structures.

Rather than run reviews of each individual chain hotel and motel in the guide, there follows a round-up of the more common chains, listed in approximate price order. Many motel chains publish free directories listing their locations; you can pick these up at any branch. While all places have individual phone numbers, you can book for any location on the numbers listed below, as well as online. However, note that reservations aren't always necessary at some of the cheaper roadside chains, especially outside of the major cities and particularly midweek, and that rates are often better if you contact the individual hotel.

If you're travelling on a whim and a budget, without either reservations or a bulging wallet, it's worth picking up free coupon books from gas stations or highway rest stops; they're full of coupons offering discounts, to walk-in customers only, on motels across the state. They're also useful simply for details on the locations of such motels: all coupons include directions, plus details of amenities. When you take a motel room, ask for one away from the highway. Many sit near busy roads, and while the majority are set far enough back to prevent disturbance, it's best to be on the safe side.

Four Seasons
1-800 819 5053/www.fourseasons.com. **Locations** 6.
St Regis
1-877 787 3447/www.starwood.com/stregis. **Locations** 3.
W Hotels
1-877 946 8357/www.starwood.com/whotels. **Locations** 4.

The smartest and, generally, most expensive of the chains. Four Seasons hotels, found in LA, San Diego, San Francisco and Santa Barbara, are plush and luxurious; St Regis resorts, in LA, Orange County and San Francisco (the latter opening in mid 2005), are even more exclusive. The small but expanding W chain, now in LA, San Diego, San Francisco and Silicon Valley, offers a kind of approachable, familiar hipness to a mix of business travellers and twenty- and thirtysomething weekend vacationers.

Hilton
1-800 445 8667/www.hilton.com. **Locations** 38.
Marriott
1-888 236 2427/www.marriott.com. **Locations** 49.
Sheraton
1-800 325 3535/www.starwood.com/sheraton. **Locations** 17.
Westin
1-800 228 3000/www.starwood.com/westin. **Locations** 12.

These four chains generally offer everything the business traveller requires: a bar, a gym and a pool, plus minibars, high-speed internet connections and on-demand movies. The service can't be faulted, though if we were travelling with this kind of money, we'd prefer to stay somewhere a little less anonymous. Hiltons and Sheratons are smart without being formal, while the style in Marriotts varies enormously: some are basic business-traveller lodgings, while others are decadent resorts, with pools, tennis courts and even golf courses. Westins are slightly more modish.

Courtyard by Marriott
1-888 236 2427/www.marriott.com. **Locations** 68.
Doubletree
1-800 222 8733/www.doubletree.com. **Locations** 23.
Fairfield Inn
1-888 236 2427/www.marriott.com/fairfieldinn. **Locations** 18.
Four Points by Sheraton
1-800 368 7764/www.starwood.com/fourpoints. **Locations** 15.
Radisson
1-800 333 3333/www.radisson.com. **Locations** 14.

These five hotel chains are concentrated in major towns and cities, and generally cater chiefly to business travellers. The rooms (and suites) in each are immaculate and modern, though a notch down from

the establishments detailed above. Facilities often include heated pools, workout rooms and high-speed internet connections; some have bars and restaurants. Expect to pay $100-$150 a night, sometimes more and very occasionally less.

Best Western
1-800 780 7234/www.bestwestern.com. **Locations** 315.
Holiday Inn & Holiday Inn Express
1-800 465 4329/www.holiday-inn.com. **Locations** *Holiday Inn* 65. *Holiday Inn Express* 118.

Two reliable chains; not luxurious, but always clean and decent. Added extras at Best Westerns, which vary from comfortable to fairly smart, and the more identikit Holiday Inns may include pay-per-view movies and/or indoor pools. This extra level of service is reflected in their rates, which in most towns are anywhere from $20 to $40 more than the likes of Motel 6 and Super 8; on average, you can expect to pay $70-$100. Holiday Inn Express removes a few of the frills from the regular Holiday Inn formula.

Days Inn
1-800 329 7466/www.daysinn.com. **Locations** 94.
Ramada
1-800 272 6232/www.ramada.com. **Locations** 74.
Howard Johnson
1-800 446 4656/www.hojo.com. **Locations** 34.

These three motel franchises are all owned by the same company, and there's not much to choose between them in terms of either service (so-so), location (most by major roads) or value (halfway between Best Western and Motel 6 in the overall price schema). Anecdotal evidence suggests that Days Inns are generally the nicest of the three. Ramadas, while safe and clean, also have a tendency towards mind-blowingly ugly furnishings; Howard Johnson motels are a very mixed bunch. You're usually looking at $40-$80/night for hotels for this trio.

Comfort Inn
1-877 424 6423/www.comfortinn.com. **Locations** 100.
Econo Lodge
1-877 424 6423/www.econolodge.com. **Locations** 59.
Motel 6
1-800 466 8356/www.motel6.com. **Locations** 175.
Red Roof Inn
1-800 733 7663/www.redroof.com. **Locations** 15.
Super 8
1-800 800 8000/www.super8.com. **Locations** 93.
Travelodge
1-800 578 7878/www.travelodge.com. **Locations** 71.

The cheapest of the motel chains, and you can usually tell why: don't expect amenities to run much beyond cable TV and a shower. Of these chains, generally clustered on the outskirts of towns, we've long found Motel 6 to be the most reliable in terms of safety and comfort: if you've only got $40/night to spend, you could do plenty worse. Comfort Inns are reliable; Super 8 and the less common Red Roof Inn are pretty basic. Econo Lodges and Travelodges, meanwhile, vary wildly: some are fine, but we've also found some in appalling condition.

Return of the Swallows

Festivals & Events

Jumping frogs? Cowboy poets? California's got the lot.

Because California is so diverse in culture, geography, climate and attitude, it's not surprising that its schedule of annual events is longer than the state's tax code. Within a two-week period, a visitor to California could attend a national rodeo, worship an agricultural crop, celebrate an ethnic tradition, witness a freakish display of urban eccentricity and bare everything in a street parade. Whatever rings your bell, folks.

The information listed below is as accurate as possible, but always check before you make plans, since every event is subject to change of dates and even location. For the most up-to-date information, call the local visitor centre or pick up a copy of one of the local newspapers, including the free alternative press.

Spring

Lake Tahoe WinterFest Gay & Lesbian Ski Week

South Lake Tahoe, California & Stateline, Nevada (1-877 777 4950/www.laketahoewinterfest.com). **Location** p320. **Date** early Mar.
WinterFest has become one of the top gay-themed ski festivals in North America, this decade-old event includes plenty of hook-up opportunities during dance parties, a comedy night, breakfast meetings, dinner events and shuttles to Lake Tahoe's solitary gay bar, Face. Men comprise about three-quarters of the attendees.

Return of the Swallows

Mission San Juan Capistrano (1-949 248 2048/ www.sanjuancapistrano.net). **Location** p214.
Date 19 Mar.
Every year on St Joseph's Day, the town of San Juan Capistrano celebrates the return of the swallows who spend most of the year in their mission before flying south for the winter. There's a big parade, and plenty of celebratory food and drink.

Santa Clarita Cowboy Poetry & Music Festival

Melody Ranch & Motion Picture Studio, Santa Clarita Valley, just north of Highway 14 (1-800 305 0755/1-661 286 4021/www.santa-clarita.com).
Date late Mar/early Apr.
Get out your dude ranch duds for this Western hoedown. Among the attractions are the Walk of Western Stars gala, horseback rides, a cowboy couture fashion show, a casino and plenty of cowboy comedy, poetry and chow. The festival is the only time that Gene Autry's ranch opens to the public.

Blessing of the Animals

El Pueblo de Los Angeles Historical Monument, Olvera Street, Downtown Los Angeles (1-213 625 5045/www.olvera-street.com). **Location** p108.
Date Sat before Easter.
Led by a flower-festooned cow, this procession of farm animals and pets (and their owners) winds its way down the oldest street in LA. At the end, each animal is blessed with holy water by a Roman Catholic cardinal. The celebration dates to the fourth century and honours animals' service to humanity.

St Stupid's Day Parade

Usually Justin Herman Plaza, Embarcadero, San Francisco (www.saintstupid.com). **Location** p232. **Date** 1 Apr.

Bishop Joey of the First Church of the Last Laugh gathers his disciples at noon to snake through San Francisco's Financial District before coming to a halt at the Pacific Stock Exchange. Sermons are given and everyone removes a sock as part of the Pacific Sock Exchange. The event usually ends in a sock fight.

International Teddy Bear Convention

Miners Foundry, 325 Spring Street, Nevada City (1-530 265 5804/www.teddybearcastle.com). **Location** p298. **Date** 1st wknd in Apr.

Dealers from around the country show and sell new and antique bears, and bear fanatics buy jewellery, furniture and clothing for their beloved Teddies. The Flying Teddy Bear Circus entertains the crowd and all bears are admitted free of charge.

Red Bluff Round-Up

670 Antelope Boulevard, Red Bluff (1-800 545 3500/1-530 527 1000/www.redbluffroundup.com). **Location** p293. **Date** Apr.

A week's worth of community events at this nice little Northern California town – including a bowling tournament, antiques shows, a chilli cook-off and the running of 100 rodeo horses down Main Street – culminates with ten rodeo competitions.

California Poppy Festival

Lancaster City Park, 43011 N 10th Street West, Lancaster (1-661 723 6077/www.poppyfestival.com). **Location** p174. **Date** mid to late Apr.

A party for California's state flower. Pick up a free map to the poppy hotspots or browse the arts and crafts expo, farmers' market and Celtic Market Square, which features sheep and dog demonstrations and an English tea house.

Stockton Asparagus Festival

Downtown Stockton waterfront (1-209 644 3740/ www.asparagusfest.com). **Location** p278. **Date** last wknd in Apr.

Vegetable buffs share their 'spear-it' for skinny green stalks at this three-day extravaganza. Cooking demonstrations, car and craft shows, and live performances are standard, but the biggest draw is Asparagus Alley, an open-air food court.

Ramona Pageant

Ramona Bowl, 27400 Ramona Bowl Road, Hemet (1-800 645 4465/1-909 658 3111/www.ramona pageant.com). **Date** late Apr-early May.

A picturesque amphitheatre provides the backdrop for this flamboyant play, a love story about the forbidden romance between a Mexican woman and her Native American suitor. Set in the 18th century, the production features a cast of around 400; back in the days before she was a famous starlet, Raquel Welch appeared in the title role.

Kinetic Sculpture Race. *See p57.*

Fiesta Broadway/Cinco de Mayo

Downtown Los Angeles & Universal City Walk, Los Angeles (1-310 914 0015/www.fiestabroadway.la). **Location** p108 & p115. **Date** last Sun in Apr.

Covering 36 square blocks, with crowds topping 500,000, this free fiesta lives up to its reputation as the largest Cinco de Mayo celebration in the world. The blowout of music, piñata-breaking, clowns and food celebrates the 1862 Battle of Puebla, in which an underdog Mexican army manged, against all odds, to fend off French invaders.

Fiesta Cinco de Mayo

Old Town, San Diego (1-619 260 1700/www. fiestacincodemayo.com). **Location** p73. **Date** 1st wknd in May.

This free event in Old Town attracts an average of 200,000 people a year for mariachi music, Mexican dance, food, stagecoach rides, horseback acrobatics and kids' activities. Costumed soldiers re-enact the Battle of Puebla.

Bay to Breakers Foot Race

Howard & Spear Streets, San Francisco (1-415 359 2800/www.baytobreakers.com). **Location** p239. **Date** 3rd Sun in May.

A number of sponsors encourage 70,000 athletes, weekend warriors, joggers-for-a-day and fleet-footed zanies to run to Ocean Beach from SoMa. The course is about 7.5 miles, a perfect length for most to make it without much training. The race is famous for its costumes, party atmosphere and nudity, as well as a school of runners dressed as salmon who attempt to run the course 'upstream'.

Calaveras Jumping Frog Jubilee

Town of Angels Camp (1-209 736 2561/www.frog town.org). **Location** p309. **Date** 3rd wknd in May.
Once the stuff of Mark Twain fiction, this event attracts 40,000 people to this old mining town for all the trappings of a traditional country fair: a junior livestock auction, demonstrations, carnival rides, parades and kids' activities. The culmination is the International Frog Jump Grand Finals, at which 50 hoppers vie for top prize and the chance to break Rosie the Ribeter's world record of 21ft 5¾in.

California Strawberry Festival

Strawberry Meadows of College Park, 3250 South Rose Avenue, Oxnard (1-888 288 9242/1-805 385 4739/www.strawberry-fest.org). **Location** p197. **Date** 3rd wknd in May.
On pizza, in shortcake, skewered, brewed, fried… if there's a way to eat a strawberry, it'll be found at this homage to the region's $230-million industry. Berries are sold by the pint; a strawberry shortcake eating contest, a tart toss and a 'build your own strawberry shortcake tent' add extra flavour.

World Championship Kinetic Sculpture Race

Arcata, Eureka & Ferndale (1-707 845 1717/www. kineticsculpturerace.org). **Location** pp375-377.
Date Memorial Day wknd.
People-powered rhinos, submarines and chocolate éclairs take to the streets for the original event on the kinetic sculpture racing circuit. Started here in 1969 by a local artist, the unusual three-day stage race takes sculptures through mud, sand and surf. The self-proclaimed 'triathalon of the art world' has spawned copycat races around the world, but not one of them could possibly rival the slapstick energy of the original.

Sacramento Jazz Jubilee

Various locations in Sacramento (1-916 372 5277/ www.sacjazz.com). **Location** p287. **Date** Memorial Day wknd.
Every summer Sacramento morphs into an inland New Orleans, enticing music lovers from near and far to come and worship jazz's Dixieland roots. With performances at more than 40 venues, the festival has grown since 1974 to become the largest traditional jazz festival in the country. Past performers include the Jim Cullum Jazz Band, which broadcasts live every weekend on NPR.

Summer

Pageant of the Masters

Festival of Arts, 650 Laguna Canyon Road, Laguna Beach (1-949 494 1145/www.foapom.com).
Location p121. **Date** early June-late Aug.
Classic paintings, statues and murals take on a new dimension as real people dress and pose to recreate original masterpieces. Helping to bring the works to life are a professional orchestra, live narration, intricate sets and lighting. Talk about life imitating art.

Youth in Arts Italian Street Painting Festival

Mission San Rafael Arcangel, San Rafael (1-415 457 4878/www.youthinarts.org). **Location** p214.
Date mid June.
Give some kids chalk and concrete and they'll etch a hopscotch grid. But here hundreds of Madonnari (street painters) of all ages transform the streets into a colour-splashed underfoot gallery of Renaissance and other masterpieces. Entertainment and regional cuisine round out the Italian experience.

Annual Crawdad Festival

Highway 160, Isleton (1-916 777 5880/www. crawdadfestival.org). **Location** p279. **Date** 3rd wknd in June.
More than 200,000 shellfish fanatics flock to this delta town every Father's Day weekend to chow down on some 22,000 pounds of crawdads and boogie to a packed line-up of cajun, creole and zydeco bands. According to local lore, an Isleton hotel guest inspired the crawdad festival with his stories of crawdads and Cajun music back home in Louisiana.

US Sandcastle Open

Imperial Beach, San Diego (1-619 424 6663/ www.usopensandcastle.com). **Location** p68.
Date July.
A weekend's worth of beachy fun (parades, concerts, fireworks) concludes on the Sunday with this prestigious competition. Some of the carefully carved creations are breathtaking.

Lambtown USA

May Fair Grounds, Highway 113, Dixon (www.lambtown.com). **Date** July.
Food vending booths, cooking demonstrations and a lamb barbecue cook-off are the most popular draws, and lambs lucky enough to go uneaten star in shearing competitions and livestock shows. Other activities include sheepdog trials, weaving demonstrations, craft shows and wool-dying workshops.

Books by the Bay

Yerba Buena Gardens, Mission Street, San Francisco (1-415 561 7686/www.booksbythebay.com).
Location p229. **Date** July.
San Francisco's reputation as a literary city is especially well deserved during this weekend of open-air events. You can browse booksellers' booths, attend author signings and participate in book panel discussions. There are also many kids' events.

Spirit West Coast Christian Music Festival

Laguna Seca Recreation Area, 1021 Monterey-Salinas Highway, Salinas (1-831 443 5399/www. spiritwestcoast.org). **Location** p218. **Date** July.
Upwards of 50 musical acts and comedians provide entertainment with a higher message at one of the largest Christian music festivals in the Western United States. Other activities include teachings, activities for all ages, camping and ministries. Come pitch your tent and praise the Lord.

Comic-Con International

San Diego Convention Center, San Diego (1-619 491 2478/www.comic-con.org). **Location** p68. **Date** July.
Freaks and geeks gather to pour over comics and graphic novels and rub elbows with revered illustrators and publishers. Science fiction and comic movies and their stars are a big draw.

Sawdust Art Festival

935 Laguna Canyon Road, Laguna Beach (1-949 494 3030/www.sawdustartfestival.org). **Location** p121. **Date** July-Aug.
This sawdust-strewn village is a great place to purchase one-of-a-kind paintings, jewellery, ceramics, photographs, sculptures and hand-blown glass from the artists who made them. Demonstrations, free art workshops, live entertainment and casual eateries add to the community feeling.

Sacramento French Film Festival

Crest Theatre, 1013 K Street, Sacramento (1-916 453 1723/www.afdesacramento.org). **Location** p287. **Date** mid July.
Francophiles may never mistake Sacramento for the City of Light, but for three days in July the glow coming from the Crest Theatre is purely French. Films cut across all genres: some are classics, some are new releases, and some have their one-and-only US showing in Sacramento.

Gilroy Garlic Festival

Gilroy, south of San Jose (1-408 842 1625/www.gilroygarlicfestival.com). **Date** last wknd in July.
For 25 years this food-and-wine fest has featured the 'stinking rose' of Gilroy: the garlic clove, made into every edible concoction you can imagine and plenty you can't. There are more than 100 craft booths and three stages of entertainers, including puppeteers, magicians and musicians.

US Open of Surfing

Huntington Beach Pier, Huntington Beach (1-310 473 0411/www.usopenofsurfing.com). **Location** p121. **Date** 1st wk in Aug.
America's largest pro surfing competition attracts the world's elite, who compete for big money while wowing 200,000 beach boys and girls. Heating up the festivities are live bands and a sports expo.

Nisei Week Japanese Festival

Little Tokyo, Downtown LA (1-213 687 7193/www.niseiweek.org). **Location** p108. **Date** late July/early Aug.
This eight-day event celebrates Japanese culture with displays of martial arts, tea ceremonies, flower arranging, calligraphy and more. It culminates with the coronation of the Nisei Week Queen (Nisei means the first generation of Japanese born in America).

Monterey Historic Automobile Races

Mazda Raceway Laguna Seca, 1021 Monterey-Salinas Highway, Salinas (1-831 648 5111/www.montereyhistoric.com). **Location** p218. **Date** Aug.
A must for racing history fans and vintage car buffs, this annual meet draws the crowds with hundreds of historic racing cars from makers such as Ferrari, Jaguar, Porsche, Bugatti and Maserati competing in 15 races. Fans have access to cars, drivers, owners and crews in an 'open' paddock.

Street Scene

Between PETCO Park and 14th Avenue, Downtown San Diego (www.street-scene.com). **Location** p68. **Date** late Aug.
For 20 years Street Scene has united disparate musical acts and fans for one of the largest urban music festivals in the nation. In 2004, it featured such acts as the Foo Fighters, Black Eyed Peas, Ludacris and Social Distortion. Tickets usually range somewhere between $40 and $70.

California State Fair

Cal Expo, 1600 Exposition Boulevard, Sacramento (1-916 263 3247/www.bigfun.org). **Location** p287. **Date** late Aug-early Sept.
One of the nation's largest state fairs has every staple of Americana and then some: fried Twinkies, livestock competitions, concerts, a carnival midway, horse racing, professional bull riding, extreme sports competitions and a nightly fireworks display.

Autumn

Apple Hill Season

Placer County, north of Route 50 (1-530 644 7692/www.applehill.com). **Location** p304. **Date** Labor Day wknd-mid Dec.
Two dozen orchards open their doors for apple, berry and pumpkin picking, wine tasting, craft fairs, petting zoos and music. Expect plenty of sweets and backed-up traffic. Every weekend in October, a free shuttle transports visitors from the Schnell School parking lot to most ranches.

How Berkeley Can You Be?

Downtown Berkeley (1-510 644 2204/www.howberkeleycanyoube.com). **Location** p269. **Date** mid Sept.
Berkeleyites showcase civic pride and spoof their history of political and social rabblerousing during this entertaining late-summer parade and festival. Pedal-powered bananas might share space with painted VW buses, gay cheerleading squads, a life-size petition to repeal the laws of gravity and groups of marching naked people.

Lodi Grape Festival & Harvest Fair

413 East Lockeford Street, Lodi (1-209 369 2771/www.grapefestival.com). **Date** mid Sept.
This festival highlights the rising status of Lodi, between Sacramento and Stockton, as a wine producing region. Besides wine from several dozen local vineyards, the festival has amusement rides, competitions, food booths and entertainment. Attendees willing to kick off their shoes and watch their feet turn purple can sign up for the 'grape stomp'.

Castro Street Fair

Market & Castro Street, San Francisco (1-415 285 8546/www.castrostreetfair.org). **Location** p230. **Date** early Oct.

Presenting the softer side of gay life here, this one-day fair, started in 1974 by Harvey Milk, features food, crafts and community activists' stalls, along with plenty of rainbow merchandise.

Reggae in the Park

Sharon Meadow, Golden Gate Park, San Francisco (1-415 458 1988). **Location** p238. **Date** early Oct.

You'll hear it from blocks away and smell the smoke long before you get there: RITP is quickly becoming one of the city's best-attended music festivals, mainly because it always seems to take place during the finest spells of autumn weather. It's a two-day event, and it attracts a mixed bag of artists and fans from all over the world.

Exotic Erotic Ball

Cow Palace, 2600 Geneva Avenue, Daly City (1-415 567 2255/www.exoticeroticball.com). **Date** late Oct.

It's obnoxious, it's exploitative, it's 25 years old and it's the bridge-and-tunnel crowd's annual excuse to pull on the latex and fishnets and party with other sex kittens at the world's largest indoor masquerade ball. Strippers, sideshows and a costume competition are among the tamer perks.

Día de los Muertos

Bryant & 24th Streets, Mission District, San Francisco (1-415 722 8911/www.dayofthedeadsf. org). **Location** p230. **Date** 2 Nov.

Hundreds of marchers gather each year to celebrate the Mexican Day of the Dead: expect to see Aztec dancers, hippie musicians, women in antique wedding dresses clutching bouquets of dead flowers. Ending in Garfield Square, people leave candles at a community altar. Wear dark, sombre clothes (the dressier the better) if you attend.

Doodah Parade

Around Pasadena (1-626 440 7379/www.pasadena doodahparade.com). **Location** p116. **Date** Sun before Thanksgiving.

This spoof on the Rose Bowl Parade (*see p60*) is mayhem. Basically, anyone is allowed to take part: all that's required is a strange idea and a sense of humour. Acts range from the political to the puerile; past participants have included the Synchronised Briefcase Marching Drill Team and the Spawn of Captain James T Kirk.

Run to the Far Side

Music Concourse, Golden Gate Park, San Francisco (1-415 759 2690/www.calacademy.org). **Location** p238. **Date** Sun after Thanksgiving.

Dress as your favourite Gary Larson character (cows, chickens, squid and cavemen are popular) for this annual footrace, a fundraiser for the California Academy of Sciences. Participants can walk or run three or six miles through Golden Gate Park.

Hollywood Spectacular

Around Hollywood (1-323 469 2337). **Location** p107. **Date** Sun after Thanksgiving.

The event that inspired Gene Autry to write 'Here Comes Santa Claus' is a glitzy presentation. First held in 1928, the parade features elaborate floats, pop stars and celebs, camels, equestrian shows and marching bands. Even with reserved bleacher seats, early arrival is a must, and parking is a nightmare.

Winter

Sawdust Art Festival Winter Fantasy

935 Laguna Canyon Road, Laguna Beach (1-949 494 3030/www.sawdustartfestival.org). **Location** p121. **Date** late Nov-mid Dec.

Held over four weekends between Thanksgiving and Christmas, the winter version of the summer festival features work from 200 artists, visits with Santa, a play area with real snow, free art classes, children's activities and live holiday entertainment.

The Nutcracker

War Memorial Opera House, San Francisco (1-415 865 2000/www.sfballet.org). **Location** p227. **Date** Dec.

The San Francisco Ballet, America's oldest ballet company, presents Tchaikovsky's beloved classic every holiday season. The company puts on dozens of performances, but be quick: it always sells out.

US Sandcastle Open. *See p57.*

Cheerleaders with beards? Only at the **Doodah Parade**. *See p59*.

Balboa Park December Nights

Balboa Park, San Diego (1-619 239 0512/www.
balboapark.org). **Location** p70. **Date** early Dec.
This two-day holiday festival features international
foods, music, dancing and, best of all, free admission
to the park's museums and cultural attractions. This
is likely to be the only place in the world where
you can sample traditional Swedish Christmas spe-
cialties like glogg and Swedish meatballs while
wearing sandals and a halter top.

Tournament of Roses Rose Parade

Pasadena (1-626 449 7673/www.tournamentofroses.
com). **Location** p116. **Date** 1 Jan.
The first Rose Parade in 1890 was staged to show
off California's sun-kissed climate. And it's still
going strong: with its elaborate floral floats, musical groups, marchers and horses, not to mention the
crowning of the fresh-faced Rose Queen, it's prime
entertainment (on TV or in person) for millions of
Americans ringing in the New Year.

Palm Springs International Film Festival

Palm Springs (1-800 898 7256/www.psfilmfest.org).
Location p158. **Date** Jan.
Hollywood shifts 80 miles east for one of the largest
film festivals in the country, which screens around
200 films from more than 60 countries.

Morro Bay Winter Birding Festival

Around Morro Bay (1-805 772 4467/www.morro-
bay.net). **Location** p206. **Date** 3rd wknd in Jan.
The return of wintering birds to Morro Bay is celebrated with guided tours, presentations by wildlife
photographers and researchers, and vendors selling
birdwatching supplies and paraphernalia.

Crab & Wine Days

Mendocino (1-707 462 7417/www.gomendo.com).
Location p371. **Date** late Jan.

Few people need an excuse to visit this upscale artist's
colony on the north coast, but those who do rely on
this tribute to Mendocino's ocean crop, the Dungeness
crab. The wine helps the more refined visitors forgive
themselves for eating with their hands.

Southwest Arts Festival

Empire Polo Club, Indio (1-760 347 0676/www.south
westartsfest.com). **Location** p166. **Date** last wknd in
Jan/1st wknd in Feb.
Over 200 artists peddle traditional and contemporary Southwest art including paper collage, bronze
and metal sculpture, glass, jewellery and pottery.

Napa Valley Mustard Festival

Around Napa Valley (1-707 259 9020/www.mustard
festival.com). **Location** p348. **Date** Feb-Apr.
As dazzling mustard plants blanket the fields of
Napa, the local community stages a handful of celebratory events, most of them in some way related to
food and (of course) wine.

Riverside County Fair & National Date Festival

Riverside County Fairgrounds, Indio (1-800 811
3247/www.datefest.org). **Location** p166. **Date** Feb.
Operators of this mega-fair offer camel races, alligator wrestling and an Arabian Nights Musical
Pageant. Lest anyone take the international influence too seriously, there are American-style truck
races, carnival rides and livestock exhibits aplenty.

Chinese New Year

Market Street, San Francisco (1-415 391 9680/www.
chineseparade.com). **Location** p223. **Date** Feb.
San Francisco's Chinese New Year is the biggest
event of its kind outside Asia, and the best parade
in the city. With beauty pageants, drumming, martial arts, mountains of food, endless fireworks and a
huge procession of dancing dragons, acrobats and
stilt-walkers, the party turns the city jubilant.

Southern California

Features

Southern California

Welcome to paradise.

Singer Albert Hammond famously posited that 'it never rains in Southern California'. He wasn't, strictly speaking, correct, but what's a few inches between friends? Southern California, for the most part, is every bit the sun-soaked idyll of popular cliché. Its cities sit under almost perpetual sunshine; its toughest deserts get less than five centimetres of rain a year.

Los Angeles (*see pp94-153*) is where most begin, and not without good reason. Mark Twain's dry observation that while LA is a great place to live, you wouldn't want to visit it proves only half-true, at least once you've figured out its geography and come to terms with its spreadeagled vastness. Further south, down the **Orange Country** coast and close to the Mexican border, **San Diego** (*see pp64-93*) is a more manageable size and a rather more relaxed place, content to live the easy life under brilliant blue skies and on inviting golden sands.

With only a few exceptions – chiefly, the **Coachella Valley** (*see pp158-166*) – the rest of Southern California is deserted desert, dotted with small towns but mostly as quiet as a church on Monday. Still, that's not to say there's nothing here: **Death Valley** and **Joshua Tree National Parks**, **Mojave National Preserve** and **Anza-Borrego Desert State Park** (*see pp154-176*) are endlessly fascinating. And then there's the preposterous desert Gomorrah of **Las Vegas** (*see pp177-194*): not in California, but so close – a crisp 35-mile drive from the Nevada border to the Strip – that we couldn't possibly not include it in this guide.

A brief logistical note: for the purposes of this guide, Southern California is taken to cover everything south of LA, plus the deserts to the east and north-east. **Santa Barbara**, seen as a Southern Californian town, is in the Central Coast chapter of the Central California section.

Climate

Average daily maximum and minimum temperatures in Southern California.

		San Diego	Los Angeles	Palm Springs	Death Valley	Las Vegas
Jan	max	62°F/17°C	68°F/19°C	69°F/20°C	65°F/18°C	58°F/14°C
	min	48°F/8°C	49°F/9°C	40°F/4°C	39°F/4°C	34°F/1°C
Feb	max	63°F/17°C	69°F/20°C	73°F/22°C	72°F/22°C	63°F/17°C
	min	52°F/11°C	59°F/10°C	44°F/6°C	46°F/8°C	39°F/4°C
Mar	max	64°F/18°C	69°F/20°C	79°F/26°C	80°F/27°C	69°F/20°C
	min	55°F/13°C	52°F/11°C	47°F/8°C	53°F/12°C	44°F/7°C
Apr	max	67°F/19°C	72°F/22°C	86°F/30°C	90°F/32°C	78°F/25°C
	min	56°F/13°C	54°F/12°C	52°F/11°C	62°F/17°C	51°F/10°C
May	max	69°F/20°C	74°F/23°C	94°F/34°C	99°F/37°C	88°F/31°C
	min	58°F/14°C	58°F/14°C	58°F/14°C	71°F/22°C	60°F/15°C
Jun	max	73°F/22°C	78°F/25°C	102°F/38°C	109°F/43°C	100°F/38°C
	min	61°F/16°C	61°F/16°C	64°F/18°C	80°F/27°C	69°F/20°C
July	max	77°F/25°C	84°F/28°C	108°F/42°C	115°F/46°C	106°F/41°C
	min	65°F/18°C	65°F/18°C	73°F/22°C	88°F/31°C	74°F/23°C
Aug	max	77°F/25°C	85°F/29°C	106°F/41°C	113°F/45°C	103°F/39°C
	min	66°F/19°C	65°F/18°C	71°F/21°C	85°F/29°C	74°F/23°C
Sep	max	79°F/26°C	83°F/28°C	102°F/38°C	106°F/41°C	95°F/35°C
	min	63°F/17°C	65°F/18°C	66°F/19°C	75°F/24°C	66°F/19°C
Oct	max	72°F/22°C	79°F/26°C	91°F/32°C	92°F/33°C	82°F/28°C
	min	59°F/10°C	60°F/15°C	57°F/13°C	62°F/17°C	54°F/12°C
Nov	max	67°F/19°C	72°F/22°C	79°F/26°C	76°F/24°C	67°F/19°C
	min	56°F/13°C	53°F/11°C	48°F/8°C	48°F/9°C	43°F/6°C
Dec	max	63°F/17°C	68°F/19°C	70°F/21°C	65°F/18°C	58°F/14°C
	min	52°F/11°C	49°F/9°C	42°F/5°C	39°F/4°C	34°F/1°C

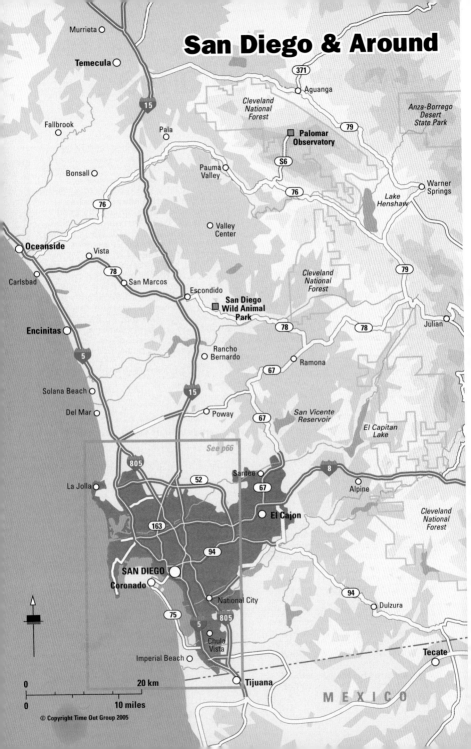

San Diego & Around

San Diego & Around

Welcome to the land of sunny Southern California dreaming.

Be beside the seaside.

San Diego

According to its official motto, San Diego is 'America's Finest City'. The boast isn't as wild as it might seem. San Diego is more manageable than Los Angeles and more approachable than San Francisco, and though it's also far less charismatic than either, few locals mind. The town still has its winning combination of sun and surf, but the cranes and building scaffolds hugging the skyline bear testament to the fact that its popularity is growing.

Still, while it's the seventh largest city in the US, San Diego doesn't feel crowded... yet. With the help of local preservationists, the new Downtown is incorporating existing historical buildings into new structures: the historic Western Metal Supply Building, for example, forms part of PETCO Park, the recently completed new home of the town's major league baseball team, the San Diego Padres.

The city's location has resulted in a culture that's heavily influenced by Mexico, with Spanish almost as widely spoken among its citizens as English. The city's Mexican and Spanish heritage is celebrated throughout the city in everything from street names to the preservation of the area's missions.

HISTORY

Humans settled this area perhaps 20,000 years ago, but San Diego's history is usually counted from the arrival of Juan Rodríguez Cabrillo on 28 September 1542, somewhere near Ballast Point in Point Loma. Although the area was home to up to 20,000 residents, mostly Indian tribes, Cabrillo claimed the area for the King of Spain and called it San Miguel. It was not until 40 years later, when Sebastián Vizcaíno was sent north from Mexico by Spain to survey and map the harbour and shoreline, that the city was renamed after Spanish saint San Diego de Alcalá. The first steps towards establishing what we now know as the city of San Diego took place on 16 July 1769, when the recently arrived Father Junípero Serra blessed Presidio Hill as the site of San Diego de Alcalá Mission, California's first Spanish mission.

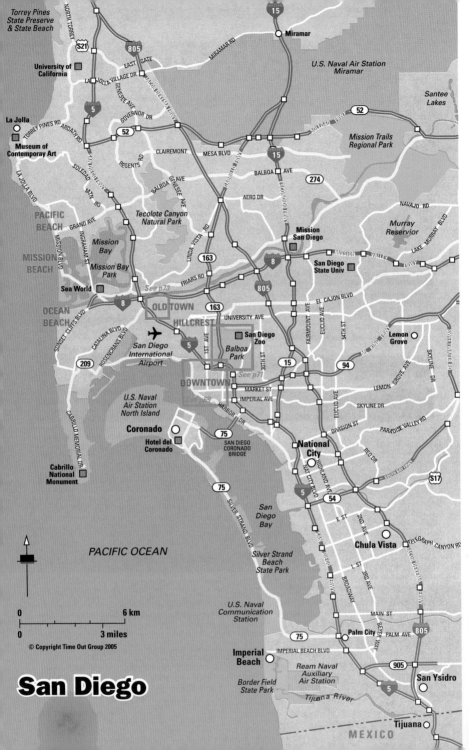

In 1821, following years of war, Mexico won its independence from Spain; over the next few years, families began building homes a little south of the Presidio, in what is now known as Old Town. The Presidio gradually fell out of regular use; the status of San Diego was changed from Mission to Pueblo (town) on 1 January 1835. The US flag was raised in San Diego by a marine detachment on 29 July 1846, but locals had to wait until 9 September 1850 for California to be admitted into the Union.

Also in 1850, William Heath Davis attempted to build a new San Diego nearer the waterfront. Where Davis failed, Alonzo Erastus Horton succeeded: steaming in from San Francisco on 15 April 1867, Horton purchased the waterfront site that provided the basis for the San Diego of today. The late 1800s proved to be a boom time in San Diego, particularly with the arrival of the first transcontinental railroad in 1886. Two years later construction started on the Hotel del Coronado (see p87) and, in 1892, John D Spreckels bought the city's transportation system, his first step in building an empire that would include the San Diego & Arizona Railroad, unveiled in 1919.

The Panama-California International Exposition of 1915-16, which celebrated the opening of the Panama Canal, proved crucial for the town. Nearly three million attended the event over two years; but, more importantly, the Exposition's fabulous new buildings made Balboa Park a glorious public amenity. Civic pride was also boosted in 1927, when Charles Lindbergh became the first person to cross the Atlantic in a non-stop flight from New York to Paris using a plane, the *Spirit of St Louis*, built in San Diego by Claude Ryan.

By 1917 San Diego was clearly developing into a military town. Rockwell Field and the Naval Air Station on North Island, in Coronado, were already open; within the year, Camp Kearny, through which thousands of GIs would pass, had been established and the construction of both the US Marine Base in Point Loma and the Naval Hospital in Balboa Park was under way. San Diego's reputation as a military town was confirmed in the 1940s by the opening of the naval Air Station and the purchase of Camp Pendleton, adjacent to Oceanside, as the site of a new marine base. Even those with misgivings about the military acknowledge the purchase was fortuitous: the area used for manoeuvres is today practically the only open space along I-5 between the border with Mexico and the northern tip of LA. The town grew further with the arrival of the Salk Institute in 1963. Based in La Jolla, the firm spearheaded what would become San Diego's major industries: software development and scientific and medical research.

The best San Diego

Things to do
You could spend several days just visiting the plethora of excellent museums in **Balboa Park** (see p70). Once you have, ddrive on out to **Coronado** (see p74) for a spell winding down on the beach. If you've kids, you're going to end up at **Legoland** (see p89) or **SeaWorld** (see p76) whether you like it or not. The olde worlde town of **Julian** (see p91) offers a dramatic change of pace, particularly outside summer season.

Places to stay
If you've money to burn, you can't beat the **Hotel del Coronado** (see p87), although **Prava** (see p86) is more stylish and central.

Places to eat
You're not short of options here. For a hearty breakfast, try the **Big Kitchen** (see p78) or the **Broken Yolk** (see p80), while the comfort food lunches at the **City Delicatessen** are always tasty (see p79). **Kitima** (see p79) also has good lunch specials. For dinner, try the **Gaslamp Stripclub** (see p78), **Bertrand at Mr A's** (see p78), chic **Chive** (see p77) or, for a real blowout, **Star of the Sea** (see p78).

Nightlife
For dance music, don't miss **On Broadway** (see p82) or **E Street Alley** (see p83). Rock fans should check the line-ups at the **Casbah** (see p85); jazz fans of all ages will love **Dizzy's** (see p85). The town's gay and lesbian scene is centred around **Hillcrest** (see p82).

Culture
Theatre is prominent here; highly respected venues include the **Old Globe Theatre** (see p85) in Balboa Park, and two Coronado theatres, the **Coronado Playhouse** and the and **Lamb's Players Theatre** (see p85).

Sports & activities
Sedentary athletes should make tracks to PETco Park, the shiny new Downtown home of the **San Diego Padres** baseball team (see p68). Those of a more active bent should note the presence of several worthwhile if less than strenuous walking trails in **Palomar Mountain State Park** (see p92), but the real sport here is the **surfing** (see p90 Surf's up).

Southern California

The last couple of decades have seen explosive building growth throughout the city, with skyscrapers seemingly sprouting up overnight, and a population boom to match. The jury is out on when more will become too much, with the city struggling to keep its identity intact as it absorbs new residents. Yet San Diego still has lots to offer, most noticeably an uncommon friendliness: citizens seem proud of their city and keen to share it with visitors.

Sightseeing

That San Diego takes tourism seriously is hardly surprising: it is, after all, the county's main industry. Bordered by Camp Pendleton to the north, Mexico to the south and the ocean to the west, **San Diego County** has a culturally mixed population. There's also the bonus of geography varied enough to make it possible, during winter months, to spend the morning in the snows of Julian before catching a wave and copping some sunburn in La Jolla.

Downtown

Downtown San Diego has been in the grip of a building boom for the past decade or thereabouts, with no end in sight. Luckily, local preservationists have been able to save some of the most notable 19th-century buildings. The result is a mix of the ultra-modern with remnants of the town's Wild West days. Happily, the combination works.

Set on the waterfront, Downtown is very pedestrian-friendly. Much of the neighbourhood activity centres along 5th Avenue, below Broadway and east of 16th Street; with lettered streets running east to west and numbered streets north to south, it's very easy to navigate. On top of its status as a tourist hotspot, though, Downtown is a flourishing business district, and the difference between its population during and after work can be as different as… well, day and night.

THE GASLAMP QUARTER

Long-time San Diego residents remember when the **Gaslamp Quarter**, boundaried by Broadway, 6th Street, Harbor Drive and 4th Street, was a sleazy neighbourhood. Built in the 19th century, the area had fallen on hard times by the 1970s. But the mid 1980s construction of **Horton Plaza**, a complex of shops spread over six lavish open-air levels that was conceived by Jon Jerde (who went on to design CityWalk at Universal Studios), signalled both a burst of building activity and a dramatic change in character.

To an extent, the Gaslamp Quarter is an illusion. A great deal of the street furniture here, such as the brick sidewalks and the mock-Victorian streetlamps from which the locale takes its name, is actually modern; many of the buildings, conversely, are original. The skill is that you can't always see the join. Also original, incidentally, are the Gaslamp Quarter's few remaining lowlifes, who've miraculously managed to survive the redevelopment and still gather in small pockets of the neighbourhood. But they're now outnumbered by tourists, who gather here to eat, drink and be merry in the area's myriad smart bars and restaurants.

An entertaining walking tour of the Gaslamp Quarter is available from the Gaslamp Historical Foundation docents on Saturdays, beginning at **William Heath Davis House** (410 Island Avenue, 1-619 233 4692, www.gaslamp.org). Built in 1850 and believed to be haunted (*see p74* **San Diego spooks**), the house is the oldest surviving structure in the new Downtown. Conducted by a guide dressed in period garb, the tour takes in such gems as the 1888 **Louis Bank of Commerce**, with its twin towers, and the Chinese-influenced roof and façade of the 1913 **Lincoln Hotel**. Sports fans will head, instead, for **PETCO Park**: opened in 2004 and home to the San Diego Padres baseball team, it dominates the skyline along 7th Avenue and has certainly added extra pep to Downtown. Call 1-619 795 5011 or check www.padres.com for game tickets or tour information.

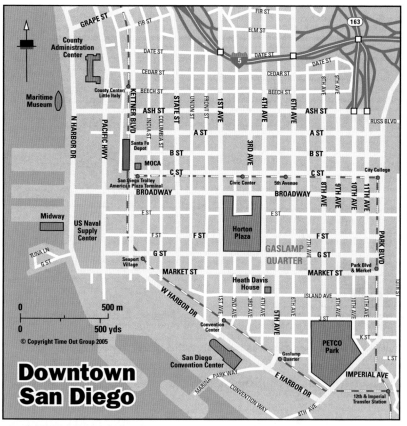

Downtown San Diego

© Copyright Time Out Group 2005

TOWARDS THE WATERFRONT

Moving west on Broadway, just a stone's throw from the waterfront stands one of San Diego's most recognisable landmarks, the **Santa Fe Depot** (1050 Kettner Boulevard). Constructed in 1915 for the Panama-California International Exposition, it's still one of the town's most important travel hubs, with Amtrak, the Coaster and the San Diego Trolley all stopping here. Built in Spanish Mission-Colonial Revival style, with twin towers looming at the south entrance, it certainly makes a striking introduction to the city and provides an excellent contrast with the **Museum of Contemporary Art** (1001 Kettner Boulevard, 1-619 234 1001, www.mcasd.org) across the street. Located in a futuristic two-storey building, it's the sister museum to the original venue in La Jolla (*see p77*), and focuses on Latin American art;

a major multimedia event on the first Thursday of each month combines music, art and film.

Continue west on Broadway and you'll reach the tree-lined pathways of the **Embarcadero**. It's very popular with the city's jogging population, but it's a scenic journey at any speed, offering panoramic views of the city and with numerous reminders of San Diego's naval history along the way. The excellent **Maritime Museum** (*see p70*) has recently been joined by **Midway: San Diego's Aircraft Carrier Museum** (*see p70*), but some visitors choose to experience San Diego's water at closer quarters. **San Diego Harbor Excursions** (1050 N Harbor Drive, 1-619 234 4111, www.harborexcursion.com) offers one- and two-hour tours from Broadway Pier, taking in all the nautical sights along the coast; the 15-minute Bay Ferry to Coronado (*see p74*), run by the same company, is a more practical and considerably cheaper alternative. A mile or so south, you'll find the shoppers' paradise of **Seaport Village** (*see p83*).

Maritime Museum

1492 N Harbor Drive (1-619 234 9153/ www.sdmaritime.com). **Open** 9am-8pm daily. **Admission** $8; $5-$6 discounts; free under 5s. **Credit** AmEx, Disc, MC, V.

The *Star of India*, a tall ship built in 1863, may be impressive standing in dock, but it's still an active vessel: sailed once a year, it is the world's oldest ship still in service. Other vessels on display include the 1898 steam ferry *Berkeley*, the 1904 steam yacht *Medea* and the 1914 harbour boat *Pilot*.

Midway

910 N Harbor Drive (1-619 544 9600/www.midway. org). **Open** 10am-5pm daily. **Admission** $13; $7-$10 discounts; free under-6s. **Credit** AmEx, MC, V.

Opening in June 2004, San Diego's newest attraction is within the aircraft carrier USS *Midway*: commissioned for the US Navy in 1945, it continued in service until after the first Gulf War. Complete with restored aircraft, flight simulators and more than 35 exhibits, the *Midway* also hosts fascinating ship tours, many led by men who served on the ship.

Balboa Park

The jewel of San Diego, lush **Balboa Park** (www.balboapark.org) covers around 1,200 acres (just under five square kilometres) at the north end of Downtown. It's possible to spend

a week here exploring a quite staggering variety of attractions: 85 cultural institutions, 15 museums, one of the best zoos in the world… and we're just getting started.

The seeds for the park were planted in 1868 when the city put the land aside for public use. Horticulturalist Kate Sessions had begun planting trees here by 1892, establishing the park's long history of supporting botanical wonders, but it wasn't until 1910 that the park was named, as the result of a competition, after the Spanish explorer Vasco Núñez de Balboa. Many of the buildings that line the Prado were built for the 1915 Panama-California International Exposition, including Cabrillo Bridge, the Spreckels Organ Pavilion and the Botanical Gardens; the California-Pacific International Exposition, held here two decades later, spurred on a fresh wave of buildings, among them the impressive Old Globe Theatre, the Starlight Bowl Theatre and the United Nations Building. The resulting mix of fine architecture and beautiful plants was deemed exotic enough for the park to play the protagonist's 'Florida' mansion Xanadu in the 1941 film *Citizen Kane*.

Start at the park's west entrance, heading along Laurel Street, across the Cabrillo Bridge, until it becomes the park's main street, El Prado. Here you'll find the first swathe of impressive museums, of which the most important is the **San Diego Museum of Art** (*see p72*).

Sail away: the *Star of India* docked at the **Maritime Museum**.

At the opposite end of the street, and a million miles away in intent, the **Reuben H Fleet Science Center** (*see p72*) lies next to the park's signature fountain. The park's main attraction, though, is slightly north of here, past the **Balboa Park Miniature Railroad** (*see p72*) and the octogenarian **Carousel** (1889 Zoo Place, 1-619 460 9000); entertaining visitors to the park since 1922, it's one of the few remaining carousels that still has a brass ring game (grab the ring, get a free ride). The carved animals on it are delightful, but it's the real things inside the **San Diego Zoo** (*see p72*) that most people are here to see.

Strolling back from the zoo towards the middle of the park, you'll come across the **Spanish Village Art Center** (1770 Village Place, 1-619 233 9050, www. spanishvillageart.com), off whose cobbled courtyard work an array of artists. The small cottages do create a village feel, although the 'village' is juxtaposed with a view of the glass-encased rear entrance to the **San Diego Natural History Museum** (1788 El Prado, 1-619 232 3821, www.sdnhm.org, $5-$9), which houses over seven million specimens from such fields of study as mineralogy, ornithology and entomology over more than 90,000 square feet (8,360 square metres) of gallery space. Keeping on El Prado, you'll come to the **Museum of Photographic Arts** (1649 El Prado, 1-619 238 7559, www.mopa.org, $4-$6), which shows works by filmmakers alongside renowned photographers. The **San Diego Hall of Champions** (2131 Pan American Plaza, 1-619 234 2544, www.sdhoc.com, $3-$6) houses sports memorabilia relating to the many famed figures who have emerged from the San Diego area.

At the park's south end, next to the Starlight Bowl, is the **San Diego Aerospace Museum** (*see p72*). Vehicles of a smaller nature are to be found in the **San Diego Automotive Museum** (2080 Pan American Plaza, 1-619 231 2886, www.sdautomuseum. org, $3-$7), where the hot wheels include a one-of-a-kind 1966 Bizzarrini, a 1924 Ford Model T Speedster and a collection of vintage

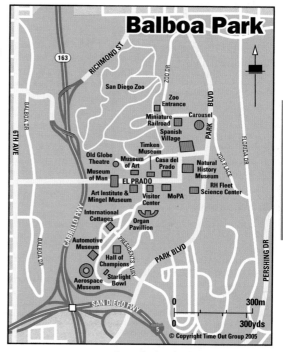

motorcycles and related ephemera. For music fans, the must-see is the **Spreckels Organ Pavilion**, which houses one of the world's largest outdoor pipe organs. Free organ concerts are held every Sunday at 2pm, but performers of all different kinds of art also use the 2,400-seat space. One of San Diego's finest theatres is also here: the **Old Globe Theatre** (*see p85*).

The park is exceptionally well maintained and, despite its initially daunting size, it's very walkable (there is also the option of a free tram, which runs every ten minutes). Food is plentiful, from roving ice-cream vendors to fine dining at the **Prado** (*see p78*), but you'd do well to bring a picnic and settle down in the area by the pond in front of the **Botanical Gardens**, a great spot for people-watching. Budget-minded visitors will want to take advantage of Balboa Park's 'Free Tuesdays' programme, which offers gratis admission to a selection of the park's museums on a monthly rotating basis. For more details on the park, call or visit the **Balboa Park Visitors Center** (1549 El Prado #1, 1-619 239 0512, www.balboapark.org), which is open daily and can provide park maps and other literature.

Hillcrest.

Lindbergh's locally-built *Spirit of St Louis* provides a contrast to the latest permanent exhibit on the Apollo space mission.

San Diego Museum of Art

1450 El Prado, at Laurel Street (1-619 232 7931/ www.sdmart.org). **Open** 10am-6pm Tue, Wed, Fri-Sun; 10am-9pm Thur. **Admission** $9; $4-$7 discounts; free under-6s. **Credit** MC, V.

The San Diego Museum of Art opened in 1926 and now supplements its sizeable and wide-ranging permanent collection (which includes Spanish and Dutch Masters, 20th-century paintings and sculpture and over 4,000 pieces of Asian art) with some high-profile temporary shows.

San Diego Zoo

2920 Zoo Drive, at Park Boulevard (1-619 234 3153/www.sandiegozoo.org). **Open** 9am-4pm daily. **Admission** $21; $14 discounts; free under-3s. **Credit** AmEx, MC, V.

Widely renowned for its work in animal conservation, the 100-acre San Diego Zoo employs pioneering techniques to create naturalistic habitats and themed areas for its residents, which include more than 4,000 rare and endangered animals. The result is a series of exhibits that together add up to the next best thing to being out in the wild. It's easy to see why the zoo has a reputation as one of the world's best.

The pandas are the zoo's most popular exhibit; visit them early to avoid the crowds. Other highlights include Tiger River, which gets you up close to hippos, okapis and tigers in a jungle setting, and the Polar Bear Plunge, with split-level viewing that allows delighted visitors to watch the bears cavort underwater. Marvel at the Rainforest Aviary; check out Gorilla Tropics, complete with its own waterfall; and be sure not to miss the flying fox enclosure and reptile house. The children's zoo appeals to kids for its petting zoo and animal hospital, and to adults for its place in pop culture history as the zoo featured on the cover of the Beach Boys' album *Pet Sounds*. The calming hummingbird aviary is the best place to avoid the crowds, and do notice the fabulous plant life: the San Diego Zoo is an accredited botanical garden in its own right. The animal shows tend to be educational: don't expect bears on unicycles.

To start, it's worth taking a 40-minute bus tour of the zoo's highlights, or the aerial Skytram gondola system that crosses the park. But after that, you're on your own, so wear comfortable shoes. During the summer, hours extend until after dark, appealing as many animals are most active at night. Dining options range from burgers to pricier sit-down restaurants, but even if you're not hungry, check the spectacular views from the Treehouse Café, which looks out over the treetops into Downtown.

Balboa Park Miniature Railroad

2885 Zoo Place, at Park Boulevard (1-619 231 1515 ext 4219). **Open** 11am-4.30pm Sat, Sun; also Mon-Fri during school holidays. **Admission** $1.75. **Credit** MC, V.

In operation since 1948, the Balboa Park Miniature Railroad is now operated by the zoo's transportation department. Holding 48 passengers, the 1:5 scale train runs only a three-minute circuit.

Reuben H Fleet Science Center

1875 El Prado, at Village Place (1-619 238 1233/ www.rhfleet.org). **Open** 9.30am-5pm Mon-Thur; 9.30am-9pm Fri; 9.30am-8pm Sat; 9.30am-6pm Sun. **Admission** $6.75; $5.50-$6 discounts; free under-3s. **Credit** MC, V.

An interactive experience containing more than 100 hands-on exhibits over two levels. The deep-sea simulator ride is popular, but the real point of pride is the domed theatre, used both as a planetarium and an IMAX cinema.

San Diego Aerospace Museum

2001 Pan American Plaza, at President's Way (1-619 234 8291/www.aerospacemuseum.org). **Open** *Summer* 10am-5.30pm. *Fall-spring* 10am-4.30pm daily. **Admission** $9; $4-$7 discounts; free under-6s. **Credit** MC, V.

Seeking to preserve San Diego's place in aviation history, the striking Aerospace Museum puts equal emphasis on those who flew or built the machines and on the aircraft themselves. Its round building is filled with all manner of planes, helicopters and spacecraft, arranged in well thought-out and evocative displays. A replica of

Hillcrest & Mission Valley

Hillcrest, located a short drive north of Downtown, is the heart of San Diego's gay and lesbian community (*see p82*), as well as a focal point for the local arts brigade. It's one of San Diego's trendier areas, though it's still hardly edgy; the locals are just too nice and mellow for such cosmopolitan shenanigans. There's nothing much to see here, but there are plenty of places to shop, especially for used clothes and books (*see p83*), and a good few spots in which to eat and drink. The neighbourhood is centred around the junction of University and 5th Avenues; once you've found a place to park, which isn't as easy as it might sound, an agreeable afternoon and evening can be spent pootling around from bookstore to bar to diner.

Just a short trip down the hill to the north, **Mission Valley** is one of San Diego's busiest commercial zones, and contains one of the city's best-kept secrets. An oasis in the concrete desert, the San Diego River runs the length of the valley, with the **San Diego River Park** (4891 Pacific Highway, Suite 114, 1-619 297 7380, www.sandiegoriver.org) a great place for hiking, birdwatching or just getting away from the urban tumult. **San Diego de Alcalá Mission** (10818 San Diego Mission Road, 1-619 281 8849, www.missionsandiego.com), founded in 1769 and the first mission in California, is also here. It's open daily, but you'll need to book ahead to join one of the tours.

Old Town & Mission Hills

Celebrating San Diego's origins, the living museum known as **Old Town State Historical Park** (1-619 220 5422, www.parks.ca.gov) preserves, recreates and celebrates San Diego life between 1821, when the Mexicans settled here, and 1872, when fire destroyed much of the area. The park contains almost two dozen historic buildings (some original, some reconstructed), all of which are open to the public and none of which charges admission; pick up a map from the visitor centre in the 150-year-old **Robinson-Rose House** (4002 Wallace Street), which also contains a model of the park and offers details on the regular tours. Note that the park can get overrun with schoolkids at times.

Among the sites worth exploring within the park are the **Seeley Stables**, named for the gentleman responsible for the city's mail and stagecoach services between 1867 and 1871. You'll find two floors of transportation items here, ranging from carriages to wagons, as well as ephemera such as saddles and slot machines. The displays of historical work implements at **Black Hawk Smithy & Stable** are also worth a stop, especially on demonstration days, whereas you can see how a typical family lived at the time (a wealthy one, at least) in **La Casa de Estudillo**. The

Mormon Battalion Memorial (2510 Juan Street, 1-619 298 3317, www.mormonbattalion.com) commemorates the longest march in military history, a 2,000-mile trek from Iowa to San Diego in 1846.

Still, Old Town is no dry re-creation; while not quite a living, breathing neighbourhood in its own right, it still has more life to it than other such historic enterprises. Many cultural events are held here (including one of the city's biggest events, Fiesta Cinco de Mayo; *see p56*); the shops of the Bazaar del Mundo (*see p84*) and a handful of restaurants, while certainly touristy, do liven things up.

The surrounding area also has numerous sites that are worth investigating, not least among them the **Heritage Park Victorian Village** (*see p74*) and, just up the hill from Old Town, Presidio Park (2811 Jackson Street). The **Junípero Serra Museum** (*see p74*) is here, surrounded by a lush green park with great views of Mission Bay and Point Loma. It's an excellent place for a picnic and there are several hiking trails.

Perched on the hills above Old Town from which it takes its name, **Mission Hills** is a quiet neighbourhoods. In many ways not much has changed here in the 19th century, with preservation of the magnificent, century-old homes a major concern. The main shopping and dining stretches can be found along Goldfinch and Washington Streets. Also adding to the community's historic flavour, **Pioneer Park** (aka Graveyard Park) is a popular picnic site, the resident tombstones creating a certain unique character (*see p74* **San Diego spooks**).

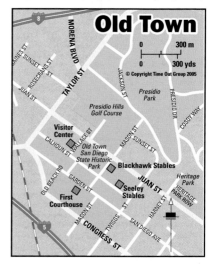

Heritage Park Victorian Village

2450 Heritage Park Row, at Hamey Street (1-858 694 3049/www.sdcounty.ca.gov). **Open** 8am-5pm daily. **Admission** free. **No credit cards.**

Heritage Park features seven homes, built between 1887 and 1896, that were moved here by local preservationists, mostly in the 1940s. In pleasantly landscaped surroundings, these homes have been completely restored; they are now used for wedding receptions, with two offering bed and breakfast.

Junípero Serra Museum

2727 Presidio Drive, Presidio Park (1-619 297 3258/ www.sandiegohistory.org). **Open** 10am-4.30pm Fri-Sun. **Admission** $5; $2 discounts; free under-6s. **No credit cards.**

Perched on a hillside, on the site of the first Spanish settlement in what was to become California, this museum contains historical displays and artefacts, including a large wine press. It is also an active archaeological site, which means that artefacts are still being unearthed.

Coronado

Though it makes great play of its isolation, the exclusive enclave of **Coronado Island** is technically not an island at all; rather, it's a peninsula. Nor is it all as picture-book pretty as it first appears: while the southern tip might be swanky, the north-western edge is dominated

by the North Island Naval Air Station. Still, most visitors will see only the glossy side of this small, ageing community: its carefully manicured lawns and parks, its proliferation of historic buildings, and the clean, serene **Silver Strand State Beach**. It certainly feels a world away from the city across the harbour.

The journey here is half the fun. Drivers get to ride in over the **Coronado Bay Bridge**, which soars spectacularly over the water; pedestrians and cyclists take the Bay Ferry, which leaves San Diego's Broadway Pier twice hourly. Once here, head for **Orange Avenue**, where you'll find a large proportion of the town's restaurants and shops.

Coronado's main attraction is the decidedly luxe **Hotel del Coronado** (*see p87*); cultural highlights include two well-respected repertory theatres (*see p85*), as well as monthly outdoor events that range from summer concerts to holiday parades. However, most come simply for the sun and the outdoor activities, which include great fishing and boating, and miles of hiking and biking trails around the beaches.

Point Loma

As the area where Spanish explorers most likely first set foot in San Diego, **Point Loma** looms large in the area's history. A large

San Diego spooks

Few places in San Diego are quite as grand as the **Hotel del Coronado** (*see p87*). But few places are quite as spooky. The hotel is inhabited by multiple ghosts: rooms 3502 and 3312 are said to be haunted by the spirits of two pregnant women who committed suicide in the late 1800s; other sightings have included a pair of small children, a caretaker and, dancing alone in the ballroom, a Victorian woman.

Cross the Coronado Bay Bridge into the Gaslamp Quarter and you'll find the **Horton Grand** (*see p85*), also popular with ghost hunters. Plagued by several spirits, the hotel even keeps a flyer on the subject ready at the front desk to sate the curiosity of inquisitive visitors. Room 309 seems to be the centre of supernatural activity, but guests have reported strange encounters throughout the building, including the sighting of a man dressed in Western clothing. Nearby **William Heath Davis House** (*see p68*), built in 1850 and one of the oldest structures in what is now Downtown, also has a spooky resident.

It's not Davis, who never occupied the house himself, but a Victorian lady who did once live here and now seems most reluctant to leave. It is claimed that on one occasion, she even started one of the tours of the building.

Heading north into Old Town, **Whaley House** (2482 San Diego Avenue, 1-619 297 751, www.whaleyhouse.org) was built on the site of a public gallows and is rumoured to have been recognised as haunted by no less authority than the US government. Many spirits have been experienced here, including a crying baby and a small dog, sometimes seen wandering the house and yard.

One way to take in San Diego's supernatural activity is on the two-hour **Ghosts and Graveyards Trolley Tour** (4010 Twiggs Street, Old Town, 1-619 298 8687). The trolley departs at twilight and includes a stop at **Pioneer Park** (1501 Washington Place, Mission Hills). The place looks innocent enough, but it was built on the site of a 19th-century cemetery, and now bears the nickname Graveyard Park...

Llama rides on **Ocean Beach**.

portion of the waterfront is used by the military – Point Loma Nazarene College is here – but what's left includes some of the most beautiful coastal scenery in San Diego.

At Point Loma's western end, you'll find **Shelter Island**. A shoreline park runs the entire south side of its access road, Shelter Island Drive. The north side is largely the domain of resort hotels, but the park itself offers trails, a great view of San Diego Harbor, and the **Tunaman's Memorial** (at the southwest end of the island) and a **Friendship Bell** (1401 Shelter Island Drive), the latter given to San Diego by the city of Yokohama in 1958.

Leaving the island and heading west, you'll pass through residential and business districts, as well as government buildings, none of which seems very promising. But press on to Point Loma's highest altitudes and the scenery makes a marked improvement. Here you'll also find one of San Diego's most striking locations: **Fort Rosecrans National Cemetery**, a beautiful if sombre tribute to the city's military heritage. The area was a burial ground as early as 1847, but became an army cemetery in 1860.

Moving past the summit on the cliffs above the Pacific, you'll enter the 160-acre **Cabrillo National Monument** (1800 Cabrillo Memorial Drive, 1-619 557 5450, www.nps.gov/cabr). It's named to commemorate the arrival of Juan Rodriguez Cabrillo here in 1542, but most come simply to enjoy the incredible view of

the harbour and surrounding ocean: it's a favourite spot for watching whales during their annual migration between December and February. The park's defining feature is the **Old Point Loma Lighthouse**, which was built in 1854 at 422 feet (129 metres) above sea level but put out of commission 35 years later. However, it's been preserved pretty much as it was in the 1800s, and now has a few displays on its history. Hiking the paths surrounding the park will take you past remains of the coastal defences erected in World Wars I and II. Locals love to head down the steep winding road on the park's western side to the marine nature reserve at the bottom, where there are tidal pools to explore.

Ocean Beach, Mission Beach & Pacific Beach

Ocean Beach, six miles north of Point Loma, was once home to a number of Portuguese fishermen, who worked the waters and lived in beachside huts. It's grown a little more affluent since then, but it's still a scruffy spot. For that, we can blame (or thank) the surfers, who loaf around the bars, restaurants, tattoo parlours and surf shops of **Newport Avenue**. North of Ocean Beach Pier are Dog Beach, so called because it is one of the few beaches on which dogs are permitted to run off the leash, and the equally nicely named Sunset Cliffs.

Food with flair at **Chive**. *See p77.*

The name of both the community and its shoreline, similarly surfer-friendly **Mission Beach** to the north offers visitors clean, wide sandy beaches, manicured parks and ample parking on all but the biggest holidays. It's also San Diego's most traditional boardwalk, recently widened to allow two-way traffic (top speed 8mph) of the bike, in-line skates and pedestrian varieties. The boardwalk is lined with typical beach community shops, restaurants and nightclubs, as is the area's main thoroughfare, Mission Boulevard.

It's **Belmont Park** (3146 Mission Boulevard, 1-858 228 9283, www.belmontpark. com), though, that really sets this piece of the waterfront apart. Built in 1925, this amusement park went through a long period of disrepair, but today it's a treasured landmark, extensively refurbished in recent years. The standout attraction is the scary, spectacular and all-wooden **Giant Dipper Rollercoaster** (1-858 488 1549, www.giantdipper.com). The new Flowrider wave platform also makes Belmont Park a must for surfers; creating a machine that simulates the ocean might seem a little odd when there's real surf a few feet away, but these man-made waves are ideal for honing skills. Also on Mission Bay is **Sea World** (*see below*), one of San Diego's main draws.

The boardwalk that begins in Mission Beach runs north to the almost stereotypically Californian neighbourhood of **Pacific Beach**. After Downtown, the area boasts San Diego's highest concentration of bars, clubs and restaurants, as well as plenty of palm trees and the most popular beach in San Diego.

Visited by 20 million people a year, its combination of ocean and nightlife seems well nigh irresistible.

The area is a casual place, but does have something of a split personality. The informal eateries are crowded during daylight with swimsuited out-of-towners, but nights see the roughly ten-block area west of Mission Boulevard fill up with barhoppers. In particular, **Garnet Avenue** can be a sea of people, with surf dudes and the babes that love them hanging around the pool halls and drinking dens. The beach itself is a wide sandy expanse, highlighted by the large gateway arch of the **Crystal Pier** (4500 Ocean Boulevard, 1-800 748 5894, www.crystalpier.com), which houses a hotel over the water but can also be accessed for the fishing or the view.

SeaWorld

500 Sea World Drive, Mission Bay (1-619 226 3901/www.seaworld.com). **Open** *Summer* 9am-10pm daily. *Winter* 10am-5pm daily. Hours vary; call to confirm. **Admission** $49.75; $39.75 discounts; free under-3s. **Credit** AmEx, Disc, MC, V.

While SeaWorld ranks alongside San Diego Zoo (*see p72*) as the city's main attraction, this is by far the more commercial enterprise. Dedicated to marine life, SeaWorld does rescue and care for injured animals, but recent years have seen the park become far more entertainment-oriented, with the addition of 3-D movies and water rides, performances from acrobats and even kiddie pop shows.

Still, it's trained animal shows that remain SeaWorld's mainstay. The park's mascot is killer whale Shamu, who shows off several times a day: the first 14 rows get soaked, so come prepared. The

Fools with Tools show is popular, using otters, sea lions and a walrus to act out a parody of television DIY shows, and children love Shamu's Happy Harbor, with contraptions, slides and a ball pond.

There's no shortage of adult-oriented fun, at least if you don't mind getting wet. Rides include Shipwreck Rapids, which transports nine passengers through watery obstacles; two recently added highlights are a new rollercoaster, Journey to Atlantis, and Wild Arctic, a motion-sensor ride that 'transports' guests to a series of animal enclosures. The park is also home to rescued manatees, otters, sharks and the Penguin Encounter, whose chilled interior and moving sidewalk are particularly popular on hot summer days; more prosaically, the Anheuser-Busch Hospitality Center offers its world-famous Clydesdale Horses and regular beer-making demonstrations. The park's peak season is summer; the winter months are far less crowded.

La Jolla & Torrey Pines

The Beverly Hills of San Diego, La Jolla is a village nestled on the coast around ten minutes north of Downtown. Surrounded by the high-end houses of Mount Soledad, **Prospect Street** is the heart of the community, bustling with restaurants, pricey boutiques and most of the 30-plus art galleries to be found in the area. It makes for an interesting juxtaposition of people, with an older, affluent crowd mixing with younger (if still pretty upscale) hipsters. The **Museum of Contemporary Art** (700 Prospect Street, 1-858 454 3541, www.mcasd. org, closed Wed, $2-$6; *see also p69*) features more than 3,000 post-1950 works, including impressive collections of pop and Latin American art. There's also a sculpture garden, the Sherwood Auditorium (for both films and live performances) and great ocean views.

Just one street west of the crowded sidewalks of Prospect Street, you'll find some of the most stunning coastal scenery in San Diego. The cliffwalk near favourite swimming spot La Jolla Cove and the adjacent Scripps Park is a particular favourite. Wanderers are rewarded at either end of the walks. At the southern end, the **Children's Pool** is now a (free) rookery for seals. Though you can only get within a few feet (the sand is roped off), it's a great place to view the aquatic mammals as the pool has a railed sea wall that provides a unique vantage point. At the north end of the cliffpath, **La Jolla Caves** (1325 Cave Street, 1-858 459 0746) give access into the cliffs for a fascinating peek at the geological structure of the coastline.

La Jolla's beaches are terrific, notably surfing spot **La Jolla Shores** and clothing-optional **Blacks Beach** (public nudity is illegal in San Diego, but the beach is sufficiently inaccessible to maintain its

reputation). The area above the waves is also a popular diversion: the cliffs provide a perfect location for the **Torrey Pines International Gliderport** (2800 Torrey Pines Scenic Drive, 1-858 452 9858, www. flytorrey.com), in operation since 1928. Whether you hang-glide or just watch, it's always exhilarating. But the area's biggest attraction is the **Birch Aquarium at Scripps Institute of Oceanography** (2300 Expedition Way, 1-858 534 3474, www.aquarium.ucsd.edu, $6.50-$10), an excellent place to get properly acquainted with marine life and the perfect antidote to the commercialism of SeaWorld.

North of the gliderport is **Torrey Pines State Reserve** (1-858 755 2063, www.torrey pine.org), the last area on the mainland in which you can see the eponymous trees, the rarest variety in America. The visitor centre (1-858 755 2063) is near the main entrance, and holds displays on the park's wildlife.

Where to eat

San Diego County is now home to more than 7,000 restaurants. Sure, fast food is everywhere, but the recent increase in quantity has been joined by a leap in quality. Downtown, La Jolla and Hillcrest have the largest selection of good eateries, but each neighbourhood has its own treasures, and in just about every price range.

Downtown

Aubergine Grill

500 4th Avenue, at Island Avenue (1-619 232 8100/ www.aubergineon4th.com). **Open** from 5pm Tue-Sun. **Average** $$$$. **Credit** AmEx, MC, V.
A nice mix of seafood and grilled items, with an extensive list of wines by the glass. A meal can be made from its appetisers or soups du jour, but you wouldn't want to miss the sublime duck with baby spinach or steak and prawns combo.

Chive

558 4th Avenue, at Island Avenue (1-619 232 4483/ www.chiverestaurant.com). **Open** from 5pm daily. **Average** $$$$. **Credit** AmEx, Disc, MC, V.
Chive's ultra-modern decor matches its flair for unusual but tasty food. The restaurant specialises in American cuisine, with such delights as spice-crusted lamb loin or, from the vegetarian set, chimichurri-grilled tofu.

Croce's

802 5th Avenue, at W F Street (1-619 233 4355/ www.croces.com). **Open** 5.30pm-midnight Mon-Fri; 8.30am-midnight Sat, Sun. **Average** $$$-$$$$. **Credit** AmEx, MC, V.
Run by the widow of singer/songwriter Jim Croce, this is one of San Diego's landmark eateries. There is memorabilia on the walls and, more importantly,

Southern California

rather fine food on the tables: the menu features international cuisine, covering pasta, fish and salads. Jazz acts play nightly.

Gaslamp Strip Club

340 5th Avenue, at K Street (1-619 231 3140/ www.cohnrestaurants.com). **Open** from 5pm Tue-Sun. **Average** $$$$. **Credit** AmEx, DC, Disc, MC, V.

Though this restaurant is well known for its Vargas Girls paintings, it's actually named after its signature New York-style strip steak. A new hang with the hipster crowd, this is the place if you like meat: you grill yours to your own satisfaction. And the Martinis are perfect.

Kansas City Barbeque

610 W Market Street, at W Harbor Drive (1-619 231 9680). **Open** 11am-2am daily. **Average** $$. **Credit** AmEx, Disc, MC, V.

Famous from the film *Top Gun* and decorated with Kansas memorabilia (the city, not the band), this is a barbecue lover's dream. Chicken and ribs are the staples, sloshed down with beer. A favourite with tourists and locals, there's nothing fancy here: just good, solid, filling chow in a casual environment.

Nectar

911 5th Avenue, at E Street (1-619 615 3146/ www.nectar.com). **Open** 11.30am-2.30pm, 5.30-11pm Mon-Fri; 5.30-11pm Sat, Sun. **Average** $$-$$$$. **Credit** AmEx, Disc, MC, V.

Located in the Prava Hotel, this chic dining spot has one defining architectural feature: a curtained circular booth in the middle of the dining room that's perfect for any romantic meal. Happy hour (4-7pm) offers up delicacies such as tiger shrimp rolls and scallops wrapped in crispy bacon to start. Mains are superb: lobster bisque, say, or roasted quail.

Sevilla

555 4th Avenue, at Island Avenue (1-619 233 5979/ www.cafesevilla.com). **Open** 5pm-2am daily. **Average** $$$. **Credit** AmEx, MC, V.

Sevilla's chef Christian Vignes has put together a wonderful menu of Spanish cuisine and seafood. A nice selection of hot and cold tapas are served in the bar, where guitarists play flamenco.

Star of the Sea

1360 N Harbor Drive, at W Ash Drive (1-619 232 7408/www.starofthesea.com). **Open** 5.30-10pm daily. **Average** $$$$$. **Credit** AmEx, DC, Disc, MC, V.

Right on the Embarcadero, this elegant restaurant offers a wonderful bay view and some of San Diego's best seafood. A cocktail lounge and award-winning wine list round out one of the city's best fine dining establishments.

Also recommended

Lunchtime pizzas and evening pastas at **Mare e Monti** (644 5th Avenue, 1-619 235 8144, www. mare-monti.com, $$-$$$); great food and gorgeous presentation at **Taka Sushi** (555 5th Avenue, 1-619 338 0555, www.takasushi.com, closed lunch, $$$$).

Balboa Park & around

Big Kitchen

3003 Grape Street, at Fern Street, South Park (1-619 234 5789). **Open** 7am-2pm Mon-Fri; 7.30am-3pm Sat, Sun. **Average** $. **No credit cards.**

This friendly vegetarian diner closes after lunch, but given that its enormous breakfasts are among the best not just in San Diego but the entire state, we think they've earned the break. A local institution.

Chicken Pie Shop

2633 El Cajon Boulevard, at Hamilton Street, Balboa Park (1-619 295 0156). **Open** 10am-8pm daily. **Average** $. **No credit cards.**

With chicken-related decor, a cafeteria-styled layout and waitresses who've known their regulars for years, the Chicken Pie Shop seems to be lost in a time warp. Let's hope it stays there: its handmade comfort food (chicken pies, sandwiches, soups) are delicious, and prices are more than reasonable.

Prado

House of Hospitality, 1549 El Prado, at Plaza de Panama, Balboa Park (1-619 557 9441). **Open** 11am-3pm Mon; 11.30am-3pm, 5-9pm Tue-Thur; 5-10pm Fri; 11am-3pm, 5-10pm Sat; 11am-3pm, 4.30-8pm Sun. **Average** $$$. **Credit** AmEx, DC, Disc, MC, V.

This intimate and casual spot in Balboa Park is perfect for getting away from the surrounding bustle. Specialising in Italian and Latin American cuisine, Prado has a patio set above the park's greenery and rooms indoors, as well as a bar where you can mull over which museum to hit next over a sangria.

Turf Supper Club

1116 25th Street, at C Street, South Park (1-619 234 6363). **Open** 5pm-midnight Mon-Thur; 5pm-2am Fri; 1pm-2am Sat; 2pm-midnight Sun. **Average** $$. **Credit** AmEx, MC, V.

Helmed by Tim Mays and Sam Chammas, this old-school bar and restaurant has a dark interior, a friendly vibe and a simple gimmick: pick your favourite slice of meat and grill it yourself. All orders come with garlic bread; non-meat eaters can enjoy portobello mushroom sandwiches and salads.

Also recommended

Old-fashioned 24/7 diner **Rudford's** (2900 El Cajon Boulevard, North Park, 1-619 282 8423, $).

Hillcrest & Mission Valley

Bertrand at Mr A's

2550 5th Avenue, at Laurel Street, Hillcrest (1-619 239 1377/www.bertrandatmisteras.com). **Open** 11.30am-2.30pm, 5.30-10.30pm Mon-Thur, Sun; 5.30-11pm Fri, Sat. **Average** $$$-$$$$$. **Credit** AmEx, DC, Disc, MC, V.

At the top of the Financial Center, Bertrand has an incredible panoramic view, pretty much at eye-level with the planes arriving at Lindbergh Field. The high-class menu is inventive modern French.

Corvette Diner

3946 5th Avenue, at University Avenue, Hillcrest (1-619 542 1001/www.cohnrestauraunts.com). **Open** 11am-10pm Mon-Thur, Sun; 11am-11pm Fri, Sat. **Average** $$. **Credit** AmEx, Disc, MC, V.
Boisterous fun. This is a family-friendly '50s-styled diner like they never really were: Marilyn and Elvis memorabilia, loud waitresses in bouffant hairdos and poodle skirts, a DJ blasting out early rock 'n' roll. Extremely popular with the younger set.

Hash House a Go Go

3628 5th Avenue, at Brookes Avenue, Hillcrest (1-619 298 4646/www.hashhouseagogo.com). **Open** 7.30am-2pm, 5.30-9pm Mon-Thur; 7.30am-2pm, 5.30-10pm Fri; 7.30am-3pm, 5.30-9pm Sun. **Average** $$–$$$. **Credit** AmEx, MC, V.
The name might inspire visions of Austin Powers, but this is an excellent diner with one of the most varied menus in town. Its motto is 'long live food', which in this case is everything from cereal for breakfast to blue crab cakes with mashed butternut squash for dinner.

Khyber Pass

523 University Avenue, at 5th Avenue, Hillcrest (1-619 294 7579). **Open** 11am-10.45pm daily. **Average** $$. **Credit** AmEx, MC, V.
This restaurant has had problems drawing clientele, probably due to the troubles in the Middle East. That's no fault of the traditional food on offer, nor the service and decor. There's a decent vegetarian platter, but it's the mantu (ground meat ravioli) and kebabs that will keep you coming back.

Kitima

406 University Avenue, at 4th Avenue, Hillcrest (1-619 298 2929). **Open** 11am-11pm daily. **Average** $$. **Credit** AmEx, DC, Disc, MC, V.
Although there are several Thai restaurants in Hillcrest, none reaches the heights of Kitima. The difference is the sauces, which have more bite without being overly hot – unless hot is what you're after. The Pa-Nang Kai (chicken in a red curry sauce) is particularly splendid, and the surroundings impressively through-designed, right down to the menus. Meat dishes can be ordered as vegetarian.

Parkhouse Eatery

4574 Park Boulevard, at Madison Avenue, Hillcrest (1-619 295 7275). **Open** 8am-2.30pm, 5-9pm Mon-Thur; 8am-2.30pm, 5-10pm Fri-Sun. **Average** $$–$$$. **Credit** AmEx, DC, Disc, MC, V.
With a giant clock towering over its front gate, you can't miss the Parkhouse. Enjoy chilaquiles, a rare Mexican breakfast treat served with scrambled eggs, crispy corn tortillas, home-made red chilli sauce and asiago cheese. It's also great for Sunday brunch and has an outdoor patio out front.

Also recommended

Northern Indian cuisine at elegant **Bombay** (3975 5th Avenue, 1-619 298 3155, www.bombayrestaurant. com, $$$); the best pie in town at **Bronx Pizza** (111 Washington Street, 1-619 291 3341, www.bronx pizza.com, closed Sun, $); comfort food and Jewish treats at the early-opening, late-closing **City Delicatessen** (535 University Avenue, 1-619 295 2747, $); highly regarded **Tapas Picasso** (3923 4th Avenue, 1-619 294 3061, closed lunch Mon, Sat & Sun, $$$).

Old Town & Mission Hills

Café Pacifica

2414 San Diego Avenue, at Conde Street, Old Town (1-619 291 6666/www.cafepacifica.com). **Open** 5-10pm Mon-Sat; 5-9.30pm Sun. **Average** $$$$. **Credit** AmEx, DC, Disc, MC, V.
If you're looking for something a little different in Old Town, try this excellent seafood restaurant, whose unusual dishes includes cultured abalone. The barbecue sauce is especially memorable.

Casa de Bandini

2754 Calhoun Street, at Juan Street, Old Town (1-619 297 8211). **Open** 11am-9.30pm Mon, Thur-Sun; 11am-10pm Fri, Sat. **Average** $$. **Credit** AmEx, DC, Disc, MC, V.
Mexican food is a staple of Old Town dining and this venerable eaterie, with its three dining rooms and an outdoor patio, has been enchanting the locals for decades. There are good seafood options on the menu, and the huge Margaritas are a party in a glass. Other decent Mexican eats can also be found at the **Old Town Mexican Café** (2489 San Diego Avenue, 1-619 297 4330, www.oldtown mexcafe.com, $$$).

Gathering

902 W Washington Street, at Goldfinch Street, Mission Hills (1-619 260 0400). **Open** 8am-10pm daily. **Average** $–$$. **Credit** AmEx, Disc, MC, V.
Despite the imposing bar smack dab in the middle of the floor, the Gathering is a cosy place, serving breakfast, lunch and dinner – accompanied in the evening by light entertainment that ranges from jazz to a roaming magician. That bar lends the place the feel of a tavern, and of course provides a better than average drink selection.

Parallel 33

741 W Washington Street, at Eagle Street, Mission Hills (1-619 260 0033). **Open** 5-10pm Mon-Thur; 5.30-11pm Fri, Sat. **Average** $$$$. **Credit** AmEx, Disc, MC, V.
Unusually, this chic restaurant only features food found 33° north of the Equator. Luckily, that's not limiting in the slightest: there is a range of dishes to choose from, from such countries as India, Japan, China, Lebanon and Morocco.

Also recommended

Coffee and ice-cream at **Gelato Vero** (3753 India Street, Mission Hills, 1-619 295 9269, $); inexpensive, impressive take-out Mexican at **El Indio** (3695 India Street, Mission Hills (1-619 299 0333, $).

Coronado

Il Fornaio

*1333 1st Street, at Marine Way (1-619 437 4911/
www.ilfornaio.com)*. **Open** 11.30am-10pm Mon-Thur;
11.30am-11pm Fri, Sat; 10.30am-10pm Sun. **Average**
$$$. **Credit** AmEx, MC, V.
Offering a view of the San Diego skyline from vir-
tually every seat, this classy restaurant serves clas-
sic Italian dishes, as well as a fine Sunday brunch.

Hotel del Coronado

*1500 Orange Avenue, at Glorietta Boulevard (1-619
522 8490/www.hoteldel.com)*. **Crown Room** Open
9am-2pm Sun. **Average** $$$$. **Palm Court** Open
6-10pm Thur-Sun. **Average** $$$$$. **Prince of
Wales** Open 5.30-9.30pm Tue-Sun. **Average**
$$$$$. **Sheerwater** Open 7am-9.45pm daily.
Average $$$$. **All Credit** AmEx, DC, Disc, MC, V.
Eating options at this historic, landmark hotel (*see
p87*) comprise a lounge and four restaurants. The
Crown Room is open for the Del's popular Sunday
brunch and teas; the Palm Court, overlooking the
Garden Patio, is an excellent choice for light meals
and pastries; and the Prince of Wales is perfect for
a special evening, with a wealth of delicious options
including pan-roasted Muscovy duck breast.

La Jolla

Alfonso's

*1251 Prospect Street, at Roslyn Lane (1-858 454
2232)*. **Open** 11am-2am Mon-Sat; 11am-10pm Sun.
Average $$$. **Credit** AmEx, Disc, MC, V.
Having celebrated its 30th anniversary, Alfonso's
continues to serve top-of-the-line Mexican food in a
warm, friendly atmosphere right on La Jolla's main
drag. The outdoor patio is perfect for watching the
street life while enjoying the delectable signature
carne asada. The chicken with mole is also amazing.

Crab Catcher

*1298 Prospect Street, at Coast Boulevard (1-858
454 9587/www.crabcatcher.com)*. **Open** 11.30am-
3pm, 5.30-10pm Mon-Thur; 11.30am-3pm, 5.30-
10.30pm Fri, Sat; 10.30am-3pm, 5.30-10pm Sun.
Average $$$$-$$$$$. **Credit** AmEx, MC, V.
As you might surmise, the Crab Catcher specialises
in shellfish, with a nice sideline in other seafood and
pasta dishes. Perched on a cliff overlooking the
coast, this is a favourite for business meetings but
is also enjoyable for more casual get-togethers, with
specialities such as the crab martini or (not for the
faint-hearted) fire shrimp perfect for a quick nosh.

India Palace

*7514 Girard Avenue, at Pearl Street (1-858
551 5133/www.indiapalace-lajolla.com)*. **Open**
11.30am-2.30pm, 5-10pm daily. **Average** $-$$.
Credit AmEx, MC, V.
One of the best Indian restaurants in town, India
Palace has high ceilings and a spacious dining room,
and features a fine lunch buffet (11.30am-2.30pm).

Its extensive tandoori selection and willingness to
modify its offerings make this an excellent choice
for discriminating tastebuds.

Marine Room

*2000 Spindrift Drive, at Roseland Drive (1-858
459 7222/www.ljbtc.com)*. **Open** 11.30am-2pm,
6-10pm Tue-Thur; 11.30am-2pm, 5.30-10pm Fri,
Sat; 11am-1.30pm, 6-10pm Sun. **Average**
$$$$-$$$$$. **Credit** AmEx, DC, Disc, MC, V.
Other restaurants claim to be near the water, but the
Marine Room tops them all. It may be a little off the
beaten track, but this fine dining establishment is
well worth the search, with windows right on the
water; indeed, waves have been known to crash
through them during winter storms. The pricey
menu features contemporary French cuisine.

Also recommended

Belly dancers at exotic Moroccan eaterie
Marrakesh (634 Pearl Street, 1-858 454 2500, $$$).

Ocean Beach, Mission Beach & Pacific Beach

Broken Yolk

*1851 Garnet Avenue, at Kendall Street, Pacific
Beach (1-858 270 9655)*. **Open** 6am-3pm daily.
Average $. **Credit** AmEx, DC, Disc, MC, V.
Eggs are, self-evidently, the house speciality at the
Broken Yolk. An amazing range of 50-plus omelettes
is available, plus burgers and sandwiches. A rooftop
patio is available for sun worshippers, but be
warned: weekends can be extraordinarily busy.

Cucina Fresca

*1851 Bacon Street, Ocean Beach (1-619 224
9490)*. **Open** noon-10pm Tue-Thur; noon-11pm Fri;
5-11pm Sat; 5-9pm Sun. **Average** $$-$$$. **Credit**
AmEx, MC, V.
Large portions and a wonderful old world atmos-
phere are the draws at this family-owned Italian
restaurant. You'll find all the basics here: the chick-
en and veal dishes are especially fine.

Guava Beach Bar & Grill

*3714 Mission Boulevard, Mission Beach (1-858
488 6688/www.guava-beach.com)*. **Open** 11.30am-
2am daily. **Average** $$. **Credit** AmEx, MC, V.
One need only note the 70 different tequilas avail-
able to realise Guava Beach has a party atmosphere.
Light fare includes a dozen appetisers; Mexican
dishes highlight the list of more filling options.
Several TVs broadcast the latest sporting events.

Hodad's

*5010 Newport Avenue, at Bacon Street, Ocean
Beach (1-619 224 4623)*. **Open** 11am-10pm
Mon-Thur, Sun; 11am-11pm Fri, Sat. **Average** $.
Credit AmEx, DC, Disc, MC, V.
Just a block from Ocean Beach Pier, this funky,
ultra-casual place is all about the burger, with four
basic types served as single or double patties.
Sandwiches, chicken burgers and veggie burgers

fill out the choices – and the choosers – and the thick and creamy shakes are just right for hot days on the beach.

Nick's at the Beach

809 Thomas Avenue, at Mission Boulevard, Pacific Beach (1-858 270 1730/www.nicksatthebeach.com). **Open** 11am-1am Mon-Sat; 9am-1am Sun. **Average** $$-$$$. **Credit** AmEx, MC, V.

A popular casual spot for couples after a romantic walk along the water, Nick's is just a block from the beach. Decorated with paintings of whales, the ground floor contains a bar and the dining room, where good seafood is served. A second level holds pool tables, a second bar and over a dozen TVs.

People's Organic Foods Co-op Deli

4765 Voltaire Street, Ocean Beach (1-619 224 1387/www.obpeoplesfood.coop). **Open** 8am-9pm daily. **Average** $. **Credit** AmEx, Disc, MC, V.

This inexpensive deli is open seven days a week for all three meals. Tofu delights, sandwiches, vegan macaroni and cheese… the menu at this deli is broad and comforting. There's both indoor and outdoor seating; travellers may also want to check out the adjacent market for some of the best produce in town. In keeping with the environmentally friendly theme, the place is even solar-powered.

Saska's

3768 Mission Boulevard, Mission Beach (1-858 488 7311/www.saskas.com). **Open** 11.30am-4pm, 5-11pm Mon-Fri; 10am-4pm, 5.30-11pm Sat, Sun. **Average** $$-$$$. **Credit** AmEx, DC, Disc, MC, V.

Steak and seafood are the signature foods at Saska's, in business for five decades, but the restaurant also offers a nice selection of salads and pasta dishes, and a fine wine list. Lunch also adds Mexican food, soups and sandwiches to the choices; the adjacent Saska's Sushi restaurant broadens the dinner menu further.

Also recommended

Meat the locals at the **Bar-B-Que House** (5025 Newport Avenue, Ocean Beach, 1-619 222 4311, $); hefty portions at the Germanic **Kaiserhof** (2253 Sunset Cliffs Boulevard, Ocean Beach, 1-619 224 0606, closed Mon, $$$); the **Mission** (3795 Mission Boulevard, 1-858 488 9060, $$, closed dinner), excellent for breakfast and lunch.

Where to drink

Downtown

Downtown, especially the Gaslamp Quarter, is good for bars, though the scene can be very touristy. Boasting the city's oldest liquor licence, the **Waterfront Bar & Grill** (2044 Kettner Boulevard, 1-619 232 9656) has for decades been one of Downtown's best neighbourhood taps. The glassless windows that face the street give the room a particularly welcoming feeling. For an old-school classic, head to **US Grant Bar** (326 Broadway, 1-619 232 3121), whose dark wood interior attracts everyone from local businessmen to students. Jazz raises the roof on weekends. While still relaxed, the **Onyx Room** (852 5th Avenue, 1-619 235 6699) is more sophisticated, serving reasonably priced drinks in the modern-retro front lounge; other good spots for an upbeat night out include **Landlord Jim's** (1546 Broadway, 1-619 233 9998), with live DJs on

Southern California

Drink to **Hillcrest**. *See p82.*

video feed, and the huge **Bitter End** (770 5th Avenue, 1-619 338 9300). Flamenco and tapas can be enjoyed at **Sevilla** (*see p78*); **Dublin Square** (554 4th Avenue, 1-619 239 5818) offers trad Irish music (good) and food (less good).

Balboa Park & around

South Park's **Whistle Stop** (2236 Fern Street, 1-619 284 6784) is big with the twentysomething crowd and known for its quirky promotions: board game nights, trivia quizzes and DJs.

Hillcrest & Mission Hills

The main grouping of bars and clubs in Hillcrest is along University Avenue east of 8th Street; the area is a favourite among locals keen to avoid Downtown. Recently renovated **Alibi** (1403 University Avenue, 1-619 295 0881) is as loud and crowded as ever, unsurprising given the 23oz Buds for $2.50. A classier choice is **Live Wire** (2103 El Cajon Boulevard, 1-619 291 7450), with its generous cocktails and a well-stocked jukebox. The retro-cool of **Nu Nu's** (3537 5th Avenue, 1-619 295 2878) – late '60s exterior, red-vinyl booths, low lighting – make it the place for scene-makers. Its location in a strip mall doesn't bode well, but **Cherry Bomb** (2237 1st Avenue, 1-619 544 1173) is as authentic a rock 'n' roll bar as you'll find in San Diego: a loud jukebox, boisterous crowds and a 25¢ pool table.

La Jolla

Tops here is the **Beach House Brewery** (7536 Fay Avenue, 1-858 456 6279), a comfortable brewpub-sports bar that also

What's on when

There are several free weekly publications, including the **San Diego Reader** and **San Diego Citybeat**, which feature extensive listings of events in San Diego County. Both run websites: respectively, www.sdreader.com and www.sdcitybeat.com. Also recommended is Thursday's 'Night & Day' insert to local newspaper the **San Diego Union Tribune**, responsible for the excellent www.signonsandiego.com site.

Discount tickets for many of the area's plays and classical events can be found at **Arts Tix**, which operates a booth in Horton Plaza Square (1-619 497 5000, www.sandiegoperforms.com).

serves fine bar food. **The Spot** (1005 Prospect Street, 1-858 459 0800) can be a noisy, hectic place, best approached for the drinks than the food. Part of the historic La Valencia Hotel, the plush **Whaling Bar & Grill** (1132 Prospect Street, 1-858 454 0771) has been a haunt for movie stars and politicians down the decades.

Ocean Beach, Mission Beach & Pacific Beach

Few beach bars boast 20 beers on tap, but that's what you'll find at friendly **Liar's Club** (3844 Mission Boulevard, Mission Beach, 1-858 488 2340). A few feet from the Crystal Pier is **Blind Melons** (710 Garnet Avenue, Pacific Beach, 1-858 483 7844), a small sports bar that stages blues, rock and reggae acts. In Ocean Beach, try the divey **Arizona Café** (1925 Bacon Street, 1-619 223 0847) or **Pacific Shores** (4927 Newport Avenue, 1-619 233 7549), a classic old-time bar with a laid-back beachy atmosphere.

Nightlife

Gay & lesbian

The heart of the gay and lesbian community in San Diego is Hillcrest, and the dance scene there is thriving. Nightspots on University Avenue include high-energy dance clubs like **Rich's** (No.1051, 1-619 215 2195), and **Flicks**, the city's first video bar (No.1017, 1-619 297 2056). The **Brass Rail** (3796 5th Avenue, 1-619 298 2233) is another option; it runs occasional drag shows, but at **Lips** (2770 5th Avenue, 1-619 295 7900), they're staged every night. A few blocks from the centre of Hillcrest stands one of the largest clubs in town, the three-level **Club Montage** (2028 Hancock Street, 1-619 294 9590). Downtown, the **Chee-Chee Club** (929 Broadway, 1-619 234 4404) is a nicely relaxed drinking den, while **Caliph** (3100 5th Avenue, 1-619 298 9495) is a piano bar that largely caters for grown-ups.

For lesbians, Hillcrest's the **Flame** (3780 Park Boulevard, 1-619 295 4163) has a cigar bar and ample dancefloor, while Old Town's **Club Bombay** (3175 India Street, 1-619 296 6789) has a stage for bands and does Sunday barbecues. The latter is also popular with gay men.

New clubs and bars open and old ones close. Check the free *Gay & Lesbian Times* and *Update* for information during your visit.

Nightclubs

Downtown, especially 5th Avenue, features the greatest concentration of clubs in San Diego. The commercial dance clubs are led by **On Broadway** (615 Broadway, 1-619 231 0011), whose line-up of resident and touring celeb DJs, spinning everything from hip hop to old-school techno draws enormous crowds. **E Street Alley** (919 4th Avenue, 1-619 231 9200) is a large multi-roomed venue beneath the streets, with a great sound system pumping out floor-fillers. Elsewhere, **L5** (203 5th Avenue, 1-619 858 2100), **Deco's** (731 5th Avenue, 1-619 696 3326) and the **5th Quarter** (600 5th Avenue, 1-619 236 1616) are big with scenesters.

Hillcrest is the more bohemian area of San Diego, with a cluster of gay clubs (*see p82*), while Pacific Beach's beach bar district is focused along Garnet Avenue, west of Mission Boulevard. Expect to find anything from reggae to hip hop, a relaxed atmosphere and plenty of opportunities for rowdy behaviour.

Shopping

If you're shopping Downtown, use **Horton Plaza** (*see p68*) for free parking. You'll need to get your parking ticket validated, but buying a pack of chewing gum is all that's really necessary to get the stamp. Street parking (when available) is usually metered, costing around $1 an hour for stays of up to two hours.

Department stores

Macy's (www.macys.com) is well represented, with the most convenient branches in Horton Plaza (No.160, 1-619 231 4747) and Fashion Valley Center (7007 Friars Road, 1-619 299 9811); classy **Nordstrom** (www.nordstrom.com) also has Horton Plaza (No.103, 1-619 239 1700) and Fashion Valley Center (1-619 295 4441) outposts; also in Fashion Valley are **Neiman Marcus** (1-619 692 9100, www.neimanmarcus.com) and **Saks 5th Avenue** (1-619 260 0030, www.saks5thavenue.com). For affordable prices, the nearest **Sears** is La Jolla's University Towne Centre mall (4575 La Jolla Village Drive, 1-858 622 9300, www.sears.com).

Malls

Downtown's **Horton Plaza** (324 Horton Plaza, 1-619 239 8180, www.westfield.com) contains the usual mix of chains, but its quirky post-modern architecture sets the mall apart from its competitors and helps make it as good a spot for people-watching as it is for shopping. Also Downtown, the **Seaport Village** (849 West Harbor Drive, 1-619 235 4014, www.spvillage.com) is a slightly cheesy outdoor mall styled to resemble an East Coast fishing village.

Mission Valley is one of San Diego's busiest commercial zones, with a freeway running through the middle of it for easy access by car.

Fashion Valley Center (7007 Friars Road, 1-619 688 9113) is the biggest mall, with over 200 speciality shops and a dozen restaurants. In La Jolla, you'll find 160 shops among the dolphin fountains of **University Towne Centre** (4545 La Jolla Village Drive, 1-858 546 8858).

Antiques & markets

Ocean Beach provides a good range of antiques on Newport Avenue. **Antique Row**, off University Avenue in Hillcrest, lives up to its name, and nearby **Adams Avenue** hosts an Antiques Street Faire each July (call 1-619 282 7329). It is also home to furniture store **Retreads** (No.3220, 1-619 284 3999, closed Wed pm) and global-minded **Back from Tomboctou** (No.3564, 1-619 282 8708).

For those who like a serious rummage, **Kobey's Swap Meet** (San Diego Sports Arena, 3500 Sports Arena Boulevard, 1-619 226 0650) is San Diego's nearest equivalent to a European flea market. It opens Friday to Sunday from 7am.

Books

Both big chains are represented here: **Borders** (668 6th Avenue, 1-619 702 4200) in the Gaslamp Quarter, and **Barnes & Noble** in the Mission Valley Center mall (1-619 220 0175). There are a few second-hand stores on Broadway near Horton Plaza, among them the triple-storey **Wahrenbrock's Book House** (No.726, 1-619 232 0132).

Hillcrest has some fine used book shops, such as **Bountiful Books** (3834 5th Avenue, 1-619 491 0664), and **Bluestocking** (3817 5th Avenue, 1-619 296 1424). La Jolla has the legendary **John Cole's Book Shop** (780 Prospect Street, 1-858 454 4766, closed Mon & Sun), with mainly specialist works on Baja California and kids' books in what was once Wisteria Cottage.

Fashion

The **Gaslamp Quarter** is the first port of call for credit card hounds, with such as **Urban Outfitters** (665 5th Avenue, 1-619 231 0102) awaiting your attention. **Hillcrest** is more sedate, but a tree-lined stretch of 5th Avenue at the intersection with University Avenue is another focal point. **Buffalo Exchange** (3862 5th Avenue, 1-619 298 4411) and **Flashbacks** (3847 5th Avenue, 1-619 291 4200) are just two of a half-dozen used clothing stores in the area. Both also have shops on Garnet Avenue in Pacific Beach (No.1007, 1-858 273 6227; No.975, 1-858 270 3582); also on Garnet, you'll find **The Buff** (No.1061, 1-858 581 2833), which caters for the costume end of the market.

Southern California

Beachside shopping for surfer threads.

Gifts

The Gaslamp Quarter offers a decent variety of shops, ranging from tourist-slanted knick-knack joints to more esoteric outlets such as the **Faerie Store** (230 5th Avenue, 1-619 234 4100), which deals strictly in items for and from elves and other mythical folk. The deeply touristy **Bazaar del Mundo** (2754 Calhoun, 1-619 296 3161) in Old Town holds 16 colourful boutiques, selling Latin American textiles, clothes and folk art. In Hillcrest don't miss **Babette Schwartz** (421 University Avenue, 1-619 220 7048): named after the owner, one of San Diego's best-loved drag queens, it's stuffed with kitsch novelties.

Music

Music junkies in Hillcrest spend hours sifting through *Mojo*-featured record store **Off the Record** (3849 5th Avenue, 1-619 298 4755). Though geared to the indie rock scene, the store features everything from rare jazz to soundtracks, both new and used recordings; vinyl makes up about half of the store.

Arts & entertainment

Comedy

For stand-up in San Diego, head to **Lestat's** (*see p85*) on a Tuesday. Occasional gigs can be seen at **Humphrey's Concerts by the Bay** (2241 Shelter Island Drive, Point Loma, 1-619 523 1010; *see p87*) and primarily music venues. La Jolla's **Comedy Store** offers nightly shows (916 Pearl Street, 1-858 454 9176).

Film

Film buffs walking the 3900 block of 5th Avenue in Hillcrest will notice an authentic old movie marquee, all that's left of the Guild Theatre. Still one of the city's best movie houses, the **Hillcrest Cinemas** (3965 5th Avenue, 1-619 819 0236), is tucked away at the north end of the same street, in the Village Hillcrest mall. For films outside the mainstream, **La Jolla Village Cinema** (1-858 453 7831) and the **Ken** (4061 Adams Avenue, 1-619 283 5909) are strong possibilities, while the **Reuben H Fleet Science Center** (*see p72*) offers the wonders of IMAX.

Galleries

Outside the museums – and, in most cases, outside buildings altogether – San Diego has **public artworks** dotted along the bay shore: www.portofsandiego.org/sandiego_publicart provides a full listing and gives a map. You'll

For casual duds – especially surf gear – head to Pacific Beach. On Mission Boulevard, men can get long shorts at **Liquid Foundation Surf Shop** (No.3731, 1-858 488 3260), while women are well catered for at **Pilar's Beachwear** (No.3745, 1-858 488 3056) and **Gone Bananas Beachwear** (No.3785, 1-858 488 4900). For surfing equipment as well as clothes, try **South Coast Surf Shops** (5023 Newport Avenue, 1-619 223 7017) or the women-only store **South Coast Wahines** (4500 Ocean Front Boulevard, 1-858 273 7600).

If money is no object, a few miles up the coast, **La Jolla** offers a wealth of trendy, and pricey, boutiques. A great locale for window-shopping, this small seaside community is like Beverly Hills on the water: expect Armani, Ralph Lauren and the like. Most of the action takes place along Prospect Avenue, though Girard Street is also worth a look.

Food & drink

Farmers' markets have a strong hold in San Diego: there are afternoon markets on Tuesday in **Coronado** (Ferry Landing Marketplace, at 1st and B Streets) and on Wednesday in **Ocean Beach** (Newport Avenue, between Bacon and Cable Streets), and morning markets on Saturday in **Pacific Beach** (Mission Boulevard, between Pacific Beach Drive and Reed Avenue) and on Sunday in **Hillcrest** (5th Avenue, at Normal Street and Lincoln Avenue).

also find several commercial galleries in the Studio Arts Complex (2400 Kettner Boulevard), among them the **Pratt** (1-619 236 0211) and **David Zapf** (1-619 232 5004) galleries, but La Jolla is the best place for art: **Prospect Avenue** is the axis for more than 35 galleries.

Music: classical & opera

The **San Diego Symphony** (www.sandiego symphony.com), saved from bankruptcy in 2002 by a daunting private $120 million donation (the largest single gift ever made to an orchestra), performs an eclectic programme each year at San Diego's **Copley Symphony Hall** (750 B Street, 1-619 235 0804) and the **California Center for the Arts** (340 N Escondido Boulevard, 1-760 839 4138) in Escondido. Its annual Summer Pops series, held on Navy Pier, is always popular. The annual Mainly Mozart Festival is hosted in La Jolla in June by the **Neurosciences Institute** (10640 John Jay Hopkins Drive, 1-619 239 0100), usually selling out. Opera buffs have two options. **San Diego Opera** stages lavish productions of the classics at the Civic Theatre (202 C Street, 1-619 533 7000), while the **Lyric Opera** (1-619 239 8836) moves from Balboa Park's **Casa del Prado Theatre** (1650 El Prado, 1-619 239 8836) to the newly retrofitted **Birch North Park Theatre** (2895 University Avenue, 1-619 294 2501) for its 2005 season.

Music: jazz & blues

You'll find jazz gigs at **Lestat's** (*see below*) and **Croce's** (*see p77*), as well as in the **US Grant Bar** and **Onyx Room** (for both, *see p81*), but the intimate, alcohol-free **Dizzy's** (344 7th Avenue, 1-858 270 7467) is *the* place for jazz aficionados. San Diego's best spot for blues is **Blind Melons** (*see p82*).

Music: rock, pop & hip hop

The **Casbah** (2501 Kettner Boulevard, 1-619 232 4355) is a fine indie-rock venue: there's a front room for the headline act, while the Atari Lounge out back caters for smaller groups. **Soma** (3350 Sports Arena Boulevard, 1-619 226 7662) has hosted the likes of the White Stripes and the Damned. Tiny **Lestat's Coffee House** (3343 Adams Avenue, Normal Heights, 1-619 282 0437) is outfitted with a mix of old movie seats and coffee tables, junk-shop chic that's matched by an eclectic bill of folk, pop and jazz. And **Java Joe's Pub** (6344 El Cajon Boulevard, 1-619 286 0400), the hub of San Diego's acoustic music scene through three previous incarnations, reopened near San Diego's State University in 2004.

For a feel of San Diego's sun-and-surf vibe, checking out some music along the beaches is a must. Music is secondary to boozing along the stretch west of Mission Boulevard in Pacific Beach, but the likes of **Cane's** (3105 Ocean Front Walk, 1-858 488 1780) and **Winston's** (1921 Bacon Street, 1-619 222 6822) both stage local acts. One of the area's best music venues is north of the city: the **Belly Up Tavern** (143 S Cedros, Solana Beach, 1-858 481 1840) is set apart by its quirky decor (including a life-size Great White shark) and its impressive line-ups.

Theatre

Jewel of San Diego's theatrical scene, the **Old Globe Theatre** (1363 Old Globe Way, Balboa Park, 1-619 234 5623) was built in 1935 to stage 50-minute versions of Shakespeare plays. The Old Globe's season comprises 12-14 plays or musicals, with the annual Summer Shakespeare Festival on the outdoor **Lowell Davies Festival Theatre** particularly noteworthy. A third theatre in the complex, the 225-seat **Cassius Carter Centre Stage**, puts on smaller-scale performances in the round.

Of the city's smaller venues, the San Diego Repertory Theatre performances at the **Lyceum Theatre** (79 Horton Plaza, 1-619 544 1000, www.sandiegorep.com) specialises in new works, and there are also performances nightly in Hillcrest's intimate **Sixth at Penn Theatre** (3704 6th Avenue, 1-619 688 9210, www.sixthatpenn.com). In Coronado, you'll find the **Coronado Playhouse** (1775 Strand Way, 1-619 435 4856, www.coronadoplayhouse.com) and the **Lamb's Players Theatre** (1142 Orange Avenue, 1-619 437 0600, www.lambs players.org).

Where to stay

Downtown has the city's largest concentration of rooms, but Mission Valley has a number of chain hotels. For a rundown of chains, *see p54*.

Downtown

Horton Grand

311 Island Avenue, at 3rd Avenue (1-619 544 1886/ 1-800 542 1886/www.hortongrand.com). **Rates** $189-$209 single/double. **Credit** AmEx, DC, MC, V.
This three-star hotel in the midst of the Gaslamp Quarter is a re-creation of Victorian architecture, formed from two existing buildings in 1986. Said to be haunted (*see p74* **San Diego spooks**), the Grand has no two rooms alike, but each contains an antique queen bed, lace curtains and a gas fireplace. Some rooms have a balcony; others have bay or city views.

Hostel International San Diego

521 Market Street, at 5th Avenue (1-800 909-4776/ 1-619 223 4778/www.sandiegohostels.org). **Rates** $17-$22.50 dorm; $44-$55 private room. **Credit** MC, V.
For the budget-minded visitor, it doesn't get much better than this. The main selling point is the Gaslamp Quarter location. Small private rooms are available in addition to the expected dorms and there's free breakfast, internet access and bike rentals next door.

Prava

911 5th Avenue, at E Street (1-619 233 3300/ www.pravahotel.com). **Rates** $139-$159 single/ double. **Credit** AmEx, DC, Disc, MC, V.
Prava is popular with the hipster crowd. All rooms are spacious and well appointed; there's also a ground-level restaurant and bar. Staff are friendly to a fault. Low-key but classy, and a quiet respite from the bustle.

US Grant

326 Broadway, at 3rd Avenue (1-619 232 3121/ www.usgrant.net). **Rates** $189-$239 single/double. **Credit** AmEx, MC, V.
Directly across Broadway from Horton Plaza (*see p68*), this renovated historic hotel retains its early 20th-century stateliness. Attracting a star clientele (Bono famously serenaded a crowd from one of its windows) the US Grant has period style rooms, with Queen Anne beds alongside modern accessories.

W Hotel

421 West B Street, at State Street (1-619 231 8220/ www.whotels.com). **Rates** $239-$399 single/double. **Credit** AmEx, DC, Disc, MC, V.
The ultra-modern W is inspired, with not only the typical restaurant and lounges, but also a rooftop outdoor beach bar (complete with sand, though without waves). Rooms are either 'wonderful' (with one king or two doubles) or 'spectacular' (the same sleeping arrangements, but with higher ceilings and views).

Balboa Park & around

Balboa Park Inn

3402 Park Boulevard, at Upas Street, North Park (1-800 9388181/1-619 298 0823/www.balboapark inn.com). **Rates** $99-$199 single/double. **Credit** AmEx, Disc, MC, V.
Within walking distance of Balboa Park, this guesthouse consists of four Colonial Revival buildings, built in 1915 for the park's opening. There are 25 themed rooms, with queen-sized beds. The 'Greystoke' room comes complete with papier-mâché animal heads.

Mission Valley

Town & Country Hotel

500 Hotel Circle North, at Camino de la Reina (1-619 291 7131/www.towncountry.com). **Rates** $175-$275 single/double. **Credit** AmEx, DC, MC, V.
Your choices at this three-star hotel are two towers or a selection of ranch-styled bungalows. The rooms are a little small and plain, but the hotel lives up to its name: surrounded by greenery, it has two pools and a golf course. Perfect for family vacations.

Coronado

Glorietta Bay Inn

1630 Glorietta Boulevard, at Orange Avenue (1-800 283 9383/1-619 435 3101/www.glorietta bayinn.com). **Rates** $160-$255 single/double. **Credit** AmEx, DC, MC, V.
Built around and including a mansion originally constructed in 1908 as the home for 'sugar baron' John D Spreckels, this ornate hotel is the definition of elegance. The Mansion contains 11 gorgeous unique bedrooms, while the Contemporary Inn has another 89 rooms surrounding the original structure, with a pool in front.

The art of the matter

The colourful murals of **Chicano Park** (between National and Logan Avenues) were ostensibly created in the early '70s as a way to cover the huge, ugly grey pylons erected in Barrio Logan to support Coronado Bay Bridge. Yet the art serves as an important forum for statements from the Mexican-American residents of the surrounding barrio. Originally ignored by the city, the murals were declared San Diego's Historical Site No.143 in 1980. Today, more than 40 of these extraordinary works remain on public display.

The murals were the brainchild of Salvador Torres, who founded the Chicano Park Monumental Public Mural Program in 1969 and oversaw the unveiling of the park's first murals five years later. Depicting a wide range of subjects, from political works like *Varrio Si. Yonke No!* ('Neighbourhood? Yes. Junkyard? No!') to their polar opposite *Cosmic Clowns*, the pictures tell stories, and none is more direct than *Chicano Park Takeover*, painted in 1978 by Roger Lucero Casteneda. Using photographs and newspaper accounts, Casteneda pieced together a collage of images to illustrate the events of 22 April 1970, when community activists took over the land to create a park. Appropriately enough, Lucero himself was granted the accolade of having a mural painted in his honour in 1993.

Hotel del Coronado

1500 Orange Avenue, at Glorietta Boulevard (1-800 582 2595/1-619 435 6611/www.hoteldel.com). **Rates** $190-$2,300 double. **Credit** AmEx, DC, Disc, MC, V.
Built in 1888, the Del is easily one of San Diego's best-known landmarks, its red-roofed turrets defining the Coronado skyline. Any number of presidents and movie stars have stayed here; the hotel was also the backdrop for Marilyn's star turn in Billy Wilder's *Some Like it Hot*, and served as inspiration for the Emerald City in L Frank Baum's *Wizard of Oz* books. These days, it's kept immaculately, though you'll pay through the nose to see for yourself.

Point Loma

Humphrey's Half Moon Inn & Suites

2303 Shelter Island Drive, at Anchorage Lane (1-800 542 7400/1-619 224 3411/www.halfmooninn.com). **Rates** $169-$499 single/double. **Credit** AmEx, DC, Disc, MC, V.
Right by the water on Shelter Island, this three-star resort is a lush tropical paradise. Tiki torches greet you at an entrance lined with palm trees, with waterfalls and a heated pool adding to the exotic ambience. There is an on-site restaurant and bar; during summer, Humphrey's hosts a concert series. Basic rooms are plain but functional; suites offer balconies.

Ocean Beach, Mission Beach & Pacific Beach

Bahia Resort Hotel

998 W Mission Bay Drive, at Ventura Place, Mission Beach (1-800 576 4229/1-858 488 0551/ www.bahiamotel.com). **Rates** $129-$525 single/ double. **Credit** AmEx, DC, Disc, MC, V.
The 321 rooms are would benefit from an update, but the 50-year-old hotel's location, Olympic-sized pool, tennis courts and 1860s paddle wheelers make it worth a visit. Beachfront rooms can be a bit noisy.

Catamaran Resort Hotel

3999 Mission Boulevard, at Braemar Lane, Mission Beach (1-800 422 8386/1-858 488 1081/ www.catamaranresort.com). **Rates** $159-$385 single/double. **Credit** AmEx, DC, Disc, MC, V.
A Polynesian-style resort (there's a waterfall in the lobby), the Catamaran is right on the sands of Mission Bay, with Mission Beach and the Pacific Ocean just a stroll away. The 313 rooms are simply appointed with king or double beds, but the Bayfront Suites are worth the extra dosh for the joy of having a door that opens on to the beach.

Ocean Beach International Hostel

4961 Newport Avenue, at Bacon Street, Ocean Beach (1-619 223 7873). **Rates** $18 dorm (with proof of international travel). **Credit** AmEx, DC, Disc, MC, V.
Just two blocks from Ocean Beach, this multi-level building might be the ticket for fans of sun and surf with limited funds. Offering free transport from the airport or train station with reservations, this lively hostel is right in the middle of things, surrounded by restaurants, bars and shops.

Pacific Shores Inn

4802 Mission Boulevard, Pacific Beach (1-888 478 7829/1-858 483 6300/www.pacificshoresinn.com). **Rates** $69-$179 single/double. **Credit** AmEx, DC, Disc, MC, V.
This centrally located hotel is also perfectly placed for the PB nightlife, though conversely, its setting in a converted Victorian-styled house makes it an ideal place in which to escape the hustle and bustle.

Pacific Terrace Hotel

610 Diamond Street, Pacific Beach (1-800 344 3370/1-858 581 3500/www.pacificterrace.com). **Rates** $260-$385 single/double. **Credit** AmEx, DC, Disc, MC, V.
Patrons here have the option of visiting the large heated pool or heading a few feet across the boardwalk to the Pacific Ocean. West-facing rooms have a panoramic ocean view; all rooms have a balcony. Amenities include everything from free newspapers to in-room Nintendo games.

Paradise Point Resort & Spa

1404 Vacation Road, at Ingraham Street, Mission Bay (1-800 34 2626/1-858 274 4630/ www.paradisepoint.com). **Rates** $195-$425 single/double. **Credit** AmEx, DC, Disc, MC, V.
A secluded getaway, this 44-acre island resort offers a huge range of leisure activities, including a tropical lagoon pool, jogging paths and an 18-hole putting course. Guests stay in single-storey bungalows, with their own patios, with each unit a family-friendly world of its own, only minutes away from the city.

La Jolla & Torrey Pines

La Valencia Hotel

1132 Prospect Street, at Herschel Avenue, La Jolla (1-800 451 0772/1-858 454 0771/ www.lavalencia.com). **Rates** $275-$3,500 single/ double. **Credit** AmEx, DC, Disc, MC, V.
This large pink Mediterranean-style building opens right on to scenic Scripps Park to the north side, while to the south, it lies alongside one of the city's best shopping districts. Dominating Prospect Street since 1926, the hotel has nearly 100 small but comfortable guest rooms and 17 suites.

Lodge at Torrey Pines

11480 N Torrey Pines Road, at High Avenue, La Jolla (1-858 453 4420/www.lodgetorreypines.com). **Rates** $375-$3,500 single/double. **Credit** AmEx, DC, Disc, MC, V.
One of only two five-star hotels in San Diego, the Lodge is located in lush greenery, high on a bluff overlooking the Pacific and next to the 18th hole of the world-class Torrey Pines Golf Course. Styled by craftsmen, it's basically an oversize mountain lodge; amenities include a 9,500sq ft spa, two restaurants and guaranteed tee times next door.

Southern California

Resources

Hospital

Hillcrest/Mission Hills *Scripps Mercy Hospital, 4077 5th Avenue (1-619 294 8111/www.scripps health.org).*
La Jolla *Scripps Memorial Hospital, 9888 Genesee Avenue (1-858 457 4123/www.scrippshealth.org).*

Internet

Downtown *Internet Coffee, 1800 Broadway (1-619 702 2233/www.internet-coffee.com).* **Open** 11am-midnight daily.
Hillcrest *Living Room, 1417 University Avenue (1-619 295 7911/www.livingroomcafe.com).* **Open** 6am-midnight daily.
Pacific Beach *Wired Cybercafé, 853 Hornblend Street (1-858 490 8060/http://wiredcybercafe.net).* **Open** 9.30am-9pm daily.

Police

Coronado *700 Orange Avenue (1-619 522 7350).*
Downtown *1401 Broadway (1-619 531 2000).*

Post office

Downtown *815 E Street (1-619 232 8612).*
La Jolla *1140 Wall Street (1-858 459 5476).*

Tourist information

Coronado *Coronado Visitor Center, 1100 Orange Avenue (1-619 437 8788/www.coronadovisitor center.com).* **Open** 9am-5pm Mon-Fri; 10am-5pm Sat; 11am-5pm Sun.
Downtown *San Diego CVB, 1040½ W Broadway, at Harbor Drive (1-619 236 1212/www.sandiego. org).* **Open** 9am-5pm Mon-Sat; 10am-5pm Sun.
La Jolla *La Jolla Visitor Center, 7966 Herschel Avenue (1-619 236 1212/www.sandiego.org).* **Open** 11am-5pm Mon-Fri; 10am-6pm Sat; 10am-4pm Sun.

Getting there

By air

San Diego International Airport (1-619 231 2000, www.san.org), aka Lindbergh Field, is a 10-mile ride on the 992 bus from Downtown San Diego.

By bus

Greyhound (1-800 229 9424, www.greyhound.com) runs over 20 direct bus services daily between Los Angeles and San Diego (average 2½-3½hrs, $15 one-way, $25 round-trip). The Greyhound station is at 120 W Broadway in Downtown San Diego.

By car

Most drivers reach San Diego on the surprisingly speedy I-5, which runs along the coast. The journey from LA should take 2-2½hrs.

By rail

Amtrak (1-800 872 7245, www.amtrak.com) runs 10-12 services a day between LA's Union Station and Santa Fe Station in San Diego (1850 Kettner Boulevard). The journey time is 2¾hrs, and the one-way fare is $26 (or $52 round-trip).

Getting around

San Diego's a smaller city than LA, but the car is still the dominant mode of transport. That said, all the individual neighbourhoods detailed earlier – the likes of Downtown, La Jolla, Hillcrest and Old Town – are pedestrian-friendly. Once you've found a parking spot (not always easy), park up and explore the place on foot.

San Diego's public transport is run by the **Metropolitan Transit System** (aka MTS; 1-800 266 6883, www.sdcommute.com). The bus network covers much of the city and is generally efficient; the trolley system, meanwhile, is most often used by visitors for the Blue Line route that runs to the Mexican border. Bus fares cost $1-$2.50, with the majority of fares in the city itself $2.25 or $2.50; trolley fares cost between $1.25 (a flat fare for all Downtown-only journeys) and $3. The 'day-tripper' pass offers unlimited travel on any given day; costing $5 for one day, $9 for a two-day pass and $12 for the three-day variety, it offers good value for money.

Around San Diego

Heading north

Solana Beach to Encinitas

North of high-class Del Mar (famous for its racetrack, if not much else), **Solana Beach** is worth a brief look for its excellent beaches. During the day, check out the **City Hall Gallery**. Surf-centric **Cardiff-by-the-Sea** boasts a 900-acre shallow-water estuary, **San Elijo Lagoon** (1-760 436 3944, www.sanelijo. org), that attracts birds and, it follows, birdwatchers. Attractions in **Encinitas**, are entirely natural: the surfing (of course); the Self-Realization Fellowship's **Meditation Garden** (215 K Street, 1-760 753 2888), with its waterfall and koi pond; the **Quail Botanical Gardens** (1-760 436 3036, www.qbgardens.com), which contain an award-winning interactive children's garden; and the colourful flower farms that dot the area just inland.

Carlsbad

San Diego's North County is overshadowed in the tourism department by the attractions to the south, but there's no shortage of places to visit. In particular, the community of **Carlsbad** has made a serious effort to attract visiting families. The beaches have drawn surfers and swimmers for years; less famous are the three local lagoons, perfect for birdwatching and hiking.

Monumental playthings at **Legoland**.

Carlsbad's major attraction for children is **Legoland** (*see below*), but if money's no object, take a flight in one of the vintage planes at **Barnstorming Adventures** (2160 Palomar Airport Road, 1-800 759 5667, www.barn storming.com). Carlsbad's famed **Flower Fields** (5704 Paseo del Norte, 1-760 431 0352, http://visit.theflowerfields.com, $5-$8) also draw crowds to see the none-more-colourful blooms; the season runs for around two months from early March. Indoor options include the **Museum of Making Music** (5790 Armada Drive, 1-877 551 9976, www.museumofmaking music.com, closed Mon, $3-$5), which has an assortment of hands-on exhibits, and the **Children's Discovery Museum** (*see below*).

Children's Discovery Museum

2787 State Street (1-760 720 0737/www.museumfor children.org). **Open** 10am-4pm Tue-Sat; noon-4pm Sun. **Admission** $6; free under-2s. **Credit** MC, V. Interactivity is the name of the game here: there's a castle in which to play, complete with princess, knight and king costumes, as well as an area for small fry to make art in different media. Lots of other lessons, disguised as playtime, are also staged.

Legoland

1 Legoland Drive, at I-5 (1-760 918 5346/www.lego.com). **Open** hours vary by season. **Admission** $43.95; $36.95 discounts; free under-2s. **Credit** AmEx, Disc, MC, V.
On paper, a theme park with almost everything built out of Lego might seem a bit much, but it's actually a heap of fun. You'll marvel at what can be constructed out of little multicoloured blocks, such as the park's centrepiece Miniland USA, a scale replica of US landmarks. The park is a work in progress, with additions made regularly. The painstakingly accurate details will impress even the most jaded visitor.

Legoland also features several small rollercoasters: try the Dragon, with its signature dragon-shaped cars, and the Coastersaurus, which moves through life-sized animated dinosaurs. (Made of Lego, of course.) Other attractions include the Aquazone Wave Racers and the Bionicle Blaster, an interactive spinning vehicle.

Most of the park is aimed at the youngest visitors, with the attractions supplemented by enough shows and educational activities to keep kids entertained for days. Adults will have fun, too, but will most likely consider a single visit plenty.

Oceanside & Vista

Bordered by Camp Pendleton to the north, **Oceanside** was not considered a holiday spot until recently, thanks to its proximity to the army base and rowdy reputation. However, things are changing: the city is actively pursuing the tourist dollar by capitalising on its handful of attractions: chiefly, the **Oceanside Museum of Art** (*see p90*), the **Mission San Luis Rey** (*see p90*) and the **California Surf Museum** (223 North Coast Highway, 1-760 721 6876, www.surfmuseum.org), where you can find out about the pioneers who helped develop the sport. The neighbouring town of **Vista**, meanwhile, is home to the enthusiastically run **Antique Gas & Steam Engine Museum** (2040 N Santa Fe

Avenue, 1-760 941 1791, www.agsem.com, $2-$3), a volunteer-run collection of old railway gear, much of it in working order.

But outdoor activities are really the thing here. The **Oceanside Pier** reaches 1,954 feet out into the water; the longest wooden pier on the West Coast, it's popular with fishermen. The **Audubon Society Nature Center** (2202 South Coast Highway, 1-760 439 2473, www.bvaudubon.org, closed Mon) has exhibits of local and migratory birds, but the best reason to visit is its lagoon: the only freshwater lagoon in California, it provides a home for dozens of species of waterfowl. Outdoor enthusiasts of the sporting stripe will also be drawn to the **Harbor**, a favourite of kayakers and jet skiers, though the four miles of sandy, palm tree-lined beach will attract anyone with a holidaymaker's bone in their body.

Mission San Luis Rey

4050 Mission Avenue, at Rancho del Oro Drive (1-760 757 3651/www.sanluisrey.org). **Open** 10am-4pm daily. **Admission** $5; $3 discounts. **No credit cards.**

Surf's up

Surfing has been part of San Diego's beach culture since at least the 1940s, becoming more ingrained with each passing generation. While the county's 50 miles of beaches don't get the huge waves of Hawaii or Bondi, they are immensely popular, for the weather as much as the surf. The largest waves tend to arrive in winter, when the use of wet suits is recommended.

Swami's in Encinitas and **Tourmaline Park** in Pacific Beach are two of the best spots to catch some waves or watch those who do; for a superior view of the action, try Ocean Beach Pier or Crystal Pier, from which you get to watch surfers carve between the support pylons from above the water level. Beginners may want to try the calmer waves of **La Jolla Shores**, **Mission Beach** or **Pacific Beach**; more experienced wave-riders should head towards **Sunset Cliffs**, where just the trek down the cliffs towards the water can be enough to separate the pros from the amateurs, or South Bay's **Tijuana Slough**. A number of schools offer lessons, among them **Surf Diva, Inc** (1-858 454 8273, www.surfdiva.com), the first all-women surfing school, and the **Surfari Surf School** (3470 Mission Boulevard, 1-858 337 3287, www.surfarisurf.com).

The 18th of the 21 missions built in California, San Luis Rey is very much in operation; it's now run by the Franciscan Friars of California. Visitors can take self-guided tours, explore the gardens, visit the museum and even attend mass if they're so minded.

Oceanside Museum of Art

704 Pier View Way, at N Ditmar Street (1-760 721 2787/www.oma-online.org). **Open** 10am-4pm Tue-Sat; 1-4pm Sun. **Admission** $5; $3 discounts. **Credit** MC, V.
Works of local artists are emphasised here, but there's also international art on display. OMA nurtures budding artists with lessons using a variety of media, and redesigns the galleries for changing exhibitions.

Where to eat, drink & stay

Not much to get excited about here. Still, in Encinitas, the Hawaiian and Polynesian food at picturesque **Kealani's** (137 West D Street, 1-760 942 5642, closed Sun, $), a surfers' favourite, is decent enough, as are the dirt-cheap Mexican snacks at **Juanita's Taco Shop Estilo Tepatitlan** (290 Highway 101, 1-760 943 9612, closed dinner, $). In Oceanside, the **101 Café** (631 Highway 101, 1-760 722 5220, www.101cafe.net, $) serves basic diner favourites.

Among the lodging options in Encinitas is the compact, comfortable **Portofino Inn** (186 North Coast Highway, 1-800 566 6654, 1-760 944 0301, www.portofinobeachinn.com, $69-$185); Oceanside places to stay include the well-situated, no-frills **Guest House Inn** (1103 North Coast Highway, 1-800 214 8378, 1-760 722 1904, www.guesthouseintl.com, $87-$195).

Resources

Hospital

Encinitas *Scripps Memorial Hospital, 354 Santa Fe Drive (1-760 753 6501/www.scrippshealth.org).*

Internet

Encinitas *E Street Café, 130 West E Street (1-760 230 2038/www.estreetcafe.com).* **Open** 6am-midnight daily.
Oceanside *The Chatroom, 3375 Mission Avenue (1-760 433 5087/www.thechatroom.us).* **Open** 10.30am-midnight daily.

Police

Encinitas *175 N El Camino Real (1-760 966 3500).*
Oceanside *3855 Mission Avenue (1-760 435 4900).*

Post office

Encinitas *1150 Garden View Road (1-760 753 1415).*
Oceanside *1895 Avenida del Oro (1-760 806 3866).*

Tourist information

Carlsbad *Carlsbad CVB, 400 Carlsbad Village Drive (1-800 227 5722/www.carlsbadca.org).* **Open** 9am-5pm Mon-Fri; 10am-4pm Sat; 10am-3pm Sun.

Slap your beach up in **Oceanside**. *See p90.*

Encinitas *Encinitas Visitor Center, 138 Encinitas Boulevard (1-760 753 6041/www.encinitaschamber. com).* **Open** 9am-5pm Mon-Fri; 10am-4pm Sat, Sun.
Oceanside *Oceanside Chamber of Commerce, 928 North Coast Highway (1-760 722 1534/www.ocean sidechamber.com).* **Open** 8.30am-4.30pm Mon-Fri.

Getting there

The **San Diego Coaster** (1-800 262 7837, www.sdcommute.com), a light rail service, links Downtown San Diego and Oceanside, making stops at (among others) Old Town, Solana Beach, Encinitas and Carlsbad. Fares run from $3.75 to $5.25. There are around a dozen trains a day during the week, but fewer on weekends.

The Back Country

Heading east and north-east of San Diego, civilisation runs out in a hurry. The most interesting town on the 110 unremarkable miles of I-15 that link San Diego and San Bernardino is **Escondido**, notable mostly for the **Wild Animal Park** (*see below*) nearby. Taking I-8 through the Cleveland National Forest is prettier, but unless you've a yen to throw money away at one of the area's casinos – the **Sycuan Casino** in El Cajon (5469 Casino Way, El Cajon, 1-800 279 2826, www.sycuancasino.com), or the **Viejas Casino** in Alpine (5000 Willows Road, 1-800 847 6537, www.viejas.com) – or are heading up towards Julian or south-east into Arizona, there's no reason to head this way.

Better, perhaps, that you should begin by driving out on I-8 but then loop out on Route 67 towards **Ramona** and one of the legendary breakfasts at the **Ramona Café** (628 Main Street, 1-760 789 8656, $–$$): try the Kitchen Sink option. From here, take Route 78 east

to Santa Ysabel, from where you have two options: east to **Julian** (*see below*), or north on route 76 to **Palomar Mountain** (*see p92*).

Wild Animal Park

15500 San Pasqual Valley Road, at W Zoo Road, Escondido (1-760 747 8702/www.sandiegozoo.org). **Open** 9am-4pm daily. **Admission** $26.50; $19.50-$23.85 discounts. **Credit** AmEx, MC, V.
The Wild Animal Park is a division of the San Diego Zoo (*see p72*), but unlike the more traditional animal enclosures in Balboa Park, a 'safari'-style set-up allows animals, from gazelles to rhinos, to roam free. This part of the San Pasqual Valley is known for its heat, which remains even when other parts of San Diego are cool; as such, it makes an ideal home for the larger nomadic animals. There's an African theme to the park as a whole, with the main area – 'Nairobi Village' – a re-creation of an African fishing hamlet constructed over a rushing waterfall. Here also is the unmissable Lorikeet Landing, always a hit with children: for a small fee, guests can have the colourful red birds land on their arms and feed on nectar.

The central area is the most typically zoo-like, with lush foliage, a petting kraal and a lagoon, as well as the Hidden Jungle, a tropical forest area that hosts the lovely Butterflies and Orchids exhibit each spring. The park's greatest treasures, though, are in the outlying areas. The Kilimanjaro Safari Walk leads you along a two-mile path that takes in great views of the animals, but the best way to get the broadest overview is to board the Wgasa Bush Line Railway for the hourlong tour. The monorail train circles the park's 1,800 acres, offering panoramic views at every turn.

Julian

The small Gold Rush town of **Julian**, which sprung up in the 1870s, is a charming place. Trouble is, it knows it, and so does everyone else. Towns like it are, well, if not quite ten a

All things bright... **Tijuana**. *See p93*.

penny in the Gold Country (*see pp295-313*), then still a running theme. Down in San Diego County, though, Julian is one of a kind, and so in summer, its sweet Victorian Main Street gets overrun by day-trippers and weekend-breakers. Wildfires in late 2003 and 2004 missed the town but burned much of the surrounding landscape, but the beautiful foliage for which the area is known has already begun to make a comeback.

The two-mile strip of **Main Street** is just a collection of nooks and crannies filled with small antique stores, gift shops and pie shops. Though the town was built on gold money, it's now famed for its apples and orchards dot the surrounding fields. The first stop for anyone wanting to explore the town's history is the **Julian Pioneer Museum** (2811 Washington Street, 1-760 765 0227, closed Mon Apr-Nov & closed Mon-Fri Dec-Mar, $1), which houses artefacts from local Indian tribes and the days of the early pioneers. The nearby **Grosskopf Family House**, whose trade was blacksmithing, is open to visitors who want a look at living conditions in the early days of the state. A self-guided walking tour (maps from the Chamber of Commerce) includes the tiny **Julian Jail**; built in 1914, it was the first building in town equipped with an indoor toilet.

Head north on C Street and you'll find the **Eagle & High Peak Mines** (North C Street, 1-760 765 0036, $1-$8), a working gold mine. Visitors can see rock and mineral displays, as well as demonstrations of how you pan for gold and the machinery used to extract minerals.

Palomar Mountain

Drive 25 indelibly pretty miles north-west of Santa Ysabel on Route 76 and you'll reach Cleveland National Forest and, eventually (up Highway S7), the **Palomar Mountain State Park** (1-760 742 3462, www.palomar. statepark.org). The big attraction is the **Palomar Observatory**, a vast white hilltop dome housing a 200-inch (508-centimetre) telescope. Definitely worth the drive for the stunning views.

Where to eat, drink & stay

The rustic **Julian Café** (2112 Main Street, Julian, 1-760 765 2712, $$) is enormously popular. Alternatively, try the terrific pie, made from apples grown in the owner's orchard, at the **Julian Pie Company** (2225 Main Street, 1-760 765 2449, $). If you're near Palomar Mountain, head for a bite at **Mother's Kitchen** (junction of S6 & S7, 1-760 742 4233, closed Tue & Wed in winter, $), a landmark eatery whose baked goods are rarely less than immaculate.

Julian is prime B&B territory. Both the central **Julian Hotel** (2032 Main Street, 1-800 734 5854, 1-760 765 0201, www.julian hotel.com, $100-$195), built in 1897, and the newer **Butterfield Bed & Breakfast** (2284 Sunset Drive, 1-800 379-4262, 1-760 765 2179, www.butterfieldbandb.com, $130-$175) are romantic places to spend the night.

Resources

Post office

Julian *1785 Highway 78 (1-760 765 2336).*

Tourist information

Julian *Julian Chamber of Commerce, 2129 Main Street (1-760 765 1857/www.julianca.com).* **Open** 10am-4pm daily.

Tijuana

Only 20 minutes from Downtown San Diego, **Tijuana** is the world's busiest border town. It's also one of the most tourist-slanted. The town is Spanish-speaking, but most residents are at least casually conversant in English and US dollars are readily accepted. American citizens who don't intend to travel beyond the border zone and/or plan to stay in Tijuana for less than 72 hours need only a form of photo ID (a driver's licence, say) to get in and out of town; everyone else should carry their passport. Phone numbers are listed below with the Mexican country code (52) and the Tijuana area code (664); to access these numbers from the US, precede them numbers with the US international access code (011).

Tijuana, be aware, is not The Real Mexico. By far the most tourist-oriented part of the city is **Avenida Revolución**, which stretches several miles through Downtown. Every inch of the place is packed with small restaurants and shops hawking straw hats, leather goods and paper flowers. Still, it could be worse; or, at least, more predictable. Over the last few years, Jack in the Box, Burger King and the Hard Rock Café have moved in, and are now doing big business catering to some of the least adventurous tourists on earth.

For a more authentic Mexican experience (and better shopping), explore the surrounding area. Once off the main street, the city reverts to the locals, often resulting in lower prices than those quoted a block or so away. Tijuana is packed with bars and nightclubs, and with a drinking age of 18, it's a major attraction for young adults. Stateside authorities do look for signs of intoxication during re-entry to the US.

Still, there is more to the place than ropey tacos and alcoholically challenged students. Built in 1928, **Agua Caliente** (Bulevar Agua Caliente) was once a fabulous resort, a Prohibition playground for the naughtiest of the rich and famous; Rita Hayworth was discovered here. It's mostly ruined now, and the few remaining bungalows are all private residences. Meanwhile, bullfights are still extremely popular in Mexico, and are held here in a pair of stadia: **El Toreo** (Bulevar Agua Caliente, +52 664 686 1510) and **Plaza de Toros Monumental** (Calle Rafael Rodríguez s/n, esq

López Mateos, +52 664 680 1808), aka the Bullring-by-the-Sea, on Sundays from May to September. Tickets are available at the gate.

Other attractions are tackier. At the seen-better-days **Mexitlán** theme park (899 Avenida Benito Juarez, Zona Rio, +52 664 638 4101, closed Mon mid May-mid-Sept & closed Mon, Tue mid Sept-mid May, $3.50), you'll find a miniature replica of Mexico, though at 150,000 square feet, it's not all that small. Celebrities stand alongside important historical figures at the **Museo de Cera**, the town's wax museum (8281 Calle 1, +52 664 688 2478, $1.50). Rising above them all is the **Centro Cultural Tijuana** (Paseo de los Héroes, +52 664 687 9650, www.cecut.gob.mx), where exhibits range from Mexican culture to anthropology studies. Lectures, concerts and dance are held in the concert hall and courtyard; the Omnimax screens daily films in English.

Where to eat & drink

Long-running **Café la Especial** (Avenida Revolución 718, +52 664 685 6654, $) offers steamed tacos and other favourites at a walk-up window; there's also a full-service restaurant. **El Rodeo** (Bulevar Salinas 1647, +52 664 686 5640, $) does the best steaks in town. Popular **Super Antojitos** (1810 4th Street, +52 664 685 5070, $) serves basic dishes, as does **La Escondida** (Santa Monica 1, +52 664 681 4457, $).

Resources

Hospital

Tijuana *Avenida Centenario 10851 (+52 664 684 0922).*

Internet

Tijuana *Bulevar Lázaro Cardenas 5100 (+52 664 626 1816).* **Open** 10am-11pm daily.

Police

Tijuana *Avenida Constitución 1616 (060).*

Post office

Tijuana *Calle 11A, at Avenida Negrete.*

Tourist information

San Ysidro *4570 Camino de la Plaza San Ysidro (1-619 428 6200).*

Getting there

By bus

From San Diego, take either the 932 bus or the Blue Line trolley to San Ysidro; central Tijuana is a short walk away. Journey time is around 20-30mins. There's a Greyhound service from San Diego to Mexico (1hr 10min, $5 one-way, $8 round-trip). If you're driving, leave your car at the border (there are several parking lots) and walk across.

Los Angeles & Orange County

Shout hooray for Hollywood, but there's more to La-La Land than the movies...

It may take you a while to get your bearings in Los Angeles. You won't a sign directing you to the city centre, because there isn't one. Greater LA is a sprawling agglomeration spread over a huge flood basin, divided by freeways and bound by ocean and mountains: on its western edge by 160 miles of Pacific coastline, and then, clockwise, by the Santa Monica, San Gabriel, San Bernadino, San Jacinto and Santa Ana Mountains. Laid over this geography is a dizzying variety of cityscapes and neighbourhoods. You won't get the hang of it straight away.

But like the triumphant post-match sportsman who, he tells the interviewer, is just trying to take it one game at a time, you'll get more out of LA and Orange County by doing less while you're here. The area as a whole is initially overwhelming and the freeway traffic frustratingly time-consuming; though LA and, to a lesser extent, OC are served by a network of buses and an expanding metro rail system, doing it without a car is essentially impossible. However, the individual cities, towns and neighbourhoods that make up LA are on an approachable scale; some are even pedestrian-friendly. Though it may be a drive away, all human life is here, and with a little forethought, you'll find LA a rather more manageable city than you might expect. Enjoy the ride.

HISTORY

The history of Los Angeles as a city dates to 1781, when the Spaniards decided they needed a settlement, or *pueblo*, in Southern California. A site was selected nine miles east of the San Gabriel mission, where the Los Angeles River widened. The new *pueblo* was a dusty cow town for decades. But by the time California entered the US in 1850, many Americans had settled there. The arrival of the railroad from St Louis in 1886, and the short-lived but influential boom that followed, really put LA on the map.

The region grew apace. Influenced by Chamber of Commerce advertisements extolling LA's sunny climate, thousands of Midwestern

farmers sold up and moved west. All the city needed was water, which led to one of the most audacious schemes ever devised to ensure a city's greatness. In 1904 a former mayor of LA named Fred Eaton went to the Owens Valley, a high-desert region north of the city, claimed he was working on a dam project for the federal government and began buying land along the Owens River. Once the land was purchased, Eaton said the federal project was dead and revealed his true purpose: to divert the Owens River through an aqueduct to LA. William Mulholland, a self-taught Irish immigrant, then accomplished one of the great engineering feats in US history; his 230-mile aqueduct from the Owens Valley to the San Fernando Valley still operates, without electrical power, entirely on a gravity system.

With the water in place, LA boomed in the 1910s and 1920s, partly on the strength of real-estate speculation, and partly on the rise of three new industries: petroleum, aircraft and, of course, movies. Inspired by the temperate climate, directors began filming in LA around 1910, and moved to Hollywood the following year. The country-wide Depression slowed

Santa Monica Beach.

> ▶ For a full survey of LA and OC, buy the 320-page *Time Out Los Angeles* guide.

The best Los Angeles & Orange County

Things to do

Where to start? The choice is overwhelming, from landmarks like **Disneyland** (*see p119*), the **Hollywood Walk of Fame** (*see p107*) and the shops of **Beverly Hills** (*see p103*), to more obscure spots such as the **Museum of Jurassic Technology** (*see p103*) and the **Norton Simon Museum** (*see p116*). Best retreat to the **fabulous beaches** (*see p110 Life's a beach*) while you make up your mind.

Places to stay

For classic decadence, try **Chateau Marmont** (*see p145*). For old-school opulence, its the **Beverly Hills Hotel** (*see p143*). For modern-day cool, head for either of the **Standard** hotels (*see p145 and p146*). And for affordable style and convenience, book into the **Banana Bungalow** or the **Farmer's Daughter** (for both, *see p145*).

Places to eat

A perfect foodie's day begins with breakfast at the **Polo Lounge** (for toffs; *see p125*) or **Millie's** (for scruffs; *see p129*). Lunch? **Roscoe's House of Chicken 'n' Waffles** (*see p128*), **Vermont** (*see p129*) or the **Apple Pan** (*see p124*). A mid-afternoon snack should be enjoyed at **Randy's Donuts** (*see p131*), **Pink's Hot Dogs** (*see p126*) or **Tito's Tacos** (*see p124*), before a blow-out dinner at **Noé**

(*see p128*), **Valentino** (*see p122*) or **Spago of Beverly Hills** (*see p125*). Still got the munchies? Head to **Fred 62** (*see p129*), open round the clock.

Nightlife

Hooray for Hollywood, especially bars like the characterful **Frolic Room** (*see p133*) and the **Avalon** and **Highlands** (*see p134*) nightclubs. In West Hollywood bars such as **Dime** and **North** (*see p132*) are joined by a big gay scene, while Silver Lake (*see p112*) is home to several fine drinking holes.

Culture

The movie industry dominates: regardless of what's playing, **Grauman's Chinese Theatre** and the **American Cinematheque** (*see p138*) should be experienced. But the real headline-maker lately has been spectacular **Disney Hall**, home to the LA Philharmonic (*see p139*).

Sports & activities

Basketball's Lakers might be the better team, but summer in LA's not summer in LA without taking in baseball's **Los Angeles Dodgers** (*see p114*). Those of a more active bent who are disinclined to go **surfing** (*see p121*) should head to **Griffith Park** (*see p113*), where there are golf courses, tennis courts, football pitches, MTB tracks and over 50 miles of hiking trails.

---

growth in LA, but only briefly. By the 1940s it was on the rise again, becoming a major military manufacturing centre and staging ground for the US fight against Japan in the Pacific. Dormitory communities sprang up to accommodate the workers, helping to establish the sprawling pattern of city development that came to characterise LA in the post-war period.

After the war, the entire LA region devoted itself to building things. Road construction soared in 1947 when California imposed an additional petrol tax to pay for it. Virtually the entire freeway system was built between 1950 and 1970. Perhaps its most important long-term effect was to open up vast tracts of land in outlying areas for urban development, especially in the San Fernando Valley and Orange County. A seminal event in this suburbanisation was the opening, in 1955, of Disneyland.

The city's population was diversifying. During the war, more than 200,000 African-Americans moved here to take advantage of job

opportunities. In need of labourers, Los Angeles again encouraged the return of the Mexicans and Mexican-Americans who had been pushed out a decade before. But, their welcome was not warm; the Zoot Suit Riots of 1943 showed Mexican dis-satisfaction with racism, while the Watts Riots of summer 1965 saw the frustrations of the black ghetto explode into one of the first and most destructive of the US's urban disturbances. By the early 1990s Los Angeles was a social tinderbox , and when a jury acquitted four LAPD police officers of the assault of Rodney King in 1992, it touched off a riot that lasted three days.

Yet despite racial tensions, an economic renaissance beginning in the mid 1990s has brought new life to LA. Political and financial scandal never seems far away, though it's hard to imagine anything could top the events of 2003, which saw California governor Gray Davis replaced by Arnold Schwarzenegger. Still, this is LA, where each blockbuster has to be bigger and better than the last one. Anything can happen.

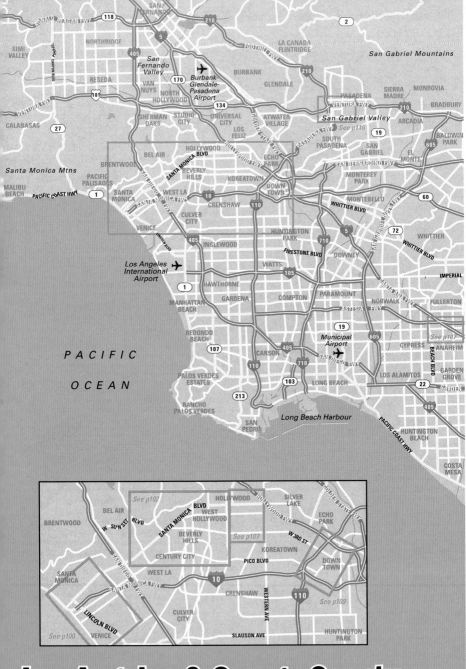

Los Angeles & Orange County

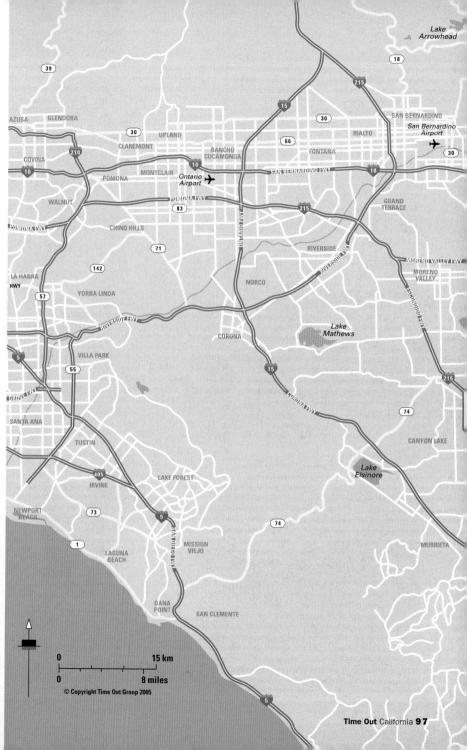

Sightseeing

When exploring LA, it doesn't necessarily pay to start first thing in the morning. Sure, an early arrival is recommended at Disneyland and Universal Studios to beat the crowds. But if you want to cross town, then an early-ish start will probably mean you get stuck in the stressful freeway rush-hour traffic.

A number of organisations offer tours around LA. **Starline Tours** (1-800 959 3131, www.starlinetours.com) offer a variety of pricey coach tours around the city, as does **LA Tours** (1-323 937 0999, www.la-tours.com). The laudable **LA Conservancy** (1-213 623 2489, www.laconservancy.org) runs a number of tours, the majority on foot, that aim to educate people on the urban architectural heritage of LA, while **Red Line Tours** (1-323 402 1074, www.redlinetours.com) offers fine tours of Downtown and Hollywood.

The beach towns

Malibu & Pacific Palisades

Malibu is not a place so much as a 27-mile stretch of the Pacific Coast Highway, north of Los Angeles, winding through some of Southern California's most magnificent coastal terrain. Parts of it are lined, on the ocean side,

Los Angeles in brief

THE BEACH TOWNS
There's more to the Westside beach towns than sun, sea and sand. Working north to south down the Pacific coast, desirable **Malibu**, affluent **Pacific Palisades** (for both, see above), comfortable **Santa Monica** (p99), arty **Venice** and tidy **Marina del Rey** (for both, p100) all have distinct characters; south of LAX is the **South Bay** (p101), made up of pleasant coast-hugging cities **El Segundo**, **Manhattan Beach**, **Hermosa Beach** and **Redondo Beach**. The beach cities are not at their best in June, when they're swathed in morning cloud known as June Gloom.

WEST LA
Moving inland, LA soon reveals itself to be the glamorous city of popular legend.

Granted, you'll have to drive through workaday **Culver City** (p105) and **Century City** (p103), but then there's wealthy, rustic **Brentwood** (p100), which adjoins, to the west, UCLA-dominated **Westwood** and, to the north, the moneyed **Bel Air** (for both, see p103).

BEVERLY HILLS
From the impossibly posh shops around Rodeo Drive to the expansive, tree-lined residential streets that surround it, **Beverly Hills** (p103) more than lives up to its highfalutin reputation.

WEST HOLLYWOOD
Separated from Beverly Hills by Doheny Drive, parts of **West Hollywood** (p105) are nearly as swanky as its neighbour to the

Downtown.

by beach houses of varying sizes and styles, with mediocre commercial buildings on the inland side nestling against the Santa Monica Mountains. It's a wealthy area and sniffy towards visitors; its residents include privacy-hungry stars and industry moguls. Malibu's treats are its beaches and canyons: within yards of the entrance to one of the many canyon trails, you can be out of view of the city and communing with coyotes and red-tailed hawks.

Between Malibu and Santa Monica lies the small residential community of **Pacific Palisades**. The perfect, shiny lawns and large bungalows of the area are straight out of *Leave It to Beaver*, but contained within its Santa Monica Mountains location are some wonderful, rugged places to visit. Among them are **Rustic Canyon Park** (1-310 454 5734), **Temescal Canyon Park** (1-310 459 5931) and **Will Rogers State Historic Park** (1-310 454 8212, www.parks.ca.gov), whose hikes are topped by the path leading to the breathtaking views of mountains and sea at Inspiration Point.

Santa Monica & Ocean Park

At first glance, **Santa Monica** appears to be a white-bread-and-mayo place, long on Starbucks, short on nightclubs and devoid of any edge. However, it's easy to see how the town, named by Spanish settlers in 1770 and taken over by Anglo pioneers in the 19th century, became the

east, albeit far denser; conversely, Beverly Hills doesn't have the nightlife to compete with the Sunset Strip.

THE FAIRFAX DISTRICT & THE MIRACLE MILE
South of West Hollywood is the **Fairfax District** (*p106*), a Jewish neighbourhood with some terrific shops. The **Miracle Mile** (*p106*) is best enjoyed for its array of museums.

HOLLYWOOD
Due east of West Hollywood is **Hollywood** itself (*p107*), whose glamorous reputation belies a ragged neighbourhood only marginally improved by a recent regeneration project.

MIDTOWN
The boundaries of **Midtown** (*p108*) can vary. But, for the purposes of this book, they include the wealthy **Hancock Park** (*p108*), earthier **Koreatown** (*p108*), and, nearer to Downtown, the down-at-heel **Westlake**, whose main landmark is MacArthur Park.

DOWNTOWN
Stretching south from the eastern end of Sunset Boulevard, **Downtown** (*p108*) is the site of the original city and home to most of LA's financial institutions, a compelling clash of comparatively old buildings with immense skyscrapers.

LOS FELIZ, SILVER LAKE & ECHO PARK
Three increasingly hip residential 'hoods that sit in an arc starting just north-east of Hollywood. **Los Feliz** (*p112*) is home to a number of funky shops and restaurants, and the vast sprawl of Griffith Park; **Silver Lake** (*p112*) is cheaper, scruffier, homier and artier; and **Echo Park** (*p112*) is most frequently visited by folks on their way to a baseball game at Dodger Stadium.

EAST LA
Located in eight square miles east of Downtown, **East LA** is the heartland of LA's Mexican community.

THE VALLEYS
The **San Fernando Valley** (*p114*) to the north-west of LA, and the **San Gabriel Valley** (*p116*) to the north-east, are ridiculed for embodying the horrors of American suburbia: hot, smoggy and covered with low-rise sprawl. This probably holds true in the San Fernando Valley, but parts of the San Gabriel Valley are very charming.

SOUTH CENTRAL
While popular cliché about South Central does stick in places (chiefly, the long-troubled **Watts**; *p117*), it's also blown out of the water in areas such as affluent **Crenshaw** and cultured **Leimert Park** (for both, *see p118*).

LONG BEACH
Drive over the majestic Vincent Thomas Bridge from **San Pedro** and you'll reach **Long Beach** (for both, *see p118*), an old US Navy port that's now a relatively cosmopolitan city of nearly 500,000.

ORANGE COUNTY
Bordering LA County to the south-east, **Orange County** (*p119*) is best known as the home of Disneyland in **Anaheim**.

Southern California

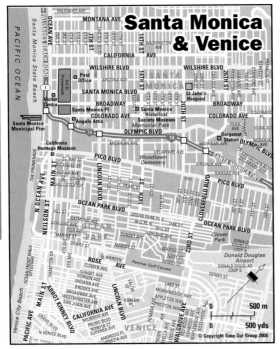

Santa Monica & Venice

© Copyright Time Out Group 2005

Avenue, the Rodeo Drive of the coast. Yoga studios and health-food markets rub shoulders with furniture shops and chi-chi restaurants, all popular with the yuppies and wealthy liberals of north Santa Monica and nearby Brentwood.

Heading south down Main Street from the Promenade will lead you into the bohemian neighbourhood of **Ocean Park**. Among the highlights are the **Edgemar Center for the Arts** (No.2437, 1-323 399 3666, www.edgemarcenter.org), a Gehry-designed sculptural mall, and the **Eames Office Gallery** (No.2665, 1-310 396 5991, www.eamesoffice.com), founded by Charles and Ray's grandson.

California Heritage Museum

2612 Main Street, at Ocean Park Boulevard (1-310 392 8537/www.californiaheritage museum.org). I-10, exit 4th-5th Street south. **Open** 11am-4pm Wed-Sun. **Admission** $5; $3 discounts; free under-12s. **Credit** *Shop only* MC, V.

This enthusiastically run operation, housed in an 1894 Summer P Hunt house, is devoted to decorative arts. The exhibits take the shape of a number of rooms decorated in period style, among them a Victorian-era dining room and a '30s kitchen.

Santa Monica Museum of Art

Building G1, Bergamot Station, 2525 Michigan Avenue, at Cloverfield Boulevard (1-310 586 6488/ www.smmoa.org). I-10, exit Cloverfield Boulevard north. **Open** 11am-6pm Tue-Sat. **Admission** free; suggested donation $3. **Credit** AmEx, MC, V.
Greater LA's best contemporary *kunsthalle* occupies a corner of Bergamot Station, a complex of art galleries, and attracts sizeable crowds to its openings and lively temporary exhibitions by local and international artists. Shows have included collages and drawings by the late Fluxus-Happenings artist Al Hansen and his grandson, singer Beck.

Venice & Marina del Rey

Despite gentrification, the touristy atmosphere, and the fact that its name long ago passed into popular cliché as a byword for hippiedom, **Venice** still retains its edge. Its most visible population is still hippies, bums, artists and students, but they've been joined by young professionals in creative industries; the

hub of LA's Westside. With the Santa Monica Mountains to the north and the Pacific to the west, the palm tree-lined cliffs and year-round sun tempered by ocean breezes, its natural surroundings couldn't be bettered. It's always summertime in Santa Monica, and if you've got a little money, the living is always easy.

There is, though, more to Santa Monica than its climate and setting: some of the best restaurants in the LA basin, thriving galleries and coffeehouses, a popular shopping circuit and, most surprisingly, some daring modern architecture. All these combine to attract a great many tourists to the town (check the plethora of beachfront hotels on Ocean Avenue), despite the fact that sights are limited to the popular **Santa Monica State Beach** (*see p110* **Life's a beach**) and a handful of small museums.

A few blocks inland from the beach sits what is, after the sand and the sea, Santa Monica's main attraction: the **Third Street Promenade**, a four-block pedestrianised stretch of shops that runs down 3rd Street from Wilshire Boulevard to Colorado Avenue. It's a handsome affair, although its range of shops is chain-heavy and conservative. Things are more interesting several blocks north on east–west **Montana**

uneasy mix here is completed by low-income black and Latino communities beset by social problems.

Venice was founded in 1904 by entrepreneur Abbot Kinney, who hoped that it would become the hub of an American cultural renaissance. In time, Venice became a successful resort. However, it wasn't until later, after its resort popularity foundered, that the area developed as a cultural hotbed. Artists were attracted by the sense of community and cheap rents. In May the Venice Artwalk offers the chance to tour more than 60 artists' studios.

Disc drive

CDs to soundtrack your journey around LA and Orange County.

Today!/Summer Days and Summer Nights The Beach Boys
Splendid two-for-one reissue of a pair of early albums by this most quintessentially Californian band. Stellar hits collection *Endless Summer* also does the trick.

Now is the Hour Charlie Haden/ Quartet West
Any of Haden's sublimely smoky, *noir*-influenced Quartet West records would work just as well, but saxophonist Ernie Watts is on particularly excellent form here. One for late-night driving.

Forever Changes Love
One of the few records from the LA rock scene of the late 1960s that's held up. And how: *Forever Changes* is a blissed-out folk-rock diamond, despite 'Bummer in the Summer'.

Ozomatli Ozomatli
Modern-day melting-pot LA: Latino rhythms meet black hip hop in an Anglo rock venue, and everyone gets on fine and dandy. One of the best live bands on earth.

Aja Steely Dan
'Black Cow', 'Deacon Blues', 'Peg'… Becker and Fagen's finest, and an LA archetype. Companion piece: *Gaucho*, the souring of the Hollywood dream.

Grand Prix Teenage Fanclub
In which four pasty Scottish lads journey to LA and come away with the sunniest rock record of the last two decades. Essential.

The World is a Ghetto War
Fearsome and funky, the sound of black LA in the early 1970s.

As in Santa Monica, the attractions of Venice are mostly commercial; unlike its neighbour, though, Venice's shops and cafés are predominantly independent. The increasingly upscale **Abbot Kinney Boulevard** holds a varied collection of galleries, shops, cafés and restaurants; **Rose Avenue**, an east–west commercial street at the north end of the area, holds a few interesting second-hand shops and, nearby, the famous **Gold's Gym** (360 Hampton Drive). Some of the iron-pumping, steroid-chomping strongmen who frequent it also show off at Muscle Beach, a small corner of the world-famous but rather wearying **Venice Beach** (*see p110* Life's a beach).

Inland, a fascinating couple of hours can be spent strolling the neighbourhood. The area west of Lincoln Boulevard has rows of clapboard beach-houses on 'walk-streets' (pedestrian-only alleyways leading to the beach) and, at the more affluent southern end, one of LA's best-kept secrets: an idyllic enclave of eclectic architecture, waterways, bridges and motormouth ducks known as the Venice Canals. The artistic bent of many of the locals is reflected in the volume and quality of murals and public artworks scattered around the neighbourhood; the most striking is Jonathan Borofsky's *Ballerina Clown*, where Main Street meets Rose Avenue.

Separating Venice from LAX is **Marina del Rey Harbor**, a resort and residential complex completed in 1965. Its picturesque artificial harbour contains eight basins named to evoke the South Seas (Tahiti Way, Bora Bora Way); all are filled with bobbing yachts, motor boats and flashy cruisers, and surrounded by low- and high-rise apartment buildings. Attractions are all recreational. Picnic, jog and cycle in the **Burton W Chace Park** and **Admiralty Park** at the northern end; fish from a dock at the west end of Chace Park or rent a boat to go ocean-fishing at **Fisherman's Village** (13755 Fiji Way, Green Boathouse); or join whale-watching excursions run during the winter.

The South Bay

South of LAX, the ambience grows calmer; something partly due to the absence of tourists. That's not to say these beach towns are unpopular; on sunny weekends, **Manhattan Beach** is mobbed by skaters, cyclists and sun worshippers, enjoying the people-watching on the strands. The surfside flavour continues southward into nearby **Hermosa Beach** and **Redondo Beach**, the latter boasting one of the area's most developed piers in the shape of the anodyne but family-friendly **King Harbor** (at the end of Portofino Way), with its shops, restaurants, fish markets and marina.

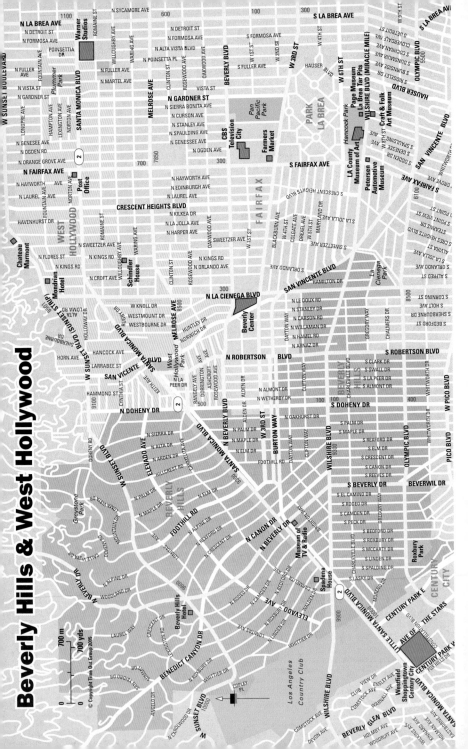

One of the best drives in Southern California is the loop around the Palos Verdes Peninsula. Take the Pacific Coast Highway (Highway 1, aka the PCH) south to Palos Verdes Boulevard (at Redondo State Beach, a mile south of the eponymous city), go south again to Palos Verdes Drive West and then Palos Verdes Drive South. On the way, stop at the glass and stone **Wayfarer's Chapel** (5755 Palos Verdes Drive South, 1-310 377 1650, www.wayfarerschapel. org), built by architect Lloyd Wright (Frank's son), and the **South Coast Botanic Garden** (26300 Crenshaw Boulevard, 1-310 544 6815, http://parks.co.la.ca.us).

West LA

Brentwood is one of LA's more exclusive neighbourhoods. Today the rustic hills north of San Vicente Boulevard house dozens of stars; in years gone by, Marilyn Monroe died a lonely death at 12305 5th Helena Drive, and OJ Simpson didn't murder Nicole Brown Simpson at a now-relandscaped condo on S Bundy Drive. However, as in the nearby hillside community of **Bel Air**, where dozens more stars make their homes, there's little to actually see or do here.

South of Bel Air, **Westwood** is dominated by the 400-acre campus of the influential University of California at Los Angeles, aka **UCLA**. The site is well worth a stroll, diverse architectural styles blending in beautifully landscaped grounds; it's also home to two museums, the ethnographic **UCLA Fowler Museum of Cultural History** (1-310 825 4361, www.fmch.ucla.edu) and the arty **UCLA Hammer Museum** (1-310 443 7000, www.hammer.ucla.edu).

Nearby Westwood Village, south of UCLA, is a good place for inexpensive, student-quality food and, south of Wilshire Boulevard, for Persian restaurants. Heading south down Westwood Boulevard, you arrive at Pico Boulevard and the **Westside Pavilion**, a classic 1980s LA mall.

Getty Center
1200 Getty Center Drive, at I-405 (1-310 440 7300/ www.getty.edu). I-405, exit Getty Center Drive. **Open** 10am-6pm Tue-Thur, Sun; 10am-9pm Fri, Sat. **Admission** free.
Los Angeles's acropolis was conceived as a home for the hitherto disparate entities of the J Paul Getty Trust and initially designed in 1984 by architect Richard Meier; however, it took 13 years, several additional designers and $1 billion to complete. The surprise is that it's a stunning building, a complex of marble and white metal-clad pavilions whose relative inaccessibility is more than compensated for by stupendous panoramic views.

It's a big place. To the west of the plaza is a café, a restaurant and the circular Research Institute. North are the other institutes (some off-limits to the public) and the Harold M Williams Auditorium. And to the south, up a grand Spanish Steps-style stairway, is the museum lobby, an airy rotunda that opens to a fountain-filled courtyard surrounded by six pavilions housing the permanent collection.

Indeed, the only real disappointment is the art. Although its acquisitions budget is huge, the Getty was a Johnny-come-lately to European art; until, say, the Vatican has a fire sale, the Getty's collections won't be much of a match for the great art museums. Still, certain selections – post-Renaissance decorative arts, photography – are magnificent, while among the paintings are notable works by Cézanne, Titian, Rembrandt and Van Gogh (*Irises*, for which the museum paid $53.9 million in 1987). Worth a visit, though not necessarily for the art.

Beverly Hills

Swimming pools, movie stars, Rolls-Royces: when it comes to Beverly Hills, all the clichés are true. Expensively manicured and policed to the point of sterility, it comes across as a theme park for the rich, where shopping, eating and looking good are the major activities.

The best way to experience Beverly Hills is to drive the residential streets that run north to south from Sunset to Santa Monica Boulevards, between Linden and Doheny Drives. The only pedestrians you'll see are street vendors hawking maps to the stars' homes in this celeb-heavy neighbourhood. North of Sunset, the hillside houses in and around Benedict and Coldwater Canyons offer a similar window into how the other half live; once you're bored of staring, head to the landmark, 55-room Tudor-style **Greystone Mansion** (905 Loma Vista Drive, 1-310 550 4796, www.beverlyhills.org); the building's closed to the public, but its 18 acres of landscaped gardens are open daily.

Most people visit Beverly Hills for the shops in the **Golden Triangle** (*see p136*), the pocket of streets bounded by Wilshire Boulevard, Canon Drive and Little Santa Monica Boulevard that includes **Rodeo Drive**, **Dayton Way** and **Brighton Way. Two Rodeo Drive**, a $200-million ersatz European cobbled walkway, is always busy with window-shopping tourists and serious spenders. Amid such highfalutin consumerism sits the fairytale folly of the 1921 **Spadena House**, also known as the Witch's House (516 N Walden Drive), a more attractive building than anything found in the nearby, office-dominated locale of **Century City**.

Museum of Jurassic Technology
9341 Venice Boulevard, at Bagley Avenue (1-310 836 6131/www.mjt.org). I-10, exit Robertson Boulevard south. **Open** 2-8pm Thur; noon-6pm Fri-Sun. **Admission** free; suggested donation $5. **No credit cards.**

After hours on **Sunset Strip**.

The Museum of Jurassic Technology, in the so-so suburb of Culver City, presents itself as a museum of curiosities, scientific wonders (a bat that can fly through walls) and artistic miracles (the 'micro-miniature' painting of Hagop Sandaldjian). The result is an enterprise that challenges the nature of what a museum is or should be, while also taking its place as one of the city's most fascinating museums.

Museum of Tolerance

9786 W Pico Boulevard, at Roxbury Drive (1-310 553 8403/www.wiesenthal.com/mot). I-10, exit Overland Avenue north. **Open** *Apr-Oct* 11.30am-6.30pm Mon-Thur; 11.30am-5pm Fri; 11am-7.30pm Sun. *Nov-Mar* 11.30am-6.30pm Mon-Thur; 11.30am-3pm Fri; 11am-7.30pm Sun. *Year-round* last entry 2-2½hrs before closing. **Admission** $10; $6-$8 discounts. **Credit** AmEx, MC, V.

While the Museum of Tolerance aims to educate people on a general concept, its primary focus is on the Holocaust. The main permanent exhibit is a programme that guides visitors through the horrors of World War II, with dioramas, photos and stories. Among other permanent displays is a map of the USA pinpointing active hate groups.

West Hollywood

West Hollywood, an independent city since 1984, was once notorious for the decadence of its nightlife and the earthiness of its locals. These days, however, it's a tidy, affluent place, still capable of letting its hair down but mostly concerned with keeping up its buff appearance.

Since it was developed in 1924, **Sunset Strip**, the stretch of W Sunset Boulevard from Doheny Drive to Laurel Canyon, has been the area's focal point. By the 1930s it was Hollywood's playground, and in the 1960s it became a focal point for the LA rock scene (led first by the Byrds and then by the Doors).

However, the nightlife is not what it was; though the Strip still has clubs (such as the Whisky A Go-Go, *see p140*), they're further from the cutting edge than ever, and the legend of the Strip is only kept alive by hotels such as **Chateau Marmont** (No.8221; *see p146*). But while the Strip has declined in recent years, nearby **Santa Monica Boulevard** still impresses. The stretch between N Doheny Drive and N Fairfax Avenue is the centre of LA's gay community, a buzzing, cruisy mix of shops, bars and nightclubs (*see p133*).

Save for the shops on **Melrose Avenue** and in the **Beverly Center** mall (*see p135*), daytime activities in West Hollywood are limited. **Sunset Plaza** (W Sunset Boulevard, east of the junction with La Cienega Boulevard) offers some people-watching and shopping. Meanwhile, the **MAK Center** (*see below*) and the **A+D Museum** (8560 W Sunset Boulevard, 1-310 659 2445, www.aplusd.org), which stages temporary architecture and design shows, draw adventurous tourists, as do the exhibits staged by MOCA (*see p110*) at the hulking **Pacific Design Center** (8687 Melrose Avenue, 1-310 657 0800, www.pacificdesigncenter.com).

MAK Center for Art & Architecture

Schindler House, 835 N Kings Road, between Waring & Willoughby Avenues (1-323 651 1510/www.mak center.com). I-10, exit La Cienega Boulevard north. **Open** 11am- 6pm Wed-Sun. *Tours* hourly 11.30am-2.30pm Sat, Sun. **Admission** $5. Free to all 4-6pm Fri. Built as a live-work space by architect Rudolf Schindler, this landmark is a dazzling combination of concrete walls, redwood partitions, rooftop 'sleeping baskets' and outdoor living rooms. Tours are offered on weekends; in keeping with Schindler's adventurousness, the building also hosts exhibitions, talks and concerts on non-mainstream themes.

Home run

Gawking at stars is a national pastime in the US. Gawking at their houses, though, is the only-in-LA equivalent. Los Angeles is rife with guided tours of celeb homes (the outside only, mind), but most cost a preposterous $30-$40 for 90 minutes spent being ferried around in a minibus by an unemployed actor with scant regard for facts. You're best off guiding yourself.

If it's a summer weekend, you'll see towel-waving vendors on every streetcorner in Hollywood (and more than a few in Beverly Hills) selling map guides to where the stars live. However, walk on by and head to newsstands or tourist shops such as **Souvenirs of Hollywood** (6800 Hollywood Boulevard, 1-323 962 8851) instead. The more money you put down, the better – ie, more accurate – map you'll receive.

Once you've got a map, plan your route. For reasons of both time and traffic, try to stick to one area, whether that's the Pacific Coast Highway (where you'll find the houses of Cher and Bruce Willis, among others), West Hollywood (home to Winona, Leonardo and Halle) or Beverly Hills (too many to mention).

You'll also need the patience and meagre expectations of one of the many folk who wait for hours to crowd along the red carpet at the Academy Awards. You'll be lucky if you catch even a glimpse of a star scurrying into a dark car. In some cases, you'll be lucky if you can spy a single brick of the property behind all the shrubbery and fencing. And wherever you go, don't linger too long, stare through binoculars, knock on doors, shout anyone's name or climb over any gates. That's one sure way to get your mug shot in the tabloids. Or, even worse, on reality TV.

The Fairfax District & the Miracle Mile

The stretch of **Fairfax Avenue** between Beverly Boulevard and Melrose Avenue, south of West Hollywood, has been Los Angeles's main Jewish drag since the 1940s. If you're shopping for a new menorah or the latest in Israeli pop music, head here. Open 24/7 is the legendary **Canter's** (No.419; *see p127*), a World War II-era restaurant, deli and bakery.

Just south of the Beverly-Fairfax intersection lies **CBS Television City**, while next door, around the junction of W 3rd Street and Fairfax Avenue, is the tag-team retail experience of the **Grove** and the **Farmers' Market**. The former, while essentially the area's answer to Universal CityWalk, is one of the more tasteful shopping centres in Los Angeles, while the latter isn't really a farmers' market at all, its stalls dealing in knick-knacks, clothes and tourist tat.

The Miracle Mile, which stretches along Wilshire Boulevard between Fairfax and La Brea Avenues, gained its nickname because of its tremendous commercial growth during the 1920s. The shops have long gone, but the street retains appeal for its assorted museums; those listed below are joined by the **Craft & Folk Art Museum** (5814 Wilshire Boulevard, 1-323 937 4230, www.cafam.org, $2.50-$3.50), LA's only showcase for functional and informal art.

Los Angeles County Museum of Art

5905 Wilshire Boulevard, at S Spaulding Avenue (1-323 857 6000/www.lacma.org). I-10, exit Fairfax Avenue north. **Open** noon-8pm Mon, Tue, Thur; noon-9pm Fri; 11am-8pm Sat, Sun. **Admission** $9; $5 discounts; free under-17s. Free after 5pm daily, & noon-8pm 2nd Tue of mth. **Credit** AmEx, MC, V.
LACMA's five funky pavilions, soon to be subject to a $100 million upgrade courtesy of Renzo Piano, house a large, diverse collection that covers everything from modern American art to ancient Islamic artefacts, incorporating an impressive sculpture garden (heavy on the Rodins), textiles, photographs and pre-Columbian, Indian, South-east Asian and Japanese art. Temporary exhibitions have included surveys of Van Gogh and Bill Viola. A block away sits LACMA West, which hosts large touring shows.

Page Museum at the La Brea Tar Pits

5801 Wilshire Boulevard, between S Stanley & S Curson Avenues (1-323 934 7243/www.tarpits.org). I-10, exit La Brea Avenue north. **Open** 9.30am-5pm Mon-Fri; 10am-5pm Sat, Sun. **Admission** $7; $2-$4.50 discounts; free under-5s. Free 1st Tue of mth. **Credit** AmEx, Disc, V.
In 1875 a group of amateur palaentologists doing research in the La Brea Tar Pits discovered the remains of a prehistoric animal. Almost 130 years later, the pros are still at work, having dragged over a million bones from the mire. Many of these specimens are now on display in this half-underground museum; outside, the pits still bubble with goo.

Petersen Automotive Museum

6060 Wilshire Boulevard, at Fairfax Avenue (1-323 930 2277/www.petersen.org). I-10, exit Fairfax Avenue north. **Open** 10am-6pm Tue-Sun. **Admission** $10; $3-$5 discounts; free under-5s. **Credit** AmEx, MC, V.

A monster pick-up truck embedded in the building marks the entrance to this impressive museum. Inside, life-size dioramas of garages, supermarkets and diners evoke the early days of the American car obsession, though it's the sleek racers and wild hot rods that everyone's here to see. Unfortunately, the site is also the place where rapper Notorious BIG was gunned down (in his SUV, no less).

Hollywood

Hollywood Boulevard

One of LA's strongest contrasts is between the dazzling Hollywood of legend and the dim Hollywood of reality. But still, Hollywood's decline isn't exactly big news. **Hollywood Boulevard** – specifically, the stretch that runs between La Brea Avenue and Vine Street – has been a tourist trap for years. Recently renamed the **Hollywood Entertainment District**, the area has been the subject of a much-ballyhooed billion-dollar makeover in recent years, yet the place seems more desperate than ever.

A case in point is the gargantuan, four-storey **Hollywood & Highland** development, which stuffs a selection of unremarkable restaurants and shops into one of the most bafflingly laid-out public spaces in the city. The complex does contain the **Kodak Theatre**, the 3,300-seat home of the annual Academy Awards (for tours, call 1-323 308 6363 or see www.kodak theatre.com), but evidence of Hollywood glamour is otherwise non-existent. The blocks either side of Hollywood & Highland are pretty tacky, a mix of so-so sights, unattractive attractions like the **Hollywood Wax Museum** (No.6767, 1-323 462 8860, www.hollywoodwax.com) and the obligatorily cheesy souvenir retailers.

Indeed, the only buildings that exude any star quality are the old ones that, you suspect, the developers are itching to trash. Indeed, the main benefit of the redevelopment was that the opulent, legendary **Grauman's Chinese Theatre** (*see p138*) got a restoration; it's just a pity that its glamour is tapered by the tour hawkers and ticket agents who clutter its handprint-covered forecourt. Almost opposite is the **El Capitan Theater** (No.6838), for whose glorious makeover we have Disney to thank; and down the road sits the historic **Egyptian Theatre** (No.6712; *see p138*), now home to the excellent American Cinematheque.

Hollywood Boulevard's other main attraction is its sidewalk between N La Brea and N Argyle Avenues, known as the **Hollywood Walk of Fame**. Its star-shaped plaques bear the names of 2,100-plus entertainment greats. Well, perhaps 1,000 entertainment greats, and 1,000-odd others with $15,000 and a decent agent. At the junction of Hollywood and Vine, surrounded by stars, sits the proposed location for the **Motion Picture Hall of Fame**, scheduled to open in 2005 (call 1-323 465 2300 or see www.filmfame.com for details).

But try not to keep your eyes to the ground the whole way along Hollywood Boulevard, for if you look up, you'll regularly spy signs, nine feet above the sidewalk that mark sites of historical or architectural significance. Taken individually, they're an interesting group; taken as a group (there are 46 in total), they make for an excellent self-guided tour. Among the sites pinpointed is the **Roosevelt Hotel** (No.7000; *see p146*), which hosted the first ever Academy Awards in 1929, and the venerable **Musso & Frank Grill** (No.6667; *see p132*). Sites omitted from the list include lingerie shop **Frederick's of Hollywood** (No.6608), home to a gloriously bizarre underwear museum.

Erotic Museum

6741 Hollywood Boulevard, between N Highland & N Las Palmas Avenues (1-323 463 7684/www.theerotic museum.com). US 101, exit Highland Avenue south. **Open** noon-9pm Mon-Thur, Sun; noon-midnight Fri, Sat. **Admission** *Over-18s only* $12.95; $9.95 discounts. **Credit** MC, V. **Map** p309 A1.
The Erotic Museum's mission statement offers its aim as 'educating the public about human sexuality by creating entertaining exhibitions regarding the broad range of mankind's erotic endeavour through the ages'; which, in effect, means everything from ancient pleasure machines and Picasso etchings to film clips of John Holmes in all his 13.5in of glory.

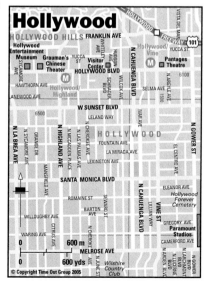

Southern California

Hollywood Entertainment Museum

7021 Hollywood Boulevard, between N Sycamore Avenue & N Orange Drive (1-323 465 7900/www. hollywoodmuseum.com). US 101, exit Highland Avenue south. **Open** *Summer* 10am-6pm daily. *Winter* 11am-6pm daily. **Admission** $10; $5 discounts; free under-5s. **Credit** AmEx, DC, MC, V.

This below-ground museum has little of its subject's pizzazz but is still the pick of the Hollywood museums, attracting groupies to its array of original TV sets (*Star Trek* and *Cheers*), Tinseltown memorabilia, an educational wing, a recording studio and a library. Temporary shows cover anything from album cover art to blaxploitation movies.

Hollywood History Museum

1660 N Highland Avenue, at Hollywood Boulevard (1-323 464 7776/www.hollywoodhistory museum.org). US 101, exit Highland Avenue south. **Open** 10am-5pm Thur-Sun. **Admission** $15; $5-$12 discounts. **Credit** AmEx, MC, V.

First known as the Hollywood Fire & Safe Building, this structure was converted in 1928 into a beauty salon by Max Factor. A refurbishment seven years later turned it into an art deco classic; a recent five-year renovation has restored it to something like its former glory. Since 2002 it's housed this museum, which surveys the last century of movie-making with costumes, props and other ephemera.

The legendary **Chinese Theatre**. See p107.

South of Hollywood Boulevard

Walking south on Vine Street from Hollywood Boulevard will take you to **W Sunset Boulevard**, which, while not as seedy as it once was (prostitutes are not as prevalent as when Hugh Grant met Divine Brown on the corner of Sunset and Courtney Avenue), still retains its edge. The corner of Sunset and N Bronson Avenue is one of the best points from which to see the **Hollywood Sign**, built in the affluent Hollywood Hills in 1923 as an ad for a real-estate development called Hollywoodland; 26 years later, the city tore down the final four 50-foot letters and kept the rest as a landmark. Nearby is the **Hollywood Forever** cemetery (No.6000, 1-323 469 1181, www.hollywood forever.com), the top place in town to star-spot: Tyrone Power, Cecil B de Mille, and Jayne Mansfield are among those buried here.

Midtown

Three very different neighbourhoods sit more or less side by side to the south and east of Hollywood, all worthy of a diversion. Bounded by Wilshire Boulevard and Van Ness, Highland and Melrose Avenues, the **Hancock Park** area is home to some of the most jaw-droppingly opulent mansions outside Beverly Hills and Bel Air. Tour it by car to avoid arousing the suspicions of the local security services, but

park up to explore **Larchmont Village**, and specifically the restaurants and antiques shops in 1920s buildings on N Larchmont Boulevard.

Torched during the 1992 riots, **Koreatown** (bordered by Wilshire and Pico Boulevards, and N Western and N Vermont Avenues) has made a stunning comeback. Businesses abound, especially along Pico and Olympic Boulevards, but the area is most popular among outsiders for its restaurants (*see p128*). At Koreatown's north-western corner sits the **Wiltern Center**, a performing arts and commercial centre; further along Wilshire Boulevard is the sadly derelict **Ambassador Hotel** (No.3400, www.theambassadorhotel.com), known to most as the site of Robert F Kennedy's assassination on the eve of the 1968 California primaries.

Downtown

By day, Downtown LA is largely a bustling centre of commerce and city politics; by night, it's anything but. Still, things are changing. In the last few years, some landmark businesses have opened, among them sports-and-music venue the **Staples Center**, the hip **Standard Downtown** hotel and Frank Gehry's stunning **Walt Disney Concert Hall**; the restaurant scene has also improved immeasurably of late. It can be argued, convincingly, that this is currently LA's most interesting neighbourhood.

Excepting Skid Row, which runs from 3rd to 7th Streets and from Main to Alameda Streets, Downtown is one of the few parts of LA that rewards the pedestrian more than the driver: everything can be seen on foot in a day.

Chinatown to Little Tokyo

Downtown's northern edge, where Broadway meets Cesar E Chavez Avenue, is marked by its small **Chinatown**, interesting to visitors for the shops and markets on N Broadway and N Spring Street. Central Plaza (947 N Broadway), constructed in 1938, was one of the nation's first pedestrian malls, complete with a statue of Republic of China founder Dr Sun Yat-Sen and an elaborate coin-toss wishing well. The row of shops on **Gin Ling Way** is good for souvenirs.

Just across Cesar E Chavez Avenue from Chinatown is **El Pueblo de Los Angeles Historical Monument**, a restored 44-acre historic park that purports to be on the site of the original settlement of LA (which was, in fact, about half a mile away); across Main Street is the **Plaza**, whose bandstand hosts shows by dancers and musicians and the annual **Cinco de Mayo** celebrations. Running off the eastern side of the Plaza is **Olvera Street**, a narrow thoroughfare of stalls selling postcards and Mexican handicrafts. Renovated in 1930 as a marketplace, it's now a tourist trap, albeit an enjoyable one. And close by is **Union Station** (800 N Alameda Street), completed in 1939 and the last of the great American train stations.

Head south down Alameda Street, past Temple Street and on to Central Avenue, and you'll reach the **Geffen Contemporary** wing of the Museum of Contemporary Art (*see p110*), in a warehouse converted by Frank Gehry. Just around the corner is the **Japanese American National Museum** (*see below*): located inside a grand plaza designed by sculptor Isamu Noguchi, it's the highlight of Little Tokyo, which begins at 1st Street and spreads to the south.

Japanese American National Museum

369 E 1st Street, at N Central Avenue (1-213 625 0414/www.janm.org). US 101, exit Alameda Street south. **Open** 10am-5pm Tue, Wed, Fri-Sun; 10am-8pm Thur. **Admission** $8; $4-$5 discounts; free under-6s. Free to all 10am-8pm 3rd Thur of mth, 5-8pm all other Thur. **Credit** AmEx, MC, V.

The brutal internment camps to which Japanese-Americans were sent during World War II inspired the creation of the modernised JANM. The museum stages impressive documentary and art exhibitions.

Civic Center & the Financial District

Many of LA's administrative and political institutions are based on and around W 1st Street, a few blocks south-east of the Plaza

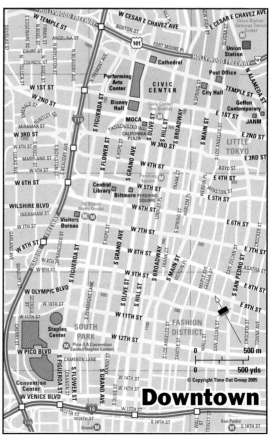

Downtown

Life's a beach

Ever since Vasco Núñez de Balboa clapped eyes on the Pacific Ocean in 1513, the world has gazed upon the Southern California coastline with wonder. With its gorgeous interface of sea and sky against a lush mountain backdrop, LA County's 30-mile stretch of beaches – from Malibu in the north, through Santa Monica and Venice, and on to the South Bay – is incomparable.

Beaches officially open at sunrise and close at sunset. Many have space and rental gear for rollerblading, cycling, surfing and volleyball, as well as refreshments, showers and toilets. Swimming is permitted on all beaches in LA County (except in exceptional circumstances; look for the signs), and lifeguards are on duty year-round. Despite LA's surf city reputation, the Pacific is chillingly cold nine months of the year; however, in July and August, the water can reach 70°F (21°C). Alcohol, pets and nudity are prohibited. Always use sunblock. For more information, call the Department of Beaches & Harbors on 1-310 305 9503, or check http://beaches.co.la.ca.us. The following are the pick of LA's beaches, from north to south.

El Matador State Beach

Six miles north of Malibu and 25 miles up the coast from Santa Monica (the approximate street address is 32350 PCH), El Matador is just past Zuma Beach, accessible via a steep gravelly path. Wear shoes and don't bring too much heavy gear. There are no lifeguards or other facilities, so you should be able to find some privacy; spread your towel in the cupped hands of the rocks. Arriving early or staying late should reward you with a memorable dawn or sunset. El Matador and nearby El Pescador and La Piedra Beaches collectively form the Robert H Meyer Memorial Beaches; all are worth a visit.

Zuma Beach

The four-mile sprawl of sand that makes up Malibu's Zuma Beach (at 30000 PCH) is ideal for surfing, swimming, volleyball, sunbathing and long walks; the water is clean and the sand is soft. Zuma can get crowded, and getting there along traffic-congested PCH can be a drag. Unless you arrive early, it's better to fork out $5 to park in a lot. There are lifeguards, toilets and showers. Ideal for families or large gatherings.

and north-east of Little Tokyo, the most striking building being the extravagant 1928 **City Hall** (200 N Spring Street). Until 1957 the tallest building in Los Angeles, its art deco lines stand out among the uninspired modern office blocks.

Several appealing buildings sit a few blocks west. It would ordinarily take a lot to overshadow the imposing new **Cathedral of Our Lady of the Angels** (555 W Temple Street), but the **Walt Disney Concert Hall** (111 S Grand Avenue; *see p108*), home of the LA Philharmonic, manages it with ease. After an epic odyssey of starts, stops, funding problems and structural concerns, the building opened in 2003, and was worth the wait; bold, brash, even sensual in its reflective glory, Frank Gehry's stunning building sits like a reclining steel butterfly atop Bunker Hill. Adjoining Disney Hall are a number of other institutions, which officially shelter under the umbrella term of the Performing Arts Center: the **Dorothy Chandler Pavilion**, which stages opera and dance, and the **Mark Taper Forum** and the **Ahmanson Theatre**, a pair of playhouses.

To the south, art meets commerce. At Grand and 3rd Street sits the **Museum of Contemporary Art** (*see p110*), part of the

billion-dollar **California Plaza**, which boasts a computer-operated fountain spraying 40-foot geysers and stages daily concerts in summer. Across the road, meanwhile, sits the **Wells Fargo Center** (333 S Grand Avenue), which heralds the start of LA's Financial District. Among the skyscrapers are some worthwhile diversions: the restful **Pershing Square**; the grand **Millennium Biltmore** hotel (*see p146*), built in 1923 and one of the grandest hotels in LA; and the **Richard J Riordan Central Library** (630 W 5th Street), refurbished with money from the developers of **US Bank Tower** (formerly Library Tower) directly opposite.

Museum of Contemporary Art & Geffen Contemporary

MOCA *250 S Grand Avenue, at 3rd Street. I-110, exit 4th Street east.* **Geffen Contemporary** *152 N Central Avenue, at 1st Street. US 101, exit Alameda Street south.* **Both** *1-213 621 6222/www.moca.org.* **Open** *11am-5pm Mon, Fri; 11am-8pm Thur; 11am-6pm Sat, Sun.* **Admission** *Combined ticket $8; $5 discounts; free under-12s. Free to all Thur.* **Credit** AmEx, MC, V.

A premier showcase for post-war art, MOCA splits its life between the Geffen Contemporary, a humongous bus barn, and a newer building a block from

Southern California

Malibu

The nicest beaches in Malibu are private. Most, by law, have public access, but finding the routes to them can be difficult. Public beaches, dotted with commercial restaurants, are nothing special but still prove popular for swimming, sunning and watching surfers at Surfrider Beach. There are also tide pools, a marine preserve and volleyball areas.

Santa Monica State Beach

This big, festive beach is usually crowded. The main attraction is Santa Monica Pier, packed with typical and endearingly low-tech distractions: pier fishing, video arcades, free twilight dance concerts in summer, fairground games, rides and a Ferris wheel. At beach level, beneath the carousel, is the **Santa Monica Pier Aquarium** (1-310 393 6149, www.healthebay.org/smpa). The posh terrace bar at **Shutters on the Beach** (*see p142*) is the place to watch the sunset.

Venice Beach

Though its reputation for eccentricity is overstated (these days, it's more like Camden-Market-on-Sea), Venice Boardwalk still entertains, whether for people-watching (skateboarders, couples, Muscle Beach's bodybuilders), lunch-munching (at the **Figtree Café**, 429 Ocean Front Walk) or book-browsing (at the excellent **Small World Books**, 1407 Ocean Front Walk). Street parking is usually jammed; try the lots at the end of Rose Avenue or Windward Avenue, off Pacific Avenue ($5-$7).

Manhattan & Hermosa Beaches

These neighbouring spots, not too far south of LAX, offer clean water, sand that stretches out of sight, small piers and all kinds of activities: volleyball, sailing and ocean-front paths for walking, cycling and rollerblading. The real charm at both is the local flavour; visitors can swim, picnic and bask in the sun alongside residents and local fishermen. Good surf too.

Huntington State Beach

More of the above, just a lot further south (Huntington Beach is about 15 miles south of Long Beach). Its chief attraction is its surfing: Huntington Beach picks up swells from a variety of directions, making for good waves.

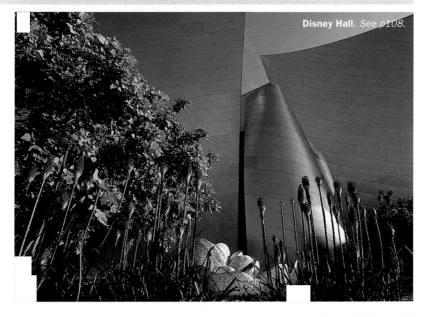

Disney Hall. *See p108.*

Rubber-necking at the **Los Angeles Zoo**. *See p113.*

the Civic Center. Upwards of half a dozen shows can be viewed at any single time between the two; MOCA stages the more mainstream exhibits, leaving the Geffen to concentrate on more esoteric art. A free bus runs between the two sites.

Broadway & further south

If you want to see what a *real* Mexican shopping street looks like, as opposed to the tourist tack of Olvera Street, head to Broadway. Running the length of Downtown, it's the most fascinating street in the area, a place where old LA meets the new, increasingly Hispanic city. Mixed in with the pulsating retail outlets, hawking clothes, trinkets, jewellery and food, are an assortment of iconic LA structures.

At 304 S Broadway sits the **Bradbury Building**, an early-20th-century masterpiece in brick and iron lacery best known for its starring role in *Blade Runner*. Close by is Sid Grauman's 2,400-capacity **Million Dollar Theatre**, built in 1918 (No.307) and left over from the brief period when Downtown was the focal point for the city's theatre scene; other similar theatres further south include the lavish **Los Angeles Theatre** (No.615) and the **Tower Theatre** (No.802). Most are closed and some are derelict, but the LA Conservancy (www.laconservancy.org) opens many briefly in the summer as part of its excellent Last Remaining Seats festival.

Also around here is the exotic, frantic **Jewelry District** (Hill Street and Broadway, between 6th and 8th Streets); directly southeast, on the blocks around Los Angeles Street

south of 7th Street, is the **Fashion District** (www.fashiondistrict.org), whose streets are filled with workers wheeling carts of sweatshop swag, and shop owners coaxing passers-by to buy flannel suits. At its northern edge is the **Los Angeles Flower Market** (on Wall Street, between 7th and 8th Streets); get here pre-dawn for an odiferous and spectacularly colourful riot of activity.

Continuing east brings you to **South Park**, which isn't a park at all. The area, such as it can be described, is anchored by the intersection of US 110 and the I-10; nestled within their arcs are two hulking monstrosities: the **Staples Center** (1111 S Figueroa Street), where you can catch major concerts and the home games of both LA's basketball teams, and the adjoining **Los Angeles Convention Center** (1201 S Figueroa Street).

Los Feliz, Silver Lake & Echo Park

Los Feliz

Studded with campy bars, hideaway eateries and fashion stores, Los Feliz is an enviably fluid melding of yuppie demand, hipster distinction and exotic ethnic influence. Drive around the blocks leading to Griffith Park and you'll find vast mansions and luscious flora; life moves at a more mellow pace here.

The stretch of Hollywood Boulevard close to Hillhurst Avenue is home to a handful of interesting shops and the low-key cultural complex known as the **Barnsdall Art Park** (at the junction with N Vermont Avenue). However, the pedestrian-friendly, shop-packed heart of Los Feliz is on N Vermont Avenue, between bustling Hollywood Boulevard and bucolic Franklin Avenue. The similarly wanderable **Hillhurst Avenue** offers plenty of ways to dawdle away a Sunday afternoon or heat up a Saturday night.

The residential streets in Los Feliz are almost entirely handsome, but a couple of properties stand out. One is the boxily exotic **Ennis-Brown House** (2655 Glendower Avenue, 1-323 660 0607, www.ennisbrown house.org), built by Frank Lloyd Wright in 1924 and now open for tours to those who book in advance (Tue, Thur, Sat; $15-$20). The other is the **Lovell House** (4616 Dundee Drive), Richard Neutra's 1929 masterpiece recognisable from *LA Confidential*.

Griffith Park

Back in 1896, mining tycoon Griffith J Griffith donated 3,015 acres of land to the city. Today, expanded by a third thanks to other donations and purchases, **Griffith Park** is the largest city-run park in the US, its vastness separating Los Feliz and the Hollywood Hills from Glendale and Burbank.

The park's attractions are manifold, from traditional ones such as the **Los Angeles Zoo** (*see p113*) to the **Forest Lawn Memorial Park** (6300 Forest Lawn Drive, 1-800 204 3131), the final resting place for the likes of Buster Keaton, Telly Savalas and Rod Steiger. Summer sees a variety of concerts in the 6,000-capacity open-air **Greek Theatre**; all year, the park is used by locals as a sporting venue (it contains four golf courses and 24 tennis courts) and a means to escape the city, via the 53 miles of hiking trails. Get details from the Ranger Station in the south-east corner (4730 Crystal Springs Drive). For more, call 1-323 913 4688 or check www.ci.la.ca.us/RAP/grifmet/gp.

Griffith Observatory

2800 E Observatory Road (1-323 664 1181/www. griffithobs.org). I-5, exit Los Feliz Boulevard west. **Open** *Observatory* closed until Dec 2005. *Satellite* 1-10pm Tue-Fri; 10am-10pm Sat, Sun. **Admission** *Observatory* call for details. *Satellite* free.
This formidable deco-modern building, currently closed for a programme of renovation and expansion, houses a triple-beam solar telescope and a 12in (30.5cm) Zeiss refracting telescope, its outside deck providing the best overview of the sprawl of LA. While it's closed, a 'satellite' operation, located in the north-east corner of Griffith Park just south of the LA Zoo's parking lot, holds a handful of astronomy displays and a *darling* mini-planetarium.

Los Angeles Zoo

5333 Zoo Drive (1-323 644 4200/www.lazoo.org). I-5, exit Zoo Drive west. **Open** *July-Labor Day* 10am-6pm daily. *Labor Day-June* 10am-5pm daily. *Last entry* 1hr before closing. **Admission** $10; $5 discounts; free under-2s. **Credit** AmEx, Disc, MC, V.
Take the Safari Shuttle on a loop of the LA Zoo before venturing on foot for a closer look; the perspective will help you (and your kids) figure out what you want to see, as trying to get around the entire 113 acres in one visit usually ends in tears. The $6.5 million Red Ape Rainforest, where orang-utans live in an imitation Indonesian rainforest, is popular, but was overshadowed in summer 2004 by a new sea lion habitat and kids' Discovery Center at the front of the zoo. Other coming attractions include new homes for its elephants, hippos and gorillas, due to open in late 2004.

Museum of the American West

4700 Western Heritage Way, Griffith Park (1-323 667 2000/www.museumofthe americanwest.org). I-5, exit Zoo Drive west. **Open** 10am-5pm Tue, Wed, Fri-Sun; 10am-8pm Thur. **Admission** $7.50; $3-$5 discounts; free under-2s. Free 5-8pm Thur. *Joint ticket with Southwest Museum (see p114)* $12; $5-$8 discounts; free under-2s. **Credit** AmEx, MC, V.
Although 2002 saw the Autry Museum of Western Heritage merge with the Southwest Museum and change its name to the Museum of the American West, it's still business as usual. The theme remains much as it's always been: the mythic, multicultural history of the American West. Temporary shows supplement the illuminating permanent displays.

Silver Lake

Where W Sunset Boulevard meets Santa Monica Boulevard, **Sunset Junction** is where much of the rapidly gentrifying but still bohemian Silver Lake neighbourhood goes about its daily life. The area is awash with many of Silver Lake's brightest and boldest independent enterprises: shops, restaurants and bars. To see the locale in all its glory, visit for the **Sunset Junction Street Fair**, held in August.

Silver Lake's namesake boulevard is worth driving for the curves around the reservoir, glittery at night and enveloped by some of the area's nicest homes. Elsewhere, Silver Lake is a bastion of refined glamour: some of the city's top architects built houses in this area in the 1920s and '30s. RM Schindler built the **Droste** and **Walker Houses**, at 2025 and 2100 Kenilworth Avenue; the same street holds two buildings by John Lautner, **Silvertop** (No.2138) and Lautner's own residence (No.2007).

Echo Park

Sometimes defined as the area to the north of US 101 and east of Alvarado Street, raffish **Echo Park** is the gateway neighbourhood to LA's Latino east side. The area around the junction of Alvarado and Sunset supports many of the 'hood's best cafés and shops; Sunset offers several funky clothing boutiques, some fine antiques stores and the area's best eating options. The park after which the area is named was laid out in the 1890s to resemble an English garden; if you've time, take a paddle-boat ride through the blossoming lotuses in the lake.

On the west side of the park is **Angelino Heights**, noted for its restored Victorian mansions; the 1300 block of **Carroll Avenue** is handsome. North-east is **Dodger Stadium**, home of the underachieving LA Dodgers baseball team (*see p140* **The sporting life**); beyond the outfield bleachers lies the vast **Elysian Park**, with worthwhile trails and picnic spots.

Southwest Museum

234 Museum Drive, at Marmion Way, Mount Washington (1-323 221 2164/www.southwest museum.org). I-110, exit Avenue 43 north. **Open** 10am-5pm Tue-Sun. **Admission** $7.50; $3-$5 discounts; free under-2s. *Joint ticket with Museum of the American West (see p113)* $12; $5-$8 discounts; free under-2s. **No credit cards.**
Located a couple of miles north-east of Elysian Park, LA's oldest museum is approaching its 2007 centenary with renewed energy. A new partnership with the Museum of the American West (*see p113*) will allow the museum to preserve its 250,000-item collection of textiles, jewellery and other Southwest-related artefacts, and also to secure the future of its building, an oversized adobe-style building on a hill.

LA for kids

No matter where you stay, you'll be within a short drive of something that will keep your kids occupied. That said, some areas are more kid-friendly than others, and with its sunkissed beaches and car-free shopping drags, Santa Monica is justifiably popular with families on vacation.

Budget permitting, and none is a cheap day out, the various LA-area theme parks are all kid-pleasers. For **Disneyland** and **Knott's Berry Farm** in Orange County, *see p119*; for **Universal Studios** and **Six Flags California** in the San Fernando Valley, *see p115*. Animal attractions are always a favourite: leaving aside the **Los Angeles Zoo** (*see p113*), the other main draws are **Santa Monica Pier Aquarium** (1-310 393 6149, www.healthebay.org/smpa, closed Mon, $1-$5) and the **Aquarium of the Pacific** in Long Beach (*see p118*). On a more educational level, Exposition Park holds the **California Science Center** and the **Natural History Museum of Los Angeles County** (for both, *see p117*).

With its picnic areas, 1920s merry-go-round and the must-see LA Zoo (*see p113*), the hills of **Griffith Park** (*see p113*) make a great one-stop outdoor experience. Almost all LA's major parks contain playgrounds; two good ones are at **Clover Park** in Santa Monica and on **Venice Beach**.

For details of what's on, check the 'Calendar' section of the Sunday *LA Times*, or the free monthly *LA Parent* (for stockists, call 1-818 846 0400 or check http://losangeles.parenthood.com).
Your concierge will be able to arrange babysitting; if you don't have one, call the **Babysitters Guild** (1-310 837 1800), LA's largest and oldest babysitting service.

East LA

East LA is the city's own Ellis Island. Many non-Anglo immigrant groups arrived here first, starting with Jews in the early 20th century, followed by Asians, blacks, Italians and, finally, Mexicans, who have dominated the area since the 1960s. Now largely a staging post for immigrants, East LA (or El Este) remains very poor and suffers from virulent gang problems. However, it's also a lively and characterful area, with a strong sense of Latino identity.

East LA ostensibly begins at Olvera Street, to the west, at the corner of Cesar E Chavez Avenue and Alameda Street in Downtown, but much of the action in East LA takes place on **1st Street**, **Whittier Boulevard** and **Cesar E Chavez Avenue**. Chavez is home to street vendors, selling bargain silver items, tapes and mangoes, and strolling musicians, who will play a bolero or two on their well-worn guitars for a fee. East of Downtown, at 1st Street and Boyle Avenue, is **Mariachi Plaza**, where freelance musicians gather and wait to be hired.

The Valleys

San Fernando Valley

The early history of the **San Fernando Valley**, fictionalised in the movie *Chinatown*, is a colourful tale. At the start of the 20th century, LA's land barons hoodwinked voters into approving bonds for an aqueduct and then diverted the water away from the city to the Valley so they could cash in on increased land values. Still, many older residents remember only a pastoral yesteryear of horses and orange groves, also forgetting the porn industry that now dominates the area's economy.

The San Fernando Valley's two main cities sit more or less side by side, north of Griffith Park. Crisply pressed **Glendale** is larger than dreary **Burbank**, but both are forgettable places that bring to mind Mark Twain's famous quote that while 'Los Angeles is a great place to live, I wouldn't want to visit there'. Glendale's main attraction is a cemetery, the **Forest Lawn Memorial Park**, (1712 S Glendale Avenue, 1-800 204 3131, www.forestlawn.com), the final resting place of Lon Chaney, Walt Disney, Nat 'King' Cole and Harold Lloyd. Burbank, meanwhile, is only worth a visit if you've got audience tickets for one of the TV shows filmed in the area (*see p142* **TV tapings**); Warner Brothers, NBC and Disney all have studios here.

Things don't get much more interesting elsewhere. North-west of Burbank sit **Mission Hills** and the **Mission San Fernando Rey de Espa**, founded in 1797 and rebuilt after the 1971 earthquake; **Sylmar** boasts the two Nethercutt museums (*see below*); a short ride up I-5, **Santa Clarita** is home to the **Six Flags** park (*see below*). To the west are **Sherman Oaks**, once Valley Girl Central but now more diverse, and not much else.

Suburbia aside, the Valley is the gateway to the **Santa Monica Mountains**, one of the country's most beautiful and environmentally fragile urban mountain ranges. Separating the Valley from the city basin and the ocean, the mountains are covered with hiking and biking trails. For more information, contact the **Santa Monica Mountains National Recreation Area** (1-805 370 2301, www.nps.gov/samo).

Nethercutt Collection

Nethercutt Museum *15151 Bledsoe Street, at San Fernando Road, Sylmar (1-818 364 6464).* **Open** 9am-4.30pm Tue-Sat. **San Sylmar** *15200 Bledsoe Street, at San Fernando Road, Sylmar* *(1-818 367 2251).* **Open** *Tours* 10am, 1.30pm Tue-Sat. Booking essential. **Both** *www.nether cuttcollection.org. I-5, exit Roxford Street east.* **Admission** free.

The collection of eccentric philanthropists Dorothy and JB Nethercutt makes for a striking pair of museums. The San Sylmar building houses a huge collection of old, fancy but functional objects, anything from Steuben Glass hood ornaments to automated musical instruments, while the Nethercutt is home to 100 of the pair's 230 classic cars.

Six Flags California

Magic Mountain Parkway, off I-5, Valencia (1-818 367 5965/www.sixflags.com). I-5, exit Magic Mountain Parkway. **Open** *Magic Mountain* Summer from 10am daily. Winter from 10am Fri-Sun. Call for closing. *Hurricane Harbor* Summer from 10am daily; call for closing. Winter closed. **Admission** *Magic Mountain* $46.99; $29.99 discounts; free under-2s. *Hurricane Harbor* $23.99; $16.99 discounts; free under-2s. *Combined* $56.99. **Credit** AmEx, Disc, MC, V.

Set on the hip of the San Fernando Mountains, this place is fun with a screamingly huge 'F'. Comprising Magic Mountain and newer watery cousin Hurricane Harbor, Six Flags California delivers for all but the most joyless (and, in summer, crowdphobic) holidaymaker. The park offers rollercoasters and water rides for every level of screamer; the most famous is the Colossus, billed as 'the tallest and fastest wooden coaster in the West'. Note that many rides have height requirements starting at about 48in (1.22m).

Universal Studios & CityWalk

100 Universal City Plaza, Universal City (1-800 864 8377/www.universalstudios.com). US 101, exit Universal Center Drive. **Open** *Studios* Summer 9am-8pm Mon-Thur; 9am-9pm Fri, Sun; 9am-10pm Sat. Winter 10am-6pm Mon-Fri; 9am-6pm Sat, Sun. *CityWalk* 11am-9pm Mon-Thur, Sun; 11am-11pm Fri, Sat. **Admission** $49; $31-$39 discounts; under-3s free. **Credit** AmEx, DC, Disc, MC, V.

Universal Studios.

Once you've run the gauntlet of CityWalk, crammed with souvenir hawkers and junk-food retailers, and made it through the gates of Universal Studios, you'll find an attraction whose entertainment value is more than the sum of its parts. The rides, while fun, aren't as exciting as one might expect; you're here for the illusion of glamour. Adults will enjoy the *Back to the Future* stomach-churner and young teens may be charmed by the entertainingly lame *Jurassic Park* ride, but the pick of the themed attractions, for both adults and kids, is the *Shrek 4-D* movie. The studio tour is cheesy but enjoyable; the rest is mush. Arrive early (especially in summer) to avoid the worst crowds.

San Gabriel Valley

Unlike the San Fernando Valley, the **San Gabriel Valley** is not part of the City of LA. This independence is reflected, by accident and design, in its neighbourhoods: it's charming, ethnically diverse and visually less homogenous.

Pasadena, first settled by wealthy retired farmers from the Midwest, is one of the most attractive towns in the area. Its focal point is **Old Town Pasadena** (centred on Colorado Boulevard and bounded by Arroyo Parkway, De Lacey Avenue and Holly and Green Streets), a 1920s-meets-1990s retail district where packs of teenagers mingle with families and couples. Chains dominate, but it's a world away from the Valley mall culture of myth and legend. The town's various museums are, without exception, fine and worthwhile operations.

Two perfectly pleasant communities adjoin Pasadena: to the north-west, the picturesque hillside town of **La Cañada Flintridge**; just south of town is the expensive suburb of **San Marino**, developed by land and railroad baron Henry Huntington at the start of the 20th century. Nearby, Pasadena's Lake Street district and the Fair Oaks area of **South Pasadena** are pleasant walking and shopping areas.

Heading east, points of interest become fewer. In **Arcadia** sits an elegant '30s racetrack, **Santa Anita Park** (285 W Huntington Drive, 1-626 574 7223), and the **LA County Arboretum & Botanical Garden** (301 N Baldwin Avenue, Arcadia, 1-626 821 3222, www.arboretum.org). The area south of Pasadena holds greater variety: the suburbs of **Monterey Park**, **Alhambra** and **San Gabriel** have largely Chinese or Chinese-American populations, and Atlantic Boulevard and Garfield Avenue contain Chinese restaurants of every stripe.

Descanso Gardens

1418 Descanso Drive, at Oakwood Avenue & Knight Way, La Cañada (1-818 949 4200/www.descanso. com). I-210, exit Gould Avenue north. **Open** 9am-5pm daily. **Admission** $6; $1.50-$4 discounts; free under-5s. **No credit cards.**

This delightful tribute to the horticultural magic of Southern California includes more than 600 varieties of camellia (best seen between mid Feb and early May). The gardens are also notable for their five acres of roses, the lilac, orchid, fern and California native plant areas, and the oriental tea house.

Gamble House

4 Westmoreland Place, at Walnut Street, Pasadena (1-626 793 3334/www.gamblehouse.org). I-10, exit Orange Grove Boulevard north. **Open** noon-3pm Thur-Sun. **Admission** $8; $5 discounts.

This stern but handsome property is perhaps the leading example of Southern California's 'Craftsman' bungalow style, influenced – in typical fashion – by both Japanese and Swiss architecture. The property received a long-awaited restoration in 2003-04.

Huntington Library, Art Collections & Botanical Gardens

1151 Oxford Road, off Huntington Drive, San Marino (1-626 405 2100/www.huntington.org). I-110, exit Atlantic Boulevard north. **Open** *June-early Sept* 10.30am-4.30pm Tue-Sun. *Sept-May* noon-4.30pm Tue-Fri; 10.30am-4.30pm Sat, Sun. **Admission** $15; $6-$12 discounts; free under-5s. Free to all 1st Thur of mth. **Credit** MC, V.

The bequest of entrepreneur Henry E Huntington is a magnet to Europhiles. The collection here runs to some serious academia and 18th- and 19th-century French and British art; Gainsborough's *Blue Boy* is on show here. The library holds six million items, the star attractions a Gutenberg Bible, several early Shakespeares and the earliest known edition of Chaucer's *Canterbury Tales*. The region's most glorious botanical gardens sit outside.

Norton Simon Museum

411 W Colorado Boulevard, between N Orange Grove Boulevard & N St John Avenue, Pasadena (1-626 449 6840/www.nortonsimon.org). I-110, exit Colorado Boulevard west. **Open** noon-6pm Mon, Wed-Sun. **Admission** $6; $3 discounts; free students, under-18s. Free 6-9pm 1st Fri of mth. **No credit cards.**

The Norton Simon's makeover in the late 1990s (courtesy of Frank Gehry) raised the museum's profile and helped it expand the range of its collection,

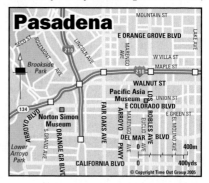

creating a more sympathetic environment in which to display it. The museum is still best known for its impressive collection of Old Masters from the likes of Rembrandt and Brueghel; French Impressionists are represented by, among others, Monet and Manet. Other valuable holdings include a generous array of Degas's ballerina bronzes, some fine modern works, and extensive collections of European prints and Buddhist artefacts. After you've filled up on the art, head into the garden, inspired by Monet's Giverny.

Pacific Asia Museum

46 N Los Robles Avenue, at E Colorado Boulevard West, Pasadena (1-626 449 2742/www.pacificasia museum.org). I-110, exit Colorado Boulevard east. **Open** 10am-5pm Wed, Thur, Sat, Sun; 10am-8pm Fri. **Admission** $7; $5 discounts. Free 4th Fri of mth. **No credit cards.**

Art and artefacts from Asia and the Pacific Rim are displayed in the historic Grace Nicholson Building, a re-creation of a northern Chinese palace with a charming Chinese Garden Court to match. Displays include both contemporary and traditional Asian arts, but the museum's most popular events are its family-oriented festival days.

Pasadena Museum of California Art

490 E Union Street, between S Los Robles & Oakland Avenues, Pasadena (1-626 568 3665/www.pmcaon line.org). I-210, exit Lake Avenue. **Open** noon-5pm Wed, Thur, Sat, Sun; 10am-8pm Fri. **Admission** $6; $4 discounts; free under-12s. **No credit cards.**

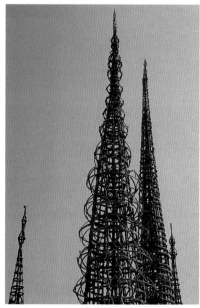

Italian by design: **Watts Towers.**

Since opening in 2002, this museum has hung work by the likes of mid 20th-century artist Edward Biberman, and modernist painter and poet Yun Gee, a Chinese émigré to San Francisco when he was 15. The PMCA's Design Biennial features the best graphics, fashion, furniture and industrial design from California; the next one is scheduled for 2005.

South Central

South Central owes its black identity to the era of restrictive covenants: legal restrictions, instituted in the early 20th century, on who could reside in a property. The laws confined African-Americans to a tight area around Central Avenue, but in the past two decades, African-Americans have vacated South Central and headed to the suburbs; Latino families have replaced them, and the area's character is subtly changing. While South Central is not necessarily dangerous, it is bleak; unrelieved by hills or sea, it seems to consist of relentless flatlands of concrete and asphalt.

Central Avenue & Exposition Park

From the 1920s to the '50s, **Central Avenue** was home to some of the first theatres and businesses set up exclusively to serve blacks: the **Dunbar Hotel** (4225 S Central Avenue), for example, was the first hotel built by and for blacks. Modern-day Central Avenue, though, is less alluring, many of its buildings in disrepair.

West of Central Avenue sits **Exposition Park**: come in spring to see the Rose Garden in full and impressive bloom. Year-round, you can visit several fine museums here, including the **California African American Museum** (600 State Drive, 1-213 744 7432, www.caam.ca.gov, closed Mon & Tue) of black history and art. Also in the park is the hulking Coliseum, host of the 1984 Olympics but these days used chiefly by the football team at the neighbouring **University of Southern California.**

Situated several miles down Central Avenue, still deprived **Watts** is notorious for the riots of 1965 and 1992, but it also contains a wonderful LA landmark. The vast **Watts Towers** (1727 E 107th Street, 1-213 847 4646, www.watts towers.net) were built between 1921 and 1954 by Italian tilesetter Simon Rodia, who fashioned a folk-art masterpiece using steel frames, glass, mirrors, rocks, ceramic tiles, pottery, marble shards and 25,000 sea shells. Don't miss it.

California Science Center

700 State Drive, between S Figueroa Street & S Vermont Avenue, Exposition Park (1-323 724 3623/IMAX 1-213 744 2019/www.casciencectr.org). I-110, exit Exposition Boulevard west. **Open** 10am-5pm daily. *Air & Space Gallery* 10am-1pm

Mon-Fri; 11am-4pm Sat, Sun. **Admission** *Museum* free. *IMAX* $7.50; $4.50-$5.50 discounts. **Credit** *IMAX* MC, V.

The permanent exhibits at this museum are split into themed wings: Creative World, which focuses on technology (and has a little catching up to do); World of Life, whose coolest feature is Gertie, a 50ft (15m) see-through lady who teaches human anatomy; and the Air & Space Gallery, which does pretty much what it says on the tin. An IMAX cinema screens the usual array of dazzling, quasi-educative films.

Natural History Museum of Los Angeles County

900 Exposition Boulevard, between S Figueroa Street & S Vermont Avenue, Exposition Park (1-213 763 3466/www.nhm.org). I-110, exit Exposition Boulevard west. **Open** 10am-5pm daily. **Admission** $9; $2-$6.50 discounts; free under-5s. **Credit** AmEx, Disc, MC, V.

Now housed in a sprawling complex of buildings, the third largest natural history museum in the US is currently planning a sizeable programme of remodelling. But until it begins (2006 looks likely), visitors get to wander 35 halls and galleries packed with birds, mammals, gems, a huge Tyrannosaurus rex skull and Native American pottery and baskets. The pre-teens' perennial favourite is the Insect Zoo.

Crenshaw to Inglewood

Crenshaw, which surrounds Crenshaw Boulevard south of the I-10, is now one of the few mainly black communities in LA County; the Hills (Baldwin Hills, Windsor Hills, Fox Hills, View Park and Ladera Heights), west of Crenshaw Boulevard around Slauson Avenue, are home to some of LA's most prominent upper middle-class blacks. So why the Japanese feel? Because, after returning from World War II internment camps, a large number of Japanese settled here and set up as landscape gardeners. Their legacy is still visible today. On the far west side of Crenshaw is the unsung **Kenneth Hahn State Recreation Area**. Named after a popular former city councilman, it's a huge, delightful place, with a fishing pond, ducks, swans and excellent views of LA.

Nearby **Leimert Park** ('Luh-murt') has undergone a cultural revolution of late, with galleries, jazz clubs, shops and restaurants springing up everywhere. In Leimert Park Village, a pedestrianised shopping area bordered by Crenshaw Boulevard, 43rd Street, Leimert Boulevard and Vernon Avenue, there's live music every night of the week.

Although it's located outside LA city limits, **Inglewood** is often considered part of South Central. It's best approached as the home of Randy's Donuts, an architectural classic on the corner of W Manchester and S La Cienega Boulevards. Trust us, you can't miss it.

Long Beach & San Pedro

Long Beach has been given short shrift by its more well-heeled neighbours to the north and south. But since the factories closed and navy work dwindled in the 1980s, it's changed , and is now more cultured than ever. The city's turnaround was heralded by the opening of the **Aquarium of the Pacific** (*see p119*) in 1998; however, it's just a part of the redevelopment of the area called Queensway Bay, now dotted with shops and restaurants. Other worthwhile diversions in the area include the small but ambitious **Long Beach Museum of Art** (2300 E Ocean Boulevard, 1-562 439 2119, www.lbma.org, closed Mon, $4-$5), where the permanent collection includes some Californian works and an extensive library of video art.

In the expensive **Naples** neighbourhood (off 2nd Street, between Bay Shore and Marina Avenues), you can take a gondola ride on one of the picturesque canals (**Gondola Getaway**,

The final frontier

Based on a 177-acre site in Pasadena and managed by NASA, the **Jet Propulsion Laboratory** has led the US's planetary space exploration for decades. In 1958 it controlled and built the satellite Explorer I, America's first foray into space; years later, it was behind the Mariner and Voyager projects, which have flown by every planet in the solar system bar Pluto. Employing 5,500 people, and equipped with an annual budget of $1.4 billion, it's the JPL that designed, built and now operates NASA's Deep Space Network, and which is responsible for the Mars Pathfinder and the recent mission to Mars, the Spirit rover. Its exploratory exploits are matched by its protective work: its satellite-mounted cameras and sensors send back vital data about our ozone and oceans.

Roughly once a week (usually Monday or Wednesday at 1pm), the JPL opens its doors to the public for tours. Demand is high, and booking is essential. Security concerns dictate that US citizens need to bring a passport or driver's licence, while citizens of other countries must declare their nationality prior to booking and bring a passport or green card on the day. For reservations, call 1-818 354 9314 six months or more in advance. For more information, check www.jpl.nasa.gov.

1-562 433 9595, www.gondolagetawayinc.com). But one big no-no is a day at the beach: pollution is a problem in this industrial town.

The port town of **San Pedro**, five miles west of Long Beach, has not gentrified at the same rate. However, there are a couple of nice little attractions: the **Cabrillo Marine Aquarium** (3720 Stephen White Drive, 1-310 548 7562, www.cabrilloaq.org, closed Mon), dedicated to California marine life, is home to a jellyfish farm and 30 ocean-life tanks, while the **Los Angeles Maritime Museum** (Berth 84, 1-310 548 7618, www.lamaritimemuseum.org, closed Mon, $1), is the largest maritime museum in California, housed in a fine 1940s Streamline Moderne structure that was once a ferry terminal.

Aquarium of the Pacific

100 Aquarium Way, at Shoreline Drive (1-562 590 3100/www.aquariumofpacific.org). I-710, exit Shoreline Drive east. **Open** 9am-6pm daily. **Admission** $18.95; $10.95-$14.95 discounts; free under-2s. **Credit** AmEx, MC, V.
This spectacular $117m aquarium has been saving parents the drive down to SeaWorld in San Diego since 1998. Inevitably, the Shark Lagoon is the most popular exhibit, with much of the rest of the aquarium divided geographically: the lovable sea lions in the Southern California section, all kinds of garish fish in the tropical Pacific area.

Queen Mary

1126 Queens Highway (1-800 437 2934/1-562 435 3511/www.queenmary.com). I-405, then I-710 south. **Open** *Summer* 10am-6pm daily. **Admission** $23-$28; $12-$25 discounts. **Credit** AmEx, DC, Disc, MC, V.
Having retired from active duty in 1967, the majestic *Queen Mary* is now a popular tourist sight and hotel. Attractions range from a low-key display of photographs outlining the boat's history to the rather more adventurous Ghosts & Legends, which plays up to the boat's reputation as a home for myriad old spooks. Steady your nerves afterwards with a Martini in the gorgeous bar.

Orange County

Anaheim

Anaheim and its surrounds are filled with some of the best-known icons of middle Americana, of which **Disneyland** (*see below*) is king. The area around it, for years known for its strip-mall seediness, has been revitalised, though at the cost of much of its wacky 1950s Googie architecture. For a traditional slice of American pie, hop over to **Buena Park**, where you'll find **Knott's Berry Farm** (*see p121*).

If you're in the area, two other shrines to the American way of life deserve a visit. The **Crystal Cathedral** in Garden Grove (12141 Lewis Street, 1-714 971 4000, www.crystal cathedral.org), an all-glass house of worship, is a marvel of sheer excess, built by Philip Johnson and John Burgee. The **Nixon Library & Birthplace** in Yorba Linda (18001 Yorba Linda Boulevard, 1-714 993 5075, www.nixon foundation.org, $2-$5.95), meanwhile, is a combination library–propaganda machine.

Disneyland

1313 S Harbor Boulevard, between Katella Avenue & Ball Road, Anaheim (1-714 781 4000/recorded information 1-714 781 4565/www.disneyland.com). I-5, exit Disneyland Drive. **Open** *Disneyland* Summer 8am-midnight daily. Winter 10am-8pm Mon-Thur; 8am-midnight Fri, Sat; 9am-9pm Sun. *California Adventure* Summer 10am-8pm Mon-Thur; 10am-9pm Fri-Sun. Winter 10am-6pm Mon-Thur; 10am-8pm Fri; 10am-9pm Sat, Sun. **Admission** *One park for one day* $50; $40 discounts; free under-3s. Combination tickets also available. **Credit** AmEx, DC, Disc, MC, V.
The Disneyland resort isn't just a set of theme parks; it's a spectacular piece of pop art that's as bright or dark as you'd like it to be. Incorporating two parks – the 50-year-old, near-mythic **Disneyland** and the five-year-old **Disney's California Adventure** – the resort calls itself 'The Happiest Place on Earth'. If you bring the right mood to it, it certainly can be.

Certainly, Disney does all it can to get you in the right mood. Disneyland is not so much a park as its own separate world; there are even three Disney-operated hotels (*see p147*) located in the resort, so you need not have the illusion shattered at the end of the day. The hotels, though, do bring to attention the main drawback to spending time here: the sheer expense. You can save hundreds of dollars staying at one of the non-Disney hotels just outside the property, and you may need to do so in order to afford the steep prices of food, drink and admission. It's worth noting, though, that ticket prices drop if you visit for multiple days, recommended if you want to get a real feel for the place and ride all the rides.

Both parks boast dozens of dining spots, with cuisine ranging from burgers and pizza to pastas and seafood. Still, you may want to dine at **Downtown Disney**, a pedestrian-only avenue of nightclubs (including a House of Blues) and restaurants between the two parks. It's not that the food is that much better, but if you're going to be paying Disney's high prices, you might as well be able to order a drink or two to soften the blow: liquor sales were banned from Disneyland by Walt himself, citing the undesirable 'carnie atmosphere' booze might have created.

The other main demerit against Disneyland is the crowds, which can be overwhelming, particularly in summer. But it can't be helped, and it's unlikely to change: Disneyland is popular for a reason.

Disneyland

Disneyland is packed with must-do attractions spread over seven 'lands', all immaculately themed in every detail. **Main Street USA** embodies turn-of-the-19th-century America, while **Frontierland** takes on Westward expansion (the John Wayne version) and **New Orleans Square** is just like its namesake, minus the booze. **Adventureland** offers thrills of the jungle variety; **Tomorrowland** is a kitschy look into the future; **Critter Country** is the wooded home of Winnie the Pooh and Br'er Rabbit; and **Fantasyland** is where Disney's animated films come to life, and is where you're most likely to find Mickey Mouse, scurrying about in Toontown.

The secret of Disneyland's charm lies in its history. Unlike the parks in Paris, Tokyo, Hong Kong and Florida, Disneyland was largely designed by Walt Disney himself, and it's the only one of the Disney Company's parks in which he ever set foot. As a result, Disneyland is practically a biography of its creator's life, if you know where to look. Try reading the names in Main Street's upper-level windows; you'll find many of Disney's collaborators and artists listed. *The Walt Disney Story* features artefacts from Disney's entertainment career. And in Frontierland, you'll find the petrified tree Walt once gave his wife as an anniversary present.

But most people, of course, are here for the rides. Among the best are **Space Mountain** (in Tomorrowland), a legitimately thrilling indoor rollercoaster ride through 'deep space'; the epic **Indiana Jones Adventure** (in Adventureland), based on the Spielberg adventure movies; **Pirates of the Caribbean** (in New Orleans Square), the basis for the hit Johnny Depp film and one of the most detail-packed and atmospheric rides in the park; and **Matterhorn** (in Fantasyland), a breakneck bobsled ride around and through a scaled-down replica of the

Swiss peak. Beyond that, there are dozens of carnival-style 'dark' rides, boat trips, rollercoasters, flume rides and Audio-Animatronics shows, each telling its own story and holding charms for young and old alike.

Disney's California Adventure

Located in the former Disneyland car park, this decent little park, while no match for Disneyland in terms of size or attention to detail, does a decent job of celebrating the geography, culture and history of its namesake state. Plus, unlike Disneyland, it serves wine, beer and cocktails, and has done so since opening day with little or no carnie interference.

While DCA doesn't have anything as engrossing as Pirates of the Caribbean, it does feature some rides that warrant a visit. The **Twilight Zone Tower of Terror**, a special effects-packed 'drop'-ride based on the classic TV show and housed in the entertaining **Hollywood Pictures Backlot** section of the park, is worth a look, as is **Soarin' Over California**, a flight simulator that's so beautifully done that it borders on the poetic. Soarin' Over California is located in the **Golden State** section, itself split up into separate areas that pay homage to (among other places) San Francisco and Wine Country. The highlight of the **Paradise Pier** section, meanwhile, is the **California Screamin'** rollercoaster, the tallest and fastest coaster ever built in a Disney park. Not every ride is suitable for kids of all ages, but very young children are welcome in **A Bug's Land**, the most family-friendly corner of the California Adventure.

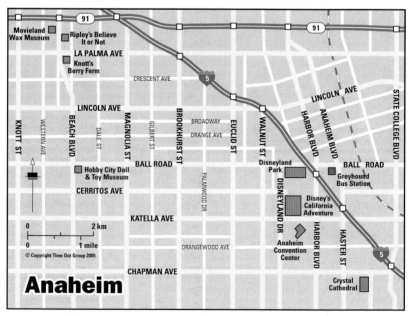

Knott's Berry Farm

8039 Beach Boulevard, at La Palma Avenue, Buena Park (1-714 220 5200/www.knotts.com). I-5, exit Beach Boulevard south. **Open** *Knott's Berry Farm* Jan-Apr, Sept-Dec 10am-6pm Mon-Fri; 10am-10pm Sat; 10am-7pm Sun. May 10am-6pm Mon-Fri; 9am-11pm; 10am-7pm Sun. June-Aug 10am-10pm Mon-Fri, Sun; 9am-11pm Sat. *Soak City USA* May-Oct 10am-7pm daily. **Admission** *Knott's Berry Farm* $43; $12.95-$35 discounts; free under-3s. *Soak City USA* $25; $10-$13 discounts. **Credit** AmEx, DC, Disc, MC, V.

Knott's Berry Farm started as a farm selling the home-made preserves of one Mrs Cordelia Knott. Although Ma Knott and her family are long gone, her jams are still on sale, but the park's a little livelier these days, with water rides, the 20-storey Sky Jump parachute ride and Montezooma's Revenge, a stomach-churning rollercoaster ride. Many of the buildings in the park have been transplanted from old mining towns, which heightens the feeling of nostalgia. Next door to the Berry Farm is **Soak City USA**, a water park with 21 rides; combination tickets are available for the two attractions. Hours for both vary throughout the year.

The Orange County coast

Seal Beach and **Sunset Beach** begin the 50-mile expanse of beach bliss that is coastal Orange County. While both are fun, the real action starts in **Huntington Beach**, aka 'Surf City'. Hang out at the pier (Main Street, off PCH) or on the sand and you'll see how the city got its nickname; from dawn to dark, surfers search for the perfect wave. The refurbished Main Street is home to numerous surf shops and bars; nearby is the **International Surfing Museum** (411 Olive Avenue, 1-714 960 3483, www.surfingmuseum.org, closed Tue & Wed in winter, $1-$2), which honours surf music, surf lifesaving and (of course) surf babes.

Newport Beach, to the south, is something else altogether. From the lavish homes overlooking Newport Harbor to the outdoor **Fashion Island** mall, Newport Beach is where the American leisured class live out their days in splendour. **Balboa Island** (Jamboree Road Bridge, near PCH) and **Balboa Peninsula** (Balboa Boulevard and PCH) are both prime walking areas; a ferry ushers visitors between the two. The island is full of shops, restaurants and homes; just off the ferry on the peninsula is a carnival with a Ferris wheel and arcade.

Laguna Beach began as an artists' colony and is the home of the **Laguna Art Museum** (307 Cliff Drive, 1-949 494 8971, www.lagunaart museum.org). **San Juan Capistrano** is famous for the swallows that return each spring to **Mission San Juan Capistrano** (*see p214* **On a mission**). At the county's end, **San Clemente** has all the sun and waves but few of the crowds of its neighbours.

Surf's up

If you really want to hook into the California lifestyle, you need to start surfing. But it ain't easy: it can take weeks just to learn to sit on the board. Most novice surfers opt for the easier-to-learn alternatives: boogie-boards (aka bodyboards), body surfing and skim-boarding.

If you're learning, choose a wide-open beach break such as **Zuma Beach** (*see p110*), **Will Rogers State Beach** (*see p96*; the surfing is best where Sunset Boulevard meets the Pacific Coast Highway), **Santa Monica Beach** (*see p100*) or El Porto at **Manhattan Beach** (*see p101*). Intermediate surfers can find excellent beach breaks at **Manhattan, Hermosa, Redondo** and **Huntington Beaches** (*see p101 and p121*); only experienced surfers should test their skill at the competitive point breaks, such as **Topanga State Beach** (near the intersection of PCH and Topanga Canyon Road), **Surfrider Beach** (by PCH and Cross Creek Road, just north of Malibu Pier), and the **Wedge**, a dangerous break at the end of Balboa and Ocean Boulevards at the top of the Balboa Peninsula in Orange County.

Plenty of places hire surfboards, among them the excellent **ZJ Boardinghouse** in Santa Monica (2619 Main Street, Santa Monica, 1-310 392 5646), **ET Surf** in Hermosa Beach (904 Aviation Boulevard, 1-310 379 7660) and **Malibu Ocean Sports** (22935 PCH, 1-310 456 6302, www.malibuoceansports.com). Expect to pay anywhere from $10 an hour up to around $25-$30 a day for board hire. For surfing and beach conditions, call the **Surfing Conditions Hotline** on 1-310 578 0478, check with the Department of Beaches & Harbors on 1-310 305 9503 or see http://beaches.co.la.ca.us.

Central Orange County

Costa Mesa, which isn't on the coast, bills itself as an arts-friendly city. However, it's really a city of commerce, notable for its malls: **South Coast Plaza** (off I-405 at Bristol Avenue, 1-800 782 8888, www.southcoast plaza.com) is one of the world's largest. North is Latino **Santa Ana**. Colourful 4th Street, between French and Ross Streets, is like a small city in Mexico. Another lively area is **Little Saigon** in Westminster, the largest Vietnamese community outside Vietnam.

Southern California

Where to Eat

LA's restaurant scene used to be more about fashion than food. Seeing and being seen is still important, but now what's on your plate matters too. Witness the birth of a new LA breed: the serious foodie, as likely to champion an unpretentious ethnic eatery as a chi-chi, celebrity-filled restaurant. And, of course, there are still plenty of the latter around: in recent years, new restaurant openings have been as star-studded as any awards ceremony.

Competition for tables in LA can be fierce, especially at the restaurants *du jour*, so make reservations if possible. If you're happy with the service, tip at least 15 per cent. Regarding dress code, remember the term 'California casual' was invented here, but don't push your luck: some eateries draw the line at shorts and jeans. Smoking is banned in all LA restaurants.

Southern California

The beach towns

Malibu

Geoffrey's

27400 Pacific Coast Highway, just west of Latigo Canyon Road (1-310 457 1519/www.geoffreys malibu.com). I-10, exit PCH north. **Open** noon-10pm Mon-Fri; 11am-11pm Sat; 11am-10pm Sun. **Average** $$$$-$$$$$. **Credit** AmEx, MC, V.

Dining on the cliffside deck, you'd swear you were on the French Riviera. But the California-centric menu and wine list, plus the Ray Ban-clad waiters, will set you straight. The good food, exceptional views and fine service make the drive worthwhile.

Also recommended

Seafood on the beach at **Gladstone's 4 Fish** (17300 PCH, 1-310 454 3474, www.gladstones.com, $$$); Cal-Asian fusion cooking at **Granita** (23725 W Malibu Road, 1-310 456 048, closed Mon, $$$$); seafood shack **Neptune's Net** (42505 PCH, 1-310 457 3095, $$); starry sushi chain **Nobu** (3853 Cross Creek Road, 1-310 317 9140, www.noburestaurants.com, $$$$$).

Santa Monica

Border Grill

1445 4th Street, between Broadway & Santa Monica Boulevard (1-310 451 1655/www.bordergrill.com). I-10, exit 4th-5th Street north. **Open** 11.30am-10pm Mon-Thur, Sun; 11.30am-11pm Fri, Sat. **Average** $$$-$$$$. **Credit** AmEx, DC, Disc, MC, V.

It's no longer as hip as it once was, but with its orange walls and vivid paintings, pulsating music and sharp Margaritas, the Border Grill is still pretty hot. The New Mexican menu is full of temptations, but it's hard to forego the green corn tamales with salsa fresca, or the pescado Veracruzano.

JiRaffe

502 Santa Monica Boulevard, at 5th Street (1-310 917 6671/www.jirafferestaurant.com). I-10, exit 4th-5th Street north. **Open** 6-9pm Mon; 6-10pm Tue-Thur; 1-11pm Fri, Sat; 5.30-9pm Sun. **Average** $$$$. **Credit** AmEx, DC, Disc, MC, V.

This acclaimed restaurant serves gourmet French food with a California twist. Owner and head chef Raphael Lunetta keeps the atmosphere down to earth and the food unpretentious; his mantra is fresh ingredients and simple preparation. His erstwhile partner Josiah Citrin now serves classic-with-a-twist Provençal fare at nearby **Melisse** (1104 Wilshire Boulevard, 1-310 395 0881, www.melisse.com, $$$$).

Lobster

1602 Ocean Avenue, at Arcadia Terrace (1-310 458 9294/www.thelobster.com). I-10, exit 4th-5th Street south. **Open** 11.30am-10pm Mon-Thur, Sun; 11.30am-11pm Fri, Sat. **Average** $$$-$$$$. **Credit** AmEx, DC, Disc, MC, V.

Housed in a glass building overlooking the pier, this award-winning restaurant is an elegant affair. It's a fine spot to watch the sunset (there's a great terrace) but it doesn't rely on its views: service and food are excellent. To whet your appetite for the sublime steamed Maine lobster, try crispy lemon calamari or romaine and endive salad with fried oysters.

Röckenwagner

2435 Main Street, at Ocean Park Boulevard (1-310 399 6504/www.rockenwagner.com). I-10, exit 4th-5th Street south. **Open** 6-9.30pm Tue-Sat. **Average** $$$$-$$$$$. **Credit** AmEx, DC, MC, V.

Located in the Edgemar Complex, the restaurant that made chef Hans Röckenwagner's name epitomises California cuisine in its marriage of eclectic food and artistic presentation. It's in two sections: a stylish restaurant, in which two tasting menus are served nightly, and a more casual brasserie.

Sushi Roku

1401 Ocean Avenue, at Santa Monica Boulevard (1-310 458 4771/www.sushiroku.com). I-10, exit 4th-5th Street north. **Open** 11.30am-2.30pm, 5.30-11.30pm Mon-Fri; noon-11.30pm Sat; 4.30-10.30pm Sun. **Average** $$$$. **Credit** AmEx, DC, Disc, MC, V.

Hip Sushi Roku is designed in a decidedly odd Zen-meets-Frank-Lloyd-Wright style: lots of gray stone, black granite and bamboo. Sushi ranges from the basics to unusual fare; say, crispy tuna sashimi spring rolls with a chilli oil and beurre blanc sauce.

Valentino

3115 Pico Boulevard, at 31st Street (1-310 829 4313). I-10, exit Centinela Avenue south. **Open** 5-11pm Mon-Thur, Sat, Sun; 11.30am-2.30pm, 5-11pm Fri. **Average** $$$$$. **Credit** AmEx, DC, Disc, MC, V. **Map** p306 C3.

Piero Selvaggio has awards coming out of his ears for his flagship restaurant, one of the best Italian restaurants in LA if not the whole of the US. Ask Selvaggio to put together a 'tasting plate' for you, and if you've got the moolah, splurge. The wine cellar's as notable as the food.

Don't kick the **Abbot's Habit**. *See p125.*

Also recommended

Cool sushi at **Akwa** (1413 5th Street, 1-310 656 9688, $$$); high-tech French-Japanese fusion at **Cinch** (1519 Wilshire Boulevard, 1-310 395 4139, www.cinch restaurant.com, closed lunch, $$$$); buzzy Chinese eaterie **Chinois on Main** (2709 Main Street, 1-310 392 3038, closed lunch Mon, Tue, Sat & Sun, $$$$); casual **Cora's Coffee Shoppe** (1802 Ocean Avenue, 1-310 451 9562, $); good food and better views at **1 Pico** (1 Pico Boulevard, 1-310 587 1717, $$$$); great Hong Kong eats at **Royal Star Seafood** (3001 Wilshire Boulevard, 1-310 828 8812, $$); LA's best Polish restaurant, **Warszawa** (1414 Lincoln Boulevard, 1-310 393 8831, closed Mon and lunch Tue-Sun, $$$).

Venice & Marina del Rey

Amuse Café

796 Main Street, at Brooks Avenue (1-310 450 1956). I-10, exit Lincoln Boulevard south. **Open** 11am-10pm Tue-Fri; 9am-10pm Sat, Sun. **Average** $$-$$$. **Credit** AmEx, MC, V.
Housed in an old worker's cottage, Amuse looks like a New England beach house, both outside (buttercup-yellow clapboard) and in (exposed beams, creaky wood floors). Highlights include seasonal salads and scrumptious onion and cheese tarte. BYOB.

Ballona Fish Market

Villa Marina Marketplace, 13455 Maxella Avenue, between Glencoe Avenue & Delray Avenue (1-310 822 8979/www.rockenwagner.com). Hwy 90, exit Mindanao Way north. **Open** 11.30am-2.30pm, 5.30-11pm Mon-Fri; 11am-11pm Fri, Sat; 4-10pm Sun. **Average** $$$$. **Credit** AmEx, MC, V.

Hans Röckenwagner recently transformed his trendy Rock restaurant into a pastiche of seaside Americana. The new menu is trad seafood with a nouvelle twist: crab cakes with lemongrass mayo, or steamed clams with spicy Italian sausage.

Joe's

1023 Abbot Kinney Boulevard, between Broadway & Westminster Avenues (1-310 399 5811/www.joesrestaurantcom). I-10, exit Lincoln Boulevard south. **Open** noon-2.30pm, 6-11pm Tue-Thur; noon-2.30pm, 6-11pm Fri; 11am-2.30pm, 6-11pm Sat; 11am-2.30pm, 6-10pm Sun. **Average** $$-$$$$. **Credit** MC, V.
Opened in 1991 by chef Joseph Miller, Joe's began life as an unassuming neighbourhood restaurant. After a slew of rave reviews and accolades, Miller has recently expanded, but the place has retained its hard-to-find, low-key feel and the French-Californian food remains exquisite. The *prix-fixe* lunch is a steal.

Also recommended

The Deep South comes to LA at **Aunt Kizzy's Back Porch** (4325 Glencoe Avenue, 1-310 578 1005, $$); Dogtown's favourite breakfast spot, the **Brickhouse** (826 Hampton Drive, 1-310 581 1639, closed dinner, $), brunch on the boardwalk at the **Figtree** (429 Ocean Front Walk, 1-310 392 4937, $$); upscale California cuisine at **Hal's Bar & Grill** (1349 Abbot Kinney Boulevard, 1-310 396 3105, $$$$); authentic Italy in Venice at **Piccolo Cipriani** (5 Dudley Avenue, 1-310 314 3222, www.piccolocipriani.com, closed lunch, $$); tapas *du jour* at **Primitivo Wine Bistro** (1025 Abbot Kinney Boulevard, 1-310 396 5353, $$$).

The South Bay

Chez Melange

Palos Verdes Inn, 1716 Pacific Coast Highway, at Prospect Avenue, Redondo Beach (1-310 540 1222/www.chezmelange.com). I-405, exit Artesia Boulevard west. **Open** 7.30am-2.30pm Mon-Thur, Sun; 7.30am-2.30pm, 5-11pm Fri, Sat. **Average** $$$-$$$$. **Credit** AmEx, Disc, MC, V.
In 1982 Michael Franks and Robert Bell walked into a bank, with no collateral, and left with a $200,000 loan to build Chez Melange; two decades later, it's still going strong. The food here is nouvelle eclectic, but it's not pretentious, and the 1950s diner decor is fab. There are also vodka, champagne and caviar bars.

Michi

903 Manhattan Avenue, at 9th Street, Manhattan Beach (1-310 376 0613). I-405, exit Hawthorne Boulevard north. **Open** 6-10.30pm Mon; 11.30am-2.30pm, 6-10.30pm Tue-Fri; 6-11pm Sat. **Average** $$$$. **Credit** AmEx, DC, MC, V.
Michi Takahashi is one of the Southland's hippest chefs, thanks to his cross-cultural culinary style that's inspired by French, Italian and Japanese cuisines. Recommendations include seafood paella for two as an entrée and anything for dessert.

Samba Brazilian Steakhouse & Bar

207 N Harbor Drive, between Beryl Street & N Pacific Avenue, Redondo Beach (1-310 374 3411/www. sambaredondo.com). I-405, exit 182nd Street west. **Open** 11am-2.30pm, 5-11pm Mon-Fri; 5-11pm Sat; 11am-3pm, 5-11pm Sun. **Average** $$$–$$$$. **Credit** AmEx, DC, MC, V.

Redondo Beach meets Rio at this lounge. There's 1960s furniture, a patio with views of the water, and Samba dancers. The food is all-you-can-eat, barbecued meat and fish cooked churrasco-style.

Also recommended

Dip into the **Crab Pot** (215 Marina Drive, Long Beach, 1-562 430 0272, $$$); posh American-French **Reed's** (2640 N Sepulveda Boulevard, Manhattan Beach, 1-310 546 3299, $$$); Med/Californian food at **Splash!** (350 N Harbor Drive, Redondo Beach, 1-310 798 5348, $$$); **Zazou** (1810 S Catalina Avenue, Redondo Beach, 1-310 540 4884, $$$) mixes Provence with Tuscany.

West LA

Apple Pan

10801 W Pico Boulevard, at Glendon Avenue, West LA (1-310 475 3585). I-10, exit Overland Avenue north. **Open** 11am-midnight Tue-Thur, Sun; 11am-1am Fri, Sat. **Average** $. **No credit cards.**

This local legend was born in 1947, when the Baker family bought a vacant lot and built the place from the ground up. The simple formula – sandwiches, burgers and pies served on paper plates and washed down with Coke, Dr Pepper or root beer – is still going strong.

Beacon

3280 Helms Avenue, at Washington Boulevard, Culver City (1-310 838 7500). I-10, exit Washington Boulevard south. **Open** 11am-2.30pm Mon, Sun; 11am-2.30pm, 5.30-9.30pm Tue, Wed; 5.30-10.30pm Thur-Sat. **Average** $$–$$$. **Credit** AmEx, DC, MC, V.

To help Culver City's bid for nouveau trendy status, Beacon is working overtime. Kazuto Matsusaka serves up steaming bowls of miso, well-priced bento boxes, sashimi or grilled hanger steak (to name but a few of his culinary tricks) to a hungry throng of locals.

La Cachette

10506 Little Santa Monica Boulevard, at Moreno Drive, Century City (1-310 470 4992/www.lacachette restaurant.com). I-405, exit Santa Monica Boulevard east. **Open** noon-2.30pm, 6-10pm Mon-Fri; 5.30-10.30pm Sat, Sun. **Average** $$$$–$$$$$. **Credit** AmEx, DC, MC, V.

This romantic, high-end restaurant serves some of LA's finest French cuisine. Chef Jean François Meteigner, who apprenticed in Michelin-starred restaurants in Paris, plies his trade with deftness and restraint. Try his provocative tasting menu.

Sunnin

1779 Westwood Boulevard, at Santa Monica Boulevard, Westwood (1-310 477 2358). I-405, exit Crenshaw Boulevard north. **Open** 11.30am-9.30pm daily. **Average** $$. **Credit** AmEx, MC, V.

Don't be put off by the cafeteria setting and fluorescent lighting: people drive miles for the cheap and delicious raw cabbage salad, spicy fava beans and kebabs at this authentic Lebanese restaurant.

Tanino

1043 Westwood Boulevard, between Weyburn & Kinross Avenues, Westwood (1-310 208 0444/ www.tanino.com). I-405, exit Crenshaw Boulevard north. **Open** 11.30am-3pm, 5-10pm Mon-Fri; 5-11pm Sat; 4-10pm Sun. **Average** $$$–$$$$. **Credit** AmEx, Disc, MC, V.

Tanino Drago, a genial thirtysomething Sicilian, presides over this elegant Westwood dining room. The more daring may care for his $48 funghi menu, four dishes (plus dessert) all based around mushrooms.

Vincenti

11930 San Vicente Boulevard, between S Bundy Drive & Montana Avenue, Brentwood (1-310 207 0127/www.vincentiristorante.com). I-405, exit Sunset Boulevard west. **Open** 6-10pm Mon-Thur, Sat; noon-2.30pm, 5-10pm Fri. **Average** $$$$$. **Credit** AmEx, MC, V.

Favoured by the local haute bourgeoisie, this contemporary Italian restaurant looks very sleek, and has rather smart food to match. The pastas are decent, but there are also excellent meat and fish dishes.

Also recommended

Darlin' **Clementine** (1751 Ensley Street, Century City, 1-310 552 1080, closed dinner, $), Annie Miler's charming café; health-conscious couture at **Coral Tree Café** (11645 San Vincente Boulevard, Brentwood, 1-310 979 8733, www.coraltreecafe.com, $); amiable Mexican **Monte Alban** (11927 Santa Monica Boulevard, West LA, 1-310 444 7736, $$); dirt-cheap **Tito's Tacos** (11222 Washington Place, Culver City, 1-310 391 5780, $); Oaxacan-meets-Californian food at **Tlapazola** (11676 Gateway Boulevard, West LA, 1-310 477 1577, closed Mon, $$).

Beverly Hills

Enoteca Drago

410 N Canon Drive, at Brighton Way (1-310 786 8236). I-405, exit Santa Monica Boulevard east. **Open** 7am-11pm Mon-Fri; 8am-11pm Sat; 8am-10pm Sun **Average** $$–$$$. **Credit** AmEx, DC, Disc, MC, V.

Celestino Drago's excellent enterprise is an *enoteca* taken up a notch. Food comes either as small plates or as regular entrées, and wine is served in measures as small as 2.5oz (74ml). Great for experimenting: a flight of oyster shots, say, or grilled octopus.

Matsuhisa

129 N La Cienega Boulevard, between Wilshire Boulevard & Clifton Way (1-310 659 9639/www. nobumatsuhisa.com). I-10, exit La Cienega Boulevard north. **Open** 11.45am-2.15pm, 5.45-10.15pm Mon-Fri; 5.45-10.15pm Sat, Sun. **Average** $$$$. **Credit** AmEx, DC, MC, V.

Chef Nobuyuki Matsuhisa's merging of Japanese and Peruvian cuisines attracts expense-account eaters and celebrities. Traditional sushi is available,

Java jive

Coffee isn't so much a drink as a religion in LA, and the coffeehouses that dot the town are nothing less than churches, each with their own faith to maintain. There's a niche for every kind of caffeinaholic, but where should you go to worship the Bean Almighty?

Hundreds of Los Angeles's coffeehouses are now owned and operated by chains; you're never far from a **Starbucks**, a **Coffee Bean & Tea Leaf** or (best of all) a **Peet's Coffee & Tea**. However, there are establishments still flying the independent flag. Many of the best are in Santa Monica and Venice: **Anastasia's Asylum** (1028 Wilshire Boulevard, 1-310 394 7113) and **Abbot's Habit** (1401 Abbot Kinney Boulevard, 1-310 399 1171) have art on the walls and music in the evenings; **Infuzion** (1149 3rd Street, 1-310 393 9985) and **Cow's End** (34 Washington Boulevard, 1-310 574 1080) offer net access.

In West Hollywood, the scene is slicker. **Buzz Coffee** (8000 W Sunset Boulevard, 1-323 656 7460) draws the young and the glamorous with its hyper-strong coffee; similarly enlivening java is served at the European-style **Kings Road Café** (8361 Beverly Boulevard, 1-323 655 9044). Cameron Diaz, meanwhile, has been known to pass the time at **Urth Caffé** (8565 Melrose Avenue, 1-310 659 0628), which has a delightful patio. It couldn't be much more different to Hollywood's earthy, shabby-chic **Bourgeois Pig** (5931 Franklin Avenue, 1-323 464 6008).

Elsewhere, Los Feliz boasts the European-style **La Belle Epoque** (2128 Hillhurst Avenue, 1-323 669 7640) and Silver Lake is home to the comfy **Back Door Bakery & Café** (1710 Silver Lake Boulevard, 1-323 662 7927). However, one of the real treats is all the way down in Inglewood. **Pann's** (710 La Tijera Boulevard, 1-323 776 3770) is a charming slice of 1950s nostalgia: from the art deco design to the waitresses who still wear the kind of pointy hats familiar from coffeehouse scenes in 1950s sitcoms, its authenticity is irresistible.

but he's most famous for the fusion dishes that use garlic, chilli and sauces in an imaginative way. Try squid 'pasta' with garlic sauce.

Nate 'n Al

414 N Beverly Drive, between Brighton Way & Santa Monica Boulevard (1-310 274 0101/www.natenal. com). I-405, exit Santa Monica Boulevard east. **Open** 7am-9pm daily. **Average** $$. **Credit** AmEx, MC, V.
Despite its slightly tawdry exterior, this 50-year-old establishment is a big industry hangout, serving excellent, traditional Jewish deli fare. The blintzes and velvety corn beef hash are particularly good.

Nic's

453 N Canon Drive, between Brighton Way & Santa Monica Boulevard (1-310 550 5707). I-405, exit Santa Monica Boulevard east. **Open** 5-10pm Mon-Thur; 6-11.30pm Fri; 5pm-midnight Sat. **Average** $$$$. **Credit** AmEx, Disc, MC, V.
Nic's sits on the edge of Beverly Hills, both geographically and metaphorically. The lounge setting has a distinctly bourgeois bohemian vibe (people are loaded here), attracting the full gamut from punks to politicians. The food is edgy, too: chef Larry Nicola calls it American with ethnic flair.

Polo Lounge

Beverly Hills Hotel, 9641 Sunset Boulevard, at N Crescent Drive (1-310 276 2251). I-405, exit Sunset Boulevard east. **Open** 7am-2am daily. **Average** $$$$. **Credit** AmEx, DC, MC, V.

A not-to-be-missed piece of Old Hollywood, where the power breakfast was invented and having a phone brought to your table became a legendary Hollywood ruse. The hotel was renovated magnificently in 1995, but the lounge was left intact. Today million-dollar deals are still sealed over eggs benedict, while romantic interludes are shared on the patio over fresh fish. The **Fountain Coffee Shop**, which offers diner staples, is almost as mythic.

Spago of Beverly Hills

176 N Canon Drive, between Clifton Way & Wilshire Boulevard (1-310 385 0880/www.wolfgangpuck. com). I-405, exit Wilshire Boulevard east. **Open** 11.30am-2pm, 6-10.30pm Mon-Thur; 11.30am-2.30pm, 5.30-11.30pm Fri, Sat; 6-10.30pm Sun. **Average** $$$$-$$$$$. **Credit** AmEx, DC, Disc, MC, V.
Wolfgang Puck, California's first celebrity chef, opened the original Spago off Sunset umpteen years ago; it closed in 2001, but this version had already opened three years earlier. It's a huge, stunning extravaganza, but the food is Puck classics: light California cuisine with Far East influences.

Also recommended

French-Vietnamese eden **Crustacean** (9646 Little Santa Monica Boulevard, 1-310 205 8990, www.an family.com, closed Sun & lunch Sat, $$$$); slick Japanese with a twist at **Kakemoto** (456 N Bedford Drive, 1-310 989 9467, $$$$); American standards at **Kate Mantilini** (9101 Wilshire Boulevard, 1-310 278 3699, $$–$$$); contemporary Asian food at **Mako**

(225 S Beverly Drive, 1-310 288 8338, www.mako restaurant.com, closed Sun & lunch Mon, Tue & Sat, $$$$); Sicilian-style pizza at **Mulberry Street** (347 N Canon Drive, 1-310 247 8100, $$); Chef Drago's **Piccolo Paradiso** (150 S Beverly Drive, 1-310 271 0030, www.giacominodrago.com, $$$).

West Hollywood

Bastide

8475 Melrose Place, between N La Cienega Boulevard & N Alfred Street (1-323 651 5950). I-10, exit La Cienega Boulevard north. **Open** 6-9pm Tue-Sat. **Average** $$$$$. **Credit** AmEx, DC, Disc, MC, V.
The light touch of French designer Andrée Putman has turned what was essentially a small California bungalow into a pared-down version of a French *bastide*, or country house. It's the perfect setting for haute cuisine, served in immaculate tasting menus.

Citrine

8360 Melrose Avenue, at N Kings Road (1-323 655 1690). I-10, exit La Cienega Boulevard north. **Open** 6.30-10.30pm Mon-Thur, Sun; 6-11pm Fri, Sat. **Average** $$$$. **Credit** AmEx, DC, Disc, MC, V.
Surrounded by sleek, minimalist decor, chef David Slatkin conjures up chic California cooking with Asian and Latin influences: sweet plantain papardella with Manila clams is a particular treat. Other highlights include applewood bacon and pan-seared foie gras; there's also an excellent sushi bar.

Dan Tana's

9071 Santa Monica Boulevard, between N Doheny Drive & Nemo Street (1-310 275 9444). I-10, exit Robertson Boulevard north. **Open** 5pm-1am daily. **Average** $$$$. **Credit** AmEx, DC, Disc, MC, V.
A local favourite since 1964, this late-night restaurant is one vivacious place, frequented by film and TV stars, sports personalities and the rank and file of the movie industry. The food is simple Italian fare and the staff have a great sense of humour.

Le Dôme

8720 W Sunset Boulevard, between N Sherbourne Drive & Sunset Plaza Drive (1-310 659 6919). I-10, exit La Cienega Boulevard north. **Open** 11.30am-3pm, 6-10.30pm Mon-Thur; 6pm-midnight Sat, Sun. **Average** $$$$$. **Credit** AmEx, DC, Disc, MC, V.
This LA institution has received a $2m restoration and is hoping to regain its place as the jewel of Sunset Boulevard. The Tuscan-style decor has been spruced up by Dodd Mitchell and there's a new menu of Californian classics by Sam Marvin.

Norman's

8570 W Sunset Boulevard, at Alta Loma Road (1-310 657 2400/www.normans.com). I-10, exit La Cienega Boulevard north. **Open** 6-10.30pm Mon-Sat. **Average** $$$$$. **Credit** AmEx, MC, V.
Miami-born Norman van Aken's eponymous restaurant in the Sunset Millennium is a wonderful excuse for getting dressed up. His exotic fusion cuisine borrows from the Caribbean and Latin America, but is

grounded in French technique. Pacing errs on the side of languid, but in such a wonderful setting, perhaps this is an inadvertent plus.

Sona

401 N La Cienega Boulevard, between Oakwood & Rosewood Avenues (1-310 659 7708/www.sona restaurant.com). I-10, exit La Cienega Boulevard north. **Open** 6-10.30pm Tue-Thur; 6-11.30pm Fri; 5.30-11pm Sat. **Average** $$$$$. **No credit cards**.
Sona's neutral design is dreamy, but the modern French food, created by David Myers, is often even better. Served on Bernadout china, it's full of lovely touches: a nasturtium leaf floats atop cold poached salmon; tapioca adorns the roasted line-caught cod.

Also recommended

See-and-be-seen hotspot **Asia de Cuba** (Mondrian Hotel, 8440 W Sunset Boulevard, 1-323 848 6000, $$$$); Charlie Palmer's lunch-only patio, **Astra West** (8687 Melrose Avenue, 1-310 652 3003, www.charliepalmer.com, closed dinner, $$$$); the **Ivy**, LA's ultimate star-spotting spot (113 N Robertson Boulevard, 1-310 274 8303, $$$–$$$$$); California cuisine with a Southern soul at **G Garvin's** (8620 W 3rd Street, 1-323 655 3888, $$$); fine French at **L'Orangerie** (903 N La Cienega Boulevard, 1-310 652 9770, $$$); healthy food and a hip crowd at the **Newsroom Café** (120 N Robertson Boulevard, 1-310 652 4444, $$); two legendary hot dog stands, **Pink's Hot Dogs** (709 N La Brea Boulevard, 1-323 931 4223, $) and **Tail-o'-the-Pup** (329 N San Vicente Boulevard, 1-310 652 4517, $); brown rice and tofu at **Real Food Daily** (414 N La Cienega Boulevard, 1-310 289 9910, $).

The Fairfax District & the Miracle Mile

AOC

8022 W 3rd Street, at S Laurel Avenue (1-323 653 6359/www.aocwinebar.com). I-10, exit Fairfax Avenue north. **Open** 6-10.45pm Mon-Fri; 5.30-10.45pm Sat; 5.45-10pm Sun. **Average** $$$$$. **Credit** AmEx, DC, Disc, MC, V.
The name stands for *Appellation d'Origine Controlée*, a system for certifying the regional origin of food and wine in France. And the food? Exquisite. Offerings might include salad of arugula, persimmon and hazelnut strewn with pomegranate seeds, or braised pork cheeks with a mustard gremolata. Book ahead.

Cobras & Matadors

7615 Beverly Boulevard, between N Curson & N Stanley Avenues (1-323 932 6178). I-10, exit Fairfax Avenue north. **Open** 6-11pm Mon-Thur, Sun; 6pm-midnight Fri, Sat. **Average** $$$. **Credit** AmEx, DC, Disc, MC, V.
Expect to wait for a table at this hip Spanish tapas bar, owned by Steven Arroyo. Inside, it's noisy but fun; outside on the sidewalk, you can dine under heat lamps. Ensure you pick up a bottle of something suitably Spanish from their its wine store.

India Sweet House

5992 W Pico Boulevard, at Stearns Drive (1-323 934 5193). I-10, exit S La Cienega Boulevard north. **Open** 11.30am-9pm daily. **Average** $$. **No credit cards.**
Indian restaurants are a dime a dozen here, but India Sweets is the cream of the crop. It's vegetarian, so don't come if you're craving a chicken tikka. The tali (mixed plate) gives you a nice sampling of the menu, and the sugary desserts are irresistible.

La Terza

8384 W 3rd Street, at S Orlando Avenue (1-323 782 8384). I-10, exit Fairfax Avenue north. **Open** 7-11pm daily. **Average** $$$$$. **Credit** AmEx, DC, MC, V.
While the environs of La Terza are uninspired and maybe even clinical, Gino Angelini's food is as good and as inventive as Italian gets in LA. The entrées of branzino steamed in white wine and the costata di bue grilled over oak and seasoned with sea salt are especially outstanding. Prices, of course, are vertical…

Versailles

1415 S La Cienega Boulevard, between W Pico Boulevard & Alcott Street (1-310 289 0392). I-10, exit La Cienega Boulevard south. **Open** 11am-10pm daily. **Average** $$. **Credit** AmEx, MC, V.
A funky no-frills Cuban joint, boasting good food and great prices – no wonder the LAPD loves it. Try the garlic chicken served with sweet raw onion and fried plantains on white rice with black beans. Service is quick and to the point.

Paladar.

Yi

7910 W 3rd Street, at N Fairfax Avenue (1-323 658 8028/www.yicuisine.com). I-10, exit Fairfax Avenue north. **Open** 6-10.30pm Mon-Thur; 6-11.30pm Fri, Sat; 6-10pm Sun. **Average** $$$$. **Credit** AmEx, Disc, MC, V.
Dramatic decor aside, the pull here is Hawaiian chef Rodelio Aglibot's bewitching menu. Nothing will disappoint, but don't leave without the seriously orgasmic organic miso and red curry bronzed black cod.

Also recommended

Ace Med cuisine at **Campanile** (624 S La Brea Avenue, 1-323 938 1447, www.campanilerestaurant.com, $$$$$); 24-hour Jewish deli **Canter's**, an LA legend (419 N Fairfax Avenue, 1-323 651 2030, $); **Du-Par's** diner (6333 W 3rd Street, 1-323 933 8446, $); new American cuisine and Liz Belkind's hot doughnut desserts at **Grace** (7360 Beverly Boulevard, 1-323 934 4400, www.gracerestaurant.com, closed Mon & lunch Tue-Sun, $$$$); sublime Mexican food at the **Loteria Grill**, a small stand at the Farmers' Market (6333 W 3rd Street, 1-323 930 2211, closed dinner Sun, $); **Meals by Genet**, the best of Fairfax's Ethiopian restaurants (1053 S Fairfax Avenue, 1-323 938 9304, www.mealsbygenet.com, $$); bistro fare at **Mimosa** (8009 Beverly Boulevard, 1-323 655 8895, www. mimosarestaurant.com, closed Mon, Sun & lunch Tue-Sat, $$$$); upscale **Table 8** (7661 Melrose Avenue, 1-323 782 8258, closed Sun & lunch Mon-Sat, $$$$$).

Hollywood

Ammo

1155 N Highland Avenue, between Lexington Avenue & Santa Monica Boulevard (1-323 871 2666). US 101, exit Highland Avenue south. **Open** 11am-3pm, 6-10pm Mon-Thur; 11am-3pm, 6-11pm Fri; 10am-3pm, 6-11pm Sat; 10am-3pm Sun. **Average** $$–$$$$. **Credit** AmEx, DC, Disc, MC, V.
Ammo's gritty location, sandwiched between photo labs and industrial manufacturing companies, lends it cred. Stylists, editors and other industry folk flock to this groovy, low-key space to munch on simple, well-prepared comfort food: turkey burgers, breakfast burritos, green salad strewn with parmesan.

Mario's Peruvian Seafood

5786 Melrose Avenue, at N Vine Street (1-323 466 4181). I-10, exit La Brea Avenue north. **Open** 11.30am-8.30pm Mon-Thur, Sun; 11.30am-10pm Fri, Sat. **Average** $$$. **Credit** MC, V.
You'll probably have to queue at this Peruvian hole-in-the-wall – the food is cheap and delicious. Highlights include siete mares (seven seas seafood soup), lomo saltado (strips of beef sautéed with onions and tomatoes, served with french fries) and a challenging hot guacamole sauce to eat with bread.

Paladar

1651 Wilcox Avenue, between Hollywood Boulevard & Selma Avenue (1-323 465 7500/www.paladar.cc). US 101, exit Vine Street south. **Open** 11am-3pm, 5.30-11pm Mon-Fri; 5.30-11pm Sat, Sun. **Average** $$$$. **Credit** AmEx, Disc, DC, MC, V.

Southern California

Hollywood hipsters have discovered Cuba and this trendy café is living proof. The elegant dining lounge has shades of Havana and so does the menu: empañadas, braised oxtail and spicy fries served in generous portions. Eat, then pop next door to bar/club **Nacional** (1645 Wilcox Avenue, 1-310 962 7712).

Roscoe's House of Chicken 'n' Waffles

1514 N Gower Street, at W Sunset Boulevard (1-323 466 7453). US 101, exit Gower Street south. **Open** 8am-midnight Mon-Thur, Sun; 8am-4am Fri, Sat. **Average** $. **Credit** AmEx, Disc, DC, MC, V.
The dimly lit, carefully under-decorated Hollywood branch of this funky Southern joint delights with its long hours and low prices, but most of all for its fantastic fried chicken. Dieters: don't even think about it.

White Lotus

1742 N Cahuenga Boulevard, between Hollywood Boulevard & Yucca Street (1-323 463 0060/www. whitelotushollywood.com). US 101, exit Gower Street south. **Open** *Restaurant* 6pm-12.30am Tue-Sat. *Nightclub* 9pm-2am Tue-Sat. **Average** $$$$. **Credit** AmEx, Disc, DC, MC, V.
In 2004 this Asian-slanted club/restaurant was one of the city's hippest spots; only time will tell if it stays that way. Certainly, it looks beautiful, and the guest list is a Hollywood who's who. The food? Cal-Asian, and impressive given the nightclub setting.

Also recommended

Gourmet organic pizzas at colourful **Cheebo** (7533 Sunset Boulevard, 1-323 850 7070, www.cheebo.com, $$); Mexican hole-in-the-wall **Lucy's Café El Adobe** (5536 Melrose Avenue, 1-323 462 9421, closed Sun, $); huevos rancheros at the **101 Coffee Shop** (6141 Franklin Avenue, 1-323 467 1175, closed dinner, $); local pizzeria **Prizzi's Piazza** (5923 Franklin Avenue, 1-323 467 0168, $$).

Midtown

Cassell's

3266 W 6th Street, between S Berendo Street & S New Hampshire Avenue, Koreatown (1-213 387 5502). I-10, exit Vermont Avenue north. **Open** 10.30am-4pm Mon-Sat. **Average** $. **No credit cards.**
Hamburgers are to Americans what pizzas are to Italians: there are endless arguments about where to get the best burger in town. Many Angelenos are faithful to this lunch-only joint, which serves up a mean and greasy burger with home-made mayo.

Las Delicias Chapinas

3731 W Pico Boulevard, between 4th & 5th Avenue, Koreatown (1-323 731 6995). I-10, exit Arlington Avenue north. **Open** 7am-10pm daily. **Average** $$. **No credit cards.**
This Guatemalan joint, a fun little neighbourhood *boîte*, entertains its customers with live marimba music. Dishes include carne asada, sausages and pork tamales; portions are sizeable and prices are extremely keen. You'll need to book at weekends.

Dong Il Jang

3455 W 8th Street, at S Hobart Boulevard, Koreatown (1-213 383 5757). I-10, exit Western Avenue north. **Open** 11am-10pm daily. **Average** $$$$. **Credit** AmEx, MC, V.
Dong Il Jang is an upmarket affair. Dine at the sushi bar, in a booth, or sitting on cushions on the floor. For Korean barbecued fare, be sure to try the galbi-marinated beef short ribs, which arrive with myriad side dishes: pickled vegetables, sweet potatoes, glass noodles and rice.

Soot Bull Jeep

3136 W 8th Street, between S Berendo & S Catalina Streets, Koreatown (1-213 387 3865). I-10, exit Vermont Avenue north. **Open** 11am-11pm daily. **Average** $$$. **Credit** AmEx, MC, V.
All the sizzling goes on right in front of you, at one of the best Korean barbecue joints in LA. Before you're seated, a waitress will scatter a trowel of glowing coals into a pit set in the middle of your table.

Also recommended

Legendary Mexican **El Cholo** (1121 S Western Avenue, 1-323 734 2773, $$); mom 'n' pop Northern Italian at **Girasole** (225½ N Larchmont Boulevard, Larchmont Village, 1-323 464 6978, $$$); casual, colourful Mexican restaurant **Guelaguetza** (3337½ W 8th Street, Koreatown, 1-213 427 0601, $); LA's best pastrami is at **Langer's Deli** (704 S Alvarado Street, Koreatown, 1-213 483 8050, closed Sun & dinner Mon-Sat, $); characterful Greek joint **Papa Cristo's** (2771 W Pico Boulevard, Koreatown, 1-323 737 2970, www.papacristo.com, closed Mon, $).

Downtown

Ciudad

445 S Figueroa Street, between W 4th & W 5th Streets (1-213 486 5171/www.ciudad-la.com). I-110, exit 9th Street west. **Open** 11.30am-3pm, 5-8.45pm Mon, Tue; 11.30am-3pm, 5-9.45pm Wed-Fri; 5-9.45pm Sat; 5-8.45pm Sun. **Average** $$$. **Credit** AmEx, Disc, MC, V.
Chefs Susan Feniger and Mary Sue Milliken researched this tribute to Latin American cuisine by touring South America. The decor is colourful and fun, and so is the lively, mouthwatering menu. Pollo Ciudad and seared monkfish are both terrific choices; try and make room for a side of plantain.

Noé

251 S Olive Street, between W 2nd & W 3rd Streets (1-213 356 4100/www.omnihotels.com). US 101, exit Broadway west. **Open** 5-10pm Mon-Thur, Sun; 5pm-midnight Fri, Sat. **Average** $$$$. **Credit** DC, MC, V.
British-born chef Robert Gadsby confirmed his status as one of the city's great culinary talents with the 2003 opening of this dining room atop the Omni Hotel. If you have the time and the money, his tasting menus (with wine) are particularly inspiring. A typical meal might include lobster salad over a roasted pear and potato agnolotti with chanterelles.

Ocean Seafood

747 N Broadway, at Ord Street (1-213 687 3088/ www.oceansf.com). I-110, exit Hill Street east. **Open** 9am-10pm daily. **Average** $3-$15. **Credit** DC, MC, V.
During the day, this Chinatown seafood restaurant in is a bustling dim sum operation. By night, the atmosphere is more relaxed. You can bet the food is fresh: diners choose their dinner from tanks of live shrimp, lobster and clams on their way in.

Patina

Walt Disney Concert Hall, 141 S Grand Avenue, between W 2nd & W 3rd Streets (1-213 972 3331/ www.patinagroup.com). I-110, exit 3rd Street east. **Open** 11.30am-1.30pm, 5-10.45pm Mon-Fri; 5-10.45pm Sat, Sun. **Average** $$$$. **Credit** AmEx, Disc, MC, V.
The outlandish building suits Joaquim Splichal's esoteric Italian cooking to a tee. Patina is certainly the best of the Disney restaurants; indeed, it's one of the best in the whole city. Mains include champagne and Tahitian vanilla bean risotto with Maine lobster tail. Splichal also runs excellent Italian restaurant **Zucca** (810 S Figueroa Street, 1-213 614 7800, $$$).

Philippe the Original

1001 N Alameda Street, at Ord Street (1-213 628 3781/www.philippes.com). US 101, exit Alameda Street north. **Open** 6am-10pm daily. **Average** $. **No credit cards.**
Pure old-school LA. Philippe Mathieu invented the French Dip Sandwich in 1908: freshly carved roast beef, lamb, pork or turkey served on a soft bun dipped in the meat's juices. The place gets packed at lunchtimes and in the early evenings, but staff keep the sandwiches coming apace.

Also recommended

Parisien jewel **Angelique Café** (849 S Spring Street, 1-213 623 8698, www.angeliquecafe.com, closed Sun & lunch Mon-Sat, $$); outstanding Cantonese-style **Empress Pavilion** (Suite 201, Bamboo Plaza, 988 N Hill Street, 1-213 617 9898, $$$); upscale steakhouse **Nick & Stef's** (330 S Hope Street, 1-213 680 0330, closed lunch Sat & Sun, $$$$$); popular Japanese **R-23** (923 E 3rd Street, 1-213 687 7178, closed Sun & lunch Sat, $$$$); Cali-French **Traxx** (Union Station, 800 N Alameda Street, 1-213 625 1999, closed Sun & lunch Sat, $$$).

Los Feliz, Silver Lake & Echo Park

Café Stella

3932 W Sunset Boulevard, between Sanborn & Hyperion Avenues, Silver Lake (1-323 666 0265). US 101, exit Silver Lake Boulevard north. **Open** 6-11pm Tue-Sat. **Average** $$$$. **Credit** AmEx, MC, V.
This casual French bistro and bar is immensely popular with locals. The menu is far from fussy nouvelle; poulet à l'estragon, excellent steak au poivre with pommes lyonnaise or translucent pommes frites and ratatouille are highlights. Booking is strongly advised.

Cha Cha Cha

656 N Virgil Avenue, at Melrose Avenue, Los Feliz (1-323 664 7723/www.theoriginalchachacha.com). I-10, exit Vermont Avenue north. **Open** 8am-10pm Mon-Thur, Sun; 8am-11pm Fri, Sat. **Average** $$$. **Credit** AmEx, DC, Disc, MC, V.
This festive restaurant is located in an insalubrious neighbourhood, but is still hugely popular; people come from across town to taste the superlative Latin American food. The jerk chicken is excellent.

Edendale Grill

2838 Rowena Avenue, between Auburn & Rokeby Streets, Silver Lake (1-323 666 2000/www.edendale grill.com). I-5, exit Hyperion Avenue west. **Open** 5.30-10pm Mon-Thur, Sun; 5.30-11.30pm Fri, Sat; 5.30-10pm Sun. **Average** $$$. **Credit** AmEx, MC, V.
Hip locals come to this former fire station as much for the atmosphere – the happening bar stays open two hours after the kitchen closes – as for the food, which tends towards hearty American fare. Typical dishes include iceberg lettuce wedges smothered in blue cheese dressing and a splendid mushroom pie.

Fred 62

1850 N Vermont Avenue, at Franklin Avenue, Los Feliz (1-323 667 0062). US 101, exit Vermont Avenue north. **Open** 24hrs daily. **Average** $$. **Credit** AmEx, DC, Disc, MC, V.
This round-the-clock Los Feliz staple from Fred Eric simply is what it is. The menu is stylised fast food with a slight health-conscious and vegetarian focus but some of LA's best meat loaf. The theme is '50s diner, but with '60s design influences and a soundtrack that runs through '70s funk and '80s alt-rock.

Millie's

3524 W Sunset Boulevard, between Maltman & Golden Gate Avenues, Silver Lake (1-323 664 0404). US 101, exit Silver Lake Boulevard north. **Open** 7.30am-4pm daily. **Average** $. **Credit** MC, V.
This quaint little diner has gone through a lot of owners since it opened in 1926, but it's settled into landmark status these days. The hearty food is tasty and cheap. For breakfast, try the Eleanor R (for Roosevelt): two eggs over easy, cheddar, salsa and sour cream on rosemary potatoes.

Vermont

1714 N Vermont Avenue, at Hollywood Boulevard, Los Feliz (1-323 661 6163/www.vermontrestaurant online.com). US 101, exit Vermont Avenue north. **Open** 11am-11pm daily. **Average** $$$. **Credit** AmEx, DC, Disc, MC, V.
Vermont serves a mishmash of American and French comfort food. The house salad, two perfectly poached eggs atop bacon and frisée, is hard to beat; also excellent is lamb shank on lentils.

Also recommended

Creole at **Cirxa** (3719 Sunset Boulevard, Silver Lake, 1-323 663 1048, $$$); hearty fare at the **Kitchen** (4348 Fountain Avenue, Silver Lake, 1-323 664 3663, closed lunch Mon-Fri; $$); Mexican **Malo** (4326 W Sunset Boulevard, Silver Lake, 1-323 664 1011, closed lunch, $$$); marvellous things are done with avocado at **Mustard Seed Café** (1948 N Hillhurst Avenue, Silver Lake, 1-323 660 0670, $$); comfort food, Latin-style at **Netty's** (1700 Silver Lake Boulevard, Silver Lake, 1-323 662 8655, closed Sun, $); Vietnamese at **Pho Café** (2841 W Sunset Boulevard, Silver Lake, 1-213 413 0888, $$); Oaxacan at **Yucca's** (2056 Hillhurst Avenue, Silver Lake, 1-323 662 1214, $$).

East LA

La Parilla

2126 E Cesar E Chavez Avenue, between Cummings & St Louis Streets, East LA (1-323 262 3434). I-10, exit Cesar E Chavez Avenue east. **Open** 8am-11pm daily. **Average** $$. **Credit** AmEx, MC, V.
In the middle of rundown Boyle Heights, this Mexican restaurant is the real thing. Its speciality is grilled meats – sweet and spicy spare ribs are delicious – as well as seafood, mole sauce and sangria. Beware of the parillada for two: it's way too large.

La Serenata di Garibaldi

1842 E 1st Street, between N State Street & N Boyle Avenue, East LA (1-323 265 2887). I-10, exit Boyle Avenue north. **Open** 11am-10pm Mon-Thur; 11am-11pm Fri, Sat; 10am-10pm Sun. **Average** $$$. **Credit** DC, MC, V.
This small place in Boyle Heights – call in advance, get directions and park in the back – serves fresh fish in exquisite sauces. The atmosphere is great: Mexican families and Downtown artists dine at tables with red-and-white-checked tablecloths.

Also recommended

Hole-in-the-wall **Tacos Clarita** (3049 E 4th Street, 1-323 262 3620, $); basic Mexican food at **Tamales Liliana's** (4619 E Cesar E Chavez Avenue, 1-323 780 0989, $); Mex mecca **El Tepeyac** (812 N Evergreen Avenue, 1-323 267 8668, $); home-made recipes at **Teresita's** (3826 E 1st Street, 1-323 266 6045, $$).

The Valleys

San Fernando Valley

Chili My Soul

4928 Balboa Boulevard, at Ventura Boulevard, Encino (1-818 981 7685/www.chilimysoul.com). US 101, exit Balboa Boulevard south. **Open** 11am-9pm daily. **Average** $. **Credit** AmEx, MC, V.
Randy Hoffman prepares over 30 different chillis. The habanero/mango chicken is the best of the trad varieties; the Irish whiskey version is better than you'd imagine. They all come with a choice of three amazing toppings, from Monterey Jack to chocolate chips.

Max

13355 Ventura Boulevard, at Nagle Avenue, Sherman Oaks (1-818 784 2915/www.max restaurant.com). US 101, exit Woodman Avenue south. **Open** 11.30am-2.30pm, 5.30-10pm Mon-Thur; 11.30am-2.30pm, 5.30-11pm Fri; 5.30-11pm Sat; 5.30-10pm Sun. **Average** $$$. **Credit** AmEx, MC, V.

Star bar: the **Frolic Room**. *See p133.*

This welcome addition to the Valley is headed up by André Guerrero, the former chef at Linq in West Hollywood. It's a noisy little place, but the California-Asian cuisine is very sophisticated.

Minibar

3413 Cahuenga Boulevard, at Universal Studios Boulevard (1-323 882 6965/www.minibarlounge.com). US 101, exit Universal Center Drive. **Open** 5.30pm-2am daily. **Average** $$$. **Credit** AmEx, MC, V.
The music and '60s mod decor works well with the international tapas-style menu at this fun place on the edge of the Valley. The food, in turn, fits sweetly with the fine cocktail and wine lists.

Sushi Nozawa

11288 Ventura Boulevard, between Tujunga & Vineland Avenues, Studio City (1-818 508 7017). US 101, exit Vineland Avenue south. **Open** 5.30-10pm Mon-Fri. **Average** $$$$. **Credit** MC, V.
Hidden away in a Studio City strip mall, in-the-know foodies frequent this café for one reason only: the superb sushi. Chef Kazunori Nozawa has a reputation as a prickly character, but when he puts up a sign reading 'tonight's special: trust me', you should.

Zeke's Smokehouse

2209 Honolulu Avenue, at N Verdugo Road, Montrose (1-818 957 7045/www.zekessmokehouse. com). I-210, exit Ocean View Boulevard south. **Open** 11am-9pm Mon-Thur, Sun; 11am-10pm Fri, Sat. **Average** $$$. **Credit** MC, V.

Zeke's is more expensive than your average barbecue joint, but the baby backs and spare ribs are lip-smackingly good, as are the pork sandwiches.

Also recommended

Much loved **Art's Deli** (12224 Ventura Boulevard, Studio City, 1-818 762 1221, $); burger landmark **Bob's Big Boy** (4211 Riverside Drive, Burbank, 1-818 843 9334, www.bobs.net, $); unpretentious French at **Pinot Bistro** (12969 Ventura Boulevard, Studio City, 1-818 990 0500, closed lunch Sat, Sun, $$$$); go game at romantic **Saddle Peak Lodge** (419 Cold Canyon Road, Calabasas, 1-818 222 3888, www.saddle peaklodge.com, closed Mon & lunch Tue-Sat, $$$$$).

San Gabriel Valley

Café Atlantic

53 E Union Street, at N Raymond Avenue, Pasadena (1-626 796 7350). I-710, exit Colorado Boulevard south. **Open** 7am-10pm daily. **Average** $$$. **Credit** AmEx, Disc, MC, V.

The setting – in Old Town Pasadena – might not scream authenticity, but the food at this reasonably priced relation of Xiomara (*see p131*) certainly does.

Celestino Ristorante

141 S Lake Avenue, between E Green & Cordova Streets, Pasadena (1-626 795 4006/www.celestino pasadena.com). I-210, exit Lake Avenue south. **Open** 11.30am-2.30pm, 5.30-10.30pm Mon-Fri; 5.30-10.30pm Sat. **Average** $$$$. **Credit** AmEx, Disc, MC, V.

Celestino is owned by Celestino Drago, just one member of a foodie family from Sicily now working in LA. Here, he serves up sophisticated but not over-complicated dishes with origins in his homeland.

Empress Harbor

111 N Atlantic Boulevard, at W Garvey Avenue, Monterey Park (1-626 300 8833/www.empress harbor.com). I-10, exit Atlantic Boulevard south. **Open** 9am-10pm daily. **Average** $$–$$$$. **Credit** AmEx, Disc, MC, V.

Empress Harbor serves what's arguably the best dim sum in the city – be quick though, as it's only served until 3pm. Other appetising possibilities from the main menu are the shark fin soup and lobster.

Also recommended

Exotic fusion at **Cinnabar** (933 S Brand Boulevard, Glendale, 1-818 551 1155, closed lunch, $$$); stylish American at **Firefly Bistro** (1009 El Centro Avenue, 1-626 441 2443, closed Mon, $$$$); sun-dappled Provençal lunch spot **Julienne** (2649 Mission Street, San Marino, 1-626 441 2299, $$); awe-inspiring café **Lake Spring Shanghai** (219 E Garvey Avenue, Monterey Park, 1-626 280 3571, $$$); New Asian **Nonya** (61 Raymond Avenue, Pasadena, 1-626 583 8398, $$$); Cali food at the **Raymond** (1250 S Fair Oaks Avenue, Pasadena, 1-626 441 3136, $$$$); nouvelle Thai at **Saladang Song** (383 S Fair Oaks Avenue, Pasadena, 1-626 793 5200, $$); more Latino at **Xiomara** (69 N Raymond Avenue, Pasadena, 1-626 796 2520, $$$$; fusion-happy **Yujean Kang's** (67 N Raymond Avenue, Pasadena, 1-626 585 0855).

South Central

Harold & Belle's

2920 W Jefferson Boulevard, between Arlington Avenue & Crenshaw Boulevard, Jefferson Park (1-323 735 9023). I-10, exit Crenshaw Boulevard south. **Open** 11.30am-10pm Mon-Thur, Sun; 11.30am-11pm Fri, Sat. **Average** $$$–$$$$. **Credit** AmEx, Disc, MC, V.

If you have a hankering for Southern food, you're in luck. Located in a distinctly down-at-heel neighbourhood, Harold & Belle's is surprisingly elegant. And the good ol' Southern hospitality is a delight.

M&M's Soul Food Café

9506 S Avalon Boulevard, at 95th Street, Watts (1-323 777 9250). I-110, exit Century Boulevard east. **Open** 8am-8pm Tue-Sat; 8am-6pm Sun. **Average** $$. **Credit** MC, V.

All the branches of this soul food chain claim to be the original – this one has been around for 30 years. With only five burgundy leatherette booths, seven stools at the counter and four tables in the middle, it's a small, basic place. People who try the newer, more user-friendly branches end up back here.

Also recommended

Unmissable **Randy's Donuts** (805 W Manchester Avenue, Inglewood, 1-310 645 4707, www.randys donuts.com, $); LA's best fried chicken at **Stevie's on the Strip** (3403 Crenshaw Boulevard, South LA, 1-323 734 6975, $).

Orange County

Aubergine

508 29th Street, at Newport Boulevard, Newport Beach (1-949 723 4150). Hwy 55, exit Newport Boulevard. **Open** 5.30-9pm daily. **Average** $$$$. **Credit** AmEx, DC, Disc, MC, V.

Simply put, Tim Goodell's sophisticated dining establishment, housed in a charming cottage, is the best thing behind the orange curtain. Dress up for this serious dining experience: the food is among the most sublime and deftly presented in California.

French 75

1464 Pacific Coast Highway, at Calliope Street, Laguna Beach (1-949 494 8444/www.culinary adventures.com). Hwy 133, exit PCH south. **Open** 5-10pm Mon-Thur, Sun; 5-11pm Fri, Sat. **Average** $$$$. **Credit** AmEx, Disc, MC, V.

This little Parisian bistro is an extremely elegant spot, with overstuffed chairs and art deco touches. If you crane your neck, you can see the ocean from the patio. Dishes run the gamut from heavenly seafood – langoustine and crayfish cappuccino – to rustic French cooking. There's jazz nightly Wed-Sat.

Hush

858 S Coast Highway, at Shadow Lane, Laguna Beach (1-949 497 3616/www.hushrestaurant.com). Hwy 133, exit PCH south. **Open** 5.30-10.30pm daily. **Average** $$$$. **Credit** AmEx, DC, Disc, MC, V.

The designer decor at Hush is beautiful, and there's even a patio, lit and heated with outdoor fireplaces, overlooking the ocean. The food is contemporary American with Asian and Mediterranean overtones.

El Misti Picanteria Arequipena

3070 W Lincoln Avenue, at Beach Boulevard, Anaheim (1-714 995 5944/www.elmisticuisine.com). I-405, exit Beach Boulevard north. **Open** 11am-8pm daily. **Average** $$. **Credit** AmEx, Disc, MC, V.
Rustic Peruvian dishes are the mainstay at this place that's as sweet as it is humble, adorned with vivid artwork depicting similar eateries around El Misti, a volcano that frowns down on Arequipa in Peru.

Napa Rose

Grand Californian Hotel, 1600 S Disneyland Drive, at Katella Avenue, Anaheim (1-714 300 7170). I-5, exit Harbor Boulevard south. **Open** 5.30-10pm daily. **Average** $$$$$. **Credit** AmEx, DC, Disc, MC, V.
The food lives up to the stunning, Frank Lloyd Wright-style setting at what is quite possibly the best restaurant in Anaheim. The lengthy California wine list is astonishing.

Where to Drink

LA will never be a drinking town, thanks chiefly to the in-built necessity to drive. But bar culture has improved in the last few years, with the ongoing hipster fascination with dive bars and the improving public transport. All bars are subject to California's alcohol laws: you have to be 21 or over to buy and consume it (take photo ID even if you look much older), and alcohol can only be sold between 6am and 2am.

The beach towns

The success of the grungey-chic **Circle Bar** (2926 Main Street, Santa Monica, 1-310 450 0508) helped spawn the **Buffalo Club** (1520 Olympic Boulevard, Santa Monica, 1-310 450 8600), a dim-lit speakeasy high on style, and **Voda** (1449 2nd Street, Santa Monica, 1-310 394 9774), a chic spot for a vodka. Other Santa Monica favourites include the **Cameo Bar** at the Viceroy (*see p142*) and the **Veranda** at the Casa del Mar (1910 Ocean Way, 1-310 581 5533); levity is provided at **Chez Jay** (1657 Ocean Avenue, 1-310 395 1741), an adorable hole-in-the-wall bar/restaurant.

In Venice, try the scene-to-be-seen at the **Brig** (1515 Abbot Kinney Boulevard, 1-310 399 7537) or **Club Good Hurt** (12249 Venice Boulevard, 1-310 390 1076), which comes with a bizarre medical motif (female bartenders dressed as nurses). In the South Bay, good bars are few and far between, but you're usually guaranteed a lively scene by the beaches.

Beverly Hills

The bars of Beverly Hills are as stylish as you'd expect. One of the area's finest spots is a hotel bar: the small, reserved **Avalon Hotel Lounge** (9400 Olympic Boulevard, 1-310 277 5221). However, the best cocktails – specifically, Martinis – are to be found at **Nic's** (453 N Canon Drive, 1-310 550 5707). Drinks and tapas are served in a vaguely boho setting at **Cobra Lily** (8442 Wilshire Boulevard, 1-310 651 5051); and there's sushi at Ben Affleck and Matt Damon's supper club buddy-venture the **Continental** (8400 Wilshire Boulevard, 1-323 782 9717). Sexy lounge **Nirvana** (8689 Wilshire Boulevard, 1-310 657 5040) allows you to imbibe on canopied beds.

West Hollywood

Between its gay scene (*see p133*), Sunset Strip and the hotels, drinking in LA gets interesting in WeHo. Hotel spots include **Bar Marmont** at the Chateau Marmont (*see p145*), overbearingly hip **SkyBar** at the Mondrian (*see p145*) and the retro-modish **Poolside Café** at the Standard (*see p145*); you'll also find a stylish crowd at the fashionable but relaxed **North** (8029 W Sunset Boulevard, 1-323 654 1313). Celeb-owned joints include Justin Timberlake's Old West meets Asian **Chi** (Hyatt, 8401 W Sunset Boulevard, 1-323 848 3884) and Ashton Kutcher's **Dolce** (8284 Melrose Avenue, 1-323 852 7174); Blink 182, Danny DeVito and assorted *Maxim*-friendly eye candy have all been seen in smoky mirrored speakeasy the **Dime** (442 N Fairfax Avenue, 1-323 651 4421). **Monroe's** (8623 Melrose Avenue, 1-310 360 0066) is a clubby roadhouse in the old Sloan's bar. Those just after a beer are best off at the **Coronet Pub** (370 N La Cienega Boulevard, 1-310 659 4583).

Hollywood

Nowhere enjoys its booze like Hollywood. While denizens of Beverly Hills sip on their drinks, and the WeHo crowd use their cocktails as accessories, Hollywood is here simply to *drink*.
With a little forethought, it's possible to plan a fine bar crawl. Start with a Martini amid the Old Hollywood ambience of the **Musso & Frank Grill** (6667 Hollywood Boulevard, 1-323 467 5123), before adjourning to slum-ming musos at legendary, dim-lit **Boardner's** (1652 N Cherokee Avenue, 1-323 462 9621). Wander down N Cahuenga Boulevard to the **Room**, so hip it doesn't need a sign (No.1626, 1-323 462 7196). Close by on Vine Street are the **Three of Clubs** (No.1123, 1-323 462 6441; look for the Bargain Clown Mart sign overhead) and the **Vine Fondue & Wine Bar** (No.1235, 1-323 960

0800), a hard-to-find-but-worth-the-effort mod revival lounge that makes a stellar Saketini. Keep walking north and you'll spy the neon of gritty **Frolic Room** (6245 Hollywood Boulevard, 1-323 462 5890), which starred in *LA Confidential*.

Other bars sit further apart. The **Cat & Fiddle** (6530 W Sunset Boulevard, 1-323 468 3800) is Hollywood's version of a Brit pub; about as convincing as the remake of *The Italian Job*, but few care. The delicious **Formosa Café** (7156 Santa Monica Boulevard, 1-323 850 9050) is as Old Hollywood as fat blonde actresses, its walls covered with photos of the stars who have swollen their livers here over 60 years.

Downtown

The aggressively hip **Rooftop Bar** at the Standard Downtown hotel (*see p146*) has helped enliven Downtown nightlife. A few hip hangs have even cropped up in 'arty' (read: dodgy) areas, like the funky/swanky **Golden Gopher** (417 W 8th Street, 1-213 623 9044) or the sushi-DJ hotspot **Zip Fusion** (744 E 3rd Street, 1-213 680 3770). The old school, though, still thrives at the **Gallery Bar** at the Millennium Biltmore (*see p146*), where the house drink, the Black Dahlia, is named for the murder victim last seen alive in the lobby. Further north, sumptuous Mao-red **Mountain Bar** (475 Gin Ling Way, 1-213 625 7500) and scruffier **Hop Louie** (950 Mei Ling Way, 1-213 628 4244) are the yin and yang of Chinatown's art scene. In the basement is **Cole's PE Buffet** (118 E 6th Street, 1-213 622 4090), which opened in 1908 and is LA's oldest bar.

Los Feliz, Silver Lake & Echo Park

Most visitors to Los Feliz take their first drink at the camp **Dresden Room** (1760 N Vermont Avenue, 1-323 665 4294), but after hearing the unspeakable noise made by house band Marty and Elayne (remember the duo in *Swingers*?), don't stay for a second. Nearby, gaudy **Good Luck Bar** (1514 N Hillhurst Avenue, 1-323 666 3524) draws a college-age crowd; scenesters prefer the **Roost** (3100 Los Feliz Boulevard, 1-323 664 7272). In truth, you're better off drinking in Silver Lake, at the Moroccan-themed, mixed-gay **Akbar** (4356 W Sunset Boulevard, 1-323 665 6810); the magically camp **Tiki-Ti** (4427 W Sunset Boulevard, 1-323 669 9381); or **Tantra** (3705 Sunset Boulevard, Silver Lake, 1-323 663 8268), like being trapped in a hookah from *Barbarella*. Echo Park's not far away either. Try kinetic **Short Stop** (1455 W Sunset Boulevard, 1-213 482 4942) or lively, Mexican **Gold Room** (1558 W Sunset Boulevard, 1-213 482 5259).

Nightlife

Gay & lesbian

In no other US city does coming out give you such instant credibility as it does in LA, at least in part because gays and lesbians make up a large chunk of the town's creative industries.

The gay districts of LA are very female-friendly. West Hollywood might be nicknamed Boys Town, but you'll find lesbians of all demographics here, from glammy cocktail swillers to soccer mums. However, few LA bars or clubs devote themselves to lesbians seven days a week; check listings in local gay magazines and pick your venue accordingly.

West Hollywood

The centre of LA's gay action is West Hollywood, where guys cruise the stretch of Santa Monica Boulevard between N Doheny Drive and N Fairfax Avenue. But while it's cruisey, it's also laid-back and fairly residential.

There are a number of bars and clubs around here, and the fierce competition means that there's usually something going on. Perhaps the quintessential West Hollywood gay club is **Rage** (8911 Santa Monica Boulevard, 1-310 652 7055, www.ragewesthollywood.com), which hosts a range of nights, though the cruisier **Here Lounge** (696 N Robertson Boulevard, 1-310 360 8455, www.herelounge.com) is also a favourite. Saturdays at the **Factory** (652 N La Peer Drive, 1-310 659 4551, www.factorynightclubla.com) are usually huge; on a more prosaic level, the two-storey **Melrose Spa** bathhouse (7269 Melrose Avenue, 1-323 937 2122, www.midtowne.com) attracts a varied clientele all week long. Lesbians are served by **Benvenuto** (8512 Santa Monica Boulevard, 1-310 659 8635) and **Palms** (8572 Santa Monica Boulevard, 1-310 652 6188), the latter the oldest lesbian bar in LA, along with **Girl Bar** every Friday at the Factory (*see above*).

It's a mystery what makes a restaurant gay, but WeHo's gay dining is excellent. First choice is **Mark's** (861 N La Cienega Boulevard, 1-310 652 5252, closed lunch Mon-Sat, $$$$), where steaks are a speciality. **Marix** (1108 N Flores Avenue, 1-323 650 0507, $$$) serves fine food and Margaritas. But the jewel is the **Abbey** (692 N Robertson Boulevard, 1-310 289 8410, $$$).

Hollywood

If you tire easily of the muscle parade on Santa Monica Boulevard, you may prefer some of the divier places in Hollywood. There's always an interesting crowd at recently remodelled dance bar **Spike** (7746 Santa Monica Boulevard, 1-323 656 9343), while **Circus Disco** (*see p134*) hosts the popular Boys Night Out every Tuesday. The divey-but-still-inviting **Spot Light Room** (1601 N Cahuenga Boulevard, 1-323 467 2425), opened back in 1963, is Hollywood's oldest gay club. **Hollywood Spa** (1650 N Ivar Avenue, 1-800 772 2582, www.hollywoodspa.com) is the best-known bathhouse in the city.

Silver Lake

After West Hollywood, Silver Lake is the best-known gay neighbourhood in LA. But the crowd here tends towards twentysomething indie kids or older men, and the leather scene is big: **Cuffs** (1941 Hyperion Avenue, 1-323 660 2649) and **Faultline** (4216 Melrose Avenue, 1-323 660 0889) are a pair of fairly full-on leather bars. Mixed-gay **Akbar** (*see p133*) is a more sedate option.

Los Angeles's love of glamour and beauty is nowhere more evident than on its nightclub circuit, especially around Hollywood and West Hollywood. Compared to other urban centres, LA's dance scene has a little catching up to do, but the scene will still be a pleasant surprise to anyone who's not visited since the late 1990s.

Most clubs open seven days in LA, but peak on Thursday to Saturday. Carry photo ID: all clubs 'card' people at the door. Admission costs $5-$20. Club owners have tightened security of late; drugs are not tolerated. Some of the upscale

clubs operate a velvet rope policy: the better you look, the more likely you are to get in. Being female, or bringing females, helps.

West Hollywood

West Hollywood's nightlife is low-key next to Hollywood's, but inviting when held up against anywhere else in LA. Head first to the **Parlour Club** (7702 Santa Monica Boulevard, 1-323 650 7968, www.parlourclub.com), which attracts a mixed clientele for its roster of intriguing nights. Also worth investigating are New York-style lounge/club **Belly** (7929 Santa Monica Boulevard, 1-323 822 9264, www.bellylounge.com) and the infamous **Viper Room** (8852 W Sunset Boulevard, 1-310 358 1880, www.viperroom.com): the low-ceilinged sweatbox in front of which River Phoenix died packs in Valley Girls on weekends, but can be interesting earlier in the week. Trendy supper club/lounge **Pearl** (665 N Robertson Boulevard, 1-310 358 9191, www.pearl90069.com) features go-go dancers writhing around in shadow boxes. And the old Sunset Strip eyesore Coconut Teaszer has re-risen as **Shelter** (8117 Sunset Boulevard, 1-323 654 0030, www.shelterla.com), an ever-evolving club.

Hollywood

Much of LA's after-hours action takes place in Hollywood, where you'll find many of the city's most chic nightclubs. They don't come any bigger than the 25,000-square-foot **Highlands** (6801 Hollywood Boulevard, 1-323 461 9800, www.thehighlandsla.com), notable more for its views than its music. However, **Circus Disco** (6655 Santa Monica Boulevard, 1-323 462 5508, www.circusdisco.com) isn't far behind it in terms of size, and hosts Saturday's ever-popular house-happy Spundae. Elsewhere, the **Ivar** (6356 Hollywood Boulevard, 1-323 465 4827, www.ivar.cc) draws beautiful LA archetypes to its quasi-futuristic interior; and **Blue** (1642 N Las Palmas Avenue, 1-323 468 3863) attracts a more alternative crowd with industrial and goth-friendly nights. As well as staging bands during the week, the **Avalon** (1735 N Vine Street, 1-323 462 8900, www.avalonhollywood.com) on Saturdays hosts house party Giant (www.giantclub.com), the club that kickstarted the LA dance scene a few years ago. The venue also holds the **Spider Club**, a modernist spin on a 1960s disco. Just because Paris Hilton is co-partner in hot club **Concorde** (1835 N Cahuenga Boulevard, 1-323 464 5662) doesn't mean the place doesn't have class... providing you make it past the door. At the opposite end of the scale, **El Centro** (1069 N El Centro Avenue, 1-323 957 1066) has no sign, but is a lively DJ spot with slumming glitter brats.

Get loved up on LA's **gay scene**.

Gay beaches

Many of Southern California's beaches are very gay-friendly. Below are three of the best, listed from north to south; they cater to both gay men and lesbians, but the scenes are male-dominated.

Will Rogers State Beach

Will Rogers State Beach: on the Pacific Coast Highway, just over two miles north of Santa Monica Pier, in front of the Beach Club. This cruisey beach is packed on sunny weekends, and it's easy to see why: it's free, it's got tons of guys playing volleyball and it lasts until sunset.

Venice Beach

Venice: see p100. Gay beach: near where Windward Avenue meets the beach, next to the wall, just down from Muscle Beach.

It figures that LA's most bohemian, liberal neighbourhood should also welcome the gay community. The quasi-legendary **Roosterfish** bar (1302 Abbot Kinney Boulevard, 1-310 392 2123) is a must-see for guys.

Laguna Beach

Laguna Beach: off PCH (US 1), 30 miles south of Long Beach. Gay beach: just past the pier; look for the rainbow flag. It's a long drive from LA, especially on congested Saturdays, but the water is clean and the beach is hot. After the beach, try the lively **Boom Boom Room** (1401 S Coast Highway, 1-800 653 2697). Among the gay-friendly restaurants in the area is the stylish **Cottage** (308 N Coast Highway, 1-949 494 3023).

Shopping

Opening hours are usually 10am to 7pm, 9pm if the shop is in a mall. Parking is usually not too difficult, but if you're visiting the more expensive shops, use their valet parking: it's a small indulgence. LA County adds an 8.25 per cent sales tax to the price of all merchandise; Orange County taxes at 7.75 per cent.

One-stop shopping

Department stores

All the big American names have a branch in LA, and some have several. At the glamour end sit **Saks Fifth Avenue** (9600 & 9634 Wilshire Boulevard, Beverly Hills, 1-310 275 4211) and **Barneys New York** (9570 Wilshire Boulevard, Beverly Hills, 1-310 276 4400), a couple of Manhattan exports famed for their designer clothes; a notch below, but still relatively upmarket, are **Bloomingdale's** (Westfield Shoppingtown Century City, 10250 Santa Monica Boulevard, Century City, 1-310 772 2100), **Neiman Marcus** (9700 Wilshire Boulevard, Beverly Hills, 1-310 550 5900) and the chic **Nordstrom** (Westside Pavilion, 10830 W Pico Boulevard, West LA, 1-310 470 6155). **Fred Segal** (8100 Melrose Avenue, West Hollywood, 1-323 655 3734) is a smaller, chicer, boutique department store where you might just rub elbows with the likes of Cameron Diaz and other stars.

Malls

The LA area is awash with malls. Santa Monica has **Santa Monica Place** (Broadway & 3rd Street, 1-310 394 1049, www.santamonicaplace.com), whose shops are less interesting than its Frank Gehry design. Moving inland, **Westside Pavilion** (10800 W Pico Boulevard, West LA, 1-310 474 6255, www.westsidepavilion.com) has a moderately upscale selection of 160-plus stores, slightly more than nearby **Westfield Shoppingtown Century City** (10250 Santa Monica Boulevard, Century City, 1-310 277 3898, www.westfield.com). The huge **Beverly Center** (8500 Beverly Boulevard, West Hollywood, 1-310 854 0070, www.beverlycenter.com) is a good all-rounder; the open-air **Grove** (189 The Grove Drive, at the Farmers' Market, 6301 W 3rd Street, Fairfax District, 1-323 900 8080, www.thegrovela.com) is LA's most pleasant and smartest malls.

Individual shops

Antiques

Most of LA's good antique shops are located in West Hollywood, along Robertson and Beverly Boulevards and La Brea Avenue, though Echo Park's Antique Row, on the 2200 block of W Sunset Boulevard, is also worth a look. The **Santa Monica Antique Market** (1607 Lincoln Boulevard, 1-310 673 7048) and the **Pasadena Antique Center** (444 & 480 S Fair Oaks Avenue, 1-626 449 7706) are both open daily, and hold a wide variety of stalls.

Southern California

Books

For general stock, there are branches of **Barnes & Noble** and **Borders** all over LA, among them the B&N at the Farmers' Market (*see p135*; 1-323 525 0270) and the Borders on the Third Street Promenade in Santa Monica (No.1415, 1-310 393 9290). The list of indie all-rounders is topped by the excellent **Book Soup** (8818 Sunset Boulevard, West Hollywood, 1-310 659 3110) and family-run **Dutton's** (11975 San Vicente Boulevard, Brentwood, 1-310 476 6263).

Meanwhile, LA has a specialist book retailer for more or less every taste. **A Different Light** (8853 Santa Monica Boulevard, West Hollywood, 1-310 854 6601) is America's most famous gay bookshop. On W 3rd Street in West Hollywood sit two fine shops: **Traveler's Bookcase** (No.8375, 1-323 655 0575) and the **Cook's Library** (No.8373, 1-323 655 3141). **Samuel French** (7623 W Sunset Boulevard, West Hollywood, 1-323 876 0570) sells just about every film script in print, while **Koma** (1228 W 7th Street, Downtown, 1-213 623 6995) is stocked with books on out-there topics. **Brand's** (231 N Brand Boulevard, Glendale, 1-818 243 4907) is LA's best used bookstore.

Fashion

DESIGNER

You'll find every designer label in LA; many are in Beverly Hills' **Golden Triangle** area, bounded by Rexford Drive, Wilshire Boulevard and Santa Monica Boulevard. The starriest streets are **Rodeo Drive** and **Brighton Way**, which hold the likes of Chanel and Prada. **Maxfield** (8825 Melrose Avenue, West Hollywood, 1-310 274 8800, closed Sun) is one of the best high fashion all-rounders.

But while the big global names have set up shop in Beverly Hills, smaller designers are scattered far and wide. They include **Eduardo Lucero** (7378 Beverly Boulevard, Fairfax District, 1-323 933 2778, closed Mon & Sun), loved by every starlet for his red carpet gowns; San Fran designer **Erica Tanov** (7938 W 3rd Street, Fairfax District, 1-323 782 1411), who started selling her simple hippie chic here in 2003; and WeHo archetype **Tracey Ross** (8595 W Sunset Boulevard, 1-310 854 1996), adored by celebs and trust fund kids alike.

GENERAL

Branches of old reliables **Gap** (1355 Third Street Promenade, Santa Monica, 1-310 393 0719), **Old Navy** (Beverly Connection, 8487 W 3rd Street, West Hollywood, 1-323 658 5292) and **Banana Republic** (357 N Beverly Drive, Beverly Hills, 1-310 858 7900) are plentiful. Likewise

Abercrombie & Fitch (the Grove, 6301 W 3rd Street, Fairfax District, 1-323 954 1500). Santa Monica's Third Street Promenade has branches of **Diesel** (1-310 899 3055) and **Urban Outfitters** (1-310 394 1404).

For a more unusual look, head to the Los Feliz-Silver Lake-Echo Park axis. **Atmosphere** (1728 N Vermont Avenue, Los Feliz, 1-323 666 8420) stocks upmarket brand names such as Juicy Couture; edgier fashions can be found at **Funky Revolution** (2170 W Sunset Boulevard, Echo Park, 1-213 484 2500), **oOo** (1764 N Vermont Avenue, Los Feliz, 1-323 665 6263), and **Show Pony** (1543 Echo Park Avenue, Echo Park, 1-213 482 7676, closed Mon & Tue), which celebrates soon-to-break designers.

VINTAGE

American Rag (150 S La Brea Avenue, Fairfax District, 1-323 935 3154) has one of the city's largest collections of vintage clothing: pick up anything from a 1960s leather mini to a designer suit. Smaller shops include two lively spots on W Sunset Boulevard in Echo Park, **The Kids are Alright** (No.2201, 1-213 413 4014) and **Luxe de Ville** (No.2157, 1-213 353 0135), and Silver Lake staple **Come to Mama** (4019 W Sunset Boulevard, 1-323 953 1275). **Decades** (8214 Melrose Avenue, Melrose District, 1-323 655 0223, closed Sun), which sells couture classics from the 1960s and '70s, is America's most glamorous vintage shop, though **Paper Bag Princess** (8700 Santa Monica Boulevard, West Hollywood, 1-310 358 1985, closed Sun), which sells clothes once worn by Hollywood legends, isn't far behind.

SHOES

All the big names have stores in LA, including **Jimmy Choo** (469 N Canon Drive, Beverly Hills, 1-310 860 9045) and neat and tidy NY chain **Kenneth Cole** (8752 W Sunset Boulevard, West Hollywood, 1-310 289 5085). **Camille Hudson** (4685 Hollywood Boulevard, Los Feliz, 1-323 953 0377) sells both international labels and her own pointy-toed flats; **Diavolina II** (334 S La Brea Avenue, Fairfax District, 1-323 936 2166) has stilettos, wedges and platforms from the likes of Alexander McQueen and Marc Jacobs.

Food & drink

LA has a number of weekly markets where you can buy seasonal produce direct from farmers. There are four in **Santa Monica**: at Arizona Avenue and 2nd Street (9am-2pm Wed); a heavily organic market at Arizona and 3rd (8.30am-1pm Sat); on Airport Avenue, at the Donald Douglas Loop (8am-1pm Sat); and at the California Heritage Museum (*see p100*) (9.30am-1pm Sun). See http://farmersmarket.santa-monica.org for

Where to shop

Southern California

THE BEACH TOWNS
While **Santa Monica**'s shopping reputation rests on the shoulders of the chain-heavy Third Street Promenade, there's more engaging shopping north on Montana Avenue, lined with upscale boutiques. South of Santa Monica, stores on Main Street in **Ocean Park** sell clothes and bric-a-brac, while in **Venice**, Abbot Kinney Boulevard has a mix of fine shops, and stalls on the Boardwalk offer everything from $2 shades to African masks.

BEVERLY HILLS, WEST HOLLYWOOD & THE MELROSE DISTRICT
Chichi City: three adjoining neighbourhoods awash with swanky boutiques and the occasional hyper-pricey design store.

HOLLYWOOD & THE FAIRFAX DISTRICT
The stretch of La Brea Avenue between Santa Monica and Wilshire Boulevards (heading south from **Hollywood**) and W 3rd Street from La Cienega Boulevard to Sweetzer Avenue (just west of the **Fairfax District**) supplement their used clothes shops with an array of furniture shops, antique boutiques and bookstores.

DOWNTOWN
The Fashion District (*see p112*) is the place to head for cheap new clothes, many knock-off designer copies. Nearby is some of LA's richest multicultural shopping, in **Little India**, **Chinatown**, Mexican-slanted **Olvera Street** and **Little Tokyo**.

LOS FELIZ, SILVER LAKE & ECHO PARK
All three 'hoods have a number of fine vintage clothing stores, as well as a few hip stores dealing in new duds.

THE VALLEYS
Shopping in the Valleys is focused at malls, though the handsome (but chain-packed) Old Town in **Pasadena** breaks the mould. Nearby is Glendale, an improving destination.

more. Also worth a trip is the bustling **Grand Central Market** (317 S Broadway, Downtown, 1-213 624 2378), which sells food from around the globe. **Erewhon Natural Foods Market** (7660 Beverly Boulevard, Fairfax District, 1-213 937 0777) is the best organic supermarket in town.

Gifts

Gallows humour meets capitalism at **Skeletons in the Closet** (2nd Floor, 1102 N Mission Road, Downtown, 1-323 343 0760, closed Sat & Sun): run by the LA County Coroner's Office it sells morbid ephemera. **Hustler Hollywood** (8920 W Sunset Boulevard, West Hollywood, 1-310 860 9009) hawks street-safe *Hustler* T-shirts. **Chic-a-Boom** (6817 Melrose Avenue, Melrose District, 1-323 931 7441) and **Cinema Collectors** (1507 Wilcox Avenue, Hollywood, 1-323 461 6516) deal in Hollywood memorabilia. The **Getty Center** (*see p103*) and **MOCA** (*see p110*) are among LA's best museum gift shops.

Health & beauty

Of all US cities, only Miami Beach matches LA in terms of its vanity. **Larchmont Beauty Centre** (208 N Larchmont Boulevard, Hancock Park, 1-323 461 0162) and **Kalologie Skin Care** (132 S Robertson Boulevard, Beverly Hills, 1-310 276 9670) are two great stores. In Tinseltown the upmarket **Aida Thibiant's European Day Spa** (449 N Canon Drive, Beverly Hills, 1-310 278 7565) offers the full range of treatments; other favourites include **Ole Henrikson** (8622A W Sunset Boulevard, West Hollywood, 1-310 854 7700, closed 1st Mon of mth).

If you need is pharmacy, head to one of the branches of **Sav-On** (5510 W Sunset Boulevard, Hollywood, 1-323 464 2172; for others, call 1-888 746 7252), **Rite Aid** (1130 N La Brea Avenue, West Hollywood, 1-323 463 8539; for others, call 1-800 748 3243) or **Walgreens** (8770 W Pico Boulevard, Beverly Hills, 1-310 275 1344; for others, call 1-800 289 2273). Many open 24 hours.

Music

Ever since **Amoeba Music** (6400 W Sunset Boulevard, Hollywood, 1-323 245 6400) opened its vast LA operation in 2002, other music stores have struggled to keep up. Still, you'll find a more personal service at Venice's legendary hippie-friendly **Benway Records** (1600 Pacific Avenue, 1-310 396 8898), Silver Lake used-CD staple **Rockaway Records** (2395 Glendale Boulevard, 1-323 664 3232), and **Vinyl Fetish** (1614 N Cahuenga Boulevard, Hollywood, 1-323 957 2290), which serves electronica and dance fans especially well (and also stocks CDs).

Arts & Entertainment

Comedy

Comedy is serious business in LA. Many of today's megastars got their start here, and still play regularly. Jay Leno and Drew Carey have weekly gigs in the city: Leno's at the **Comedy & Magic Club** (1018 Hermosa Avenue, Hermosa Beach, 1-310 372 1193, www.comedy andmagicclub.com) every Sunday, while Carey joins other *Whose Line* stars at the **Improv** (8162 Melrose Avenue, 1-323 651 2583, www. improv.com) on Thursdays. However, stars show up all over the place, often unbilled.

Many big venues are located in Hollywood and West Hollywood; among them are the top-notch **Groundlings Theatre** (7307 Melrose Avenue, 1-323 934 4747, www.groundlings. com), the enjoyable **Improv Olympic West** (6366 Hollywood Boulevard, 1-323 962 7560, www.iowest.com) and the fading **Comedy Store** (8433 W Sunset Boulevard, 1-323 656 6225, www.thecomedystore.com). Diners usually get first dibs on the best seats; it's often worth booking ahead, especially for big clubs.

Dance

LA hasn't got a major ballet company, but no matter: famous troupes visit regularly, particularly in fall and winter. The Dorothy Chandler Pavilion at the **Performing Arts Center of Los Angeles County** (135 N Grand Avenue, Downtown, 1-213 972 7211, www.musiccenter.org) is a popular dance venue, while the **Redcat Theatre** at the Walt Disney Concert Hall (631 W 2nd Street, at Hope Street, Downtown, 1-213 237 2800, www.redcat web.org), has quickly established itself as the hot venue for avant-garde dance.

The city also boasts its own crop of dancers. For purists, Burbank's **Media City Ballet** (www.mediacityballet.org) dances in the style of the Ballet Russe de Monte Carlo. For modern dance, try the edgy **Lula Washington Dance Theatre** (www.lulawashington.com), or avant-garde **Praxis Collective** (www.kindance.org).

Film

It's the capital of the global movie industry; do you need to know anything else? As long as your taste isn't too European (only the big hits make it here), this a great town in which to catch a movie.

The town is full of multiplexes, many of them a cut above the usual metropolitan standard. The pick of them are both in Hollywood: the recently renovated 15-screen **ArcLight** (6360 W Sunset Boulevard, Hollywood, 1-323 464 1478, www.arclightcinemas.com) and the legendary **Grauman's Chinese Theatre** (6925 Hollywood Boulevard, Hollywood, 1-323 464 8111). Artier fare is screened by the Laemmle chain, which runs the **Sunset 5** (8000 W Sunset Boulevard, 1-323 848 3500, www.laemmle.com); the **Magic Johnson Theatres** (4020 Marlton Avenue, Crenshaw, 1-323 290 5900, www.magicjohnsontheatres.com) specialise in African-American films; faith in old movies is kept by **American Cinematheque**, at the beautifully restored Egyptian Theatre (6712 Hollywood Boulevard, Hollywood, 1-323 466 3456, www.americancinematheque.com).

There are endless preview screenings in LA; hang around Hollywood or Universal Studios long enough, and you'll be accosted by studio recruiters offering free tickets. Such screenings are often used for audience testing.

Gold-card territory: **Rodeo Drive**. *See p136.*

LA has innumerable film festivals all year round, from small, weekend-long events to the large **AFI Los Angeles International Film Festival** (www.afifest.com) in November and June's excellent **Last Remaining Seats** event (www.laconservancy), which runs films in many classic old movie palaces on Broadway in Downtown LA. Check listings for details.

Galleries

The LA gallery scene has evolved of late, partly because LA is wealthier than ever: where there's cash, artists are likely to congregate. Two monthly directories, *Art Scene* and *Art Now Gallery Guide*, available at the galleries they list, provide a briefing on LA's spaces.

Santa Monica holds a large number of LA's galleries, the majority in 'art malls' such as **Bergamot Station** (2525 Michigan Avenue, 1-310 829 5854, www.bergamotstation.com). This sprawling site, formerly a trolley station, an ice-packing plant and a factory, holds some 30 galleries that present contemporary art of every stripe. The artist-run exhibition, performance and media spaces of the **18th Street Arts Complex** (1639 18th Street, 1-310 453 3711, www.18thstreet.org) are also worth a look.

The galleries of **Beverly Hills** are the most prestigious in the city; **Spencer Jon Helfen Fine Arts** (Suite 200, 9200 W Olympic Boulevard, 1-310 273 8838, www.helfenfinearts.com) specialises in California modernist art of the 1930s, while **Gagosian** (456 N Camden Drive, 1-310 271 9400, www.gagosian.com) is where to come for notable post-war painting, sculpture and photography. N La Brea Avenue, between Santa Monica Boulevard and W 3rd Street, is dotted with photography galleries. Silver Lake and Echo Park hold sparkier, funkier spots such as **La Luz de Jesus** (4633 Hollywood Boulevard, 1-323 666 7667).

Music

Classical & opera

Under the baton of dynamic Finn Esa-Pekka Salonen, the **LA Philharmonic** (1-323 850 2000, www.laphil.org) has consolidated an already impressive reputation. With the opening of Frank Gehry's stunning **Walt Disney Concert Hall** (111 S Grand Avenue, Downtown, 1-213 972 7211), it at last has a venue good enough to match. From June to September, the Phil moves outdoors to the venerable **Hollywood Bowl** (2301 N Highland Avenue, Hollywood, 1-323 850 2000), which also stages rock concerts. Disney Hall is also home to the **Los Angeles Master Chorale** (1-213 972 7282, www.lamc.org).

What's on when

Your first port of call to find out what's on in LA should be the **Los Angeles Weekly**: published every Thursday, this vast alternative weekly details more or less everything in town. It's not easy to use (the listings are organised somewhat chaotically), but the information is all here and can be found online at **www.laweekly.com**. Its main competition comes from the skimpier **LA Citybeat** (also online at www.lacitybeat.com). The **Los Angeles Times** publishes *Calendar*, a fine culture insert, on Sundays; its website, **www.calendarlive.com**, is also a good resource.

The Phil's old home, the **Dorothy Chandler Pavilion** (135 N Grand Avenue, Downtown, 1-213 972 7211, www.performingartscenterla.org) is still used by the **Los Angeles Opera** (1-213 972 8001, www.losangelesopera.com), which performs works old and new. Other ensembles include the **Los Angeles Chamber Orchestra** (1-213 622 7001, www.laco.org) and the **Pasadena Symphony** (1-626 793 7172, www.pasadenasymphony.org).

Jazz

Of all the jazz venues in Los Angeles and Orange County, the thoroughly civilised **Catalina Bar & Grill** (6725 W Sunset Boulevard, Hollywood, 1-323 466 2210, www.catalinajazzclub.com) attracts the heaviest hitters: Jimmy Smith, McCoy Tyner and Pharoah Sanders play here on a semi-regular basis. There are also good line-ups at the not-for-profit **Jazz Bakery** (3233 Helms Avenue, Culver City, 1-310 271 9039, www.jazzbakery.org) and the hardcore **World Stage** (4344 Degnan Boulevard, Leimert Park, 1-323 293 2451, www.theworldstage.org), founded by drummer Billy Higgins. However, the city's jazz circuit is scattered from pillar to post: many bars, hotels and restaurants host local jazz acts, often top Hollywood sessioneers spending the nights playing as much for pleasure as for pay.

Rock, pop & hip hop

LA has reigned as the music industry capital of the US since the early 1970s. When it comes to new music, the city has been on the decline since the 1980s, when hair metal ruled the Strip. Still, LA's an important stop on any touring artist's itinerary, and the city's giant populace ensures that lack of variety isn't a problem.

Really big acts play in the acoustically unimpressive **Staples Center** (1111 S Figueroa Street, Downtown, 1-213 742 7340, www.staples center.com). A notch down in terms of capacity is the open-air **Greek Theatre** in Griffith Park (1-323 665 1927); smaller still is the art deco **Wiltern** (3790 Wilshire Boulevard, Koreatown, 1-213 388 1400, www.thewiltern.com).

The days when the Sunset Strip clubs ruled the scene are long gone. The indie-friendly **Roxy** (9009 W Sunset Boulevard, 1-310 276 2222, www.theroxyonsunset.com) does all right, and the newer **House of Blues** (8430 W Sunset Boulevard, 1-323 848 5100, www.hob.com) is an impressive set-up with a varied programme, but the **Whisky A Go-Go** (8901 W Sunset Boulevard, 1-310 652 4202, www.whiskyagogo. com) seems long ago to have lost the plot.

The **Troubadour** (9081 Santa Monica Boulevard, West Hollywood, 1-310 276 6168, www.troubadour.com) puts music made by acts of taste and substance through one of the best sound systems in town. **Largo** (432 N Fairfax Avenue, Fairfax District, 1-323 852 1073, www.largo-la.com) specialises in singer-songwriters, with one-man-band Jon Brion a perennial hot ticket on Fridays. The LA offshoot of New York's **Knitting Factory**

The sporting life

SPECTATOR SPORTS

LA owns an abundance of athletic franchises. At one end of the spectrum sits Kobe Bryant and the **Los Angeles Lakers** (1-800 462 2849, www.nba.com/lakers), who are to the National Basketball Association (NBA) what the New York Yankees are to Major League Baseball. At the other are the laughable **Los Angeles Clippers** (1-800 462 2849, www.nba.com/clippers), who've not had a winning season since 1991-92. Both the Lakers and the Clippers, along with mediocre National Hockey League franchise the **Los Angeles Kings** (1-888 546 4752, www.lakings.com), play Downtown at the **Staples Center** (1111 S Figueroa Street). The NBA and NHL seasons run from October to April, followed by two months of playoffs.

The LA area's two baseball teams, who play from April to October, have both found success of late: the **Los Angeles Dodgers** (who play at lovely Dodger Stadium, 1000 Elysian Park Avenue, 1-323 224 1448, www.dodgers.com) won the NL West in 2004, and the **Anaheim Angels** (Angel Stadium of Anaheim, 2000 Gene Autry Way, 1-888 796 4256, www.angelsbaseball.com) were crowned World Series champions in 2002.

PARTICIPATORY SPORTS

LA's sprawl and thick traffic mean that you'll see few rollerbladers and cyclists. But there are still opportunities. Cyclists keen on off-roading would do well to head to the **Santa Monica Mountains**, **Topanga State Park** in Topanga (1-310 454 8212) and **Malibu Creek State Park** in Calabasas (1-818 880 0367); **Griffith Park** also has more than 14 miles of bike trails, some MTB-accessible

only. Both cyclists and rollerbladers are welcome on the **South Bay Bicycle Trail**: commonly known as the **Strand**, it runs 22 miles from Will Rogers State Beach to Torrance. Many oceanfront stalls in Santa Monica and Venice rent beach bikes.

There's great (and free) public fishing at the piers of many local beaches: try **Santa Monica Pier**, **Seal Beach**, **Redondo Beach** or **Manhattan Beach** – a licence is not required. Horse-riders should try **Sunset Ranch** in the Hollywood Hills (3400 Beachwood Drive, 1-323 469 5450). And hikers are best served contacting the **Sierra Club** (1-213 387 4287, http://angeles. sierraclub.org), which runs an astonishing 4,000 hikes each year in the area.

Golfers are spoiled for choice. The City of LA runs 13 municipal courses around the city. To book a tee time in advance, you'll need a registration card ($35 non-residents), available at any public course. Among the courses are a short nine-holer in **Los Feliz** (reservations not required; 3207 Los Feliz Boulevard, 1-323 663 7758), and two courses in Griffith Park (1-323 663 2555).

FITNESS

There are gyms all over LA, including in many of the hotels listed on *pp141-147*. A number of other gyms are open to non-members, among them bodybuilders' mecca **Gold's Gym** (360 Hampton Drive, Venice, 1-310 392 6004), the recently renovated **Spectrum Club** (2250 Park Place, Manhattan Beach, 1-310 643 6878) and various branches of **24-Hour Fitness** (including one at 8612 Santa Monica Boulevard, West Hollywood, 1-310 652 7440; see www.24hourfitness.com for others).

(7021 Hollywood Boulevard, Hollywood, 1-323 463 0204, www.knittingfactory.com) offers alternative acts across three stages.

Over in Silver Lake, hip local bands and hot touring tickets run through **Spaceland** (1717 Silver Lake Boulevard, 1-323 661 4380, www.clubspaceland.com); further east in Echo Park, the **Echo** (1822 W Sunset Boulevard, 1-213 413 8200, www.attheecho.com) is a good place in which to hear edgy rap, reggae and electronica acts. For folk and singer-songwriters, head to **McCabe's Guitar Shop** (3101 Pico Boulevard, Santa Monica, 1-310 828 4497, www.mccabesguitar.com); get the blues at **Babe & Ricky's Inn** (4339 Leimert Boulevard, Leimert Park, 1-323 295 9112).

Theatre

Thanks to the movies, theatre will always be the red-headed stepchild of LA's entertainment scene. That said, there's still decent theatre here; to find out what's on, check the *LA Times*, *LA Weekly*, or www.LAplayZ.com.

The town's main venue is the **Performing Arts Center of Los Angeles County** (135 N Grand Avenue, Downtown, 1-213 972 7211, www.musiccenter.org); it's home to the 2,000-seat Ahmanson Theatre, which stages many big musicals, and the 760-seat Mark Taper Forum, which features plays by the likes of August Wilson. In Hollywood, the modern **Kodak Theatre** (6801 Hollywood Boulevard, 1-323 308 6363, www.kodaktheatre.com) and the breathtaking, art deco **Pantages Theatre** (6233 Hollywood Boulevard, 1-323 468 1770, www.nederlander.com) stage big budget shows.

Among the smaller venues are the 284-seat **Coronet Theatre** (366 N La Cienega Boulevard, West Hollywood, 1-310 657 7377, www.coronet-theatre.com); the Gehry-designed **Edgemar Center for the Arts** (2437 Main Street, Santa Monica, 1-310 399 3666, www.edgemarcenter. org); and the **Santa Monica Playhouse** (1211 4th Street, Santa Monica, 1-310 394 9779, www.santamonicaplayhouse.com).

Also worth checking are the town's 99-seat theatres, whose prevalence stems from a union agreement that means theatres with fewer than 100 seats needn't pay full Equity wages. Some attract big names who don't need the money but could use the cred; others deal in edgier works. The **Actors' Gang Theatre** (6209 Santa Monica Boulevard, 1-323 465 0566, www.theactorsgang.com), the four **Hudson Theatres** (6539 Santa Monica Boulevard, 1-323 856 4252, www.hudsonontheatre.com) and the **Met Theatre** (1089 N Oxford Avenue, 1-323 957 1152, www.themettheatre.com), all in Hollywood, are among the best.

Where to Stay

It's always done the glamour thing very well. But a few years into the 21st century, the range of hotels in LA has never been broader. The bad news? It's not cheap. Expect to pay up to $100 for a double room in a budget hotel, $100-$250 for a room in a mid-priced property, and anything over $250 – and we mean *anything* – at the top end. Worse, these rates exclude sales tax (12 to 15 per cent), and parking, up to $30 a night. Outside peak season, many hotels offer cut-price rooms; whenever you travel, prices will be lower the further you stay from the beach. In addition to the hotels listed below, LA is awash with chain hotels and motels; *see p54*.

The beach towns

Santa Monica

Ambrose

1225 20th Street, between Wilshire Boulevard & Arizona Avenue (reservations 1-877 262 7673/front desk 1-310 315 1555/www.ambrosehotel.com). I-10, exit 4th-5th Street north. **Rates** $155-$245 single/ double. *Parking* free. **Credit** AmEx, DC, Disc, MC, V.
This boutique hotel is a mixture of sturdy Craftsman tradition and Asian chic; the living-room lobby, with its crackling fire, is typical of the cosy atmosphere. Guestrooms, some with terraces and fireplaces, combine luxury with oriental panache: dark woods, green tea tones. This being Santa Monica, there's a healthy bent: yoga, room service by Celestine Drago and minibars packed with Chinese elixirs.

Bayside

2001 Ocean Avenue, at Bay Street (1-310 396 6000/ www.baysidehotel.com). I-10, exit 4th-5th Street south. **Rates** $79-$179 single/double. *Parking* free. **Credit** AmEx, DC, Disc, MC, V.
Located across from the beach, the Bayside is a steal. For an elderly motel, its rooms are surprisingly comfy. Each has been dressed with plush hand-me-downs from the Beverly Hills Hotel (*see p143*); some have kitchens, while others come with balconies and ocean views. The bathrooms, with original 1950s tiles, are deliciously retro. South-facing rooms have a/c; the rest rely on ceiling fans and sea breezes.

Channel Road Inn

219 W Channel Road, between PCH & Rustic Road (1-310 459 1920/www.channelroadinn.com. I-10, exit PCH north. **Rates** $185-$295 single/double. *Parking* free. **Credit** AmEx, MC, V.
Situated at the mouth of Santa Monica Canyon, the rustic Channel Road Inn is just as easy on the eye. Built in 1915, the 14-room inn features four-poster and sleigh beds and private bathrooms (book ahead for room six, with its living room and jacuzzi, or room three, with fireplace and whirlpool for two).

Southern California

TV tapings

LA is the best place on earth for TV junkies to get their fix. What's more, tickets are free: you can score them from clipboard-toting 'brokers' on Venice Beach, Universal CityWalk or Hollywood Boulevard, or by writing to the studios. But the easiest way to snag a seat is on the internet from **Audience Associates** (1-323 653 4105, www.tvtix.com), which has tickets to shows such as The Price is Right and The Tonight Show with Jay Leno; **Audiences Unlimited** (1-818 753 3470 ext 810, www.tvtickets.com), which doles out tickets to more than 30 shows during peak season (Aug-Mar); and **Hollywood Tickets** (1-818 688 3974, www.hollywoodtickets.com). Allow up to three or four hours of taping time. All shows have minimum age requirements.

Fairmont Miramar

101 Wilshire Boulevard, at Ocean Avenue (reservations 1-800 441 1414/front desk 1-310 576 7777/www.fairmont.com). I-405, exit Wilshire Boulevard south. **Rates** $249-$299 single/double; $279-$1,399 bungalow/suite. *Parking* $26. **Credit** AmEx, DC, Disc, MC, V.

Through wrought-iron gates, behind an ancient fig tree and up a cobbled driveway lies Santa Monica's oldest hotel. Built in 1889, Fairmont Miramar, former estate of city father John P Jones was frequented by royalty of both Hollywood (Garbo, Harlow) and the Beltway (JFK, Clinton). Renovation in 1999, and recent work on the 32 bungalows spruced it up no end; a wall of photos celebrates the building's history. The Ocean Tower rooms offer unobstructed views but lack the clubby charm of those in the Palisades Tower.

Hostelling International LA

1436 2nd Street, at Santa Monica Boulevard (reservations 1-800 909 4776 ext 105/front desk 1-310 393 9913). I-10, exit 4th-5th Street north. **Rates** $28-$31 dorm bed; $69-$73 single/double. *No parking.* **Credit** MC, V.

Book far in advance for this huge Santa Monica hostel, whose great location two blocks from the beach ensures demand is always high. The rooms cover the basics: dorms sleep between four and ten; private rooms come with mirrors and dressers. The place is spotless, though you might want to bring flip-flops for the shower (all bathrooms are shared).

Shutters on the Beach

1 Pico Boulevard, at Ocean Avenue (reservations 1-800 334 9000/front desk 1-310 458 0030/ www.shuttersonthebeach.com). I-10, exit 4th-5th Street south. **Rates** $405-$650 single/double; $905-$2,500 suite. *Parking* $26. **Credit** AmEx, DC, Disc, MC, V.

Once a cool retreat for hot Hollywood stars, this old hotel reopened in 1993 as a chic resort. The lobby is all whitewashed wood, picture windows and shabby-chic couches. On foggy days, two fireplaces keep the guests warm. All 198 rooms have balconies and whirlpool tubs. Minibars are stocked with reflexology socks and, bizarrely, disposable thongs.

Viceroy

1819 Ocean Avenue, at Pico Boulevard (reservations 1-800 670 6185/front desk 1-310 260 7500/www.viceroysantamonica.com). I-10, exit 4th-5th Street south. **Rates** $259-$450 single/double; $339-$1,500 suite. *Parking* $22. **Credit** AmEx, DC, Disc, MC, V.

It's easy to miss this newcomer, which whispers its arrival with a bland '60s façade, but then that's the way the tragically hip like their boutiques. Mere mortals will have their work cut out trying to get a table at acclaimed Whist; likewise, it's hard to find breathing room at the Cameo Bar, where leggy models and wannabes strike poses until they ache. The hotel's 'British urban' design pokes fun at tradition.

Also recommended

Deco landmark the **Georgian** (1415 Ocean Avenue, 1-800 538 8147, www.georgianhotel.com, doubles $200-$280); the **Hotel California**, such a lovely place (1670 Ocean Avenue, 1-866 571 0000, www. hotelca.com, doubles $179-$189); the airy **Loews Santa Monica** (1700 Ocean Avenue, 1-800 235 6397, www.loewshotels.com, doubles $250-$500).

Venice

Cadillac

8 Dudley Avenue, at Speedway Street & Ocean Front Walk (1-310 399 8876/www.thecadillachotel. com). I-10, exit 4th-5th Street south. **Rates** $89-$110 single/double; $130-$160 suite. *Parking* free. **Credit** AmEx, MC, V.

Built in 1905, this low-rise hotel used to be Charlie Chaplin's summer home. Its pink and turquoise façade is striking, and it's got a buzzy location: outside the front door is the Venice freak show. The hotel is a popular hangout for young travellers: they love its common areas, which include a sun deck and lounge with pool table.

Venice Beach House Historic Inn

15 30th Avenue, at Speedway Street (1-310 823 1966/www.venicebeachhouse.com). I-10, exit 4th-5th Street south. **Rates** $130-$195 single/double. *Parking* $10. **Credit** AmEx, DC, MC, V.

This landmark Craftsman-style inn was the summer home of Venice Beach founder Abbot Kinney. Surrounded by a lush garden with cosy patio, the rustic bungalow is a quiet sanctuary from the Venice circus, though the beach is just at its back door. The nine rooms are named for famous guests; each comes with antiques, and most have private bathrooms.

Bad but beautiful: the **Chateau Marmont**. *See p145.*

West LA

Hilgard House

927 Hilgard Avenue, at Le Conte Avenue (reservations 1-800 826 3934/front desk 1-310 208 3945/www.hilgard house.com). I-405, exit Wilshire Boulevard east. **Rates** $165 single/double; $179-$279 suite. *Parking* free. **Credit** AmEx, DC, Disc, MC, V.

This cheery, European-style hotel offers one of the best deals in Westwood; these prices, and its location right by the UCLA campus, make it popular with visiting academics. Three penthouse suites, each with full kitchen, living room and dining areas, are ideal for long-term stays. No pool or bar, but the rates do include free continental breakfast.

Hotel Bel-Air

701 Stone Canyon Road, at Bellagio Road (reservations 1-800 648 4097/front desk 1-310 472 1211/www.hotelbelair.com). I-405, exit Sunset Boulevard east. **Rates** $385-$550 single/double; $725-$3,500 suite. *Parking* $20. **Credit** AmEx, Disc, MC, V.

After the Sultan of Brunei bought the Beverly Hills Hotel (*see below*) in 1987, his brother decided he wanted a pink palace of his own. Five years later, he snapped up this Mission-style 1920s hotel and gave it a $16m facelift. Set amid 12 acres of luxurious gardens and dotted with fountains and flowers, the 91 guestrooms and suites are decorated in an understated French country style, but the signature oval pool is pure Hollywood. If you can't afford a room, come for high tea at the Terrace.

Beverly Hills

Avalon

9400 W Olympic Boulevard, at S Canon Drive (reservations 1-800 670 6183/front desk 1-310 277 5221/www.avalonbeverlyhills.com). I-10, exit Robertson Boulevard north. **Rates** $199-$259 single/double; $295-$395 suite. *Parking* $22. **Credit** AmEx, MC, V.

The city's first (and arguably best) boutique hotel, the former Beverly Carlton is, with the Viceroy and Maison 140, part of a group of hotels owned by Brad Korzen and designed by his wife, Kelly Wearstler. It's a low-key remodel of a mid-20th-century building, with a kitschy motor court, fabulous boomerang façade and kidney-shaped pool. The 88 rooms are tastefully appointed with vintage furnishings. The owners are also responsible for the similarly stylish but slightly cheaper **Maison 140**, also in Beverly Hills (140 S Lasky Drive, 1-800 432 5444, www. maison140beverlyhills.com).

Beverly Hills Hotel & Bungalows

9641 Sunset Boulevard, at N Crescent Drive (reservations 1-800 283 8885/front desk 1-310 276 2251/www.thebeverlyhillshotel.com). I-405, exit Sunset Boulevard east. **Rates** $380-$470 single/double; $820-$3,300 suite. *Parking* $25. **Credit** AmEx, DC, Disc, MC, V.

Every screen legend from Valentino to Arnie has slept in this fabled hideaway or held court in its Polo Lounge. The pink stucco façade, manicured grounds and sumptuous guestrooms look as fresh and fanciful as they did over 90 years ago. The big draw are the 21 bungalows: No.5 has its own pool; No.7 is decorated to Marilyn's tastes. The standard rooms are furnished with overstuffed chairs, fine bed linens and bathrooms the size of garages.

Beverly Terrace

469 N Doheny Drive, at Rangeley Avenue (reservations 1-800 842 6401/front desk 1-310 274 8141/www.beverlyterracehotel.com). I-10, exit Robertson Boulevard north. **Rates** $95-$125 single; $115-$145 double; $165 suite. *Parking* free. **Credit** AmEx, DC, Disc, MC, V.

This hotel has retro prices to match its '50s stylings, which explains its clientele: a mix of bargain hunters and bohemians. The Beverly Terrace has replaced its mid-20th-century decor with a contemporary Asian theme. Some rooms have balconies, kitchens or views of the palm-fringed courtyard pool; all come with en suite bathrooms. Free continental breakfast in the restaurant.

Crescent

403 N Crescent Drive, at Brighton Way (1-310 247 0505/www.crescentbh.com) I-405, exit Santa Monica Boulevard east. **Rates** $145-$225 single/double. *Parking* $18. **Credit** AmEx, DC, Disc, MC, V.

This new Beverly Hills boutique has gained a hip following since LA designer *du jour* Dodd Mitchell reworked the old 1926 building in 2003. It's best known for Boe, a Californian indoor-outdoor resto-bar that serves 'street food' to Hollywood deal-makers and trendies. The small, pleasant rooms are stocked with Italian linens, plush robes, wireless internet and flat-screen TVs.

Peninsula Beverly Hills

9882 Santa Monica Boulevard, between Wilshire & Charleville Boulevards (reservations 1-800 462 7899/front desk 1-310 551 2888/www.peninsula.com). I-405, exit Santa Monica Boulevard east. **Rates** $395-$525 single/double; $550-$3,500 suites/villas. *Parking* $28. **Credit** AmEx, DC, Disc, MC, V.

This French renaissance palace, possibly LA's most luxurious hotel, lures a stream of stars, moguls and power brokers with its white glove service, award-winning cuisine and proximity to Rodeo Drive. Rooms and villas include marble baths and 24-hour personal valets, plus a chauffered Rolls-Royce anywhere in Beverly Hills. A magnificent 60ft (18m) pool, the Roof Garden restaurant and the state-of-the-art spa all overlook the city and Hollywood Hills.

Raffles L'Ermitage Beverly Hills

9291 Burton Way, at N Foothill Road (reservations 1-800 800 2113/front desk 1-310 278 3344/www. lermitagehotel.com). I-405, exit Wilshire Boulevard east. **Rates** $418-$448 single/double; $895-$3,800 suite. *Parking* $24. **Credit** AmEx, DC, Disc, MC, V.

Hollywood bigwigs and fashionistas adore the sleek L'Ermitage: its privacy, business perks, gigantic guestrooms and Asian-influenced decor. The 124 rooms double as offices, with multi-line phones, faxes and personalised business cards (with private, direct-dial numbers). The French fusion restaurant serves its famous $45 salad anywhere you wish – at the rooftop pool, in the VIP cigar lounge or in the spa.

Also recommended

The **Luxe Hotel Rodeo Drive**, an aptly named star magnet (360 N Rodeo Drive, 1-866 589 3411, www.luxehotels.com, doubles $189-$350).

West Hollywood

Argyle

8358 Sunset Boulevard, at N Sweetzer Avenue (reservations 1-800 225 2637/front desk 1-323 654 7100/www.argylehotel.com). I-10, exit La Cienega Boulevard north. **Rates** $225-$325 single/double; $289-$1,299 suite. *Parking* $22. **Credit** AmEx, DC, MC, V.

It's almost worth getting a room here for the privilege of standing outside, pointing up at the gorgeous art deco façade and yammering 'I'm staying there!' to passing strangers. The surprise is that the Argyle hasn't been a hotel for long: built as a posh apartment building, it lay derelict for years before being

Farmer's Daughter. *See p145.*

rescued in the 1980s. A terrific job they did, too: the rooms here are sympathetic to the building's origins, and the bar/restaurant Fenix is no less chic.

Banana Bungalow Hollywood

7950 Melrose Avenue, at N Hayworth Avenue (reservations 1-800 446 7835/front desk 1-323 655 1510/www.bananabungalow.com). I-10, exit La Cienega Boulevard north. **Rates** $15-$20 dorm bed; $43-$91 private room. *No parking.* **Credit** MC, V.

This popular hostel recently moved to this trendy stretch on the edge of West Hollywood, and its new location, in the old *Jetsons*-style Orbit Hotel, suits its retro ethos down to the ground. All 32 rooms are done up in funky colours; dorms have six beds per room with closets and baths or showers. There's a mod lounge with late-night jukebox parties.

Chateau Marmont

8221 W Sunset Boulevard, between N Harper Avenue & Havenhurst Drive (reservations & front desk 1-323 656 1010/www.chateaumarmont.com). I-10, exit La Cienega Boulevard north. **Rates** $295 single/double; $415-$2,500 bungalow/cottage/suite. *Parking* $25. **Credit** AmEx, DC, MC, V.

This legendary 1929 hotel has always had a reputation for celebrity bad behaviour. But it's survived: after all, it was built as an earthquake-proof imitation of the Loire Valley's Château Amboise. In 1990 celebrity hotelier Andre Balazs restored it and today, it's a paparazzi-free zone for famous regulars, who hang in the plush lobby lounge, lush gardens, guest-only outdoor dining patio and Bar Marmont.

Grafton on Sunset

8462 W Sunset Boulevard, between N Olive Drive & N La Cienega Boulevard (reservations 1-800 821 3660/front desk 1-323 654 4600/www.graftonon sunset.com). I-10, exit La Cienega Boulevard north. **Rates** $149-$349 single/double; $279-$539 suite. *Parking* $20. **Credit** AmEx, DC, Disc, MC, V.

Formerly a speakeasy and a transvestite hotel, the Grafton was given a huge makeover prior to reopening in 2000. Now it's a sleek, chic hotel, but its four suites pay homage to Hollywood troublemakers of yore: the Rat Pack is a swingin' bachelor pad, while the Jane is dressed with come-hither satin sheets and pink pillows. Other rooms are decorated in South Beach limes, yellows and peaches.

Mondrian

8440 W Sunset Boulevard, at N Olive Drive (reservations 1-800 606 6090/front desk 1-323 650 8999/www.mondrianhotel.com). I-10, exit La Cienega Boulevard north. **Rates** $255-$335 single/double; $285-$2,600 suite. *Parking* $24. **Credit** AmEx, DC, Disc, MC, V.

Philippe Starck's decor at this Ian Schrager landmark, minimalist with a quirky humour, is not for everyone. His rooms are both luxurious and unsettling: a glaring white, with eyeball decals on the chairs and subliminal messages painted over beds. The Agua Spa, however, is gorgeous. Celebs and wannabes keep the attitude alive at invite-only SkyBar.

Secret Garden B&B

8039 Selma Avenue, at Laurel Canyon Boulevard (reservations 1-877 732 4736/front desk 1-323 656 8111/www.secretgardenbnb.com). I-10, exit Fairfax Avenue north. **Rates** $95 single/double; $165 cottage. *Parking* free. **Credit** AmEx, MC, V.

LA's best B&B is located a block from Sunset Strip, but inside, the 1923 Spanish-style inn is pure serenity. Run by Raymond Bilbool, former maître d' of the legendary Chasen's restaurant, the hotel offers five individually decorated rooms and a fairytale garden setting. Only two rooms are en suite, but robes are provided for journeys down the hall. The guest cottage – with sleigh bed! – is very private.

Standard Hollywood

8300 W Sunset Boulevard, at N Sweetzer Avenue (1-323 650 9090/www.standardhotel.com). I-10, exit La Cienega Boulevard north. **Rates** $135-$225 single/double; $450 suite. *Parking* $18. **Credit** AmEx, DC, Disc, MC, V.

In 1998, at the height of *Austin Powers* mania, the Standard was converted from a '60s retirement home to a tongue-in-chic shag pad, and still draws ironic hipsters with its Jetsonian decor. The International Man of Mystery would feel at home among the cottage cheese ceilings and groovy lobby carpeting. The bright bedrooms come with mini-bars peddling condoms; bathrooms are a blinding acid orange.

The Fairfax District & the Miracle Mile

Beverly Laurel Motor Hotel

8018 Beverly Boulevard, between S Laurel & S Edinburgh Avenues (reservations & front desk 1-323 651 2441). I-10, exit La Cienega Boulevard north. **Rates** $90 single; $94 double. *Parking* free. **Credit** AmEx, DC, MC, V.

This '50s-era motel is one of the best buys on Beverly, its location making it popular with young movers and shakers. The rooms are funky, with black vinyl chairs and groovy '50s tables. Some have kitchens; all have microwaves and fridges. Potted plants spruce up the tiny pool area. The motel's coffee shop, Swingers, serves a mean burger and malt.

Farmer's Daughter

115 S Fairfax Avenue, at W 1st Street (reservations 1-800 334 1658/front desk 1-323 937 3930/www.farmersdaughterhotel.com). I-10, exit Fairfax Avenue north. **Rates** $104-$115 single; $109-$125 double. $169 suite. *Parking* free. **Credit** AmEx, MC, V.

Charlize Theron stayed here when she first arrived in LA. Back then, it was downmarket, but these days, it's a gingham-giddy motor lodge. The rooms and suites are duded up in blue and yellow checks and denim bedspreads; barnyard humour abounds, with alarm clocks that cry 'cock-a-doodle-doo'. Perks include DVD players and a small pool.

Hollywood

Hollywood Bungalows

*2775 N Cahuenga Boulevard, between Mulholland
Drive & Franklin Avenue (reservations 1-888 259
9990/front desk 1-323 969 9155). US 101, exit
Highland Avenue north.* **Rates** $17 dorm bed; $57
private room. *Parking* free. **No credit cards.**

The Hollywood Bungalows recently redecorated in
a festive tropical jungle theme. It's only a brisk walk
down to the attractions and nightlife of nearby
Hollywood, but daily shuttles will ferry you there if
you can't be bothered. The well-kept bungalows,
each with their own bathroom, sleep four to six.

Magic Castle

*7025 Franklin Avenue, between N Sycamore Avenue
& N Orange Drive (reservations 1-800 741 4915/
front desk 1-323 851 0800/www.magiccastlehotel.
com). US 101, exit Highland Avenue south.* **Rates**
$129-$239 single/double. *Parking* $8. **Credit** AmEx,
Disc, DC, MC, V.

It was only a matter of time before this apartment-
style hotel in the Hollywood foothills, once a fave
among struggling actors and screenwriters, became
a trendy boutique. All the spacious rooms have been
redone in the Old Hollywood style, complete with
smart bathrooms and luxury linens. Most rooms
have balconies overlooking the pool.

Roosevelt

*7000 Hollywood Boulevard, at N Orange Drive
(reservations 1-800 950 7667/front desk 1-323
466 7000/www.hollywoodroosevelt.com). US 101,
exit Highland Avenue south.* **Rates** $109-$159
single/double; $229-$299 suite. *Parking* $18.
Credit AmEx, DC, MC, V.

Thanks to a lavish restoration by designer Dodd
Mitchell in 2003, this 1927 landmark is back on the
A-list. The large rooms have all been feng shuied,
and the triple-paned windows keep out the noise.
Most rooms are decorated with Chinese Theatre-
style concrete slabs of handprints and autographs
of the stars. The pool bar, a new Asian fusion restaurant and the revived Feinstein's Cinegrill cabaret
have lured back Hollywood's big hitters.

Also recommended

Two good-value hotels on Franklin Avenue:
the movie-themed **Best Western Hollywood
Hills** (No.6141, 1-800 287 1700, www.bestwestern.
com, double $109-$149) and the clean and tidy
Highland Gardens (No.7047, 1-800 404 5472,
www.highlandgardenshotel.com, doubles $69-$79).

Downtown

Hotel Figueroa

*939 S Figueroa Street, between W 9th Street &
W Olympic Boulevard (reservations 1-800 421 9092/
front desk 1-213 627 8971/www.figueroahotel.com).
I-110, exit 9th Street east.* **Rates** $94-$128 single;
$108-$148 double; $165-$195 suite. *Parking* $8.
Credit AmEx, DC, MC, V.

This striking hotel is a dramatic mix of Morocco and
Mexico, and oozes the kind of quirky but authentic
character for which boutique hotel designers strive.
Built in 1925 as a YWCA, the Figueroa is now more
exotic but still a bargain. The hotel's airy lobby is a
pot-pourri of Moroccan chandeliers, huge cacti and
woven rugs. Rooms vary in size, and are done out in
funky casbah chic with Mexican-tiled bathrooms.

Millennium Biltmore

*506 S Grand Avenue, at W 5th Street, Los Angeles,
CA 90071 (reservations 1-800 245 8673/front desk
1-213 624 1011/www.thebiltmore.com). I-110, exit
6th Street east.* **Rates** $169-$259 single/double; $239-
$2,000 suite. *Parking* $22. **Credit** AmEx, Disc, MC, V.

Built in 1923, the Biltmore is the oldest hotel in
Downtown, and it still maintains the Italian-Spanish
renaissance elegance that enticed such dignitaries as
Winston Churchill and JFK. The ground level is stunning, gorgeous rooms peeling off the exquisite lobby.
Sadly, the guestrooms can't compete, but they're comfortable enough. Downstairs is a Roman-style pool.

Standard Downtown

*550 S Flower Street, between W 5th & W 6th Street
(1-213 892 8080/www.standardhotel.com). I-110,
exit 6th Street east.* **Rates** $95-$325 single/double;
$450-$500 suite. *Parking* $25. **Credit** AmEx, MC, V.

The Downtown version of the Sunset Strip shag pad
(*see p145*) pokes fun at jet-setting '60s bachelors and
James Bond culture, the slick lobby setting the tone.
The swinger-style rooms come equipped with platform beds, tubs for two and peek-a-boo showers. The
rooftop bar – with vibrating waterbeds, DJs and ace
views – is a tough ticket on weekends for non-guests;
you'd do as well to hang in the ground-level bar.

Also recommended

The newly restored **Cecil Hotel**, Downtown's
largest budget hotel (640 S Main Street, 1-213 624
4545, doubles $45-$52); the **Inn at 657**, one of LA's
best B&Bs (657 & 663 W 23rd Street, 1-800 347 7512,
www.patsysinn657.com, doubles $125).

The Valleys

San Fernando Valley

Sportsmen's Lodge

*12825 Ventura Boulevard, at Coldwater Canyon
Avenue (reservations 1-800 821 8511/front desk
1-818 769 4700/www.slhotel.com). US 101, exit
Coldwater Canyon Avenue south.* **Rates** $115-$175
single/double; $175-$275 suite. *Parking* free. **Credit**
AmEx, DC, Disc, MC, V.

Relaxed and retro, this Valley landmark is popular
with families and famous faces, thanks to its prime
location near all major studios (and free shuttle to
Universal). The rooms are clean and comfortable,
with flowery bedspreads and country pine furniture.
Bathrooms are on the smallish side, but the Olympic-
sized pool is a showstopper, and the '50s-era coffee
shop dishes out hearty, all-American breakfasts.

Orange County

Candy Cane Inn

1747 S Harbor Boulevard, at Katella Avenue, Anaheim (1-800 345 7057/front desk 1-714 774 5284/www.candycaneinn.net). I-5, exit Harbor Boulevard south. **Rates** $82-$149 single/double. **Parking** free. **Credit** AmEx, DC, Disc, MC, V.

There's hardly a stripe to be found at this hotel, a three-minute walk from Disneyland's main gate. However, it consistently wins Anaheim's most beautiful hotel award: set amid romantic gardens, it's deliciously nostalgic, with cobblestone driveways, old-fashioned street lamps and a hint of 1950s flair. The comfy rooms are similarly old-fashioned.

Disneyland hotels

Disney's Grand Californian Hotel *1600 S Disneyland Drive, between Ball Road & Katella Avenue (reservations 1-877 700 3476/front desk 1-714 635 2300).* **Rates** $275-$350 double; $510-$590 suite. **Disneyland Hotel** *1150 W Magic Way, between Ball Road & Katella Avenue, Anaheim, CA 92802 (reservations 1-714 520 5005/front desk 1-714 778 6600).* **Rates** $225-$300 single/double; $450-$2,000 suite. **Disney's Paradise Pier Hotel** *1717 Disneyland Drive, at Katella Avenue, Anaheim, CA 92802 (1-714 999 0990).* **Rates** $195-$295 single/double; $350-$450 suite. **All** *www.disney.com. I-5, exit Disneyland Drive.* **Credit** AmEx, DC, Disc, MC, V.

The **Grand Californian**, Disney's entrance into the luxury hotel market, celebrates California's redwood forests, mission pioneers and Plein Air painters. The grand lobby is a Lloyd Wright-inspired gem, with stained-glass doors, wood panelling and a three-storey walk-in hearth with roaring fire. All rooms are equipped with bunk beds, trundles and sleeping bags for rugrats; some overlook the park.

The **Disneyland Hotel** and **Paradise Pier** offer similar services at similar prices; both have had recent refits. The main change wrought by the Disneyland Hotel makeover is the huge new pool complex, complete with 110ft (33m) water slide. The boardwalk-themed pool area at Paradise Pier is less expansive, but the hotel still charms with its beachy theme.

Montage Resort & Spa

30801 South Coast Highway, Laguna Beach (reservations 1-866 271 6953/front desk 1-949 715 6000/www.montagelaguna beach.com). I-405, exit PCH south. **Rates** $475-$735 single/double; $1,100-$5,500 suite. **Parking** $25-$29. **Credit** AmEx, DC, Disc, MC, V.

No expense was spared in building this dreamy resort overlooking the Pacific. Yet its luxury is understated: a romantic blend of wood and stone, gables and porches, and beach-chic furnishings. Rooms have private balconies with commanding ocean views and all the luxury trimmings you'd expect.

Ritz-Carlton Laguna Niguel

1 Ritz-Carlton Drive, at PCH, Dana Point (reservations 1-800 241 3333/front desk 1-949 240 2000/www.ritzcarlton.com). I-5, exit Crown Valley Parkway west. **Rates** $345-$695 single/double; $595-$3,200 suite. **Parking** $25. **Credit** AmEx, DC, Disc, MC, V.

The signature hotel of California's Riviera. Situated atop a cliff, the hotel's biggest selling point is its private beach. It draws a moneyed crowd who gather in the lounge for the dazzling sunsets. All rooms feature balconies and large marble bathrooms.

Resources

Hospitals

Anaheim *Anaheim Memorial Hospital, 1111 W La Palma Avenue, at N West Street (1-714 774 1450). I-5, exit La Palma Avenue north.*
Huntington Beach *Huntington Beach Medical Center, 17772 Beach Boulevard, at Newman Avenue (1-714 843 5011/www.hbhospital.com). I-405, exit Beach Boulevard south.*
Long Beach *Pacific Hospital of Long Beach, 2776 Pacific Avenue, at E 27th Street (1-562 997 2000/www.phlb.org). I-405, exit Pacific Avenue south.*
Santa Monica *St John's Health Center, 1328 22nd Street, at Santa Monica Boulevard (310 829 5511/www.stjohns.org). I-10, exit Cloverfield Boulevard north.*
West Hollywood *Cedars-Sinai Medical Center, 8700 Beverly Boulevard, at George Burns Road (1-310 423 3277/www.csmc.edu). I-10, exit La Cienega Boulevard north.*

Internet

Hollywood *Cyberjava, 7080 Hollywood Boulevard, at N la Brea Avenue (1-323 466 5600/www.cyberjava.com). US 101, exit Hollywood Boulevard west.* **Open** 7am-11.30pm daily.
Long Beach *The Library Coffee House, 3418 E Broadway, at Redondo Boulevard (1-562 433 2393). I-405, exit 7th Street south.* **Open** 9am-11pm daily.
Midtown *Infuzion, 1149 3rd Street, between California Avenue & Wilshire Boulevard (1-310 393 9985). 1-10, exit 4th-5th Street north.* **Open** 6.30am-9pm Mon-Fri; 7am-9pm Sat; 8am-6pm Sun.
Venice *Cow's End, 34 Washington Boulevard, at Pacific Avenue (1-310 574 1080). I-10, exit 4th-5th Street south.* **Open** 6am-midnight daily.
West Hollywood *Kinko's, 7630 W Sunset Boulevard, at N Stanley Avenue (1-323 845 4501/www.fedex.com). I-10, exit Fairfax Avenue north.* **Open** 7am-midnight Mon-Thur; 7am-10pm Fri; 8am-10pm Sat, Sun. **Note:** Kinko's has branches all over the LA and Orange County area. Call 1-800 254 6567 for details of your nearest.

Police

Anaheim *425 S Harbor Boulevard, at E Broadway (1-714 765 1900). I-5, exit Lincoln Avenue east.*
Beverly Hills *464 N Rexford Drive, at Santa Monica Boulevard (1-310 285 2100). I-405, exit Santa Monica Boulevard east.*

Burbank *200 N 3rd Street, at E Orange Grove Avenue (1-818 238 3200). I-5, exit Olive Avenue east.*
Downtown *251 E 6th Street, at Wall Street (1-213 485 3294). I-110, exit 6th Street east.*
Huntington Beach *2000 Main Street, at W Yorktown Avenue (1-714 960 8811). I-405, exit Beach Boulevard south.*
Long Beach *100 Long Beach Boulevard, at E 1st Street (1-562 570 7301). I-710, exit Shoreline Drive east.*
Pasadena *207 N Garfield Avenue, at E Walnut Street (1-626 744 4241). I-210, exit Marengo Avenue south.*
Santa Monica *333 Olympic Boulevard, at 7th Street (1-310 458 8431). I-10, exit Lincoln Boulevard north.*
West Hollywood *720 N San Vicente Boulevard, at Santa Monica Boulevard (1-310 855 8850). I-405, exit Santa Monica Boulevard east.*

Post offices

Anaheim *701 N Loara Street, at W North Street (1-714 520 2649). I-5, exit Euclid Street north.*
Beverly Hills *325 N Maple Drive, between Burton Way & W 3rd Street (1-310 247 3470). I-10, exit Robertson Boulevard north.*
Downtown *505 S Flower Street, at W 5th Street (1-213 629 5460). I-110, exit 6th Street east.*
Huntington Beach *6771 Warner Avenue, at Edwards Street (1-714 843 4200). I-405, exit Bolsa Avenue west.*
Long Beach *300 Long Beach Boulevard, at W 3rd Street (1-562 494 2298). I-710, exit Shoreline Drive east.*
Santa Monica *1248 5th Street, at Arizona Avenue (1-310 576 6786). I-10, exit 4th-5th Street north.*
West Hollywood *820 N San Vicente Boulevard, at Santa Monica Boulevard, West Hollywood (1-323 654 8236). I-10, exit Fairfax Avenue north.*

Tourist information

Anaheim *Anaheim/Orange County Visitor & Convention Bureau, 800 W Katella Avenue, at N Batavia Street (1-714 765 8888/www.anaheimoc.org).* **Open** *8am-5.30pm Mon-Fri.*
Beverly Hills *Beverly Hills Visitors Bureau, 239 S Beverly Drive, between Charleville Boulevard & Gregory Way (1-800 345 2210/1-310 248 1015/www.beverlyhillscvb.org). I-10, exit S Beverly Drive north.* **Open** *8.30am-5pm Mon-Fri.*
Hollywood *Hollywood Visitor Information Center, 6801 Hollywood Boulevard, at N Highland Avenue (1-323 467 6412/www.lacvb.com). US 101, exit V ine Street south.* **Open** *10am-10pm Mon-Sat; 10am-7pm Sun.*
Huntington Beach *Huntington Beach Visitors Bureau, 301 Main Street, at Olive Avenue (1-800 729 6232/www.hbvisit.com). I-405, exit Bolsa Avenue west.* **Open** *9am-5pm Mon-Fri.*
Long Beach *Long Beach CVB, 1 World Trade Center, at E Ocean Boulevard (1-800 452 7829/www.golongbeach.org). I-710, exit Shoreline Drive east.* **Open** *8am-5pm Mon-Fri.*

Downtown *Los Angeles CVB, 685 S Figueroa Street, at Wilshire Boulevard (1-213 689-8822/www.lacvb.com). I-110, exit 6th Street east.* **Open** *9am-5pm Mon-Fri.*
Malibu *Malibu Chamber of Commerce, Suite 100, 23805 Stuart Ranch Road, at Civic Center Way (1-310 456 9025/www.malibu.org). I-10, exit PCH north.* **Open** *10am-4pm Mon-Fri.*
Pasadena *Pasadena CVB, 171 S Los Robles Avenue, at Cordova Street (1-800 307 7977/www.pasadenacal.org). I-210, exit Los Robles Avenue south.* **Open** *8am-5pm Mon-Fri; 10am-4pm Sat.*
San Fernando Valley *San Fernando Valley CVB, 5121 Van Nuys Boulevard, between Magnolia Boulevard & Otsego Street, Sherman Oaks (1-818 379 7000/www.valleyofthestars.org). US 101, exit Van Nuys Boulevard north.* **Open** *9am-5pm Mon-Fri.*
Santa Monica *Santa Monica Visitor Center, 1400 Ocean Avenue, at Santa Monica Boulevard (1-310 393 7593/www.santamonica.com). I-10, exit 4th-5th Street north.* **Open** *10am-4pm daily.*
West Hollywood *West Hollywood CVB, Pacific Design Center, Suite M38, 8687 Melrose Avenue, at N San Vicente Boulevard (1-800 368 6020/1-310 289 2525/www.visitwesthollywood.com). I-405, exit Santa Monica Boulevard east.* **Open** *8.30am-5.30pm Mon-Fri.*

Getting There

By air

Los Angeles International Airport (LAX; 1-310 646 5252, www.lawa.org) is located on the west side of LA. The cheapest way to reach your hotel from LAX is by public transport. From the airport, take either the C or G free shuttle buses. The C will ferry you to the MTA Bus Center at Vicksburg and 96th; the G heads to the Aviation station on the Metro's Green Line.

Shuttles flit between LAX and LA, 24 hours a day. Most will drop you at your hotel; fares start at around $25; pick them up outside the arrival terminals. Many of the same companies will pick you up from your hotel and take you back to LAX when you leave, with 24 hours' notice. Among the firms serving LAX are Golden West Express (1-800 917 5656).

Taxis can be found outside all terminals. All fares from LAX come with a $2.50 surcharge. If you're staying on the Westside, a taxi from LAX will cost $20-$25 plus tip. If you're heading to Hollywood or beyond, you should expect to pay twice that. There's a flat rate of $38 ($40.50 with surcharge) between LAX and Downtown.

If you're flying from a US airport, you may fly into **Burbank-Glendale-Pasadena Airport** (1-818 840 8840, www.burbank

Millennium Biltmore. *See p146.*

airport.com). There are many ways in which you can travel from Burbank to your hotel: by public transport (there is a free shuttle that will take you to the MTA bus stop at Hollywood Way and Thornton Avenue; the airport is also served by Metrolink rail), by shuttle (such transport firms are numerous) and by taxi.

By bus

Los Angeles's main **Greyhound** (1-800 229 9424, www.greyhound.com) station is located Downtown, at 1716 E 7th Street. However, buses to LA stop at several smaller stations around town.

By rail

Trains to Los Angeles terminate at **Union Station** (800 N Alameda Street, Downtown). From here, you can take the Red or Gold lines on the Metro (see *p150*) to your destination, or connect with one of the myriad buses that stop at or very near the station.

Getting Around

By car

Driving in LA presents its own challenges. Those used to driving in towns or smaller cities may initially blanche at the five-lane freeways; but you'll quickly get used to it. An essential aid is the *Thomas Bros Street Guide to Los Angeles & Orange Counties*, an easy-to-use, annually updated map to the region published by Rand McNally, it costs about $35. KFWB 980 AM runs traffic updates every ten minutes.

LA is subdivided by numerous freeways and a loose grid of large arteries, the boulevards and avenues (aka surface streets). When planning a journey, find out the nearest cross-street; for example, Hollywood and Highland, or Sunset and San Vicente. If you're taking the freeway, find out the exit nearest to your destination. In this chapter, we've included cross-streets and a freeway exit for every listed establishment.

Freeways in LA are referred to by their numbers (10, 110, 405, etc) but also, fairly often, by their names. Among the most common are the **Golden State Freeway** (I-5), which scythes up through Anaheim, Downtown and the San Fernando Valley; the **Santa Monica Freeway** (I-10), which runs east to west across LA; the **Hollywood Freeway** (US 101), which parallels I-5 through Hollywood; and the self-explanatory **Long Beach Freeway** (I-710).

Public transport

LA's public transport system is run by the **Metropolitan Transportation Authority** (MTA). Its telephone operators (1-800 266 6883) can plan your journey, including connections, if you tell them where you are and where you want to go. The same information is available online at www.metro.net, and at MTA information centres at Union Station (800 N Alameda Street) and on the Miracle Mile (5301 Wilshire Boulevard).

Buses

The main mode of public transport in LA are the 2,000-plus white-and-orange **MTA buses**, which cover over 180 routes. The fare on all MTA routes is $1.25; a further 25¢ is required

Standard Downtown. *See p146.*

trip costs $1.25; trains run approximately 5am to 12.30am daily. The system is colour-coded; the three most useful lines are as follows:

Red The Red Line starts at Union Station, crosses Downtown and forks into two branches at Wilshire-Vermont. One continues west to Wilshire-Western, while the other heads north through Hollywood and to Universal Studios.

Gold The Gold Line begins at Union Station (where it connects with the Red Line) and heads north-east through Monterey Hills and Pasadena to Sierra Madre.

Blue Starting at the Red Line station at 7th and Figueroa in Downtown, the Blue Line heads south through South Central to Long Beach.

Taxis

Because of the city's size, taxis are not a cheap way of getting around LA. Nor are they convenient (you can't hail taxis on the street) or straightforward (you may have to give the driver directions). The basic fare is $2; each additional mile will cost you a further $2. Large, licensed firms include Bell Cab (1-800 666 6664) and Yellow Cab (1-800 200 1085).

for a transfer to a bus run by a separate agency (*see below*). An all-day pass is $3. The following are LA's most useful bus routes:

2 Runs more or less the entire length of Sunset Boulevard, from its junction with the PCH via West Hollywood, Hollywood, Silver Lake and Echo Park to Downtown.

4 Runs along Santa Monica Boulevard from Santa Monica to the junction with Sunset Boulevard in Silver Lake, whereupon it follows the same route as the 2.

20 Runs along Wilshire Boulevard from Santa Monica to Downtown, whereupon it takes 6th Street (east) or 7th Street (west).

156 Runs from the Vermont-Santa Monica Metro station west along Santa Monica Boulevard, then north up Highland Avenue and Cahuenga Boulevard (past the Hollywood Bowl and Universal Studios).

A number of smaller bus networks serve individual communities. Culver City and Santa Monica have their own bus routes, and the DASH services (www.ladottransit.com) are useful for short hops, especially Downtown.

Metro

LA's Metro subway system covers a limited area of the city, but it can be a convenient way to get around, especially from Downtown. One

Beyond LA & OC

Santa Catalina Island

The most Mediterranean island in North America, **Santa Catalina Island** (or Catalina, as it's commonly known) juts above the Pacific Ocean by more than 2,000 feet (610 metres) at its highest point. Its 54 miles of rocky shoreline, steep drop-offs and relatively dry climate disguise the fact that it's a mere 22 miles off the coast of the industrial port city of Long Beach. Privately owned for two centuries and now 86 per cent owned and administered by the **Santa Catalina Island Conservancy** (125 Claressa Avenue, Avalon, 1-310 510 2595, www. catalinaconservancy.org), Catalina is protected from overdevelopment in perpetuity. Relaxing on a Catalina beach in a quiet cove, looking over the blue ocean as waves lap the pebbly beach, it's hard not to imagine yourself lost among the Grecian Archipelago or the coast of Turkey. Count this geographic trick as one of the most valuable attractions of the island, home to just 3,300 permanent residents.

The Catalina most know is the Catalina of the day-tripper, ferried from mainland Southern California on speedy, comfortable catamarans.

Up to 7,000 day-trippers arrive every day, but it takes a little planning to get the best out of the island in a small timespan. Most day-trippers limit themselves to the tourist activities, and thus never get a chance to really relax into the island's pace of life. Better that you should take a weekend, an extension that offers you the opportunity to dramatically extend your vista.

Chief among these is the very short (and quickly exhausted) stroll along the quaint shops and restaurants of **Crescent Avenue** in the town of **Avalon**, likely to be the first main street you walk on reaching Catalina. Crescent Avenue curves along Avalon's postcard-perfect small boat harbour towards the magificent domed art deco **Casino** building, which houses a theatre, a ballroom and the **Santa Catalina Island Museum** (1 Casino Way, Avalon, 1-310 510 2414, $1-$3). Crowded **Crescent Beach**, a tiny, urban populist beach (without waves), is also a big draw, as are the variety of boat trips on glass-bottomed boats or semi-submersible subs over crystal-clear waters teeming with colourful sea life. For details, call **Discovery Tours** (1-800 626 1496, www.scico.com).

There's much to see beyond Crescent Avenue, though. Most obviously, you can stroll (or take the low-cost shuttle that departs from the kiosk at the north end of Crescent Avenue) one and a half miles along Avalon Canyon to the picturesque 38-acre grounds of the **Wrigley Memorial & Botanical Gardens** (1400 Avalon Canyon Road, 1-310 510 2288, $3). The 1934 memorial recognises Chicagoan chewing gum magnate William Wrigley, Jr, who bought the island in 1915 and is most responsible for its current state of conservancy. The memorial's architecture has the stately feel of a mausoleum (though Wrigley's body is not buried here) combined with the laid-back vibe imparted by hand-painted tiles for which the island is famous. The harbour view is stunning.

Elsewhere, the **Descanso Beach Club** (1-310 510 7410, closed Nov-Apr) is a relaxing, green retreat at the beachside terminus of Descanso Canyon, a ten-minute walk north along Via Casino from Avalon. The Descanso Beach Club charges a small access fee ($1.50) that buys sun worshippers a slightly upscale, country-clubby ambience (volleyball nets, beachside patio bar and restaurant, sea kayak instruction). It can be a pleasant alternative to packed Crescent Beach.

Catalina offers a trove of outdoor activities. You'll need a permit from the Conservancy to either bike or hike outside Avalon or Two Harbours, the rustic settlement at the island's northern isthmus; hiking permits are free, but

mountain biking on the island's dirt tracks costs $60 (or $85 family), a permit that's valid for a year. There's impressive diving, too, both for scuba and skin divers; try **Catalina Divers Supply** (1-800 3535 0330, www.catalinadivers supply.com). The less adventurous can enjoy a private (and pricey; $495 for a half-day, covers up to six people) four-wheeler tour of the island, led by the Catalina Island Conservancy. Reservations are required; call 1-310 510 2595. You can also take an open-sided bus tour of the island's largely inaccessible 42,000-acre interior to catch glimpses of the herd of 400-plus buffalo (left here after the filming of the 1925 adaptation of Zane Grey's *The Vanishing American*), the unspoiled countryside, and stunning vistas of the Pacific Ocean. Call 1-800 626 1496 or check www.scico.com for details.

But the main reason to spend more than a quick day-trip here is to enjoy the benefits of the Catalina evening. Take a nap and a shower before a relaxing, harbour-view dinner as the sun, in another geographic trick, dips behind you rather than on the horizon. Cap your day with a romantic moonlit stroll or, during summer, a horse-drawn carriage ride.

Where to eat & drink

Almost all eating options on Catalina are in tiny Avalon, and you may saunter past nearly every joint in town in the first hour you're there. Dress code is California casual (denim is fine); booking are suggested at weekends for dinner.

For the best fresh fish at fair prices, nothing beats **Armstong's Seafood** (306 Crescent Avenue, 1-310 510 0113, $$–$$$) right on the harbour; you'll often see local fishermen plying their catch to the chef. Those seeking an elegant meal will find it at the continental **Channel House** (205 Crescent Avenue, 1-310 510 1617, $$$–$$$$) or the Italian **Ristorante Villa Portofino** (101 Crescent Avenue, 1-310 510 0508, closed lunch, $$$$), both with nice ocean views. Mexican is also popular here; the **Catalina Cantina** is good, and very popular thanks to its indoor/outdoor seating facing the harbour (313 Crescent Avenue, 1-310 510 0100, $$), but we prefer the food at **Mi Casita** (111 Claressa Avenue, 1-310 510 1772, $$).

Among the relaxed options on Catalina, the dockside **Busy Bee** (306 Crescent Avenue, 1-310 510 1983, $) is the locals' fave, featuring a huge menu that includes some vegetarian specialities, and **Sally's Waffle Shop** (505 Crescent Avenue, 1-310 510 0355, breakfast only, $) is a cheap, happy place for brekkie. Off the beaten path, the **Catalina Country Club** offers a delicious Sunday brunch (1 Country Club Drive, 1-310 510 0327, $$$). Want to know where everyone is scoring those saliva-inducing, ice-cream packed waffle cones? **Big Olaf's** (220 Crescent Avenue, 1-310 510 0798).

Bars? Join the pleasantly rowdy crowd at the vaguely tiki-themed **Luau Larry's** for a night of rum-fuelled singalong with 'human jukebox' Gil Torres, or dancing at the island's only disco, the rudimentary **Chi Chi Club**, where suntanned partiers approximate, island style, the mating rituals of nightclubs worldwide. The **Blue Parrot** (1-310 510 2465), an upstairs island-styled restaurant, has a very comfortable bar that will have tiki aficionados drooling.

Where to stay

As with everything on Catalina, lodging can be expensive; hotels also fill, especially on summer weekends, up to a year in advance. You'll pay dearly to be in the centre of it all, but the casual European elegance of **Hotel Vista del Mar** (1-800 601 3836, $105-$350), steps from the beach, is worth it. There's a peaceful courtyard where you can escape the beach madness downstairs. Down Crescent Avenue is the nicely renovated, mid-century modern **Pavilion Lodge** (1-800 626 1496, $94-$279), a classic motor court without the motors. If cost is of no concern, look into the **Inn at Mt Ada** (1-310 510 2030, $320-$675), a six-room inn 350 feet (107 metres) above the harbour that was formerly the home of William Wrigley, Jr. Backpackers will find that Catalina's five campgrounds are more than worth the effort. **Hermit Gulch** is the only one with proximity to Avalon (reservations/permits required; call 1-310 510 8368, pitches $12); for the others, such as the stunning seaside hike-in at **Little Harbour**, call 1-310 510 0303 (www.scico.com).

Resources

Post office

Avalon *118 Metropole Street (1-310 510 2850).*

Tourist information

Avalon *Catalina Island Chamber of Commerce & Visitors Bureau, 1 Green Pleasure Pier, Avalon (1-310 510 1520/www.catalina.com).* **Open** 8am-5pm Mon-Sat; 9am-3pm Sun.

Getting there

For the hour-long boat journey from Long Beach or San Pedro, call **Catalina Express** (1-800 481 3470, www.catalinaexpress.com). For the 75-minute trip from Newport Beach, call the less regular **Catalina Flyer**, 1-949 673 5245, www.catalinainfo.com). Fares are around $23-$25 one-way and $44-$50 return; reservations are recommended.

Beyond the San Gabriel Valley

The San Gabriel Valley grows progressively less interesting the further east you go; by the time you've driven outside it, through or near the likes of **Pomona**, **Ontario** and **Rancho Cucamonga** and on to **San Bernardino**, you're really in forgettable, mall-dominated suburbia. However, there is one perk to the area: a long and uninterrupted stretch of **Route 66** (*see p32*). South of San Bernardino are a number of similar no-mark 'burbs, although **Riverside** does at least boast the University of California's interesting **Museum of Photography** (3824 Main Street, 1-951 784 3686, closed Mon & Sun, $1).

However, this general area, about 60 miles east of LA, is notable mostly as a stepping-off point. Taking I-10 or Highway 60 east will bring you to Palm Springs; I-215 south leads to San Diego (*see p64*). From San Bernardino, meanwhile, I-215 north soon hooks up with I-15 en route to Las Vegas, while Highway 18 runs to **Lake Arrowhead** and the San Bernardino National Forest.

Lake Arrowhead

Nestled atop one of Southern California's few mountain ranges, two small towns and a handful of scattered neighbourhoods make up the community of Lake Arrowhead. **Blue Jay**, a town at the west side of the region, is made up of a number of small but, with the exception of luxury grocers Jensen's (1-909 337 8484), rather forgettable shops. **Lake Arrowhead Village**, meanwhile, offers a gathering of gift and outlet shops on a peninsula surrounded by water.

Though the narrated tours on the **Arrowhead Queen** (1-909 336 6992, $7.50-$12) offer a little history, sightseeing in Lake Arrowhead is largely usurped by the sports and activities. In summer, water sports are king. **McKenzie's Water Ski School** in the Village (1-909 337 3814, http://mckenzie skischool.com, closed Oct-Apr) is the oldest water-ski school in the US, and offers lessons. In summer, sailing and water-ski races that can be viewed from the Village or around the lake. The main disappointment, apart from the plethora of speedboats, is the lack of swimming: the lake is privately owned, and so unless you're staying at the **Lake Arrowhead Resort** (*see p153*), which has private access, swimming is not allowed.

Hikers are in luck. The mile-long **Seely Creek Trail** and the marginally longer **Crab Flats Trail** are two straightforward trails in the area; pick up a map and a permit ($5) from the Lake Arrowhead Visitor Center (*see p153*).

If you've got young children, the **Children's Forest**, off Highway 18 at Keller Peak Road, is an easier bet.

Winter sees skiers descend on the area. The Arrowhead Ranger Station (1-909 337 2444) can offer guidance, maps and details on current conditions for cross-country skiing and snow-shoeing. About ten miles up from Lake Arrowhead on US 18 is the **Snow Valley** resort (1-800 680 7669), where you can buy a range of ski and snowboarding passes. The resort is located at a low altitude, but makes its own snow to ensure that the slopes are always in service. Nearby, there's cross-country skiing at **Rim Nordic Ski Area** (1-909 867 2600, www.rimnordic.com).

Where to eat & drink

Variety is limited in this small town but if you're looking for something quaint and home cooked, try the tiny, family-owned **Casual Elegance** (26848 Hwy 189, 1-909 337 8932, closed Mon, Tue & lunch Wed-Sun, $$$$). The **Belgian Waffle Works** (28200 Hwy 189, 1-909 337 5222, closed dinner, $), a Victorian waffle house, is as impressive for its views as much as its breakfasts. **Casa Coyotes' Grill & Cantina** (28200 Hwy 189, 1-909 337 1171, www.casacoyotes.com, $$), a locals' hangout, offers Mexican fare and a full bar, with music on weekends.

Where to stay

The most notable of Lake Arrowhead's few B&Bs is the **Fleur de Lac European Inn** (285 Hwy 173, 1-909 336 4612, $139-$199), a quaint little place decorated in a French country motif that's only steps away from the lake. The **Lake Arrowhead Resort** (27984 Hwy 189, 1-866 794 3732, www.laresort.com, $139-$209) is a large hotel near the Village. For an inexpensive alternative, try the charming **Storybook Inn** (28717 Hwy 18, 1-909 337 0011, www.storybookinn.com, $89-$189), on the way to Snow Valley.

Big Bear Lake

A mountain community 90 minutes east of Lake Arrowhead, **Big Bear Lake** offers a less charming and more mountainous experience than its near-neighbour. There's also a greater variety of activities here year-round, and no need to rely on the fake snow often required at Lake Arrowhead. From around 1860, people began settling in Big Bear in search of gold. Today gold still exists in the San Bernardino Mountains, and the **Big Bear**

Discovery Center (Hwy 38 between Fawnskin and Stanfield Cutoff, 1-909 866 3437) offers guided tours. But as at Lake Arrowhead, the sporting opportunities are the main attraction here.

Unlike at Arrowhead, Bear Lake authorities allows visitor to swim in it. The lake is also a first-rate fishery, where you can find rainbow trout, large and small mouth bass, catfish and blue gill. The lake is stocked with 2,000 pounds of rainbow trout every two weeks. Many hiking trailheads are easily accessible and many offer panoramic views. The **Big Bear Lake Visitor Center** (*see below*) offers maps and advice.

From November to April, **Snow Summit** (1-800 232 7686, www.bigbearmountainresorts. com) is one of the most popular ski/snowboard resorts in Southern California. In summer, the resort converts its East Mountain Express high-speed chairlift into the **Scenic Sky Chair** (rates 1-800 232 7686); running to an 8,200-foot (2,500-metre) summit, it offers a magnificent view of the San Gorgonio Mountains.

Where to eat & drink

Mandarin Garden Chinese (501 W Valley Boulevard, 1-909 585 1818, $-$$), located at the small regional airport, is a good bet. The restaurants along Big Bear Boulevard include **Marisco's La Bamba** (40199 Big Bear Boulevard, 1-909 866 2350, $-$$), which specialises in Mexican seafood. For cocktails with a lakeside view, try the **Tail of the Whale** at Whaler Pointe (350 W Aeroplane Boulevard, 1-909 866 5514).

Where to stay

Many people enjoy the traditional B&Bs around the lake, such as the **Windy Point Inn** (39015 North Shore Drive, 1-909 866 2746, www.windypointinn.com, $145-$265). The **Boulder Creek Resort** (760 Blue Jay Road, 1-800 244 2327, $69.95-$100) is a great choice for those who prefer to spend the day on the slopes as opposed to the bedroom. A variety of hotel and motel chains can be found Downtown; *see p54* for some suggestions.

Resources

Tourist information

Big Bear Lake *Big Bear Lake Visitor Center, 630 Bartlett Road (1-909 866 6190/ www.bigbear.com)*. **Open** 8am-5pm Mon-Fri; 9am-5pm Sat, Sun.
Lake Arrowhead *Lake Arrowhead Chamber of Commerce, 28200 Hwy 189 (1-909 337 3715/ www.lakearrowhead.net)*. **Open** 9am-5pm Mon-Fri.

Southern California

The Deserts

NEVADA

Big Pine

Beatty

Death Valley
National Park

Panamint Range

Amargosa Valley

Sequoia
NP

Lone Pine

136

190

Death Valley
Junction

Amargosa Range

Las Vegas

Winchester

Paradise

Henderson

Boulder City

Overton

Lake Mead NRA

Lake
Mead

Desert National
Wildlife Refuge

See p175

395

178

Shoshone

160

Searles Valley

127

Ridgecrest

Randsburg

Johannesburg

Red Rock
Canyon SP

California
City

Mojave

Rosamond

Lancaster

Palmdale

Wrightwood

Victorville

Hesperia

Mojave Desert

Baker

Cima

Kelso

Mojave National
Preserve

Calico Town

Afton

Barstow

Boron

Bagdad

Amboy

Big Bear

San Bernardino

Los Angeles

Anaheim

Riverside

Yucaipa

Joshua Tree

Yucca Valley

Twentynine
Palms

Desert Hot Springs

Palm Springs

Joshua Tree
National Park

Eagle Mountain

San
Bernardino
National
Forest

Indio

Palm Desert

Coachella

Chiriaco
Summit

Blythe

Long
Beach

Costa Mesa

Avalon

Vista

See p158

Salton
Sea

Niland

Calipatria

Chocolate Mountains

Oceanside

Escondido

Borrego Springs

Julian

Anza-Borrego
Desert
State Park

Brawley

Poway

San Diego

El Cajon

La Mesa

Chula Vista

El Centro

Calexico

MEXICALI

Yuma

San Luis

Rosarito

MEXICO

San Luis

93

95

15

93

95

Lake
Mohave

Bullhead City

40

Needles

95

62

177

10

111

86

78

78

8

14

58

395

15

14

138

5

15

0   45 km

0   20 miles

© Copyright Time Out Group 2005

Mexico

The Deserts

Empty? We don't think so.

Nature played a cruel trick on the early Western pioneers. Just where the barrier of the Sierras peters out in the south, a great desert swathe cuts to the coast. Technically, much of southern California is desert, receiving fewer than ten inches of rain a year. Were it not for irrigation, air-con and the automobile, large areas would be close on uninhabitable for modern man; **Palm Springs** and the **Coachella Valley**, in fact, could not exist in their current form.

Inhospitable, maybe, but given present-day comforts, also beautiful. Starved of rain except in rare, cathartic storms, and sculpted by extreme winds, the land is left bare, its forms decorated by minerals swept down from the mountains by the weather and a survivalist ecology that is rich and complex, but remains graspable. Human endeavour also stands out against the blank canvas. Traces of the early Native American inhabitants and the 19th-century settlers remain side by side, along with the ongoing incursions of the present: military and mining companies occupy huge tracts, only occasionally visible from the highway.

This chapter covers the area east of a line drawn, roughly, along the route of US 395, which runs north–south from Bishop to the LA massif. It includes the geologically spectacular Death Valley and Joshua Tree National Parks, along with the less newsworthy but scarcely less interesting Anza-Borrego Desert State Park, the largest in the contiguous USA, and the wilderness Mojave National Preserve. It also covers resort towns, from the flourishing Palm Springs to the backwater Borrego Springs and the defunct Zzyzx, along with more functional desert towns such as Baker, inalienable from its 'World's Tallest Thermometer'.

Three of the four types of North American desert are represented in California. The Great Basin, characterised by sagebrush, spills over from Nevada in the northern state. In the area covered by this chapter, two major deserts abut on a line that runs through Joshua Tree National Park, each with a characteristic indicator plant: the Mojave and its iconic, arms-akimbo Joshua tree, and the Sonoran (aka, in California, Colorado), where the thorny sprays –

The best Deserts

Things to do
Aside from exploring the wilderness of the assorted national and state parks, of which **Death Valley** (*see p173*) is surely the most interesting, the deserts' main treat is the architecture of **Palm Springs** (*see p158*).

Places to stay
Lodgings in the desert run the gamut. Among the highlights: the luxurious **Furnace Creek Inn** in Death Valley (*see p176*); Borrego Springs' lovingly restored **Palms at Indian Head** resort (*see p158*); the impossibly cute **Hotel Nipton** (*see p173*); and the legendary **Joshua Tree Inn** (*see p169*).

Places to eat
The restaurant at the **Furnace Creek Inn** in Death Valley National Park (*see p176* is surprisingly impressive, but otherwise, your best dining options in the deserts are all in or around Palm Springs: **Bit of Country** (*161*) for

breakfast, **Shermans Deli & Bakery** (*see p163*) for lunch and **Riccio's** (*see p163*) for dinner.

Nightlife
Unless you're gay, in which case **Palm Springs** (*see p158*) should be your destination, there isn't much out here.

Culture
The lounge culture of **Palm Springs** (*see p163*) can be fun, but there's not a stranger theatre in California than the **Amargosa Opera House** at Death Valley Junction (*see p176*).

Sports & activities
Death Valley (*see p174*) and **Anza-Borrego** (*see p156*) parks contain a number of worthwhile hikes, while **Mojave National Preserve** (*see p169*) is a mecca for 4WD fanatics. The **Coachella Valley** is packed with golf courses; for the best, *see p37*.

fire-tipped in spring – of ocotillo proliferate. The ecosystems are robust, remote and often preserved, but they suffer increasingly from pollution and smog. Treat them carefully, and respect them, too. Desert precautions for your car are covered in **On the Road** (*see p31*) and for your body in **Resources A-Z** (*see p401*).

The desert is beautiful to fly over and, thrillingly so, from the driving seat. But engaging with it more closely pays dividends. Go on an interpreted or ranger-led trail to familiarise yourself with some of the basics of geology, flora and fauna. *A Sierra Club Naturalist's Guide to the Deserts of the Southwest* by Peggy Larson and the National Audubon Society's *Deserts* are good field guides. A worthwhile planning resource is www.desertusa.com.

The Anza-Borrego Desert

Driving up – and we mean *up* – S22 from San Diego, passing condo developments and high-country orange groves, you crest a mountain ridge and without warning find yourself looking down over a vast desert bowl. The change in terrain is dramatic, the geology naked: canyons, ridges, mountains in various shades of ochre, changing with the light. You have just crossed the mountain barrier that blocks moisture from coming any further inland, creating instant desert.

Anza-Borrego Desert State Park is the largest state park in the continental US, at 600,000 acres. It contains a remarkable variety of terrains – a desert primer of high mountains, palm-studdedd oases, badlands, washes, flood plains, slot canyons, mesas, mudhills and rock formations – among which flourish rich plant and animal communities. You might see desert bighorn sheep ('borrego' in Spanish; Anza was the name of an early Spanish explorer), jackrabbits, coyotes, red-tailed hawks, golden eagles, roadrunners and hummingbirds, or wander among creosote, yucca, a dozen cacti, desert willow, ironwood, elephant tree and sprays of ocotillo, the signature plant of the Colorado Desert. Its human inhabitants have built roads and railways, mined mines, pecked petroglyphs and abandoned homesteads: preserved in the dry heat, remnants lie exposed. There aren't many folks around these days; the odds are you'll have the trails to yourself.

Though the size of many national parks, Anza-Borrego is a state park, which implies certain differences. It is less controlled, so – responsibly – you can camp wild, walk at will, mountain-bike and horseback-ride on marked trails, and drive 500 miles of 4WD tracks. It also means that a degree of commercial development is permitted. Indeed, there's an entire town in the middle of it: the charmingly low-key resort of **Borrego Springs**, which was intended to develop into an alternative to Palm Springs but never quite made it. These days, though, it's welcomed as one by visitors who appreciate a lack of pretension; witness its grapefruit festival in the third week of April.

The park's primary roads are **S22**, which runs east to west, and **S2**, which diverges from it in the west to cut 60 miles south-east before joining I-8. The main **visitor centre**, a stone-built building set into the ground to minimise its environmental impact, is on S22, just west of Borrego Springs. It's a well-kept place,

Anza attractions: teddy bear cholla and the pool at the **Palms at Indian Head** (*see p158*).

refitted in 2005, with lots of maps, guides and volunteers who run a programme of walks and talks (most between November and April). Near here are two enjoyable leaflet-guided trails. The easiest is to **Borrego Palm Canyon Falls** (3.0-mile round-trip), which takes you past a variety of flora and up a year-round stream to an incongruously verdant grove of California palms (most palms you see in the state are not local varieties). Slightly tougher, but otherwise not too dissimilar, is the hike to **Maidenhair Falls** (5.0-mile round-trip). The visitor centre can provide details of the park's other hikes.

Twelve miles east on S22, you can turn right up a dirt road (fine for 2WD) to reach the **Fonts Point** viewpoint over the Borrego Badlands, a sort of mini Zabriskie Point; a few miles further on go left up Calcite Mine Road to explore some dramatic slot canyons. S22 leads on to **Ocotillo Wells State Vehicular Recreation Area**, a 4WD tear-it-up paradise, and then to Salton City and the **Salton Sea**, a lot less interesting than it sounds. Formed in 1905-7, when Colorado River irrigation overflowed a dyke into the prehistoric Salton Basin, it shrinks, expands and leaves a rimy margin depending on evaporation. There's a state recreation area here (www.parks.ca.gov), popular for angling and water-skiing.

Other 2WD-accessible park highlights are **Split Mountain Road** and **Fish Creek**, accessible via Highway 78. You'll see beautiful

sedimentary rock formations, including an anticline, and can hike a mile up to some wind-eroded caves. The S2 road is a lovely drive, with several easily hiked-to diversions, both human and geological.

To make the desert flower, just add water. Anza-Borrego's trump card is its particularly stunning spring display. Rain depending, this runs from mid March to early April; the park's website and wildflower phone line (1-760 767 4684) give updates. Plants everywhere will be in flower; for carpets of purple sand verbena and waxy evening primrose, try driving the Borrego Springs rectangle, around Henderson Canyon and Peg Leg roads. Rangers will be able to point you to other blooms of interest.

Anza-Borrego is preposterously hot in summer, and you should follow the usual desert precautions; carry plenty of water at all times, particularly if you're planning on walking one of the park's trails. If the heat is too much, head for higher elevations.

Where to eat & drink

Though there are independent eating options in the town of Borrego Springs – **Kendall's Café** (The Mall, Country Club Drive, 1-760 767 3491, $), for example, a basic place that's good for breakfast – the finest restaurants in the area are tied to hotels. Despite the grating name, the **Krazy Koyote**, at the Palms at

Indian Head (*see below*; closed lunch & Mon, Tue, $$$), serves an appetising menu of Cal-American favourites. You'll need to wear a jacket and tie to eat in the Butterfield Room at **La Casa del Zorro** (*see below*; $$$$), which offers a sturdier menu in a sophisticated setting. Both resorts have bars; those after an earthier atmosphere should seek out the **Iron Door** (Split Mountain Road, no phone), an isolated shack that serves 'em cold.

Where to stay

The lap of desert luxury is provided at prim, proper **La Casa del Zorro** (3845 Yaqui Pass Road, 1-800 824 1884, www.lacasadelzorro. com, $270-$505). The splendid guestrooms are supplemented by 18 private casitas, some with their own pools; public facilities include restaurants (*see above*), six tennis courts, a putting green and five swimming pools, none of which is anything like as nice as the 25-metre beauty at the **Palms at Indian Head** (1-800 519 2624, 1-760 767 7788, www.thepalmsat indianhead.com, $60-$189). The resort was the first in Borrego Springs: opening in 1947, it attracted the likes of Marilyn Monroe before burning to the ground in 1958. Rebuilt in the international modern style, it served time as a prison before revitalised a few years ago. The airy rooms and cottages are decorated in a delightfully sympathetic style.

Those travelling with less cash have a number of choices, of which the nicest is the plain, peaceful **Borrego Valley Inn** (405 Palm Canyon Drive, 1-800 333 5810, 1-760 767 0311, www.borregovalleyinn.com, $110-$250), a southwestern-themed hotel built in 1998. Rooms at the **Borrego Springs Resort** (1112 Tilting T Drive, 1-888 826 7734, 1-760 767 5700, www.borregospringsresort.com, $94-$135) are pretty plain, but the place does have its own golf course. Motels include **Hacienda del Sol** (610 Palm Canyon Drive, 1-760 767 5442, www.haciendadelsol-borrego.com, $70-$130) with a sweet pool and classic neon sign, and the smaller, slightly less appealing **Oasis Motel** (366 Palm Canyon Drive, 1-760 767 5409, www.oasismotelborrego.com, $65-$95).

Resources

Tourist information
Anza-Borrego Desert State Park Visitor Centre *200 Palm Canyon Drive, Borrego Springs (1-760 767 4205/www.anzaborrego.statepark.org).* **Open** *Oct-May* 9am-5pm daily. *June-Sept* 9am-5pm Sat, Sun.
Borrego Springs Chamber of Commerce *786 Palm Canyon Drive, Borrego Springs (1-760 767-5555/1-800 559 5524).* **Open** 9am-4pm Mon-Fri; weekend opening planned for winter.

The Coachella Valley

Palm Springs

Tucked into an abutment of the San Jacinto and Santa Rosa mountain ranges like a sapphire in the crook of a giant's elbow, **Palm Springs** is a treasure that remains unappreciated by most Southern Californians. The common view of the city tends to be as a sort of God's waiting room for wealthy retirees, or a sleepy resort town with little to recommend it other than its expensive golf courses and its legendarily warm climate: 350 days of blue skies a year, and a mercury level that rarely drops below 70°F (21°C) during the day. The truth, however, is rather more complex and alluring.

Because of its dry climate, fresh air and scenic beauty, Palm Springs first found fame as a destination for the infirm and the tubercular, who were able to soothe their aches and pains at the town's eponymous natural springs. But Hollywood began filming silent westerns and Arabian-themed romances (think Rudolph Valentino's *The Sheik*) in the deserts during the 1920s, and Palm Springs quickly transformed itself into a popular winter playground for the Hollywood elite. By the 1950s and '60s, nearly every major American entertainer owned a home in Palm Springs, but the next few decades were far from kind. As long-time residents like Frank Sinatra decamped to more lavish spreads in nearby Palm Desert and Rancho Mirage, Palm Springs became a tawdry tourist trap best known for its rowdy spring-break bacchanals and its preponderance of elderly residents.

Though late mayor Sonny 'I Got You Babe' Bono tends to get most of the credit for turning around the town's increasingly sleazy reputation with his visionary 'no thongs' policy, Palm Springs' recent resurgence is really due to the combination of a healthy economy and an active gay community. Renewed popular interest in mid-century modernist architecture and the opulent trappings of the leisure-obsessed Rat Pack era has also proved a welcome shot in the arm: Palm Springs has them both in spades.

Still, the future of the city remains somewhat cloudy. Current mayor Ron Oden, the first openly gay mayor of any American city, has been portrayed (with some accuracy) as having never met a developer he didn't like; under his tenure, the city council has signed off one ugly, sprawling housing development after another, destroying many of Palm Springs' scenic vistas in its desperation to appear 'business-friendly'. The year-round population of the Coachella Valley (which also includes destinations such as Rancho Mirage, Palm Desert and La Quinta) is swelling, and the number of Palm Springs residents is expected to double within the next ten years, yet the city council has so far made no contingencies to improve the town's already overtaxed water, power, traffic and security systems. Thankfully, the non-profit Palm Springs Modern Committee (www.psmodcom. com) has been actively sounding the alarm about these issues, as part of its continuing mission to preserve Palm Springs' modernist architectural aesthetic and keep the still lovely city from mutating into yet another ugly, anonymous Riverside Country exurb.

Sightseeing

For most visitors, a sojourn in Palm Springs consists of idling around the pool, cocktail in hand. And while that sort of behaviour has much to recommend it, there's plenty to do. The city itself consists simply of a commercial spine: **N Palm Canyon Drive**, where most of the eating and drinking is done, and where a healthy amount of motels, art galleries and souvenir shops are to be found. Groovy mid-century antiques shops abound on Palm Canyon and N Indian Canyon Drive; while bargains are

no longer easy to find, you can still score a lucite table or an Eames-style chair for less than you would pay on LA's Beverly Boulevard.

Though it takes less than an hour to traverse the lengths of Palm Canyon and Indian Canyon by car, it's worth deviating from the main drags. Nearly every turn reveals another eye-popping mountain view, as well as stunning examples of mid-century modern architecture, from simple tract homes with angular 'butterfly' roofs to Jetsonian structures; for more on architecture, *see p162* **Built to last**. It's even worth leaving the car behind entirely, especially on breezy winter days when you can stroll N Palm Canyon Drive or hike the surrounding mountains without ever breaking much of a sweat.

The only thing more pleasing to the eye than Palm Springs' mid-century buildings are the mountains and deserts that surround them. There are hundreds of hiking trails to be found throughout the San Jacintos and Santa Rosas, but the **Indian Canyons** (1-760-325-3400, www.indian-canyons.com), located five miles south of Downtown on S Palm Canyon Drive, are a must-see. Owned and preserved by the Agua Caliente Indians, the Canyons have miles of hiking trails, ranging from the very easy to the extremely arduous, that wind through an

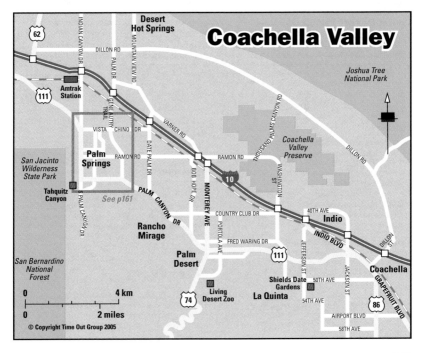

unspoiled wilderness of palm groves, barrel cacti, waterfalls and dramatic rock formations. Be on the lookout for everything from brightly coloured lizards to moody bighorn sheep.

For a total change of ecosystem, and a breathtaking view of the entire Coachella Valley, take the **Palm Springs Aerial Tramway** (1-760 325 1391, www.pstramway.com, $14-$21) to the crest of San Jacinto. The rotating tram cars, allegedly the world's largest, lift you 85,016 feet (25,900 metres) through four different 'life zones' into a lush pine forest where the temperature is typically 30°F to 40°F (18°C to 24°C) cooler than it is back on the desert floor. Aside from the sheer scenic beauty of the destination, it's also worth making the journey just to enjoy a drink or a meal at E Stewart William's **Tramway Mountain Station**, a structure whose exterior and interior have changed little since it was built in the early '60s. From this alpine spot, you can also walk a mile to Idyllwild, a mountain retreat housing a small artsy community and school.

Every Thursday (except holidays), the city blocks off N Palm Canyon from Baristo Road to Amado Road for **Palm Springs VillageFest**, a street party featuring a farmers' market, a variety of arts and crafts vendors and live entertainment. For more, call 1-760 320 3781.

Living Desert Zoo & Gardens

47-900 Portola Avenue, Palm Desert/Indian Wells (1-760 346 5694/www.livingdesert.org). **Open** *Sept-14 June* 9am-5pm daily. *15 June-Aug* 8am-1.30pm daily. **Admission** *Sept-14 June* $10.95; $8.75-$9.50 discounts. *15 June-Aug* $8.75; $4.75-$6.50 discounts. Free under-3s. **Credit** AmEx, MC, V.
This 1,200-acre wildlife and botanical park features rare and endangered animals from both local and African deserts, as well as hundreds of amazing desert plants.

Moorten Botanical Gardens

1701 S Palm Canyon Drive, Palm Springs (1-760 327 6555). **Open** 9am-4.30pm Mon, Tue, Thur-Sat; 10am-4pm Sun. **Admission** $2.50; $1 discounts; free under-5s. **No credit cards.**
An internationally famous (and wilfully eccentric) living museum featuring nature trails, sculpture, rusted-out cars, dinosaur footprints... oh, and 3,000 varieties of cacti, succulents and flowers.

Shields Date Gardens

80-225 Highway 111, Indio (1-760 347 0996). **Open** *Sept-May* 8am-6pm daily. *June-Aug* 9am-5pm daily. **Admission** free.
The Coachella Valley is the self-proclaimed 'Date Capital of the World', and a visit to Shields Date Gardens is one of the area's oldest tourist traditions. Stop by for a tour (featuring the steamy documentary 'The Sex Life of the Date') and try a delicious (if highly calorific) date shake.

Palm Springs Air Museum

745 North Gene Autry Trail, Palm Springs (1-760 778 6262/www.palmspringsairmuseum.org). **Open** *Oct-May* 10am-5pm daily. *June-Sept* 9am-3pm daily. **Admission** $8; $4-$7 discounts; free under-5s. **Credit** AmEx, Disc, MC, V.
Located across the runway from the Palm Springs International Airport, this museum boasts an impressive collection of propeller-driven World War II aircraft, many of which are still in flying condition. Old aviation films are screened in the 60-seat Buddy Rogers Theatre of the Air, and old-timers and collectors alike regularly take their old jalopies up for demonstration flights.

Tahquitz Canyon

500 W Mesquite, Palm Springs (1-760 416 7044). **Open** *Oct-May* 7.30am-5pm daily. *Tours* Oct-May 8am, 10am, noon, 2pm. **Admission** $12.50; $6 discounts; free under-3s. **Credit** AmEx, MC, V.
This beautiful and sacred Agua Caliente refuge has recently reopened for guided tours. It's a nice way to experience the natural beauty of the area without wearing out your legs, though even here you're in for a moderately strenuous hike.

Village Green Heritage Center

221 South Palm Canyon Drive, Palm Springs (1-760 323 8297/1-760 327 2156). **Open** *Mid Oct-Apr* noon-3pm Wed; 10am-4pm Thur-Sat; noon-3pm Sun. **Admission** $1. **No credit cards.**
Sitting incongruously amid the boutiques and restaurants of Palm Canyon Drive is this humble collection of buildings that hark back to the days before air-conditioning, when white pioneers first settled in Palm Springs. Attractions include the McCallum Adobe, which was built in 1885 from native soil, and Miss Cornelia White's house, which was built from railroad ties in 1893. There's also Ruddy's General Store Museum, which recreates the look and stock of a general store from the 1930s and '40s.

Where to eat

The last half-decade has seen improvements in Palm Springs' cuisine, but many restaurants still seem geared towards an elderly local clientele who have long since smoked their tastebuds into oblivion. Mediocre Mexican food dominates, but there are also more lousy Italian joints than you can shake a breadstick at. Those looking along Palm Canyon should remember that just because a restaurant is crowded, it doesn't mean the food is any good. Many Palm Springs restaurants and bars close during July, August and September.

Al Dente Pasta

491 N Palm Canyon Drive (1-760 325 1160/www.aldente-palmsprings.com). **Open** 11am-4pm, 4.30-10.30pm daily. **Average** $$$. **Credit** DC, MC, V.
This Tuscan trattoria might not have the Rat Pack atmosphere you'd perhaps expect from a Palm Springs Italian restaurant, but the incredible food

Palm Springs

W SAN RAFAEL RD
N PALM CANYON DR
VISTA CHINO
INDIAN CANYON DRIVE
PALM CANYON DR
AVENIDA CABALLEROS
TACHEVAH RD
TAMARISK RD
Palm Springs Air Museum
ALEJO RD
FARRELL DR
O'Donnell Golf Course
AMADO RD
SUNRISE WAY
TAHQUITZ CANYON WAY
Palm Springs Desert Museum
BARISTO RD
RAMON RD
EL CIELO
SUNNY DUNES RD
MESQUITE AVE
111
SONORA RD
E PALM CANYON DR
Moorten Botanical Gardens
LAVERNE WAY

0   1 km
0   0.5 mile
© Copyright Time Out Group 2005

Palm Springs Aerial Tramway. *See p160.*

more than makes up for any perceived shortcomings on the atmosphere score. Don't miss the crab-filled ravioli with brandy-cream sauce.

Bit of Country
418 S Indian Canyon Drive (1-760 325 5154).
Open 6am-2pm daily. **Average** $. **Credit** Disc, MC, V.
The tourists may go to IHOP down the street, but locals know that the Bit of Country offers the best-value breakfast in town. Expect friendly staff, good people-watching, and the most addictive biscuits and gravy this side of the Rio Grande.

Blame It On Midnight
777 E Tahquitz Canyon Way (1-760 323 1200/ www.blameitonmidnight.com). **Open** 5-10pm Mon-Thur, Sun; 5-11pm Fri, Sat. **Average** $$. **Credit** AmEx, MC, V.
Imagine a gay Bennigan's or Appelby's, with a large black woman singing disco soul karaoke in the corner, and you'll have some idea what to expect from this Palm Springs institution. The food (burgers, chicken strips and the like) is actually quite good, and straights are as welcome as the ubiquitous friends of Dorothy.

Blue Coyote Grill
445 N Palm Canyon Drive (1-760 327 1196).
Open 10am-10pm Mon-Thur, Sun; 10am-11pm Fri, Sat. **Average** $$$. **Credit** AmEx, DC, MC, V.
A perennial favourite with the tourist crowds, Blue Coyote actually serves pretty decent Southwestern cuisine. Of course, after a couple of their Margaritas, you wouldn't mind if they served you shoe leather with jalapeño sauce.

Davey's Hideaway
292 E Palm Canyon Drive (1-760 320 4480).
Open 5-9.30pm daily. **Average** $$$. **Credit** AmEx, DC, Disc, MC, V.
This old-school purveyor of American comfort food is favoured by locals who come back time after time for the thick steaks and the convivial piano bar.

The Deck
262 S Palm Canyon Drive (1-760 325 5200). **Open** 11.30am-10pm Mon-Thur, Sun; 11.30am-midnight Fri, Sat. **Average** $$$. **Credit** AmEx, DC, Disc, MC, V.
Located upstairs from the rather pedestrian and overpriced Chop House, the Deck is one of the best places in town to meet someone for a late afternoon or early evening cocktail. Grab a seat on the patio, and watch the lights come up on Palm Canyon as the sun sets over Mount San Jacinto. Excellent fried calamari, too.

Kaiser Grille
205 S Palm Canyon Drive (1-760 323 1003/www.kaisergrille.com). **Open** 11.30am-3.30pm, 5-10pm daily. **Average** $$$. **Credit** AmEx, DC, Disc, MC, V.
One of the more reliable establishments along Palm Canyon, the Kaiser serves excellent and inexpensive continental favourites in a setting that's both sleek and comfortable. The well-appointed, roomy bar is a pleasant place to wait for an open table, should you have to.

Lyons English Grille
233 E Palm Canyon Drive (1-760 327 1551).
Open Oct-May 4.30-10pm daily. **Average** $$$. **Credit** AmEx, DC, MC, V.

Built to last

It has been said that what art deco did for Miami Beach in the 1980s, modernism is today doing for Palm Springs. Paradise for lovers of mid-century architecture, the city can make you feel like you've travelled 40 or 50 years back in time. Though many of the city's great structures have been razed or remodelled beyond recognition, you can still find gems by such modernist architects as William Cody, Richard Neutra, John Lautner, Donald Wexler, E Stuart Williams and Albert Frey in the area. Indeed, Frey's classic 1963 **Tramway Gas Station**, a dramatically angled structure at the town entrance that has come perilously close to demolition, has recently been renovated to serve as the Palm Springs Bureau of Tourism's Visitor Information Center (*see p166*).

It's far from the only must-see modernist site, however. The upside-down arches of E Stewart Williams' **Washington Mutual Bank** (499 S Palm Canyon Drive) were built in 1961 across the street from Rudy Baumfeld's blue-tiled 1959 **Bank of America Building** (588 S Palm Canyon Drive). William Cody's sensually curved **St Theresa's Church** (2800 E Ramon Road), built in 1968, almost makes church-going seem cool, and is just a quick drive from the equally fantastic **Palm Springs City Hall** at 3200 E Taqhuitz Canyon Way (Albert Frey, 1952) and the nearby **Palm Springs International Airport** (Donald Wexler, 1965).

A map to over 50 significant mid-century residential and commercial structures is available from the **Palm Springs Modern Committee** (www.psmodcom.com). But it's also fun to just get lost in the winding streets of the ritzy Las Palmas and Little Tuscany locales west of Palm Canyon Drive at the foot of Mount San Jacinto, where hundreds of ranch-style modern mansions have been preserved in all of their space-age glory. Celebrity homes can be difficult to identify, but the most famous ones are Frank Sinatra's **Twin Palms** (1148 E Alejo Road), where Ol' Blue Eyes lived and fought with Ava Gardner, and Liberace's Spanish-style **Casa de Liberace** (501 N Belardo Road), still adorned with the pianist's trademark 'L' logo.

From top: Rudy Baumfeld's **Bank of America Building**; **Palm Springs City Hall**, designed by Albert Frey; **Washington Mutual Bank**, by E Stewart Williams.

A Palm Springs institution, Lyons may have seen better days but it's still a reliable place for a steak, a scotch and the sort of dark, clubby atmosphere that Dean Martin would no doubt have appreciated.

More Than a Mouthful

134 E Tahquitz Canyon Way (1-760 322 3776). **Open** 7.30am-2.30pm Mon, Wed-Sun. **Average** $$. **Credit** MC, V.

A welcome recent addition to the Downtown dining scene, this small café specialises in breakfast and lunch dishes that, like the name implies, will keep your jaw working overtime. The service can be a bit curt, but the food is excellent.

Riccio's

2155 N Palm Canyon Drive (1-760 325 2369/ www.riccios-palmsprings.com). **Open** 11.30am-2.30pm, 5pm-midnight Tue-Sat. **Average** $$$$. **Credit** AmEx, DC, Disc, MC, V.

With old Palm Springs favourites Sorrentino's and Banducci's now sadly gone, Riccio's is one of the last true old-school Italian joints in the Coachella Valley. The menu is extremely pricey, but you get your money's worth from the dark, romantic atmosphere, the delicious pasta and seafood, and a staff right out of *Goodfellas*.

Shermans Deli & Bakery

401 E Tahquitz Canyon Way (1-760 325 1199). **Open** 7am-9pm daily. **Average** $. **Credit** AmEx, MC, V.

Those craving hot pastrami, creamed herring or bagels and lox are hereby directed to this desert standby, which has been serving New York-style Jewish soul food since the 1960s.

Thai Smile Restaurant

651 N Palm Canyon Drive (1-760 320 5503). **Open** 11.30am-4pm, 5-10pm daily. **Average** $. **Credit** AmEx, MC, V.

The best Thai restaurant in a town that's nearly over-run with them, Thai Smile gets the nod for friendly service, expansive portions, and designated 'spicy' dishes that will blow your head off, in a good way.

Tyler's

149 S Indian Canyon Drive (1-760 325 2990). **Open** 11am-4pm Mon-Sat. **Average** $$. **No credit cards**. The best hamburgers in town – and possibly in all of California – are served at this converted bus station in the heart of downtown Palm Springs. Try their Sliders, which are far, far superior to the White Castle items of the same name.

Where to drink

Though the local Chamber of Commerce likes to boast that Palm Springs 'comes alive at night', the sad fact is that the town generally goes pretty quiet around 9pm. The **Village Pub** (266 S Palm Canyon Drive, 1-760 323 3265) features live country and alternative music and gets pretty rowdy, while the Casablanca

Lounge at **Ingleside Inn** (*see p164*) is good for Rat Pack-style lounge entertainment. The **Atlas Restaurant & Dance Club** (200 S Palm Canyon Drive, 1-760 325 8839, closed Mon & Tue) seems to be the only place on earth that hasn't heard that the swing music revival is dead, which may be why the once-hopping club is often woefully empty. **Zeldaz** (169 N Indian Canyon Drive, 1-760 325 2375, closed Mon-Wed & Sun) packs in the singles with upbeat Latin sounds and promotions like bikini contests.

Gay & lesbian nightlife

In truth, Palm Springs nights belong to the city's gay contingent. Happening homo bars include **Badlands** (200 S Indian Canyon, 1-760 778 4326), **Hunter's Video Bar** (302 E Arenas Road, 1-760 323 0700), the tropical-themed **Toucan's Tiki Lounge** (2100 N Palm Canyon Drive, 1-760 416 7584) and the leather-intensive **Tool Shed** (600 Sunny Dunes Road, 1-760 320 3299). Though these establishments tend to be patronised primarily by locals, the gay tourist dollar is very strong in Palm Springs.

Two of Southern California's biggest gay parties take place each year in the Palm Springs area: the **LPGA Nabisco Golf Tournament** (aka the Dinah Shore Tournament) and the **White Party**. The former, held each March at the Mission Hills Country Club in Rancho Mirage, is the lesbian social event of the year. The latter was started in the late '80s by Jeffrey Sanker as a spring getaway for his gay male friends, but has grown into a city-wide weekend party that attracts upwards of 15,000 gay men each April. Over the years, city officials have tried to put the kibosh on the event, but they've never managed to gain widespread support. Mayor Ron Oden, on the other hand, authored an official proclamation in 2004, commending the party's 15th anniversary, which means it's probably here to stay for the foreseeable future.

Arts & entertainment

Sure, there's plenty of golf art to be found in Palm Springs, and the oddly proportioned bronze statues of Lucille Ball and Sonny Bono along Palm Canyon Drive aren't exactly on a par with Auguste Rodin. But that said, there's still a decent amount of bona fide culture here. Palm Canyon Drive has a variety of galleries, with the pop-oriented **M Modern Gallery** (448 N Palm Canyon Drive, 1-760 416 3611, www.mmoderngallery.com, closed Mon-Thur) and the Southwestern/Latin-leaning **Adagio Galleries** (193 S Palm Canyon Drive, 1-760 320 2230, www.adagiogalleries.com, closed Tue & Wed) offering the most consistently interesting shows. On N Palm Canyon, many galleries and antiques shops celebrate the first Friday of the month by staying open until the decadent hour of 9pm; some offer free refreshments and stage live music. There's also the **Palm Springs Desert Museum** (101 Museum Drive, 1-760 325 7186, www.psmuseum.org, closed Mon, $3.50-$7.50), housed in an appealing mid 1970s structure designed by E Stewart Williams.

If you want to catch a movie, the **Camelot Theatres** (2300 E Baristo Road, 1-760 325 6565, www.camelottheatres.com), which hosts January's Palm Springs International Film Festival, offer an intriguing array of arthouse and low-budget films. **Courtyard 10** (789 E Tahquitz Canyon Way, 1-760 322 3456) leans more towards the commercial. The nearby **Desert IMAX Theatre** (68-510 E Palm Canyon Drive, Cathedral City, 1-760 324 7333), runs large-format films (and is housed in one of the valley's ugliest buildings).

Considering the town's ties with the entertainment world, it's not surprising that a great many showbiz types have retired here – or that, once retired, they would seek new outlets for their performing abilities. Hence the **Fabulous Palm Springs Follies**, an old-time vaudeville revue featuring musicians, jugglers, acrobats, comedians and dancing chorus 'girls'. The revue runs November to May at the **Historic Plaza Theatre** (128 S Palm Canyon Drive, 1-760 327 0225, www.psfollies.com).

Where to stay

Palm Springs has no shortage of lodging options, from a variety of chain motels (*see p54*) to the last word in luxury resorts. Some are less child-friendly than others, while many are geared to a gay clientele; as always, it pays to phone ahead or check online.

Ballantines Movie Colony

1420 N Indian Canyon Drive (1-760 320 1178/ www.ballantineshotels.com). **Rates** $149-$265 double. **Credit** AmEx, DC, MC, V.
This retro-style hotel on the western edge of the old Movie Colony neighbourhood was built in the 1930s by Albert Frey, and features 17 uniquely designed theme rooms. Most are cool, but some – such as the Marilyn Monroe room – are nauseatingly kitsch.

Caliente Tropics Resort

411 E Palm Canyon Drive (1-760 327 1391/ www.calientetropics.com). **Rates** $149-$205 double. **Credit** AmEx, Disc, MC, V.
A must for tiki worshippers, the Caliente Tropics is a faux-Polynesian playground built in 1963, and renovated in 2001 after a period of neglect. Imposing tiki figures guard the pool and parking lot, both of which are lit up at night by (of course) tiki torches. The Reef Tiki Bar is open at weekends.

East Canyon Hotel & Spa

288 E Camino Monte Vista (1-760 320 1928/ www.eastcanyonhotel.com). **Rates** $149-$229 double. **Credit** AmEx, MC, V.
The only gay men's hotel in town with its own full-service spa, this luxurious spot is also famed for its excellent breakfast buffet.

Ingleside Inn

200 W Ramon Road (1-760 325 0046/ www.inglesideinn.com). **Rates** $100-$165 double. **Credit** AmEx, DC, Disc, MC, V.
Built in 1925 as a private residence and a favourite with celebs since 1975, Mel Haber's Ingleside Inn (also home to Melvyn's restaurant and the Casablanca

Send yourself into **Orbit**. *See p165.*

Lounge) features 30 suites, mini-suites and private villas. The decor may be too frou-frou for many, but the place's comfort and service are legendary.

Inndulge
601 Grenfall Road (1-760 327 1408/www.inndulge. com). **Rates** $115-$149 double. **Credit** AmEx, DC, Disc, MC, V.
A clothing-optional gay men's resort in the heart of the Warm Sands neighbourhood. Pool and 'ten-man' jacuzzi are open 24 hours daily. Several all-male porn films have reputedly been shot on the premises.

Korakia
257 S Patencio Road (1-760 864 6411/www. korakia.com). **Rates** $129-$289 double. **Credit** AmEx, MC, V.
This ornate Arabian Nights fantasy actually incorporates two villas into its sumptuous grounds: one Moroccan in style, the other Mediterranean. A favourite with the current crop of Hollywood movers and shakers, this is the place to go for some serious star treatment, even if you aren't one.

Orbit In Oasis & Hideaway
1-760 323 3585/www.orbitin.com.
Oasis *562 W Arenas.* **Rates** $139-$289 double.
Hideaway *370 W Arenas.* **Rates** $119-$269 double.
Both **Credit** AmEx, DC, Disc, MC, V.
These two mid-century sister motor court hotels are within walking distance of each other. Both have been expertly renovated and appointed with stunning modern furniture by Eames, Noguchi et al. The Oasis, which has a small outdoor bar next to its swimming pool (and free 'Orbitinis' at happy hour…), is the livelier of the two. Both offer gorgeous mountain views and free bicycle rental, so you can pedal around nearby downtown Palm Springs.

Orchid Tree Inn
261 S Belardo Road (1-760 325 2791). **Rates** $79-$95 double. **Credit** AmEx, Disc, MC, V.
Nestled peacefully in the wind-sheltered area of the Tennis Club Historic District, the historic Orchid Tree is a charming and tranquil Spanish-style desert garden retreat. Its cluster of tile-roofed Spanish bungalows was built in 1934.

Palm Springs Riviera Resort
1600 N Indian Canyon Drive (1-760 327 8311/ www.psriviera.com). **Rates** $69-$169 double.
Credit AmEx, DC, Disc, MC, V.
This massive 24-acre complex features 476 rooms, three buildings and two large pools. It was the location for the 1963 film *Palm Springs Weekend*, starring Connie Stevens and Stefanie Powers, and the home away from home of the Los Angeles (then California, then Anaheim) Angels when they used to hold spring training in Palm Springs.

The Willows
412 W Tahquitz Canyon Way (1-760 320 0771/ www.thewillowspalmsprings.com). **Rates** $250-$575 double. **Credit** AmEx, DC, Disc, MC, V.

Hope Springs *(p166)*: cool digs, hot pools.

Built in 1927, this attractive eight-room Spanish-style inn was the scene of Carole Lombard and Clark Gable's honeymoon, and is still incredibly romantic.

Other towns

Cathedral City

Conveniently located on the eastern border of Palm Springs, **Cathedral City** was once home to an impressive assortment of dives, casinos and brothels: the sort of things Palm Springs residents didn't want in their own city, but were happy to patronise in someone else's. These days, the excitement has faded, but the tawdriness remains; if you've heard of Cathedral City, it's probably because episodes of the reality TV show *Cops* were filmed here. The two biggest attractions are the **Desert IMAX**

Theatre (*see p164*) and the **Desert Memorial Park** cemetery (69-920 E Ramon Road), where Frank Sinatra and Busby Berkeley are buried.

Desert Hot Springs

Desert Hot Springs has long been a poor relation to its southern neighbour. True, there isn't much to do here, but the place is so named for a reason, and that reason is enough to draw many people here to soak in its recuperative waters. The best places to do this are **Two Bunch Palms** (67425 Two Bunch Palms Trail, 1-760 329 8791, www.twobunchpalms.com, $175-$295), the **Desert Hot Springs Resort** (10805 Palm Drive, 1-760 329 6000, www.dhsspa.com, $89-$139) and, especially, the chic, stylish **Hope Springs** motel (68075 Club Circle Drive, 1-760 329 4003, www.hopespringsresort.com, $160-$185). If you don't require a soak check the **Desert Hot Springs Motel** (cnr of Yerxa Road & San Antonio, 1-760 288 2280, www.lautnermotel.com, $135-$170), a lovingly restored treasure built in 1947 by John Lautner.

Indian Wells

One of the richest cities in California, this enclave of gated communities, golf courses and tennis courts hosts the Tennis Master Series Indian Wells Tournament every March. Top lodgings include the **Miramonte Resort** (45000 Indian Wells Lane, 1-760 341 2200, www.miramonteresort.com, $89-$229) and the **Renaissance Esmeralda Resort** (45-400 Indian Wells Lane, 1-760 773 4444, www.renaissancehotels.com, $99-$339).

Indio

Originally founded as a Southern Pacific Railroad distribution point in the late 1800s, Indio is now home to a thriving date industry, as well as the popular Native American-owned **Fantasy Springs Casino** (84-245 Indio Springs Drive, 1-760 342 5000) and two polo grounds. The latter is the location of the **Coachella Music Festival**, a two-day orgy of alternative sounds that attracts over 50,000 music fans. Other festivities include the **Indio International Tamale Festival** (first week in December), the **National Date Festival** (*see p60*) and the **Indio Desert Circuit Horse Show**, six weeks beginning in January.

La Quinta

Comfortably nestled inside a bend of the Santa Rosa mountain range, La Quinta is famous for its dark nights (local ordinances forbid bright lights), its golf courses and tennis courts, and the opulence of the **La Quinta Resort** (49-499 Eisenhower Drive, 1-760 564 4111, www.laquintaresort.com, $135-$395), which was built in 1926 and still retains an aura of Hollywood's Golden Age.

Palm Desert

Palm Desert comes off like a cross between the San Fernando Valley and Beverly Hills, at least from a commercial standpoint. Not only does it boast more big strip malls and chain stores than anywhere else in the Valley, but it also has **El Paseo**, the region's ritzy answer to Rodeo Drive, which features dozens of ridiculously high-priced boutiques and jewellery stores. The less materialistic can visit the **Living Desert Zoo & Gardens** (*see p160*) or the **Desert Holocaust Memorial at Palm Desert Civic Center Park** (San Pablo Avenue, at Fred Waring Drive).

Rancho Mirage

Home of the Betty Ford rehabilitation centre, Rancho Mirage has a lot of beautiful mansions and not much else. But since you'll probably be driving through it at some point on your way to Palm Desert or Indio, keep your eye out for **Haleiwa Joe's** (69-934 Highway 111, 1-760 324 5613, $). The Hawaiian-fusion food isn't much to write home about, but the building (designed in 1968 by Kendrick Bangs Kellogg) looks a bit like a UFO that's crash-landed into the side of a hill.

Resources

Hospital
Palm Springs *Desert Regional Medical Center, 1150 N Indian Canyon Drive (1-760 323 6511/ www.desertmedctr.com).*

Internet
Palm Springs *Log-On, 1775 E Palm Canyon Drive (1-760 325 0077).* **Open** 9am-9pm Mon-Fri; 9am-6pm Sat, Sun.

Police
Palm Springs *200 S Civic Drive (1-760 323 8116).*

Post office
Palm Springs *333 E Amado Road (1-760 322 4111).*

Tourist information
Palm Springs *Palm Springs Visitor Information Center, 2901 N Palm Canyon Drive (1-800 347 7746/1-760 778 8418/www.palm-springs.org).* **Open** 9am-5pm Mon-Thur, Sun; 9am-5.30pm Fri, Sat.

Joshua Tree

Joshua Tree National Park

North of Palm Springs, the desert valley gives way to massive granite monoliths and strange, jagged trees with spiky blooms. These are Joshua trees, a form of cactus named by early Mormon settlers after the prophet Joshua, which they believed pointed the way to the Promised Land. The trees lend their name to **Joshua Tree National Park**, a mecca for modern-day explorers that's home to wildlife, 17 different types of cactus, palm-studded oases, ancient petroglyphs and spectacular rock formations.

The 794,000-acre park straddles two desert ecosystems, the Mojave and Colorado. The remote eastern half, once inhabited by the Pinto tribe, is dominated by cholla cactus, small creosote bushes and some adrenaline-pumping 4WD routes. The cooler and wetter western section, with its trademark rocks and twisty trees, is what the Joshua Tree tourists come to see. And it's a stone's throw from three pit stops – Yucca Valley, Joshua Tree village and Twentynine Palms – along Highway 62 (aka Twentynine Palms Highway).

William F Keys, a cattleman and mining partner of Walter Scott (aka Death Valley Scotty), discovered the beauty of the area in 1910, when he was hired to run the Desert Queen Mine. After it closed in 1917, Keys homesteaded 160 acres and called it Desert Queen Ranch. Tours lasting 90 minutes chronicle 60 years of Key family history in this rocky canyon (reservations essential; 1-760 367 5555).

Now known as **Hidden Valley** and **Wonderland of Rocks,** the area is a virtual candy shop of climbs, hikes and picnic spots stretching as far as the eye can see. More than 100 million years ago, seismic activity from the nearby San Andreas Fault shaped this part of the park. Molten liquid oozed upwards from the earth's crust and cooled below the surface. Flash floods eventually washed away the ground cover, exposing towers, domes and spires of monzogranite that draw millions of would-be Spidermen today. The most popular of the park's 4,500 climbing routes are located here. **Sports Challenge Rock** is a favourite of experienced climbers; **Echo Rock** is where rookie rappellers test their mettle. One Saturday a month, near the new moon, the Andromeda Astronomical Society hosts a stargazing party at the Hidden Valley picnic area.

For walking, hiking or scrambling, more than 12 nature trails revisit remnants of the gold mining era. The one-mile **Hidden Valley** loop winds around a dramatic, rock-enclosed valley, used by cattle rustlers in the 1800s. Nearby **Barker Dam Trail** leads to a lake built by early ranchers, and Native American petroglyphs. At dusk, it's possible to spot rare bighorn sheep taking a sip. Feast your eyes on

Southern California

Joshua Tree National Park.

some of the park's most fascinating formations, hiking all or part of the 16-mile **Boy Scout Trail**. Down the road, 5,461-foot (1,665-metre) **Ryan Mountain** delights peak-baggers with a strenuous three-hour trek topped off by views of Mount San Jacinto and Mount San Gorgonio.

Keys View, due south of Hidden Valley, is worth a side trip; on a clear day, you can see all the way to Mexico. Here you can also pick up 18-mile **Geology Tour Road** (high clearance vehicles are a must) showing off some of Joshua Tree's most dramatic landscapes. Off-road adventures continue on **Berdoo Canyon Road**, which intersects Geology Tour Road and passes the ruins of a camp constructed in the '30s by builders of the California Aqueduct. During the sizzling days of summer, head south to the Cottonwood Visitor Center. The 3.7-mile **Lost Palm Oasis Trail**, a lush, leafy grove with trickling water, offers welcome relief. The challenging, 20-mile **Pinkham Canyon** 4WD road also starts here, and ends at a service road along I-10.

From Yucca Valley, **Covington Flats Road** takes you to the park's largest Joshua trees; toward the end, the road gets fairly steep and offers excellent views of Palm Springs and the Morongo Basin. Some 35 miles of the **California Hiking and Biking Trail** start from adjacent **Black Rock Canyon campground.** Some 253 miles of horseback-riding paths also criss-cross the park.

Getting there

Joshua Tree can be reached from the south via I-10, or from the north via Highway 62 in the towns of Joshua Tree and 29 Palms. Admission is $10 per vehicle and is good for one week.

Yucca Valley

This sprawling suburban town named after the local desert plant is the gateway to **Pioneertown** (www.pioneertown.com) a better-than-average tourist trap about five miles off Highway 62. Originally a set for movies and TV (*The Cisco Kid* was filmed here) and now a working, if tiny, Main Street, it retains an Old West feel, and its dirt roads make you realise why so many cowboys were called Dusty. There are occasional gunfight demonstrations near the old post office, and a bowling alley/saloon/arcade built for Roy Rogers.

Yucca Valley is also home to the **Hi-Desert Nature Museum** (57-116 Twentynine Palms Highway, 1-760 369 7212, www.yucca-valley. org/visitors/museum/museum.html, closed Mon), which features a number of interesting dioramas and exhibits about the area's wildlife

and history. Those who prefer their nature unmediated will be more inclined towards the **Pipes Canyon Preserve** outside of town, owned by a private conservation group and every bit as wild as a national park. Ask at the visitor centre (*see p170*) for information about cougars, bears and bobcats, petroglyphs and active springs. Admission is free.

Where to eat & drink

Once a cantina set for numerous westerns, **Pappy & Harriet's Pioneertown Palace** (53688 Pioneertown Road, 1-760 365 5956, closed Tue & Wed, $$) is now a popular local hangout serving heaped portions of mesquite BBQ and live country music. For quieter tunes with a cup o' joe, try **Water Canyon Coffee Co** (55844 Twentynine Palms Highway & Pioneertown Road, 1-760 365 7771, $). **Stefano's Giardino** (55509 Twentynine Palms Highway, 1-760 228 3118, closed lunch Sun, $$), a gem of an Italian restaurant, is heavy on atmosphere and garlic.

Where to stay

The **Pioneertown Motel** (Pioneertown Road, 1-760 365 4879, $55-$200) once hosted movie stars such as Barbara Stanwyck when they worked on films out here. Its 22 rooms recently got a much-needed makeover under new owners Scott and Stacy Samuels.

Joshua Tree Village

Joshua Tree is one of the smaller national parks, but it's big with rock climbers... and rock stars. The 2003 release of *Grand Theft Parsons*, a caper movie about the demise of singer Gram Parsons at the nearby **Joshua Tree Inn**, brought renewed fame to this desert town after its first starring role in U2's *The Joshua Tree*.

In nearby **Landers**, a different sort of music plays in the acoustically perfect **Integratron** (2477 Belfield Boulevard, 1-760 364 3126). UFO pioneer George Van Tassel built the domed tabernacle in the '60s as a healing and time machine that, to this day, invites curious customers to take a 'sound bath'. Van Tassel was also known for leading séances at **Giant Rock**, a 23,000-ton boulder and energy vortex, three miles away. Legend has it a cave under the rock was 'home' to a gold-rush-era prospector.

Where to eat & drink

Locals swear by the **Crossroads Café** (61715 Twentynine Palms Highway, 1-760 366 5414, closed Wed, $$), a Woodstock-style eatery that serves huge salads, veggie burgers and smoothies. **Tommy Paul's Beatnik Café** (61597 Twentynine Palms Highway, 1-760 366 2090, $$) is better known for its music than its food, but it does serve 'designer pizzas' named after local musicians. Newcomer **Park Visitor Café** (6554 Park Boulevard, 1-760 366 3622, $) is a great place to stock up on take-out (the coriander tabouleh is to die for) for a hike or evening picnic in the park.

Where to stay

Spanish hacienda-style **Joshua Tree Inn** (61259 Twentynine Palms Highway, Joshua Tree, 1-760 366 1188, www.joshuatreeinn.com, $75-$145) was built in the 1950s as a getaway for silver-screen stars, but rock star guests put it on the map. The Byrds, the Rolling Stones and the Eagles all stayed here in their heyday; room 8 is where Gram Parsons spent his final hours, and is supposedly haunted. **Rosebud Ruby Star** (1-877 887 7370, 1-760 366 4676, www.rosebudrubystar.com, $140-$155) is a jewel of a B&B near the park entrance with two artist-decorated rooms and an original homestead cabin for groups. In the national park, there are nine campsites, but only two with water. **Hidden Valley** and **Jumbo Rocks** (near the Twentynine Palms entrance) are most popular and fill up early in high season (October to May). Fees are $5-$10; some sites accept reservations (call 1-800 365 2267), while others are first-come, first-served.

Twentynine Palms

The small, uninteresting town of **Twentynine Palms** is one of those places where clusters of mailboxes testify that most things go on off the highway. It's home to the world's largest Marine base and the **Oasis of Mara**, a lush desert spring that stretches across part of the national park and nearby **Twentynine Palms Inn** (*see p170*). Originally inhabited by the Chemehuevi and Serrano Indians, the oasis was discovered by US military surveyor Colonel Henry Washington in 1855 and later by homesteaders. The area's rich history is depicted in 17 gigantic paintings (the **Oasis of Murals**, www.oasisofmurals.com) on walls throughout Downtown.

From town, it's just five miles to the park's **Jumbo Rocks** campgrounds, where locals often go to stargaze. For something truly different, get a modern haircut surrounded by beauty equipment dating back to the 1800s at kitschy **Beauty Bubble Salon & Museum** (1-760 361 5617) in nearby Wonder Valley. It opens Wednesday and Thursday, as well as Saturdays by appointment.

Mojave National Preserve. *See p170.*

Where to eat & drink

You won't have trouble finding an edible meal here, but tracking down a memorable one might prove tougher. **Twentynine Palms Inn** (*see below*; $$$) is the best bet for steaks, chops and veggies from its own garden (yes, in the desert). Locals line up for finger-lickin' goodies at the **Rib Company** (72183 Twentynine Palms Highway, 1-760 367 1663, closed lunch, $$) and greasy burritos at **Santana's Mexican Food** (73680 Sun Valley, 1-760 361 0202, $). The **Wonder Garden Café** (73511 Twentynine Palms Highway, 1-760 367 2429, $) is the place to come for a healthier class of sandwich.

Where to stay

Skip the plain-vanilla motels on Highway 62 in favour of quirky **Twentynine Palms Inn** (73950 Inn Avenue, 1-760 367 3505, www.29palmsinn.com, $50-$295). Owned by the same family since 1928, the hotel features adobe bungalows, historic cabins, a funky poolside bar/restaurant and plenty of local colour. Old Frame 1&2, a cabin hideaway on the pond, is a favourite. The charming **Homestead Inn B&B** (74153 Two Mile Road, 1-877 367 0030, 1-760 367 0030, www.joshuatreelodging.com, $95-$160) has six tastefully decorated rooms, all with private baths. The 1950s-style **Harmony Motel** (711661 Twentynine Palms Highway, 1-760 367 3351, www.harmonymotel.com, $60-$100) doesn't look like much, and it isn't, but the place where U2 stayed while recording *The Joshua Tree* offers cheap sleep with a little nostalgia. Six hilltop rooms and one cabin are sparsely decorated with jute rugs and minimalist etchings.

Tourist information

Pipes Canyon Preserve *51010 Pipes Canyon Road (1-760 369 7105).* **Open** dawn to dusk.
Twentynine Palms *Joshua Tree National Park Visitor Center (1-760 367 5500/www.nps.gov/jotr).* **Open** 8am-5pm daily. There's a smaller visitor centre (8am-4pm daily) at the Cottonwood Spring entrance to the park.

Mojave National Preserve

Covering a gigantic rectangle bordered by I-15 to the north and I-40 to the south, the 2,500-square-mile **Mojave National Preserve** is something of a Cinderella park: it has no honeypot attractions, low visitorship and few facilities. Rather, it is a giant and fascinating desert sampler. The meeting point of three of the four types of North American desert – Mojave, Great Basin and Sonoran – it contains a variety of terrains, geological features and ecosystems, including the human. Because its protected status is relatively recent (it was upgraded from a Scenic Area to a National Preserve in 1994), historical relics of inhabitants and would-be conquerors from early man through to 20th-century ranchers, dreamers and miners dot the landscape. Spanish explorers, western pioneers and routefinders, soldiers, navvies and settlers passed this way, leaving behind roads and railroads still in use today, along with historic buildings well preserved in the dry, warm air.

Mojave National Preserve has been developed only minimally, with just three marked trails and gas and accommodation available only

The snake-oil saint

Just west of Baker, a short road dead-ends into the park. The fact that it's called Zzyzx Road should tip you off that it doesn't lead to any normal destination. At the end is **Soda Springs**, home to the usual Mojave characters plus, from 1944 to 1974, Dr Curtis Springer. It was Springer who founded the lavish Zzyzx resort, which at its peak contained a 60-room hotel, a church, a castle and an airstrip called Zyport. Purveying healthful mineral baths (in indoor baths and a cruciform pool) and the word of God (via the resort radio station, picked up by 200 broadcasters nationwide), the white-clad Curtis made such a packet from the enterprise that the tax authorities got a little too interested, as did the American Medical Association and later the Bureau of Land Management over his land rights. Springer died in exile from his Shangri-La still bitterly contesting his eviction.

Zzyzx is now a Desert Studies Center, but is Mojave National Preserve land, so you can wander around freely. The resort's structures are visible on either side of Springer's Boulevard of Dreams, now a dirt road to nowhere. It is worth noting that most of the nostrums that sent Springer down as a quack contained celery, carrot and parsley juice.

The highway that's the best

The town of **Barstow**, like a number of its neighbours, grew up around its railroad. Trains run through here even now, but as is the case with most former railroad towns, the majority are mile-long monsters shipping commercial goods across the country, crawling through the Californian night with a hoot and a holler. An Amtrak passenger service still stops in Barstow, but these days, it's hard to imagine anyone disembarking at its station for anything other than a journey-breaking piss.

Barstow was a thriving town a half-century or so ago; those travellers not riding trains through the town were driving into it on Route 66. Even people who'd never visited the place knew its name from its appearance, between Kingman and San Bernardino, in the lyrics to Bobby Troup's much-covered ode to the Mother Road. But as the railroad network faded and the interstate system grew, Barstow struggled to adjust. Drivers today use I-15 instead of Route 66, which is now known only as Main Street and has faded dramatically since its glory days. Back before rock 'n' roll, people heading through Barstow were full of hope, the promise of a better life in sunny California fuelling their one-way westward journey. These days, such optimism is absent; the couple of dozen people hanging around along Main Street in the heart of Saturday night have lost what little pep they once had, and seem to be here only because they've no particular place to go.

The prefab motels on Main, it follows, no longer draw their trade from ambitious Midwesterners. The buildings that have survived the wrecking ball stay afloat chiefly thanks to customers who rent their now-tatty rooms by the month; casual travellers head, instead, for the familiarity of the Best Westerns and Days Inns that have arrived in force over the last couple of decades, leaving their rooms only for a late dinner at Denny's and an early breakfast at International House of Pancakes. The revitalised **Route 66 Motel** (195 W Main Street, 1-760 256 7866, www. route66motelbarstow.com) has a glorious neon sign, a classic old motor parked out front and a selection of Mother Road memorabilia in the forecourt that's part exhibition and part installation. But it's also a dozen blocks from the intersection with I-15, far enough that only a handful of casual travellers even discover it's there. A similar fate sadly befalls the **Route 66 Mother Road Museum** (681 N 1st Avenue, 1-760 255 1890), which collates an assortment of 66abilia, and the **Western American Railroad Museum** next door (681 N 1st Avenue, 1-760 256 9276).

In 1941, iconoclastic composer/musician/inventor Harry Partch wrote a piece called *Barstow*, based on eight phrases scribbled by hitchhikers at the side of Route 66. The graffiti has long since been rubbed away, but the sentiment of number eight is not difficult to appreciate. 'The best of luck to you,' it reads. 'Why in hell did you come, anyway?'

on its borders. Its four paved roads are of good quality, and though the signs at entry points warning of 'no services' are a reminder of how hostile the desert can be, drivers are unlikely to run into trouble if they keep an eye on the fuel gauge, have plenty of water in the trunk and stick to paved roads and recommended dirt roads only. You can see plenty this way, combined with short side walks. But for those with 4WD it's an off-road paradise: numerous unpaved roads include the 140-mile east–west Mojave Road, a Native American track developed by successive users (the best reference is the *Mojave Road Guide* by Dennis Casebier). Go off-road, and you take your safety into your own hands. Don't do it alone or without adequate planning and equipment. The best times to visit are spring or autumn; it's brutally hot here from mid May to mid September, with temperatures spiralling

over 110°F (43°C). But do stay into the late afternoon, when the shadows are long and the mountains at their most beautiful.

A good starting point for exploring the Mojave from I-15 is the small town of **Baker**, whose Desert Information Center (*see p173*), located under the world's tallest thermometer, has maps, books and updates on road conditions. Fill up on gas and drinking water while you're here. If you've only a few hours, a 67-mile triangular drive from Baker, via the Kelbaker Road, Kelso-Cima Road and Cima Road, to rejoin I-15 at the end of the trek, is a good introduction to the sights.

You pass the reddish humps of over 30 young volcanic cones before reaching Kelso, which used to be a major passenger stop on the Union Pacific Railroad; now only freight trains pass through. The grand, Spanish Mission-style depot, built in 1924 and closed in 1985, is in the process of being turned into a visitor centre, due to open some time in 2005; when it does, the Desert Information Center in Baker will close.

If you want to detour to the 500-foot (150-metre) Kelso sand dunes, continue south from Kelso on the Kelbaker Road and turn right after about seven miles on to a signed dirt road. These 10,000- to 20,000-year-old dunes support a remarkable variety of plant and animal life, including the rarely seen desert tortoise. You may hear the dunes 'booming' as dry sand slides down the steep upper slopes.

Back in Kelso, turn left towards Cima, passing the 7,000-foot-high (2,130-metre) Providence Mountains en route. At Cima, little more than a collection of wooden shacks, you have a choice. Either take Cima Road towards I-15, past the gently swelling Cima Dome, which has the largest stand of Joshua trees in the world, or go up Morning Star Mine Road to Nipton Road up the Ivanpah Valley, then either take a left to I-15 or a right to tiny **Nipton** (population 40), just outside the preserve's northern edge. Here you'll find a railroad crossing, an old-fashioned country store/souvenir shop, a town hall and the charming **Hotel Nipton** (*see p173*). If you go on towards Vegas from Nipton via Searchlight, you'll pass an impressive forest of Joshua trees.

If you're approaching the Mojave National Preserve from I-40, the Kelbaker Road takes you to Kelso. Alternatively – and recommended during the heat of summer – you could take the Essex Road to the Providence Mountains State Recreation Area, which is far cooler than the desert floor. Multi-branched cholla, spiky Mojave yucca, round barrel cactus, spindly Mormon tea and the flat pads of prickly pears share the upland slopes with juniper and piñon trees, creating a stunning geometric display. There are great views south from the visitor centre. This park within a park also houses the dramatic limestone **Mitchell Caverns**, which remain a cool 65°F (18°C) year round, good to know in summer. There are tours of the caves ($4 adults, $2 children) daily from Labor Day to Memorial Day, and Saturday and Sunday the rest of the year; call 1-760 928 2586 for details.

Another diversion from I-40 is a stretch of old Route 66, featuring the kind of bleak desert landscapes beloved of cinematographers and the similarly iconic astro-googie Americana of photogenic **Amboy**, notably Roy's Motel & Café (whose future was uncertain in late 2004, partly because the whole town was up for sale). To the east, 66 crosses I-40 and dips back into the preserve to visit **Goffs**, a lonely spot despite – or perhaps because of – being 'the Desert Tortoise Capital of the World'.

Where to eat, drink & stay

There's not a lot up close. Most visitors either pass through en route to somewhere else or day-trip in from the chain motels of Barstow or Needles. On the edge of the park cute little Baker has a clutch of pretty basic non-chain motels including the **Royal Hawaiian** (200 West Baker Boulevard, 1-760 733 4326, $37-$55), but

Fore!

One of the most peculiar features in Death Valley, a park full of geological oddities, is the **Devil's Golf Course**. Reached via a shaky drive south from Furnace Creek, and about as close as the public are allowed to get to the lowest point of elevation in the Western Hemisphere (nearby Badwater), it's a disturbing and hypnotic sight. The landscape in front of you, acre upon acre, is topped with crystallised rock salt, sculpted by the elements into shapes alternately spherical and sharp. The area was so named because, it was said, only Lucifer himself would dare play golf upon it.

It is not, though, the park's only golf course. In 1925, a caretaker at Greenland Ranch, a series of living spaces built for the miners who once harvested borax here, decided to build three golf holes on the property, which sits 214 feet (65 metres) below sea level. Five years later, the course grew to nine holes, and was expanded to the full complement of 18 in 1968. In the meantime, Greenland Ranch became the resort now known as **Furnace Creek Ranch** (*see p176*).

Renovations in 1997 added a new irrigation system that now keeps the course green, and open, all year round. The spring providing the water for the showers and the pools also feeds the golf course, to the tune of half a million gallons daily. And so, confronted with one of the country's most extraordinary and mysterious natural environments, spread across an area of over 5,000 square miles, the visiting leisure classes are able to spend four hours clubbing a ball around these unnaturally green pastures so they can go home and tell their friends they've played the lowest golf course in the world. The American pursuit of the superlative can rarely have been placed into such sharply absurd focus.

Red Rock Canyon (*see p174*) and the costume cowboys of Calico (*see p173*).

the pick of the park-side accommodation is the **Hotel Nipton** (1-760 856 2335, www.nipton. com, $64-$74), an early-century hotel in splendid desert isolation (except, that is, for its wi-fi), and the nearby **Whistle Stop Oasis** (1-760 856 1045, $), serving good Italian-American food, breakfast included. But the landmark grub is back in Baker, at the rammed and rated **Mad Greek Diner** (1-760 733 4354, $), where fast food both Greek and American is served up. It is a criminal offence to leave without ordering the strawberry milkshake. South, you could try **Roy's** (1-760 733 4263, www.rt66roys.com) in Amboy, but check before going out of your way. Otherwise, there's damn all between Barstow and Needles, except a gas station at Fenner.

In the preserve itself, the new visitor centre at Kelso will have a lunch counter. Of the two campgrounds ($12, no reservations), **Mid-Hills** is usually cooler than **Hole-in-the-Wall**, and always much prettier. You'll need to drive some reliable but not always comfortable dirt roads to get here; Hole-in-the-Wall is accessible on blacktop from I-40.

Resources

Baker *Desert Information Center, 72157 Baker Boulevard (1-760 733 4040).* **Open** 9am-5pm daily. This office near the big thermometer will close in 2005, in favour of a spiffy new information centre at the old Kelso depot. You can also pick up advice and information from the **California Desert Information** office in Barstow (831 Barstow Road, 1-760 255 8760, 9am-5pm Mon-Fri).

Death Valley

Those heading north towards Death Valley from Mojave National Preserve and/or Baker have but one choice of road, the classic desert driving of Highway 127. Some 85 miles north of Baker is **Death Valley Junction**, home only to the **Amargosa Opera House** (*see p176*); from here, it's a further 29 miles to Furnace Creek Visitor Center (*see p176*) in Death Valley itself.

The drive to Death Valley north from LA at least offers a choice. The more popular of the two options is to leave LA north on I-15, which throws up a handful of Californian curiosities to divert the restless traveller. In dusty, isolated **Helendale**, off I-15 via old Route 66, is **Exotic World USA** (29053 Wild Road, 1-760 243 5261, www.exoticworldusa.org), a celebration of the history of burlesque run by former artiste Dixie Evans; each June, it hosts the Miss Exotic World USA pageant, which is exactly as sassy and saucy as you might expect.

Depressing **Barstow**, meanwhile, is home to a couple of interesting museums relating to the history of travel in the West; *see p171* **The highway that's the best**. And east of Barstow is **Calico Ghost Town** (1-760 254 2122, www.calicotown.com, $6), deserted only during the heat of summer and the rest of the time populated by costumed gunslingers and crowds of family holidaymakers. Half regional park and half roadside attraction, it comprises a museum, some turn-of-the-century buildings

Death Valley, tamed (Scotty's Castle) and wild (sand dunes). *See p175.*

and a lot of saloons and fudge shops. The same mineral seams that yielded the silver and borate that made Calico rich are beatifully exposed in **Rainbow Basin Natural Area** (1-760 252 6000). From Barstow, it's just over 60 miles to Baker along I-15, whereupon you can either head north to Death Valley (*see p173*) or continue east to **Las Vegas** (*see pp177-194*).

The alternative route from LA to Death Valley, though, is more beguiling. Leave LA on I-5, I-210 or I-405, then pick up Highway 14 north of Sylmar. From here, it's 35 miles north to **Edwards Air Force Base** (1-661 277 8050, www.edwards.af.mil) in **Palmdale**, home of *The Right Stuff* and occasional space shuttle landings. Security worries mean the base's museum is closed, and the annual open house and air show (usually in October) was cancelled in 2004. It's a further 35 miles from Palmdale north to **Mojave**, a barely extant town seemingly populated by more planes (decommissioned by airlines and stored here until they find buyers) than people. Get gas here: you won't have another chance for a while.

The road north from **Mojave** to Death Valley is desert driving at its best (*see p32*). Around 30 miles north, you'll pass the erosion-carved formations of **Red Rock Canyon State Park** made famous by *Jurassic Park*. If you're in a hurry to get to Death Valley, you can head east

on Highway 178 via Ridgecrest, but continuing north for around 65 miles and instead taking Highway 190 is the more scenic drive.

Death Valley National Park

Enlarged and redesignated as a national park under the 1994 Desert Protection Act, Death Valley is now the largest national park outside Alaska, covering more than 5,156 square miles. It's also, more famously, one of the hottest and driest places on the planet. The park's website calmly offers that 'Death Valley is generally sunny, dry and clear throughout the year'. Uh, yeah. There's usually less than two inches of rain a year, and with air temperatures regularly topping 120°F (49°C) in July and August (the ground temperature can be 50 per cent higher) and lows averaging 90°F (32°C), it's apparent how the park got its name; though, in point of fact, only one pioneer died trying to cross it.

The drive in from Death Valley Junction takes you past the turn-off to **Dante's View**, reached via a winding 13-mile road. The landscape, some 5,475 feet (1,669 metres) above sea level, is drab and barren yet oddly beautiful. Returning to Route 190, you'll pass **Zabriskie Point**, famed among cinephiles for the eponymous 1970 Antonioni film but recognisable to all by its ragged, rumpled appearance.

Five miles down the road, you'll reach
the Death Valley Visitor Center (*see p176*)
at **Furnace Creek**, a compulsory stopping
point for its excellent bookshop, decent
exhibits, useful orientation film and excellent
staff. Stop in for advice on current weather and
road conditions (some tracks are only accessible
to 4WD vehicles), and pay your fee of $10 per
car. And take the opportunity to fill up the car
at one of three expensive gas stations. While
it is reassuring to know that all the major car
manufacturers test their vehicles in the extreme
conditions here, keep an eye on the gauges;
roadside storage tanks hold radiator water.

From Furnace Creek, you've two choices.
Taking the road south will take you first past
Golden Canyon, a straightforward two-mile
round-trip hike. It's best walked in the late
afternoon sunlight: you'll see how the canyon got
its name. Continuing south, the landscape gets
plainer. Nine miles down the road is the **Devil's
Golf Course**, a striking, scrappy landscape
formed by salt crystallising and expanding; a
few miles further is bleak, eerie **Badwater**, just
two miles as the crow flies from Dante's View
but over 5,000 feet (1,524 metres) lower. Nearby
but inaccessible is the lowest point in the
Western Hemisphere, 282 feet (86 metres) below
sea level. It's only 85 miles from the highest point

in the US, the 14,494-foot (4,420-metre) Mount
Whitney, in the Sierra Nevada. An annual
bicycle race takes place between the two.

Heading north from Furnace Creek offers a
greater variety of sights. The remains of the
Harmony Borax Works have been casually
converted into a short trail; there's a similarly
simple walk, less historic but more aesthetically
pleasing, at nearby **Salt Creek** (look out for
pupfish in the stream in spring). Following the
road around to the left will lead you past the
eerie **Devil's Cornfield**, the thoroughly
frolicable **Sand Dunes**, which rise and dip in
100-foot (30-metre) increments, and on to the
small settlement at **Stovepipe Wells**; taking a
right and driving 36 miles will take you to the
extravagant **Scotty's Castle** (1-760 786 2392),
built in the 1920s for Chicago millionaire Albert
Johnson but named after Walter Scott, his
eccentric chancer of a friend. Costumed rangers
tell the story during 50-minute tours from 9am
to 5pm, usually hourly ($8; $4-$6 discounts).

It's often too hot to hike in Death Valley,
but there are plenty of trails, short and long.
Among the options is the 14-mile round-trip
to the 11,000-foot (3,353-metre) summit of
Telescope Peak, a good summer hike (the
higher you climb, the cooler it gets). Starting at
Mahogany Flat campground, you climb 3,000

Southern California

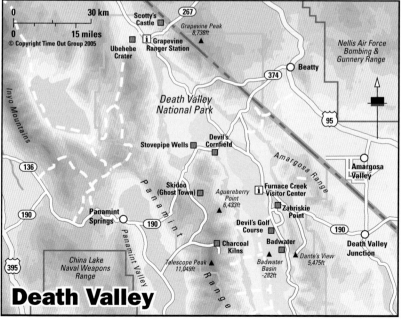

Death Valley

feet (914 metres) for spectacular views of Mount Whitney. In winter only experienced climbers with ice axes and crampons should attempt it.

The Death Valley area is also littered with ghost towns and abandoned mines (watch your step). If you're heading back on Highway 178, drop in on the tiny ghost town of **Ballarat**, on the edge of the beautiful Panamint Valley.

Where to eat & drink

Unsurprisingly, culinary pickings are a bit slim in these parts – there are restaurants at Furnace Creek Ranch, Stovepipe Wells Village and Panamint Springs – and the food tends to be fairly ordinary. The exception is the dining room at the **Furnace Creek Inn** (*see below*; closed mid May-mid Oct, $-$$$), where the upscale Californian food is considerably better than it has any right to be. The Inn also has a handsome bar; the watering hole at the related **Furnace Creek Ranch** is fun but more basic.

Where to stay

Set into the hillside above Furnace Creek Wash, 1930s **Furnace Creek Inn** (1-760 786 2345, www.furnacecreekresort.com, closed mid May-mid Oct, $240-$370) is the luxury option. **Furnace Creek Ranch** (closed mid May-mid Oct, $89-$149) has 200 motel-style rooms and cabins, with a pool, tennis and golf (*see p172* Fore!). **Stovepipe Wells Village** has 83 rooms (1-760 786 2837, www.stovepipewells. com, closed May-mid Oct, $75-$95).

Most of the park's nine campgrounds cost $10 a night; Furnace Creek (1-800 365 2267) and a few others are open all year.

Resources

Tourist information

Death Valley *Death Valley Visitor Center, Furnace Creek (1-760 786 3200/www.nps.gov/deva).* **Open** 8am-6pm daily.

A night at the opera

It's not your archetypal ghost town, Death Valley Junction. It was settled not by travelling pioneers or gold-hungry prospectors, but by the Pacific Coast Borax Company, which built it in the mid 1920s to house its workers. They didn't stick around, and the town crumbled. Until, that is, a fortysomething ballet dancer named Marta Becket, disillusioned with her life in New York, arrived in 1967.

The **Amargosa Opera House**, at Death Valley Junction, is her life's work. Its creaky building was the town's derelict community hall when Becket chanced upon it. Deciding to renovate it as her own theatre, she turned coffee-cans into spotlights, painted an audience on the walls – which made performing in an empty hall, as she often did, easier to bear – and filled the room with garden chairs.

Renovations continued, and word spread. Despite the building's none-more-awkward location, people travelled to see Becket's theatre and her self-devised and slightly peculiar performance pieces. Becket finally bought the property in the early 1980s, continuing to paint and renovate and perform; audiences, fascinated by this tale of devotion and self-imposed isolation, continued to come.

Becket's in her eighties now, but the show must go on. And it does, with Saturday performances, staged October through mid May, supplemented by Monday shows from February to April (tickets $15, booking essential on 1-760 852 4441; for more, see www.amargosa-opera-house.com). Becket, it seems, will dance until she drops, for her own American dream is still very much alive.

Las Vegas

Bones, broads and all-night boozing.

Perhaps 15 miles after you cross the border into Nevada on I-15, you'll detect an almost eerie glow. Soon the city edges into focus, illuminated in rainbow neon. Arrive at night for the full effect; then, before you do anything else, exit I-15 at Russell Road and drive the length of the Strip, three of the loudest, most overwhelming miles on the planet. Welcome, as the sign says, to fabulous Las Vegas, Nevada.

Everything you've read about Vegas is true. *Everything.* It's just up to you what you want to believe. Glorious or ugly? Thrilling or tedious? Crazy or predictable? Romantic or loveless? Pretty much depends which side of the bed you stepped from this morning. What's a given, though, is that nowhere does excess quite like Vegas. The gambling carries on 24-7 (helped on by a total absence of clocks and windows in all the casinos), the bars never holler last call, breakfast is served at 8pm and dinner at 8am, and you can work out, watch strippers or get married at any time of the day you damn well please. It is America *reductio ad absurdum.*

HISTORY

Las Vegas celebrates its centennial in 2005. However, the early foundations were laid in 1903, when the San Pedro, Los Angeles and Salt Lake Railroad arrived, and what we now know as Las Vegas began to take shape. And by New Year's Day 1906, 1,500 optimistic, boom-town pioneers called Las Vegas home.

But the initial boom was short-lived. Only the construction in the 1930s of the Hoover (née Boulder) Dam saved Vegas. The population soared to 5,000, many of them construction workers; thousands more passed through en route to the soon-to-be-tamed Colorado River. Vegas didn't just survive: it began to thrive.

However, it was the statewide legalisation of wide-open casino gambling in 1931 that really transformed Vegas. Casino operators migrated here in droves; vice-starved visitors streamed into town to partake in the naughtiness. The prosperity of the early 1940s ushered in new casinos: the El Cortez in Downtown, and the Last Frontier and El Rancho Vegas resorts on the Los Angeles Highway, soon to be known as the Las Vegas Strip.

It wasn't long before the Mob moved in on the action. In 1947 Benjamin 'Bugsy' Siegel was the first to arrive and, though his dalliance with the casino world ended in his assassination, the die was cast. Vegas, as we know it today, began with Mob money: the opening of the Flamingo, which Siegel helped establish, led to a ten-year hotel-building boom, all funded by black money that came pouring in from the underworld power centres across the country.

> ► For an expanded survey of Las Vegas, buy the 320-page *Time Out Las Vegas* guide.

The **Bellagio**. *See p180.*

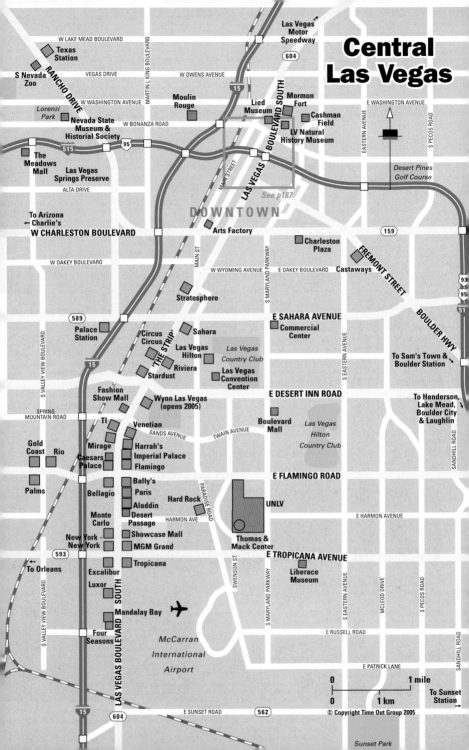

America's moral majority hated Vegas. But despite such criticism (or, in all likelihood, because of it), people still came. The late 1950s and early 1960s were the glamour years: crap shooters rolled the bones elbow to elbow with hit men, comps flowed as easily as champagne, and Frank, Dean, Sammy et al performed at the Sands. Another dozen hotel-casino resorts opened between 1968 and 1973, but then, as corporate America moved in, Mob involvement petered out, and so did the town's popularity. Vegas in the '80s was a fairly ordinary place.

But nothing here stays static for long. In November 1989, a 47-year-old casino chairman called Steve Wynn opened a 3,000-room, $650 million pleasure palace called the Mirage in the heart of the Strip. Its size, style and price tag stunned the old guard, but the enthusiasm with which the public greeted the Mirage galvanised the industry. Excalibur, a medieval-themed casino-resort, opened in June 1990, followed by the great pyramid Luxor, the pirate-technic Treasure Island and the huge MGM Grand. The late 1990s saw another wave of construction: New York–New York, the Bellagio, Mandalay Bay and the $1.5 billion Venetian.

Wynn and his followers have, essentially, rebuilt the town from scratch; Vegas has never been more popular, or more lucrative, than it is today. And yet the reinvention hasn't stopped: Wynn's latest project, the conspicuously non-themed **Wynn Las Vegas**, is due to open in spring 2005. There are now over 120,000 hotel rooms in Las Vegas (no other city in the world has even 100,000), with 37 million visitors a year losing more than $6 billion on the casino floors and leaving another $6 billion in non-gambling expenses. There's nowhere else on earth even remotely like it.

Sightseeing & Resorts

Throw traditional notions of sightseeing out of the window. Las Vegas's attractions are its hotel-resorts, for in them are also the overwhelming majority of its best restaurants, bars, nightclubs, shows and – of course – casinos. A handful of the town's attractions

The best Las Vegas

Things to do

Walk the Strip under the cloak of darkness, your path lit by a gazillion megawatts of neon radiance. Take a **rollercoaster**, either at New York–New York or the Sahara. Oh, and **lose a heap of money** in a casino playing a game you barely understand. Everyone else does.

Places to stay

If you've money to burn, take your pick: the **Venetian** (see p182), the **Bellagio** (see p180) and **Mandalay Bay** (see p181). For the lighter of wallet, try **New York–New York** (see p184) and **Bally's**. If you're really on a budget, try **Binion's Horseshoe** (see p187) or the **Sin City Hostel** (see p193).

Places to eat

Every hotel-casino on the Strip has at least one respectable eaterie; some have several gems. Start the day by feasting on a classic Vegas buffet: during the week, try the **Bellagio** (see p180), and on Sundays, go for **Bally's Sterling Brunch** (see p183). No one does lunch like the French: look no further than **Mon Ami Gabi** at Paris Las Vegas (see p182). For dinner, push the boat out at **Aureole** at Mandalay Bay (see p181) or **Bradley Ogden**

at Caesars Palace (see p180), or count the pennies at the **Pink Taco** at the Hard Rock Hotel (see p189) or the **Mediterranean Café** (see p189). Then satisfy those late night/early morning food cravings at **Mr Lucky's 24/7** at the Hard Rock (see p186) or the Venetian's wonderful **Grand Lux Café** (see p182).

Nightlife

For live music, the most eclectic bookings are at the **House of Blues** (see p181). Also, look up the **Joint** at the Hard Rock (see p186) or the divey **Double Down Saloon** (see p190); the latter is also among the town's best bars. The city's nightclub scene is thriving: **Tabú**, at the MGM Grand, and **Rain**, off-Strip at the Palms (for both, see p191), are the best.

Culture

Don't expect much high culture in Vegas. Do expect to be overwhelmed by showbiz and scale. If you only see one big show, make it a **Cirque du Soleil** production (see p192).

Sports & activities

For reservations at many of the area's best golf courses, contact **Las Vegas Preferred Tee Times** (1-877 255 7277, www.lvptt.com).

are stand-alone enterprises; for these, *see p190*
Beyond the casinos. But in truth, you're likely to spend almost all your time in Vegas in one or more of the 30-odd hotel-casino resorts on Las Vegas Boulevard South, aka the Strip.

Competition between resorts is phenomenally fierce. But once a resort has attracted a customer to stay overnight, then the real battle – keeping him or her on the premises to spend even more money – has only just begun. Every major resort boasts at least ten eating options, some swanky and some snacky: almost everywhere has a steakhouse, restaurants serving Italian, Chinese and Mexican food, an anything-goes buffet, and a 24-hour coffeehouse. Most resorts also have at least one showroom, a number of which contain big-budget spectaculars that play nightly. Handsome bars and chic nightclubs are other popular attractions.

Go on a weekend and you'll pay handsomely for the privilege of staying on the Strip, but head to Vegas midweek and you'll find prices in some casinos have fallen through the floor: a room that costs $250 on Friday can often be had for $50 two days earlier. And whenever you arrive in Vegas, be aware that there are bargains galore to be had if you know where to look: free drinks in casinos for anyone gambling, heavily discounted show tickets with a flyer or a coupon, two-for-one meals... The Cheapo Vegas website (www.cheapovegas.com) is a good resource.

The Strip

These days the **Strip**, aka Las Vegas Boulevard South, more or less *is* Vegas. Aside from the journey to and from McCarran Airport, most tourists never leave the Strip for the duration of their stay. It's easy to see why. Here you'll find the vast majority of Las Vegas's best gaming, dining and sleeping options, as well as its biggest and brashest entertainments.

It's a hypnotic place, glorious and horrible and glamorous and shocking (and many other things) all at once. Assuming the weather allows (it gets absurdly hot here in summer), every visitor should walk the length of it once, from the iconic 'welcome' sign at its southern tip all the way north to Sahara Avenue, where the street life suddenly gets a whole lot seedier.

Expensive

Bellagio
3600 Las Vegas Boulevard South, at W Flamingo Road (reservations 1-888 987 6667/front desk & casino 1-702 693 7111/restaurants 1-702 693 7223/ box office 1-888 488 7111/www.bellagio.com).
Rates $159-$799 single/double; $325-$7,000 suite.
Credit AmEx, DC, Disc, MC, V.

The epitome of new Vegas luxury, the Bellagio is meant to evoke a Lake Como villa, complete with 8-acre lake fronting the Strip, a lush garden conservatory and pools set into a formal, old world Italian garden. The rooms are large and luxurious, the ambience elegant (if, in the casino itself, a bit vulgar). Under-18s are not permitted on the property unless accompanied by grown-ups.

Restaurants
The Bellagio raised the city's culinary profile with its host of celebrity chefs. The best of its restaurants are Julian Serrano's French/Mediterranean **Picasso** (closed Tue & lunch Wed-Mon, $$$$$), hung with nine of the artist's paintings; **Prime** (closed lunch, $$$$$), Jean-Georges Vongerichten's superior chophouse; and **Michael Mina**'s seafood-driven menu (closed lunch, $$$$). The hotel's **Buffet** ($–$$), predictably, is one of the city's best.

Entertainment & nightlife
The free **fountain show** outside the Bellagio, in which a string of computer-choreographed fountains 'dance' to a soundtrack of anything from Frank Sinatra to Lee Greenwood, is justly one of Vegas's most popular attractions. The fountains spring into action every quarter-hour during the evenings. There's more water inside, as a cast of dancers, musicians, clowns, acrobats, divers, swimmers and aerialists takes to the watery stage in **O** (tickets $93-$150), the stunning spectacle from Cirque du Soleil. Sleek **Caramel** (1-702 693 8300) is one of the Strip's most attractive bars; nightclub **Light** (1-702 693 8300) is exclusive and snooty, but undeniably chic; the **Fontana Lounge** offers live music.

Caesars Palace
3570 Las Vegas Boulevard South, at W Flamingo Road (reservations 1-800 634 6001/front desk & casino 1-702 731 7110/restaurants 1-877 346 4642/ box office 1-877 423 5463/www.caesarspalace.com).
Rates $89-$500 single/double; $300-$1,300 suite.
Credit AmEx, DC, Disc, MC, V.

Caesars is an icon of classic Sin City decadence, a meld of affluence, nonsense and glamour. Though its craziest kitsch has been toned down, the resort remains a monument to ancient Greece and Rome, with marble columns, arches, colonnades and costumed centurions. Key to its continuing allure is the ever-expanding **Forum Shops**, a pioneering mall fashioned after an ancient Roman streetscape. Standard rooms are expansive; the highest of high rollers are comped into the luxurious Pool Villas.

Restaurants
Bradley Ogden's chic American eaterie ($$$$$) and Jean-Marie Josselin's Euro-Asian-Pacific Rim restaurant **808** (closed lunch, $$$$$) are the best of the offerings. In the Forum Shops, along with steakhouse the **Palm** ($$$–$$$$$), *über*-chef Wolfgang Puck is represented by Asian eaterie **Chinois** ($$$$) and trend-setting **Spago** ($$$–$$$$$). At the **Stage Deli** ($$), portions and prices are huge.

Entertainment & nightlife
The new 4,000-seat Colosseum is home to the lame Céline Dion production **A New Day** (tickets $87.50-$225). When she's on vacation, Elton John takes over with his show **The Red Piano** (tickets $100-$250). The **Shadow Bar** is a plush lounge with flair bartenders and silhouetted beauties dancing behind lit screens. A vast new underground nightclub is due to open in 2005.

Mandalay Bay
3950 Las Vegas Boulevard South, at E Hacienda Avenue (reservations 1-877 632 7000/front desk & casino 1-702 632 7777/restaurants 1-877 632 5300/ box office 1-877 632 7400/www.mandalaybay.com). **Rates** $99-$599 single/double; $149-$599 suite. **Credit** AmEx, DC, Disc, MC, V.

It's always high tide at the South Seas island-themed Mandalay Bay, one of the town's most luxurious resorts. Accommodation here is impressive (the standard rooms are the largest on the Strip); more memorable is the 11-acre water park at the centre of the resort, complete with sandy beach, wave pool and jogging track. And Mandalay's sister tower, THEhotel, is as close to metro-modern as Vegas gets.

Restaurants
Mandalay Bay is unusual in that it locates many of its eateries away from the casino, so you can dine without seeing – or, just as crucially, hearing – a single slot machine. The vast **Aureole** (closed lunch, $$$$$) is the best option; Wolfgang Puck's expensive Italian **Trattoria del Lupo** (closed lunch Mon-Fri, $$$) and nouveau Mexican **Border Grill** ($$; for the LA version, *see p122*) also impress. You'll have to venture into the casino to sample the Cajun cooking at **House of Blues** ($$$).

Entertainment & nightlife
A 'walk-through' aquarium, Mandalay Bay's **Shark Reef** is filled with 100 species of underwater life, including rays, jellyfish, eels and, of course, 11 varieties of sharks. The main attraction at night is all-conquering Abba musical **Mamma Mia!** (tickets $45-$100), but the 12,000-seat **Mandalay Bay Events Center** and the smaller **House of Blues** stage one-off concerts. Bar- and clubwise, striking **Rumjungle** draws a young, pretty crowd with its pounding Latin/Caribbean beats.

Mirage
3400 Las Vegas Boulevard South, between Spring Mountain Road & W Flamingo Road (reservations 1-800 374 9000/front desk & casino 1-702 791 7111/restaurants 1-866 339 4566/box office 1-800

See p184.

963 9634/www.themirage.com). **Rates** $109-$459 single/double; $275-$2,500 suite. **Credit** AmEx, DC, Disc, MC, V.

Steve Wynn's $650 million tropical island hotel set the industry standard for modern megaresorts when it opened in 1989. It looks dated these days, but it's still a draw for high rollers and those who just want to enjoy the exploding volcano, the 90ft (27m) rainforest atrium and the much-imitated 20,000-gallon aquarium behind the main desk. The pool area has a series of blue lagoons, inlets and waterfalls.

Restaurants

Chef Alessandro Stratta's take on southern French cuisine at **Renoir** (closed Mon, Sun & lunch Tue-Sat, $$$$$) is highly impressive, which is more than can be said for the other eating options. For quick dining, try the **California Pizza Kitchen** ($$).

Entertainment & nightlife

Siegfried & Roy may have been necessarily forced into retirement, but with their **Secret Garden & Dolphin Habitat** (the former a small zoo), their name remains in evidence at the Mirage. Since Roy's on-stage mauling by one of their tigers, unimpressive impressionist **Danny Gans** (tickets $100) has been holding the fort. The bars are nothing special.

Paris Las Vegas

3655 Las Vegas Boulevard South, at E Flamingo Road (reservations 1-888 266 5687/front desk & casino 1-702 946 4222/www.parislasvegas.com). **Rates** $79-$400 single/double; $300-$1,219 suite. **Credit** AmEx, DC, Disc, MC, V.

Transatlantic tensions haven't dampened the appeal of Paris Las Vegas, which offers some of the glamour of gay Paree without – cue cheering from middle America – any of the actual Parisians. PLV incorporates reproductions of Paris landmarks, starting with its 34-storey tower of 2,916 rooms modelled after the Hotel de Ville and ending with the half-scale replica of the Eiffel Tower that plunges into the casino. Sounds absurd? It works pretty well.

Restaurants

JJ's Boulangerie ($) and **La Creperie** ($) are the value options here. Those with a little more cash to splash would do well to try streetside brasserie **Mon Ami Gabi** (1-702 944 4224, $$$$); sophisticates prefer the haute cuisine offered at the **Eiffel Tower Restaurant** (1-702 948 6937, closed lunch, $$$$$), located on the tower's 11th floor.

Entertainment & nightlife

Stupendously terrible Queen musical **We Will Rock You** (tickets $80.50-$113.50) is the staple entertainment at Paris. Late nights, the party people are swamping **Risqué** (1-702 946 4589), a chic lounge with DJs spinning house music nightly until the early hours.

Venetian

3355 Las Vegas Boulevard South, at Sands Avenue (reservations 1-877 283 6423/front desk & casino 1-702 414 1000/www.venetian.com). **Rates** $119-$1,299 single/double. **Credit** AmEx, DC, Disc, MC, V.

On the site of the Sands, the Rat Pack's old stomping ground, this version of Venice is surprisingly convincing. Owner Sheldon Adelson tried to recreate the real city of canals with accurate, to-scale replicas of many of its landmarks, along with indoor and outdoor chlorinated canals traversed by singing gondoliers. The exterior is a showstopper, but the ornate interior is equally impressive. One big draw is **Grand Canal Shoppes**, a meandering mall with flowing canals and cobblestone streets.

Restaurants

The roster reads like a who's who of top chefs. Both Wolfgang Puck and Emeril Lagasse are present, with upscale Med-American café **Postrio** (1-702 796 1110, $$$$$) and Cajun steakhouse **Delmonico** (1-702 414 3737, $$$$$); Joachim Splichal's **Pinot Brasserie** (1-702 414 8888, $$$$) serves California cuisine. The excellent 24-hour **Grand Lux Café** (1-702 414 3888, $$$) is the best option for those who want to save their cash for the casinos.

Entertainment & nightlife

Purchase your tickets at St Mark's Square, then take a **gondola ride** on canals that weave through replica Venetian architecture. It's a lot more fun than **Madame Tussaud's** collection of ropey waxworks. The hotel's real after-hours hotspot is **V Bar** (1-702 414 3200), a chic, minimalist New York-style lounge; **Venus** (1-702 414 4870) pulses with beautiful people and quaintly old-fashioned house music. Opening in 2005: an outpost of NYC fave **Tao**.

Drai's, at the Barbary Coast. *See p185.*

Vegas for kids

Las Vegas's appetite for reinvention worked in favour of young 'uns a decade ago, when the casinos decided to pitch themselves as family-friendly resorts. Pretty soon, though, it occurred to the execs that kids don't gamble, and the town reverted to its adult-oriented ways. That's not to say kids here are unwelcome: a handful of casinos go out of their way to accommodate them.

Circus Circus and **Excalibur** (for both, *see p185*) offers kid-friendly entertainments; the rides and amusements at the **Luxor** (*see p183*) and **New York–New York** (*see p184*) please ankle-biters; and the **MGM Grand** (*see p183*) even has a Youth Activity Centre, with toys, games and a full menu.

If you'd rather shove coins into a video game than a slot machine, **GameWorks** (3785 Las Vegas Boulevard South, 1-702 432 4263), a huge madhouse on the Strip, is for you. Games cost 50¢-$5; you save money by paying by the hour. The gentler **Scandia Fun Center** (2900 Sirius Avenue, 1-702 364 0070) is home to a miniature golf course, go-karts and bumper boats.

Other options

Treasure Island (3300 Las Vegas Boulevard South, 1-800 288 7206, www.treasureisland.com, $79-$329) has morphed into a hotel for young adults called TI. Its streetside piratefest has become the wannabe-saucy *Sirens of TI*; new bar/club Tangerine offers brief, teasing burlesque shows each evening.

Mid range

Bally's

3645 Las Vegas Boulevard South, at E Flamingo Road (reservations 1-888 742 9248/front desk & casino 1-702 739 4111/restaurants 1-702 967 7999/ www.ballyslv.com). **Rates** $49-$400 single/double; $325-$1,500 suite. **Credit** AmEx, DC, Disc, MC, V.
Don't let the garish, incongruous exterior of moving sidewalks and pulsating neon hoops colour your impression of what is one of the most elegant Vegas resorts. The sunken rectangular casino floor seems downright Monaco-like; the small shopping arcade features 20 unique boutiques (no chain stores here), and there's also a spa and a wedding facility.

Restaurants
Bally's restaurant selection is like the rest of the resort: a throwback to old-school subtlety (or, to be harsh, obscurity). **Al Dente** ($$$$) offers contemporary Italian food, and the New England-style **Steakhouse** ($$$$$) does grilled beef and seafood right.

Entertainment & nightlife
Only two big-stage feathers-and-sequins spectaculars remain in Vegas, and **Donn Arden's Jubilee** (tickets $55-$79) is one of them. The **Indigo Lounge** is a fine place for a cocktail.

Luxor

3900 Las Vegas Boulevard South, between W Tropicana Avenue & Russell Road (reservations 1-888 777 0188/front desk & casino 1-702 262 4000/box office 1-800 557 7428/www.luxor.com). **Rates** $69-$599 single/double; $169-$800 suite. **Credit** AmEx, DC, Disc, MC, V.
Stark black glass pyramid, high-intensity light shooting skyward from its top (yes, it's visible from space), sphinx guarding the entrance… Welcome to the Luxor. Thirty storeys high, with a 9-acre base, the pyramid is a scale reproduction of the one at Giza. The homage to Egypt continues inside: the campest elements have been tidied up, but the lobby replica of the Temple Abu Simbel remains. Deeply silly, but damn good fun, and family-friendly to boot.

Restaurants
Pharaoh's Pheast ($–$$) gets the gold star for the most inventive buffet decor: it serves all the typical fare, but does so in the midst of an archaeological dig, complete with ropes, pulleys and ladders. More upscale is the clubby **Luxor Steakhouse** (1-702 262 4778, dinner only, $$$$); less pricey is the Mexican **La Salsa** ($$).

Entertainment & nightlife
The flagship attraction is the **King Tut Museum**, a full-size re-creation of Tutankhamen's burial chamber and his golden throne and sarcophagus, but **In Search of the Obelisk**, one of Vegas's better motion-simulators, runs it a close second. Since opening in 2000, **Blue Man Group** (tickets $65-$75) has wowed audiences with its unique and peculiar mix of art, comedy, music and science. The **Luxor IMAX Theatre** (1-702 262 4629) screens documentaries and pop features; for adults, there's the **Midnight Fantasy** topless revue (tickets $29.95). Club-hoppers will want to check out the silvery, *Stargate*-like **Ra** (1-702 262 4949).

MGM Grand

3799 Las Vegas Boulevard South, at E Tropicana Avenue (reservations & box office 1-877 880 0880/ front desk & casino 1-702 891 7777/www.mgm grand.com). **Rates** $99-$349 single/double; $199-$15,000 suite. **Credit** AmEx, DC, MC, V.
The MGM Grand lives up to its name: with well over 5,000 rooms, it's the largest hotel in the world, and looks like it. Admittedly, what it has in size it lacks in character, being defined purely by its huge size. That said, the standard of accommodation is high, and the vast casino floor an impressive sight.

Restaurants
Though no slouch before, the MGM has done much to upgrade its dining options during 2004. Noisy, brash and exciting **Craftsteak** (1-702 891 7318, closed lunch, $$$$) serves what might be the best

Beating the odds

Gambling virgin? Worry not. But don't take to the tables right away. A little tuition always helps, and many casinos offer lessons that teach beginners the basics of blackjack, craps and other popular games. Lessons tend to take place in the morning; call your casino for a schedule.

If you'd prefer to learn at your leisure, there are many books offering instruction. The finest are published by Huntington Press (www.huntingtonpress.com); the best place to buy such books, and a staggering variety of other gambling ephemera, is the **Gamblers General Store** (800 S Main Street, 1-702 382 9903). But, for now, here are five tips that should help you cut your losses a little...

● The house edge at blackjack is virtually nil, provided you play correctly. Pick up a strategy card from the Gamblers General Store, which outlines when you should hit and when you should stand, and stick to it.
● Craps isn't as tough as it looks: you'll with a little concentration, you'll pick it up in no time. Conversely, you'll need to know a little more than just the rules if you want to hang on to your shirt playing poker: unless you know what you're doing, it's easy to lose a lot of money very quickly.
● Keno is a simple game. It's also the worst-value bet in the casino. Don't even contemplate playing it. The edge offered by many slot machines is almost as bad.
● Ask for comps when you play table games (drinks, maybe a buffet meal later); look out for coupons offering betting perks (free bets, first-card-is-an-ace at blackjack).
● Always check the payouts before playing video poker: they're indicated at the top of the machine. On basic 'jacks or better' games, for example, look for payouts of 9 for 1 on a full house and 6 for 1 on a flush – these are known as 9/6 machines. For the varieties of 'bonus poker' machines, our best advice is simply to shop around.

steaks in all of Vegas; newly remodelled **Emeril's** ($$$$) conjures up an array of Cajun and Creole dishes, in lively fashion. Michael Mina's **SeaBlue** (1-702 891 3486, closed lunch, $$$$) offers some of the freshest seafood in town, while an outpost of NYC's **Fiamma** (1-702 891 7600, closed lunch, $$$$) serves tasty Italian. Casual options include the **Wolfgang Puck Bar & Grill** ($$$$) and the **Grand Wok** ($$), which shares a kitchen with the 24-hour coffeeshop.

Entertainment & nightlife

The MGM's main resident show is new Cirque du Soleil production **Kà** (tickets $99-$150); also here is **La Femme** (tickets $59), a showy topless revue that plays twice nightly. Other entertainment comes courtesy of a series of headliners who play one- or two-week engagements: among the regulars in the 740-seat **Hollywood Theatre** are Carrot Top, Tom Jones and David Copperfield. The after-hours choice is between optimistically monikered nightclub **Studio 54** (1-702 891 7254) and calmer **Tabú** (1-702 891 7183), an incomparably sleek lounge.

New York–New York

3790 Las Vegas Boulevard South, at W Tropicana Avenue (reservations 1-888 693 6763/front desk & casino 1-702 740 6969/box office 1-866 606 7111/ www.nynyhotelcasino.com). **Rates** $99-$249 single/ double; $599-$2,500 suite. **Credit** AmEx, Disc, MC, V. The city that never sleeps comes to the city that *really* never sleeps. There isn't a more colourful, eye-catching example of Vegas-style theming in the city than this place, which has been called the largest piece of pop art in the world. Along with a mini-New York Harbor, a scaled-down Brooklyn Bridge and a giant Statue of Liberty, the resort's skyline includes a dozen of the Big Apple's most famous landmarks. Inside, along with representations of Times Square, Central Park, Greenwich Village and Wall Street, you'll find every New York cliché in the book: a subway station, graffitied mailboxes, steam rising from manhole covers. It's an absolute blast.

Restaurants

There's good culinary variety at New York–New York – a posh steakhouse, a bargain deli, burger joints and ice-cream stands – but nothing about which to get particularly excited.

Entertainment & nightlife

Cirque du Soleil's newest Vegas production, the adult-oriented **Zumanity** (tickets $95-$165), opened here in 2003, and has played to packed houses ever since. **Rita Rudner** (tickets $63.50) performs her likeable stand-up routine nightly in the Cabaret Theatre. Daytime entertainment comes from the **Coney Island Emporium**, a lively amusement arcade, and the **Manhattan Express**, a spectacular rollercoaster. The most popular watering hole is the **Bar at Times Square**, where duelling piano players face off nightly in a rowdy, singalong atmosphere; the ghastly **Coyote Ugly** nightclub draws single men determined not to go to bed alone.

Other options

Harrah's (3475 Las Vegas Boulevard South, 1-800 392 9002, www.harrahsvegas.com, $60-$300) is a middlebrow place whose greatest assets are its mid-Strip location and Clint Holmes, its likeable headline act. The family-friendly **Monte Carlo** (3770 Las Vegas Boulevard South, 1-888 529 4828, www. monte-carlo.com, $69-$499) appeals to those after an approximation of high style at hoi polloi prices; the main attraction is the wonderful but pricey French restaurant André's.

Budget

Barbary Coast

3595 Las Vegas Boulevard South, at E Flamingo Road (reservations 1-888 227 2279/front desk, casino & restaurants 1-702 737 7111/www.barbary coastcasino.com). **Rates** $39-$199 single/double; $200-$400 suite. **Credit** AmEx, DC, Disc, MC, V.

The Barbary Coast, done up like fin-de-siècle San Francisco, occupies a sliver of space between the Flamingo hotel and Flamingo Road.

Restaurants

Michael's ($$$$$) has earned a reputation as one of the best gourmet/continental rooms in town. In the basement, the high-class French eaterie **Drai's** ($$$$$) has been one of Vegas's in-the-know restaurants since it opened in 1997.

Entertainment & nightlife

There's music in the lounge, but those in the know head for the after-hours party at Drai's (*see above*).

Circus Circus

2880 Las Vegas Boulevard South, at Circus Circus Drive (reservations 1-877 224 7287/front desk & casino 1-702 734 0410/www.circuscircus-lasvegas.com). **Rates** $39-$250 single/double. **Credit** AmEx, DC, Disc, MC, V.

The city's first family-friendly casino, opened in 1966, is a phantasmagoria of sights, sounds and colours that gnash together blindingly. The place is low-roller heaven: Vegas enigma Howard Hughes complained that it brought 'the poor, dirty, shoddy side of circus life' to the Strip. There's plenty for older children to do while the parents are pumping the slots, including the **Adventuredome Theme Park** and circus acts on the carnival mezzanine.

Restaurants

The **Steak House** (1-702 794 3767, $$$$$) is a high-quality dining room. Cantina-like **Blue Iguana** ($$) does cheap 'n' cheerful Mexican.

Entertainment & nightlife

The only entertainment here comes from the circus performers on the mezzanine level.

Other options

Excalibur (3850 Las Vegas Boulevard South, 1-877 750 5465, www.excalibur.com, $60-$350) is good for kids but not for adults. The 1955-vintage **Riviera** (2901 Las Vegas Boulevard South, 1-800 634 6753, www.theriviera.com, $29-$195) has some good shows: the tits-and-feathers clichés of Splash, and the edgy magic of the Amazing Johnathan. The **Stardust** (3000 Las Vegas Boulevard South, 1-866 642 3120, www.stardustlv.com, $60-$250) boasts one of the last remaining classic neon signs, good-value rooms and headline act Wayne Newton. The 1,149ft (350m) tower topping the **Stratosphere** (2000 Las Vegas Boulevard South, 1-888 236 7495, www.stratlv.com, $39-$219) is only worth approaching for the views from its tower and the ass-clenching Big Shot, which shoots passengers up 160ft (49m) to the tip of the tower. The best thing about the Moroccan-themed **Sahara** (2535 Las Vegas Boulevard South, 1-888 696 2121, www.saharavegas.com, $55-$285) is Speed: The Ride, the rollercoaster that zips around the hotel.

Off-Strip

Their location away from the madding crowd means the handful of big resorts that make their home away from the Strip have to work hard to attract visitors. This is, of course, in the visitors' favour: you get more for your money in

See p187.

Southern California

Nobu, at the Hard Rock Hotel.

terms of accommodation. Off-Strip is also where you'll find the two hippest casinos in Vegas: the **Hard Rock Hotel** and the **Palms**.

Mid range

Hard Rock Hotel

4455 Paradise Road, at Harmon Avenue (reservations & box office 1-800 473 7625/front desk & casino 1-702 693 5000/www.hardrockhotel.com). **Rates** $99-$300 single/double; $250-$750 suite. **Credit** AmEx, DC, Disc, MC, V.

If you want to rock and roll all night and party every day, look no further than the city's only rock 'n' roll casino (you'll recognise it by the huge Stratocaster jutting from the porte cochère). It draws a glittery, funseeking crowd to its 11-storey white deco-style property and circular casino. Though other casinos catering to the Gen-X crowd have opened since, the Hard Rock remains the city's premier party place.

Restaurants

You can't really go wrong with any of the eateries, from the sublime sushi at **Nobu** (1-702 693 5090, closed lunch, $$$$$) and upscale comfort food at **Simon** (1-702 693 4440, closed lunch, $$$$$) to **Mr Lucky's 24/7** ($), the city's finest diner.

Entertainment & nightlife

Entertainment comes courtesy of the acts who regularly play at the 3,000-capacity **Joint**. For celebrity- and gorgeous-people-watching, nowhere beats the **Center Bar** or the pulsating **Viva Las Vegas Lounge**. Opened in 2004, **Body English** is the hotel's requisite nightclub, a velvety rock star underground situated two storeys below the hotel.

Palms

4321 W Flamingo Road, at S Valley View Boulevard (reservations 1-866 942 7770/front desk & casino 1-702 942 7777/www.palms.com). **Rates** $69-$509 single/double; $109-$600 suite. **Credit** AmEx, DC, Disc, MC, V.

Opened by the sports-franchisee Maloof brothers in November 2001, the 470-room Palms has a nondescript, low-key desert resort vibe, attracting silver-haired gamers by day (slot payouts are the best in town) and the bold and beautiful by night. As the site of MTV's *Real World Las Vegas*, the Palms has racked up numerous coolness points in the collective Gen-X and -Y consciousness: the hip, beautiful and famous turn out in droves.

Restaurants

There are several choices here, all of them excellent. Up in the penthouse is André Rochat's **Alizé** (1-702 951 7000, closed lunch, $$$$$), where the views of the Strip are excellent and the French food even better. Downstairs, there's **Little Buddha** (1-702 942 7778, closed lunch, $$$$), where you can dine on Asian dishes with a French twist or nosh with the beautiful people at the sushi bar. And from Chicago comes **N9ne** (1-702 933 9900, closed lunch, $$$$$), a steakhouse and champagne/caviar bar.

Entertainment & nightlife

Rain (1-702 992 7970) is giving House of Blues and the Joint some competition as a live music venue, but where it shines is as a proper nightclub. High above it all (and with an equally lofty attitude) is the white-on-white **Ghostbar** (1-702 942 7777), kind of Los Angeles East. When the queues at both are too long (and they will be), there's the **Lounge**, which features DJs more or less nightly, or the bar at **N9ne** (*see above*), which can get pretty crowded on its own.

Rio

3700 W Flamingo Road, at Valley View Boulevard (reservations 1-800 746 7153/front desk & casino 1-702 777 7777/box office 1-888 746 7784/ www.playrio.com). **Rates** $59-$1,500 suite. **Credit** AmEx, DC, MC, V.

Thanks to its off-Strip location, its range of attractions and its friendly vibe, the Rio once had a lock on attracting tourists and locals in nearly equal numbers. The Palms opened across the street in 2001, but the Rio has worked hard, and successfully, to hang on to its popularity. One of the moves, during summer 2003, was to replace all existing servers with 'bevertainers', cocktail waitresses who sing and dance between bringing over the drinks.

Restaurants

There's little to excite here: the Rio's array of restaurants is fine, but rather predictable.

Entertainment & nightlife

The Rio's shows range from good to excellent. Entertainment family the **Scintas** ('shin-tas'; tickets $59.95) are a Vegas success story; the off-kilter comedic magic of **Penn & Teller** (tickets $70) runs in the Samba Theatre. For something different, try the live interactive comedy theatre of **Tony and Tina's Wedding** (tickets $78.95), a (now rare) dinner show wherein guests attend the ceremony and reception… and join in the scoffing and boozing. The nightlife, though, is weak: the **VooDoo Lounge** offers terrific views from the 51st floor, but staff are snooty and the crowd is loud and obnoxious.

Downtown

In 1906, one year after the railroad land auction made Vegas an official city and decades before Bugsy Siegel thought to go south, people were gambling in what is now Downtown. A lack of space meant the hotel-casinos on these tightly packed blocks were unable to expand, so this is still the closest you'll get to classic Vegas: old neon signs turn night to day, and casinos offer fewer sideshows (read: no entertainment) to distract from serious gambling. Indeed, this is a better place for the serious gambler: house rules are often more liberal than on the Strip, but minimum bets also tend to be lower.

Mid range

Binion's Horseshoe

128 Fremont Street, at Casino Center Boulevard (reservations 1-800 622 6468/front desk & casino 1-702 382 1600/ www.binions.com). **Rates** $29-$199 single/double. **Credit** AmEx, DC, Disc, MC, V.
For much of its storied history, this Downtown landmark was considered a home for serious gamblers. This reputation faded slightly after founder Benny Binion died in 1989, but the Downtown landmark is still home to the **World Series of Poker** every spring. Despite expanding in the late 1980s, the Horseshoe retains its old-school charm, not

least in the casino itself, a low-lit, smoky affair. The hotel's steak specials remain legendary: try the $9.95 deal in the **Coffee Shop**.

Golden Nugget

129 E Fremont Street, at Casino Center Boulevard (reservations 1-800 846 5336/front desk & casino 1-702 385 7111/www.goldennugget.com). **Rates** $49-$399 single/double; $275-$675 suite. **Credit** AmEx, DC, Disc, MC, V.
The Nugget has been a fixture since 1946, and you'll see its formerly OTT neon sign on nearly every postcard of Downtown. Steve Wynn remodelled it into a Vegas-style celebration of class and restraint in 1987, which it remains. However, in 2003, it was bought by a pair of thirtysomething guys, who are rebranding it into a classic *Swingers*-type Vegas vibe. Above-average eating options are headed by the **Buffet**, which beats its Strip competitors hands down for value; a revitalised programme in the 400-seat theatre has included acts such as Tony Bennett.

Budget

Fremont

200 E Fremont Street, at Casino Center Boulevard (reservations 1-800 634 6182/front desk 1-702 385 6244/casino 1-702 385 6222/www.fremontcasino. com). **Rates** $40-$100 single/double. **Credit** AmEx, DC, Disc, MC, V.
Built in 1956, the Fremont was Downtown's first carpet joint, meaning it had carpet on the floors rather than the wood found in 'sawdust joints'. Its block-long neon sign today helps light up the Fremont

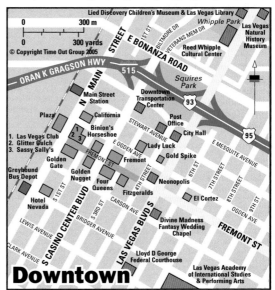

Street Experience. The hotel courts visitors from the Pacific Rim, hence the surprising **Second Street Grill**: an unexpectedly upscale and risk-taking fusion-focused dining room.

Golden Gate

1 Fremont Street, at Main Street (reservations 1-800 426 1906/front desk 1-702 385 1906/www.golden gatecasino.net). **Rates** $32-$69 single/double. **Credit** AmEx, Disc, DC, MC, V.

The 1906 Golden Gate is the city's oldest hotel still in operation, and offers a rare glimpse of Vegas before it became a spectacle. While the 106-room premises have been modernised, the hotel retains much of its historic charm. Even if you don't stay here, swing by the 24-hour **Bay City Diner**, a Downtown institution that still draws politicos, journalists and sundry Vegas characters.

Where to Eat

Ten years ago, Las Vegas's culinary reputation rested on the value offered by its buffets. No more. Almost every casino still has a buffet, offering a variety of food at one all-you-can-eat price, but they've been usurped by a wave of upscale restaurants. While there are holes in the variety (there's little in the way of high-quality, high-value ethnic neighbourhood eateries, for example), it's no exaggeration to say that Las Vegas is now one of the top dining destinations in the United States.

The majority of Vegas's best restaurants are in its hotel-casino resorts. In our individual reviews of these resorts, we've pinpointed the best eating options; here's a round-up of the town's finest restaurants by cuisine, including the best of the local non-casino restaurants.

American

Prime steakhouse at the Bellagio (*see p180*), chic **Bradley Ogden** at Caesars Palace (*see p180*), low-key high-roller heaven **Michael's** at the Barbary Coast (*see p185*) and **Aureole** at Mandalay Bay (*see p181*) form the quartet that rules the high end; the cheaper **AJ's Steakhouse** at the Hard Rock Hotel (*see p186*) is also worth the trip. The best diner in town is the open-all-hours **Mr Lucky's 24/7** (*see p186*), also at the Hard Rock. Off-Strip, head to the immaculate **Rosemary's Restaurant** (W Sahara Promenade, 8125 W Sahara Avenue, 1-702 869 2251, $$$$$), arguably the best non-casino eaterie in town, while the no-nonsense **Big Mama's Rib Shack** (2230 W Bonanza Road, 1-702 597 1616, $) offers stellar barbecue. Lastly, try the casual, friendly **Coffee Pub** (2800 W Sahara Avenue, 1-702 367 1913, $), which is tops for brunch.

Asian

Japanese eaterie **Nobu** at the Hard Rock (*see p186*) leads the field by a mile here. **Hamada of Japan** (365 E Flamingo Road, 1-702 733 3005, $$$) is cheaper; **Lotus of Siam** (Commercial Center, 953 E Sahara Avenue, 1-702 735 3033, $$) is an outstanding Thai restaurant; **Togoshi Ramen** (855 E Twain Avenue, 1-702 737 7003, $) is a bargain-basement noodle shack par excellence. Or if you fancy a plain old Indian, try Gandhi (4080 Paradise Road, 1-702 734 0094, www.gandhicuisine.com) and Shalimar (3900 Paradise Road, 1-702 796 0302, $$), two basic but tasty curry houses within a block of each other, or for a more upscale curry, make your way to Gaylord's in the Rio (*see p186*; 1-702 777 2277, $$$).

Buffets

Almost every hotel-casino in Vegas has a buffet, serving breakfast (typically $5-$10), lunch ($7-$13) and dinner ($10-$25) to a crowd with inestimably large appetites. Your one-off fee buys you as much food as you can eat, and the choice is usually immense: at least 50 food selections in a variety of cuisines. They're all much of a muchness, but a few stand out. The best regular buffet in town is at the **Bellagio** (*see p180*); the finest one-off buffet is **Bally's** Sterling Brunch, served only on Sundays (*see p183*); and the **Golden Nugget** (*see p187*) is Downtown's most impressive option.

French

Drai's at the Barbary Coast (*see p185*) is a surefire winner, as is the daring, exciting **Picasso** at the Bellagio (*see p180*). **Mon Ami Gabi** brasserie at Paris Las Vegas (*see p182*) offers better value. Local star chef André Rochat has three French eateries to tempt: the original **André's** in a quaint Downtown bungalow (401 S 6th Street, 1-702 385 5016, $$$$$), the upscale outpost of the same in the Monte Carlo (*see p184*), plus the city's best-view room, **Alizé** at the Palms (*see p186*).

Italian

Highly regarded **Canaletto** at the Venetian (*see p182*) and Wolfgang Puck's more approachable **Trattoria del Lupo** at Mandalay Bay (*see p181*) are both excellent, not to mention good value; Puck is also behind the welcoming Italian-fusion eaterie **Spago** at Caesars (*see p180*), which is especially good for lunch. If you're dining Off-Strip, try heading to the **Bootlegger** (7700 Las Vegas Boulevard South, 1-702 736 4939, www. bootleggerlasvegas.com, $$$), a glorious old Italian hangout with live entertainment: go for Off the Cuff on Fridays or Saturdays.

Latin American & Southwestern

The pan-American **Border Grill** at Mandalay Bay (*see p181*) has a terrific reputation; the artful, lively Mexican eats at the **Pink Taco** at the Hard Rock Hotel (*see p186*) are excellent value. Out of the casinos, the **Florida Café** (1410 Las Vegas Boulevard South, 1-702 385 3013, $$) dishes up no-nonsense Cuban food at bargain prices, while **Doña Maria's** (910 Las Vegas Boulevard South, 1-702 382 6538, $) serves the best tamales in town.

Middle Eastern

Two Middle Eastern places stand out in Vegas: **Marrakech** (3900 Paradise Road, 1-702 737 5611, $$$), which specialises in Moroccan cuisine, and the pioneering **Mediterranean Café** (4717 S Maryland Parkway, 1-702 731 6030, $$), where you'll find the best falafel and kebabs in town.

Seafood

The trend towards seafood in the Mojave Desert may seem odd. But remember: this is a city dedicated to excess and, in Vegas, there's nothing money can't buy. And the boast that fresh fish is flown in twice daily has become the hallmark of the city's best seafooderies. Formerly known as Aqua, the Bellagio's stuffy **Michael Mina's** (*see p180*) has long been thought the best. Now, however, there's the Venetian's hipper **AquaKnox** (1-702 414 3772, $$$$) to consider, while Mina competes for the glitterati at MGM's **SeaBlue** (*see p184*). Want to dine with the Hollywood hipsters? Make a booking at the Palms' **N9ne** (*see p186*), but do so far in advance.

Where to Drink

As with everything here, the Vegas drinking scene splits into two categories: bars in casinos, bars outside casinos. The former tend to be slick operations, carefully run and often pricey; the latter are usually a bit careworn, and many come with the not inconsiderable advantage that they stay open 24 hours a day, seven days a week. Drinkers unfussy about atmosphere should note that free booze is customarily

Southern California

It's strictly **Tabú**... *See p191.*

handed out to anyone gambling in a casino. Look out for a waitress, and don't forget to tip her: she'll be back that much quicker next time.

The Strip

Every casino has a classic lounge: a smart and comfortable place to have a drink, not far from the casino floor and often with live music to drown out the gaming machines. Among the nicer ones are the **Houdini Lounge** at the Monte Carlo (*see p184*), the **Indigo Lounge** at Bally's (*see p183*), **La Scena** at the Venetian (*see p182*) and the **Starlight Lounge** at the Stardust (*see p185*). Don't miss the Bellagio's **Fontana Lounge** (*see p180*), where properly mixed drinks and good live music meet.

However, it's the new breed of hotel bars that really grab the attention. Every opening sees another round of one-upmanship, as casino moguls try to make their new baby the slickest, smartest and most fashionable joint in town. The newest addition is the MGM Grand's **Teatro** (*see p183*), which stands out as having all the style, atmosphere and quality booze of **Tabú** (*see p184*) but without the attitude; other success stories include **Caramel** at the Bellagio (*see p180*), the **Shadow Bar** at Caesars Palace (*see p180*), adventurous **Rumjungle** at Mandalay Bay (*see p181*) and the **V Bar** at the Venetian (*see p182*). For all these joints (Teatro excepted), look sharp and pack plenty of cash: you may need the latter just to get past the doorman, much less fork over for the inevitably expensive cocktails.

Off-Strip

Of the Off-Strip casinos, the Hard Rock Hotel (*see p186*) boasts the **Center Bar**, a perpetually buzzing hangout in the middle of the casino floor, and the **Viva Las Vegas Lounge**, just off to the side but no less bustling. The bar at the Hard Rock's trendy

Simon eaterie is a grand alternative, but gets crowded at weekends. The Palms, meanwhile, offers the terrifyingly fashionable **Ghostbar** (*see p186*).

Downtown, the recently opened **Ice House** (650 S Main Street, 1-702 315 2570), a two-floor bar/restaurant with DJs and other special events, has taken over from the less homely but still comfortable **Saloon** (450 Fremont Street, 1-702 388 4116) as the watering hole of choice.

The rest of the city throws up an intriguing variety of bars, though you'll have to drive a little way to find a few of them. The legendary **Double Down Saloon** (4640 Paradise Road, 1-702 791 5775) is a deliberately scruffy hangout where the music is loud, the lighting is dim and the house cocktail is called Ass Juice. **Dino's** (1516 Las Boulevard South, 1-702 384 3894) is a fine neighbourhood bar, pure and simple; **Champagnes Café** (3557 S Maryland Parkway, 1-702 737 1699) serves a similar purpose, but with gorgeous flock wallpaper and a killer jukebox. The '70s live on at the **Dispensary Lounge** (2451 E Tropicana Avenue, 1-702 458 6343), whose Stealer's Wheel soundtrack and revolving waterwheel are straight out of Tarantino. Homesick Brits will find solace at the **Crown & Anchor** (1350 E Tropicana Avenue, 1-702 739 8676).

Nightlife

Gay & lesbian

Despite the city's visual flamboyance and anything-goes decadence, Vegas is far from a gay mecca. The scene here is small and centred around two areas, the main one being the Gay Triangle (or 'Fruit Loop'), whose epicentre is around the junction of Naples Drive and Paradise Road (just south of the Hard Rock Hotel). The town's two best gay nightclubs are

Beyond the casinos

Few attractions try to compete with the might of the Strip's hotel-casinos, and those that do fall feebly short. Leave the Strip, though, and there are a few attractions for which it's worth making a diversion. Just west of the Strip stands the **Elvis-a-Rama Museum** (401 S Industrial Road, 1-702 309 7200, $9.95), which claims the largest collection of Elvisabilia outside Graceland; east of the action is the **Liberace Museum** (1775

E Tropicana Avenue, 1-702 798 5595, $8-$12), the kitschiest attraction in America. But the real curio lies north of Downtown. The **Old Las Vegas Mormon Fort Historic Park** (500 E Washington Avenue, 1-702 486 3511) is Vegas's pioneer settling site. Although only remnants of the original 1855 building remain, guides are on hand to fill in the blanks, and the whole thing is a fascinating contrast to the neon excess down the road.

Fashion Show Mall. *See p191.*

here: **Gipsy** (4605 Paradise Road, 1-702 731 1919), a long-popular sweatbox that still draws big crowds with its mixed programme of music and cabaret, and **Free Zone** (610 E Naples Drive, 1-702 794 2310), where the highlights include a drag show on Saturday and the city's best lesbian night every Tuesday. Also here are a handful of gay bars, among them Levi-leather hangout **Buffalo** (4640 Paradise Road, 1-702 733 8355) and **Get Booked** (4640 Paradise Road, 1-702 737 7780), which sells magazines, cards, videos and gifts in addition to literature.

The other main gay area is around the Commercial Center mall at 953 E Sahara Avenue. Tenants here include the transsexual-friendly **Las Vegas Lounge** (1-702 737 9350), and the two top cruising spots in town: **Apollo Health Spa** (1-702 650 9191) and the more youthful **Hawk's Gym** (1-702 731 4295).

Nightclubs

Vegas's dance scene is in a perennial state of flux, as the hotel-casinos on the Strip – which is, of course, where most of the best nightclubs are located – constantly try to outdo each other. Indeed, a nightclub is rarely a nightclub in Sin City: it's an ultralounge, or a megaclub, or some other ridiculous marketing-led aphorism. This boosterism extends to the exclusivity of many clubs. You'll need to look good and carry cash to get beyond the velvet rope that fronts many venues, and even that may not be enough.

A few places will be jumping regardless of what's happening elsewhere. **Rumjungle** at Mandalay Bay (*see p181*) converts from restaurant to nightclub after 10pm, drawing a frisky crowd with music that's heavy on the Latin house. **Tabú** opened at the MGM Grand (*see p184*) in 2003 and shows little sign of losing popularity. **Ra** at the Luxor (*see p183*) has survived for eight years, perhaps because the emphasis here is more on dancing than at other spots. **Light** at the Bellagio (*see p180*) is exclusive, upscale and chic; **Rain** at the Palms (*see p186*) attracts the young and the beautiful.

Shopping

Along with restaurants and nightclubs, shopping is the big growth area in the world of Vegas casinos. The last decade has seen the shopping on the Strip improve immeasurably, in terms of both quality and variety.

Caesars Palace's pioneering, sizeable **Forum Shops** arcade (*see p181*) is still one of the best malls on the Strip, especially since expansion in late 2004. Mid-range staples such as Gap and Banana Republic are mixed in with the smarter likes of Christian Dior and DKNY, with variety coming from toy store FAO Schwarz and music retailer Virgin Megastore. Close behind is the stylish **Grand Canal Shoppes** at the Venetian (*see p182*), which mixes chains and classier one-off shops to impressive effect.

Via Bellagio at the Bellagio (*see p180*) contains only the smartest designer names (Chanel, Armani, Hermès. The hipper **Mandalay Bay Shops** (*see p181*), meanwhile, include an Urban Outfitters and – hurrah! – an arty bookstore. But the headline-maker on the

Strip is the **Fashion Show Mall** (3200 Las Vegas Boulevard South, 1-702 369 0704, www.thefashionshow.com): here, you'll find seven department stores, including Neiman Marcus, Saks Fifth Avenue and Nordstrom, plus some 200 other stores. Check out the Strip-front piazza covered by a giant floating 'cloud' that looks for all the world like a spaceship.

Arts & Entertainment

Casino entertainment

The best live entertainment in Vegas is to be found in the variety of shows staged by the resorts. These are big-budget spectaculars, their cost reflected in the ticket prices: expect to pay anywhere from $50 for the big evening shows.

Big production shows

The king of Vegas is Cirque du Soleil. The company has four shows in competing casinos, and there's not much to pick between them in terms of quality. However, themes and styles differ: **O** at the Bellagio (*see p180*) is pure extravagance, **Mystère** at Treasure Island (*see p183*) is light-hearted, and **Zumanity** at New York–New York is pretty saucy. Also worth catching are the old-time Vegas thrills and spills of **Splash** at the Riviera (*see p185*); the incomparable blend of art, science, comedy, music and spectacle staged by the **Blue Man Group** at the Luxor (*see p183*); and the Vegas production of Abba musical **Mamma Mia!** at Mandalay Bay (*see p181*).

Magicians

Since Siegfried and (especially) Roy had a little local difficulty with one of their tigers, the Strip has been missing its most iconic magicians. Still, **David Copperfield** is a relatively regular visitor to the MGM Grand (*see p183*). The best of the residents are two subversive magic acts: **Penn & Teller** give away the secrets of magic nightly at the Rio (*see p186*), but crucially keep a few to themselves; while the **Amazing Johnathan**'s mix of eyes-out trickery and gross-out comedy at the Riviera (*see p185*) appeals to an adult crowd.

Singers

A mixed bunch. **Céline Dion**'s regular show at Caesars Palace (*see p180*) is a disappointment, especially given the vast ticket price (**Elton**

John, who appears in the same showroom when Dion is on a break, is a far better bet), and much-hyped Mirage (*see p181*) variety act **Danny Gans** isn't much better. You're better off with Harrah's resident **Clint Holmes** (tickets $59.95, from 1-702 392 9002), who charms despite patchy material; **Gladys Knight** (tickets $65-$75, from 1-702 733 3333), whose hit-packed show is the best reason to visit the Flamingo; and the legendary **Wayne Newton** (tickets $54.95, from 1-866 888 3427), still going and still swingin' at the Stardust. For more on music at the MGM Grand, the Hard Rock Hotel and Mandalay Bay, *see p193*.

Afternoon bargains

Several casinos add an afternoon show into their mix, mainly as a bid to lure customers on to casino floors at what's usually a quiet time of day. It's worth bearing in mind, though, that despite the fact that tickets for these shows are almost always cheap by Vegas standards (less than $20), if you flick through local magazines or check the leaflets at the front desk and/or the LVCVA (*see p194*), you'll find coupons entitling you to discounted (two-for-one) or even free entry. The pick of the afternoon shows are **Mac King**'s magic show at Harrah's (*see p184*), ventriloquist **Ronn Lucas** at the Rio (*see p186*), and the vaudeville-and-burlesque jollity of **Bottoms Up!** at the Flamingo (3555 Las Vegas Boulevard South, 1-888 308 8899).

Zumanity.

Film

The nicest multiplex near the Strip is the shiny **Brenden Las Vegas 14** at the Palms (*see p186*; 1-702 507 4849), which, along with screening the latest blockbusters, also boasts one of the city's two IMAX screens. Downtown, **Crown Theatres** also offers 14 screens of entertainment at Neonopolis (450 E Fremont Street, 1-702 383 9600).

Galleries

Thanks to Steve Wynn, whose casino-made fortune led him to start buying art, Vegas now has a few galleries staging big-name temporary exhibitions: the **Bellagio Gallery of Fine Art** (Bellagio, 3600 Las Vegas Boulevard South, 1-702 693 7871) has been followed by Wynn's own **Wynn Collection** (3145 Las Vegas Boulevard South, 1-702 733 4100) and the flash 'n' fancy **Guggenheim Hermitage** at the Venetian (3355 Las Vegas Boulevard South, 1-702 414 2440). For the Downtown galleries, *see p194* **The culture club**.

Music

The unimpressive classical scene in Vegas is dominated by the **Las Vegas Philharmonic** (1-702 258 5438, www.lasvegasphilharmonic. com), which plays a little over a dozen concerts a year at UNLV's Artemus W Ham Concert Hall (4505 S Maryland Parkway). Big-name rock acts can be found at the enormous **MGM Grand Garden Arena** (*see p183*), the almost-as-big **Mandalay Bay Events Center** (*see p181*) and a trio of smaller venues: the **Joint** at the Hard Rock Hotel (*see p186*), the **House of Blues** at Mandalay Bay (*see p181*) and **Rain** at the Palms (*see p186*). Smaller travelling acts of the alt-rock variety play the **Huntridge Theatre** (1208 E Charleston Boulevard, 1-702 471 6700, www.thehuntridge.com), currently having a much-needed renovation, and the shambolic **Double Down Saloon** (*see p190*).

Where to Stay

The vast majority of guestrooms in Vegas are housed in the town's hotel-casino resorts; for a full rundown of these, *see pp179-187*. However, there are a number of other options if you'd like to steer clear of the madness for at least part of your stay. Easily the plushest is the **Four Seasons** (3960 Las Vegas Boulevard South, 1-877 632 5000, www.fourseasons.com, $310-$4,000), which adjoins Mandalay Bay and boasts some of the most luxurious guestrooms

What's on when

To find out what's on in Las Vegas when you're in town, then log on and get online: **www.vegas.com** is a mine of information, as are the websites run by the *Las Vegas Review-Journal* (**www.lasvegas.com**), the LVCVA (**www.vegasfreedom.com**) and *What's On* (**http://ilovevegas.com**).
  Of the town's print publications, the **Las Vegas Review-Journal** includes *Neon*, an entertainment guide, in its Friday edition, while three free alternative weeklies, **Las Vegas Weekly**, **CityLife** and the **Las Vegas Mercury**, contain listings and reviews. The town's other free magazines, led by **What's On: The Las Vegas Guide**, contain hopelessly uncritical reviews and features that are best ignored, but do have listings for events in the town's major resorts.

anywhere in town. Cheaper, Off-Strip options include two Marriott-related enterprises: **Courtyard by Marriott** (3275 Paradise Road, 1-800 321 2211, www.courtyard.com, $69-$290) and the **Residence Inn** (3225 Paradise Road, 1-800 331 3131, www.residenceinn.com, $65-$300), popular with conventioneers. The town's only hostel is the **Sin City Hostel** (1208 Las Vegas Boulevard South, 1-702 868 0222, $17.50). The motels on Las Vegas Boulevard are a fairly mixed bunch, which you're best off avoiding.

As mentioned earlier, the main thing to remember when booking accommodation is to shop around. Prices vary wildly from day to day and from resort to resort. If you're not planning to spend much time in your room, you might as well hole up somewhere cheap but central and save money for your waking hours.

Try to avoid visiting town during a big convention, as room availability nosedives and prices skyrocket: the LVCVA lists all major conventions on its website (www.lvcva.com). Whenever you visit Vegas, staying Downtown will be cheaper than staying on the Strip.

Resources

Hospital

University Medical Center *1800 W Charleston Boulevard (1-702 383 2000/www.umc-cares.org).*

Internet

Cyberstop Café *3743 Las Vegas Boulevard South (1-702 736 4782/www.cyberstopinc.com).* **Open** 7am-2.30am daily.

The culture club

The creation of a viable arts district in Vegas has long seemed an impossible ambition. For every hardy soul who opened a gallery, café or studio, another one shut up shop. The problem was simple: how to get the word out without help from the Vegas hype machine.

But **First Friday**, created by a couple of local storeowners and modelled on similar events in other US cities, has had a stunning effect. On the first Friday of each month, galleries and other cultural retail outlets in the area stay open late, sponsor a variety of performances and generally cross-pollinate. From quiet beginnings, the event has become a social staple in Vegas for the arty crowd.

First Friday takes as its focal point the **Arts Factory** (101-109 E Charleston Boulevard, 1-702 676 1111, www.theartsfactory.com),

a two-storey gallery complex just south of Downtown that contains a variety of artists, designers and galleries, but it stretches north to the **Ice House** bar/restaurant (*see p190*) and south to the **Funk House** antiques store and gallery (1228 S Casino Center Boulevard, 1-702 678 6278). Main Street, just to the west, is slowly coming into play, with the fine **Dust** gallery (1221 S Main Street, 1-702 880 3878) relocating here and leading the way.

If you're in town on the first Friday of the month, the event will come as a more than welcome break from the glitz and dazzle of the nearby Strip. But even if you miss First Friday, the Arts Factory and its neighbouring establishments are worth a visit, if only to see that Vegas's reputation as a town that's all commerce and no art is a false one.

Police
400 Stewart Avenue (1-702 795 3111).

Post office
1001 E Sunset Road (1-800 275 877). **Open** 7.30am-9pm Mon-Fri; 8am-4pm Sat.

Tourist information
Las Vegas Convention & Visitors Authority (LVCVA) *3150 Paradise Road, opposite Convention Center Drive (1-702 892 0711/www.lvcva.com).* **Open** 9am-5pm daily.

Getting There

By air
McCarran International Airport (1-702 261 5211, www.mccarran.com) is now just five minutes from the south end of the Strip. Among the airlines that fly to Vegas daily from both LA and San Francisco are America West, American Airlines, Northwest Airlines and US Airways.

By bus
Greyhound (1-800 229 9424, www.greyhound.com) runs 10-15 direct bus services daily between Los Angeles and Las Vegas (average 5-7hrs one-way, around $75 return), and 4-5 direct services from San Francisco to Las Vegas (average 15hrs one-way, around $130 return). The Greyhound station is at 200 S Main Street in Downtown Las Vegas.

By car
Your quickest route to Vegas from California will inevitably involve a lengthy drive on I-15. To steer clear of traffic, avoid driving during peak times: the Friday run from LA to Vegas can be horrific, as can the Sunday commute the other way. The only

exception to the I-15 route is travellers heading to Vegas from Death Valley, who should take Highways 190 and 160 via Pahrump.

Getting Around

If you're content to just stay on the Strip, you won't need to use your car. Indeed, on busy Friday and Saturday nights, it's quicker (and, in many ways, more fun) to walk than drive on Las Vegas Boulevard South.

Public buses, which cover much of the city, are run by **Citizens Area Transit** (CAT). The most popular route is 301, which runs the length of Las Vegas Boulevard and is the best way of travelling between the Strip and Downtown. For information on routes, call 1-702 228 7433, check www.rtcsouthernnevada. com/cat, or visit the Downtown Transportation Center at the junction of Stewart Avenue and Casino Center Boulevard. Fares are $1.25 on all routes except the 301, which costs $2.

A daring recent addition to the Vegas map is the Robert N Broadbent Las Vegas Monorail, which opened in July 2004. The monorail currently runs between the Sahara and the MGM Grand, making assorted stops along the way. A single fare is $3 and an all-day pass costs $10; for more, see www.lvmonorail.com.

Taxis are prevalent in Vegas, but they're forbidden by law from collecting passengers in the street. All hotel-casinos on the Strip have cab ranks; otherwise, bar and restaurant staff are happy to call one for you. To call one yourself, phone 1-702 873 2000.

Central California

Features

Central California

Stunning scenery and a buzzing city define the heart of the state.

First, a caveat: Central California doesn't really exist, at least not in the way that Southern California and Northern California exist. While the former lives up to its sun-bleached legend, and the latter is, on the whole, as rugged as its reputation suggests, Central California's extreme diversity prevents easy pigeonholing.

One thing's for sure. Though you're best off leaving the car in park during your stay in thrilling **San Francisco** (*see pp219-259*), arguably the most vital city in California and certainly the one with the most useful public transport network, the region that this guide denotes as Central California rewards the driver. The Pacific-side road that links Los Angeles and San Francisco along the **Central Coast** (*see pp197-218*) is among the most dazzling drives in the country, but is also home to a trio of very visitable small towns, extraordinary **Hearst Castle** and some fantastic hiking.

There's plenty more of the latter in the **Sierra Nevada** (*see pp314-342*). The landmark attraction here is undoubtedly **Yosemite National Park** (*see pp324-331*); south are two neighbouring national parks, **Sequoia** and **Kings Canyon** (*see pp339-342*), whose scenery is less spectacular but whose visitor numbers are more comfortable. To the north of Yosemite, meanwhile, is **Lake Tahoe** (*see pp316-322*), popular year-round.

Separating the Sierra Nevada from the Central Coast is the Central Valley, here split into two halves. The **Sacramento Valley** (*see pp286-294*) includes the unassuming but likeable state capital; the **San Joaquin Valley** (*see pp278-285*) ebbs south through dusty agricultural towns. Central California's hidden gem? The **Gold Country** (*see pp295-313*), a succession of adorable Gold Rush towns set in beautiful, becalmed countryside.

Climate

Average daily maximum and minimum temperatures in Central California.

		S Barbara	San Fran	Fresno	Sac'mento	Nevada City	S.L.Tahoe	Y'mite Vlly
Jan	max	64°F/17°C	56°F/13°C	54°F/12°C	53°F/11°C	51°F/10°C	37°F/2°C	49°F/9°C
	min	40°F/4°C	46°F/8°C	37°F/2°C	38°F/3°C	32°F/0°C	17°F/–8°C	26°F/–3°C
Feb	max	65°F/18°C	60°F/15°C	62°F/16°C	60°F/15°C	53°F/11°C	39°F/4°C	55°F/13°C
	min	43°F/6°C	48°F/9°C	40°F/4°C	41°F/5°C	33°F/1°C	18°F/–7°C	28°F/–2°C
Mar	max	65°F/18°C	61°F/16°C	67°F/19°C	64°F/17°C	56°F/13°C	43°F/6°C	59°F/15°C
	min	45°F/7°C	49°F/9°C	43°F/6°C	43°F/6°C	36°F/2°C	22°F/–5°C	31°F/–1°C
Apr	max	68°F/20°C	63°F/17°C	75°F/23°C	71°F/21°C	62°F/16°C	50°F/10°C	65°F/18°C
	min	47°F/8°C	50°F/10°C	48°F/8°C	46°F/7°C	39°F/4°C	26°F/–3°C	35°F/2°C
May	max	69°F/20°C	64°F/17°C	83°F/28°C	80°F/26°C	70°F/21°C	59°F/15°C	73°F/23°C
	min	50°F/10°C	51°F/10°C	54°F/12°C	50°F/10°C	45°F/7°C	32°F/0°C	42°F/5°C
Jun	max	72°F/22°C	66°F/19°C	91°F/32°C	87°F/30°C	79°F/26°C	69°F/20°C	82°F/28°C
	min	53°F/11°C	53°F/11°C	60°F/15°C	55°F/13°C	51°F/10°C	37°F/2°C	48°F/9°C
July	max	74°F/23°C	66°F/19°C	98°F/36°C	93°F/33°C	86°F/30°C	79°F/26°C	90°F/32°C
	min	57°F/13°C	54°F/12°C	65°F/18°C	58°F/14°C	56°F/13°C	43°F/6°C	54°F/12°C
Aug	max	75°F/23°C	66°F/19°C	96°F/35°C	91°F/32°C	86°F/30°C	78°F/25°C	90°F/32°C
	min	58°F/14°C	54°F/12°C	63°F/17°C	58°F/14°C	55°F/13°C	42°F/5°C	53°F/11°C
Sep	max	75°F/23°C	70°F/21°C	90°F/32°C	88°F/31°C	80°F/26°C	70°F/21°C	87°F/30°C
	min	56°F/13°C	56°F/13°C	59°F/15°C	56°F/13°C	51°F/10°C	38°F/3°C	47°F/8°C
Oct	max	73°F/22°C	69°F/20°C	80°F/26°C	78°F/25°C	70°F/21°C	58°F/14°C	74°F/23°C
	min	51°F/10°C	55°F/13°C	51°F/10°C	50°F/10°C	44°F/7°C	31°F/–1°C	39°F/4°C
Nov	max	69°F/20°C	64°F/18°C	65°F/18°C	64°F/17°C	56°F/13°C	47°F/8°C	58°F/14°C
	min	44°F/6°C	51°F/10°C	42°F/5°C	43°F/6°C	36°F/2°C	25°F/–3°C	31°F/–1°C
Dec	max	65°F/18°C	57°F/14°C	54°F/12°C	53°F/11°C	50°F/10°C	40°F/4°C	48°F/9°C
	min	40°F/4°C	47°F/8°C	37°F/2°C	38°F/3°C	32°F/0°C	20°F/–6°C	26°F/–3°C

Central California

The Central Coast

Ritzy resorts, smart restaurants and some of the most beautiful scenery in the US.

Where to start? You've seen it already: in photos, movies and commercials. Still, it bears repeating: the Pacific Coast Highway running along the central coast of California is awe-inspiring, beautiful, magical. Add the stunning natural environment to the fact that the road links California's two greatest cities while also taking in three of its nicest smaller towns and its most extraordinary tourist attraction, and it's no surprise that this is such a popular spot.

Which, of course, creates problems; indeed, of all California's destinations (with the arguable exception of Death Valley, almost unvisitably hot in summer), the quality of any Central Coast vacation is most affected by the time of year you visit. If possible, avoid summer, Memorial Day to Labor Day. The traffic on the two-lane highway, especially along Big Sur, can be paralysingly slow, which both frustrates the driver and spoils the view. Hitting the road first thing is one way to beat the traffic, but with fog often shrouding the coast on summer mornings, you're hardly getting the best of the place. Then, when you get off the roads, the area's greatest asset – its isolation – is tougher to find. Head here, instead, in April, May, September or October, when the area is generally a lot quieter and the Central Coast makes a convincing case for itself as California's greatest destination.

LA to Santa Barbara

Towards Oxnard & Ventura

The drive north from LA is a gorgeous one, however you choose to begin it. If you take US 101 from Hollywood, cut down through the untamed **Santa Monica Mountains**. Taking route N1 (aka Las Virgenes Road) will bring you down via the start of the Las Virgenes View Trail: this two and a half-mile uphill hike, which begins at the junction of N1 and the Mulholland Highway, affords gorgeous vistas.

But it's the coastal road that really appeals. The stretch of **Route 1** from Malibu to Oxnard is dotted with surfer-friendly beaches. **Leo Carillo State Beach** is popular, as are the beaches that form rugged **Point Mugu State Park** (1-818 880 0350, www.parks.ca.gov): Sycamore Cove, where you'll find the visitor centre, is especially magnificent.

Happily, **Oxnard** is nothing like as ugly as it first appears when approached from the south, dominated by a vast naval base. Still, nor is it a must-see destination. The impression left by the grand neo-classical building housing the **Carnegie Art Museum** (424 South C Street,

The Central Coast

1-805 385 8157, closed Mon-Wed, $1-$3) is spoiled by the disconsolate apartment building that now sits opposite; the **Cultural Heritage District**, some delightful old houses in the area between 2nd, 6th, F and C Streets, is a nice walk.

Ventura, though, is a handsome little place, a largely unspoilt piece of Middle America by the sea. The attractions are led by the **Mission San Buenaventura** (211 E Main Street, 1-805 643 4318, 50¢-$1), whose buildings date from 1815; a statue of Father Junípero Serra guards the entrance to **City Hall** (501 Poli Street, 1-805 658 4726). The **Ventura County Museum of History & Art** (100 E Main Street, 1-805 653 0323, closed Mon, $1-$4) is worth a look for the bizarre collection of figurines crafted by Ojai artist GS Stuart. But the real reason to stop here is to wander Downtown, between well preserved old buildings – pick up a leaflet from the visitor centre – and a handful of browsable bookshops.

Where to eat, drink & stay

Ventura beats Oxnard for food. **71 Palm** (71 N Palm Street, 1-805 653 7222, closed Sun, lunch Sat, $$$$) dishes up solid French cuisine; the **Anacapa Brewing Company** (472 E Main Street, 1-805 643 0350, $$) offers bar food to go with the brews. But maybe the best food in town is the barbecue to go at **It's in the Sauce** (2050 E Main Street, 1-805 652 1215, closed Mon, $).

Unless you fancy camping at Sycamore Canyon or one of the other campgrounds in **Point Mugu State Park** (1-800 444 7275, www.reserveamerica.com), the best lodgings are in Ventura. There are several chains present (*see p54*), but the largest independent spot is **Bella Maggiore** (67 S California Street, 1-800 523 8479, $75-$175), a cosy European-style hotel. B&Bs include the **Victorian Rose**, an old Gothic church (896 E Main Street, 1-805 641 1888, www.victorian-rose.com, $99-$175).

The Channel Islands

Straggled out in an offshore line from Point Conception to LA, the Channel Islands are a largely unspoiled wilderness home to more seals, seabirds and pelicans than humans. Five of the islands, and the surrounding ocean, make up **Channel Islands National Park**, a haven for those after an isolated marine experience involving such pursuits as diving, hiking, fishing, kayaking and wildlife observation.

Santa Rosa is the best island for an extended stay; closer to the shore, a 90-minute boat trip away, is tiny, dramatic **Anacapa**, a good day-trip option. If you can't be bothered to schlepp out that far, join the crowds at the mainland visitors' centre in Ventura (1901 Spinnaker Drive, 1-805

658 5730, www.nps.gov/chis) to watch live-dive relays from Anacapa (Tue & Thur May-Sept). Some 300,000 visitors come here annually, ten times the number who set foot on the islands.

Boat transport from here to the islands is organised by **Island Packers Cruises** (1-805 642 1393, www.islandpackers.com). No supplies are available on the islands: bring all food and water with you. Note that while temperatures are mild, it can be very foggy and windy.

The Ojai Valley

At first glance, **Ojai** looks to be nothing more than a delightful village in a gorgeous setting. But a keen eye spots a few signs that all is not quite as it seems. The cinema is flanked by a psychic; there are two racks of New Age CDs at Blue Sky Music. For Ojai is one of those towns to which people come to find themselves; and, perhaps, lose the real world into the bargain.

Ojai's big industry – though its practitioners would be appalled to hear it described as such – is spirituality. The town has long attracted

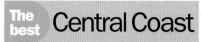

The best Central Coast

Things to do

The grandiose dreamworld of **Hearst Castle** (*see p207*), the **Monterey Bay Aquarium** (*see p216*), the **Paso Robles** wineries (*see p208*) and myriad **missions** (*see p214*).

Places to stay

Rough it at **Kirk Creek Campground** (*see p211*), live in luxury at the **Post Ranch Inn** (*see p211*), or go through the looking glass at the **Jabberwock Inn** (*see p217*).

Places to eat

Too many to mention: **Big Sky Café** in San Luis Obispo (*see p204*), **Stokes** in Monterey (*see p217*), and… oh, about a half-dozen restaurants in **Santa Barbara** (*see p201*).

Nightlife

Concentrated in two towns: **Santa Barbara** (*see p202*) and **San Luis Obispo** (*see p205*).

Culture

Again, **Santa Barbara** comes out ahead, though keen readers should detour to Salinas's **Steinbeck Center** (*see p218*).

Sports & activities

Surfing is excellent in places (*see p44*). But there are also some marvellous **hikes** in the state parks of Big Sur (*see p209*).

Central California

those who believe that we're not living in the 21st century but the Age of Aquarius. Perhaps it's something to do with the sunsets: locals talk with awe about the nightly 'pink moment', when the sun dips over the Pacific and its dying light reflects towards Ojai off the mountains.

Whatever the reason, the influence of the spiritually inclined is in evidence all over Ojai: in the galleries of **Ojai Avenue**, but also in the esoteric businesses on the fringes of the town. The Krotona Institute of Theosophy has been here for years; five miles east of Downtown along Reeves Road sits **Meditation Mount**, where you'll find spiritually inclined events (and, perhaps more pertinently, great views).

Still, there are other entertainments here. At joyously chaotic **Bart's Books** (302 W Matilija Street, 1-805 646 3755), piles of used books sit on every available surface, many in shelves outside the shop. And in June, there's the **Ojai Music Festival**, a long weekend of high-quality classical music presented under clear skies (1-805 646 2053, www.ojaifestival.org).

Where to eat, drink & stay

Though there are worthwhile restaurants on Ojai Avenue in the middle of town, among them relaxed, French-esque **Suzanne's Cuisine** (No.502, 1-805 640 1961, closed Tue, $$$), the

Disc drive

CDs to soundtrack your journey up or down the Central Coast.

California Dreaming Wes Montgomery
The jazz guitarist is backed by an orchestra on this easygoing, unsung delight.

Five Leaves Left Nick Drake
The singer-songwriter's 1970 debut, and the best balance he struck between beauty and melancholy in a pitifully brief career.

The Melody at Night, With You Keith Jarrett
Ten songs ('I Loves You, Porgy', 'Shenandoah'), delivered on solo piano with grace, tenderness and humility.

Ten Easy Pieces Jimmy Webb
'MacArthur Park', 'Galveston', 'Wichita Lineman'... you know more Webb songs than you realise. Here, armed with a piano, the backroom boy takes to the spotlight.

Zuma Neil Young & Crazy Horse
Young and comrades are at their most epic on the immense *Zuma*.

most esteemed eatery in town is a short drive from the centre: the **Ranch House** (S Lomita Avenue, 1-805 646 2360, closed Mon, $$$$), where a stream of in-the-know locals dine on high-class Californian cuisine in a delightful outdoor setting. The town's healthy vibe is increased by **Rainbow Bridge** (211 E Matilija Street, 1-805 646 6623, $), a food store and deli.

Lodgings are above par. The cottages at the **Emerald Iguana** (Blanche Street, 1-805 646 5277, www.emeraldiguana.com, $189-$289) are individually decorated and pleasingly private; the same owners run the **Blue Iguana** (11794 N Ventura Avenue, 1-805 646 5277, www.blue iguanainn.com, $95-$199), slightly more of a traditional hotel. With a spa, a golf course and some of the most comfortable rooms in the area, the **Ojai Valley Inn & Spa** (905 Country Club Road, 1-888 697 8780, www.ojairesort.com, from $195) offers unmatched luxury, presumably all the more so since a $70 million expansion and renovation, due to be completed in early 2005.

Santa Barbara

The fabled resort town of **Santa Barbara**, the 'American Riviera', is almost too perfect to be true. And boy, does it know it. A well heeled conservative coterie works hard to keep it that way: the only edge you'll get here is the oceanfront. But that's fine. You don't come here for urban thrills, but history, culture, top-end eating and shopping, and an old-world aesthetic.

The city's first kick is its benevolent setting. Sheltered between towering green mountains and deep blue ocean, it's always been sought-after land. The local Chumash Indians lived here for 5,000 years, provided for so liberally by nature that despite being hunter-gatherers, they had a settled society. It was, though, doomed by the ambitions of the Spanish missionary monks, who set up here in 1786.

Though the brothers had an interest in saving souls, they must have saved a bit of cash to boot. Santa Barbara's wealth is reflected in its park-studded layout, handsome residential areas and attractive public buildings. When its centre was devastated by an earthquake in 1925, a uniform Spanish style, copied later by many coastal towns in Southern California, was imposed and subsequently policed by preservation-oriented building regulations. It's now a pleasant place to wander, with, unusually, a real outdoor life.

Sightseeing

The story begins at the **Santa Barbara Mission** (2201 Laguna Street, 1-805 682 4713, www.sbmission.org, $4), one of the most attractive of the chain. The current building and courtyard date from 1870 and are still an active Catholic Church, though they are part-presented as a museum. The mission's elevated perch provides the perfect lookout over Santa Barbara, its red tiled roofs a striking contrast to the deep blue sea beyond.

For another perspective on the region, try the **Museum of Natural History** (2559 Puesta del Sol Road, 1-805 682 4711, www.sbnature.org, $4-$7), where the flora and fauna are most explicitly detailed, or go Downtown to visit the **Santa Barbara Historical Society** (100 E De La Guerra Street, 1-805 966 1601, www.santa barbaramuseum.com, closed Mon). Down De la Guerra Street is **De la Guerra Plaza**, site of the raucous Old Spanish Days Fiesta (first weekend in August). This historic town square is flanked by **City Hall** and **Casa de la Guerra** (11-19 E De la Guerra Street, 1-805 965 0093, http://sbthp.org/casa.htm, closed Mon-Wed), the early 19th-century home of city father José de la Guerra. Near here is what's left of the **Presidio**, now a state park (123 E Canon Perdido, 1-805 965 0095) in the process of restoration.

Perhaps the finest example of the town's Spanish-Moorish colonial architecture is the **County Courthouse** (11 Anacapa Street, www.sbcourts.org, closed Sat & Sun), a veritable castle complete with lofty towers, muralised interior and sprawling grounds. Take the elevator to the top and breathe in the billion-dollar views, from the 4,000-foot tips of the Santa Ynez Mountains all the way to the beach.

Two blocks away is the main drag of **State Street**, a strip of uppity boutiques, decent restaurants and upscale bars. The Paseo Nuevo shopping courtyard is an outdoor ode to the credit card. Near the top of the Downtown core is the **Museum of Art** (1130 State Street, 1-805 884 6476, www.sbmuseart.org), a worthwhile display of cutting-edge and ancient creativity. The ivy-filled galleries, brass sculptures and turtle-filled fountain of **La Arcada** would be worth a wander even without its restaurants.

State Street ends at **Stearns Wharf**, with wine tasting, seaside dining and views galore. Up the coast is **Leadbetter Beach**, where soft waves make the perfect playground; down the coast is sandy, comfortable East Beach. If it happens to be a Sunday, don't miss the weekly

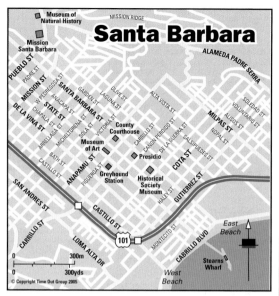

Arts & Craft Show (9am-5pm) on E Cabrillo Boulevard, jam-packed with the output of local painters, photographers, sculptors, jewellers, potters, yo-yo makers and lawn ornamenteers.

For all its urbanity, the town has a wilder face. For kayak rentals, try **Paddle Sports** (100 State Street, 1-805 899 4925); for wind-powered ocean expeditions, call the **Santa Barbara Sailing Center** (1-805 962 2826, www.sbsail. com) in the harbour; and for fishing, cruises and jet skis, try **Sea Landing** (301 W Cabrillo Boulevard, 1-805 963 3564). The affordable and flexible bike, kayak, climbing and hiking tours from **Santa Barbara Adventure Company** (1-805 452 1942, www.sbadventureco.com) reveal the most hidden of coastal treasures.

Where to eat

It's often said that Santa Barbara has one of the highest number of restaurants per capita of any town in the world. Whether this is actually true or not is probably unknowable, but there's plenty of variety here. **Bouchon** (9 W Victoria Street, 1-805 730 1160, closed lunch, $$$$) and **Downey's** (1305 State Street, 1-805 966 5006, $$$$) both serve upscale menus of Californian cuisine with a number of local wines; at **Sage & Onion** (34 E Ortega Street, 1-805 963 1012, closed lunch Mon-Thur & Sun, $$$$), British chef Steven Giles serves what he describes as European-American cuisine with an English twist; the old-fashioned dining room at the

Santa Barbara's Cabrillo Field houses Chromatic Gate, by local artist Herbert Bayer.

El Encanto Hotel (1900 Lasuen Road, 1-805 687 5000, $$$$$) has a terrace with lovely views. At the harbour, long-time fave **Brophy Bros** (119 Harbor Way, 1-805 966 4418, $$$$) turns out fresh fish and a celebrated clam chowder.

Other restaurants offer fine food at more affordable prices. A good place to start is **Roy** (7 W Carrillo Street, 1-805 966 5636, closed lunch, $$$), where the service is quick and the American food is memorable. In the same range, check homegrown and mellow **Dish** (138 E Canon Perdido, 1-805 966 5365, closed Sun & lunch Sat, $$$). Down another price rung are hamburgers from the **Habit** (628 State Street, 1-805 892 5400, $) and the **Italian-Greek Deli** (636 State Street, 1-805 682 6815, $).

Since the US's environmental movement began in Santa Barbara after the 1969 oil spill, a trip here wouldn't be complete without a visit to the organic old-timers' fave the **Sojourner** (134 E Canon Perdido Street, 1-805 965 7922, closed Sun, $), or the new, **SpiritLand Bistro** (230 E Victoria Street, 1-805 966 7759, dinner only, closed Mon & Tue, $), which is emerging as a formidable competitor. And try N Milpas Street for Mexican food. **La Super-Rica** (No.622, 1-805 963 4940, $) draws the raves and the crowds, but our favourite is **Julian's** (No.421, 1-805 564 2322, $).

Where to drink

State Street and its surroundings are home to the highest concentration of bars on the Central Coast. The loudest joints play to the college-age crowd, at party bars such as **Sharkeez** (416 State Street, 1-805 963 9680) and **Madison's** (525 State Street, 1-805 882 1182). But there are more sophisticated venues, such as **Blue Agave** (20 E Cota Street, 1-805 899 4694). A louche local

crowd converges at the retro-chic **Wildcat Lounge** bar/dance club (15 W Ortega Street, 1-805 962 7970). For the best of Santa Barbara's drinkers' bars, start with a happy-hour appetiser at **Joe's Café** (536 State Street, 1-805 966 4638), head up to **Jimmy's Oriental Gardens** (126 E Canon Perdido, 1-805 962 7582), and then drive the nail into the coffin of your hangover with a nightcap at the **Sportsman** (20 W Figueroa Street, 1-805 564 4411).

Arts & entertainment

For live music, **SOhO** (1221 State Street, 1-805 962 7776) has an eclectic schedule: reggae to folk, hip hop to salsa. **Velvet Jones** (423 State Street, 1-805 965 8676) attracts a younger crowd with alternative bands, electronica and hip hop. For one-off events, check the **Santa Barbara Bowl** (www.sbbowl.com) and the **Lobero Theatre** (www.loberotheatre.com).

The **Ensemble Theatre Company** (www.ensembletheatre.com) performs all year at the historic **Alhecama** (914 Anacapa Street, 1-805 965 6252); the **Contemporary Arts Forum** (653 Paseo Nuevo, 1-805 966 5373, www.sbcaf.org) frequently offers shows; both **UCSB** (www.dramadance.ucsb.edu) and **Santa Barbara City College** (www.sbcc.edu) stage student productions. To get the buzz on shows and performances, check out the **Santa Barbara Independent** weekly freesheet.

Where to stay

The options are many but the prices are high. Unless you're staying at the **Santa Barbara Tourist Hostel** (134 Chapala Street, 1-805 963 0154, www.sbhostel.com, rooms $44-$55), or camping at **Carpinteria** or **El Capitán State**

Beaches (1-800 444 7275, www.reserve america.com), expect to spend a healthy sum. The best spot Downtown is the **Hotel Santa Barbara** (533 State Street, 1-800 549 9869, www.hotelsantabarbara.com, $139-$259), within walking distance of the beach and plush enough to warrant its prices.

If moonlit walks on the beach sound good, there are three options. First are the inns of West Beach, where quaint hoteliers jockey for customers and sometimes drop rates on a slow weekend. Second are the resorts of East Beach: the **Doubletree** (633 E Cabrillo Boulevard, 1-805 564 4333, $249-$325) and **Radisson** (1111 E Cabrillo Boulevard, 1-805 963 0744, $259-$319) chains. And then there's the ritzy **Biltmore** (1260 Channel Drive, 1-805 969 2261, www.fourseasons.com, $500-$600), adjacent to Butterfly Beach, the region's choicest cove.

You'll find better deals further out of town. Try **El Prado Inn** (1601 State Street, 1-805 966 0807, $65-$200) or other spots further along State. You can even decamp to **Goleta**, ten miles or so west, which, though considered the ugly suburban duckling to Santa Barbara's civilised extravagance, isn't so bad after all.

Resources

Hospital

Santa Barbara *Santa Barbara Cottage Hospital, Bath & Pueblo Streets (1-805 682 7111/www.sbch.org).*

Internet

Santa Barbara *Kinko's, 1030 State Street (1-805 966 2700/www.kinkos.com).* **Open** 7am-10pm Mon-Thur; 7am-9pm Fri; 9am-7pm Sat; 10am-8pm Sun.

Police

Santa Barbara *215 E Figueroa Street (1-805 897 2300).*
Ventura *1425 Dowell Drive (1-805 339 4400).*

Post office

Santa Barbara *836 Anacapa Street (1-805 564 2226).*
Ventura *675 E Santa Clara Street (1-800 643 3057).*

Tourist information

Ojai *Ojai Visitors Bureau, St Thomas Aquinas Chapel, 150 W Ojai Avenue (1-805 646 8126/ www.ojaichamber.org).* **Open** 9.30am-4.30pm Mon, Wed-Fri; 10am-4pm Sat, Sun.
Oxnard *Oxnard CVB, 200 W 7th Street (1-800 269 6273/1-805 385 7545/www.visitoxnard.com).* **Open** 8.30am-12.30pm, 1.30pm-5.30pm Mon-Fri.
Santa Barbara *Santa Barbara CVB, 1 Garden Street (1-805 966 9222/www.sbchamber.org).* **Open** 9am-5pm Mon-Sat; 10am-5pm Sun.
Ventura *Ventura Visitors & Convention Bureau, Suite C, 89 S California Street (1-800 483 6214/ 1-805 648 2075/www.ventura-usa.com).* **Open** 9am-5pm Mon-Sat; 10am-4pm Sun.

Solvang to San Simeon

North to Avila Beach

The coastal route north from Santa Barbara is predictably attractive: after taking in mellow **El Capitán State Beach** and delightful **Refugio State Beach**, the road makes a northerly turn after rugged, oceanside **Gaviota State Park** (for all: 1-805 968 1033), where there are several good trails. But Highway 154, aka San Marcos Pass Road, is no ugly beast, winding steeply through quietly dazzling scenery. When the option arises, take Highway 246 towards Santa Ynez rather than Highway 154 to Los Olivos: the scenery isn't as alluring, but there are a few diversions along the way. Three miles west of Santa Ynez is the silly gingerbread village of **Solvang** (*see p204* **Grate Danes**); just beyond it, at **Buellton**, is the 80-year-old **Pea Soup Andersen's** (1-805 688 5581), a twee landmark not shy about advertising its house speciality.

From here, you've another choice: north on US 101, or west on Highway 246. On the former route sit a handful of wineries; the latter leads to **Lompoc** (rhymes with Coke), a sweet, hard-working town whose attractions include the lovely, relatively undiscovered **Ocean Beach County Park** and, from June to August, 1,500 photogenic acres of flower fields. The **Lompoc Museum** (200 South H Street, 1-805 736 3888, closed Mon) offers exhibits on the Chumash Indians (*see p200*). Also here is one of the more visitor-friendly of the missions, **La Purisima** (2295 Purisima Road, 1-805 733 3713, www.la purisimamission.org). The mission is open

Whale-watching

The annual whale-watching season off the Southern California coastline is in winter (December to March), following the migratory habits of the gray and wright whales; in **Santa Barbara**, whale-watching reaches its peak in summer, ending in mid September. Most marinas have boats offering trips and many operate on a 'sightings guaranteed' basis: if you don't see any whales, your money is refunded, or (more often) you're given a pass to go free on a subsequent trip. Among firms offering tours is **Sea Landing** (1-805 963 3564, www.condorcruises.com).

Central California

daily, but you should take one of the guided tours (2pm daily, also 11am Sat & Sun) to get the most from the place, rebuilt in 1812 after an earthquake destroyed the original. A new visitor centre and museum opens in 2005.

Continue north past the **Vandenberg Air Force Base**, a pair of fabulous steakhouses (*see p205*), the unheralded **Guadalupe Dunes Preserve** (guided walks are organised by the Dunes Center in Guadalupe, 1-805 343 2455, www.dunescenter.org) and the beautiful **Point Sal State Beach** (take Brown Road just south of Guadalupe), and you'll reach **Pismo Beach**, a fairly scruffy little seaside resort with not entirely unfulfilled aspirations to better itself. Still, the beaches are at least quieter than the sand in **Oceano** to the south. There is a public beach here, but most people take to the sand in 4WDs or ATVs: **Oceano Dunes State Vehicular Recreation Area** (1-805 473 7230, http://ohv.parks.ca.gov) is the only beach in California that allows vehicles, and is hugely popular with experienced off-roaders, novice teenagers and thrill-seeking tourists. It's crass but sneakily enjoyable; if you didn't bring your own vehicle, firms such as **Angelo's** (307 Pier Avenue, 1-805 481 0355) and **BJ's** (197 W Grand Avenue, 1-805 481 5411) are happy to rent you one. Rates start around $25 an hour.

The beaches and small towns further north, around the San Luis Obispo Bay, are nicer. **Shell Beach** is quiet, rugged and stately, but the best of the lot is **Avila Beach**. Oil contamination from the nearby Unocal Refinery almost finished the tiny resort in the 1990s. However, after years of campaigning, a clean-up and general remodelling of the beach began; it's now a tidy, well maintained little spot. You can fish off **Harford Pier**, but some prefer to pick their own from ready-caught selections sold by sun-bleached sea dogs.

Where to eat & drink

The Danish cafés of **Solvang** (*see below* **Grate Danes**) are good for a snack; **Pea Soup Andersen's** (*see p203*) is a local landmark, despite the fact that the soup isn't to everyone's taste; and the eateries of **Pismo Beach**, with the exceptions of upscale seafood joint **Steamers** (1601 Price Street, 1-805 773 4711, $$$$) and **Giuseppe's** Italian restaurant (891 Price Street, 1-805 773 2870, $$$, closed lunch Sat & Sun), are largely forgettable. However, all is not lost: there's fine American fare at **Gardens of Avila**, at the Sycamore Springs resort ($$$$; *see p205*), and two stellar Cali-cowboy steakhouses back down the coast.

Grate Danes

The town of **Solvang** was settled by a group of adventurous Danes in the early 20th century, their plan to set up a school in which to educate their kids in Scandinavian traditions. The school didn't pan out, for the Danes soon savvily realised that they were sitting on a potential goldmine: themselves. Education fell by the wayside, and a tourist industry grew up in its place; travelling Americans became fascinated by the relative exoticism of the Danish way of life, rendered in approachable soft-focus and dubbed in English.

The initial trickle of visitors soon became a whitewater river; today, Solvang is a living, breathing theme park, only with no admission charge and free parking. Bakeries and gift shops, souvenir stores and restaurants: all are housed in a string of immaculately maintained chocolate-box buildings you feel guilty about touching. The Best Western has a gabled roof; the Days Inn has a windmill. It's all deeply silly. But Solvang's also a fine place to stop for a snack: there are decent bakeries here, of which the best is probably **Olsen's** (1529 Mission Drive, 1-805 688 6314).

The **Hitching Post** (3325 Point Sal Road, Casmalia, 1-805 937 6151, $$$, closed lunch) is the more casual of the pair; the **Far Western Tavern** (899 Guadalupe Street, Guadalupe, 1-805 343 2211, $$$) is a little smarter and calmer, though it's all relative. Both serve terrific cuts of meat in convivial atmospheres.

Where to stay

Pismo Beach contains a good deal of choice in the lodgings stakes, but not much variety. The **Kon-Tiki Inn** (1621 Price Street, 1-888 566 8454, 1-805 773 4833, www.kontikiinn.com) has a prime, view-hogging spot by the beach, for which you'll pay a price; better value, perhaps, are the basic rooms at the sweet little **Pismo Beach Inn** (371 Pismo Street, 1-877 733 7966, 1-805 773 1234, www.pismobeachinn.com). A good bet for families is the **Pacific Plaza** (444 Pier Avenue, 1-800 300 0903, 1-805 473 6989, www.pacificplazaresort.com, $85-$165) in Oceano, 56 one- and two-bed suites available to rent by the day or week. Further north is **Sycamore Springs Resorts** (1215 Avila Beach Drive, 1-800 234 5831, 1-805 595 7302, www.sycamoresprings.com, $145-$195), an upscale hotel, spa and spiritual retreat.

Both **El Capitán** and **Refugio State Beaches** have small campgrounds, as does **North Beach** in Pismo Beach; book on 1-800 444 7275 or at www.reserveamerica.com.

San Luis Obispo

California Polytechnic State University doesn't dominate quite as completely as it might. But make no mistake about it: **San Luis Obispo** is still a college town, and a very likeable one at that. As yet undiscovered by the majority of tourists, who head straight for ritzier Santa Barbara, San Luis Obispo has kept its small-town feel, helped by a smallish population (fewer than 50,000) and a Downtown that's tidily laid out and easy on the eye.

The giveaway signs to the town's collegiate status are varied. The small Downtown, centred around Chorro and Higuera Streets, is dotted with good-value restaurants; posters outside bars threaten of imminent bands or DJs. **Copeland's**, a block-long megastore, offers clues as to Cal Poly's sporting prowess; alumni include John Madden and Ozzie Smith. On nearby Monterey Street, **Boo Boo Records** (No.978, 1-805 541 0657) and the **Phoenix** bookshop (No.990, 1-805 543 3591) hawk stimulants for ear and intellect; down on Higuera Street, **Decades** (No.785, 1-805 546 0901) does a roaring trade in used clothing, sold at premium prices.

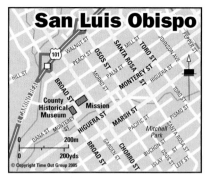

Yet there's more to the town than its college. There is, inevitably, a mission here: **Mission San Luis Obispo de Tolosa** (751 Palm Street, 1-805 781 8220, www.missionsanluis obispo.org), beautifully situated by the gentle San Luis Obispo Creek. The plaza is a lovely place to while away a couple of hours with a good book, though there are other attractions. The **San Luis Obispo County Historical Museum** (696 Monterey Street, 1-805 543 0638, www.slochs.org), housed in a century-old former library, does what you might expect; the **San Luis Obispo Art Center** (1010 Broad Street, 1-805 543 8562, www.sloartcenter.org) offers small shows, often by local artists.

Around it all, Downtown San Luis Obispo is a handsome place, one that wears its history casually. A short walking tour, grandly named the Path of History (leaflets from the visitor centre), maps the more interesting buildings, and is well worth wandering. But the town's main attraction is its atmosphere: academic but not oppressively so during the day, lively but never deafening at night. Nice place.

Where to eat & drink

Lots here, much of it very good. The menu at the **Mission Grill** (1023 Chorro Street, 1-805 547 5544, $$$$) rings the usual Cal-American bells (pork chops, piñon-crusted salmon), but the execution impresses. Dinners are good; lunch or Sunday brunch out on the patio is even better. The **Big Sky Café** (1121 Broad Street, 1-805 545 5401, $$$) is more colourful and more casual, but the food's just as great. American dishes served simply and with skill. Moving out of the US, **Le Fandango** (717 Higuera Street, 1-805 544 5515, closed lunch Sun & Mon, $$$) cooks up a lively menu of French specialities; **Oasis** (675 Higuera Street, 1-805 543 1155, $$$) offers curries and tagines in a room whose decor is best described as mall-exotic; smart-casual **Buona Tavola** (1037 Monterey Street,

1-805 545 8000, closed lunch Sat & Sun, $$$) has an all-Italian menu; and **Pepe Delgado's** (1601 Monterey Street, 1-805 544 6660, closed Mon, $) rather overcooks the Mexican theming in terms of its appearance, but the food is fine.

This being a college town, (1) there are bars galore, and (2) they're generally pretty darn loud. Time your visit right, and you can sample some of the fine beers at **SLObrew** (geddit?), the town's microbrewery, in relative peace (1119 Garden Street, 1-805 543 1843); otherwise, try **McCarthy's**, a kind of polite, Irish-themed dive (1019 Court Street, 1-805 544 0268).

Where to stay

There's nowhere quite like the **Madonna Inn** (100 Madonna Road, 1-800 543 9666, 1-805 543 3000, www.madonnainn.com, $147-$330), a riot of kitsch absurdity. The hotel was built in the 1950s by Alex Madonna, but designed by his wife Phyllis, who had a thing about the colour pink. The 109 rooms all have different themes: some are bland, but others – the horse-themed Tack Room, the exotic Caveman Room – are titanically OTT. If you can't stay, do at least stop by for a slice of cake in the Copper Café and a wander around the garish steakhouse.

More sedate accommodations are available at the delightful **Garden Inn** B&B (1212 Garden Street, 1-805 545 9802, www.gardenstreetinn. com, $145-$205), a stone's throw from the action but still private. The cluster of motels north of Downtown on Monterey Street include chains (such as **Holiday Inn**, No.1800, 1-805 544 8600; *see p54*) and independents. **La Cuesta** (No.2074, 1-800 543 2777, 1-805 543 2777, www.lacuesta inn.com, $89-$169) is a smart, business-like operation; the **Apple Farm** (No.2015, 1-800 374 3705, 1-805 544 2040, www.applefarm.com, $119-$329) brings on the corporate country chintz. Also here is the currently closed site of the first ever motel in the United States.

Morro Bay, Cambria & San Simeon

The hills above **Morro Bay** are quite a sight: smart houses, stacked one on top of the other, all staring expectantly towards the ocean like spectators at the theatre. Damn shame, then, that their view is blighted by what must be, given context and architecture, the ugliest building in California. The Morro Bay Power Plant isn't just a blot on the landscape: it's a view-hogging monster. It takes quite a building to lure the eyes away from the immense **Morro Rock**, an almost mystical 576-foot-tall (176-metre) volcanic rock at the northern edge of the bay, but the power plant manages it.

The town itself isn't much, just a cluster of gift shops and restaurants. But a nice drive south of the town will lead you through **Morro Bay State Park** (1-805 772 7434, www.parks. ca.gov), which contains a fine golf course (1-805 782 8060) and some campsites, to a marina where you can grab a drink as the sun goes down. Further south is the craggy **Montaña de Oro State Park** (1-805 528 0513, www.parks. ca.gov), home to a nice beach at Spooner's Cove.

Route 1 north of Morro Bay leads you to **Cambria**, either an adorable little village or a perfectly dreadful parade of over-cutesy gift shops and B&Bs. We'll leave it to you to decide on which side of the fence you sit, but if you have time, make the brief detour away from the main drag to **Nitt Witt Ridge**. This amazing three-storey property, built into the hillside by local dustman Art Beal using nothing but materials he salvaged from the trash, is now a California State Landmark. Driving up to the house (north-west of Main Street; take Cornwall Road and then Hillcrest Drive to No.881) will give you some idea of Beal's achievement, but tours ($5) are also offered of the property; call 1-805 927 2690 to make the required reservation.

Beyond Cambria, signs of life grow sparse. Past Cambria's pretty **Moonstone Beach** and the imposing **San Simeon State Park** (1-805 927 2020) is the turn-off to **Hearst Castle** (*see p207* **The king of all he surveys**); just by it is **William Randolph Hearst Memorial State Beach** (1-805 927 2020), great for picnics. From here, it's only a few miles to the shoreline of **Piedras Blancas**, popular both with kitesurfers and with elephant seals; there's even a viewpoint, five miles north of Hearst Castle, set aside for curious visitors to spy on them (the elephant seals, not the kitesurfers).

Where to eat, drink & stay

Though the waterfront restaurants in Morro Bay offer ocean views, Cambria has the best food. The **Sow's Ear** (2248 Main Street, 1-805 927 4865, closed lunch, $$$$) offers a cultured take on classics such as chicken-fried steak and steak sandwiches, while the **Moonstone Beach Bar & Grill** (6550 Moonstone Beach Drive, 1-805 927 3859, $$$$) deals from a pricey menu dominated by pastas and seafood in front of a sea view. **Linn's Main Binn** (2277 Main Street, 1-805 927 0371, $$), as its name suggests, is a little more low-key.

Among the motels and resorts of Morro Bay are a couple of B&Bs: the surprising **Baywood Inn** (1370 2nd Street, 1-805 528 8888, www. baywoodinn.com, $90-$170), housed in an old office building but nicer than that description suggests, and the more traditional, four-room

The king of all he surveys

With his father, he visited the Central Coast of California often as a youngster, and adored its rugged, untamed and isolated hill country. He also, aged ten, went on a grand tour of Europe, an extended vacation he never forgot.

Fast forward to the 1920s, by which time newspaper mogul William Randolph Hearst – whom you may also know as Citizen Kane – was among the wealthiest men on the planet. It was time, he decided, to build his dream home: located on the inhospitable Pacific-side hills he grew to love as a kid, but recreating the European culture he recalled from his holiday. Hearst called it 'the ranch', in that singular way the ludicrously wealthy have of downscaling the excessive to miniature. But a half-century after his death, his former home is now officially called the Hearst San Simeon State Historical Monument and semi-officially known as **Hearst Castle**, a 165-room estate styled after all kinds of notable, memorable and forgettable European buildings and crammed to bursting with heady Old Masters, immaculate furnishings and fittings, and an eye-boggling, brain-scrambling array of design flourishes.

Believe the tour guides, and the place is a stunning monument to a fascinating man. Which it is. But it's more than that; for anyone approaching it from a distance, whether geographical or cultural, Hearst Castle is also a microcosm of American ambition, American excess and, yes, the American dream. Witness the guts and gall that drove its planning; this is not land on which it's easy to pitch a tent, let alone build a series of mansions. Witness the perfectionism that defined its construction; Hearst changed his mind almost weekly, extending the time it took to build the castle to almost three decades. Witness, too, the generous absorption of and/or shameless pilfering from faraway cultures, the co-option of others' cultural history, and the posthumous egalitarianism that led its owner to bequeath the property to the state of California and open it to visitors. (The fact that the castle has not so much preserved as enhanced Hearst's place in history is, of course, entirely coincidental.)

It matters not whether Hearst had good taste in the ancient architectural styles he chose to mimic. It matters not whether, when it came to the centuries-old art and antiquities that fill every room of his dream home, he was a collector or an accumulator. As with

Hearst's newspaper empire, the thing that matters most about Hearst Castle – indeed, the only thing that really matters about it – is its scale. Hearst brought Europe to America in a manner entirely without precedent.

Hearst Castle is now open to the public for excellent guided tours. Most choose to take tour no.1, highlighted by visits to the main house (aka Casa Grande) and two stunning pools. The tour, which provides a good overview of Hearst and his abode, begins with a movie that provides background to the house's construction. Tours 2, 3 and 4, held less often than tour 1, offer access to other parts of the house; the even more infrequent tour no.5 is held at night, with costumed docents adding extra ambience. Reservations are recommended for all tours, and are more or less essential at peak times. Be sure to arrive in time for your tour: the only way to travel from the visitor centre to the house itself is by bus, and if you miss your ride, you may not get on a later tour. For details of tour times, call 1-805 927 2020; for reservations, try 1-800 444 4445. There's further information at www.hearstcastle.org.

Marina Street Inn (305 Marina Street, 1-888 683 9389, 1-805 772 4016, www.marinastreetinn. com, $110-$160). Cambria also contains some B&B-type lodgings, many near the water on Moonstone Beach Drive. **Moonstone Hotels** operate a number of pricey but reliable hotels with countrified themes and ocean views: www.moonstonehotels.com lists them. There's better value away inland; try the **Olallieberry Inn** (2476 Main Street, 1-888 927 3222, 1-805 927 3222, www.olallieberry.com, $115-$182).

There's camping at **Montaña de Oro**, **Morro Bay** and **San Simeon State Parks** (Morro Bay, closed until April 2005), and at **Morro Strand State Beach**; reservations, required in summer, can be made on 1-800 444 7275 or www.reserveamerica.com.

Paso Robles & around

Napa and Sonoma Counties gain the majority of the visitors, but there are other wine-producing regions in California that go about their business in rather quieter and more affordable fashion. The most visitor-friendly of them is just off the Central Coast at the southernmost tip of the Salinas Valley, a gorgeous drive east on Highway 46 from just south of Cambria.

The action is centred around the tidy little town of **Paso Robles**. A leaflet produced by the **Paso Robles Vintners & Growers Association** (1-805 239 8463, www.pasowine. com) and available from the **Paso Robles Visitor & Conference Bureau** (*see p209*) details the wineries' locations; most are on or near Highway 46, and offer daily tastings. Wineries west of Paso Robles include **York Mountain** (7505 York Mountain Road, 1-805 238 3925, www.yorkmountainwinery.com, closed Tue & Wed), seven miles from Paso Robles and the oldest winery in the area, and the **SummerWood Winery** (cnr Highway 46 and Arbor Road, 1-805 227 1365, www.summer woodwine.com), home to a luxurious B&B. East of town, try **Martin & Weyrich** (1-805 238 2520, www.martinweyrich.com), which stages regular concerts, and well regarded **Eberle** (1-805 238 9607, www.eberlewinery.com), which offers lovely views from its picnic-friendly gardens. Tours ($25) are by appointment only.

East of the wineries, about a half-mile before Highway 46 forks off into Highway 41, is a real curiosity. It was around here, on 30 September 1955, that a speeding James Dean crashed Little Bastard, his affectionate nickname for the Porsche Spyder, into the Ford of ironically named San Luis Obispo student Donald Turnupseed. Dean died in the crash, and is remembered with an artful silver memorial outside the **Jack Ranch Café** (1-805 238 5652).

Where to eat, drink & stay

There are a cluster of good-value chain motels around the edge of Paso Robles near US 101, among them a **Holiday Inn Express** (2455 Riverside Avenue, 1-805 238 6500, $99-$119), plus a few cheaper independents such as the **Adelaide Inn** (1215 Ysabel Avenue, 1-805 238 2770, www.adelaide.com, $50-$89), but if you've got the money, head for the **Paso Robles Inn** (1103 Spring Street, 1-800 676 1713, 1-805 238 2660, www.pasoroblesinn.com, $115-$175). The handsome guestrooms are scattered over a number of buildings, some right by a tiny spa; several rooms have their own spas that utilise water from the area's hot springs. Deals are offered out of peak season.

The Paso Robles Inn also provides two of the town's best eating options: the circular **Coffee Shop** ($), good for breakfast and lunch, and the **Steakhouse** ($$$), which does what you might expect. There are fab smoothies and to-die-for baked goods at the **Old Mission Coffee House** (1102 Pine Street, 1-805 237 0095, $); **Panolivo** (1344 Park Street, 1-805 239 3366, closed dinner Tue, $$$) serves affordable French food. More basic eating options are on the edge of town, among them **Big Bubba's BBQ** (1125 24th Street, 1-805 238 6272, $$); if the food doesn't give you indigestion, the mechanical bull will. South, in Templeton, is **McPhee's Grill** (416 Main Street, 1-805 434 2304, 1-805 434 3204, $$$), which serves excellent casual Californian cuisine.

Resources

Hospital
San Luis Obispo *Sierra Vista Regional Medical Center, 1010 Murray Avenue (1-805 546 7600/ www.sierravistaregional.com).*

Internet
San Luis Obispo *Kinko's, 894 Monterey Street (1-805 543 3363).* **Open** 6am-10pm daily.

Police
Morro Bay *850 Morro Bay Boulevard (1-805 772 6225).*
Paso Robles *900 Park Street (1-805 237 6464).*
San Luis Obispo *1042 Walnut Street (1-805 781 7317).*

Post office
Morro Bay *898 Napa Avenue (1-805 772 2361).*
Paso Robles *800 6th Street (1-805 237 8342).*
San Luis Obispo *893 Marsh Street (1-805 541 9138).*

Tourist information
Lompoc *Lompoc Valley Chamber of Commerce, 111 South I Street (1-800 240 0999/1-805 736 4567/ www.lompoc.com).* **Open** 9am-5pm Mon-Fri.

Pfeiffer Falls. *See p210.*

Morro Bay *Morro Bay Chamber of Commerce, 845 Embarcadero Road, Suite D (1-800 231 0592/1-805 772 4467/www.morrobay.org).* **Open** 10am-6pm Mon-Fri; 10am-4pm Sat.
Paso Robles *Paso Robles Visitors & Conference Bureau, 1225 Park Street (1-800 406 4040/ www.pasorobleschamber.com).* **Open** 9am-5pm Mon-Fri; 10am-4pm Sat.
San Luis Obispo *San Luis Obispo Chamber of Commerce, 1039 Chorro Street (1-805 781 2777/ http://visitslo.com).* **Open** 10am-5pm Mon; 8am-5pm Tue, Wed; 8am-8pm Thur; 8am-7pm Fri; 10am-7pm Sat; 11am-5pm Sun.

Big Sur

There are other indelible images of Californian travel: the winding roads of Wine Country, the Hollywood sign, Zabriskie Point in Death Valley, the cable cars of San Francisco, El Capitan in Yosemite. But ultimately, nothing quite compares with the soaring, swooping **Big Sur** coastline, as iconic as California gets.

The area was first settled 3,000 years ago by the Esselen Native American tribe, but when the Spanish arrived in the late 18th century, most of them had gone: disease is the most common explanation, but it's possible that they simply fled. Either way, it was the Spanish who gave the place its name. 'El Pais Grande del Sur', they called it, or 'The Big Country to the South' of Carmel, where they had established a mission. (The region now known as Big Sur is generally taken to be the stretch of coastline between Carmel and San Simeon.) It wasn't until the late 19th century that people began to settle here, courageous homesteaders set on taming this isolated wilderness.

Astonishingly, the isolation remains. Highway 1, completed in 1937 after a painstaking two-decade building project, may have provided a link – and a spectacular one at that – between Monterey Bay and Cambria, but few took, or have since taken, the opportunity to settle here. It wasn't until 1950 that Big Sur got electricity; a half-century on, you still won't get a cellphone signal, and will find the vast majority of lodging options lacking the TVs and telephones obligatory in almost every other Californian hotel.

Still, despite the fact that fewer than 1,500 people make their home along this stretch of coast – you'll catch envious glimpses of their houses – you're not alone often in Big Sur. Highway 1 ought not to be driven at any great pace even with a clear road ahead: partly because of its fierce twists and turns, and partly because the scenery is too breathtaking to pass apace. However, during summer, you may not get a choice of speeds as you drive. It's never gridlock on Highway 1, but the view is considerably less affecting when seen from behind an RV pottering absent-mindedly along at 15mph. Add in the fog that descends during summer, wreaking its righteous revenge on the thousands of tourists who haven't done their research, and it's clear that the best time to visit Big Sur is in the weeks leading up to Memorial Day and the weeks following Labor Day.

Above all else, the area is hikers' paradise. There are countless outstanding hikes in the area, too many to detail here. The best printed resource is *Day Hikes Around Big Sur: 80 Great Hikes* by Robert Stone (Day Hikes, $14.95); the rangers at **Big Sur Station** (*see p211*) can also provide details of suitable hikes.

San Simeon to Partington Point

The scenery grows steadily more photogenic on the drive north from San Simeon. A few miles north of **Ragged Point**, home to a tidy hotel and handy gas station, is the beginning of a moderately tough but relatively untrodden trail to dramatic **Salmon Creek Falls** (4.2-mile round-trip), a 100-foot (30-metre) waterfall. Not far north is **Gorda**, near where you'll find **Jade Cove**, named for the semi-precious stone found here by the adventurous and the fortunate, and briefly diverting **Sand Dollar Beach**. There's cove access at **Mill Creek**; **Plaskett Creek**, **Kirk Creek** and **Limekiln Creek State Park** all have scenic campgrounds (*see p211*).

A bit further north is **Julia Pfeiffer-Burns State Park** (1-831 667 2315, www.parks.ca. gov), one of two state parks named after members of the Pfeiffer family, who moved to the area in 1869. This one's most commonly approached for the popular hike to **McWay Falls** (0.6-mile round-trip), a surprising waterfall hidden at the end of a straightforward trail, but the **Partington Cove** (0.9-mile round-trip) and **Tan Bark** (6.4-mile round-trip) trails are almost as scenic and a lot less busy.

Pfeiffer Big Sur State Park to Point Lobos

The area around **Pfeiffer Big Sur State Park** (1-831 667 2315, www.parks.ca.gov) is easily the busiest stretch of Big Sur coast, well stocked with hotels and restaurants. Also here is the **Henry Miller Library** (1-831 667 2574), not a library at all but rather a freeform memorial – have a coffee, read a book, surf the net – to the writer who lived in this area during the '40s and '50s. Talks are held regularly, though the place open more sporadically than its official hours (11am-6pm Mon & Wed-Sun in summer) would suggest.

Partly by dint of its location, Pfeiffer Big Sur State Park is one of the more popular stop-offs on Big Sur. As such, while the trails here are indubitably pretty, they're not as gloriously solitudinous as those you'll find up or down the coast. The most favoured hike is actually a combination of two short trails: the hike to sweet little **Pfeiffer Falls**, and the slightly steeper **Valley View Trail** through woodland to a fine, verdant viewpoint. Combine the two into a 1.5-mile walk that'll take 60-90 minutes.

Despite the slightly casual signposting – the entrance, a half-mile south of Big Sur Station, is marked only by two yellow markers warning drivers of RVs and vehicles over 20 foot in length not to bother – **Pfeiffer State Beach** proves a justly popular destination. The surf here can be dramatic, but the sand is crisp and frolicable; no small wonder it always seems popular with families and couples.

Andrew Molera State Park (1-831 667 2315, www.parks.ca.gov) is a rather plainer beast, and thus less of a draw. However, the hike to the beach here is rewarding: the flat trail itself, along the edge of quiet Big Sur River, is nothing spectacular, but the unvarnished beach appeals. If you decide to loop around the park outside of summer, you'll have to wade across the river.

North of Andrew Molera State Park, the Big Sur driving is arguably at its most spectacular. Highly engaging tours of the **Point Sur Lightstation State Historic Park** (1-831 625 4419) are offered on weekends year-round, with additional tours in summer and on half-a-dozen evenings each year (reservations not accepted); you'll see whales if you're lucky. Not far away is the photogenic **Bixby Creek Bridge**, a concrete construction that stretches 714 feet (218 metres) above the water. And only a short distance up the coast is **Garrapata State Park** (1-831 649 2866), which holds two excellent and relatively undiscovered trails.

Shortly before Carmel (or shortly after it, depending on your direction) is one of the highlights of the whole journey. **Point Lobos State Reserve** (1-831 624 4909, www.ptlobos. org), an extraordinary jutting outpost whose natural attributes, shaped by the wind and waves of endless millennia, are now delicately preserved by a state parks system well aware that this 1,250-acre plot is special. Wildlife and plant life is varied and highly visible: grey whales hang offshore from December to May; sea lions honk out a nagging disturbance to the windy silence; cormorants populate Bird Island in summer; pelicans, deer and seals all call the area home. Numerous trails run around the park; if you've time and stamina, the 6.0-mile Perimeter Hike is a highly rewarding one.

Where to eat & drink

The vast majority of places to eat are attached to hotels (*see p211* for contact details). Both the big hitters have esteemed restaurants serving Californian cuisine: the Ventana Inn & Spa has **Cielo** ($$$$$), while the Post Ranch Inn's restaurant, pricey at night but very affordable at lunchtime, goes under the name of **Sierra Mar** ($$$–$$$$$). The cosy restaurant at **Deetjen's** ($$$$) serves appetising breakfasts – a favourite among the locals, always a good sign – in addition to a dinner menu. The **Big Sur River Inn** ($$) and the **Fernwood Motel** ($) have eateries serving wholesome comfort food (burgers, pastas and so on); the latter also has an agreeable bar.

The most heralded independent eaterie is elevated **Nepenthe** (1-831 667 2345, $$); while the burgers are very ordinary and come at far from ordinary prices, the views from high above the Pacific are spectacular. Still, if a view's what you're after, lunch at Sierra Mar is a better bet. Also, try the **Big Sur Bakery & Restaurant** (1-831 667 0520, closed Mon & dinner Sun, $$$), which offers delicate pizzas (lunch), more substantial American cuisine (dinner) and immaculate take-out baked goods.

Where to stay

Whether your budget is $11 or $1,100 a night, there's something for you here. The latter is what you'll pay for a house with an ocean view at the 30-room **Post Ranch Inn** (1-831 667 2200, www.postranchinn.com, $495-$1,085), south of Pfeiffer Point, but, from an awe-inspiring 1,200 feet (366 metres) above the Pacific, *what* a view. The rooms, some in treehouses, are gorgeous inside and out: the height of good taste, both in the way the interiors exude calm and the exteriors blend into their secluded, woody surroundings. Just across Route 1 is the **Ventana Inn & Spa** (1-800 628 6500, 1-831 667 2331, www.ventanainn.com, $429-$579), a similarly spreadeagled and immaculate establishment that lacks the oceanside views in comparison to its near-neighbour but does boast two pools (one clothing-optional).

There are plenty of more affordable lodgings along Big Sur, though you'll generally pay a premium for location, location, location. There's no more characterful spot on the coast than the adorable **Deetjen's Big Sur Inn** (1-831 667 2377, www.deetjens.com, $75-$195): built by Norwegian immigrant Helmuth 'Grandpa' Deetjen, who moved here in the 1930s, the inn's collection of small log cabins are charming in the extreme, free of modern trappings such as central heating and locks. The Creek House is split into two floors, perfect for families. Less unique but a good option is the **Ragged Point Inn** (1-805 927 4502, www.raggedpointinn.com,

$99-$259), a dozen miles north of San Simeon: the rooms overlook the ocean in a kind of budget version of the Post Ranch experience.

Other hotels are rather more basic, but provide the budget traveller not predisposed towards camping the chance to stay on this stretch of coast. Among them are **Ripplewood Cabins** (1-831 667 2242, www.ripplewood resort.com, $109-$135), the **Fernwood Motel** (1-831 667 2422, www.fernwoodbigsur.com, $89), the **Glen Oaks Motel** (1-831 667 2105, www.glenoaksbigsur.com, $69-$160) and the **Big Sur River Inn** (1-800 548 3610, 1-831 667 2700, www.bigsurriverinn.com, $85-$140). None are luxurious, but all are clean.

Two of the more popular places to camp are in **Pfeiffer Big Sur State Park** and the slightly more developed **Julia Pfeiffer Burns State Park**; for reservations, call 1-800 444 7275 or check www.reserveamerica.com. **Andrew Molera State Park** has some very basic pitches; the privately operated **Ventana Campground** (1-831 667 2712) offers luxury in comparison. Two great walk-in options lie down the coast at **Kirk Creek** and **Plaskett Creek**.

Resources

Post office
Big Sur *47500 Highway 1 (1-831 667 2305).*

Tourist information
Big Sur *Big Sur Station, Big Sur (1-831 667 2315/www.parks.ca.gov).* **Open** 8am-4.30pm daily.

Big Sur.

The Monterey Peninsula

Carmel-by-the-Sea

It could be a really nice little town, **Carmel**. It probably was in the early 20th century, when Sinclair Lewis, Robinson Jeffers and Ansel Adams turned the place into an artists' colony of sorts. A glimpse of this history is visible at the **Carmel Heritage Society** (6th Avenue and Lincoln Street, 1-831 624 4447, www.carmelheritage.org, closed Mon & Tue), which also runs tours every Saturday morning.

However, as the years went by, rich exiles from the Bay Area bought into the area's idyllic reputation. Prices shot up, making it impossible for artists to settle here. Inevitable, really. The problem is that the wealthy new residents brought with them attitudes that can politely be described as bloody-minded and impolitely be pinned as isolationist, haughty and snobbish.

Pretension is everywhere. Some works in the town's favour: there are no street lights, which makes the village's thin streets, bisected by the main drag of **Ocean Avenue**, atmospheric at night. Some is harmlessly amusing: there are no traffic lights and no sidewalks. And some of it is bewildering, laughable contrarianism: none of the properties in the centre have street numbers (how uncouth!), and home delivery of mail is outlawed (God forbid we should live on streets lined with ugly, new-fangled mailboxes!).

The town looks postcard-cute; it's easy to see why this is such a popular stop on the tourist trail. But if Carmel proves one thing, it's that money doesn't buy good taste. The shops that cram into the skinny streets and passageways in and around the Doud Arcade hawk prissy clothes, pricey accessories and preposterous gifts. Chains are largely confined to Carmel Plaza (it's a mall! Admit it! A *mall*!!! Whatever).

Worse, the galleries for which the town is famed are not galleries but stores. Sure, the line between exhibition space and retail space is blurred at most commercial galleries. But here, where the staff ask if you need help within seconds and American Express is proudly accepted, the line is erased. You're not here to look, only to buy, whether garish portraiture and florid landscapes in hues so loud they could cure the colourblind, or cutesy mantlepiece statues of errant golfers and beaming children. The art, for the most part, is unchallenging, ersatz and comically ghastly. You will stop laughing when you see the price tags.

However, while a walk around Carmel's centre is a maddening experience, the village's undeniable aesthetic charm excised by the pomposity of its residents, the town does have a number of things to recommend it. There are two splendid beaches: **Carmel Beach**, at the western end of Ocean Avenue, and, down the coast, the less crowded and more pleasant **Carmel River State Beach** (1-831 649 2836), which also includes a bird sanctuary. A word of warning: both beaches might look idyllic, but tides can be lethal. Swimming is a bad idea.

Those who've travelled the coast ticking off missions will want to stop at the **Mission San Carlos Borroméo de Carmelo** (3080 Rio Road, 1-831 624 3600, www.carmelmission.org, $1-$4), the final resting place of Father Junipero Serra. Mass is celebrated several times daily. Also worth a look is **Robinson Jeffers Tor House** (26304 Ocean View Avenue, 1-831 624 1813, www.torhouse.org, closed Sun, $2-$7). The poet had a hand in building the house, largely from granite boulders from the cove below. Book for the Friday and Saturday tours.

Where to eat & drink

The marvellous **Flying Fish Grill**, tucked away in the Carmel Plaza (1-831 625 1962, closed lunch, $$$$), has a seafood-heavy menu; **Little Napoli** (Dolores Street, at 7th Avenue, 1-831 626 6335, closed lunch, $$$) dishes up Italian staples with enthusiasm; and **Casanova** (5th Street, at Mission Avenue, 1-831 625 0501, $$$$), while not cheap, is a reliable bet for a high-quality Italian dinner. Other eateries are less vital. At **Anton & Michel** (Mission Street,

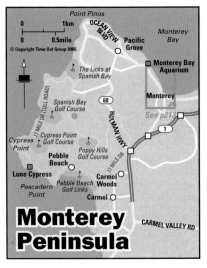

Point Pinos

0   1km
0   0.5mile
© Copyright Time Out Group 2005

OCEAN VIEW BLVD

Pacific Grove

Monterey Bay

The Links at Spanish Bay

Monterey Bay Aquarium

Spanish Bay Golf Course

68

Monterey

17 MILE DR (TOLL ROAD)

HOLMAN HWY

See p213

Cypress Point

Cypress Point Golf Course

Poppy Hills Golf Course

17 MILE DR

1

Pebble Beach

Lone Cypress

Pescadero Point

Pebble Beach Golf Links

Carmel Woods

Carmel

Monterey Peninsula

CARMEL VALLEY RD

at Ocean Avenue, 1-831 624 4395, www.
carmelsbest.com, $$$$), the upscale French food
doesn't live up to its prices; and at the **Village
Corner** (Dolores Street, at 6th Avenue, 1-831
624 3588, www.carmelsbest.com, $$$$), which
has a nice patio, so-so food is supplemented by
blasé service. Drown your disappointment at
Jack London's (Dolores Street, at 5th Avenue,
1-831 624 2336), a woody, convivial tap room.

Where to stay

The best bet is the **Mission Ranch** (26270
Dolores Street, 1-800 538 8221, 1-831 624 6436,
www.missionranchcarmel.com, $110-$290):
owned by Clint Eastwood, formerly the town's
mayor, it offers lovely, country-style lodgings
over several buildings. The rates are very
reasonable, particularly when held up against
the prices charged by some of the motels in the
town's centre; book well in advance. There's
also a popular restaurant and piano bar here.

Other options are nearer the action, and vary.
The **Coachman's Inn** (San Carlos Street, at
7th Avenue, 1-800 336 6421, $99-$350) and the
Village Inn (Ocean Avenue, at Junipero
Avenue, 1-800 346 3864, $79-$189) are both
basically motels: the former's smart and very
tidily maintained, while the latter is more basic.
The **Pine Inn** (Ocean Avenue, at Monte Verde
Street, 1-831 624 3851, $135-$260), a rambling
property in the middle of town, works hard to
create a British-toff vibe; the **Cobblestone Inn**
(Junipero Avenue, between 7th and 8th Street,
1-800 833 8836, $125-$250), one of several Four
Sisters Inns in the Monterey area, brings on the
country chintz in cutesy but agreeable fashion.

Lodgings here are expensive, but if you're
visiting midweek outside peak season, you can
usually get a good deal on the day of arrival.
Call around, and don't be afraid to haggle.

Pebble Beach & the 17-Mile Drive

Thought Carmel was a bit snooty? You ain't seen
nothing yet. The stretch of road up the coast is
so posh you have to pay just to drive it. Still, it's
testament to the scenery around the Monterey
Peninsula that it's almost worth the toll, which
won't leave you much change from $10.

The **17-Mile Drive**, which loops around
large, privately owned portions of the Monterey
Peninsula, was established in 1881, becoming a
toll road two decades later. Then, the landscape
here was entirely rugged and unspoiled; parts of
it, indeed, still are. But once the **Pebble Beach
Golf Links** (see p38) and its concomitant lodge
were completed in 1919, the area grew into a
rich man's playground. The construction of two

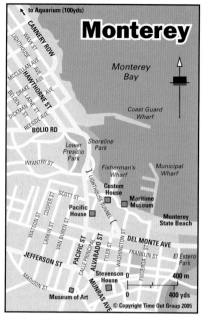

further golf courses, **Spyglass Hill** in 1966 (see
p38) and the **Links at Spanish Bay** in 1987,
only increased the mystique. The area is now one
of the most highfalutin resorts in the country.

The 17-Mile Drive, accessible via five gates
(one at Carmel, two each in Monterey and Pacific
Grove) takes in all three golf courses, and some
thrilling coastal scenery. Your entrance fee
includes a leaflet that maps points of interest:
among them are **Bird Rock**, home to birds
and sea lions; **Cypress Point Lookout**,
which offers breathtaking views; and the **Lone
Cypress**, a dramatically located tree by the
ocean. Roadside parking is discouraged, but
if there's not much traffic (avoid peak times,
especially in summer), you can usually get away
with it for long enough to take a picture or two.

Where to eat, drink & stay

Lodging and dining within the confines of the
17-Mile Drive is contained within three swanky
properties: the traditional **Lodge at Pebble
Beach**, the cultured **Inn at Spanish Bay** and
the Mediterranean **Casa Palmero**. Bookings
for all three are made via 1-800 654 9300; www.
pebblebeach.com has information. If you have
to ask how much a room costs, you can't afford
one; suffice to say, though, that the cheapest
room on any of the properties clocks in at $475.

On a mission

'With the best theological intentions in the world,' argued Carey McWilliams in his book *Southern California: An Island on the Land*, 'the Franciscan padres eliminated Indians with the effectiveness of Nazis operating concentration camps.' During the Spanish conquest of California, the Spanish missionary monks, led by Father Junípero Serra, founded a string of 21 missions from San Diego in the south to Sonoma, north of San Francisco. The first, San Diego de Alcalá, was established in 1769, the last, San Francisco Solano, came into existence in 1823. Just 25 years later, the mission system had come to an end.

The aim behind the missions was to convert the tribal peoples and establish self-sustaining communities. They succeeded only in creating productive, wealthy farms; all the while, the forced Native American converts died from a combination of depression, disease and malnutrition. In the late 19th century, the missions were reinvented as an icon of tradition and romance, for the zealous Spanish padres had also left a legacy of mission architecture: white, sometimes Moorish buildings, with bougainvillea-shaded quadrangles and simple, solid interiors. This revised image spawned Mission-style architecture and decor, a popular and influential branch of Californian design.

It is possible to tour the Californian missions, many of which have been renovated or reconstructed and now function as Catholic parishes. The 21 missions are all located near US 101, which loosely follows the old El Camino Real ('Royal Road') named in honour of the Spanish monarchy that financed the colonising expeditions. (The stretch of US 101 from San Diego to Los Angeles is now I-5.)

The first mission, **San Diego de Alcalá** (*see p73*), was founded in what is now San Diego; a few miles north, just east of Oceanside on Highway 76, sits the 18th, **San Luis Rey de Francia** (*see p90*). The remains of **San Juan Capistrano** (1-949 234 1300, www.mission sjc.com) lie in San Juan Capistrano, 40 miles south of Long Beach. Every year, on 19 March, the town celebrates the return of the cliff swallows from Argentina (*see p55*).

In Los Angeles County, you can visit **San Gabriel** (428 S Mission Drive, San Gabriel, 1-626 457 3035), formerly one of the wealthiest missions. **San Fernando Rey de España** (15151 San Fernando Mission Boulevard, Mission Hills, 1-818 361 0186) is the largest free-standing adobe structure in California. Just north of LA in Ventura is the mission of **San Buenaventura** (*see p199*).

Touring the Central Coast, you can see **Santa Barbara** (*see p200*), **Santa Inés** in Solvang (1760 Mission Drive, 1-805 688 4815, www.missionsantaines.org) and **La Purisima Concepcion** in Lompoc (*see p203*). **San Luis de Obispo de Tolosa**, whose chapel was built of logs, is north in San Luis Obispo (pictured; *see p205*); further north still is **San Miguel Arcangel** (775 Mission Street, San Miguel, 1-805 467 3256, www.missionsan miguel.org). Beyond it are **San Antonio de Padua** (Mission Creek Road, Jolon, 1-831 385 4478, www.missionsanantoniopadua.com); **Nuestra Señora de la Soledad** (36641 Fort Romie Road, Soledad, 1-831 678 2586); the Moorish **San Carlos Borroméo de Carmelo**, where Junípero Serra is buried (*see p212*); and, finally, **San Juan Bautista** (2nd & Mariposa Streets, San Juan Bautista, 1-831 623 4234, www.oldmission-sjb.org).

Monterey & Pacific Grove

Settled by Spanish explorer Sebastián Viscaíno in 1602, **Monterey** wasn't colonised until 168 years later with the arrival of Junípero Serra, who established the second of his 23 missions here (it moved the following year to Carmel). For the Spanish, the town was a crucial settlement; it was named by them as the capital of Alta ('upper') California, a swathe of land that covered all of California, Nevada and Utah, as well as parts of several other states. The town remained important when the Mexicans seceded from Spain in 1822 and assumed stewardship over California; it was at **Custom House** (*see below*) 24 years later that the American flag was raised in California for the first time with any degree of permanency (an invasion in 1842 had lasted just two days).

Monterey's unlikely journey from capital of Alta California to sardine capital of the world took several generations, during which the town, and neighbouring **Pacific Grove**, briefly became popular resorts. The fishing industry drove the economy for the first part of the 20th century; when the fish and the money both ran out, the fishermen left the place to the tourists, and Monterey is now one of the most popular towns on the left coast. Arrive outside summer to avoid the crowds and the infamous traffic.

Downtown, Monterey SHP & Fisherman's Wharf

Downtown Monterey is a pleasant place. Its low-key attractions are scattered all around its fringes, meaning that **Calle Principal** and **Alvarado Street**, the two main drags, are populated chiefly by restaurants and shops. The most notable of the latter is the sizeable but somewhat understocked Bay Books; for the former, *see pp216-217*. Stroll south, and you'll find the **Monterey Museum of Art** (559 Pacific Street, 1-831 372 5477, www.monterey art.org, closed Mon & Tue, $5), whose august permanent collection contains pieces by Ansel Adams. Continuing north along Alvarado, meanwhile, leads towards the water; dodge a hulking hotel, and you'll reach the main clutch of buildings forming part of the spreadeagled **Monterey State Historic Park** (1-831 649 7118, www.parks.ca.gov).

Once you've found the pedestrianised plaza, head for the visitor centre inside the hulking **Stanton Center** to pick up a map of the area's assorted historic buildings. Among them are the **Custom House**, an adobe building dating back over 175 years; **Pacific House**, whose chequered history has included stints as a hotel,

Monterey Bay Aquarium. *See p216.*

a bar, a courthouse and its present use as a museum; the **First Brick House** in the town; and the **Larkin House**, a curious but unquestionably attractive structure built by a Yankee merchant in the late 1840s. You can see as many or as few of these buildings as you choose as part of the two-mile **Path of History** self-guided walk, for which leaflets are dispensed at the Stanton Center. The Center can provide details of the docent-led tours of Old Monterey itself and of some of the park's individual properties; if you only have time for one, the Larkin House tour is a good choice. The Stanton Center also runs a short film offering a little background on the area's history.

Adjoining **Fisherman's Wharf** is smaller than the version in San Francisco, but is just like it in one regard: it fails to live up to its name. The fishermen who once drove the town's economy long ago drew in their nets for the final time, leaving their former base to the tourists. Fisherman's Wharf is now merely a collection of shops and restaurants, working a tired spell on a steady stream of easily impressed visitors.

Cannery Row

Some choose to drive from Fisherman's Wharf over to Monterey's Cannery Row, perhaps with a stop at the **Presidio of Monterey Museum** (1-831 646 3456, closed Tue & Wed): on the site of the town's original fort but housed in an building formerly used as an ammunitions lock-up, it details the military history of the area. But if you've already parked in one of the lots just to the east of Fisherman's Wharf, you're best served leaving your car there. For one thing, the drive west is complicated by a tunnel, and while the signage is good, it's not perfect, For another, the walk along the waterfront, assuming friendly weather, is a splendid one.

Thought Fisherman's Wharf was touristy? You're going to be in for the most dreadful shock when you get to **Cannery Row**. This stretch of waterside road was once home to the town's fishing industry, immortalised by John Steinbeck (*see p218*) in a 1945 novel. *Cannery Row* didn't romanticise the area, exactly, but it left the reader in no doubt that Steinbeck was fascinated by it. He'd be appalled to see the place now, its old buildings converted into bars, gift shops and hokey attractions that trade off his name in a variety of inventively crass ways. (Runs one storefront narration: 'Hello. I'm John Steinbeck. Step forward and join me in the **Spirit of Monterey Wax Museum**'; we're paraphrasing, but barely.) However, there is one redeeming feature: the celebrated **Monterey Bay Aquarium**.

Monterey Bay Aquarium

886 Cannery Row (1-831 648 4800/www.mbayaq. org). Open Memorial Day-Labor Day 9.30am-6pm daily. Labor Day-Memorial Day 10am-6pm daily. **Admission** *$19.95; $8.95-$17.95 discounts; free under-3s.* **Credit** *AmEx, MC, V.*
Striking the perfect balance between education and entertainment, the Monterey Bay Aquarium pulls off the enviable trick of appealing to adults as much as kids. Two decades after its opening, it's never looked better: a new entrance hall has alleviated some of the chaos that ensues on busy mornings, and though the Skywalk is less grand than its name suggests, the gangway linking the two halves of the aquarium – the original buildings and the Outer Bay Wing – has made navigation easier.

The centrepiece of the museum is still the vast **Kelp Forest** exhibit, crammed with marine life both prosaic and exotic. However, it's fast being usurped in the popularity stakes by the exhibits in the Outer Bay Wing. On the ground floor is **Sharks: Myth & Mystery**, which supplements the crowd-pleasing fish (including some funky hammerheads and a very neat stingray exhibit; we won't spoil the surprise) with displays on a more cultural tack. Above it, on the second floor, is the **Outer Bay**, a breath-taking collection of fish in a tank that holds a cool million gallons of water. Get here to see feeding time. Among the other inhabitants of the building are the perennially cute sea otters. However, it's all change in the original wing, with a number of the exhibits being revamped into a new gallery named **Ocean's Edge**, scheduled to open in summer 2005.

Incidentally, if any of the exhibits look a bit murky, there's a good reason: the water in many of the exhibits comes in direct from the Pacific. The water is filtered during the day to increase visibility but unfiltered out of hours; either way, cloudiness varies.

Pacific Grove

While Carmel wears its village status loudly, proudly and crassly, **Pacific Grove** is content simply to go about its business. As such, it's a far nicer place, its Downtown (around the junction of Lighthouse Avenue and Forest Street) largely unencumbered by gift shops and galleries, its restaurants no more expensive than they need to be. Pick up a walking tour leaflet from the Chamber of Commerce (*see p218*) for details on the histories of the town's delightful, century-old private residences.

The **Pacific Grove Museum of Natural History** (165 Forest Avenue, 1-831 648 5716, www.pgmuseum.org, closed Mon & Sun) contains an interesting exhibit on the monarch butterflies that spend winters here (November to February; ask at the visitor centre for details of where to see them). The town wears its nickname, Butterfly Town USA, with pride.

However, Pacific Grove's main year-round attraction is its craggy coastline. Catch it on a grey day, and the coast hugging Ocean View Boulevard is awesome, waves beating furiously against the rocks. On bluer days, it's more serene; several parks and viewpoints offer the chance to picnic while watching sea lions laze the day away. If you blanche at the idea of paying to skirt the **17-Mile Drive** (*see p213*), Ocean View Boulevard and Sunset Drive offer a beguiling alternative. Similarly, if the $400 green fee at Pebble Beach seems steep, you can play 18 holes for around a tenth that amount at the municipal **Pacific Grove Golf Links** (1-831 648 5777), whose greens are not quite so immaculate but whose coastal views, briefly, are as good.

The road wanders west towards **Point Pinos Lighthouse** (1-831 648 5716, closed Tue & Wed, $1-$2): the oldest working lighthouse in California, it's now open to the public. From here, head south along Sunset Drive towards **Asilomar State Beach** (1-831 372 4076), home to beaches, tidepools, wildlife and, incongruously, a conference centre. Close by is one of the entrances to the 17-Mile Drive.

Where to eat & drink

While it doesn't always do the tourist thing with the greatest regard to taste, Monterey does food better, at least away from Cannery Row. Your best bet Downtown is chic **Montrio** (414 Calle Principal, 1-831 648 8880, closed lunch, $$$$), whose Californian cuisine lives up to the stylish room in which it's served. It's an egalitarian place, too, popular with the Gold Card crew but also with local couples and tourists. **Stokes** (500 Hartnell Street, 1-831 373 1110, closed lunch Mon-Fri, $$$) has retained its favoured status with locals for two reasons: one, it's off the beaten path for tourists, despite being housed in a gorgeously converted 170-year-old adobe house, and two, the Mediterranean cuisine is wonderfully flavourful.

The food at Fisherman's Wharf is better than you might expect: while **Café Fina** (1-831 372 5200, $$$) has the best reputation, it's worth clocking the Italian menu of perfectly respectable **Domenico's** (1-831 372 3655, $$$) before making your choice. And buzzing **Tarpy's Roadhouse** (Highway 68 and Canyon del Rey, 1-831 647 1444, $$$$) is worth the drive from town for its take on American favourites. The **Old Monterey Café** (489 Alvarado Street, 1-831 646 1021, closed Mon, $) serves immensely satisfying breakfasts and lunches.

There's a high hit-rate of quality to quantity in Pacific Grove. You'll find daisy-fresh fish creations at smart-casual **Passionfish** (701 Lighthouse Avenue, 1-831 655 3311, closed lunch, $$$$); the more formal **Old Bath House** (guess what it used to be; 620 Ocean View Boulevard, 1-831 375 5195, closed lunch, $$$$$) supplements its traditional American cuisine with views over Lovers' Point. There are more fine views at the **Tinnery** (631 Ocean View Boulevard, 1-831 646 1040, $$$) to distract from the pastas and burgers. Affordable **Peppers** (170 Forest Avenue, 1-831 373 6892, closed Tue & lunch Sun, $$) serves cracking Mexican food.

Monterey's nightlife is more mixed. The bars of Cannery Row are loud and tacky; those after confirmation that there are few things in life more depressing than an empty nightclub will find it here early in the week. That said, **Sly McFly's** (700 Cannery Row, 1-831 649 8050) is popular among locals, chiefly for live music. Downtown offers few enticing alternatives, but visitors who've never set foot in the UK may be charmed by the various British-themed bars: the **Crown & Anchor** (150 W Franklin Street, 1-831 649 6496) goes for a country-pub feel. Off the beaten track is **Ocean Thunder** (214 Lighthouse Avenue, 1-831 643 9169), a friendly little dive popular with bikers and pool sharks.

Where to stay

Monterey is awash with budget motels, on **Fremont Street** on the edge of town or on **Munras Avenue** nearer the centre. Among others, Fremont has two **Best Western**s, the newer of which is the Best Western De Anza (No.2141, 1-831 646 8300, $69-$219), plus a

Motel 6 (1-831 646 8585, $56-$96); Munras holds a smaller variety. For more, check the Monterey CVB's website; *see also p54.*

There are a number of more individualistic lodgings closer to Downtown. The largest is the **Monterey Plaza** (400 Cannery Row, 1-800 368 2468, 1-831 646 1700, www.woodsidehotels.com/ monterey, $190-$550), a plush oceanside hotel-spa that strikes a decent balance between comfortable luxury and corporate efficiency. The most appealing is the **Old Monterey Inn** (500 Martin Street, 1-800 350 2344, www.old montereyinn.com, $180-$450), an immaculate B&B set on a quiet street. Also worth a look is the elegant **Spindrift Inn** (475 Cannery Row, 1-800 841 1879, 1-831 646 8900, www.spindriftinn. com, $179-$409), which bears nary a trace of its former incarnation as a whorehouse. But the best bargain is the century-old **Monterey Hotel** (406 Alvarado Street, 1-800 966 6490, 1-831 375 3184, www.montereyhotel.com, $97-$249), good value given its central location.

Over in Pacific Grove, hotels are on a smaller scale. The Four Sisters group (www.foursisters. com) have two B&Bs here, both of which play to a chintzily Victorian tune: **Gosby House** (643 Lighthouse Avenue, 1-800 527 8828, $100-$200) and the **Green Gables Inn** (301 Ocean View Boulevard, 1-800 722 1774, $120-$260). Better is the **Martine Inn** (255 Ocean View Boulevard, 1-831 373 3388, 1-800 852 5588, www.martineinn. com, $139-$359). Owned by Don Martine, who spends his spare time restoring classic cars (he's happy to show them off), the hotel has over 20 rooms with unique antique fixtures, and we mean unique: the Jenny Lind room has a wardrobe on which is carved a bust of the singer.

The area is also home to the **Jabberwock Inn** (598 Laine Street, 1-888 428 7253, 1-831 372 4777, www.jabberwockinn.com, $145-$265), a fab B&B in a century-old mansion that's gently themed around the works of Lewis 'Alice in Wonderland' Carroll. Copies of Carroll's books are scattered around the house; there's fun to be had in the handsome rooms spotting other tributes to the author. Great breakfasts, too.

Resources

Hospital
Monterey *Community Hospital of the Monterey Peninsula, 23625 Holman Highway (1-831 624 5311/www.chomp.org).*

Internet
Monterey *Kinko's, 799 Lighthouse Avenue (1-831 373 2298/www.kinkos.com).* **Open** 24hrs daily.

Police
Carmel *Junipero & 4th Avenues (1-831 624 6403).*
Monterey *351 Madison Street (1-831 646 3800).*

Post office
Carmel *Dolores Street, at 5th Avenue (1-831 625 9529).*
Monterey *565 Hartnell Street (1-805 372 4063).*

Tourist information
Carmel *Carmel Chamber of Commerce, San Carlos Street, between 5th & 6th Streets (1-800 550 4333/1-831 624 2522/www.carmelcalifornia.org).* **Open** 9am-5pm Mon-Fri.
Monterey *Monterey Visitor Center, Lake El Estero, at Franklin & Camino El Estero (1-888 221 1010/1-831 649 1770/www.montereyinfo.org).* **Open** *Apr-Oct* 9am-6pm Mon-Sat; 9am-5pm Sun. *Nov-Mar* 9am-5pm Mon-Sat; 10am-4pm Sun. There's also a smaller visitor centre in the Stanton House.
Pacific Grove *Pacific Grove Chamber of Commerce, cnr Central & Forest Avenues (1-800 656 6650/1-831 373 3304/www.pacificgrove.org).* **Open** 9am-5pm Mon-Fri.

The Salinas Valley

Salinas

John Steinbeck didn't much like **Salinas**. He left, aged just 17, to study at Stanford University; when he returned to California permanently in 1930, around a decade later, he settled in quieter, more cultured Pacific Grove.

After a period of decided ambivalence, though, Salinas now likes John Steinbeck. So much, in fact, that the town have built an entire tourist industry around their most famous son. Unless your visit coincides with the four-day **California Rodeo** in July (1-800 771 8807, 1-831 775 3100, www.carodeo.com), the only reason to swing by this plain agricultural town is to stop by the **National Steinbeck Center**.

National Steinbeck Center
1 Main Street (1-831 796 3833/www.steinbeck.org). **Open** 10am-5pm daily. **Admission** $10.95; $5.95-$8.95 discounts. **Credit** AmEx, Disc, MC, V.
Hard to imagine what the author's reaction would have been to this gleaming, $10m project; probably a kind of amused embarrassment. Still, while it is a little gimmicky in places, and while there is something strange about seeing an author built up to a level of reverential celebrity rarely bestowed on even the most famous and renowned of Hollywood stars, the Center does offer a tasteful and insightful tour around Steinbeck's life, with an assortment of exhibits both plain and interactive.

Heading south

Save for the wine-growing territory around **Paso Robles** (*see p208*), the Salinas Valley is not a trail well trod by tourists. With the San Francisco Bay Area to the north and Big Sur

directly east, this is unsurprising. Certainly, the locals around here, aware of what they're up against, make few attempts to attract visitors.

The landscape unexciting and the towns small, your main diversions will come in the form of the few missions. In the unbecoming town of **Soledad** sits the **Mission Nuestra Señora de la Soledad**; beyond it, a 20-minute drive off US 101 along either route G17 (if you're heading south on 101) or G16 (if you're driving north), is **Mission San Antonio de Padua**; and in San Miguel, just north of Paso Robles, is **Mission San Miguel Arcangel**. For all, *see p214* **On a mission**.

But the real reason to swing by this way is to take in the striking, unexpected rock formations of **Pinnacles National Monument**. The 24,000-acre monument, accessible either from Highway 25 or US 101 by taking Highway 146, was formed from the remains of a volcano over 20 million years ago, huge rock formations that now draw rock-climbers looking for adventure. However, there are also some fine hikes in Pinnacles. The **Condor Gulch/High Peaks Loop Trail** (5.0-mile round trip) offers an up-close-and-personal look at the park's rocks and wildlife; the wearying climb to **North Chalone Peak** (8.4-mile round-trip) yields the park's finest views. For something a little different, though, take the trail to **Balconies Cave** (2.4-mile round-trip), but bring a torch if you want to see anything at all when you reach it.

Head to the **Bear Gulch** Visitor Center (1-831 389 4485 ext 0), on the west side, when you get here to collect maps and other literature. There's no camping in the park, but there is a campground outside the eastern entrance (1-831 389 4462, www.pinncamp.com, $7 per person); reservations are usually required in summer.

Resources
Tourist information
Salinas *119 E Alisal Street (1-831 424 7611/ www.salinaschamber.com).* **Open** 8.30am-5pm Mon-Fri; 9am-3pm Sat.

Getting Around

Drivers must choose between scenic, coastal **Highway 1** or the quicker inland **US 101**. Train travellers on the Central Coast also get a choice: **Amtrak** (1-800 872 7245, www.amtrak.com) runs the new **Pacific Surfliner** and the older, slower **Coast Starlight** (*see p395*). For buses, the major towns all have **Greyhound** (1-800 229 9424, www.greyhound. com) stations, but **Monterey-Salinas Transit** (1-831 899 2555, www.mst.org) and **Central Coast Area Transport** (1-805 541 2228) also run pretty extensive services.

San Francisco

A small town strapped into big-city shoes, and much the better for it.

San Francisco could have been made for visitors. Bounded by the Pacific to the west, with San Francisco Bay curving around it from the east, the city has been saved by geography from aping the daunting sprawl of other Californian cities. Instead it squeezes pretty much everything you'll want into an area only seven miles by seven miles. Even if the city's notorious hills get too steep for tired limbs, there's a comprehensive and, with the historic cable cars and streetcars, beautiful public transport system.

A word for the neophyte. Don't expect blue skies and a *Baywatch* tan. The city's heedless topography creates a variety of microclimates. To the west, where the city is comparatively flat, there's little to prevent that famous fog rolling in off the ocean over Richmond, Golden Gate Park and Sunset, thence to the Western Addition. The city's central hills protect the Mission, the Castro, Noe Valley and North Beach, often leaving them warm and sunny. Fisherman's Wharf to the north and the Financial District in the east of the city are frequently windy. Dress in layers, and the perfidious weather becomes a happy distraction.

You can also leave the aerobicised babe and bouncing beefcake aesthetic to the south. San Francisco's pace is a steady walk: take that on board and the city soon unfolds around you.

HISTORY

Hunter-gatherers known as the Ohlone were the region's first inhabitants. Fortunately for them, the early European navigators spent more time failing to notice the mile-wide opening into the San Francisco Bay than exploring it. Juan Bautista de Anza was the first European to build in the area, establishing a *presidio* on the southern point of the Golden Gate around the 1770s. Three miles south-east, Mission Dolores was set up by Father Junípero Serra in 1776. And the Ohlone? By the mid 19th century, hard labour and smallpox had halved their numbers.

San Francisco's development was kickstarted by an unscrupulous entrepreneur named Sam Brannan. It was Brannan who publicised the discovery of gold at Sutter's Mill by waving a bottle of gold dust in the town square, sparking the Gold Rush. (Brannan's motivations were

The best San Francisco

Things to do

Hang off the running boards of a **cable car** (*see p259*), getting off to sip the caffeinated air of **North Beach** (*see p225*). Admire the 20th-century masters at **SFMOMA** (*see p229*), then take an evening tour to **Alcatraz** (*see p233*).

Places to stay

For sheer class, look no further than the **Clift** (*see p255*), but for luxury with a sense of humour, try the **Argonaut** (*see p257*). Paupers who plan ahead can enjoy fabulous views from **Fisherman's Wharf Youth Hostel** (*see p257*).

Places to eat

Your problem isn't where to eat, it's where to start: very special occasions call for **Asia de Cuba** (*see p241*); for brunch, perhaps North Beach institution **Mama's** (*see p240*); vegetarians love their **Greens** (*see p244*); while for traditional seafood **Swan Oyster Depot** (*see p241*) can't be beat.

Nightlife

Julip Cocktail Lounge (*see p246*) and **Six** (*see p247*) are fun and friendly, but the one for dancing is **Sublounge** (*see p247*). Fans of kitsch love **Sno-Drift** (*see p247*).

Culture

For films, there's nowhere more atmospheric than the **Castro Theatre** (*see p250*); the same can be said of the alt-music at **Hemlock Tavern** (*see p252*). The **San Francisco Ballet** (*see p250*) may be a venerable company, but their performances are bang up to date.

Sports & activities

For spectators, a summer visit to the ballpark to watch the **San Francisco Giants** (*see p252 The sporting life*) is a must. Anyone who wants to do rather than be done to should head to **Golden Gate Park** (*see p238*) for an automobile-free Sunday skate, cycle or a plain old leisurely stroll.

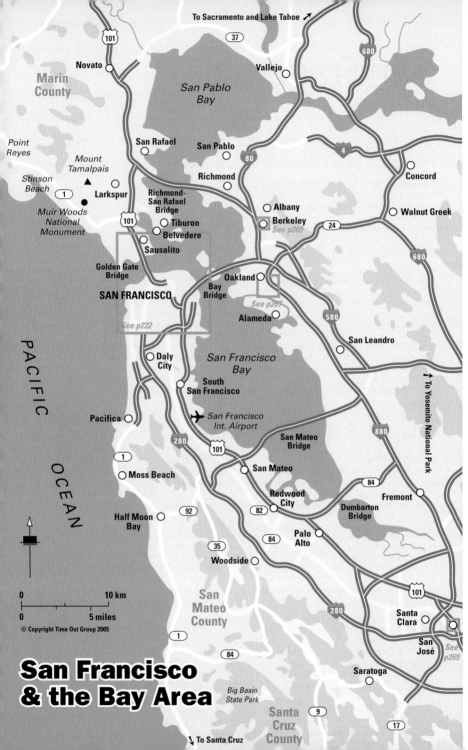

Disc drive

CDs to soundtrack your journey around San Francisco.

Reveille Deerhoof
Stereolab meet Gang of Four. Restless new music from the city that loves nothing better than to mash stuff up.

Dick's Picks Vol.IV The Grateful Dead
The archetypal Haight band, caught live at Fillmore East in 1970. Rarely bettered.

The Essential Sly & the Family Stone
This double CD of multi-ethnic rockin' funk surely takes you higher.

High Contrast Gabor Szabo
Szabo's gypsy jazz melancholy, paired with Bobby Womack's funky licks. Like summer in San Francisco – a treacherous beast.

Swordfishtrombones Tom Waits
The long-time local could be defining San Francisco in the fog on 'Shore Leave'.

entirely selfish; he'd already bought up every piece of mining equipment in the area, and went on to sell them at a huge profit to desperate Gold Rushers.) The port town in which many prospectors arrived was a lawless place. By the 1870s the waterfront, known as the Barbary Coast, was notorious. Gamblers fleeced drunken sailors and gangs kidnapped immigrant women, forcing them to work as prostitutes.

It was at this time that the seeds of the city's present-day multiculturalism were sown, as immigrants arrived from all over. Italians baked in North Beach; Chinese arrived to work on the transcontinental railroad; a Bavarian named Levi Strauss started using rivets to strengthen the pockets of miners' jeans. By 1900 the city was the ninth largest in the Union, with a population of more than 300,000.

Shortly after 5am on 18 April 1906, San Francisco was struck by the first ripples of a huge earthquake. A terrible blaze followed, and only a change of wind and the onset of rain brought an end to the three days of devastation. Never people to sit around bemoaning their fate, the San Franciscans started to rebuild. The new City Hall was completed in 1915, its dome deliberately, boastfully designed to be taller than its model: the Capitol in Washington, DC.

▶ For a full survey of San Francisco, buy the 320-page *Time Out San Francisco* guide.

Despite the Wall Street Crash, San Francisco gained a new Opera House in 1932 and, in 1935, the San Francisco Museum of Modern Art became the first West Coast museum to feature solely 20th-century work. The '30s also saw the completion of the Bay and Golden Gate Bridges.

After World War II, a slew of writers and artists who would become known as the Beat Generation, among them Allen Ginsberg and Jack Kerouac, descended on the city, articulating an unfocused dissatisfaction with mainstream America. But their arrival was as nothing compared to the events of a decade or so later, when around 8,000 hippies showed up in search of kindred spirits and readily available LSD. Over half stayed, occupying the dilapidated Victorian houses around Haight-Ashbury (dubbed the 'Hashbury'). The San Franciscan laissez-faire attitude combined with the drugs and an explosion of psychedelic music to give rise to the fabled Summer of Love, but it was their opposition to the Vietnam War and campaigning for Civil Rights that gave the hippies a political edge the Beats lacked.

The city had long lived under the threat of another major quake; in October 1989 it arrived. The Loma Prieta earthquake registered 7.1 on the Richter scale (the 1906 quake was an estimated 7.8), and damaged or destroyed 19,000 homes in only 15 seconds. Some 62 people died and 12,000 others were displaced. Another seismic shift was soon to begin: just to the south of the city, the internet revolution was starting in Silicon Valley. It soon morphed into San Francisco's cash-rich dotcom boom; the city's new-found affluence was reflected in a welter of new building projects during the 1990s; the crash that followed failed to reverse the gentrification of the city.

Yet some things remain the same: the city's reputation for militant liberalism was enhanced in 2003 by massive protests against the Iraq war, and by a huge vote against Arnold Schwarzenegger in California's gubernatorial elections. Visitors who consider San Francisco quintessentially Californian are mistaken. San Francisco is uniquely, defiantly itself.

Sightseeing

The concentration of hotels, shops and transport alternatives around Union Square means most visitors spend far too much time there. Don't make the same mistake. Ditto the inexplicably popular Fisherman's Wharf in the north of the city. San Francisco is made up of individualistic neighbourhoods, each with their own distinct flavour. You should sample as many of them as you can.

Central California

If you've got limited time at your disposal, you could do worse than orientate yourself with a touristy bus tour: **Gray Line** (1-415 558 9400, www.graylinesanfrancisco.com, $17-$79) is probably the best. If you're driving yourself, try the **49-Mile Scenic Drive** (*see p32*). Pedestrians and cyclists should check in at the **Visitor Information Center** (*see p223*), for self-guided walks, or **City Guides** (1-415 557 4266, www.walking-tours.com), for free tours led by keen volunteers.

Around Union Square

Union Square

Right in the middle of San Francisco's retail heartland, **Union Square** takes its name from pro-Union rallies held on the eve of the Civil War, though the 97-foot (30-metre) Corinthian column in its centre confusingly celebrates

Admiral Dewey's 1898 victory in the Philippines. The square's $25 million redesign, completed in July 2002, duly replaced the homeless with tourists and shoppers who perch on the oversized steps along the southern edge fanning their dazed credit cards back to life.

Architectural landmarks include Frank Lloyd Wright's **Folk Art International** (140 Maiden Lane, 1-415 392 9999), with its swooping circular interior, and the **Phelan Building** (on Market Street, between Stockton and O'Farrell), the largest of the city's 'flat-iron' structures. However, the most important attraction hums along under **Powell Street**: these are the cables that steadily haul San Francisco's fabulous cable cars uphill. The Powell Street turnaround, usually with a huge queue of tourists in attendance, is at the foot of Market Street. When you arrive, take a detour to the Powell Street BART station, at the lower level of Hallidie Plaza; you'll find the helpful

Visitor Information Center (corner of Market and Powell, 1-415 391 2000, www.sfvisitor.org) and loads of free maps, brochures and coupons.

The Financial District

Neighbouring Union Square to the east, the **Financial District** has been the business and banking hub of the American West since the Gold Rush, its northern edge now guarded by the 853-foot (260-metre) **Transamerica Pyramid** (600 Montgomery Street). Completed in 1972, San Francisco's tallest building provoked public outrage when its design was unveiled, but has long since taken its rightful place in the city's affections. The pyramid sits on giant rollers that allow it to rock safely, and ensured the building wasn't damaged by the 1989 quake. The pyramid's current owners do not offer public access, unlike the owners of the imposing **Bank of America** (555 California Street): the Carnelian Room (1-415 433 7500) on the 52nd floor becomes a cocktail lounge and upscale restaurant between 3pm and 11pm.

During business hours, pop into the **Wells Fargo History Museum** (420 Montgomery Street, 1-415 396 2619, www.wellsfargo history.com, closed Sat & Sun) or the Union Bank of California's **Museum of the Money of the American West** (400 California Street, 1-415 765 0400) for collections of Californiabilia: an 1859 Concord stagecoach is the highlight of the former; three-dollar bills are among the quirky pleasures of the latter. Huge art deco sculptures mark the front of the **Pacific Coast Stock Exchange** (301 Pine Street, 1-415 285 0495); they're an appropriate introduction to *Allegory of California*, the vibrant Diego Rivera mural on the tenth floor. Free guided tours (3pm on the first Wednesday of each month) are the only way to see the work; book well in advance. Another curiosity is ornate, lion-headed **Lotta's Fountain** on Market Street (at the intersection with Kearny and Geary Streets), since 1906 the annual gathering place on 18 April for earthquake survivors.

On the northern fringe of the Financial District, **Jackson Square Historical District** is a last vestige of San Francisco's Barbary Coast, that swamp of low-life bars and sex clubs of uncommon depravity. Stroll along **Jackson Street** and **Hotaling Street** to see the only neighbourhood that pre-dates San Francisco's ubiquitous Victorian style; these few blocks of 1850s brick buildings, housing upmarket antiques shops and lovingly restored offices, are now far from the waterfront, but their foundations rest on the hulls of ships scuttled to make room for more boatloads of gold-seekers. The four-mile self-guided

Transamerica Pyramid by night.

Barbary Coast Trail, marked by bronze medallions showing a miner and clipper ship, connects some 20 sites, including Jackson Square, a Barbary Coast saloon and Hyde Street Pier (*see p233*). A concise guide to the route can be bought at the Visitor Information Center.

Chinatown

There has been a Chinese community in San Francisco since the Gold Rush. Even today the crowded streets and dark alleys of Chinatown – with laundry fluttering overhead, restaurants serving duck's feet, herbalists grinding up love potions – can seem wonderfully atmospheric.

Dragon-topped **Chinatown Gate**, a couple of blocks north-east of Union Square, marks the district's southern entrance. Through the gate is **Grant Avenue**, Chinatown's main thoroughfare – and arguably the city's oldest. Dragon streetlamps line the street, a reminder of the '20s tourist boom when Chinatown was one of America's most-visited attractions, not least because of its exotic reputation for opium and prostitutes. No such luck these days; the shops sell only T-shirts and jewellery. The buildings are fairly undistinguished, apart from the gaudy chinoiserie of **Ying On Labor Association** (Nos.745-7) and the balconies and pagoda-style roof of **Sai Gai Yat Bo Company** (No.736). Half a block east of Grant, **Portsmouth Square** (733 Kearny Street) was where Sam Brannan precipitated the Gold Rush by announcing the discovery of gold at Sutter's Mill. Now elderly Chinese congregate to practise t'ai chi or argue over Chinese chess.

At 743 Washington Street, the pagoda-like **Bank of Canton** is one of Chinatown's most photographed buildings. The present structure was built in 1909 for the Chinese American Telephone Exchange, where multilingual phone operators routed calls throughout Chinatown by memory alone, as no phone directory existed for Chinese residents. An alley just off Washington Street contains the **Golden Gate Fortune Cookie Factory** (56 Ross Alley, 1-415 781 3956), where you can watch cookies being made by hand.

The **Kong Chow Temple** (855 Stockton Street) was established in 1857, moving to its current fourth-floor location in 1977. From its fabulous altar, a statue of the god Kuan Ti looks out on the bay. Picturesque Waverly Place is the site of the **Tien Hau Temple** (4th floor, 125 Waverly Place), which people visit to answer important questions by shaking bamboo sticks, just as they do all across Asia.

Those who want to learn a bit more about the area would do well to take one of Wok Wiz's daily **Chinatown Tours** (1-415 981 8989, 1-650 355 9657, $28-$85). There are also bilingual displays at the **Chinese American National Museum & Learning Center** (965 Clay Street, 1-415 391 1188, closed Mon, $3).

North Beach

At the northern edge of Chinatown, **North Beach** was the hub of the city's Italian community in the 1920s and '30s. In the 1950s this European aura – and the low rents – attracted the jazz-loving Beats; comedy clubs and punk venues appeared over the ensuing decades. And yet the original residents remained: these days North Beach is still home to elderly Italians playing *bocce* or nibbling *cannoli* in an array of coffeehouses.

Much of North Beach's history and many of its treasures lie along **Columbus Avenue**. Just up the hill from **Columbus Tower**, a turreted green building on the corner of Columbus and Kearny, is the **City Lights** bookshop (*see p248*); the surprisingly jaunty sign of **Vesuvio** (*see p245*) is right next door. Yet North Beach is as well known for its sex shows as its linguine and literature. **Broadway** is lined with clubs offering floor shows, and history was made at the Condor Club (300 Columbus Avenue) in 1964 when buxom Carol Doda descended from the ceiling on a white baby grand in a topless bathing suit. Condor is now a sports bar, but the owners have retained the set of neon nipples that once marked the place.

To the north, **Washington Square** is the heart of North Beach. Marilyn Monroe and Joe DiMaggio had their wedding photos taken here,

in front of the white stucco Romanesque Church of St Peter and St Paul. The park is a lovely place to watch people walk their dogs and play frisbee.

While no visit to San Francisco is complete without having an espresso in North Beach, **Coit Tower** (1-415 362 0808) is the area's only bona fide attraction. The 210-foot (64-metre) concrete turret on Telegraph Hill, the site of the West Coast's first telegraph, was gifted to the city by eccentric Lillie Hitchcock Coit. Saved from a fierce fire as a child, the benefactress was a lifelong fan of firemen; coincidentally, the tower ended up looking like the nozzle of a hose. As well as offering spectacular views from the top (the lift costs $3.75), the tower contains some amazing murals, created under Diego Rivera's supervision.

Russian Hill

Named after a group of wayward Russian sailors whose graves were discovered here in the 1840s, **Russian Hill** is quiet, residential and very pricey – quite a contrast to the tourist ferment of Fisherman's Wharf (*see p233*) below. Its most celebrated landmark is **Lombard Street**, the world's 'crookedest' road (meaning most photographed). All summer, tourists queue for the thrill of driving down the nine hairpin bends between Hyde Street and Leavenworth, to the annoyance of local residents. More exciting

Barbary Lane

Armistead Maupin's *Tales of the City* column appeared in the *San Francisco Chronicle* from 1976, but gained fame as a series of popular novels. The books offer a convincingly realistic snapshot of queer and straight life here, but the apartment at their centre – Anna Madrigal's abode at 28 Barbary Lane – is a chimera. The 'narrow, wooded walkway' is supposed to be found off Leavenworth, between Union and Filbert, but the inquisitive find there only the pretty gardens of Havens Street.

Maupin has claimed the real inspiration behind Barbary Lane was a block away: the miraculously secluded **Macondray Lane**. One of San Francisco's 400 unmarked and overgrown public stairways, it has rickety wooden stairs and gives, through the idiosyncratic houses that line one side, tantalising views of the bay. Its signpost is hard to spot (look for the name imprinted in the kerb), but you'll find it just north of Green Street, between Taylor and Jones.

Clear your mind. Rest your soul.

hotel nikko san francisco

travel to a different place

for the cognoscenti is driving the city's steepest street: from Hyde to Leavenworth, Filbert Street has a whopping 31.5 per cent gradient.

Active visitors will enjoy exploring the area's quaint stairways and alleys: **Macondray Lane** has the literary heritage (*see p225* **Barbary Lane**), but don't miss the Willis Polk-designed **Vallejo Street Stairway** (between Jones and Mason), which forms the apex of Russian Hill. For a breather, drop in on the pretty open-air courtyard of the **San Francisco Art Institute** (800 Chestnut Street, 1-415 771 7020, www.san franciscoart.edu, closed Mon & Sun, $6), then take in *The Making of a Fresco*, one of the several murals Rivera completed in San Francisco in the 1930s. Russian Hill also boasts one of the city's oldest dwellings: **Feusier Octagon House** (1067 Green Street, near Leavenworth), one of two survivors of a brief craze for octagonal houses.

Nob Hill

Overlooking Union Square from the north, **Nob Hill** is a short but steep jaunt up California Street. After the cable car started operating in the 1870s, the once-barren hill began to attract wealthy residents: so-called 'nabobs', hence the name of the hill. Of the many mansions, only the 1886 home of James C Flood survived the earthquake and fire of 1906; later remodelled by Willis Polk, the squat brownstone mansion is now the private **Pacific-Union Club** (1000 California Street). Next to it is fastidious **Huntington Park**, while the architectural extravaganza of **Grace Cathedral** (1100 California Street) lies on the other side of the park. This Episcopalian house of worship has a façade modelled on Notre Dame in Paris and impressive gilded bronze portals. Within you'll find an altarpiece by Keith Haring in the AIDS Interfaith Chapel and a meditational labyrinth. Grandiose hotels surround the park and club, and the **Cable Car Museum** (*see below*) lurks downhill to the north.

Cable Car Museum

1201 Mason Street, at Washington Street (1-415 474 1887/www.cablecarmuseum.com). Bus 1, 12, 30, 45, 83/cable car Powell-Hyde or Powell-Mason. **Open** *Jan-Mar, Oct-Dec* 10am-5pm daily. *Apr-Sept* 10am-6pm daily. **Admission** free.
The only mobile landmark in the US, the cable cars have been in operation since 1873. Earthquakes, fires and automobiles almost finished them off: by 1947 the city had proposed replacing the last three lines with diesel buses. However, outraged citizens forced the federal government to declare the remaining lines a National Historic Landmark. The museum enables you to watch the 10ft (3m) winding turbines reel in the underground cables at a steady 9.5mph. The cars themselves look more like trolley buses than conventional cable cars. Each has a two-person crew, comprising a gripman, who works the cranks and levers that grab and release the perpetually moving underground cable, and a conductor, to take fares and ding the bell.

Polk Gulch & the Tenderloin

Just west of Union Square, the **Tenderloin** is one of the ropier areas of San Francisco. Hungry folk push shopping carts around; encountering panhandlers is a given. Yet things are beginning to look up: in September 2003 the city's Board of Supervisors declared the two blocks of Larkin Street between O'Farrell and Eddy to be 'Little Saigon', recognising a steadfast local community.

Alongside the Tenderloin, **Polk Gulch** is threatening to push itself on to the visitor's itinerary with a growing number of shops and bars. It was a genuine gay ghetto before the Castro became the more salubrious focus for San Francisco's many queers, but there's little by way of sightseeing unless your idea of fun is watching hollow-eyed transvestites.

Civic Center

San Francisco's **Civic Center** is a complex of imposingly handsome government buildings and immense performance halls, centred on the Civic Center Plaza's expansive and well-tended lawn. The homeless gather in the plaza, in the shadow of the magnificent **City Hall** (1 Dr Carlton B Goodlett Place/Polk Street, 1-415 554 4000). Built in 1915 to designs by Arthur Brown and John Bakewell, it is the epitome of the Beaux Arts style that characterises the whole Civic Center. Extensively retrofitted to forestall damage from future earthquakes, the building has a system of rubber-and-steel 'base isolators' that allow it to move 3.5 feet in any direction. There are free tours of the building daily (1-415 554 6023).

In the plaza's south-east corner is the **Main Library** (100 Larkin Street, 1-415 557 4400, www.sfpl.org), whose 1996 reconstruction by architectural firm Pei Cobb Freed added a healthy dash of modernism to six beautiful storeys of Beaux Arts architecture. **United Nations Plaza**, north of the library, celebrates the 50th anniversary of the founding of the UN here in June 1945. The resplendent Gae Aulenti redesign of the former library, now the **Asian Art Museum** (*see p229*), opened here in 2003.

Across Van Ness Avenue is a trio of grand edifices. The multi-storey, curved glass façade of the **Louise M Davies Symphony Hall** (*see p251*) is enhanced by reclining Henry Moore bronzes, while the **War Memorial**

Central California

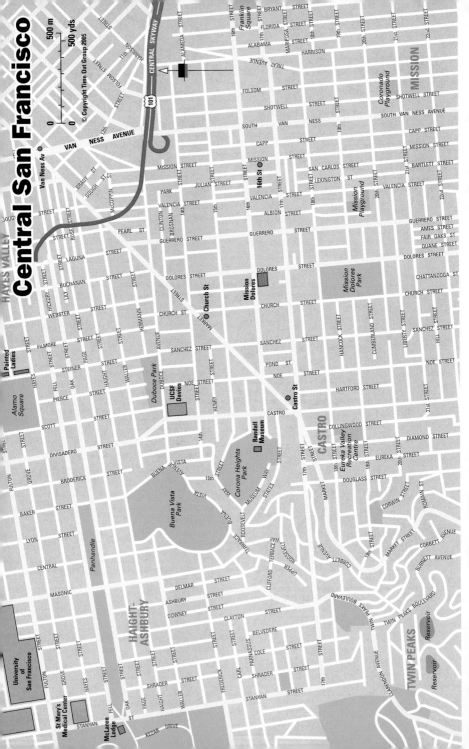

Central San Francisco

HAYES VALLEY

0   500 m
0   500 yds

© Copyright Time Out Group 2005

MISSION

CASTRO

TWIN PEAKS

HAIGHT-ASHBURY

University of San Francisco

St Mary's Medical Center

McLaren Lodge

Alamo Square

Painted Ladies

Buena Vista Park

Corona Heights Park

Duboce Park

UCSF Davies

Randall Museum

Mission Dolores

Mission Dolores Park

Mission Playground

Coronado Playground

Eureka Valley Recreation Centre

Panhandle

Reservoir

Opera House (*see p251*) is a companion piece to City Hall, designed by the same architect in the same style. The third structure is the **Veterans' Memorial Building**, containing the magnificent Herbst Theatre (*see p253*) and diminutive San Francisco Art Commission Gallery and **San Francisco Performing Arts Library & Museum** (1-415 255 4800, www.sfpalm.org).

Asian Art Museum

200 Larkin Street, at Fulton Street (1-415 581 3500/ www.asianart.org). BART Civic Center/Muni Metro F, J, K, L, M, N/bus 5, 6, 7, 9, 19, 21, 66, 71. **Open** 10am-5pm Tue, Wed, Fri-Sun; 10am-9pm Thur. **Admission** $10; $6-$7 discounts.

Beautifully redesigned by Gae Aulenti, famous for the Musée d'Orsay conversion in Paris, the Asian Art Museum has one of the world's most comprehensive collections of Asian art. Spanning 6,000 years of Asian history, the 15,000-plus objects range from Japanese buddhas to sacred texts. There's a café on the first floor and a well-stocked gift shop.

South of Market

SoMa

For most of its life, this area was an industrial wasteland, but over the last decade, it's grown increasingly prominent in San Francisco's cultural life; what used to be dowdy old 'South of Market' is now SoMa. Part of a city-funded revitalisation project, the showpiece **Yerba Buena Gardens Complex** is a maze of attractions, gardens and businesses in a complex that's half above ground and half below. The lovely urban park has shady trees and sculpture walks, including a waterfall built in 1993 in memory of Martin Luther King Jr. On one side, the **Yerba Buena Center for the Arts** (*see p253*) is an architectural beauty that puts on challenging performances and art expos, while the **Metreon Center** (*see p248*) is on the other. Rooftop at Yerba Buena Gardens offers the hands-on, child-friendly, high-tech attractions of **Zeum** (*see p230*). There's even a 1906 carousel, hand-carved by Charles Looff ($2 gets you two rides), and an ultra-cool interactive sculpture by Chico Macmurtrie: sit on the middle pink bench and your weight moves the metal figure.

Across 3rd Street from the gardens, you can't miss the stunning **San Francisco Museum of Modern Art (SFMOMA)** (*see below*). The **Museum of the African Diaspora** or **MoAD** (90 New Montgomery Street, 1-415 358 700, www.moadsf.org) is scheduled to open here in autumn 2005, pairing African oral traditions with new technology to re-examine the history and celebrate the culture of African-descended people. Another important newcomer

is only here until autumn 2008: the **California Academy of Sciences** (*see below*) stays in SoMa until renovations are complete in its Golden Gate Park home.

The **Cartoon Art Museum** (*see below*) has opened in place of the lamented Friends of Photography/Ansel Adams Center, while just across the street the **California Historical Society** (678 Mission Street, 1-415 357 1848, www.californiahistoricalsociety.org, closed Mon, Tue & Sun, $1-$3) and nearby **Seymour California Pioneers Museum** (300 4th Street, 1-415 957 1849, www.californiapioneers. org, closed Mon, Tue, Sat & Sun, $1-$3) have small collections on early settler history.

South Park was San Francisco's first gated community, but suffered a string of misfortunes: burnt down in the early 20th century, it was killed off by the appearance of those new-fangled cable cars, which whisked the South Park millionaires up to Nob Hill (*see p226*). An African-American enclave after World War II, South Park was neglected until coders and creatives blew in to create Multimedia Gulch. Now the green oval makes a calm picnic spot.

California Academy of Sciences

875 Howard Street, between 4th & 5th Streets (1-415 750 7145/www.calacademy.org). BART Powell or Montgomery/Muni Metro F, J, K, L, M, N/bus 9, 15, 30, 45, 76. **Open** 10am-5pm daily. **Admission** $7; $4.50 12-17s, students, seniors; $2 4-11s; free under-4s. Free 1st Wed of mth.

Although smaller than the original site, the temporary venue currently being used by the 150-year-old California Academy of Sciences and Steinhart Aquarium holds an impressive array of live animals and fish, from ants and giant sea bass to penguins. Visitors can experience different habitats (arid dust, the salinity of the water tanks), and there's a range of international serpents in SSsssnake Alley. Upstairs, the Astrobiology section explores life on other planets through the study of earth's extreme environments (ocean-floor geysers, for example).

Cartoon Art Museum

655 Mission Street, between 3rd & New Montgomery Streets (1-415 227 8666/www.cartoon art.org). BART Montgomery/Muni Metro F, J, K, L, M, N/bus 9, 14, 15, 30. **Open** 11am-5pm Tue-Sun. **Admission** $6; $4 discounts; $2 6-12s.

This is the only museum in the Western US dedicated to cartoons. The camera used to create the first TV animation ('Crusader Rabbit', produced in 1949-51, trivia buffs) is here, along with more than 5,000 pieces of cartoon and animation art and a library.

San Francisco Museum of Modern Art (SFMOMA)

151 3rd Street, between Mission & Howard Streets (1-415 357 4000/www.sfmoma.org). BART Powell or Montgomery/Muni Metro F, J, K, L, M, N/bus 9, 15, 30, 45, 76. **Open** *Memorial Day-Labor Day* 10am-6pm

Mon, Tue, Fri-Sun; 10am-9pm Thur. *Labor Day-Memorial Day* 11am-6pm Mon, Tue, Fri-Sun; 11am-9pm Thur. **Admission** $10; $6-$7 discounts; free under-12s; half price 6-9pm Thur. Free 1st Tue of mth. **Credit** *Café & shop only* AmEx, MC, V.

Opened in 1995 and the second largest museum in the US devoted to modern art, SFMOMA reaps approval as much for Swiss architect Mario Botta's $60m red-brick building as for the art. That's not to decry the art, though: the four floors of galleries that rise above the stunning black marble reception area house an important permanent collection. The range is formidable: Koons to Kiefer, Mondrian to Duchamp (*Fountain*, naturally). Don't miss the spectacular catwalk just beneath the skylight.

Zeum

221 4th Street, at Howard Street (1-415 777 2800/www.zeum.org). BART Powell or Montgomery/Muni Metro F, J, K, L, M, N/bus 9, 15, 30, 45, 76. **Open** 11am-5pm Wed-Sun. **Admission** $7; $6 discounts; $5 4-18s. **Credit** AmEx, MC, V.

Zeum is an art and technology centre aimed at eight-to 18-year-olds, which means parents can expect a headache. Exhibits are, of course, interactive, with kids directing their own videos, creating sculptures or experimenting with computer-aided animation.

The Mission

The Mission is the city's oldest neighbourhood, with fascinating **Mission Dolores** (*see below*) a vivid reminder of the area's earliest European settlement. This adobe building, officially Misión San Francisco de Asis, gave the city its name.

The Mission district is now, though, home to a dazzling array of political and spiritual wall art. There are more than 200 murals in the area, celebrating the struggles and achievements of its predominantly Hispanic residents. The best-known street for murals is **Balmy Alley** (from 24th to 25th Streets, between Harrison Street and Treat Avenue), but you'll find others near 24th Street, between Mission and Potrero. **Precita Eyes Mural Arts & Visitors Center** (2981 24th Street, 1-415 285 2287) runs tours.

The Mission has two arterial corridors, Valencia and Mission Streets, that demonstrate its changing character. **Valencia** is fairly well chock-a-block with quirky boutiques and bars catering to urban hipsters, while **Mission Street** retains its longstanding working-class Hispanic flavour. Mission Street is packed with taquerias, but Valencia Street is a better bet for boho cafés, especially between 16th and 24th Streets, and book-browsing.

Mission Dolores

3321 16th Street, at Dolores Street (1-415 621 8203/www.missiondolores.citysearch.com). BART 16th Street/Muni Metro J/bus 22. **Open** 8am-4pm daily. **Admission** $3; $1 discounts. **Credit** (groups only) AmEx, MC, V.

Though the original mission became an expansive outpost, housing over 4,000 monks and Indian converts, today only the tiny old church remains; it's now the oldest standing structure in the city, having survived the 1906 earthquake unscathed. Small wonder that the cool, dim interior looks and feels authentic: almost everything is original, from the redwood roof supports to ornate altars. A small museum offers tours and access to a cemetery containing a mass grave of 5,000 Costanoan Indians.

The Castro

Bordered by Market, Church, 20th and Diamond Streets, the **Castro** is one of the few places in the world where being gay is the norm. Straights aren't excluded, but they do experience the unusual sensation of being in the minority.

A huge rainbow flag flies over **Harvey Milk Plaza** (the Muni stop at Market and Castro), named for the camera-shop owner who in 1977 became California's first openly gay elected official – he was later assassinated. The other landmarks are on Castro Street. **Twin Peaks Bar** (No.401, 1-415 864 9470) shattered taboos by becoming one of the first gay bars in the US with large, pavement-facing windows – back in 1973, when homosexuality was still a felony. Then there's the dazzling art deco **Castro Theatre** (*see p250*) and **Skin Zone** (No.575), the site of Milk's camera shop and campaign HQ.

In truth, the Castro seems somnolent during the day, far from the hotbed of debauchery and febrile politics you might have imagined. To pep it up, join lesbian raconteur Trevor Hailey's gossipy four-hour **Cruisin' the Castro** tour (1-415 550 8110, $40 with lunch). Weekends and the run-up to Pride each June see the place lively itself up a bit; whatever the day, leather chaps and buffed biceps and leathery chaps with buffed biceps are as comfortably at home as Armani suits.

For a great view of the Castro from above, get lunch to go and wander up to **Corona Heights**. Along with beautiful vistas, you'll see plenty of Castro pooches and their human pets. If you've got little children in tow, visit the small petting zoo at **Randall Museum** (199 Museum Street, 1-415 554 9600, www.randall museum.org, closed Mon & Sun).

Central neighbourhoods

The Haight

The Haight's ornate Victorian properties, many emblazoned with peace signs or painted funky colours, are a reminder of the area's beginnings as a 19th-century resort town and its reincarnation as the birthplace of free love.

Built by middle-class tradesmen in the Mission and Lower Haight, the signature terraced houses have wooden frames decorated with mass-produced ornamentation. The Italianate Victorians (tall cornices, neo-classical elements, add-on porches) are well represented in the Lower Haight, notably on Grove Street.

When the middle classes began fleeing the inner cities for the suburbs in the 1950s, student bohemians moved in to the rambling houses and the hippie commune was born, with the likes of the Grateful Dead (710 Ashbury Street) and Janis Joplin (124 Lyon Street) moving in. Four decades later, runaways still gravitate to **Haight Street** from their suburban purgatory, yet on Tuesdays and Saturdays, the **Flower Power Walking Tour** (1-415 863 1621, $15) helps you find out what those who were really there in the '60s can't remember for themselves.

Shoe stores and clothing boutiques line the main drag, but shops selling drug paraphernalia and Eastern esoterica still give the place a carnival atmosphere at weekends. Most people enjoy the mellow bars and coffee houses, but few can help but be disappointed to discover the world-renowned **Haight-Ashbury** is merely the corner where Haight and Ashbury Streets meet. At the western end of Haight Street, you can cross Stanyan Street to enter **Golden Gate Park** (*see p238*); the park's grand entrance, the Panhandle, is a couple of blocks north. The eastern half of Haight Street is known as the **Lower Haight**. Focused on the intersection of Haight and Fillmore, it's hipper, harsher and more interesting than its neighbour.

The Western Addition

The Western Addition was the city's first multicultural neighbourhood, but most tourists visit only for **Postcard Row**. These tidy pastel Victorians on Steiner Street along the east side of Alamo Square Park are more remarkable for the view of Downtown behind them than the buildings themselves, which are merely the most-photographed of more than 14,000 examples of the city's architectural vernacular.

After the 1906 earthquake and fire, the **Fillmore District** at the heart of the Western Addition sprang to life as displaced residents began moving in. **Japantown** grew there, covering more than 20 blocks, but its residents were interned after Pearl Harbor. The lack of the covenant laws that prevented African-Americans owning land elsewhere in the US meant that they were able to move into the Fillmore, although now, after years of demolition under the guise of 'urban renewal', there are few signs of their presence. Instead, most visitors head to the **Japan Center** to check out the Peace Pagoda.

Chinatown. *See p223.*

Pacific Heights & Cow Hollow

Pacific Heights is home to the city's high society: billionaire socialites Gordon and Ann Getty have a house here; Danielle Steel lives in the ornate **Spreckels Mansion**, on the block between Jackson, Gough, Washington and Octavia Streets. The stretch of Broadway between Divisadero Street and the Presidio affords some of the best architecture, although the curious blue-and-white 1861 **Octagon House** (2645 Gough Street, 1-415 441 7512, open 2nd & 4th Thur & 2nd Sun of mth) is on the other side of the hill. **Haas-Lilienthal House** (*see p232*) provides a point of departure

The rocking, rolling stock of San Francisco's **cable cars**. *See p259*.

for the architecturally inclined **Pacific Heights Walking Tour** (1-415 441 3000, $5-$8). Below Pacific Heights is the former dairy pasture still known as **Cow Hollow**. Chic bars and restaurants centre on **Union Street**, but the onion domes of the century-old **Vedanta Temple** (2963 Webster Street, 1-415 922 2323) are of more interest.

Haas-Lilienthal House

2007 Franklin Street, between Washington & Jackson Streets (1-415 441 3000). Bus 1, 12, 19, 27, 47, 49. **Open** noon-3pm Wed, Sat; 11am-4pm Sun. **Admission** $8. **Credit** AmEx, MC, V.
Built in 1886 by Bavarian William Haas, this Victorian exemplifies the extravagant Queen Anne style, with elaborate wooden gables and a circular tower. The 28 rooms and six (count 'em) bathrooms have been fully restored, and the house contains photos documenting its history and that of the family that lived here until 1972.

The bay shore

The Embarcadero

The **Embarcadero** stretches along the waterfront from China Basin and the SBC Park baseball stadium in the south all the way up to Fisherman's Wharf. For years it was marred by the freeway, but once that had been polished off by the 1989 Loma Prieta earthquake, the Embarcadero re-emerged as a graceful, palm-lined boulevard. At the foot of Market Street, opposite Justin Herman Plaza, its centrepiece is the stately, recently renovated **Ferry Building**; it bustles every weekend with the Ferry Plaza Farmers' Market (*see p249*), its Grand Nave full to bursting with foodies and day-trippers about to hop on their homeward ferry.

Walk south from the Ferry Building along the Embarcadero to Howard and you'll see an immense bow in gold, complete with a silver-and-red arrow. This is Claes Oldenburg and Coosje Van Bruggen's *Cupid's Span*, installed in 2002 in a field of native grass. It's also an ideal viewpoint for the **Bay Bridge**, which might be less famous than its sister span (*see p236*) but is far more useful; crossing it westbound there are wonderful cityscape views, but you're not allowed to stop the car. Divided into two by dramatic Yerba Buena Island, the Bay Bridge is three separate spans linking into a single bridge more than eight miles across. Completed a year before the Golden Gate Bridge in 1936, the Bay Bridge was more of a challenge because of the greater distances. The solution was to build a concrete pylon of inconceivably massive proportions in the middle of the bay, and use it as an anchor point for two different suspension spans. This central pylon draws little notice (it's mostly underwater), but it is one of the largest structures in California.

Inland, the art deco **Rincon Center** (101 Spear Street, 1-415 243 0473) has a lobby containing impressive WPA-style murals by incorrigibly badly behaved Russian-born artist Anton Refregier. Nearby, the **Contemporary Jewish Museum** (121 Steuart Street, 1-415 788 9990, www.thecjm.org, closed Fri & Sat, $4-$5) runs temporary exhibitions throughout the year. The museum has a new home planned next to Yerba Buena Gardens, in a Willis Polk power substation that will be transformed by superstar architect Daniel Libeskind. It should be open in 2007.

North of the Ferry Building, the Embarcadero becomes a long, gently curving promenade, extending to the tomfooleries of Fisherman's Wharf (*see below*). Along the way, Pier 7 offers lovely views of **Treasure Island**: built on the shoals of neighbouring Yerba Buena Island for the 1939 Golden Gate International Exposition, it became a US naval station during World War II. The views from the island are spectacular.

Fisherman's Wharf

Now the commercial shipping and fishing have moved elsewhere, **Fisherman's Wharf** is an inexplicably popular tourist purgatory, with day-trippers descending in thousands from the terminus of the Powell-Hyde cable car line. Except as a departure point for ferry trips to **Alcatraz** (*see below*) and **Angel Island** (*see p259*), the area is best avoided. Jefferson Street is the main drag, 'boasting' the **Wax Museum** (No.145, 1-415 202 0402, 1-800 439 4305, $6.95-$12.95) and **Ripley's Believe It Or Not! Museum** (No.175, 1-415 771 6188, $7.95-$12.95). Sidewalk crab stalls, seafood restaurants and street performers provide distraction. The east end of Jefferson has **Pier 39** (*see p248*) and the **Aquarium of the Bay** (*see below*). Offshore from Pier 39's H Dock, **Forbes Island** (1-415 951 4900) is a man-made, engine-propelled, floating lighthouse and restaurant.

You can visit two fully restored survivors of World War II, docked along **Pier 45**: the submarine **USS Pampanito** (1-415 775 1943, www.maritime.org, $7) and the **SS Jeremiah O'Brien Liberty Ship** (1-415 544 0100, www. ssjeremiahobrien.com, $4-$7). This is also the new home of the unhinged **Musée Mécanique** (*see p235*). Behind the Cannery, you'll find a shiny red 1955 Mack fire engine that whisks you from Beach Street, through the Presidio across the Golden Gate Bridge and back in 75 minutes, clanging its bell. Always popular,

Fire Engine Tours & Adventures (1-415 333 7077, www.fireenginetours.com, $20-$35) need to be booked in advance.

West of Fisherman's Wharf, **Hyde Street Pier** (*see below*) has a fleet of historic ships. The pier is under the same administration as the **San Francisco Maritime National Historical Park Museum Building** (Beach Street, 1-415 556 3002, www.maritime.org), the white art deco building opposite Ghirardelli Square. The museum describes whaling, steamboating and perilous journeys around the Horn using archive photos and models. Between Hyde Street and Van Ness Avenue, **Aquatic Park** offers a fine panorama of the Golden Gate Bridge, Alcatraz, windsurfers, sailing boats, dogs catching frisbees and fishermen catching nothing from the Municipal Pier. This is where the **Golden Gate Promenade** begins.

Alcatraz

www.nps.gov/alcatraz. Blue & Gold ferry from Pier 41, Embarcadero (Blue & Gold Fleet: recorded information 1-415 773 1188/tickets 1-415 705 5555/ www.blueandgoldfleet.com). **Tickets** $8.25-$11.50. *Audio tour* $10.75-$16. *After-dark tours* (4.20pm Thur-Sun) $14.25-$23.50. **Credit** AmEx, Disc, MC, V. The West Coast's first lighthouse was built here in 1854, but it was soon decided that the island's isolated setting made it perfect for a prison. It became a military jail in the 1870s, but it wasn't until 1934 that it became the high-security federal penitentiary of popular legend. In operation for only three decades, the Rock remains fixed in the imagination as the ultimate penal colony, serving as a final stop for Al Capone, 'Machine Gun' Kelly and the infamous 'Bird Man', Robert Stroud (you can enter his cell). Visiting Alcatraz is a must: the audio guide is great, weaving in interviews with former inmates, and the after-dark tours are sensational.

Aquarium of the Bay

Pier 39, at Beach Street, Fisherman's Wharf (1-888 732 3483/www.aquariumofthebay.com). Muni Metro F/bus 10, 15, 39, 47. **Open** *Summer* 9am-8pm daily. *Winter* 10am-6pm Mon-Fri; 10am-7pm Sat, Sun. **Admission** $12.95; $6.50 3-11s. **Credit** MC, V. The Aquarium gives you a diver's-eye view of the bay through transparent underwater tunnels. It's an amazing place to spy on crabs and sharks, touch bat rays and watch the slow combat of octopuses.

Hyde Street Pier

At Hyde Street, Fisherman's Wharf (1-415 561 7100/www.maritime.org). Muni Metro F/bus 19, 30, 42/cable car Powell-Hyde. **Open** 10am-5pm daily. **Admission** free ($5 for vessels). **No credit cards**. Fans of maritime history and children love the eight historic vessels permanently docked here. They include the 1886 full-rigged *Balclutha*, built to carry grain from California to Europe; the *CA Thayer*, an 1895 sailing ship that carried timber along the West Coast; and the 1890 commuter ferry *Eureka*.

Musée Mécanique

Pier 45, at Taylor Street, Fisherman's Wharf (1-415 346 2000/www.museemecanique.citysearch.com). *Bus 18, 38.* **Open** 10am-7pm daily. **Admission** free. An arcade housing over 170 old-fashioned coin-op gizmos, ranging from fortune-telling machines to player pianos, some dating to the 1880s. Best of all is larger-than-life Laughing Sal.

The Marina

The vast sloping lawns of **Marina Green** (Marina Boulevard, between Scott and Webster Streets) are a considerable attraction: locals come to fly kites, jog or picnic, as visitors suck in terrific views of the Golden Gate Bridge and the bay. At the end of the harbour jetty to the west of the green is the amazing **Wave Organ**, an underwater artwork whose pipes and benches make eerie tones as the waves rush in under the organ and through its tubes.

At the eastern edge of the Marina, **Fort Mason** (*see below*), a former US Army command post, houses museums and exhibition spaces. Between here and Fort Point (*see p237*), a mile-long strip of temporary structures was erected for the 1915 Panama-Pacific Exposition. When the fair was over, this fantastical city-within-a-city was torn down, leaving just one reminder: the **Palace of Fine Arts** (Lyon Street, 1-415 567 6642, www.palaceoffinearts.org). Set in a little park at the Marina's western edge, only the shell of Bernard Maybeck's neo-classical domed rotunda was left after demolition in 1964. For the 1969 opening of the adjacent **Exploratorium** (*see below*), the original plaster was expensively converted to concrete so as to preserve this atmospheric spot.

Exploratorium

3601 Lyon Street, at Marina Boulevard (1-415 563 7337/www.exploratorium.edu). Bus 22, 28, 30, 41, 43, 45, 76. **Open** 10am-5pm Tue-Sun. **Admission** $12; $9.50 13-17s, discounts; $8 4-12s; free under-4s. Free 1st Wed of mth. **Credit** AmEx, MC, V.
This quirky science museum invites hungry young brains to learn about static electricity, Tesla coils and sound waves, with more than 700 hands-on experiments based around perception, weather, botany, mechanics and the physics of sound and light. A favourite is the Tactile Dome, a geodesic hemisphere of total blackness in which you try to identify objects; you'll have to book in advance (1-415 561 0362), but the additional $15 admission is worth it.

Fort Mason

Marina Boulevard, at Buchanan Street (1-415 441 3400/www.fortmason.org). Bus 10, 22, 28, 30, 47.
These ex-military buildings house a bevy of cultural institutions. In Building C, the African-American Historical and Cultural Society Museum (1-415 441 0640) is across the hall from the Museo ItaloAmericano (1-415 673 2200). Shows at the Museum of Craft and Folk Art (1-415 775 0991) in Building A range from bookbinding to handmade furniture. The airy SFMOMA Artists' Gallery (Building A, 1-415 441 4777) deals in contemporary works by Northern Californians. Fort Mason houses the Magic Theatre and Greens Restaurant (*see p244*). Museums close Mon, with only MoCFA open Tue; all offer free admission on the first Wed of the month.

San Francisco Museum of Modern Art. *See p229.*

Chorus to the bridge

The **Golden Gate Bridge** (linking the Toll Plaza near the Presidio to Marin County, 1-415 921 5858, www.goldengatebridge.org) may not be the longest in the world, but it is among the most beautiful and certainly the most recognisable. Completed in 1937, the bridge's statistics alone are impressive – the towers are 746 feet (227 metres) high, the road is 1.75 miles long, and enough cable was used in its construction to encircle the globe three times – but raw statistics can't convey the grandeur of the bridge, especially up close. Drive, walk or catch a bus to the Toll Plaza, and head out on foot along the pedestrian walkway to enjoy the sensation of it thrumming beneath your feet. The bridge's distinctive orange colour was an accident of fate: San Franciscans were so delighted by the reddish primer paint that they stuck with that rather than painting it silver.

A pugnacious engineer named Joseph Strauss did more than anyone to make the bridge a reality, but it was freelance architect Irwin F Morrow who actually designed it. Reputedly five times stronger than necessary, the bridge is designed to sway 21 feet and sag ten feet, withstanding winds up to 100mph and supporting bumper-to-bumper traffic across all six lanes along with shoulder-to-shoulder pedestrians on the walkways. When the massive 1989 earthquake devastated the Marina, the Golden Gate Bridge survived unscathed, but the virtual certainty of another such destructive quake prompted officials to undertake a vast seismic retrofitting project, due for completion in 2005. This, in turn, was taken as the justification for a vehicle toll hike from $3 up to $5, which is charged on southbound journeys only.

The Golden Gate

The narrow strait that opens out into San Francisco Bay is officially known as the Golden Gate. It was named in 1846 by Captain John Fremont (one of the city's more prominent and idealistsic frontiersmen), who saw it as similar to the Golden Horn in Istanbul; thus, contrary to common belief, the famous bridge takes its name from the strait, not the other way round.

The Presidio

Called 'the prettiest piece of real estate in America', the **Presidio** is situated perfectly at the northemrn tip of the city, overlooking the bay, the ocean and the bridge. A military base for 220 years, it was handed over to the Park Service in 1994, with the US Army unable to afford the upkeep. It is now managed by a confusing welter of agencies, one of which –

the controversial Presidio Trust – has allowed a massive complex to be built that will house George Lucas's Industrial Light & Magic and LucasArts operations. Set to open in 2005, annual rent will be around $5.8 million. Battles between developers and conservationists are likely to keep the Presidio in its current state of arrested decay: a great boon for visitors. There are 11 miles of hiking trails, 14 miles of bicycle routes and three miles of beaches.

The gate from Pacific Heights on Presidio Avenue and Jackson Street leads into fairytale woods, often shrouded in mist, but the centre of the Presidio is the **Main Post**. Here you'll find a visitor centre (Building 50, 1-415 561 4323), two 17th-century Spanish cannons on Pershing Square and rows of Victorian-era military homes along Funston Avenue. In the **San Francisco National Cemetery** (Lincoln Boulevard) lie the remains of several notables, including many 'Buffalo Soldiers', African-American servicemen.

The northern edge of the Presidio is **Crissy Field**. Originally dunelands, it was paved over and served as a military airfield until 2001, when – after extensive work – it was opened to the public. Some of the original marshland and coastal dunes have been restored; the rest is a beautiful and apparently endless lawn and beachfront. At the western edge, forming the northernmost tip of the Presidio, you'll find **Fort Point** (Marine Drive, 1-415 556 1693, www.nps.gov/fopo), open to the public from Friday to Sunday. Built between 1853 and 1861 to protect the city from a sea attack that never came, it now houses military exhibitions. Climb on to the roof for a fabulous view of the underbelly of the bridge.

Baker Beach, along the Presidio's Pacific edge, is a favourite getaway. None of the beaches around San Francisco is great for swimming (the water is cold beyond refreshing), but their beauty makes for joyous strolling, picnicking and loafing. The south end of Baker is reserved for clothed beach-goers, but more liberated folk quite literally hang out to the north of the 'Hazardous Surf' sign at what is the most-visited urban nude beach in the US.

Pacific Coast

Richmond

In the north-west corner of the city, bordering the northern edge of Golden Gate Park, the **Richmond** is largely residential. Most visitors get the bus straight to Land's End promontory to admire the fabulous **California Palace of the Legion of Honor** (*see below*), but there are other attractions: just north of the Palace's car park is George Segal's haunting **Jewish**

Holocaust Memorial, while the peculiar **Columbarium** (1 Loraine Court, off Anza Street, 1-415 752 7891) is at the area's easterly edge. The latter is a round, domed neo-classical rotunda, honeycombed with niches containing richly decorated urns, alternately dignified and flamboyantly whimsical. The niches house the remains of many of the city's first families.

Hidden between Land's End Beach and Baker Beach (*see above*) in the exclusive Seacliff neighbourhood, you'll find the exquisitely sheltered James D Phelan Beach. Better known as **China Beach**, it takes its nickname from the Chinese fishermen who would camp here in the 19th century. Many locals consider it the finest of San Francisco's beaches: catch it at sunset and you'll probably agree.

Perched on the verge of the city is the touristy and recently remodelled **Cliff House** (*see below*), the brainchild of silver baron Adolph Sutro. Below the Cliff House to the north are the ruins of **Sutro Baths**. Built by Sutro in 1896, these were once the world's biggest swimming baths. Fed by the Pacific, seven pools holding a total of 1,375,578 gallons (6,253,500 litres) could be filled or emptied by the tides in an hour. Destroyed by fire in 1966, the ruins are strangely photogenic. Extending south from Cliff House past the city limits, **Ocean Beach** (*see p239*) is by far San Francisco's biggest: a three-mile sandy strip.

California Palace of the Legion of Honor
Lincoln Park, at 34th Avenue & Clement Street (1-415 863 3330/www.thinker.org). Bus 1, 2, 18, 38. **Open** 9.30am-5pm Tue-Sun. **Admission** $8; $6 seniors; $5 12-17s; free under-12s. Free every Tue. **Credit** AmEx, MC, V.
Built by architect George Applegarth in homage to the Palais de la Legion d'Honneur in Paris – of which it is a three-quarter scale adaptation – this is San Francisco's most beautiful museum. A memorial to Californians who died in World War I, it stands in a wood overlooking the Pacific, its neo-classical façade and Beaux Arts interior virtually unchanged since 1924. A glass pyramid acts as a skylight for galleries that contain works of art spanning 4,000 years, with emphasis on Europeans (El Greco, Rembrandt, especially Rodin). The expanded garden level houses temporary shows. Bus 18 goes directly to the museum.

Cliff House & Camera Obscura
1090 Point Lobos Avenue, at the Great Highway (1-415 386 3330/www.cliffhouse.com). Bus 18, 38. **Open** *Bar* 11am-2am daily. *Restaurant* 9am-10.30pm Mon-Fri; 8.30am-10.30pm Sat, Sun. *Walkways* 24hrs daily. **Admission** *Museum* $2. **Credit** *Bar & restaurant* AmEx, MC, V.
After fire in 1894, the original Cliff House was replaced by a splendid, turreted Victorian palace... which itself burned down, a year after surviving the

1906 quake. Then restored into rather a muddle of architectural modes, it underwent another round of extensive renovations that were completed in 2004. A new wing was added and the building returned (more or less) to its 1909 neo-classical roots, but the place is still pretty touristy. No matter: superb views compensate for the crowds. The 19th-century camera obscura was saved from demolition by public outcry – for which, be grateful. It's an optical marvel, projecting an image of the outside world on to a giant parabolic screen. The National Park Service maintains a visitor centre (1-415 556 8642) for the Golden Gate National Recreation Area here.

Golden Gate Park

Golden Gate Park is one of the largest man-made parks in the world, encompassing 1,017 acres (over 4 million square metres) of forest, meadow and landscaped garden on what were once barren sand dunes. Civil engineer William Hammond Hall prepared the initial design for the park in 1870, but the father of Golden Gate Park is the eccentric John McLaren, who spent more than 50 years as park superintendent, planting more than a million trees.

Meandering from the easterly entrance of the park along the pedestrian footpaths beside John F Kennedy Drive to the Pacific Ocean is a fine way to spend an afternoon. The **Panhandle** is the grand entrance to the park, designed with paths wide enough to accommodate carriages. Entering here brings you out at the **McLaren Lodge**, the park's visitor centre ((1-415 831 2700, closed Sat & Sun). Sharon Meadow to the south contains the **Children's Playground**, with its 1912 Herschel-Spillman Carousel, and **Hippie Hill**, which has been attracting hippies, alt-lifestylers and an unending stream of bongo players ever since 25,000 people gathered in the nearby Polo Fields for the 1967 Human Be-In.

Heading west, you'll encounter the **National AIDS Memorial Grove**, where the names of some of the city's nearly 20,000 dead are engraved in stone amid redwoods, oaks and maples (for tours, call 1-415 750 8340). The gleaming **Conservatory of Flowers** (*see below*) stands on the north side of JFK Drive, from which leafy walkways head south via the **John McLaren Rhododendron Dell** – all agapanthus, raspberries and, of course, rhododendrons – to the looming **California Academy of Sciences** complex, closed until 2008 (for the temporary premises, *see p229*). The new **MH de Young Memorial Museum** (*see below*) is due to open here in 2005, while the **Music Concourse**, complete with its grand arch, and parts of the ever-popular and delightful **Japanese Tea Garden** (including

the teahouse, open daily) are remnants of the Exposition. The **Strybing Arboretum & Botanical Gardens** (*see p239*) are just south.

From here, concrete stairs lead up to **Stow Lake**. Standing on Strawberry Hill island in the middle of Stow Lake, the **Chinese Pavilion** was a gift from the people of Taipei in 1981, shipped to the city in 6,000 pieces and reassembled; the views from Strawberry Hill itself make it well worth the climb. The Pioneer Log Cabin is situated on the far side of the lake near the Boathouse. In the western half of the park, you'll find the famous **Buffalo Paddock**, where a small herd of bison roam, as well as **Queen Wilhelmina's Tulip Gardens** and the **Dutch Windmill**, both given to the city by the eponymous Dutch monarch in 1902.

Right on the edge of Golden Gate Park, the Willis Polk-designed **Beach Chalet** (1-415 751 2766, www.beachchalet.com) is a good end for any park adventure. The main floor is a visitor centre (open 9am-6pm daily), but the restaurant upstairs (1-415 386 8439) makes a perfect spot for sunset cocktails: the views across Ocean Beach are simply staggering. The **Park Chalet** – on the same level as the visitor centre – also opened recently. A mostly outdoor garden restaurant, it looks out to the windmill, woods and meadows.

Conservatory of Flowers

John F Kennedy Drive, Golden Gate Park (1-415 666 7001/www.conservatoryofflowers.org). Bus 5, 7, 21, 71/Muni Metro N. **Open** 9am-5pm Tue-Sun, last entry 4.30pm. **Admission** $5 adults; $3 12-17s, over-64s, students with ID; $1.50 5-11s; free under-4s. Free 1st Tue of mth. **Credit** AmEx, Disc, MC, V.
Badly damaged in a storm in 1995, the magnificent Conservatory of Flowers reopened to considerable excitement in 2003 after an eight-year, $25m restoration. Modelled on London's Kew Gardens, it's the oldest glass and wood Victorian greenhouse in the Western Hemisphere, and home to more than 10,000 plants from all over the world, including an outstanding orchid collection. Head to the west wing for seasonal flowering plants or the east wing for aquatic plants and plants from the tropics.

MH de Young Memorial Museum

75 Tea Garden Drive, Golden Gate Park (1-415 682 2481). **Open** 10am-4.45pm Tue-Sat. **Admission** free.
The de Young is due to reopen in autumn 2005 in a new copper-covered building designed by Herzog & de Meuron. The museum will have entrances on all four sides, making it accessible from anywhere in the park, plus a 144ft (44m) education tower. The collections include more than 1,000 American paintings from the 17th to the 20th centuries, an impressive textile collection, rare Yoruba pots, contemporary crafts and treasures from the South Pacific that were exhibits at the original Exposition.

Strybing Arboretum & Botanical Gardens

9th Avenue, at Lincoln Way, Golden Gate Park (1-415 661 1316/www.strybing.org). **Open** 8am-4.30pm Mon-Fri; 10am-5pm Sat, Sun. **Admission** free.

Begun as a WPA project in the 1930s, the Strybing Arboretum now houses some 7,000 species from diverse climates around the world, arranged by country and connected by a boardwalk path. There's also a fragrant garden for the visually impaired and a particularly appealing moon-viewing garden. Volunteers lead free guided walks at 1.30pm daily.

Sunset

The Sunset district, south of Golden Gate Park, usually belies its name: it's habitually swathed in fog from June to September, and often in other months. The area's main attractions are **San Francisco Zoo** (*see below*) and **Ocean Beach**, which widens here into dunes and plateaus, making it great for a blustery wander or as a place to watch surfers battling rip tides and chilly water. But look, don't taste: tremendous waves come thundering ashore when the weather's up, and even on seemingly calm days, the tides and currents can be lethal.

San Francisco Zoo

Sloat Boulevard, at 47th Avenue (1-415 753 7080/ www.sfzoo.org). Muni Metro L/bus 18, 23. **Open** *Main zoo* 10am-5pm daily. *Children's zoo* mid June-Labor Day 10.30am-4.30pm daily. Labor Day-mid June 11am-4pm daily. **Admission** $10; $7 12-17s, discounts; $4 3-11s. **Credit** AmEx, MC, V.

Situated on a 100-acre site next to the Pacific, San Francisco Zoo is the largest in Northern California. It opened a new African Savanna habitat in 2004, looking to emulate conditions in the wild by combining zebras, giraffes, antelopes and a variety of birds in a single three-acre area. There are more than 900 species gathered in the zoo, including gorillas, koalas and penguins. Kids clamour for the Lipman Family Lemur Forest – elevated walkways bring visitors up to the level of the five endangered species that are kept here – and for petting and egg-gathering at the Family Farm. There are also rides to be had on the Little Puffer mini-steam train and on the hand-carved Dentzel Carousel.

Where to Eat

San Franciscans are pretty much obsessed with food, and thus the quality, quantity and variety of places to eat are staggering. The region's mild weather and rich soil conspire with the wide ocean and wild woods to ensure the very best ingredients – vegetable and animal – are within arms' reach of any chef, and the city's broad ethnic mix enables culinary globe-trotters to find every cuisine here, from Afghan to Italian, Vietnamese and Korean to Mexican. The '90s dot-com bust, however, had mixed effects on the city's dining scene. Restaurants now open and close with an astonishing rapidity, but the absence of recklessly spending expense accounters has forced new establishments to refocus on quality service and value for money.

Around Union Square

Union Square

Fifth Floor

Hotel Palomar, 12 4th Street, at Market Street (1-415 348 1555). BART Powell/Muni Metro F, J, K, L, M, N/bus 5, 6, 7, 9, 21, 31, 66, 71/cable car Powell-Mason. **Open** 7-10am, 5.30-9.30pm Mon-Thur; 7-10am, 5.30-10.30pm Fri; 8-11am, 5.30-11pm Sat; 8-11am Sun. **Average** $$$$$. **Credit** AmEx, DC, Disc, MC, V.

An idyllic blend of romance and chic, all the way up from the zebra-print rug under your feet, this dining room boasts the triple Michelin star talents of chef Laurent Gras. Aesthetic and gustatory perfection.

Masa's

648 Bush Street, between Stockton & Powell Streets (1-415 989 7154/www.masas.citysearch.com). Bus 2, 3, 4, 76/cable car California. **Open** 5.30-9.30pm Tue-Sat. **Average** $$$$$. **Credit** AmEx, DC, Disc, MC, V.

Fine dining in San Fran was pretty much invented at Masa's, enhancing the best of Californian cooking with French service standards. The estimable Ron Siegel has moved on to the Ritz-Carlton (*see p255*). Expect a more classic French approach from his replacement, Richard Reddington, but still using only the freshest of local, seasonal ingredients.

Michael Mina

Westin St Francis Hotel, 335 Powell Street, at Geary Street (1-415 397 9222). BART Powell Street/Muni Metro F, J, K, L, M, N/bus 2, 3, 4, 15, 30, 38, 45, 76/cable car Powell-Hyde or Powell-Mason. **Open** 5.30-10pm Mon-Thur, Sun; 5.30-11pm Fri, Sat. *Afternoon tea* 1.30-3.30pm daily. **Average** $$$$$. **Credit** AmEx, DC, Disc, MC, V.

This was the most anticipated restaurant opening of 2004, a dazzling $4.5m collaboration between Mina, his partner Andre Agassi (yes, that one) and top-notch designer Barbara Barry. The attention to detail – design and cooking – is staggering, with dishes meticulously presented. The trademark is trios: three different preparations of the principal ingredient, served on three separate, immaculately arranged plates. As much theatre as it is dining.

Also recommended

Cosmopolitan bistro-style **Café de la Presse** (352 Grant Avenue, 1-415 398 2680, $$); brunch at **Dottie's True Blue Café** (522 Jones Street, 1-415 885 2767, $$).

Central California

Cortez Restaurant & Bar. *See p241.*

The Financial District

Kokkari Estiatorio

200 Jackson Street, at Front Street (1-415 981 0983/www.kokkari.com). BART Embarcadero/ bus 1, 12, 42, 83. **Open** 11.30am-10pm Mon-Thur; 11.30am-11pm Fri; 5-11pm Sat. **Average** $$$$. **Credit** AmEx, DC, MC, V.

This authentic Hellenic cuisine may command lofty prices but it's always a treat. The *pikilia* (an appetiser plate comprising three dips with fresh pitta bread) is a good place to warm up before they bring on the swordfish, lamb chops and moussaka mains.

Also recommended

Steaks and chops at **500 Jackson** (500 Jackson Street, 1-415 772 1940, closed lunch, $$$$); 130 years of the superb Hangtown Fry at **Sam's Grill** (374 Bush Street, 1-415 421 0594, closed Sun, $$$$).

Chinatown

San Fran's best Chinese food is found in the Richmond (*see p237*) but **R&G Lounge** (631 Kearny Street, 1-415 982 7877, $$$), **Dol Ho's**

(808 Pacific Avenue, 1-415 392 2828, $$$) and tiny **Yuet Lee** (1300 Stockton Street, 1-415 982 6020, $$), open until 3am, are worth a look.

Alfred's Steak House

659 Merchant Street, between Kearny & Montgomery Streets (1-415 781 7058/www.alfreds steakhouse.com). Bus 1, 15, 41, 42. **Open** 5.30-9.30pm Mon, Sun; 11.30am-9.30pm Tue-Thur; 11.30am-9pm Fri; 5.30-9pm Sat. **Average** $$$$. **Credit** AmEx, DC, Disc, MC, V.

Alfred's trademark sign was over the Broadway tunnel for decades, but when it moved to near the Chinese Cultural Center, the loyal patrons eagerly followed. In other words, this is still possibly the best steakhouse in town, and is certainly the best steakhouse experience. A bit of San Francisco gone by.

Imperial Tea Court

1411 Powell Street, at Broadway (1-415 788 6080/ www.imperialtea.com). Bus 15, 30, 39, 41, 45/cable car Powell-Mason). **Open** 11am-6.30pm Mon, Wed-Sun. **Average** $. **Credit** AmEx, MC, V.

Birds chirp in cages. Soothing Chinese lute music plays. And the waitress gently instructs you in the art of the *gaiwan* tea presentation. There are only nibbles (cookies and pistachios) to eat, but then it's the tea that you come for (and take away, with a huge range available for purchase). A branch opened in 2004 in the Ferry Building (1-415 544 9830).

Also recommended

House of Nanking (919 Kearny Street, at Jackson Street, 1-415 421 1429, $$): too touristy for most locals, but the food never disappoints.

North Beach

The Helmand

430 Broadway, between Kearny & Montgomery Streets (1-415 362 0641). Bus 12, 15, 30, 41, 83. **Open** 5.30-10pm Mon-Thur, Sun; 5.30-11pm Fri, Sat. **Average** $$$. **Credit** AmEx, MC, V.

Still the city's only Afghan restaurant, the Helmand serves cheap and deliciously aromatic food, with highlights including the speciality baked baby pumpkin and spiced own-made yoghurts.

Mama's on Washington Square

1701 Stockton Street, at Filbert Street (1-415 362 6421). Bus 15, 30, 39, 41, 45. **Open** 8am-3pm Tue-Sun. **Average** $$. **No credit cards.**

The weekend wait is part of the fun at this homely North Beach fixture. Once seated, you'll be faced with such temptations as a giant made-to-order 'm'omelette' or the Monte Cristo sandwich.

Sodini's

510 Green Street, at Grant Avenue (1-415 291 0499). Bus 15, 30, 41, 45. **Open** 5-10pm Mon-Thur; 5-11pm Fri, Sat. **Average** $$$. **Credit** MC, V.

Small and dark, with romantically flickering candle lanterns, Sodini's serves decent food but it's the terrific atmosphere that makes it stand out. Tiny premises mean patrons are jammed tightly together: arrive early, sign the waiting list and drop over to a neighbouring bar while you wait for a table.

Also recommended

Beat landmark espresso bar **Caffe Trieste** (609 Vallejo Street, 1-415 982 2605, $), complete with Saturday afternoon opera sessions; people-watching or a late-night caffeine fix (it's open until 3am) at **Steps of Rome** (348 Columbus Avenue, 1-415 397 0435, www.stepsofrome.com, $$$).

Russian Hill

Sushi Groove

1916 Hyde Street, between Union & Green Streets (1-415 440 1905). Bus 41, 45/cable car Powell-Hyde. **Open** 5.30-10pm Mon-Thur, Sun; 5.30-10.30pm Fri, Sat. **Average** $$$$. **Credit** AmEx, Disc, MC, V.
An inventive, highly charged sushi restaurant, with rich, postmodern decor. The stylish clientele sit elbow-to-elbow in a dining room the size of a postage stamp, happy to be able to scoff fresh crab, sea urchin and eel. The impressive saké selection alone would make the trip worthwhile.

Also recommended

Comfort food at neighbourly prices at **Tablespoon** (2209 Polk Street, 1-415 268 0140, closed lunch, $$$); top Spanish scran at **Zarzuela** (2000 Hyde Street, 1-415 346 0800, $$$).

Get stuffed

In the window of a Mexican restaurant on New York's Upper West Side is a sign that boasts of 'San Francisco Mission-style Burritos'. They're that good? They're really that good.

Often imitated but seldom matched, the Mission burrito is as much of an attraction as the Golden Gate Bridge or a cable car ride. Indeed, some of them are bigger than cable cars. The big burrito is actually more Californian than Mexican, but its roots remain strong in the authenticity of ingredients: everything from grilled steak (*carne asada*) and refried beans (*frijoles*) to shrimp (*camarones*) and black beans, wrapped in huge, fresh-made tortillas.

The taquerias that serve these monsters are typically unassuming places, with basic Latin American decor, tiled floors and open-grill kitchens flanked by a counter and a cash register. And though every San Franciscan will argue for their favourite, you won't regret starting at **Taqueria la Cumbre** (*see p242*).

Polk Gulch

Bob's Donut Shop

1621 Polk Street, at Sacramento Street (1-415 776 3141). Bus 1, 19, 42, 47, 49/cable car California. **Open** 24hrs daily. **Average** $. **No credit cards**.
Neither the regulars nor the premises are about to win prizes, but leave the aesthetics at home and enjoy the city's finest doughnut, round the clock.

Swan Oyster Depot

1517 Polk Street, between California & Sacramento Streets (1-415 673 1101). Bus 1, 19, 42, 47, 49, 76/cable car California. **Open** 8am-5.30pm Mon-Sat. **Average** $$$. **No credit cards**.
Half fish market, half counter-service hole in the wall, the Depot is an institution. Visit between November and June, when the local Dungeness crab is in season, but at any time the selections are straight-from-the-water fresh. One not to miss.

Also recommended

Cuban, circa 1948, at **Habana** (2080 Van Ness Avenue, 1-415 441 2822, www.habana1948.com, closed lunch, $$$$); fine wine and excellent Italian food at unassuming **Acquerello** (1722 Sacramento Street, 1-415 567 5432, www.acquerello.com, closed lunch, Mon & Sun, $$$$$); a Californian twist on French dining at **La Folie** (2316 Polk Street, 1-415 776 5577, www.lafolie.com, closed lunch, Sun, $$$$$); local speciality cioppino at **Pesce** (2227 Polk Street, 1-415 928 8025, closed lunch Mon-Fri, $$$).

The Tenderloin

Asia de Cuba

Clift Hotel, 495 Geary Street, at Taylor Street (1-415 929 2300/www.clifthotel.com). Bus 2, 3, 4, 27, 38, 76. **Open** 7am-1am daily. **Average** $$$$$. **Credit** AmEx, DC, MC, V.
Ultra-swanky destination dining at sky-high prices. The fun and interesting Chinese-Hispanic menu is good for groups, with many dishes designed for sharing. Rich, sweet sauces and a richly sauced clientele.

Also recommended

Small plates for sharing at **Cortez Restaurant & Bar** (Adagio Hotel, 550 Geary Street, 1-415 292 6360, closed lunch, $$$$); the prix-fixe five-course tasting menu at **Fleur de Lys** (777 Sutter Street, 1-415 673 7779, www.fleurdelyssf.com, closed lunch, Sun, $$$$$); hearty, quality vegetarian at the Savoy's **Millennium** (580 Geary Street, 1-415 345 3900, www.millenniumrestaurant.com, closed lunch, $$$$).

Civic Center

Also recommended

All-rounder **Soluna** (272 McAllister Street, 1-415 621 2200, www.solunasf.com, $$$), which turns into a stylishly casual hangout with DJs at night; lauded Cal-Ital at **Zuni Café** (1658 Market Street, 1-415 552 2522, closed Mon, $$$$).

Central California

SoMa

BrainWash Café & Laundromat

1122 Folsom Street, at 7th Street (1-415 861 3663/www.brainwash.com). Bus 12, 19, 27, 42. **Open** 7am-11pm daily. **Average** $. **Credit** MC, V.
BrainWash is launderette, bar and café, in one quirky industrial package. The menu is simple (soups, salads, burgers) but most nights see young hipsters gather for bands, comedians or DJs. And to do their laundry.

Caffe Centro

102 South Park, at Jack London Place, between Bryant & Brannan Streets (1-415 882 1500/ www.caffecentro.com). Bus 15, 30, 42, 45, 76. **Open** 7am-4.30pm Mon-Fri; 8am-2.30pm Sat. **Average** $$. **Credit** AmEx, MC, V.
The queues of dot-commoners have gone from this splendid SoMa hangout, leaving the friendly service and fresh snack food (much of it organic) to a quirky mix of local residents and creatives. Large windows open on to South Park.

Also recommended

Microbrewery **21st Amendment** (563 2nd Street, 1-415 369 0900, www.21st-amendment.com, $$); French bistro **Le Charm** (315 Fifth Street, 1-415 546 6128, www.lecharm.com, closed lunch Sat & Sun, $$$).

The Mission

Atlas Café

3049 20th Street, at Alabama Street (1-415 648 1047/www.atlascafe.net). Bus 27. **Open** 7am-10pm Mon-Fri; 8am-10pm Sat; 8am-8pm Sun. **Average** $. **No credit cards.**
The Mission at its egalitarian best. A daily menu of grilled sandwiches, soups and salads is chalked on the wall; order and grab a seat on the back patio. There's live music on Thursdays and Saturdays.

Taqueria la Cumbre

515 Valencia Street, at 16th Street (1-415 863 8205). BART 16th Street/bus 14, 22, 26, 33, 53. **Open** 11am-10pm Mon-Sat; noon-9pm Sun. **Average** $. **No credit cards.**
La Cumbre is jealously defended by locals as offering the city's top burritos. Try the vast *carne asada*.

Truly Mediterranean

3109 16th Street, at Valencia Street (1-415 252 7482). Bus 6, 7, 33, 43, 66, 71. **Open** 11am-midnight Mon-Sat; 11am-10pm Sun. **Average** $. **Credit** MC, V.
Truly Mediterranean has two city locations (the original is in North Beach: 627 Vallejo Street, 1-415 362 2636), but this one has beer on tap and much better people-watching. The menu's heavy on falafels, houmous and baba ganoush.

Universal Café

2814 19th Street, between Bryant & Florida Streets (1-415 821 4608). Bus 27. **Open** 5.30-10pm Tue-Thur; 5.30-11pm Fri; 9am-2.30pm, 5.30-11pm Sat; 9am-2.30pm Sun. **Average** $$$$. **Credit** AmEx, DC, MC, V.
One of the first upmarket spots to open in this area, Universal Café has an understated, industrial-look dining room and fresh, interesting food. It's great for a weekend breakfast; dinner brings higher prices, but an appetising menu too.

Also recommended

Decent prices for comfort food at **Luna Park** (694 Valencia Street, 1-415 553 8584, www.lunaparksf. com, $$$) or Italian at sister place **Last Supper Club** (1199 Valencia Street, 1-415 695 1199, www. lastsupperclubsf.com, $$$); classic films with your oysters at **Foreign Cinema** (2534 Mission Street, 1-415 648 7600, www.foreigncinema.com, closed lunch Mon-Fri, $$$$).

The Castro

Blue

2337 Market Street, at 16th Street (1-415 863 2583). Muni Metro F, K, L, M/bus 24, 35, 37. **Open** 11.30am-11pm Mon-Thur; 11.30am-11.30pm Fri; 10am-11.30pm Sat; 10am-10pm Sun. **Average** $$$. **Credit** AmEx, MC, V.
Slide into a smooth black booth, stare at the beautiful people and tuck into gourmet macaroni cheese, meat loaf or pork chops.

Chow

215 Church Street, at Market Street (1-415 552 2469). Muni Metro F, J, K, L, M/bus 22, 37. **Open** 11am-11pm Mon-Thur; 10am-midnight Fri; 10am-11pm Sat, Sun. **Average** $$. **Credit** MC, V.
A simple, no-gimmicks spot, with a vivacious clientele, Chow keeps 'em happy with great food at low prices: roast chicken and burgers share the menu with Asian bok choi noodles. Portions are huge.

Mecca

2029 Market Street, at Dolores & 14th Streets (1-415 621 7000). Muni Metro F, J, K, L, M/bus 37. **Open** 6-11pm Tue-Thur, Sun; 5.45pm-midnight Fri, Sat. **Average** $$$$. **Credit** AmEx, DC, MC, V.
Big, bustling and fashionable, this restaurant has become the de facto HQ of Castro cuisine. Stephen Barber's world-influenced menu features wonderfully flavourful spare ribs, a divine seared ahi and one of the best New York strip steaks in town.

Samovar

498 Sanchez Street, at 18th Street (1-415 626 4700). Metro Muni F, J, K, L, M/bus 24, 33, 35. **Open** 9am-10.30pm Mon-Thur, Sun; 9am-11pm Fri, Sat. **Average** $. **Credit** AmEx, MC, V.
The Castro's only tearoom, this tranquil oasis quickly became a hit with locals seeking a Zen-like refuge. There are over 100 teas, as well as affordable and healthy Asian-inspired small plates.

Gary Danko.
See p244.

Casual but classic, the Grind is populated with hip and ratty denizens of the Lower Haight, who are likely to be spending the morning leafing through Sartre or sweating off a hangover.

Thep Phanom

400 Waller Street, at Fillmore Street (1-415 431 2526). Bus 6, 7, 22, 66, 71. **Open** 5.30-10.30pm daily. **Average** $$$. **Credit** AmEx, DC, Disc, MC, V.
Possibly the best Thai in San Francisco. You'd be wise to book in advance: few can resist the *tom ka gai* (coconut chicken soup) and 'angel wings' (fried chicken wings stuffed with glass noodles).

Also recommended

Garlic and rosemary roasted chicken or grilled lobster risotto at **RNM** (598 Haight Street, 1-415 551 7900, www.rnmrestaurant.com, closed lunch, Mon & Sun, $$$$); heaps of café culture and flannel hash at **Kate's Kitchen** (471 Haight Street, 1-415 626 3984, closed dinner, $$), where long queues are a clue to the quality that characterises Kate's cooking.

The Western Addition

Café Abir

1300 Fulton Street, at Divisadero Street (1-415 567 7654). Bus 5, 24. **Open** 6am-12.30am daily. **Average** $$. **No credit cards**.
Abir is a large café, organic grocery store, coffee roastery, international newsstand and bar. With friendly staff and well-chosen house music, it's as much about nightlife as smelling the coffee.

Mifune

Japan Center, 1737 Post Street, between Webster & Buchanan Streets (1-415 922 0337). Bus 2, 3, 4, 22, 38. **Open** 11am-9.30pm Mon-Thur, Sun; 11am-10pm Fri, Sat. **Average** $$. **Credit** AmEx, DC, Disc, MC, V.
The noodle is the thing to order here – it comes in 30 different varieties. Good for kids, great for vegetarians, Mifune is what fast food should be: quick, inexpensive and delicious.

Also recommended

Boisterous brasserie **Absinthe** (398 Hayes Street, 1-415 551 1590, www.absinthe.com, closed Mon, $$$$); hip pastries and full meals at **Citizen Cake** (399 Grove Street, 1-415 861 2228, www.citizencake.com, closed Mon, $$$).

Pacific Heights

Ella's

500 Presidio Avenue, at California Street (1-415 441 5669/www.ellassanfrancisco.com). Bus 1, 3, 4, 43. **Open** 7-11am, 11.30am-9pm Mon-Fri; 8.30am-2pm Sat, Sun. **Average** $$. **Credit** AmEx, MC, V.
Famed for its French toast, Ella has equally famous queues (be prepared to wait for your plate). But the chicken hash with eggs and toast or potato scramble with pea sprouts, mushrooms, roasted garlic and manchego cheese make it all worthwhile.

2223 Restaurant & Bar

2223 Market Street, between Noe & Sanchez Streets (1-415 431 0692). Muni Metro F, K, L, M/bus 24, 35, 37. **Open** 5.30-9.30pm Mon-Thur; 5.30-11pm Fri; 11am-2pm, 5.30-11pm Sat; 10.30am-2pm, 5.30-9.30pm Sun. **Average** $$$$. **Credit** AmEx, DC, MC, V.
The most upscale restaurant in the Castro, 2223 is a popular place for queers with something to celebrate. The excellent cuisine has Mediterranean, Mexican and Caribbean influences.

Also recommended

Seafood at **Catch** (2362 Market Street, 1-415 431 5000, $$$); the 24hr **Bagdad Café** (2295 Market Street, 1-415 621 4434, $$).

Central neighbourhoods

The Haight

Grind Café

783 Haight Street, at Scott Street (1-415 864 0955). Bus 6, 7, 66, 71. **Open** 7am-8pm daily. **Average** $$. **No credit cards**.

Harris'

*2100 Van Ness Avenue, at Pacific Avenue (1-415
673 1888/www.harrisrestaurant.com). Bus 12, 42,
47, 49, 83.* **Open** 5.30-9.30pm Mon-Fri; 5-10pm Sat;
5-9pm Sun. **Average** $$$$. **Credit** AmEx, DC,
Disc, MC, V.
Harris' is all about classy old-style dining: strong
cocktails, a textbook Caesar salad, prime steaks.

Also recommended

Ceviche and other Peruvian cuisine at **Fresca** (2114
Fillmore Street, 1-415 447 2668, $$$).

The bay shore

The Embarcadero

Globe Restaurant

*290 Pacific Avenue, at Battery Street (1-415 391
4132). Bus 12, 42, 83.* **Open** 11.30am-1am Mon-Fri;
6pm-1am Sat; 6-11.30pm Sun. **Average** $$$$. **Credit**
AmEx, MC, V.
This is where local chefs eat: a testament to the late
opening hours, the excellent California cuisine and
the sublime freshness of ingredients. Standards
include wood-oven pizzas, grilled salmon with but-
tery pasta and watercress and a T-bone for two.

Ozumo

*161 Steuart Street, at Mission Street (1-415 882
1333/www.ozumo.com). Muni Metro F/bus 1, 2, 6,
7, 9, 14, 21, 31, 66, 71.* **Open** 11.30am-midnight
Mon-Fri; 5.30pm-midnight Sat, Sun. **Average** $$$$.
Credit AmEx, DC, Disc, MC, V.
A beautiful restaurant for beautiful people. There's
an exhaustive menu of teas and sakés, great views
of the Bay Bridge and a storied robata grill.

Slanted Door

*1 Ferry Plaza, at Market Street (1-415 861 8032/
www.slanteddoor.com). Muni Metro N.* **Open** *Lunch*
11.30am-2.30pm daily. *Dinner* 5.30-10pm Mon-Thur,
Sun; 5.30-10.30pm Fri, Sat. **Average** $$$$. **Credit**
AmEx, MC, V.
Chef Charles Phan moved to deluxe bayside digs in
the Ferry Building in 2004. The shaking beef is his
signature dish, an excellent take on Vietnamese street
food. His original location (540 Valencia Street) should
reopen in 2005.

Yank Sing

*Rincon Center, 101 Spear Street, at Mission
Street (1-415 957 9300/www.yanksing.com).
BART Embarcadero/Muni Metro F, J, K, L, M,
N/bus 1, 2, 6, 7, 9, 14, 21, 31, 66, 71.* **Open**
11am-3pm Mon-Fri; 10am-4pm Sat, Sun.
Average $$$. **Credit** AmEx, DC, MC, V.
Many San Franciscans consider Yank Sing the only
place for dim sum, with non-English-speaking waitresses rolling out an endless array of dumplings.

Also recommended

Pan-Asian, bay views at **Butterfly Embarcadero**
(Pier 33, 1-415 291 9481, www.butterflysf.com, $$$).

Fisherman's Wharf

A Sabella's

*3rd floor, 2766 Taylor Street, at Jefferson Street
(1-415 771 6775/www.asabella.com). Muni Metro
F/bus 39, 42.* **Open** 5-10pm daily. **Average** $$$$.
Credit AmEx, DC, MC, V.
Family-owned for four generations, A Sabella has a
huge dining room with great views and serves ter-
rific fresh Dungeness crab and lobster, or the local
speciality cioppino. What's more, this is a friendly,
comfortable place for kids too.

Gary Danko

*800 North Point Street, at Hyde Street (1-415 749
2060/www.garydanko.com). Bus 19, 30, 42/cable car
Powell-Hyde.* **Open** 5.30-10pm daily. **Average**
$$$$$. **Credit** AmEx, DC, Disc, MC, V.
Lauded by the critics, Gary Danko has made his
restaurant a glorious place for fine dining. Seasonal
tasting menus are the best way to make the very
most of the man's culinary gifts, but you can also
eat at the bar (probably your only option unless you
book in advance).

Also recommended

Sourdough bread, invented in San Francisco, is
worth a try at **Boudin Sourdough Bakery &
Café** (2890 Taylor Street, 1-415 776 1849, www.
boudinbakery.com, $).

The Marina

Greens Restaurant

*Building A, Fort Mason Center, Marina Boulevard,
at Buchanan Street (1-415 771 6222). Bus 28.* **Open**
5.30-9pm Mon-Sat; 10.30am-2pm Sun. **Average** $$$.
Credit AmEx, Disc, MC, V.
Service can be a little disengaged, but Greens pro-
duces award-winning vegetarian food, including
mesquite-grilled vegetables and wood-fired pizzas.
There's also a takeaway counter for picnickers.

Pacific Coast

Richmond

Kabuto

*5121 Geary Boulevard, between 15th & 16th
Avenues (1-415 752 5652). Bus 2, 28, 38.* **Open**
Lunch 11.30am-2pm daily. *Dinner* 5.30-10.30pm
Tue-Sat; 5.30-10pm Sun. **Average** $$$. **Credit**
MC, V.
Kabuto's sushi is a favourite with restaurateurs and
chefs. There are few tables, so sit at the sushi bar
and watch miracles being performed.

Also recommended

Dim sum at noisy, busy, family-oriented **Mayflower**
(6255 Geary Boulevard, 1-415 387 8338, $$);
traditional gypsy hakka at **Ton Kiang** (5821 Geary
Boulevard, 1-415 387 8273, $$); great comfort food at
tiny **Q** (225 Clement Street, 1-415 752 2298, $$).

Sunset

Ebisu

1283 9th Avenue, between Irving Street & Lincoln Way (1-415 566 1770/http://ebisu.citysearch.com). Muni Metro N/bus 6, 43 44, 66. **Open** 5-10pm Mon-Fri; 11.30am-11pm Sat, Sun. **Average $$$. Credit** AmEx, DC, MC, V.

Many argue for Ebisu as the best sushi joint in town, so no grumbling as you put your name on the waiting list and head into the bar. House specialities include the 'pink Cadillac' (salmon) and '49er roll.

Java Beach Café

1396 La Playa Boulevard, at Judah Street (1-415 665 5282). Muni Metro N/bus 18. **Open** 5.30am-9.30pm Mon, Tue; 5.30am-10pm Wed, Fri; 5.30am-9pm Thur; 6am-10pm Sat, Sun. **Average $. Credit** MC, V.

The wetsuits and the grand Pacific view make this the quintessential Ocean Beach caff. Sunshine or not.

Where to Drink

San Franciscans spend more than twice the national average on alcohol, so you know this is a good city in which to get drunk. It isn't about the quality of the booze (high, thanks to several microbreweries and fine cocktail hangouts), nor is it about the quantity: it's all about variety, from out-of-time boozers to of-the-minute cocktail lounges, hip DJ bars and downhome pubs. The only drawback is that San Francisco isn't a dusk-till-dawn kind of town: last orders vary between 1.15am and 1.30am, with staff obliged to confiscate drinks after 2am.

Around Union Square

Boozehounds don't spend vast amounts of time around Union Square, although if you can find dodgy-looking **Tunnel Top** (601 Bush Street, 1-415 986 8900) – Stockton Tunnel being the one it's on top of – you'll find DJs on the balcony and films playing on the walls. The Financial District empties out at night, but discreetly located **Bix** (56 Gold Street, 1-415 433 6300, www.bixrestaurant.com) appeals with its Jazz Age supper-club feel, and the Bank of America **Carnelian Room** (52nd floor, 555 California Street, 1-415 433 7500) combines fine cocktails with stunning views.

North Beach maintains its reputation as a great place for drinking. You can stroll from bar to bar past the strip joints on Broadway, but Columbus offers better options. Beers for a dollar (4-6pm, midnight-1am) make the **San Francisco Brewing Company** (No.155, 1-415 434 3344) hard to pass up, but the ghosts of Dylan Thomas and Jack Kerouac that linger

at **Vesuvio** (No.255, 1-415 362 3370), a funky old saloon with a stained-glass façade right next to City Lights (*see p248*), keep folk coming back. **Spec's** (William Saroyan Place, off Columbus, 1-415 421 4112) is a quintessential old-school bar – part North Beach boho, part Wild West saloon – while **Tosca Café** (No.242, 1-415 986 9651) maintains a bada-bing ambience with Caruso on the jukebox, movie stars in the back room and a fabulous house speciality cappuccino. On a neglected strip between North Beach and Chinatown, drop in on charmingly tatty **Rosewood** (732 Broadway, 1-415 951 4886) hasn't even got a sign outside, which means fine cocktails and lounge DJs without unwieldy crowds. In Chinatown, drop in on charmingly tatty **Li Po** (916 Grant Avenue, 1-415 982 0072), designated by a cave front and battered Chinese lantern. Up on Nob Hill, **Top of the Mark** (Mark Hopkins Inter-Continental Hotel, 1 Nob Hill, 999 California Street, 1-415 392 3434) pairs a '100 Martinis' menu with spectacular views from the 19th floor. Arrive early to avoid the dress code.

The Tenderloin offers some great boozers. If you want character, **C Bobby's Owl Tree** (601 Post Street, 1-415 776 9344) seems to have found it at some point in the 1950s. Every available perch features stuffed owls,

Belly up to the bar at **Tosca Café**.

Central California

carved owls, owl paintings… The **Edinburgh Castle** (950 Geary Street, 1-415 885 4074), Korean-owned but Scottish-operated, hosts bands, DJs and plays or readings, while the electric green façade of the **Julip Cocktail Lounge** (839 Geary Street, 1-415 474 3216) introduces an exemplary DJ bar. Given a dancefloor the size of a handkerchief, it's just as well the natives are friendly.

South of Market Street

Butter (354 11th Street, 1-415 863 5964) matches chill-room vibe (complete with DJ) with trailer-trash aesthetics, all corn dogs, Twinkies and Pabst Blue Ribbon. For good beer (and tidy tapas), try the **Thirsty Bear** brewpub (661 Howard Street, 1-415 974 0905). For something truly suave, the two bars at the **W Hotel** (181 3rd Street, 1-415 777 5300) are packed with beautiful people, though the atmosphere can be a little competitive.

With the exception of North Beach, drinkers are going to have the best fun in the Mission, especially around Valencia Street. **Zeitgeist** (199 Valencia Street, 1-415 255 7505), 'twixt SoMa and the Mission, is one of the hippest bars in town, its giant beer garden popular with people from every walk of alternative life. The **Argus Lounge** (3187 Mission Street, 1-415 824 1447) is far enough down Mission Street to escape the gentrifying masses, allowing a happy crowd to enjoy the superlative jukebox and pool table. Bric-a-brac salvaged from a Long Island hair salon makes cocktailing in the **Beauty Bar San Francisco** (2299 Mission Street, 1-415 285 0323) an unusual experience, with a free manicure on offer with cocktails from Wednesday to Saturday. Oenophiles who like a natter will enjoy **Hotel Biron** (45 Rose Street, alley between Market and Gough, 1-415 703 0403), where the impressive wine list offers 80 possibilities including 30-plus by the glass.

In the Castro, **Lucky 13** (2140 Market Street, 1-415 487 1313) is dark, spacious and always busy, with pinball, pool and foosball, plus an excellent selection of German beers.

Central neighbourhoods

The 'Victorian punch bar' **Hobson's Choice** (1601 Haight Street, 1-415 621 5859) does itself a disservice: in fact, there's a selection of 60 varieties of rum, plus a ropey bar band most nights. But apart from that, don't waste your time in Haight-Ashbury. Instead, make tracks to the earthy Lower Haight. Hobson's choice at **Toronado** (No.547, 1-415 863 2276) is beer: a huge range of draughts, slanted in favour of the Belgian. **Noc Noc** (No.557, 1-415 861 5811) is

mellow like the day after the apocalypse, kept in near darkness and enjoyably multi-ethnic. With the renegade exception of **Place Pigalle** (520 Hayes Street, 1-415 552 2671), a laid-back place with an eclectic crowd, Hayes Valley is a little upmarket for boozing. But try the long-lost recipes at the bar at **Absinthe** (*see p243*).

Bay shore

Both **Equinox** (Hyatt Regency, 5 Embarcadero Center, 1-415 788 1234) and **Pier 23** (Pier 23, 1-415 362 5125) offer outstanding views, the former from Northern California's only revolving rooftop cocktail lounge, the latter from a deck outside. Guess which of them has the dress code.

Nightlife

Gay & lesbian

The free newspapers, notably the *Bay Times* and *Bay Area Reporter* (*BAR*), are good for listings. Local queer-about-town Larry-Bob Roberts regularly updates the 'event listings' at www.holytitclamps.com, while scene magazines *Odyssey* and *Gloss* carry up-to-the-minute details of good nights out. The best clubs for queer/straight nights are glossy **Mezzanine**, a big hit with the boys, and **Six** (for both, *see p247*), for serious dancing.

The Castro

The noughties saw the gay dance scene quieten down a little. There isn't much in the Castro, the city's queer heartland, these days: the tiny, steaming **Café** (2367 Market Street, 1-415 861 3846) remains the most popular, maybe because entry is often free; it's less male-dominated than other haunts. There are a number of cruisey bars in the area, including **Badlands** (4121 18th Street, 1-415 626 9320) and the **Midnight Sun** (4067 18th Street, 1-415 861 4186), while leather fans should head to **Daddy's** (440 Castro Street, 1-415 621 8732). Those who fancy something upmarket can get cocktails at the art deco **Orbit Room** (1900 Market Street, 1-415 252 9525) or the elegantly romantic **Whiskey Lounge** (4063 18th Street, 1-415 255 2733). Queer jocks love **The Mix** (4086 18th Street, 1-415 431 8616), where fans gather for Giants or '49ers games and burgers from the terrace grill.

If you want to stay in San Francisco's queer heartland, there is a good range of quality B&Bs: the handsomely restored Edwardian **Inn on Castro** (321 Castro

Street, 1-415 861 0321, www.innoncastro2.com,
$85-$185); **24 Henry Guesthouse & Village
House**, a pair of refurbished Victorians (24
Henry Street, 1-415 864 5686; 4080 18th Street,
1-415 864 0994; 1-800 900 5686, www.24henry.
com, $65-$119) and the **Parker Guest
House** (520 Church Street, 1-888 520 7275,
1-415 621 3222, www.parkerguesthouse.com,
$119-$199), a renovated 1909 Edwardian
mini-mansion with garden and steam room.
For something less tasteful, **Beck's Motor
Lodge** (2222 Market Street, 1-415 621 8212,
$89-$109) is the quintessential motel.

SoMa

The range of nightlife is much wider in SoMa.
For back-to-back partying, the **Endup** (401
6th Street, 1-415 357 0827) is the only choice:
it's been turning Saturday night into Sunday
morning since 1973. **The Stud** (399 9th Street,
1-415 252 7883) is another SF institution, but
the location deep in SoMa makes a cab ride to
and from the club advisable. Also in the district,
Cherry Bar & Lounge (917 Folsom Street,
1-415 974 1585) makes up for the paucity of
women's clubs in the city with the sleekest
night for gals: Girl Spot on Saturdays. There is
also a concentration of gay bars in SoMa, with
a thriving leather scene at the **Eagle Tavern**
(398 12th Street, 1-415 626 0880) and **Loading
Dock** (1525 Mission Street, 1-415 864 1525).
Gen-X queers compare tattoos or play pool at
dive bar **Hole in the Wall** (289 8th Street,
1-415 431 4695).

The Mission

The bars here tend to be less sceney than those
in the Castro or SoMa. Try **Esta Noche** (3079
16th Street, 1-415 861 5757) for a spectacular
lip-synching Latino drag show (11.30pm Mon-
Thur) or the warm and funky **Lexington Club**
(3464 19th Street, 1-415 863 2052) – no men
allowed unless accompanied by women. **Wild
Side West** (424 Cortland Avenue, 1-415 647
3099), in lesbian heartland Bernal Heights,
has pool and a great jukebox. It's totally het-
friendly. The Mission also offers dykes the
joys of Rebel Girl DJing at **26 Mix** (3024
Mission Street, 1-415 826 7378) and the
great salsa party at **El Rio**.

Nightclubs

San Francisco's nightlife is still suffering a dot-
com economic hangover. The '90s high-tech
explosion brought in audiences, but rocketing
rents forced out many less commercially
minded creators. In SoMa, 11th Street is a

shadow of its former clubbing self, although
DNA Lounge (375 11th Street, 1-415 626 1409)
is going strong after reopening in 2001. Nearby
Paradise Lounge (1501 Folsom Street, 1-415
621 1911) ditched the live stages and is now a
two-storey jumpathon. 6th Street, one of the
nastier bits of the city, is host to a couple of fine
clubs: trendy **Arrow** (No.10, 1-415 255 7920),
which has a tiny cave-like dance area and a
neon hydra over the bar, and **Six** (No.60, 1-415
863 1221, www.clubsix1.com), a combination of
high-ceilinged chill room/bar and low-ceilinged
dancefloor. **Mezzanine** (444 Jessie Street, 1-415
625 8880) is a huge club-cum-gallery with two
long bars bordering the ample dancefloor.

If you like '60s kitsch, Alpine-themed cocktail
lounge **Sno-Drift** (1830 3rd Street, 1-415 431
4766) could be the glamour pad for you. Come
early if you don't like crowds. But the city's
best dance club is **Sublounge** (628 20th Street,
1-415 552 3603). The supercool decor includes
light installations and aeroplane seats with
gaming consoles. The Tenderloin's
Bambuddha Lounge (Phoenix Hotel, 601
Eddy Street, 1-415 885 5088) is also worthy of
note, combining conversational nooks and a
roaring fireplace with pan-Asian minimalism,
a discreet DJ booth and a cabana-style pool.

The Mission offers some good options:
Amnesia (853 Valencia Street, 1-415 970 0012)
draws a friendly, multi-ethnic crowd and **Pink**
(formerly Liquid, 2925 16th Street, 1-415 431
8889) is a favourite for lovers of mixology,
notwithstanding the crowded bar and small

Boys will be girls at **The Stud**.

dancefloor. The gay and straight clubbing scenes are unusually well integrated in San Francisco, so – with the exception of the harder-edged S&M clubs and cruiser places – straights or gays should feel at home at most clubs. Clubs that run excellent queer nights, like **Cherry Bar** and **Stud** (*see p247*), run excellent nights period.

North Beach and the Haight are not so well equipped with clubs. North Beach's **Blind Tiger** (787 Broadway, 1-415 788 4020) plays hip hop, house and breaks, though the floor isn't for swinging cats. On Haight Street the best options are **Milk** (No.1840, 1-415 387 6455), a cool place to catch local hip hop, and converted dive the **Top** (No.424, 1-415 864 7386), where you'll see some impressive DJing.

Many clubs stay open well past last orders, but by law they can't serve alcohol between 2am and 6am, nor can a venue that serves alcohol admit anyone under 21.

Shops

Shops in San Francisco are generally open 10am to 6pm; many, particularly those around Union Square, have extended hours in the run-up to Christmas. For quirkier shops, it's always wise to ring ahead. Don't forget that local sales tax (currently 8.5 per cent) will be added to all purchases. Parking is a nightmare, so use public transport or hail a taxi.

One-stop shopping

Department stores

For department stores, you won't have to look much further than Union Square. **Gump's** (135 Post Street, 1-415 984 9439) is the city's original emporium of good taste, selling wedding gifts, china and various baubles to the well-heeled since 1861. **Neiman Marcus** (150 Stockton Street, 1-415 362 3900) and **Nordstrom** (San Francisco Centre, 865 Market Street, 1-415 243 8500) also sell luxury items, as well as designer and diffusion labels, to wealthy spenders. **Saks Fifth Avenue** (384 Post Street, 1-415 986 4300) is great for designers such as Marc Jacobs; all-rounder **Macy's** (170 O'Farrell Street, 1-415 397 3333) is more affordable.

Malls

San Francisco doesn't make such a big deal out of malls as other parts of California. Near Union Square, **Crocker Galleria** (50 Post Street, 1-415 393 1505, www.shopatgalleria.com) is an open-ended arcade combining individual shops with designer chains (Ralph Lauren, Versace),

while the more impressive **San Francisco Centre** (865 Market Street, 1-415 512 6776, www.westfield.com) is arranged vertically, with spiral escalators drawing shoppers through the mid-priced chains (Abercrombie & Fitch, BCBG and Club Monaco) towards mighty Nordstrom (*see above*). South of Market Street is the **Metreon** (4th Street, 1-415 369 6000, www.metreon.com), a passé technology-themed mini-mall with a 15-screen multiplex. Down by the Ferry Building is the **Embarcadero Center** (Sacramento Street, Financial District, 1-415 772 0700, www.embarcaderocenter.com), with the likes of Banana Republic, Gap, Victoria's Secret and Pottery Barn.

Following the Embarcadero round to the north, you'll find the worst of collaborations between commerce and tourism: the hurly-burly tourist traps of **Pier 39** (Beach Street and the Embarcadero, 1-415 705 5500) and **Fisherman's Wharf** (Jefferson Street, 1-415 626 7070). Pier 39 does have a working carousel and some very fishy sea lions – its sole redeeming features, unless you suffer an addiction to egregious tourist trash. At the other end of Beach Street from Pier 39, **Ghirardelli Square** (Beach Street, 1-415 775 5500) is the home of the eponymous chocolate factory.

Individual shops

Antiques

The sheer size of **The Butler & the Chef** (1011 25th Street, 1-415 642 6440, www.thebutlerandthechef.com) makes it fun to browse, but be warned: the antique furniture here doesn't come cheap. Other pricey antiques shops are clustered in the **Jackson Square Historical District** (call 1-415 296 8150 for the Jackson Square Art & Antique Dealers Association); the antiques veer more towards curios in the shops in **Hayes Valley** near Gough and Market. Be sure to visit the **Alemany Flea Market** (100 Alemany Boulevard, 1-415 647 2043), held each Sunday from 8am under the US 101 & I-280 intersection east of Bernal Heights.

Books

If any bookshop on earth qualifies as a tourist destination, it's **City Lights** (261 Columbus Avenue, North Beach, 1-415 362 8193). Founded by Lawrence Ferlinghetti in 1953, it's still a fine shop, though the Beat poets and small-press ranters in the upstairs Poetry Annex draw the serious pilgrims. The European literature selection is also strong, and the occasional readings are real events.

The city's oldest (est.1923) and largest independent bookshop, **Stacey's** (581 Market Street, Financial District, 1-415 421 4687), is worth a look. For queer literature, head to the Castro and **A Different Light** (489 Castro Street, 1-415 431 0891). Other specialists include thrillers and pulp at **Kayo Books** (814 Post Street, Tenderloin, 1-415 749 0554); African-American and African writers at **Marcus Book Stores** (1712 Fillmore Street, Western Addition, 1-415 346 4222); and travel books and maps at **Get Lost** (1825 Market Street, Upper Market, 1-415 437 0529) and **Rand McNally** (595 Market Street, Financial District, 1-415 777 3131). If you're looking for a decent cluster of browsable used bookshops, your best bet is the Mission. On Valencia Street you'll find homely **Abandoned Planet** (No.518, 1-415 861 4695) and the excellent **Modern Times Bookstore** (No.888, 1-415 282 9246). Yet the best second-hand bookshop is miles away: **Green Apple** (506 Clement Street, Richmond, 1-415 387 2272).

Fashion

DESIGNER

Around Union Square you can trip in one high-end designer boutique (Chanel, Prada, Gucci), fall into the next (Armani, Hermès) and end up nursing your credit card bruises in a third (Ralph Lauren, Versace). Locals, though, love the places you can't find elsewhere, and are unimpressed by the kind of attitudinising folks might get away with in LA. The warmth and tact you'll experience shopping at Cow Hollow's **Workshop** (2254 Union Street, 1-415 561 9551), Noe Valley's sparkly chic **Rabat** (4005 24th Street, 1-415 282 7861) or the Haight's **Ambiance** (1458 Haight Street, 1-415 552 5095) could become addictive, even if the clothes weren't so special. Also uncommonly friendly is **Heather** (2408 Fillmore Street, Pacific Heights, 1-415 409 4410), with the right ideas whether you're dressing up or down.

In Hayes Valley, Hayes Street boasts the skittish **Azalea Boutique** (No.411, 1-415 861 9888), everything from jeans to fine tailoring at **Dish** (No.541, 1-415 252 5997) and decadent scanties at **Alla Prima** (No.539, 1-415 864 8180). North Beach's Grant Avenue is another good focal area: the terrific range of to-the-minute jeans at **AB Fits** (No.1519, 1-415 982 5726) is matched by great jewellery and other accessories. Super-girlie cardigans and skirts are available at the colossal **Anthropologie** (880 Market Street, Union Square, 1-415 434 2210). For handbags, try **Coach** (190 Post Street, Union Square, 1-415 392 1772); the best sparklers in town can be tracked down at **De Vera** (29 Maiden Lane, Union Square, 1-415 788 0828).

GENERAL

If it's the monoliths you're looking for, the chains pretty much all have flagship stores on Union Square: the city presence of **Banana Republic**, **Gap** and **Old Navy** is measured by the block more than the store. Stylish sub-designer chains such as **Express**, **Bebe**, **Club Monaco** and **French Connection** are scattered around the area. There's a three-floor **Diesel** (101 Post Street, 1-415 982 7077), and you can get your true blues in the city that invented them: **Levi's Jean Store** (300 Post Street, 1-415 501 0100, www.levi.com) may be brash, but it is home. Collegiate-friendly **Urban Outfitters** (80 Powell Street, 1-415 989 1515) is affordable and has some finds.

VINTAGE

Fertile hunting grounds for worn clothing include Haight Street, where you'll find **Aardvark's Odd Ark** (No.1501, 1-415 621 3141), **Crossroads Trading Company** (No.1519, 1-415 355 0555) and **Wasteland** (1660 Haight Street, 1-415 863 3150), and the Mission, where **Schauplatz** (791 Valencia Street, 1-415 864 5665) is the self-consciously selected high end and **Goodwill** (1580 Mission Street, 1-415 575 2240) is anything but. Fillmore Street – home to another **Crossroads** (No.1901, 1-415 775 8885) – and **GoodByes** on Sacramento Street (No.3464, 1-415 346 6388; No.3483, 1-415 674 0151) offer most chance of finding a designer bargain.

SHOES

In the San Francisco Centre, **Nordstrom** (*see above*) has a wonderful shoe department, but **Gimme Shoes** (50 Grant Avenue, Union Square, 1-415 434 9242) is the local favourite. The emphasis is on big or pointy fun along Haight Street at **Shoe Biz** (No.1446, 1-415 864 0990) and **Super Shoe Biz** (No.1420, 1-415 861 0313), while the **Subterranean Shoe Room** (877 Valencia Street, Mission, 1-415 401 9504) is *über*-trendy. Gents prefer **Kenneth Cole** (166 Grant Avenue, Union Square, 1-415 981 2653), for shoes with social conscience.

Food & drink

After ten years of transient existence, **Ferry Plaza Farmers' Market** (Ferry Building, on Embarcadero at Market Street, each Saturday) is now a foodie attraction in its own right. The new shops inside the building are open daily. Luxury grocers include the **Bi-Rite Market** (3639 18th Street, Mission, 1-415 241 9773) and **Whole Foods** (1765 California Street, Pacific Heights, 1-415 674 0500; 399 4th Street, SoMa, 1-415 618 0066; www.wholefoodsmarket.com), where temptation is beyond mortal power to resist.

Central California

Gifts

Hayes Valley isn't just a fashion parade: it makes for good gift shopping too. Along Hayes Street funky lifestyle accessories, many by local designers, and a variety of desirable *objets* can be found at the likes of **Propeller** (No.555, 1-415 701 7767), **BUU** (No.506, 1-415 626 1503) and **Alabaster** (No.597, 1-415 558 0482, www.alabastersf.com).

If you avoid the tat, Chinatown can be good for quirky finds. **Sam Bo Trading Co** (51 Ross Alley, 1-415 397 2998) sells Buddhist and Taoist religious items; and **Clarion Music** (816 Sacramento Street, 1-415 391 1317) is a Pandora's Box of clangour, from H'mong jaw harps and thumb bells to erhu and $1,200 pipa. In and around the Mission, **Paxton Gate** (824 Valencia Street, 1-415 824 1872) is dedicated to 'treasures and oddities inspired by the garden'. From esoteric to erotic: **Good Vibrations** (603 Valencia Street, 1-415 522 5460) has been referred to as the Blockbuster of vibrators, among its wares the exciter seen (and used) on *Sex and the City*. The best of the museum shops is at **SFMOMA** (*see p229*).

Health & beauty

Apothecary **Scarlet Sage Herb Co** (1173 Valencia Street, Mission, 1-415 821 0997) and Chinese herbalist **Vinh Khang Herbs & Ginsengs** (512 Clement Street, Richmond, 1-415 752 8336) can provide you with myriad alternative remedies. Another great place, with homeopathic remedies and other natural products, is Cole Valley's **Pharmaca Integrative** (925 Cole Street, 1-415 661 1216). More normal potions are available round the clock from **Walgreens** (3201 Divisadero Street, Marina, 1-415 931 641; 498 Castro Street, Castro, 1-415 861 6276).

If the only repair you need is a long soak, **Kabuki Springs & Spa** (Japan Center, 1750 Geary Boulevard, Western Addition, 1-415 922 6000) and women-only **Osento** (955 Valencia Street, Mission, 1-415 282 6333) fit the bill. For skincare and cosmetics, try New York import **Kiehl's** (2360 Fillmore Street, Pacific Heights, 1-415 359 9260) or **Sephora** (33 Powell Street, Union Square, 1-415 392 1545), where you can touch, smell and try on most of the premier perfumes and make-up brands without suffering the hard-sell.

Music

Once a bowling alley, **Amoeba Music** (1855 Haight Street, Haight-Ashbury, 1-415 831 1200) now packs its 25,000 square feet of space with every imaginable type of recorded music, new and used, as well as hosting free gigs. The Lower Haight is paradise for fans of vinyl. Along Haight Street you'll find **Tweekin Records** (No.593, 1-415 626 6995), **Future Primitive Sound** (No.597, 1-415 551 2328) and **Rooky Ricardo's** (No.448, 1-415 864 7526). Close by you'll also find **Open Mind Music** (342 Divisadero Street, 1-415 621 2244) and, for jazz and country, **Jack's Record Cellar** (254 Scott Street, 1-415 431 3047).

Arts & Entertainment

Dance

Founded in 1933, the **San Francisco Ballet** (1-415 865 2000, www.sfballet.org) is the longest-running professional ballet company in the US. Based in the War Memorial Opera House (*see p251*), its season runs from February to May. Other notable companies include **LINES Ballet** (1-415 863 3040, www.linesballet.org); ethnic dance is represented by the likes of **Transit** (1-415 621 6063, www.transitdance.com), the **Lily Cai Chinese Dance Company** (1-415 474 4829, www.ccpsf.org) and **Fat Chance Belly Dance** (1-415 431 4322, www.fcbd.com).

Film

There used to be a dozen grand movie palaces in San Francisco, but these days only two remain: the **United Artists Metro** (2055 Union Street, Cow Hollow, 1-415 931 1685) and the **Castro Theatre** (429 Castro Street, 1-415 621 6120, www.thecastrotheatre.com). The latter is gorgeous: deliciously rococo, with painted murals and ceilings that shimmer with gold. Rep programmes are enhanced by tunes banged out on a Wurlitzer.

Other notable cinemas include the Richmond's **Balboa Theater** (3520 Balboa Street, 1-415 221 8184) and two independent rep houses, the **Roxie** (3117 16th Street, Mission, 1-415 863 1087, www.roxie.com) and the worker-owned and -operated **Red Vic** (1727 Haight Street, Haight-Ashbury, 1-415 668 3994, www.redvic moviehouse.com. The **SF Cinematheque** (1-415 522 1990) remains the major force behind leftfield film culture. Festivals include the prestigious **San Francisco International Film Festival** (Apr/May, www.sfiff.org) and the **San Francisco International Lesbian & Gay Film Festival** (late June, www.frameline.org).

Galleries

The city boasts a rich and provocative art scene. Commercial galleries are mostly clustered within a few blocks of **Union Square**, some stacked within single buildings. 49 Geary Street houses several galleries, including photography-oriented **Robert Koch** (1-415 421 0122, www.kochgallery.com); 760 Market Street also houses several galleries. Sutter Street is home to **Hackett-Freedman** (No.250, 1-415 362 7152, www.realart.com) and its stable of Bay Area artists. **Modernism** (685 Market Street, Financial District, 1-415 541 0461) shows amazing work in a less than hospitable atmosphere. One of the city's first grassroots galleries was the **Luggage Store** (1007 Market Street, Tenderloin, 1-415 255 5971), which shows works in the *arte povera* tradition.

Cutting-edge work is often found away from the Downtown galleries, and especially in SoMa. **SoMarts Gallery** (934 Brannan Street, 1-415 552 2131, www.somarts.org) is one of the city's longest-lived alt-art spaces, hosting shows in a cavern-like space and providing the HQ from which the ever-popular **Open Studios** are run on weekends in October. Also noteworthy is **111 Minna Street** (1-415 974 1719, www.111minnagallery.com), which combines a gallery with a nightclub. A new addition to the city's art scene is the intimate and playful **Linc Real Art** (1632C Market Street, Hayes/Castro, 1-415 503 1981).

San Francisco Bay Area Gallery Guide, *Art Now Gallery Guide* and *San Francisco Arts Monthly* (www.sfarts.org) are all good sources of information. Many galleries open late for **First Thursdays** (first Thursday of the month), enticing punters with wine and cheese.

Music

Classical & opera

The Civic Center is the hub of classical music activity in San Francisco, containing the multi-tiered, curved-glass **Louise M Davies Symphony Hall** (201 Van Ness Avenue, 1-415 864 6000, www.sfsymphony.org) and the 3,176-seat **War Memorial Opera House** (301 Van Ness Avenue, 1-415 864 3330, www.sfopera. com). The **San Francisco Symphony** (1-415 864 6000, www.sfsymphony.org) gives regular performances here, as does the **San Francisco Opera** (1-415 864 3330, www.sfopera.com).

Yet part of the joy of classical music here is the combination of world-class venues and less formal spaces, among them SoMa's coolly modernist **Yerba Buena Performing Arts Theater** (701 Mission Street, 1-415 978 2787, www.yerbabuenaarts.com) and a number of city churches such as **St Patrick's** (lunchtime concerts each Wednesday; 756 Mission Street, 1-415 777 3211). Many venues offer cut-price tickets, with 'Rush' tickets for the Davies good value: available a couple of hours before the performance, they are a comparative bargain, priced at only $15-$20.

Jazz & blues

Once known as 'the Harlem of the West', the Fillmore district played host to Billie Holiday, Ella Fitzgerald and Duke Ellington, but nowadays things are less exciting. Fillmore Street has the **Boom Boom Room** (No.1601, 1-415 673 8000, www.boomboomblues.com), a classy take on the traditional blues joint. Otherwise, head to modernised Mission supper club **Bruno's** (2389 Mission Street, 1-415 648 7701, www.brunoslive.com) or North Beach's bluesy **Saloon** (1232 Grant Avenue, 1-415 989 7666): built in 1861, it has the claim to fame of being the oldest beer hall to have stayed in continuous operation in the city.

Rock, pop & hip hop

Though the high-tech boom and bust darkened a number of local venues, only New York and LA attract more bands than San Francisco, in part due to the city's association with bands such as the Grateful Dead and Sly and the Family Stone. The lovely Beaux Arts **Avalon Ballroom** (1268 Sutter Street, Tenderloin, 1-415 847 4043, www.morningspringrain.com) is where Janis Joplin first performed with Big Brother and the Holding Company, while Bill Graham's **Fillmore Auditorium** (1805 Geary Boulevard, 1-415 346 0600, www.thefillmore. com) has staged every major modern musician from Tina Turner to eccentric jazz legend Rahsaan Roland Kirk.

Notwithstanding its floor-to-ceiling pillars, a busy schedule makes **Slim's** (333 11th Street, SoMa, 1-415 255 0333, www.slims-sf.com) one

What's on when

For up-to-date information, the **San Francisco Chronicle**'s Sunday 'Datebook' section – look for the pink pages – has extensive listings. It's also accessible online at **www.sfgate.com**. Free weeklies the **Bay Guardian** and **SF Weekly** also run reviews and listings; **www.sfstation.com** is good for background.

The sporting life

SPECTATOR SPORTS

The **San Francisco Giants** play their baseball at magnificent SBC Park (24 Willie Mays Plaza, South Beach, 1-415 972 2000, www.sfgiants.com), where wonderful views of the glittering bay are matched by the exploits of legendary leftfielder Barry Bonds. Already only the third player ever to hit 700 home runs, the indefatigable Bonds seems set to beat Hank Aaron's all-time record of 755 at some point early on in the 2006 season (which runs April-October).

The glory days for the **San Francisco 49ers** were the '80s and '90s, when they won a record five National Football League Super Bowls. And even though they failed (once again) to make the play-offs in 2004, tickets are very hard to come by. Brave the scalpers outside windy 3Com Park (Giants Drive, Bayview, 1-415 656 4900, www.sf49ers.com)

or (whisper it) head across the bay and watch the Oakland Raiders instead.

PARTICIPATORY SPORTS

This peninsular city can't sprawl like most others and (given that hills can go down as well as up) cycling is pretty much the best way to get about. Cycle lanes criss-cross in every direction, but be wary of the traffic – eco-ironies are a commonplace, notably aggressive Hummers and SUVs. Cycling or skating in **Golden Gate Park** (*see p238*) is hard to beat: the beach at one end, sunny meadows along the way and, on Sunday, no automobiles are allowed in. Rent from nearby **Golden Gate Park Skate & Bike** (3038 Fulton Street, Richmond, 1-415 668 1117) or **Surrey Bikes & Blades** (50 Stow Lake Drive, Golden Gate Park, 1-415 668 6699). Skaters have been pretty thoroughly eliminated from public walkways, but plenty of downtown concrete ramps remain to tempt dedicated rats. **DLX** (1831 Market Street, Mission, 1-415 626 5588, www.dlxsf.com) is the doyen of stores.

For runners, **Crissy Field** is a gorgeous destination, with the Golden Gate Promenade heading right to Fort Point under the golden bridge; the **Embarcadero** offers a lovely route beneath the city's other bridge. The city's two

of San Francisco's most important venues. More leisurely evenings can be had at the handsome 1922 **Warfield Theater** (982 Market Street, Union Square, 1-415 775 7722, www.thefillmore.com/warfield.asp) and the **Great American Music Hall** (859 O'Farrell Street, Tenderloin, 1-415 885 0750, www. musichallsf.com), a former bordello with lavish mirrors, rococo woodwork and gold leaf trim. **Bimbo's 365 Club** (1025 Columbus Avenue, North Beach, 1-415 474 0365) is a regular stop on many bands' touring circuit; the cavernous **Bill Graham Civic Auditorium** (99 Grove Street, Civic Center, 1-415 974 4060,

www.billgrahamcivic.com) hosts not-quite-arena rock, which is generally undermined by the venue's disappointingly poor acoustics.

San Francisco is famously welcoming to new music. The best places to investigate the not-quite-yet are the indie-rock dive **Bottom of the Hill** (1233 17th Street, Potrero Hill, 1-415 621 4455, www.bottomofthehill.com) and the coolly wigged-out **Hemlock Tavern** (1131 Polk Street, Tenderloin, 1-415 923 0923, www.hemlocktavern.com). Atmospheric former Castro speakeasy **Café du Nord** (2170 Market Street, 1-415 861 5016, www.cafedunord.com) also puts on terrific gigs.

San Francisco also has a welter of smaller spaces. The Tenderloin theatre district contains **EXITheater** (156 Eddy Street, 1-415 931 1094, www.sffringe.org), the central 'theaterplex' for the city's Fringe Festival in early September; the Mission contains the long-established **Intersection for the Arts** (446 Valencia Street, 1-415 626 2787) and the **Marsh** (1062 Valencia Street, 1-415 826 5750, www.the marsh.org). More conventional work can be seen at **Yerba Buena Center for the Arts** (701 Mission Street, SoMa, 1-415 978 2787).

This being San Francisco, there are also two 'only in' offerings. One is **Audium** (1616 Bush Street, Pacific Heights, 1-415 771 1616, www. audium.org), a theatre of 169 speakers that create multi-dimensional audio sculptures. The second is North Beach's **Beach Blanket Babylon** (Club Fugazi, 678 Green Street, 1-415 421 4222), a campy show that enters its fourth decade in 2005 and is the longest-running revue in history.

major annual foot races are the seven-mile **Bay to Breakers** fun run (3rd Sun of May) and the **San Francisco Marathon** (1st Sun of Aug).

The ocean is too chilly and turbulent for comfortable swimming, but the city is very popular as a windsurfing centre (provided, of course, you're not falling in all the time). There are more than 30 launch sites, including **Candlestick Point**, **Coyote Point** and **Crissy Field**. Seasoned windsurfers head to **City Front Boardsports** (2936 Lyon Street, Cow Hollow, 1-415 929 7873, www.boardsports.com) for gear, while **Wise Surfboards** (800 Great Highway, Ocean Beach, 1-415 750 9473) caters for their wingless brethren, even hosting a 24-hour surf info line (1-415 273 1618).

Theatre

For mainstream theatre or musicals, try the deceptively unglam Tenderloin. Along Geary Street, you'll find the **American Conservatory Theater** (ACT; No.415, 1-415 834 3200) and the **Curran Theater** (No.445, 1-415 551 2000), with the **Golden Gate Theater** (1 Taylor Street, 1-415 551 2000) nearby. Closer to the Civic Center, the **Orpheum** (1192 Market Street, 1-415 551 2000) is vast, but overshadowed by the smaller **Herbst Theatre** (Veterans' Memorial Building, 401 Van Ness Avenue, 1-415 621 6600), decorated with Beaux Arts murals.

Where to Stay

Most of San Francisco's hotels are to be found Downtown, clustered around Union Square, the Tenderloin, Nob Hill and SoMa. Those we've listed have character, great facilities, impeccable service or some other aspect that sets them apart from the corporates. We've included places in all price ranges, but for those whose wallets are more tight than snug there are nearly two dozen hostels in the city; check **www.hostels.com/us.ca.sf.html**.

Low occupancy rates post-9/11 made for appealing room prices, but prices were slowly creeping up again in 2004 and the St Regis and Hotel Vitale projects in SoMa, both due for completion in 2005, suggest growing confidence in the tourism sector. Our advice? Always ask if there are any discounts available. There's still nowhere much to stay in the vibrant Mission (though the Metro, see p257, isn't far away). Places in the queer Castro, most of which welcome straight visitors, are listed on p230.

Around Union Square

Union Square

Hotel Cosmo
761 Post Street, at Jones Street (1-800 252 7466/ 1-415 673 6040/www.hotel-cosmo.com). Bus 2, 3, 4, 27, 76. **Rates** $89-$199 single/double. **Credit** AmEx, DC, Disc, MC, V.
Refashioning itself for an artsier crowd, the Cosmo has monthly art showings and a lobby full of local works. The 17 storeys lack intimacy and, when we

last visited, the remnants of the former flowery decor undermined the more interesting new scheme, all '50s art moderne. Still, stunning views put the corner suites among the best bargains in town.

Hotel Metropolis

25 Mason Street, at Turk Street (1-800 553 1900/ 1-415 775 4600/www.hotelmetropolis.com). BART Powell/Muni Metro F, J, K, L, M, N/bus 27, 31/cable car Powell-Hyde or Powell-Mason. **Rates** $89-$149 single/double. **Credit** AmEx, DC, Disc, MC, V.
A great mid-price hotel, with nice attention to detail and a pleasingly eco-friendly slant. Themed after the four elements, there's a small library, a children's suite (bunk beds, a chalkboard, Nintendo) and a small library, plus cable TV in the rooms. Some tenth-floor rooms have terrific views.

Hotel Nikko

222 Mason Street, at O'Farrell Street (1-800 645 5687/1-415 394 1111/www.hotelnikkosf.com). BART Powell/Muni Metro F, J, K, L, M, N/bus 27, 38/cable car Powell-Hyde or Powell-Mason. **Rates** $139-$350 single/double; $500-$2,000 suite. **Credit** AmEx, DC, Disc, MC, V.
Incredibly popular with Japanese visitors, the Nikko's many rooms are all large and bright, furnished with luxurious fabrics and light wood furniture. The design is clean, tranquil and elegant, and amenities include an indoor swimming pool, gym and sauna.

Hotel Rex

562 Sutter Street, between Powell & Mason Streets (1-800 433 4434/1-415 433 4434/www.thehotel rex.com). **Rates** $129-$149 single; $149-$249 double; $269-$339 suite. **Credit** AmEx, DC, Disc, MC, V.
Named after San Franciscan pacifist poet Kenneth Rexroth, this is one of the city's most appealing small hotels. Books are scattered throughout, walls are adorned with literary caricatures, and the business centre is full of antique typewriters – and modern amenities. The hotel's tiny bistro was once the hotel's bookshop, but you can still catch a reading by a local literary luminary in the bar or back salon.

Hotel Triton

342 Grant Avenue, at Bush Street (1-800 800 1299/ 1-415 394 0500/www.hoteltriton.com). Bus 2, 3, 4, 15, 30, 45, 76. **Rates** $149-$299 single/double; $299-$359 suite. **Credit** AmEx, DC, Disc, MC, V.
This avant-garde hotel aims to make all of its 140 rooms into EcoRooms by the end of 2004 – organic cotton sheets and so on – the hotel already hosts on-site yoga classes and tarot readings, as well as providing 'Zen Dens', with incense, books on Buddhism and daybeds. Not '60s enough for you? Try the suites designed by Jerry Garcia and Carlos Santana.

The Financial District

Mandarin Oriental

222 Sansome Street, between Pine & California Streets (1-800 622 0404/1-415 276 9888/ www.mandarinoriental.com). BART Montgomery/
Muni Metro F, J, K, L, M, N/bus 10, 15, 41/cable car California. **Rates** $475-$725 single/double; $1,400-$3,000 suite. **Credit** AmEx, DC, Disc, MC, V.
Few hotels can boast such extraordinary views nor such a decadent means of enjoying them. The Mandarin Oriental's lobby is on the ground floor of the 48-storey First Interstate Building, but its 158 rooms are on the top 11 floors, affording breathtaking vistas. Some rooms have glass baths by the windows.

Chinatown

Grant Plaza Hotel

465 Grant Avenue, at Pine Street (1-800 472 6899/ 1-415 434 3883/www.grantplaza.com). Bus 15, 30, 45/cable car California. **Rates** $69-$105 single/ double. **Credit** AmEx, DC, Disc, MC, V.
In the middle of Chinatown, the Grant Plaza has immaculate (if small) rooms, with contemporary furniture, private bath, TV and phone. Corner rooms on the higher floors are the largest and brightest.

North Beach

Hotel Bohème

444 Columbus Avenue, between Vallejo & Green Streets (1-415 433 9111/www.hotelboheme.com). Bus 15, 30, 39, 41, 45. **Rates** $149-$175 single/double. **Credit** AmEx, DC, Disc, MC, V.
This charming hotel is overflowing with beatnik-abilia, and justifiably so: Allen Ginsberg spent some of his last years in Room 204, tapping away on his laptop in the bay window. The rooms are tiny.

San Remo Hotel

2337 Mason Street, at Chestnut Street (1-800 352 7366/1-415 776 8688/www.sanremohotel. com). Bus 15, 30, 39/cable car Powell-Mason. **Rates** $65-$175 single/double. **Credit** AmEx, DC, MC, V.
The San Remo, a meticulously restored Italianate Edwardian, is great value. Shower rooms are shared, the rooms are small and immaculate, and there are no telephones or televisions, but if you get a room on the upper floor, you'll have no complaints.

Washington Square Inn

1660 Stockton Street, at Filbert Street (1-800 388 0220/1-415 981 4220). Bus 15, 30, 39, 41, 45/cable car Powell-Mason. **Rates** $145-$245 single/double. **Credit** AmEx, DC, Disc, MC, V.
A convivial inn in a quiet section of lovely North Beach. The interior is lovely: each of the 15 rooms is decorated with French antiques. Excellent service.

Nob Hill

Commodore International Hotel

825 Sutter Street, between Jones & Leavenworth Streets (1-800 338 6848/1-415 923 6800/www. thecommodorehotel.com). Bus 2, 3, 4, 27, 76. **Rates** $69-$159 single/double; $149-$225 suite. **Credit** AmEx, DC, Disc, MC, V.

Justly named, the Commodore follows a '20s ocean liner theme: the colourful lobby is a Lido Deck, complete with chaises longues. The postmodern deco rooms have custom furnishings by local artists.

Ritz-Carlton San Francisco

600 Stockton Street, at California Street (1-800 241 3333/www.ritzcarlton.com). Bus 1, 30, 45/cable car California. **Rates** $375-$495 single/double; $395-$5,200 suite. **Credit** AmEx, DC, Disc, MC, V.

Among the fine hotels on Nob Hill, the Ritz deservedly gets the attention. The 1909 neo-classical landmark reopened as the Ritz-Carlton in 1991 and has been pampering guests ever since. Amenities include an indoor spa with gym and swimming pool, award-winning French cooking at the Dining Room (1-415 773 6198), daily piano performances and phalanxes of capable valets. Jazz brunches are held on a sunken roof terrace each Sunday.

White Swan Inn

845 Bush Street, between Taylor & Mason Streets (1-800 999 9570/1-415 775 1755/www. jdvhospitality.com). Bus 2, 3, 4, 76/cable car Powell-Hyde or Powell-Mason. **Rates** $139-$259 single/double; $229-$309 suite. **Credit** AmEx, Disc, DC, MC, V.

There are several cosy English-style bed and breakfasts lining Bush Street, but the somewhat fusty White Swan is undoubtedly the best, boasting fresh-baked cookies and a gas fireplace in each room, as well as a big parlour hearth.

The Tenderloin

Adagio Hotel

550 Geary Street, between Taylor & Jones Streets (1-415 775 5000/www.thehoteladagio.com). Bus 27, 38. **Rates** $139-$209 single/double; $795-$895 suite. **Credit** AmEx, DC, Disc, MC, V.

The remodelled Adagio combines muted colours and arty photos to create a hotel that's comfortable as well as chic, smart without being too business-like. Having Pascal Rigo's Cortez (*see p241*) as the hotel bar and breakfast room is no minor recommendation; ethernet links and slick room service complete the picture.

The Andrews

624 Post Street, between Jones & Taylor Streets (1-800 926 3739/1-415 563 6877/www.andrews hotel.com). Bus 2, 3, 4, 27, 38, 76. **Rates** $89-$165 single/double; $139-$175 suite. **Credit** AmEx, MC, V.

Originally the opulent Sultan Turkish Baths, the Andrews is now a comfortable and convenient hotel. From the lobby's grandfather clock and the cage elevator to musty hallways and small, old-fashioned rooms, it feels like the set of a classic film noir.

Clift Hotel

495 Geary Street, at Taylor Street (1-800 652 5438/ 1-415 775 4700/www.clifthotel.com). Bus 2, 3, 4, 27, 38, 76. **Rates** $325-$385 single/double; $950-$2,025 suite. **Credit** AmEx, DC, Disc, MC, V.

Hotel Triton. *See p254.*

Since its reopening in 2001, the Clift has staked a claim as the city's trendiest hotel. Designed by the darling of the hip hotel, Philippe Starck, the Clift is the definition of grand: through the sleek glass entryway, you'll find over-the-top decor and not entirely welcoming staff. The rooms are less intense, with soft, relaxing colours and comfy sleigh beds. The Redwood and Asia de Cuba (*see p241*) are further attractions.

Hotel Bijou

111 Mason Street, at Eddy Street (1-800 771 1022/ 1-415 771 1200/www.hotelbijou.com). Muni Metro F, J, K, L, M, N/bus 27, 31. **Rates** $79-$149 single/double. **Credit** AmEx, DC, Disc, MC, V.

Adagio Hotel. *See p255.*

The Bijou is covered in photos of old cinema marquees, posts details of the films showing locally on a board and has a 'film hotline' giving the locations of any movie shoot in town. The comfortably stylish rooms are named after movies, but there's not much to distinguish *Vertigo* from *Mrs Doubtfire* (except, of course, for the film stills on the walls). Rather handily, too, Market Street is located just around the corner.

Hotel Monaco
501 Geary Street, at Taylor Street (1-866 622 5284/ 1-415 292 0100/www.monaco-sf.com). Bus 2, 3, 4, 27, 38, 76. **Rates** $179-$369 single/double; $229-$489 suite. **Credit** AmEx, DC, Disc, MC, V.
This 1910 Beaux Arts building underwent a $24m facelift in 1995 and few of the city's hotels can match it now for sheer, larger-than-life, romantic indulgence: hand-painted ceiling domes, grandiose murals, canopied beds. Its slightly cheaper sister property, the Spanish Revival-style Serrano (1-877 294 9709), sits right next door. The sumptuous Grand Café next door has the feel of a Parisian train station in the '20s, albeit somewhat contradicted by a three-storey bunny sculpture.

Phoenix Hotel
601 Eddy Street, at Larkin Street (1-800 248 9466/ 1-415 776 1380/www.thephoenixhotel.com). Bus 19, 31. **Rates** $99-$149 single/double; $149-$209 suite. **Credit** AmEx, DC, Disc, MC, V.
The Tenderloin might be funky in the old sense, but the Phoenix is funky in the new. The 44 rooms are in tropical style, with bamboo furniture and herbiage to enhance the oasis feel. The adjoining Bambuddha restaurant and cocktail lounge (*see p247*) pulls in punters from all over town. Some of the more illustrious names to have been scribbled in the register here include John F Kennedy Jr, Johnny Depp and Pearl Jam.

South of Market

SoMa

The Mosser
54 4th Street, between Mission & Market Streets (1-415 986 4400). BART Powell/Muni Metro F, J, K, L, M, N/bus 9, 30, 45. **Rates** $99-$179 single/double; $189-$249 suite. **Credit** AmEx, DC, Disc, MC, V.
Affordable and stylish, the Mosser was formerly the Victorian Mosser (despite the fact that the building was built in 1911, making it an Edwardian structure) until it was extensively updated in 2001 by the designer of the **W** (*see p246*). Many quirky details – ornate stained glass, antique phone booths, cage elevator – remain, giving the place a Gothic feel. Rooms are small and a bit dark, and some have shared baths, but there are cool amenities: good linens, the latest gadgets, soothing colours. There's also Annabelle's Bistro next door.

Palace Hotel
2 New Montgomery Street, at Market Street (1-800 325 3589/1-415 512 1111/www.sfpalace.com). BART Montgomery/Muni Metro F, J, K, L, M, N/bus 2, 3, 4, 5, 9, 10, 15, 21, 30, 45, 71. **Rates** $499-$559 single/double; $775-$4,400 suite. **Credit** AmEx, DC, Disc, MC, V.
Long one of the grandest hotels in the world, the Palace has welcomed in the past such famous guests as Winston Churchill, Thomas Edison and Franklin D Roosevelt. And a $160-million restoration in 1991 made sure the dignitaries kept coming. The 553 rooms are relatively modest, but the dining rooms are extraordinary, with 80,000 panes of stained glass used in the Garden Court's ceiling dome, and the hotel's covered swimming pool is the best in the city. Can't afford to stay? Take afternoon tea (2pm-4pm Tue-Sat) accompanied by a harp.

Central neighbourhoods

The Haight

Red Victorian

1665 Haight Street, between Clayton & Cole Streets, Haight-Ashbury (1-415 864 1978/www.redvic.com). Muni Metro N/bus 7, 33, 37, 43, 66, 71. **Rates** $72-$126 single/double; $200 suite. **Credit** AmEx, Disc, DC, MC, V.

The Red Vic is not merely Haight Street's only hotel, it feels like a portal into the '60s. The 18 wildly decorated rooms include the rainbow-coloured Flower Child and tie-dyed Summer of Love rooms. Owner Sami Sunchild has also made space for a Peace & Arts Gallery and a Meditation Room. Rooms don't have TVs and the hotel is no smoking throughout.

Stanyan Park Hotel

750 Stanyan Street, at Waller Street, Haight-Ashbury (1-415 751 1000/www.stanyanpark.com). Muni Metro N/bus 7, 33, 43, 66, 71. **Rates** $130-$180 single/double; $259-$315 suite. **Credit** AmEx, DC, Disc, MC, V.

This stately, three-storey Victorian on the edge of Golden Gate Park is on the National Register of Historic Places. Its rooms are filled with antiques, down to the drapes and quilts. Large groups may fancy the six big suites with full kitchens, dining rooms and living spaces. No smoking throughout.

The Western Addition

Archbishop's Mansion

1000 Fulton Street, at Steiner Street (1-800 543 5820/1-415 563 7872). Bus 5, 22, 24. **Rates** $165-$205 single/double; $235-$345 suite. **Credit** AmEx, DC, Disc, MC, V.

Built for the Archbishop of San Francisco in 1904, this opulent French château is on historic Alamo Square Park, facing the 'Painted Ladies'. Its belle époque style is more magisterial than cosy, but there are pleasant idiosyncrasies: the Don Giovanni suite has a seven-headed shower, one to wash away each of the seven deadly sins.

Metro Hotel

319 Divisadero Street, between Oak & Page Streets (1-415 861 5364). Bus 6, 7, 22, 24, 66, 71. **Rates** $66-$120 single/double. **Credit** AmEx, DC, Disc, MC, V.

The Metro is a convenient base, somewhat off the tourist track (it feels more Haight – two blocks away – than Western Addition). It's all a bit basic, but there are rooms overlooking the charming back garden. Bare-bones two-room studio apartments with kitchenettes can be rented for around $100 a night.

Radisson Miyako Hotel

1625 Post Street, at Laguna Street (1-800 533 4567/1-415 922 3200). Bus 2, 3, 4, 22, 38. **Rates** $89-$189 single/double; $189-$299 suite. **Credit** AmEx, DC, Disc, MC, V.

This is a pagoda-style corporate hotel, with fountains, Zen gardens and two serene tatami suites, complete with futons, sliding shoji screens and deep tubs. Even Western-style rooms have Japanese bathing stools and tubs a foot deeper than the usual.

Pacific Heights

Jackson Court

2198 Jackson Street, at Buchanan Street (1-800 738 7477/1-415 929 7670/www.jacksoncourt.com). Bus 12, 24. **Rates** $150-$175 single/double; $205-$225 suites. **Credit** AmEx, MC, V.

Not many people have discovered this superb 19th-century brownstone mansion. Located on a calm residential stretch, Jackson Court has ten rooms, each with private bath. Request the Library Room, with its brass bed and working fireplace.

Cow Hollow

Hotel del Sol

3100 Webster Street, at Greenwich Street (1-877 433 5765/1-415 921 5520/www.thehoteldelsol.com). Bus 22, 43, 76. **Rates** $149-$199 single/double; $189-$199 suite. **Credit** AmEx, DC, Disc, MC, V.

Each room at this funky '50s motor hotel is decorated with bright, splashy tropical colours, even the clock radios wake guests to the sound of waves. The family suite has bunk beds, toys and games, and guests can choose their own pillows at the Pillow Library. Free parking and an outdoor pool are additional attractions. No smoking throughout.

The bay shore

Fisherman's Wharf

Argonaut Hotel

495 Jefferson Street, at Hyde Street (1-800 790 1415/1-415 563 0800/www.argonauthotel.com). Muni Metro F/bus 10, 30, 47/cable car Powell-Hyde. **Rates** $169-$229 single/double; $489-$629 suite. **Credit** AmEx, DC, Disc, MC, V.

A fruit-packing warehouse converted into a luxury hotel. The blue-and-yellow maritime decor is clearly aimed at the kids, but there's a classy lobby with enclosed fire, stripped wood and bare bricks nicely offset by chirpy nautical props. Rooms have all mod cons and the staff are helpful and friendly to a fault. For a sea view, get a third-floor room facing north.

The Marina

Fisherman's Wharf Youth Hostel

Building 240, Fort Mason, at Bay & Franklin Streets (1-415 771 7277/www.norcalhostels.org). Bus 10, 28, 30, 47, 49. **Rates** $22-$29 dormitories; $67.50-$73.50 private rooms. **Credit** MC, V.

The regal view from this humble hostel can be yours, if you book at least 24 hours in advance, for

San Fran for kids

The sea and the sea lions, Golden Gate Park, a plethora of discovery centres... the City by the Bay is certainly very child-friendly. Among the keynote attractions are the **Aquarium of the Bay** (*see p233*) and the **San Francisco Zoo** (*see p239*), along with the hands-on exhibits at the **Exploratorium** (*see p235*) and the noisy **Zeum** (*see p230*). However, a number of other less visible kid-pleasers are also worth tracking down. **San Francisco Library** (*see p227*) has half a floor given over to kids, with a storytelling room and a creative centre for crafts and performances. The **Randall Museum** (*see p230*) has displays on earthquakes and a petting zoo. And out in Oakland, there's **Children's Fairyland** (*see p266*) and the **Oakland Zoo** (*see p267*).

As well as the permanent attractions, look out for special events and workshops listed under 'Children's events' in the Sunday pink section of the *San Francisco Chronicle*. If you want an adults-only evening, contact the **Bay Area Childcare Agency** (1-415 309 5662), a reliable babysitting option for 50 years.

---

less than $30 per night. Sleeping 170 people in rooms of three to 24 people, it also has a pool table, dining room, coffee bar, complimentary movies and free parking. There's no curfew, and no smoking.

Resources

Hospitals

Haight *California Pacific Medical Center, Castro Street (1-415 600 6000)*.
Nob Hill *St Francis Memorial Hospital, 900 Hyde Street (1-415 353 6300)*.
Sunset *UCSF Medical Center, 505 Parnassus Avenue (1-415 476 1000)*.

Internet

Polk Gulch *Quetzal, 1234 Polk Street (1-415 673 4181/www.quetzal.org)*. **Open** 6.45am-10pm daily.

Police

North Beach *766 Vallejo Street (1-415 315 2400)*.
SoMa *850 Bryant Street, Suite 525 (1-415 553 0123)*.

Post offices

Civic Center *101 Hyde Street (1-415 563 7284)*.
Mission *1198 S Van Ness Avenue (1-415 648 0155)*.
SoMa *1600 Bryant Street (1-415 431 3407)*.

Tourist information

San Francisco *San Francisco Visitor Information Center, lower level, Hallidie Plaza (1-415 391 2000/www.sfvisitor.org)*. **Open** 9am-5pm Mon-Fri; 9am-3pm Sat, Sun.

Getting there

By air

San Francisco Airport (SFO) (1-650 821 8211, www.flysfo.com) is 14 miles south of the city, near US 101. The International terminal is airy, spacious and well served with shops and eating places, with artworks and exhibition cases dotted about and even a charming Aviation Museum. A new **BART** train station opened here in 2003, allowing you to get Downtown in half an hour for only $4.95. Otherwise, there are the SamTrans KX and 292 **buses**, which run every 30 minutes between the airport's lower level and the Transbay Terminal (1st & Mission Streets). The 292 costs $1.25 and takes just over half an hour; the KX costs $3.50 and takes 30 minutes, but you can take only one small carry-on bag. You can also take a **passenger van**, an improvement on the bus or BART because it offers door-to-door service. Tickets can be bought from the driver and cost $10-$20 per person. The passenger vans leave about every quarter hour from the upper level of the terminal at specially marked kerbs. Companies include **Lorrie's Airport Service** (1-415 334 9000), **SuperShuttle** (1-415 558 8500) and **Bay Shuttle** (1-415 564 3400). **Taxis** are the most expensive option, but may be the only choice if you arrive in the wee hours: expect to pay about $37 plus tip, but be sure to haggle for a flat rate. Taxis are found outside the baggage claim area in a zone marked with yellow columns, or you can try **Luxor** (1-415 282 4141), **National** (1-415 648 4444) or **Yellow** (1-415 626 2345).

By bus

Greyhound (1-800 231 2222, www.greyhound.com) buses stop at the Transbay Terminal (425 Mission Street, SoMa, 1-415 495 1569). For buses to San Francisco from East Bay, contact **AC Transit** (1-415 817 1717, www.actransit.org); from Marin and Sonoma, try **Golden**

Gate Transit (1-415 923 2000, www.
goldengate.org); and from San Mateo County
to the south get **SamTrans** (1-800 660 4287,
www.samtrans.com).

By rail

There's no Amtrak service to San Francisco. If
you want to get here by train, you'll have to get
the shuttle bus from the Amtrak station across
the bay in **Oakland** (*see p266*).

Getting around

By car

You're thinking of driving in San Francisco?
Forget it. There's no free street parking (private
parking costs up to $15/hr) and the steep hills
are as bad for your nerves as your clutch. If you
do use a car, though, the speed limit is 25mph
almost everywhere, cable cars get right of way
and you must always kerb your wheels and set
the handbrake when parking.

Public transport

San Francisco has a comprehensive and efficient
public transport network. Buses, streetcars and
cable cars are all run by **Muni** (1-415 673 6864,
www.sfmuni.com), which sells a Muni Street &
Transit map – you can also get one online. If
you plan to use Muni often, get a **Passport**
(one day, $9; three days, $15; seven days, $20)
or **FastPass** (one month, $45). Additional
options include the flashy **BART** (Bay Area
Rapid Transit) trains and the **ferries**.

BART

BART (1-415 989 2278, www.bart.gov) is a $5
billion network of high-speed rail lines. Almost
everything is automated, with passengers
feeding money into machines that dispense a
reusable ticket. As you exit, the cost of the ride
is deducted, so save your ticket and use any
remaining value on your next trip. Easily the
best way to explore the East Bay, BART is of
limited use within San Francisco itself.

Ferries

Blue & Gold Fleet (1-415 773 1188) runs
tourist boats to Sausalito, Alcatraz and Angel
Island from Pier 41 at Fisherman's Wharf, as
well as East Bay commuter services from the
Ferry Building. **Golden Gate Transit** (1-415
923 2000) runs ferries to Marin.

Muni

Buses

Muni's orange-and-white buses are the city's
number one mode of public transport, able to
get you to within a block or two of almost
anywhere. Fares are cheap at $1.25 adults and
35¢ for seniors, disabled and kids. Unless you
have a Muni pass (*see above*), you'll need to put
exact change into the automatic toll-taker to get
a ticket, which also dispenses a free transfer for
up to two changes within 90 minutes. Buses run
every 5-10 minutes during peak hours on busy
lines; a skeleton crew operates the Owl Service
on certain lines between midnight and 5am.
Bus stops are marked in various ways, notably
a large white rectangle painted on the street.

Cable cars

San Francisco's cable cars may not be the
quickest ride in town, but they are the most
enjoyable. The cars travel three lines:

California   Runs straight along California
                   Street from the Embarcadero
                   to Van Ness Avenue.
Powell-Hyde   Climbs Powell Street before
                   heading to Fisherman's Wharf.
Powell-Mason Heads up Powell and past
                   Chinatown to North Beach.

Powell-Hyde has the best views and hence
the most tourists; California is the quietest.
Use your Muni pass or buy a $3 one-way ticket
from the conductor (under-fives go free, but no
transfers are accepted). And hold on tight: cars
lurch around on the precipitous hills.

Streetcars

Muni Metro runs handsomely restored vintage
streetcars on the F line, along Market Street
north up the Embarcadero to Fisherman's
Wharf; the J, K, L, M and N lines run under
Market Street (making the same stops as the
BART) then above ground as they branch off
towards the Mission, Castro or Sunset. The 3rd
Street Light Rail extension should take Muni
down to the Bayshore CalTrain station by 2005.
Fares are the same as for the buses.

Taxis

As San Francisco is so small, getting around
in a taxi is fairly cheap. Fares average $10-$15,
with a base fee of $2.85 and $2.25 for each
additional mile (there's an additional $2 exit
fee from the airport). Finding a cab isn't always
easy – especially in the outlying areas – so
it's best to book one in advance: try **Yellow**
(1-415 626 2345, www.yellowcabssf.com) or
Luxor (1-415 282 4141, www.luxorcab.com).

The Bay Area

San Francisco gets the headlines, but there's plenty on its doorstep too.

Head for the hills: driving across the Golden Gate Bridge to the **Marin Headlands**.

The Golden Gate Bridge sometimes seems the only link between bustling San Francisco and languid **Marin County**. The city's wealthy northern neighbour, Marin extends up from Sausalito to Bodega and inland to Novato, with the protected parkland that sprawl across the county rendering it immune to overpopulation. Of the county's towns, those on the east side (Tiburon, Sausalito, Mill Valley) tend to be well heeled and staid, while those on the western coast (Stinson Beach, Point Reyes Station and, notoriously, Bolinas) are more bohemian.

Sausalito is a quarter-hour by car from San Francisco, but for a visit to **East Bay**, you won't need to drive: Oakland and Berkeley are easily reached by public transport. The former is rougher edged and funkier; the latter makes much of its radical past but is really a comfortable collection of museums and parkland, plus that illustrious university. In both places, you'll eat well: this is where California cuisine was born. East Bay temperatures run an average ten degrees higher than at the Golden Gate; when the gloomy fogs of July hit San Francisco, a quick jaunt east can bring your sunshine out again.

The **South Bay** is a loosely defined area, and its towns and cities a varied bunch: those in Silicon Valley (notably, San Jose and Palo Alto) get the headlines, but the quiet coastal towns of San Mateo County and militantly kookie Santa Cruz make great stop offs.

Marin County

Sausalito to Larkspur

The first exit north of the Golden Gate Bridge, **Vista Point**, is a good initial stop. In addition to the spectacular view of San Francisco, you'll find the **Bay Area Discovery Museum** (557 McReynolds Road, 1-415 339 3900, www.bay kidsmuseum.org, closed Mon, $7.50-$8.50), an interactive museum geared towards youngsters that's snuggled in Fort Baker at the northern foot of the bridge. Just north, the **Marin Headlands** offer nearly endless opportunities for outdoor activity, as well as breathtaking views of the city and the wide-open Pacific Ocean. Here, too, is the **Marine Mammal Center** (1-415 289 7325, www.tmmc.org), a sanctuary for injured seals and sea lions.

Sausalito, the southernmost Marin County town, is not as quaint as its reputation suggests, but it is picturesque, with a maze of tiny streets stretching from the shoreline all the way up to US 101. Originally a fishing village, Sausalito is now home to prosperous artist-types, yacht owners and well-off businessfolk, and is famous for its elaborate houseboats. The ferry from San Francisco's Pier 41 or Ferry Building, which provides great views of the Golden Gate Bridge and Alcatraz from the top deck, docks Downtown, all manicured gardens and pretty bungalows. Along North Bridgeway, opposite Spring Street, is the turn-off for the **San Francisco Bay Model Visitor Center** (*see below*). From May to October, the town's other attraction is the **Hawaiian Chieftain** (1-415 331 3214, www.hawaiianchieftain.com, $40-$55), a replica late 18th-century sailing ship that you can help to sail.

Across Richardson Bay is tiny downtown **Tiburon**. Again, there are no real sights, just the temptation to enjoy a lingering meal at one of the harbour-view restaurants on Main Street (aka Ark Row, in honour of Tiburon's original houseboat-dwelling denizens) and the fact that the ferry to **Angel Island** (*see p265* **Angelology**) docks here.

Marin County lacks a real centre: though sizeable, Marin City, Corte Madera and Fairfield are not very interesting unless you're shopping for a BMW or a hot tub. It is, however, worth taking the North San Pedro Road exit off US 101 towards **San Rafael**. On the north side of the city is Frank Lloyd Wright's grand **Marin Civic Center** (Avenue of the Flags, 1-415 499 6400, www.marincenter.org), fondly nicknamed 'Big Pink', while a post-war replica of **Mission San Rafael Arcangel** sits on 5th Avenue. Smaller than the 1817 original, the mission has a cemetery that contains the mortal remains of once-rebellious, then-contrite Chief Marin.

From there, head to **Mill Valley**, at the bottom of Mount Tamalpais, where yuppies enjoy charming boutiques and restaurants, and a prestigious autumn film festival (1-415 383 5256, www.cafilm.org). You'll also find picnic-friendly **Tennessee Beach** (1-415 331 1540), easily accessible from Highway 101. Take the Mill Valley/Shoreline Highway exit towards Stinson Beach, then turn left on Tennessee Valley Road, which ends in the parking area a mile from the beach. The **Miwok Livery Stables** (701 Tennessee Valley Road, 1-415 383 8048, www.miwok stables.com) are also here. **Larkspur** is little frequented by tourists, though it's still visited more often than nearby **San Quentin Prison**.

San Francisco Bay Model Visitor Center

2100 Bridgeway, at Olive Street, Sausalito (1-415 332 3870/www.spn.usace.army.mil/bmvc/bmvcinfo. htm). **Open** *Labor Day-Memorial Day* 9am-4pm Tue-Sat. *Memorial Day-Labor Day* 9am-4pm Tue-Fri; 10am-5pm Sat, Sun. **Admission** free.

This two-acre 1:5 scale hydraulic model of San Francisco Bay and delta was built in 1957 as a means of demonstrating how navigation, recreation and ecology interact. As such, it prevented the construction of various dams that would have disastrously altered the bay's tidal range. There are walkways over the model, from which you can watch a complete lunar day in under 15 minutes. Improved upstairs exhibits opened in 2003.

The best Bay Area

Things to do
Nature boys and girls love **Point Reyes** and **Bolinas Nature Reserve** (for both, *see p263*), while occultists dig the **Rosicrucian Egyptian Museum** (*see p274*).

Places to stay
Manka's Inverness Lodge (*see p264*) and **Berkeley City Club** (*see p271*) are both very classy, but outdoor types will want to camp out on **Angel Island** (*see p265* **Angelology**).

Places to eat
They invented Cal cuisine here, you know: at Berkeley's **Chez Panisse** (*see p271*), to be precise. In Oakland, **Bay Wolf** does upscale and **Flints** does ribs (for both, *see p268*). But, for fresh produce, don't pass up shellfish straight from the ocean at **Johnson's Oyster Company** (*see p264*) or the speciality soup at **Duarte's Tavern** (*see p273*).

Nightlife
Stumble from the **Hotsy Totsy** (*see p272*), get down at the **Ruby Room** (*see p268*) or get with it to the finest jazz at **Yoshi's** (*see p268*).

Culture
Find bibliophilia writ large – writ every way – at **Moe's** and **Cody's Books** (*see p270*). Then pop into **Berkeley Art Museum** (*see p270*).

Sports & activities
For baseball and football, Oakland's Coliseum (7000 Coliseum Way) hosts the **Oakland A's** (1-510 568 5600, www.oaklandathletics.com) and the **Raiders** (1-510 569 2121, www. raiders.com). Elsewhere, participation's the thing: horse-riding with **Miwok Livery Stables** (*see p261*), mountain-biking on **Mount Tam** (*see p262*) or surfing – beginners head to **Bolinas Beach** (*see p263*), nutters go to **Mavericks** (*see p273*).

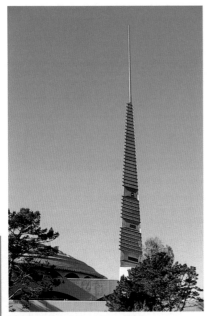

Marin Civic Centre. *See p261.*

Where to eat & drink

Bridgeway, Sausalito's main drag, proffers
the bargain early-bird specials and set meals
of **Christophe** (No.1919, 1-415 332 9244, closed
lunch, $$$) and seafood at popular **Horizons**
(No.558, 1-415 331 3232, $$$). In **Tiburon**, Main
Street is the place. Most people come to eat,
drink Margaritas and take in the view from
Guaymas (No.5, 1-415 435 6300, $$$) or for
the excellent weekends-only brunch at **Sam's
Anchor Cafe** (No.27, 1-415 435 4527, $$–$$$),
which invites you to accompany some hard
liquor on to the waterfront deck.

Larkspur's highly regarded **Lark
Creek Inn** (234 Magnolia Avenue, 1-415 924
7766, closed lunch Sat, $$$–$$$$$) is a lovely
Victorian house with giant sloping skylights,
in a grove of redwoods. Its organic salads and
vegetables come straight from the farmers'
market. **Left Bank** (507 Magnolia Avenue,
1-415 927 3331, $$$) is a Bay Area take on the
Parisian bistro. The first-rate **Marin Brewing
Company** (1809 Larkspur Landing Circle,
1-415 461 4677) is a good spot for a brew.

If you're in Mill Valley, visit ski-lodge-style
Buckeye Roadhouse (15 Shoreline Highway,
1-415 331 2600, $$$), which offers all-American
food, or old-time favourite **La Ginestra** (127

Throckmorton Avenue, 1-415 388 0224, closed
Mon & lunch Tue-Sun, $$$) for the linguine
with clams and own-made ravioli. Also in
Mill Valley, **Sweetwater** (153 Throckmorton
Avenue, 1-415 388 2820) stages gigs regularly,
and offers all pints at $3.50 before 7pm.

Mount Tamalpais & Muir Woods

Mount Tamalpais State Park covers 6,200
acres on the western and southern slopes of
the peak. Visible from as far away as Sonoma,
the mountain itself soars to nearly 2,600 feet
(almost 800 metres), but its dramatic rise is so
steep it seems far taller. Beautiful at any time
of day, it's truly magnificent at sunset. The
roads that snake over Mount Tam, though
steep, are great for hiking and for bicycling;
indeed, the mountain bike was invented here.
The **Mount Tamalpais Interpretive
Center** (1-415 258 2410, www.mttam.net)
offers organised group hikes. If you're really
feeling adventurous, call the **San Francisco
Hanggliding Center** (1-510 528 2300,
www.sfhanggliding.com).

Nearby **Muir Woods National
Monument** (1-415 388 2595, www.visitmuir
woods.com, $3) contains majestic groves of
towering coastal redwoods, many over 500
years old. You'll find several miles of trails
here, one of which (the mile-long Main Trail
Loop) is accessible to the disabled. Redwood
Creek is lined with madrone and big-leaf maple
trees, wildflowers (even in winter), ferns and
wild berry bushes. Deer, chipmunks and a
variety of birds live peacefully among the
redwoods, while the creek is a migratory route
for steelhead trout and silver salmon. To avoid
crowds, visit on weekday mornings and late
afternoons. While you're in the area, take a
spin on Panoramic Highway (*see p263*).

Where to eat, drink & stay

The restaurant at the English-styled **Pelican
Inn** (10 Pacific Way, 1-415 383 6000, closed
dinner Mon, $$$) is not great, but it's the best
eating option near the beach. It's also a fine
hotel (rates from $201): quaint rooms have
canopied beds, balconies and private
bathrooms. Rugged travellers should try
the 100-year-old **West Point Inn** (1-415 646
0702, $35), a collection of five rustic cabins two
miles up Mount Tam from **Pantoll Ranger
Station** (1-415 388 2070). Guests bring their
own sleeping bags and cook grub in a
communal kitchen. There's no electricity,
but nothing beats the views.

Stinson & Bolinas Beach

The drive from Mill Valley to Stinson Beach along **Panoramic Highway** is long and filled with dangerous hairpin bends, with deer apt to make appearances frighteningly close to the road. Nonetheless, the route is gorgeous, with redwoods casting shadows on to the road and ferns dotting the ground along the way, and takes you to affluent and pleasantly new age **Stinson Beach**. Stinson was only connected to Sausalito by a dirt road in 1870; prior to that, sole access was by boat, and there's still a delicious sense of isolation. Stinson is home to **Shakespeare at Stinson** (1-415 868 1115), a theatre company that puts on shows in a 155-seat outdoor theatre from May to October.

A good reason to visit is the **beach**, prettier and much warmer than San Francisco's Ocean Beach. Lifeguards are on duty May through October, and there's a 51-acre park with more than 100 picnic tables. All-nude **Red Rock Beach** (www.redrockbeach.com) is a bare half mile south of downtown. Just north of Stinson Beach is the pristine **Bolinas Lagoon Preserve** (4900 Highway 1, 1-415 868 9244, www.egret.org). The Alice Kent Trail leads to an observation point, from which you can see egrets and great blue herons.

Between the lagoon and the Pacific is **Bolinas Beach**, a beachside hamlet far enough off the beaten track for locals to find it worthwhile binning road signs to dissuade outsiders. But if you can, navigate your way into town and to the beach, which has small enough waves to be a great spot for novice surfers: try **Bolinas Surf Lessons** (2 Mile Surf Shop, 22 Brighton Avenue, 1-415 868 0264). The water is also excellent for kayaking and fishing; camping, campfires and dogs are allowed on the beach. The town is a haven for writers and artists, as the **Bolinas Museum** (48 Wharf Road, 1-415 868 0330, www.bolinasmuseum.org, closed Mon-Thur) makes clear. At the banding station of nearby **Point Reyes Bird Observatory** (900 Mesa Road, 1-415 868 1221 ext 307, www.prbo.org), the public can watch biologists catch and release birds, using special 'mist' nets, on Wednesday, Saturday and Sunday mornings.

Where to eat & drink

The thing to eat in Stinson is, of course, seafood: try the **Stinson Beach Grill** (3465 Highway 1, 1-415 868 2002, $$$) for white-tablecloth-and-pinot-noir dining or the lunches at **Sand Dollar Restaurant** (3458 Highway 1, 1-415 868 0434, $$). The **Parkside Café** (43 Arenal Avenue, 1-415 868 1272, $$) is the spot for a casual outdoor pizza.

Bolinas only has a few choice spots: on Wharf Road, try the **Coast Café** (No.46, 1-415 868 2224, $$) or the **Blue Heron Inn** (No.11, 1-415 868 1102, reservations only, closed Tue & lunch Wed-Mon, $$$). For a pint, the **Saloon at Smiley's** (*see below*) has been in the business for more than 150 years, and claims to be the second oldest bar in California.

Where to stay

In Stinson, the cute and simple **Sandpiper** (1 Marine Way, 1-877 557 4737, 1-415 868 1632, www.sfbay.net/sandpiper, $95-$195) has rooms and cabins within walking distance of the waves, while the funky **Stinson Beach Motel** (3416 Highway 1, 1-415 868 1712, www.stinson beachmotel.com, $85-$200) is in the town centre. **Redwoods Haus** (Belvedere & Highway 1, 1-415 868 9828, 1-415 868 9828, www.stinson-beach.com, $110-$160) and **Ocean Court Motel** (18 Arenal Avenue, 1-415 868 0212, www.oceancourt.ws, $95-$125) are other recommended options in the area.

If you'd like the comforts of home by the beach in Bolinas, go ahead and rent one: phone ahead for the address of the **Beach House** (1-415 927 2644, www.bolinasbeach.net), where up to four people can be accommodated for $190-$200 a night. Otherwise, try the friendly **Thomas' White House Inn** (118 Kale Road, 1-415 868 0279, www.thomaswhitehouseinn. com, $110-$121) for great sunset views, or **Smiley's Schooner Saloon & Hotel** (41 Wharf Road, 1-415 868 1311, $74-$84).

Central California

Disc drive

CDs to soundtrack your journey around the Bay Area.

***Silicon Valleys* Benge**
Plinky-plonk future nostalgia.

***Journey in Satchidananda* Alice Coltrane**
Perfect for those crinkly coastlines: majestic, mystical jazz from John Coltrane's widow.

***Fresh Fruit for Rotting Vegetables* The Dead Kennedys**
The debut album by the premier West Coast punks still sounds furious 25 years on. California über alles, indeed.

***Anticon Label Sampler: 1999-2004* Various Artists**
Oakland-based collective keeps the wilful eclecticism of early hip hop alive. Beautiful.

Port authority: **Tomales Bay**.

Point Reyes National Seashore

If you head north from Stinson Beach on Highway 1, you'll come to the **Bear Valley Visitor Center** (*see p265*) near Olema. This center acts as the entry point for the most famous parcel of land in these parts: the vast wilderness of **Point Reyes National Seashore**. This protected peninsula is an extraordinary wildlife refuge, with sea mammals and waterfowl, waterfalls and campsites, and miles of unspoilt beaches. From the visitor centre, you can either head west towards the coast for **Drake's Beach**, or go north via Inverness to the tip of the peninsula: **Point Reyes Lighthouse** (1-415 669 1534) is a perfect lookout for whale-watching. Several trails also start here, including the popular Chimney Rock. Nearby **Inverness** is picturesque, with many homes still owned by the families that built them, while tiny **Point Reyes Station** bustles with energy along its three-block Downtown.

Make a note to check in at the **Cowgirl Creamery** (80 4th Street, 1-415 663 9335), where you can try some fine cheeses.

Natural historians and those with more energy than is good for them should press on along Highway 1 to **Tomales Bay**. There Blue Waters Kayaking (12938 Sir Francis Drake Boulevard, 1-415 669 2600, www.bwkayak.com) offers half- or full-day paddle trips, and (by appointment) romantic full-moon tours.

Where to eat, drink & stay

No matter the sometimes grumpy owner, **Vladimir's Czech Restaurant** (12785 Sir Francis Drake Boulevard, Inverness, 1-415 669 1021, closed Mon, Tue & lunch Wed-Sun, $$$) is one of a kind: try the roast duckling, wiener schnitzel and delicious apple strudel. Also on Sir Francis Drake Boulevard, **Johnson's Oyster Company** (No.17171, 1-415 669 1149, $$$) hasn't changed in almost 50 years: same location, same family, same buildings, even the same Japanese method of farming oysters. In Point Reyes Station, the **Station House Café** (Main Street, 1-415 663 1515, closed Wed, $$–$$$) is a mellow place that serves California cuisine, while the **Pine Cone Diner** (60 4th Street, 1-415 663 1536, $) is a sweet retro spot for breakfast or lunch.

Built as a hunting and fishing lodge, **Manka's Inverness Lodge** (30 Callender Way, Inverness, 1-415 669 1034, www.mankas. com, closed Jan, $185-$515) serves as both a terrific restaurant (dinner only) and a lodging place, with eight rooms, a suite, two cabins and a dramatic 1911 boathouse over the water. Since 1876 Olema has been home to the charming **Olema Inn** (10000 Sir Francis Drake Boulevard, 1-415 663 9559, www.theolemainn. com, $145-$185). In Point Reyes, try art-heavy **Abalone Inn** (12355 Sir Francis Drake Boulevard, 1-415 663 9149, 1-877 416 0458, www.abaloneinn.com, $90-$150) or **Knob Hill** (40 Knob Hill Road, 1-415 663 1784, $70-$160).

Police

Mill Valley *1 Hamilton Drive (1-415 389 4100).*
San Rafael *1400 5th Avenue (1-415 485 3000).*
Sausalito *300 Locust Street (1-415 289 4170).*

Post office

Inverness *12781 Sir Francis Drake Boulevard (1-415 669 1675).*
Point Reyes *11260 Highway 1 (1-415 663 1305).*
San Rafael *40 Bellam Boulevard (1-415 459 6643).*
Sausalito *150 Harbor Drive (1-415 332 0227).*
Stinson Beach *15 Calle del Mar (1-415 868 1504).*

Tourist information

Mill Valley *Mill Valley Chamber of Commerce, 85 Throckmorton Avenue (1-415 388 9700/www.mill valley.org).* **Open** 10am-3pm Mon, Wed, Fri.
Mount Tamalpais *Mount Tamalpais State Park (1-415 388 2070).* **Open** 8am-5.30pm daily.
Muir Woods *Muir Woods Visitor Center (1-415 388 2595/www.visitmuirwoods.com).* **Open** 9am-4.30pm daily.
Point Reyes National Seashore *Bear Valley Visitor Center (1-415 464 5100/www.nps.gov/pore).* **Open** 9am-5pm Mon-Fri; 8am-5pm Sat, Sun. *Lighthouse Visitor Center Point (1-415 669 1534/ www.nps.gov/pore).* **Open** 10am-4.30pm Mon, Thur-Sun, weather permitting.
Sausalito *Sausalito Chamber of Commerce & Visitor Center, 10 Liberty Ship Way, Bay 2, Suite 250 (1-415 331 7262/www.sausalito.org).* **Open** 9am-5pm Mon-Fri.

By boat

Golden Gate Transit ferries run daily from the Ferry Building on the Embarcadero to **Sausalito** and **Larkspur**; the **Blue & Gold Fleet** sails to **Tiburon** from the Ferry Building and to **Sausalito** and **Angel Island** from Pier 41 on Fisherman's Wharf.

By bus

Golden Gate Transit buses link San Francisco to Marin County. For **Sausalito**, take bus 22, 107 or 143; for **Tiburon**, bus 8 or 15; for **Mill Valley**, you need bus 4 or 10; and for **Larkspur**, take bus 97. Buses start from the Transbay Terminal at Mission and 1st Streets, but there are other pick-up points in the city. (The schedules are at www.goldengate.org.) Golden Gate Transit bus 63 goes from Marin City to **Stinson Beach** and local trailheads (mid Mar-mid Dec), and to **Audubon Canyon Ranch** (Mar-July).

By car

The main highway, US 101, heads across the Golden Gate Bridge and north through the heart of Marin County. For **Sausalito**, take the Alexander Avenue or Spencer Avenue exit; for **Mill Valley** and **Larkspur**, take the East Blithedale exit (you can also reach Larkspur by the Paradise Drive or Lucky Drive exits); for **Tiburon**, turn off at the same point as for Mill Valley, but right on to Highway 131. Highway 1 passes lesser-known Marin County gems like **Muir Woods** as it weaves along the coast all the way to **Point Reyes**.

Angelology

The largest island in the San Francisco Bay, **Angel Island** is a delightful, wild place. But its history hardly predicts such pleasures. Camp Reynolds, in the east of the island, was established in 1863 by Union troops to protect the bay against a Confederate attack and the west of the island became, from 1910 to 1940, the site of a US government immigration station, set to screen immigrants under the terms of the 1882 Chinese Exclusion Act. Known as 'the Ellis Island of the West', Angel Island was notorious. Boatloads of Chinese immigrants were detained for months so officials could interrogate them; many of them were eventually sent home, never having touched the mainland. During World War II, Angel Island was an equally unwelcome home to German and Japanese POWs. The military remained in control through the '50s and '60s, when the island served as a Nike missile base (still closed to the public), but in 1963 the land was finally ceded to the government as a state park.

Ayala Cove, where the ferry docks, has a visitors' centre (1-415 435 1915). It also marks the beginning of the five-mile **Perimeter Trail**, which will take you past the immigration station, wooden Civil War barracks and other military remnants hidden among the trees. At 797 feet (243 metres), the peak of **Mount Livermore** affords a panoramic view of the bay from the island's centre. There's a wonderful diversity of bird and animal species on the island, from deer to seals, pelicans to hummingbirds. You'll also find **Quarry Beach**, a sheltered sunbathing strip popular with kayakers. Those who don't want to walk can take the tram tour and anyone who wants to stay overnight can pitch up at the campsite. For details of camping, guided tours and bike or kayak rental, see www.angelisland.org; if you do want to camp, book well in advance.

The Angel Island **ferry** (1-415 435 2131, $7.50-$10 return) runs from Tiburon, daily in summer and weekends only in winter. Schedule information can be found at www.angelislandferry.com.

East Bay

Oakland

Named after its almost-vanished oak forests, San Francisco's stepsister (with a population of 400,000, it's more than half the size of San Francisco itself) has had image problems since it made headlines in the 1960s as the base of both the radical Black Panthers and the mobhanded Hell's Angels. The murder rate still runs high – a headache for mayor Jerry Brown, known as 'Governor Moonbeam' for his quirky-left politics when in charge of California in the 1970s – but the once-notorious Panthers are now the subject of a two-and-a-half-hour **Black Panther Legacy Tour** (1801 Adeline, 1-510 986 0660, $15-$25) on the last Saturday of each month. Oakland's earliest fame, though, was as the western terminus of the transcontinental railway. After the 1906 earthquake, thousands of displaced San Franciscans moved here (Glen David Gold's novel *Carter Beats the Devil* tells the tale); today many residents commute from the lower rents of Oakland across the Bay Bridge or through the BART tunnels.

On the waterfront, **Jack London Square** (at Broadway and Embarcadero) is named after the noted local author, who used to carouse at **Heinhold's First & Last Chance Saloon** (*see p268*). The bells of passing freight trains are strangely evocative of Oakland's blue-collar heritage. For kids, the **Oakland Museum of Children's Art** (538 9th Street, 1-510 465 8770, www.mocha.org, closed Mon) is to the north of the square, while Franklin Delano Roosevelt's 'floating White House', the **USS Potomac**, is docked to the west. The visitors' centre (540 Water Street, 1-510 627 1215, www.uss potomac.org) arranges tours and bay cruises.

Having undergone huge redevelopment, Oakland's Downtown is more inviting nowadays. **Chinatown** covers liess south of Broadway around 7th to 9th Streets, and while less tourist-focused than its San Francisco counterpart, it's still packed with places to eat and shop. The **Oakland Museum of California** (*see p267*) is a great place to learn about the state, and is worth negotiating the unpleasant road that separates it from **Lake Merritt**. Here you'll find the largest collection of gondolas outside Venice (1-510 663 6603, $45, advance booking required). Tots go dewy-eyed over Little Miss Muffet and her crew at **Children's Fairyland** (699 Bellevue Avenue, 1-510 452 2259, www.fairyland.org, $6), as do grown-ups at the 1926 **Grand Lake Movie Theater** (3200 Grand Avenue, 1-510 452 3556, www. renaissancerialto.com, $6-$9).

West of Lake Merritt is the **Paramount Theatre** (2025 Broadway, 1-510 465 6400, $6), an art deco movie house built by renowned Bay Area architect Timothy L Pflueger in 1931. As well as screening classic movies (complete with the Mighty Wurlitzer), it's home to the **Oakland Symphony** (1-510 444 0801, www.oebs.org) and the **Oakland Ballet** (1-510 452 9288, www.oaklandballet.org).

Oakland's best shopping area is the stretch of College Avenue in the ritzy **Rockridge** district to the north. As well as home accessories and high-end clothes shops, you'll find the **Market Hall** (5665 College Avenue, 1-510 655 7748), catering to local yuppies with a butcher, wine shop, bakery, cheese shop, florist and café.

East Oakland merits a visit for the **Chabot Space & Science Museum, Oakland Zoo** (for both, *see p267*) and **Redwood Regional Park** (7867 Redwood Road, 1-510 562 7275, www.ebparks.org), a sprawling 1,836 acres of partially wild park with horseback riding, 150-foot (46-metre) redwoods and hiking trails.

Oakland Museum of California.
See p267.

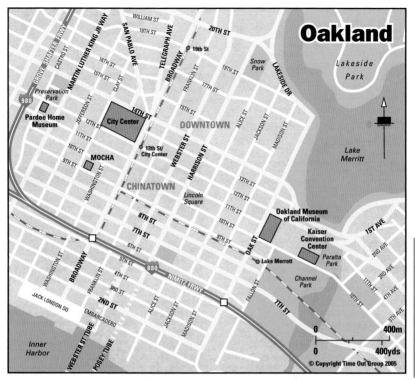

Chabot Space & Science Museum

10000 Skyline Boulevard (1-510 336 7300/www. chabotspace.org). **Open** 10am-5pm Wed-Thur; 10am-10pm Fri, Sat; 11am-5pm Sun. **Admission** (incl Planetarium) $13; $9 4-12s, seniors. *MegaDome Theater* $6; $5 4-12s, seniors. **Credit** MC, V.

High in the Oakland Hills, the Chabot combines a state-of-the-art planetarium with an observatory and film theatre; the latter runs 70mm projections of the internal workings of the human body or the cosmos, seen at the largest scale and at the submolecular level. The three telescopes here include a 36in (91cm) reflector telescope housed in the rotating roof observatory; you can look through the trio most Fridays and Saturdays, weather permitting.

Oakland Museum of California

1000 Oak Street, at 10th Street (1-510 238 2200/ www.museumca.org). **Open** 10am-5pm Wed-Sat; noon-5pm Sun. **Admission** $8; $5 discounts. **Credit** AmEx, DC, MC, V.

Divided into art, history and natural science sections, the Oakland Museum provides a fine overview of California life. The art includes pioneers' sketches and pictures from the Gold Rush, along with modern Bay Area works. The Hall of California Ecology uses stuffed mammals, reptiles and birds to explain the state's extraordinary range of habitats, while the Cowell Hall of California History houses curiosities dating back to the Spanish colonial era.

Oakland Zoo

9777 Golf Links Road, off I-580 (1-510 632 9525/ www.oaklandzoo.org). **Open** 10am-4pm daily. **Admission** $9; $5.50 2-14s, discounts; free under-2s. **Credit** MC, V.

Situated in Knowland Park, the formerly cramped Oakland Zoo has over the last few years put effort into creating decent-sized naturalistic habitats for its more than 400 species, including lions and tigers, chimps, elephants, tarantulas and snakes, ibis and toucans. There are also the CP Huntington miniature train, a carousel and the Sky Ride, a chair lift that takes you over the bison and elk on the 'North American Range'. The popular Children's Zoo reopens in spring 2005.

Where to eat

Oakland has a dizzying array of food: as well as the obligatory posh French and California cuisine, you'll find Vietnamese, Chinese, Ethiopian, Peruvian and Caribbean restaurants.

Intimate and well-reputed **À Côté** (5478 College Avenue, 1-510 655 6469, closed lunch, $$$) serves French food at moderate prices, despite its Rockridge location, while revered **Bay Wolf** (No.3853, 1-510 655 6004, closed lunch Sat & Sun, $$$–$$$$) has occupied a converted Victorian on pretty Piedmont Avenue for the last 28 years, serving Tuscan-, Basque- and Provençal-inspired California cuisine.

For great Vietnamese, head to cavernous **Le Cheval** (1007 Clay Street, 1-510 763 8495, closed lunch Sun, $$), jam-packed with locals from every walk of life. Chinatown is teeming with possibilities for dim sum: try **Tsing Tao Seafood Restaurant** (200 Broadway, 1-510 465 8811, $$$) or **Tin's Tea House** (701 Webster Street, 1-510 832 7661, $$). Telegraph Avenue's **Addis** (No.6100, 1-510 653 3456, $$) and acclaimed **Cafe Eritrea d'Afrique** (No.4069, 1-510 547 4520, $$) are great for African eats. For *huevos rancheros* in the morning and tequila by night, try **La Estrellita** (446 E 12th Street, 1-510 465 7188, $$). Oakland is also famous for its barbecue joints: old-school **Flints** (3114 San Pablo Avenue, 1-510 658 2668, $) and **Everett & Jones** (1955 San Pablo Avenue, 1-510 548 8261, $) are the pick of the pack.

Where to drink

In recent years, the hipster quotient in the East Bay City has grown, with escalating rents driving arty types out of San Francisco. The **Stork Club** (2330 Telegraph Avenue, 1-510 444 6174) is a prime example of this nightlife renaissance, a funky, two-room bar whose busy roster showcases the best local punk, hardcore and indie acts. For DJs and a tats-and-piercings crowd, head to friendly **Ruby Room** (132 14th Street, 1-510 444 7224): too hip to have a sign, you'll have to look out for the red floodlights and pack of smokers outside the front door. For something a bit more suave, dabble in saké at **Grasshopper** (6317 College Avenue, 1-510 595 3557). Oakland is also proud home to the Bay Area's premier jazz house: **Yoshi's at Jack London Square** (510 Embarcadero West, 1-510 238 9200, www.yoshis.com).

For something altogether more traditional, **Heinhold's First & Last Chance Saloon** (56 Jack London Square, 1-510 839 6761) was built from the timbers of a whaler. Opening in 1883, it got its name from the seamen's tradition of taking a last drink here before leaving port, and a first on their return. **5th Amendment** (3255 Lakeshore Avenue, 1-510 832 3242) and the **Alley** (3325 Grand Avenue, 1-510 444 8505) are also worth a look. Cosy and welcoming **White Horse Inn** (6551 Telegraph Avenue,

1-510 652 3820) is the city's longest-standing gay bar: with pool, dancing and a crowd nicely mixed between male, female, gay and straight.

Where to stay

The '50s-style **Jack London Inn** (444 Embarcadero West, 1-510 444 2032, 1-800 549 8780, www.jacklondoninn.com, $89) is handily placed on Jack London Square. If you fancy staying in a private home, contact Mary at the friendly **Bed & Breakfast Network** (1-510 547 6380): the list includes some 20 different properties, with doubles averaging $85-$175.

Around Oakland

Emeryville, near the entrance to the Oakland Bay Bridge, was once a slaughterhouse district with Prohibition gambling issues (*see p270* **Get carded**). Now it has a marina, overspill commuters and Pixar Animation Studios, and the big-box stores shunned by nearby Berkeley (*see p269*). Still, quality jazz at **Kimball's East** (6005 Shellmound, 1-510 658 2555), found inside a strip mall, makes a visit worthwhile.

Once notable only for its naval air station, **Alameda** was shell-shocked when the end of the Cold War saw its military installations shut down. Recent years have seen steady recovery, with the new **Alameda Marketplace** (1650 Park Street, 1-510 522 1462) a foodie highlight: the bakery and deli are perfect for picnic stuffs. Alameda became an island in 1902 when a tidal canal, dug to link San Leandro Bay with the Oakland harbour, separated it from the mainland. With the legendary Neptune Beach amusement park long-since buried under the naval station, Alameda's main attractions now focus on the bay. The 2.5 miles of **Crown Memorial State Beach** (8th Street and Otis Drive, 1-510 521 7090) make for warmer swimming than elsewhere on the bay, due to the gently shelving sand, and there are fine views and trails. Explore the **Elsie Roemer Bird Sanctuary** to the east and **Crab Cove Marine Reserve**, complete with visitor centre (1252 McKay Street, 1-510 521 6887), to the north. The naval base is itself home to the **USS Hornet** (*see p269*) and Northern California's largest antiques market, the 800-stall **Alameda Point Antiques & Collectibles Faire** (2700 Saratoga Street, 1-510 522 7500, $5-$15), held from 6am on the first Sunday of the month.

Fremont, around 30 miles south of Oakland, is home to a growing population of Indian, Pakistani and Afghan immigrants, but the city is an uninspiring series of strip malls, enlivened by the impressive **Mission San Jose**. Founded in June 1797, it was the most successful of the

Northern California missions, grazing thousands of sheep, cattle and horses, as well as running a 30-piece orchestra of local Ohlone Indians. The chandeliers and trompe l'oeils within reflect this prosperity, but it's all a reconstruction: the original was destroyed by an 1868 earthquake. You'll also find one of the area's few working farms here: **Ardenwood Historic Farm** (34600 Ardenwood Boulevard, 1-510 796 0199, closed Mon) demonstrates how land was farmed in the 1870s. If you're around for the October Harvest Festival, you can even ride the steam tractor.

USS Hornet Museum

Pier 3, Alameda Point, Alameda (1-510 521 8448/ www.uss-hornet.org). **Open** 10am-5pm Mon, Wed-Sun; 10am-3pm Tue. **Admission** $14; $12 seniors; $6 5-17s; free under-5s. **Credit** AmEx, DC, MC, V. Launched in 1943, the 'Grey Ghost' saw active service in the Pacific, surviving nearly 60 air attacks, with its 80 fighters destroying 1,410 Japanese planes. In peacetime, it recovered the astronauts from the Apollo 11 and Apollo 12 missions. Reopened as a museum in 1998, the four levels of displays and memorabilia include an F/A-18 flight simulator ($4, closed Mon-Tue in winter), while the impressive flight deck grants terrific views of San Francisco. On Tuesdays the entry fee drops to $5, but no one is admitted after 1.30pm and access is limited.

Where to eat, drink & stay

Almost making the trip to Emeryville worth it all by itself, **Doug's BBQ** (3600 San Pablo Avenue, 1-510 655 9048, closed Mon, $) is an under-the-freeway dive, serving first-rate Texas-style barbecue delicacies. For great skinny fries and walls decorated with waitress Barbie dolls, check out the **Can't Fail Cafe** (4081 Hollis Street, 1-510 594 1221, $). **Trader Vic's** (9 Anchor Drive, 1-510 653 3400) is fun for pricey tiki cocktails. The Alameda sister to San Francisco's **Lucky 13** (1301 Park Street, 1-510 523 2118) is a good no-nonsense boozer, while the **Tied House Cafe & Brewery** (Pacific Marina, 1-510 521 4321), which reopened in August 2004 after a remodel, revels in fine views over the tidal canal. For a room, try the **Holiday Inn Bay Bridge** (1800 Powell Street, 1-800 465 4329, 1-510 658 9300, www.holidayinn.com, $129-$139).

Berkeley

Berkeley works hard to live up to its reputation as a hotbed of avant-garde arts, leftist politics and revolutionary food: its irreverent and self-effacing annual autumn parade is called How Berkeley Can You Be? The answer, it seems, is Berkeley enough to ride a banana bike or hop aboard the Gandhi peace float.

Near the Downtown Berkeley BART station, bustling coffeehouses confirm the proximity of students. The campus of the **University of California** (known locally as Cal), only a short distance east, was the birthplace of America's youth revolution 30 years ago, with students back from the Civil Rights campaigns in the South fomenting protests against the Vietnam War and establishing the Free Speech Movement. These days, the sprawling campus of creeks and redwood groves is generally calm.

As well as the 307-foot (94-metre) **Sather Tower** (there's a lift most of the way if you fancy taking in the views), you'll find museums dedicated to art, anthropology, palaeontology and many other disciplines, prime among them the **Berkeley Art Museum** (*see p270*); the associated **Pacific Film Archive** (2575 Bancroft Way, 1-510 642 1124), just off the campus, screens some 650 films a year. Berkeley Symphony Orchestra (1-510 841 2800, www.berkeleysymphony.org), led by Kent Nagano, is based at the **Zellerbach Hall** (1-510 642 9988), which also hosts the **Berkeley Opera** (1-510 841 1903, www.berkeleyopera. org), while the 8,000-seat **Hearst Greek Theater** (Piedmont and Hearst Avenue, 1-510 642 9988) is the city's premier venue for live music. **Lawrence Hall of Science** (*see p270*), above the campus on Centennial Drive, is a fascinating museum with commanding views. Drop in on the **Visitors' Center** (University Hall, 2200 University Avenue, 1-510 642 5215, closed Sat & Sun) for maps and information.

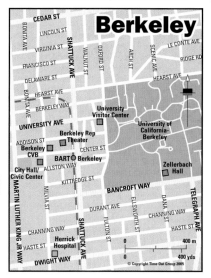

Central California

Red hot poker

Sidle into Emeryville's **Oaks Card Club** (4097 San Pablo Avenue, 1-510 653 4456) after hours and you might not realise you're entering a piece of history. MC Hammer, whose dad was once casino manager here, was probably still in the charts when the main floor was last remodelled. But the Oaks can trace its card-playing history back to 1895, which makes it one of Northern California's oldest poker rooms.

Emeryville has changed a bit since then. The California Jockey Club is gone, taking with it not only the horses but also the car racing that used to pull in 1,000s of spectators. The Oakland Oaks, who played baseball here for half a century, would now find Pixar Studios where their stadium once stood. Once dubbed 'the rottenest city on the Pacific Coast', Emeryville has also lost almost all

of its 20 or 30 gambling dens: King Midas, the Bank Club, the Avalon Card Room have all gone leaving only the Oaks intact. True, the poker room on the corner of San Pablo and Park was originally Conger's Tavern. But the Oaks Card Club opened on the self-same site in the mid 1930s, so the claim to more than a century of continuous card playing is justified. Indeed, current owner John Tibbetts and his forebears have been in charge of the place for as long as it's been the Oaks.

Inside there's a full bar and restaurant, plus a raised and railed walkway around the 40 tables that enables you to have a look at the action before you join in. Games are played against fellow players, which means there's no house edge. The Oaks simply takes a fee (around $2.50, depending on the game) for each half-hour you sit at the table.

Berkeley is a city of book lovers. **Telegraph Avenue**, spiking southwards from the campus, has the city's two essential bookshops: **Moe's** (No.2476, 1-510 849-2087), which has 100,000 volumes spread over four floors, and **Cody's Books** (No.2454, 1-510 845 7852), since 1956 one of the most staunchly independent bookstores in the US and now one of the more successful. You'll find second-hand books at **Shakespeare & Company** (No.2499, 1-510 841 8916) and nearby **Revolution Books** (2425C Channing Way, 1-510 848 1196). **Rasputin** (No.2401, 1-510 848 9004) and **Amoeba Records** (No.2455, 1-510 549 1125) are terrific for music.

To take in the daytime student vibe head for the cafés lining the university's southern limit: good choices are **Café Strada** (2300 College Avenue, 1-510 843 5282) and **Café Milano** (2522 Bancroft Way, 1-510 644 3100); in the evening, typical hangouts include world-music institution **Ashkenaz** (1317 San Pablo Avenue, 1-510 525 5054). At weekends, mooch around the corner of Ashby Avenue and Martin Luther King Jr Way for the **Berkeley Flea Market**. The town is also home to the state's finest rep theatre: **Berkeley Repertory Theater** (2025 Addison Street, 1-510 845 4700, www.berkeleyrep.org).

Berkeley's outlying districts also repay exploration. South Berkeley has the **Judah L Magnes Museum** (2911 Russell Street, 1-510 549 6950, www.magnes.org, closed Fri & Sat), a large mansion bursting at the seams with Jewish history and culture, as well as many California Craftsman-style homes. But many people visit Berkeley just for its hills: the lovely

and magnificently wild **Tilden Regional Park** (1-510 525 2233) offers hiking, nature trails and pony rides, a farm and a steam train, while those who manage the trek up to Inspiration Point or Wildcat Peak are rewarded with 180-degree views. For a more leisurely take on nature, the **UC Berkeley Botanical Garden** (200 Centennial Drive, 1-510 6432 3755, http://botanicalgarden.berkeley.edu, $1-$3), below Tilden Park, has cacti and orchids.

Berkeley Art Museum

2626 Bancroft Way, at Bowditch Street (1-510 642 0808/www.bampfa.berkeley.edu). I-80, exit University Avenue. **Open** 11am-5pm Wed, Fri-Sun; 11am-7pm Thur. **Admission** $8; free under-12s. Free 1st Thur of mth. **Credit** AmEx, DC, MC, V.

Opened in 1970, this dramatic exhibition space is arranged in terraces so visitors can see the works from various vantage points. The collection's strength is 20th-century art, be it sculpture, painting, photography or conceptual work, but there's also a good collection of Asian pieces. Ten galleries and a bookstore occupy the upper level, while a sculpture garden and café share the lower floor.

Lawrence Hall of Science

Centennial Drive, nr Grizzly Park Boulevard (1-510 642 5132/www.lhs.berkeley.edu). **Open** 10am-5pm daily. **Admission** $7; $5 5-18s, discounts; $3 3-4s; free under-3s. **Credit** Disc, MC, V.

Perched on the hills facing the bay (a great spot for daytime views and evening star-gazing), this science museum has computers to explore the inside of your brain, a Young Explorers Area and a huge DNA model to scramble over. Don't miss the telescope and the wind-driven organ pipes at the back.

Where to eat

To paraphrase resident novelist Michael Chabon, Berkeley is where people think they can save the world by eating well. The Gourmet Ghetto, a stretch of Shattuck Avenue in North Berkeley, is prime witness for the prosecution, providing a home for the place that started all the fuss in 1971: Alice Waters' **Chez Panisse** (No.1517, 1-510 548 5049, closed Sun, $$$$$). A sparkling example of California Craftsman-style architecture, the building houses a restaurant, which serves a meticulously organised daily prix-fixe (reservations required), and a popular upstairs café that provides cheaper à la carte ($$$$). For something that requires less advance planning, pop into the **Cheese Board Collective** (No.1504, 1-510 549 3191), a workers' co-operative that sells a wealth of gourmet cheeses and bakery goods; its offshoot, **Cheese Board Pizza** (No.1512, 1-510 549 3055, closed Mon & Sun), is run on the same principles, but serves just a single type of vegetarian pizza ($2.25). Next door to Chez Panisse, **César** (No.1515, 1-510 883 0222, $$$) does great tapas until late, while **Cha Am** (No.1543, 1-510 848 9664, $$) does tasty Thai. Some have hailed the coffee just around the corner at the original **Peet's** (2124 Vine Street, 1-510 841 0564) as the world's best: opened in 1966, this was where the founder of Starbucks got his training. Make of this what you will.

Beyond the Ghetto, there are killer salads and own-made bread at **Café Intermezzo** (2442 Telegraph Avenue, 1-510 849 4592, $) and Wendy Brucker's French-inspired dishes at little **Rivoli** (1539 Solano Avenue, 1-510 526 2542, closed lunch, $$$$). For those chocolate cravings, **Café Cacao** (914 Heinz Street, 1-510 843 6000, closed dinner Mon, $$$) serves such craziness as unsweetened chocolate pasta.

There is an abundance of great Indian cuisine in Berkeley. Corner shop/café **Vik's Chaat Corner** (726 Allston Way, 1-510 644 4412, closed Mon & dinner Tue-Sun, $) serves the best cheap lunch in town; **Ajanta** (1888 Solano Avenue, 1-510 526 4373, $$$) is more upscale. The **Thai Buddhist Temple Mongholratanaram** (1911 Russell Street, 1-510 849 3419, $) throws a mean Sunday brunch, with the iced tea, mango sticky rice, hot noodle soup and pork skewers perfect against a backdrop of gongs, bells and incense.

Where to drink

Berkeley's best boozer is the **Albatross Pub** (1822 San Pablo Avenue, 1-510 843 2473). Open until 2am, it combines a homely atmosphere and diverse crowd with multiple distractions: a good range of beers, darts, pool, free popcorn, regular live music and a terrific pub quiz. Try Shattuck Avenue for **Jupiter** (No.2181, 1-510 843 7625) or the relaxed **Starry Plough** (No.3101, 1-510 841 2082, free-$6), where there's live music from national cult figures and great local bands. A local institution for more than 50 years, **Blake's** (2367 Telegraph Avenue, 1-510 848 0886, closed Sun, free-$6) has a studenty restaurant (burgers, pizzas), but live music and DJs in the dingy basement are the real draw. Non-boozers will be grateful for the **Freight & Salvage Coffee House** (1111 Addison Street, 1-510 548 1761), where you'll catch music ranging from American roots to trad Irish.

Where to stay

The **Claremont Resort & Spa** (41 Tunnel Road, 1-800 551 7266, 1-510 843 3000, www. claremontresort.com, $270-$410) is a decadent hillside palace, sprawling across the Berkeley-Oakland border, both architectural landmark and indulgent splurge. Even if you can't afford to stay, experience a cocktail in the Paragon Bar. Closer to campus, the **Bancroft Hotel** (2680 Bancroft Way, 1-510 549 1002/1000, www.bancrofthotel.com, $129) is charming in an Arts and Crafts style, and the **Berkeley City Club** (2315 Durant Avenue, 1-510 848 7800, www.berkeleycityclub.com, $120-$125) is a baroque-deco wonder, designed by Julia Morgan, Hearst Castle's architect. For something less highfalutin, check out the **Bed & Breakfast Network** (*see p268*).

North of Berkeley

The tiny city of **Albany**, nestled into Berkeley's north side, may now be famous for excellent schools and a tidy Downtown, but it was once renowned for the strip clubs and seedy bars that lined San Pablo Avenue. The clubs have vanished, but some kick-ass watering holes remain (*see p272*). And not all birds have flown: between bay shore and Buchanan Street, **Albany Mudflats** is paradise for wading birds. Heading north, you enter an industrial zone. Its shipbuilding industry gone, **Richmond** is now sustained by an oil refinery: the route to Marin County (*see p260*) via the Richmond-San Rafael Bridge passes through it.

To the north-east are the Carquinez Straits. **Rodeo**, a tiny town dwarfed by the adjacent oil refinery, is home to the most fabulous vintage clothing store known to humanity (*see p273* **Prime vintage**), while former C&H Sugar company town **Crockett** has contrived to maintain the charms of small-town life – its population is only about 3,000 people – despite being but a 15-minute drive north of Downtown Berkeley. Crockett nestles in the hillside over the brand-spanking-new **Alfred Zampa Memorial Bridge**, the first large suspension bridge built in the US since 1964. Providing access to Wine Country (*see pp346-362*), it's the first major bridge to have been named after a blue-collar worker: Al Zampa worked on all the major bay bridges, including the one his namesake bridge replaced. From here, signs mark a meandering road east to tiny **Port Costa**, once thriving as a gateway town for the Sacramento River delta. There's little to see other than passing boats, the Warehouse Café (*see below*) and funky gallery-cum-shop **Theatre of Dreams** (11 Canyon Lake Drive, 1-510 787 2164), where Wendy Addison concocts modern-day Victoriana from old paper dolls, sheet music, bird's nests and glitter.

Where to drink

Albany has a fine reputation for serious boozing. The prime establishments are on San Pablo Avenue: the **Hotsy Totsy** (No.601, 1-510 524 1661), **Club Mallard** (No.752, 1-510 524 8450) and the **Ivy Room** (No.858, 1-510 524 9299), with the Bay Area's best roots jukebox. The **Albany Bowl** (No.540, 1-510 526 8818) contains a cocktail lounge: waitresses bring libations straight to your lane. For something a little more esoteric, beautiful teahouse **Celadon Fine Teas** (1111 Solano Avenue, 1-510 524 1696, closed Mon) serves and sells some 60 varieties. Port Costa's **Warehouse Café** (5 Canyon Lakes Drive, 1-510 787 1827) is the mellowest biker bar you'll find, with a stuffed polar bear and 400 beers to keep you company.

Resources

Hospital

Oakland *Highland General, E 31st Street (1-510 437 4800/www.acmedctr.org/highland.htm).*

Internet

Alameda *Alameda Free Library, 2200A Central Avenue (1-510 747 7713/www.alamedafree.org).* **Open** 1-9pm Mon, Wed; 9.30am-5.30pm Tue, Thur-Sat; 1-5pm Sun.
Berkeley *Eudemonia, 2154 University Avenue (1-510 883 0814/www.eudemonia.net).* **Open** 11am-11pm Mon-Thur, Sat; 11am-2am Fri.
Oakland *Main Library, 125 14th Street (1-510 238 3134/www.oaklandlibrary.org).* **Open** 10am-5.30pm Mon, Tue; noon-8pm Wed, Thur; noon-5.30pm Fri; 10am-5.30pm Sat; 1-5pm Sun.

Police

Alameda *1555 Oak Street (1-510 337 8340).*
Berkeley *2100 Martin Luther King Jr Way (1-510 981 5900).*

Oakland *455 7th Street (1-510 238 3455).*
Richmond *401 27th Street (1-510 620 6655).*

Post office

Alameda *2201 Shoreline Drive (1-510 748 4156).*
Albany *1191 Solano Avenue (1-510 649 6718).*
Berkeley *2515½ Durant Avenue (1-510 649 6762); 1521 Shattuck Avenue (1-510 649 6763).*
Oakland *201 13th Street (1-510 251 3127); 490 Lake Park Avenue (1-510 251 3103).*
Richmond *1025 Nevin Avenue (1-510 232 3937).*

Tourist information

Berkeley *Berkeley CVB, 2015 Center Street (1-800 847 4823/1-510 549 7040/www.visitberkeley.com).* **Open** 9am-5pm Mon-Fri.
Emeryville *Emeryville Chamber of Commerce, 5858 Horton Street, Suite 130 (1-510 652 5223/www.emeryvillechamber.com).* **Open** 8am-noon, 1-5pm Mon-Fri.
Oakland *Oakland CVB, 463 11th Street (1-510 839 9000/www.oaklandcvb.com).* **Open** 8.30am-5pm Mon-Fri.

Getting there

By air

Tiny **Oakland International Airport** (1-510 563 3300, www.oaklandairport.com) is connected by Air-BART shuttle to the Coliseum/Oakland BART station, which runs every 10-15mins ($2). You can also take the Super Shuttle (1-800 258 3826, www.supershuttle.com) or a very expensive taxi/limousine ride.

By boat

The **Alameda/Oakland Ferry** (1-510 522 3300, www.eastbayferry.com) runs from the Ferry Building in San Francisco to Alameda and Oakland several times a day.

By bus

AC Transit (1-415 817 171, www.actransit.org) runs a number of buses between San Francisco's Transbay Terminal and East Bay destinations, although it's worth checking out County Connection (1-925 676 7500, www.cccta.org) for Contra Costa County. For longer journeys, get a bus from the **Greyhound** station (1-800 231 2222, www.greyhound.com), which is in a sketchy bit of north Oakland.

By car

Cross Bay Bridge on the I-80. Take the I-580 for **Oakland**, turning off on to the I-980 then the 12th Street exit for Jack London Square and Downtown. For **Berkeley**, come off I-80 on University Avenue.

By train

The **BART** (1-415 989 2278, www.bart.gov) is by far your most convenient way to explore East Bay: fast, efficient and with well placed stops in Oakland, Berkeley, Richmond and Fremont.
The Oakland **Amtrak** train station (1-800 872 7245, www.amtrak.com) is near Jack London Square, connected to San Francisco by a free shuttle bus from beside the Ferry Building.

South Bay

Half Moon Bay & the coast

Half Moon Bay is a small, easygoing seaside town with a rural feel. Quaint Main Street is a good browse, with bookshops, health-food stores, florists and antiques shops, but the town is most famous for its Hallowe'en pumpkins and Christmas trees. If you're on Highway 84, drop in on **San Gregorio General Store** (1-650 726 0565) eight miles south of Half Moon Bay. Serving the local community since 1889, it's a hybrid bar, music hall and gathering place.

Continuing south from Half Moon Bay, you'll find probably the best of the region's beaches: **San Gregorio State Beach**, a strip of white sand distinguished by sedimentary cliffs. At Half Moon Bay and Highway 1, the **Sea Horse & Friendly Acres Ranch** (1-650 726 9903, $30-$50) offers beach rides for all levels of experience. Another 15 miles down the coast are the historic buildings and rolling farmland of quaint **Pescadero**, with locals still tending their artichoke fields and strawberry patches. Then there's **Mavericks**: right in the middle of Half Moon Bay and about half a mile offshore, it's one of the 'gnarliest' big-wave surf spots in the world (*see p44*).

Where to eat & drink

In Half Moon Bay, cosy **Pasta Moon** (315 Main Street, 1-650 726 5125, $$) serves elegant dishes of own-made pasta. Alternatively, there's the deli at **San Benito House** (356 Main Street, 1-650 726 3425, closed dinner, $), a gleaming old-fashioned saloon with brass chandeliers. On Main Street, old-school **Main St Grill** (No.435, 1-650 726 5300, closed dinner, $) and the bistro fare at **Rogue Chefs Culinary Company & Market** (No.730, 1-650 712 2000, closed Mon & Sun, $$$) are both excellent. **Half Moon Bay Brewing Company** (390 Capistrano Avenue, Princeton-by-the-Sea, 1-650 728 2739, $$) boasts views of ocean and harbour, plus excellent burgers and own-brewed ale. Enjoy a beer and a bowl of artichoke soup at historic **Duarte's Tavern** (202 Stage Road, 1-650 879 0464, $$), Pescadero's most celebrated saloon.

Where to stay

There's no shortage of places to stay in and around Half Moon Bay. The grandest is the 261-room **Ritz-Carlton** (1 Miramontes Point Road, 1-800 241 3333, 1-650 712 7000, www.ritz carlton.com, $295-$875), situated on a bluff

Prime vintage

If you're on your way from Berkeley up the I-80 to the Napa Valley, you won't immediately twig any reason for stopping in nondescript Rodeo (*see p271*). But there definitely is one: **Vintage Silhouettes** (190 Parker Avenue, 1-510 245 2443, www.vintagesilhouettes.com, closed Mon), Janene and Art Fawcett's extraordinary vintage clothes store. We're not talking overpriced, sweat-stained '70s disasters here, just sartorial perfection from the 1850s through to the 1960s. If you found big-budget weepie *Titanic* at all bearable, thank Vintage Silhouettes: it supplied the costumes. In fact, the firm has provided clothes for more than 100 films, starting with *The Age of Innocence* and running up to *Seabiscuit*.

Drop in and ask to see the secret front room: you'll be confronted by hundreds of authentic Victorian frocks, kept in almost perfect condition and lined up, rack after rack. Or visit the bank vault, where hundreds of vintage men's suits are just hanging out. You might be able to introduce yourself to a pair of size 11 Florsheim Alligator Two-Tones or some genuine '50s blue suede shoes, or check out cufflinks in the shape of sunglasses. And if you really behave yourself, Art may let you go upstairs to his custom hat-making workshop...

overlooking the rugged coastline. More affordable are the 12 rooms at **San Benito House** (*see above*; $80-$176): nine are en suite, but some are rather small. For more, check the Chamber of Commerce's website (*see p277*).

About 25 miles south of Half Moon Bay, **Costanoa Coastal Lodge & Camp** (2001 Rossi Road, 1-877 262 7848, 1-650 879 1100, www.costanoa.com) is more rustic resort than campground: there are individual wooden cabins ($115-$175), a 40-room lodge ($155-$235) and canvas cabins ($65-$130), but you can also pitch a tent for a small fee.

Silicon Valley

Silicon Valley runs south-east from the base of San Francisco Bay. Routinely dismissed as mere sprawl, it actually offers fine strolling in the pretty downtowns of upscale **Los Altos**, **Los Gatos** and **Saratoga**. More substantial pleasures are found in **Palo Alto**, the site of

Central California

Stanford University. Here the 20 bronzes that comprise the on-campus **Rodin Sculpture Garden**, associated with the Cantor Arts Center (328 Lomita Drive, 1-650 723 4177, tours 11.30am Sat, 3pm Sun), make a neat diversion.

Despite all the concrete, **San Jose** is the most appealing Silicon Valley town for visitors. Attractions include the interactive **Children's Discovery Museum** (180 Woz Way, 1-408 298 5437, www.cdm.org, closed Mon, $7) and nearby **Monopoly in the Park** (Guadalupe River Park, West Fernando Street, 1-408 995 6487, www.monopolyinthepark.com). The latter, a 930-square-foot (86-square metre) version boardgame, is one of San Jose's newest attractions, and the closest ordinary people get to buying property in Silicon Valley; you'll have to reserve a game in advance. The **San Jose Museum of Art** (110 S Market Street, 1-408 271 6840, http://sjmusart.org, closed Mon) has a collection of nearly 1,400 pieces, most from the latter 20th century. There's good shopping, too, with S Bascom Avenue boasting **Streetlight Records** (No.980, 1-888 330 7776) and, for pop-culture collectibles, **Time Tunnel Toys** (No.532, 1-408 298 1709, closed Mon & Sun).

Rosicrucian Egyptian Museum & Planetarium

1342 Naglee Avenue, at Park Avenue (1-408 947 3636/www.egyptianmuseum.org). **Open** 10am-5pm Tue-Fri; 11am-6pm Sat, Sun. *Planetarium shows* 2pm Tue-Fri; 2pm, 3.30pm Sat, Sun. **Admission** $9, $5-$7 discounts. **Credit** AmEx, MC, V.

Located in Rosicrucian Park, this museum has the biggest Egyptian collection on the West Coast. There are six real mummies, a collection of more than 4,000 ancient artefacts and full-scale replica tombs. The planetarium reopened in March 2004: its free 35-minute show explores 'The Mithraic Mysteries', connecting the Roman cult to modern astronomy.

Winchester Mystery House

525 South Winchester Boulevard (1-408 247 2101/www.winchestermysteryhouse.com). **Open** Oct-May 9am-5pm daily. June-Sept 9am-7pm daily. **Admission** free. *Tours* $16.95-$24.95; $13.95-$21.95 discounts. **Credit** Disc, MC, V.

Haunted by the ghosts of those killed by the namesake rifle, widow-heiress Sarah Winchester took 38 years to build this 160-room mansion to placate the malevolent spirits. Flashlight tours on Friday the 13th or Hallowe'en maximise the creepiness, but at any time the oddity of the place (a staircase heads into a bare ceiling, a window is set in the floor) is impressive. Still, the on-site museum celebrating the gun might be seen, given the widow's fears, to be a little insensitive.

Where to eat, drink & stay

Given the concentration of expense accounts, it's no surprise to find quality restaurants across Silicon Valley. Palo Alto offers new American cuisine at **Zibibbo** (430 Kipling Street, 1-650 328 6722, $$$$) and a **Spago** (265 Lytton Avenue, 1-650 833 1000, closed Sun & lunch Sat, $$$$); in San Jose, try venerable **AP Stumps** (163 W Santa Clara Street, 1-408 292 9928, $$$$) or French-style **La Foret** (21747 Bertram Road, 1-408 997 3458, closed Mon & lunch Tue-Sun, $$$$$).

At the other end of the eating scale, San Jose's **Falafel Drive In** (2301 Stevens Creek Boulevard, 1-408 294 7886, $) has the kind of enticing mid-century spacey flair outside that always marks the work of maestros within, while the family diner **Happy Hound** (15899 Los Gatos Boulevard, 1-408 358 2444, $) in Los Gatos defies you to master two pounds of fries (that's nearly a kilo). At San Jose's 4th Street Bowl, **The Lounge** (1441 N 4th Street, 1-408 453 5555) is a one-stop shop for boozy bowlers, and nothing says 'happy hour' like free hot dogs and meat loaf at the **South Side Café** (7028 Santa Teresa Boulevard, 1-408 226 5424). The small **Blank Club** (44 S Almaden Avenue, 1-408 292 5265) showcases punk and hard rock in a sparse black interior.

If want to stay, downtown San Jose has a **Ramada Inn** (455 S 2nd Street, 1-888 298 2054, 1-408 298 3500, www.ramada.com, $105-$147) and the classy **Hotel De Anza** (233 W Santa Clara Street, 1-800 843 3700, 1-408 286 1000, www.hotel deanza.com, $129-$179), in whose Hedley Club Lounge you can sit fireside and take in piano jazz.

San José

Making waves in **Santa Cruz**.

Santa Cruz

Established as a mission at the end of the 18th century, **Santa Cruz** is now a beach town well known for being easygoing and politically progressive. The **University of California at Santa Cruz** takes the lead, with its clothing-optional campus and refusal (until a few years back, at least) to give its students letter grades. Drop in to the robustly independent **Bookshop Santa Cruz** (1520 Pacific Avenue, 1-831 423 0900) to tune in to the town's fiercely protective attitude towards its reputation for wackiness: owner (and ex-Santa Cruz mayor) Neil Coonerty has been waging a war on local mediocrity with 'Keep Santa Cruz Weird' merchandise.

All that remains of Misión la Exaltación de la Santa Cruz is the Neary-Rodriguez Adobe in **Santa Cruz Mission State Historic Park**; commonly known as **Mission Adobe** (1-831 425 5849, closed Mon-Wed in winter, $1-$2), it once housed the mission's Native American population. Down the street is **Mission Plaza** (1-831 426 5686, closed Mon), a complete 1930s replica. The **Santa Cruz Museum of Natural History** (1305 East Cliff Drive, 1-831 420 6115, www.santacruzmuseums.org, closed Mon, $1.50-$2.50) contains info about the Ohlone people who once populated the area. The culturally inclined can visit the **Santa Cruz Museum of Art & History** (*see p276*), while pop-culture fans will be unable to resist the **Mystery Spot** (465 Mystery Spot Road, 1-831 423 8897, $5), a few miles north of the city in the woods off Highway 17. It's a 150-foot (46-metre) patch of earth that has been confounding the laws of physics and gravity since its discovery in 1939. Kitsch nonsense.

Bang on the beach, the **Santa Cruz Beach Boardwalk** (400 Beach Street, 1-831 423 5590, closed Mon-Fri Sept-May) is an amusement park that hails back to the city's 19th-century heyday and contains a vintage carousel and classic wooden rollercoaster. Admission is $25.95; tickets for the rides are an additional 64¢, with each ride requiring between three and six tickets. The Boardwalk's **Cocoanut Grove Ballroom** (1-831 423 2053) is another remnant, with live music for weekends and holidays bringing it back to life. Continuing the beach theme, the lighthouse contains the engaging **Surfing Museum** (West Cliff Drive, 1-831 420 6289, www.santacruzsurfingmuseum.org, closed Tue in summer, Tue & Wed in winter), while right outside the lighthouse is **Steamer Lane**, one of the best surfing spots in the state. (For more on surfing, *see p43*.) The presence of students makes for a lively arts scene, including gigs at the non-profit **Kuumbwa Jazz Center** (320 Cedar Street, 1-831 427 2227).

Fans of towering redwoods should head north into the Santa Cruz Mountains to **Big Basin Redwoods State Park** (21600 Big Basin Way, Boulder Creek, 1-831 338 8860, www.bigbasin.org) or **Henry Cowell Redwoods State Park** (101 North Big Trees Park Road, Felton, 1-831 335 4598), which has a tree you can drive through. Also to the north, a mile past Western Drive on Highway 1, you'll find the 4,500 acres of former dairy farm **Wilder Ranch State Park** (1-831 423 9703). Centred on a quaint compound of historic Victorian houses and gardens, the park also has 34 miles of trails. Just south of Santa Cruz, you can see the ruins of a Chinese labour camp, as well as the epicentre of the Loma Prieta earthquake, in the **Forest of Nisene Marks** (Aptos Creek Road, Aptos, 1-831 763 7063).

Some 50 wineries are scattered across the area, most open to the public but free of the crowds that put some off Wine Country (*see pp346-362*). The best of the Santa Cruz-based wineries are **Bonny Doon** (10 Pine Flat Road, 1-831 425 3625) and award-winning **Storrs Winery** (303 Potrero Street, 1-831 458 5030).

Santa Cruz Museum of Art & History (MAH)

McPherson Center, 705 Front Street, at Cooper Street (1-831 429 1964/www.santacruzmah.org). **Open** 11am-5pm Tue-Sun. **Admission** $5; $3 students, seniors; $2 12-17s; free under-12s. Free 1st Fri of mth. **Credit** MC, V.

This fair art museum features rotating exhibitions, as well as a permanent display of early Santa Cruz artefacts. There's also a historical library. The museum also offers tours of the Evergreen Cemetery, one of the region's first Protestant burial grounds.

Where to eat

High above Santa Cruz Yacht Harbor, the **Crow's Nest** (2218 East Cliff Drive, 1-831 476 4560, $$) offers magnificent views and great seafood. Downtown has a world of options: hip **Mobo Sushi** (105 S River Street, 1-831 425 1700, $$$); the county's premier Mexican **El Palomar** (1336 Pacific Avenue, 1-831 425 7575, $$$); inviting **Ristorante Italiano** (555 Soquel Avenue, 1-831 458 2321, $$$); and the excellent **Thai House** (353 Soquel Avenue, 1-831 458 3546, $$). On the Westside, the Szechuan/California cuisine at **O'mei** (2316 Mission Street, 1-831 425 8458, closed lunch Sat & Sun, $$$) is a must-try, while **Riva Fish House** (500 Municipal Wharf, 1-831 429 1223, $$) combines great seafood and excellent sea views.

The Eastside has more laid-back options: **Pink Godzilla** (830 41st Avenue, 1-831 464 2586, closed Mon, $$) puts you and your sushi but a chopstick's distance from your neighbour; there's fabulous wood-fired pizza at **Engfer Pizza Works** (537 Seabright Avenue, 1-831 429 1856, closed Mon, $), as well as a ping pong table and an exotic array of old-time, little-known sodas; and quirky local institution the **Crepe Place** (1134 Soquel Avenue, 1-831 429 6994, $$) makes a snazzy after-hours joint.

You're also spoilt for cheap choices. **Saturn Café** (145 Laurel Street, 1-831 429 8505, $$) is the kind of vegetarian meat-eaters like, and serves an outlandishly huge chocolate dessert. **Taqueria Vallarta** (1101A Pacific Avenue, 1-831 471 2655; 608 Soquel Avenue, 1-831 457 8226; 893 41st Avenue, 1-831 464 7022; $) and the **Bagelry** (320 Cedar Street, 1-831 429 8049, $)

are quick and terrific. But you'll have to wait for the best breakfast in town: the sidewalk line at **Zachary's** (819 Pacific Avenue, 1-831 427 0646, closed dinner, Mon, $) is fun, as regulars anxiously await their weekly dose of Mike's Mess (scrambled egg plus) or corned-beef hash.

Where to drink

For blues, **Moe's Alley** (1535 Commercial Way, 1-831 479 1854) is terrific; divey hole-in-the-wall **529** (529 Seabright Avenue, 1-831 426 5898) isn't, but cheap drinks and pool on locals' night (Tuesday) make it popular. Pacific Avenue boasts gay- and lesbian-friendly **Blue Lagoon** (No.923, 1-831 423 7117), which is the place for dancing; **Club Dakota** (No.1209, 1-831 454 9030), another stylish, queer-friendly bar/dance club; the **Asti Cafe** (No.715, 1-831 423 7337); and the **Catalyst** (No.1011, 1-831 423 1336), the city's main music venue. Legendary for retaining Neil Young and Crazy Horse as its house band, the Catalyst is a cavernous venue, but bands often play for free in the atrium. On Cedar Street, the smallish **Red Room** (No.1003, 1-831 426 2994) gets packed at weekends.

Being a university town means throngs of young minds in need of caffeine and somewhere to crack a laptop. Based in a converted Victorian, **Cafe Pergolesi** (418 Cedar Street, 1-831 426 1775) is a hangout for local eccentrics, students and pierced rockers, while **Lulu Carpenters** (1545 Pacific Avenue, 1-831 429 9804) is distinguished by its stylish brick

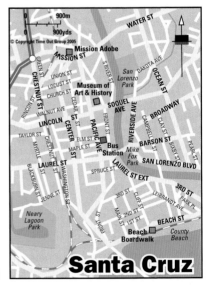

Santa Cruz

Even jogging seems fun with scenery like this.

interior, a perfect setting for jazz, folk and blues. Converted warehouse **120 Union** (120 Union Street, 1-831 459 9876) puts on live music and, on Mondays, an open mic night.

Where to stay

Most hotels in Santa Cruz are motels, but there are some charming spots. The **Babbling Brook Inn** (1025 Laurel Street, 1-800 866 1131, 1-831 427 2437, www.babblingbrookinn.com, $179-$235) is surrounded by an acre of gardens with redwoods and an appropriately garrulous watercourse. Overlooking the sea, the **Pleasure Point Inn** (2-3665 East Cliff Drive, 1-877 557 2567, 1-831 469 6161, www.pleasurepointinn. com, $198-$265) is modern, upscale and very well appointed, with four bedrooms and an eight-person rooftop jacuzzi. The **Darling House** (314 West Cliff Drive, 1-831 458 1958, www.darlinghouse.com, $85-$260) is a block from the ocean. The beautifully restored Gothic Victorian **Compassion Flower Inn** (216 Laurel Street, 1-831 466 0420, www.compassion flowerinn.com, $115-$175) created quite a stir by becoming a medical-marijuana-friendly B&B. The decor uses hemp products and users get a ten per cent discount – with a doctor's note.

Resources

Hospital
San Jose *Regional Medical Center, 225 N Jackson Avenue (1-408 259 5000/www.regionalmedical sanjose.com).*

Internet
San Jose *Dr Martin Luther King Jr Library, 150 E San Fernando Street (1-408 808 2000/ www.sjlibrary.org).* **Open** 8am-10pm Mon-Thur; 8am-6pm Fri; 9am-6pm Sat; 1-7pm Sun.
Santa Cruz *Westside Coffee Company, 849 Almar Avenue (1-831 427 1300).* **Open** 5.45am-6pm daily.

Police
Half Moon Bay *537 Kelly Avenue (1-650 726 8288).*
Palo Alto *275 Forest Avenue (1-650 329 2406).*
San Jose *201 W Mission Street (1-408 277 5339).*
Santa Cruz *155 Center Street (1-831 420 5800).*

Post office
Half Moon Bay *500 Stone Pine Road (1-650 726 4015).*
Palo Alto *2085 E Bayshore Road (1-650 321 1423).*
San Jose *1750 Lundy Avenue (1-408 437 6690).*
Santa Cruz *850 Front Street (1-831 426 0144).*

Tourist information
Half Moon Bay *Half Moon Bay Coastside Chamber of Commerce, 1st floor, 520 Kelly Avenue, Half Moon Bay (1-650 726 8380/www.hmbchamber.com).* **Open** 9am-5pm Mon-Fri.
San Jose *San Jose CVB, 408 Almaden Boulevard (1-408 295 9600/1-800 726 5673/www.sanjose.org).* **Open** 9am-5pm Mon-Fri.
Santa Cruz *Santa Cruz County CVB, 1211 Ocean Street, nr Washburn Avenue (1-831 425 1234/ 1-800 833 3494/www.scccvc.org/index.html).* **Open** 9am-5pm Mon-Fri; 10am-4pm Sat, Sun.

Getting there

By air
Tiny **San Jose Airport** (1-408 277 4759, www.sjc. org) is connected half hourly to CalTrain (1-510 817 1717, $5.50 one-way) by Santa Clara Transit bus 10.

By bus
Greyhound leaves San Francisco for Santa Cruz about four times a day.

By car
Half Moon Bay is 30 miles south of San Francisco on Highway 1, about a 45min drive. **Pescadero** is 18 miles further south, and signposted off Highway 1. San Jose is 50 miles south of San Francisco on US 101. **Santa Cruz** is 74 miles south of San Francisco on I-280 (take Highway 17 to I-85 to get to I-280).

By train
From San Francisco, either take a BART train to Daly City (15min journey), pick up SamTrans bus 110 to Linda Mar and transfer to bus 294 for **Half Moon Bay**, or take CalTrain to Hillsdale and then take bus 294. SamTrans bus 15 runs between Half Moon Bay and **Pescadero**. CalTrain (1-650 817 1717, $5.50 one-way) travels every 30min from San Francisco to **San Jose**, making several stops along the way, including **Palo Alto**; CalTrain also runs the Baby Bullet commuter train from SF to San Jose. Amtrak shuttle buses link San Jose and **Santa Cruz**.

The San Joaquin Valley

Feelin' hot, hot, hot...

The southern portion of California's Central Valley, stretching from south of Sacramento all the way to Bakersfield, is not on many tourists' maps. There's a good reason for this. To the west lies the grandeur of Yosemite, Sequoia and King's Canyon. To the east, eventually, is the justly heralded Central Coast. When faced with such glories on either side, the area simply can't compare or compete. It doesn't really try.

The main industry here is agriculture. The flat land and the climate help; in summer, it gets viciously hot under the unrelenting sun. But the boon for farmers is the water. Controversially, the San Joaquin River was diverted to feed the region, which also draws its water from smaller rivers leading from the Sierra Nevada. Ever since the influx of Okies, economic migrants who headed west in search of work during the Depression, the valley has been dominated by farming (encouraged by financial breaks offered to big corporations) and, while the large cities that dot the region are not without appeal for travellers, most carry only curiosity value.

Stockton & the Delta

It once thrived, but the port city of **Stockton** is now a desperately dreary place, bleaker even than its depiction by Leonard Gardner in his tough 1969 novel *Fat City*. Downtown is a forlorn place; the campus of the University of the Pacific is only briefly inspiring (notice the grand, Anglicised Robert E Burns Tower).

The drive into the **California Delta** along Route 4 will come as some surprise. Suburbia gives way not to unforgiving dustbowl, but to welcoming greenery. The Delta forms where the Sacramento and San Joaquin Rivers converge, and is kept in check by a network of canals and levees built in the 1920s and 1930s.

Few tourists bother with the Delta, which is both understandable (there's not a great deal to see or do here) and a pity (it's an interesting place in which to see or do nothing). Working north to south on Route 160, which follows the Sacramento River, you'll pass through the adjacent towns of **Locke** (*see p280* **Locked in**) and **Walnut Grove**, whose combined population is less than 800. Three miles south sits tiny **Ryde**, named by Englishman Judge Williams, one of the first to settle here, after his Isle of Wight home town. South is **Isleton**, Manhattan next to its dozing neighbours.

Where to eat, drink & stay

In Locke, try **Al the Wops** (*see p280* **Locked in**) for beer and a steak; down the road in Walnut Grove, **Giusti's** (1-916 776 1808, closed Mon, $$–$$$) dishes up Italian favourites. **Ernie's** in Isleton (1-916 777 6510, closed dinner Tue & Wed, $$) has garnered a reputation for its crawdads (aka crayfish). The town even stages a weekend-long event devoted to the little blighters: the Crawdad Festival, held over Father's Day weekend (mid June).

The best San Joaquin Valley

Things to do
Whatever you do, make time for the **Forestiere Underground Gardens** in Fresno (*see p283*).

Places to stay
The lovely, historic **Ryde Hotel** (*see p281*) wins the prizes here.

Places to eat
In Fresno, try the **609 Grill** or **Echo** in the Tower District (*see p283*); in Bakersfield, head to **TL Maxwell's** (*see p285*).

Nightlife
The area's most characterful bar is its most isolated: **Al the Wops** (*see p280* **Locked in**).

Culture
Any kind of music as long as it's country: **Buck Owens' Crystal Palace** and **Trout's**, both in Bakersfield (*see p284* **Buck stops here**) will keep you entertained in very different ways.

Sports & activities
Not much doing, but Modesto and Bakersfield both have minor-league baseball teams.

Locked in

Two identical roadside signs announce to drivers that they are in the town of **Locke**. One is at the north end, for the benefit of those going south on River Road; the other sits at Locke's southern tip, offering guidance to drivers heading in the opposite direction. The two signs are perhaps 200 yards apart. Never a big place, Locke is now barely a town at all. The seven or eight tightly packed wooden buildings that front on to River Road appear to be held up by nothing more than goodwill; one ill-timed sneeze would level the lot.

Locke dates back a century, to a time when exclusionary laws forbade local Chinese-American farmhands from owning land in California. Rather than set up stable homes for themselves, the workers were forced to rent land from their employers and live in cheap, hastily erected houses; whenever their landlord wanted to use the land for something else, the workers would simply have to pack

up and move on. One such settlement arose in 1915 on ten acres leased from local farmowner George Locke, who was kind enough to lend the town his name.

Most communities of this type, and there were once quite a few here, were gone within a decade. Not this one. For whatever reason, Locke not only survived but thrived, its population levelling out at around 500 by the time of the Depression. What's more, Locke's community remained largely Chinese for years, even after farming ceased to be a reliable source of employment. The town's Chinese school remained open until the late 1970s, with some parents sending their kids to it each day after they returned from receiving their English-language education in nearby Walnut Grove.

By then the town was shrinking. Now almost all of its Chinese residents have moved away and Locke grows smaller almost every year; depending on whom you ask, the population is somewhere between 50 and 70. A surprising number of tourists, including the occasional Chinese coach party, boost the takings at **Al the Wops** (1-916 776 1800), a thoroughly salty boozer that's been pouring beers and frying steaks for seven decades. One building houses a gallery dealing in local art; another, formerly a gambling house, is a small museum (1-916 776 1661). But that's it.

Locke is the only remaining settlement in the US built by Chinese-Americans for Chinese-Americans, and the sole rural Chinatown in the country. It is on the National Register of Historic Places. And yet there are no plaques in the town, no carefully mapped walking tour. For the most part, visitors are left to find their own stories amid the wreckage, communing with the spirits in a ghost town that's not quite dead.

But the real curio is the **Ryde Hotel** (1-888 717 7933, 1-916 776 1318, www.rydehotel.com, $85-$180). Built during Prohibition, the hotel and speakeasy was renovated in 1998 and is open year-round; the restaurant, though, only serves Sunday brunch. The other overnight option, outside of the various chain motels in Stockon, are the campsites at **Brannan Island State Recreation Area** (1-800 444 7275, $15).

Resources

Tourist information
Stockton *Stockton Chamber of Commerce, 445 W Weber Avenue (1-209 547 2770/www.visitstockton. org).* **Open** 9am-noon, 1-5pm Mon-Fri.

Modesto & around

The sign that greets visitors to **Modesto**, arching over the road at 9th and I Streets, reads 'Modesto: Water Wealth Contentment Health'. The faucets work, so they got one out of four, but signs of affluence are conspicuous by their absence in this blue-collar town, and smiles on the faces of weatherbeaten locals just as rare.

Modesto's claim to fame is its most famous son, a film director who based his first movie on his time growing up here. After *American Graffiti*, George Lucas went on to bigger things and has barely returned; Modesto's influence on the *Star Wars* series is hard to detect. Nor is the car-cruising culture he adored as a kid now part of the city: the practice was outlawed a decade ago after cruising became a little too tied up with bruising. Still, the city does have a statue of two lads and an old Chevy at **Lucas Plaza** (junction of McHenry Avenue and 17th Street).

Tidy Downtown Modesto doesn't reward the pedestrian. On K Street between 10th and 11th Streets is the **Modesto Flower Clock**, the most colourful timepiece in California. A walk away is the **McHenry Mansion** (906 15th Street, 1-209 577 5344, closed Sat), a Victorian property that's been redecorated to suit the period; close by is the **McHenry Museum** of local history (1402 I Street, 1-209 577 5366, closed Mon).

There's little to do nearby, though **Oakdale** has the sweet **Oakdale Museum** (212 West F Street, 1-209 847 9229, closed Sat & Sun), detailing local history. From here, it's not far to the Gold Country (*see pp295-313*), a drive that grows increasingly pretty along its 30-odd miles.

Where to eat, drink & stay

The clean-up of once-scruffy Downtown has added above-par eateries. The nicest is **Galletto** (1101 J Street, 1-209 523 4500, $$$–$$$$), where you can chow on Italian dishes (and ace Sunday brunch) in a former bank. **Tresetti's** (927 11th Street, 1-209 572 2990, $$$) dishes up solid mains and fine wines. Good bars are limited to a by-rote brewpub (**St Stan's**, 821 L Street, 1-209 524 2337). Nightlife, lively on weekends, centres on clubs such as the **Fat Cat** (930 11th Street, 1-209 524 1400), which offers DJs, comics and bands.

The Downtown-dominating **Doubletree Hotel** (1150 9th Street, 1-209 526 6000; *see p54*) is the smartest place to stop. Cheaper options include a **Holiday Inn Express** (4100 Salida Boulevard, 1-209 543 9000; *see p54*).

Resources

Hospital
Modesto *Memorial Medical Center, 1700 Coffee Road (1-209 526 4500).*

Internet
Modesto *Nexus, 1024 11th Street (1-209 523 6392).* **Open** noon-2am daily.

Police
Modesto *600 10th Street (1-209 572 9500).*

Post office
Modesto *715 Kearney Avenue (1-209 523 5094).*

Tourist information
Modesto *Modesto CVB, Suite C, 1150 9th Street (1-888 640 8467/1-209 526 5588/ww.visitmodesto. com).* **Open** 8am-5pm Mon-Fri.

Merced

There's a surprising amount to do in bleary-eyed **Merced**, certainly more than you'd expect from a town that modestly advertises itself only

Disc drive

CDs to soundtrack your journey around the Central Valley.

***Down Every Road* Merle Haggard**
Oildale native Haggard re-recorded his hits in the '90s: it's these renditions that fill most best-ofs that bear his name. Instead, get this four-disc retrospective, which has all the originals; disc two's the best.

***The Very Best of Buck Owens, Volume One* Buck Owens**
The definitive single-disc survey of the leading proponent of the Bakersfield Sound.

***California Country* Wynn Stewart**
Honky-tonk classics – 29 of 'em – by one of country music's greatest nearly men.

as the 'Gateway to Yosemite'. The town was named after El Rio de la Mercedes (the River of Mercy), the title given to a nearby river by thirsty Spanish explorers two centuries ago, and built up when the railroad arrived in the 1870s. A little of this history is still standing in endearing Downtown, which edges out from the junction of 21st and N Streets; here you'll find the 130-year-old former courthouse, converted into the **Merced Courthouse Museum** (1-209 723 2401, www.mercedmuseum.org, closed Mon & Tue) and host to history displays. The area's agricultural past is brought into focus at the **Merced Agricultural Museum** (4498 E Highway 140, 1-209 383 1912, closed Mon), but most kids – and a fair few adults – prefer the **Castle Air Museum** (1-209 723 2178, $6-$8), seven miles north in Atwater. It's home to a variety of classic aircraft and the **Challenger Learning Center**, which forgoes planes in favour of another kind of flight: space travel.

Where to eat, drink & stay

At least until a huge UCLA campus opens here in late 2005, Merced is lacking in decent places to eat and drink. The trad **Branding Iron** (640 W 16th Street, 1-209 722 1822, $$$) serves steak dinners; the **Bar-B-Q Pit** (1720 G Street, 1-209 383 2366, $) has cheaper meats. For hotels, read sub-$80-a-night motels: two **Best Westerns** and a **Holiday Inn**, among others; see p54.

Resources

Tourist information

Merced *Merced CVB, 710 W 16th Street (1-209 384 7092).* **Open** 8.30am-5pm Mon-Fri.

Fresno

Poor **Fresno** has spent decades trying to live down Johnny Carson's crack about it being 'the gateway to Bakersfield'. In truth, it's not the unutterably ghastly industrial shitpit of popular legend. Not *quite*. But it's still a town where the leaving is more enjoyable than the arriving. Opportunities offered by the town's agriculture industries keep 450,000 people here, farming cattle, cotton and especially fruit, but the casual visitor finds less to detain them.

Certainly, the town's appearance does it few favours. The polite way of looking at Fresno is that it's an Everyman town; the flip side is that could be Anytown, USA. **Downtown**, centred around the County Courthouse at the junction of Tulare and Van Ness Avenues, is a forgettable collection of office blocks, scruffy shops and the **Fresno Metropolitan Museum** (*see p283*).

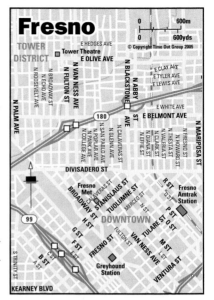

Worse is to come when you leave Downtown to head north along the town's main commercial thoroughfare. **Blackstone Avenue** is a microcosm of modern American ugliness, a seemingly endless trail of strip-mall anonymity lining an arrow-straight road to nowhere. Aside from the occasional dry-cleaner and adult video store, almost every shop, eaterie and motel is either part of a chain or looks like it should be.

Still, there are charms here. A couple of century-old houses offer a window on to a time when this was a more handsome city. The 1889 **Meux Home Museum** (1007 R Street, 1-559 233 8007, closed Mon-Thur, $3-$5) is the nicer of the two, though the **Kearney Mansion** (7160 W Kearney Boulevard, Kearney Park, 1-559 441 0862, closed Mon-Thur, $2-$4) is also of interest. This grand structure was not a family home at all: amazingly, Theo Kearney built it in 1903 for his caretaker, then dropped dead before his own presumably palatial dwellings were completed.

Other diversions are smaller. Latino culture is celebrated with exhibits and concerts at **Arte Américas** (1630 Van Ness Avenue, 1-559 266 2623, www.arteamericas.org). The temporary shows at the **Fresno Art Museum** (2233 N 1st Street, 1-559 441 4221, closed Thur, $2-$4) may be worth a look, as is its sculpture garden; the exhibits at the **American Historical Society of Germans from Russia** (3233 N West Avenue, 1-559 229 8287, closed Sat afternoon & Sun) are of more marginal interest.

Fresno's **Tower Theatre**.

West of Blackstone Avenue sits the **Tower District**, a small area where the independent shops, restaurants and bars strike a nice contrast to the homogeneity nearby. Fresno's nightlife is concentrated around here, the landmark **Tower Theatre** providing the axis around which the neighbourhood revolves.

Forestiere Underground Gardens
5021 W Shaw Avenue (1-559 271 0734/www. undergroundgardens.com). **Open** noon-2pm Sat, Sun. **Admission** $6-$9. **No credit cards**.
The extraordinary Forestiere Underground Gardens are the work of one man. An immigrant Sicilian who moved to California in the early 20th century, Baldasare Forestiere was immediately overwhelmed by the heat. His solution? This extravagant network of underground rooms, tunnels and (of course) gardens, built entirely by Forestiere over 40 years, using nothing but hand tools. Unmissable.

Fresno Metropolitan Museum
1515 Van Ness Avenue (1-559 441 1444/www. fresnomet.org). **Open** 11am-5pm Tue, Wed, Fri-Sun; 11am-8pm Thur. **Admission** $7; $3-$4 discounts. **Credit** AmEx, MC, V.
Fresno would like author William Saroyan to do for their town what John Steinbeck has done for Salinas (*see p218*). Sadly, while Salinas has built an entire industry around its most famous son, Saroyan gets just an annual festival (May), a short walking tour and a series of exhibits in this decent museum. Other galleries hold paintings, photographs and a delightful collection of jigsaws.

Where to eat, drink & stay

There are decent restaurants around the city, but the Tower District has the best options. The **609 Grill** (609 E Olive Avenue, 1-559 442 5883, closed Mon & Sun, $$$-$$$$), which serves a variety of American classics, and the adjacent **Echo** (1-559 442 3246, dinner only, closed Mon & Sun, $$$$) are fine dinner options, though the set menus at the smart **Daily Planet** (1211 N Wishon Avenue, 1-559 266 4259, $$$) offer tempting value. The polite **Sequoia Brewery** (777 E Olive Avenue, 1-559 264 5521, $) has bar food to go with its own-brewed beers. Other drinking options are spotty: the hard-to-locate **Avalon** (1064 N Fulton Street, 1-559 495 0852) tries to be both pool hall and nightclub and doesn't full succeed at either, but woody **Livingstone's Pub** (831 E Fern Avenue, 1-559 485 5198) is a cosy spot to hole up for the night.

Lodgings are uninspiring. The smartest place is the **Radisson** (2233 Ventura Street, 1-559 268 1000, www.radisson.com, $120-$184), located Downtown. Many motels lie on Blackstone Avenue, among them the **Best Western** (No.3110, 1-800 722 8878, 1-559 226 2110, $49-$69; *see p54*) and a **Days Inn** (No.4061, 1-800 441 3297, 1-559 222 5641, $44-$65; *see p54*).

Resources

Hospital
Fresno *Community Medical Center, 2823 Fresno Street (1-559 459 6000/www.communitymedical.org).*

Internet
Fresno *Fresno County Public Library, 2420 Mariposa Avenue (1-559 488 3195/www.fresno library.org).* **Open** 9am-9pm Mon-Thur; 9am-6pm Fri, Sat; 1-6pm Sun.

Police
Fresno *2323 Mariposa Mall (1-559 621 2000).*

Post office
Fresno *1900 E Street (1-559 497 7566).*

Tourist information
Fresno *Fresno CVB, Water Tower, 2430 Fresno Street (1-559 237 0988/www.fresnocvb.org).* **Open** *June-Aug* 9am-5pm Mon-Fri; 10am-3pm Sat. *Sept-May* 10am-4pm Mon-Fri; 11am-3pm Sat.

South from Fresno

If you're in a hurry to leave Fresno (and, not to labour a point, most people are), head south on US 99. However, if you've time, there's plenty to see on the smaller roads east of town, especially during spring via US 180. Leaflets available from the CVB (*see above*) detail the **Fresno County Blossom Trail** (late Feb-late Mar)

Central California

and the related **Fresno County Fruit Trail**, a loose amalgamation of roads that run through endless parades of orchards. Peaches, plums, cherries and nectarines sit on trees by the roadside, ripe for plucking. However, such theft isn't looked upon kindly; wait until you run into one of the many stalls that dot the area.

Aside from being a pleasant drive, the Fruit Trail takes you through or near a number of small, dusty towns. **Sanger** is home to the **Sanger Depot Museum** (1770 7th Street, 1-559 875 4720, closed Mon-Thur & Sun, 25¢-$1), which outlines the beginnings of this little town with a replica of Main Street as was. Sweet **Reedley** is a small-town archetype. The land around **Selma** yields around 90 per cent of all the state's raisins, a fact celebrated at the annual Raisin Festival in late April/early May.

Close by is a cutesy cousin to Solvang on the Central Coast. While Solvang plays up its Danish ancestry, **Kingsburg** makes its Swedish heritage the USP: the town was settled by Swedes in the 1880s. While Kingsburg is less overwhelmingly Scandinavian than Solvang, it's still exaggerated: buildings on Draper Street have been tweely remodelled in a bid to increase the town's tourist appeal. Even if you don't stop, make a point of looking out of your car window as you go past on US 99: that huge, quaintly decorated coffee pot towering over everything is actually the town's 122-foot-tall water tower.

Continuing south, things get less interesting. It's as if the oppressive heat has sent the area to sleep. Still, **Visalia** is an attractive city, especially once you get to its mellow, handsome Downtown (junction of Court and Main Streets).

Buck stops here

He wasn't the first country musician to break out of Bakersfield. There's an argument, often propounded by fans of Oildale native Merle Haggard, that he wasn't even the biggest. But no musician defines the Bakersfield Sound like **Buck Owens**, and not just because, in the four decades since his first hit, he's been nothing less than an ambassador for the city.

He wasn't, though, born here. Owens' parents were sharecroppers in Texas when they gave birth to a son, Alvis Edgar, in 1929. However, as John Steinbeck chronicled in *The Grapes of Wrath*, times were tough in the Dust Bowl during the Depression. When the work dried up, the Owens family joined the mass migration west.

By 1951, when Buck arrived in Bakersfield via an Arizonan childhood, the town had developed a thriving country scene; Owens found work playing guitar for Bill Woods and Tommy Collins, two of the circuit's leading lights. Before long, he was cutting his own records, initially without success. But in 1959, now resident in Washington, Owens hit the country charts with 'Under Your Spell Again', and moved back to Bakersfield with high hopes of building a career.

They were fulfilled, and how. While Collins, Fern Husky and Wynn Stewart, locals all, enjoyed only fleeting success, Owens and his band – called, inevitably, the Buckaroos – stacked up hit after hit during the '60s. That they managed it without the help of all-powerful Nashville is down to the fact that the band's sound was very different to the string-soaked sentimentality at that time emerging

from Music Row. Owens' music was pure, straightforward honky-tonk, born of the Dust Bowl he left behind. Well-drilled, certainly, and shrewdly tailor-made for AM radio thanks to the trebly twang of Owens' trademark Telecaster. But this was honky-tonk music all the same.

Though he continued to make hit records in the 1970s, when he found even greater fame hosting country variety show *Hee Haw*, it's '60s hits such as 'Act Naturally' (covered by the Beatles, with Ringo on vocals) and 'I've Got a Tiger by the Tail' that really stand as his legacy – and that of the Bakersfield Sound. It's a legacy that found new life in the late 1980s and 1990s, as acts such as Dwight Yoakam and Dale Watson aped his sound to a greater or lesser degree.

It's also a legacy that can be relived at **Buck Owens' Crystal Palace** (2800 Buck Owens Boulevard, 1-661 328 7560, www.buckowens.com), the singer's cheesy monument to himself. Illness has got the better of Owens lately, and his turns at the club (scheduled for Fridays and Saturdays) have become less frequent; call ahead to check. If you've time, there's also a nice museum here (closed Sun). But for somewhere a little more authentic, only **Trout's** in Oildale (805 N Chester Avenue, 1-661 399 6700) will do. This gruff little club has been staging country acts for over 55 years; local legend Red Simpson usually plays on Mondays. The crowd of no-nonsense roughnecks who call the place their local are friendlier than they might first appear.

Where to eat, drink & stay

In Reedley, stop at **Intermezzo** for a coffee; in Kingsburg, try some Swedish scran at **Diane's** (1332 Draper Street, 1-559 897 7460, closed Sun, $). Visalia is home to the venerable, old-school **Vintage Press** (216 N Willis Avenue, 1-559 733 3033, $$$$), but the best place to eat in Visalia is the cheapest: **Mearle's Drive-In** (604 S Mooney Boulevard, 1-559 734 4447, $), which has been dishing up fine burgers and spectacular milkshakes for over 60 years.

Need somewhere to stay? Downtown Visalia boasts a **Radisson** (300 S Court Street, 1-559 636 1111, $91-$179; *see p54*); there's also a **Best Western** (623 W Main Street, 1-877 500 4771, 1-559 732 4561, $83-$85, *see p54*).

Bakersfield & around

The reputation of industrial **Bakersfield** rests on the shoulders of one man: for more on Buck Owens, *see p284* **Buck stops here**. Those brought out in a rash by country music don't usually find much worth writing on a postcard home, but you may be momentarily surprised. Downtown is a good-looking place, dotted with characterful old buildings. However, it's also very small; once you leave the centre, Bakersfield reveals itself to be just as unbecoming as its bleak reputation suggests.

A few museums enliven proceedings, none more so than the **California Living Museum** (10500 Alfred Harrell Highway, 1-661 872 2256, closed Mon, $2.75-$4), a little combination zoo-botanical garden. Highlights at the **Buena Vista Museum of Natural History** (2018 Chester Avenue, 1-661 324 6350, closed Mon-Wed & Sun, $1.50-$3) include a collection of artefacts related to the Native American Yokut tribe who settled in the area 10,000 years ago. And try to make time for the **Kern County Museum** (3801 Chester Avenue, 1-661 852 5000, $5-$8), its highlight a collection of old relocated buildings from the town's past.

The fact that the town a few miles north of Bakersfield goes by the name of **Oildale** is redolent both of the oil industry's pre-eminence around these parts and the area's absurdly plain-speaking attitude. The crappy little town of **Taft**, south-west of Bakersfield, has the **West Kern Oil Museum** (1168 Wood Street, 1-661 765 6664, closed Mon).

Where to eat, drink & stay

Fine dining begins and ends at **TL Maxwell's** (1421 17th Place, 1-661 323 6889, closed Mon & Sun, $$$-$$$$), which offers a cultured take on American cuisine in a clubbable atmosphere.

Time for tea in **Kingsburg**. *See p284.*

Nearby, **Gumbeaux's** (1804 Chester Avenue, 1-661 325 5542, $$$) dishes up Cajun cuisine that's better than the overexuberant decor; for lunch, sample the diner fare at relaxed **24th Street Café** (1415 24th Street, 1-661 323 8801, closed dinner, $). The town is noted for its Basque restaurants, where you can fill up on some of the sturdiest food in California: **Chalet Basque** (200 Oak Street, 1-661 327 2915, closed Mon & Sun, $$-$$$) is a favourite.

Bakersfield boasts no above-average hotels, but all the chains have franchises (most off US 99). The **Best Western Crystal Palace** (2620 Buck Owens Boulevard, 1-800 424 4900, 1-661 327 9651, $58-$75; *see p54*) is adjacent to Buck Owens' Crystal Palace and thus charges more than its rivals, which include a **Courtyard by Marriott**, two **Holiday Inn**s and no fewer than four **Motel 6**s (for all, *see p54*); all have rooms for under $100 a night.

Resources

Hospital
Bakersfield *Bakersfield Memorial Hospital, 420 34th Street (1-661 327 1792).*

Police
Bakersfield *1601 Truxtun Avenue (1-661 327 7111).*

Post office
Bakersfield *1730 18th Street (1-661 861 4383).*

Tourist information & internet
Bakersfield *Bakersfield CVB, 515 Truxtun Avenue (1-661 325 5051/www.bakersfieldcvb.org).* **Open** 8.30am-5pm Mon-Fri.

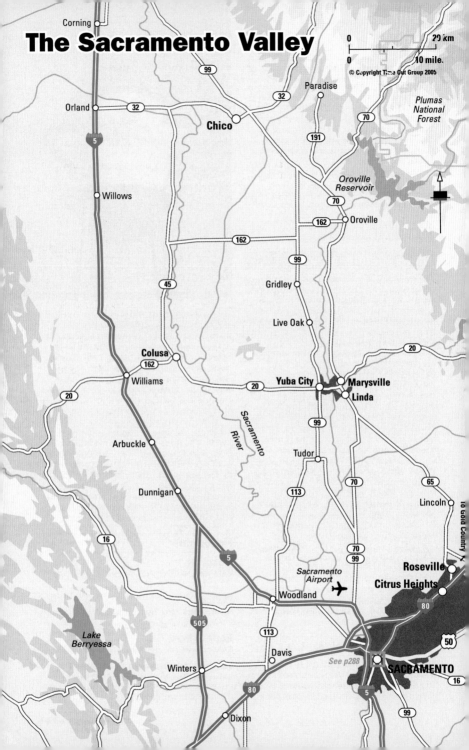

The Sacramento Valley

Where culture meets agriculture for a cold beer.

The northern part of the Central Valley differs from the San Joaquin Valley to the south in attitude, but not enormously in appearance. The 150-odd miles north of the city of Sacramento, following the Sacramento River, is flat, plain and given over, for the most part, to agriculture. It doesn't, to be blunt, look very appealing.

But while the San Joaquin Valley is strictly blue collar, rough around the edges and proud of it, the main towns of the Sacramento Valley are more cultured. State capital **Sacramento** is still dominated by its resident politicos, but not to the same degree as it was a few years ago; **Red Bluff** is a sleepy but attractive little place; and in **Davis** and **Chico**, the area boasts two highly attractive college towns.

Sacramento

The agricultural plains of the Central Valley, where temperatures often top 100ºF (38ºC) and fresh manure is a common aroma, seems an improbable place for the capital of the most populous and wealthy of the United States. Yet the city of **Sacramento** is suited to its role. It's the nexus of the two Californias: the city may have worn the cow-town label for

decades, but evidence of cultural maturation is everywhere, from eclectic restaurants to the influx of Bay Area residents seeking a less hectic way of life. It has some of the vitality of California's 'big three' cities, but on a smaller scale: cosmopolitan but quietly so, lively but not overwhelming. And yes, when the wind's blowing the right way, you might still catch a whiff of manure in the air.

Sightseeing

Old Sacramento

The proliferation of kitschy general stores and candy shops in Old Sacramento, which are located near where the American River meets the Sacramento River, belies its important and often rather odd history. The heart of commerce during the Gold Rush, this was the western terminus of the Pony Express and the transcontinental railroad. Gun battles and drunken brawls were commonplace in the raucous, sawdust-scattered saloons of the city, and disaster routinely struck: huge floods swallowed the city in 1850, 1861 and 1862, and massive fires levelled most of Old Sacramento in 1852 and 1854.

The best Sacramento Valley

Things to do
Old Sacramento (see p287) is more than a little hokey but still worth a look; however, Sacramento's most impressive sight is its **Capitol** building (see p289). Chico's **Bidwell Park** (see p293) is a real delight.

Places to stay
It might be slightly cheesy, but it's hard to deny the appeal of the 44 staterooms on board the **Delta King**, moored in Old Sacramento (see p288).

Places to eat
For variety and value, you can't beat the assortment of spots in Downtown **Davis** (see p291), though if you've money to spend, head to **Biba** in Sacramento (see p290).

Nightlife
If in doubt, head to Midtown **Sacramento** (see p290), and check the News & Review for details of what's on in town.

Culture
In just two years, Davis's new **Mondavi Center** (see p293) has established itself as one of the strongest performing arts venues in the state, while the university town of **Chico** (see p292) is a bustling mini-hotbed of culture.

Sports & activities
There's decent hiking to **Bidwell Park** in Chico (see p293), but the really outstanding sports are played by the **Sacramento Kings** basketball team (see p291).

The map labels:

Railroad Museum · Sacramento Amtrak Station · Old Sacramento SHP · Military Museum · Greyhound Bus Station · Governor's Mansion · Crocker Art Museum · Capitol · Capitol Gardens · California State History Museum · Sutter's Fort Park · Towe Auto Museum · South Side Park · CAPITOL AVE · CAPITOL MALL · 0 800m · 0 800yds · © Copyright Time Out Group 2005

Street labels: 12TH ST, 15TH ST, C ST, D ST, E ST, F ST, G ST, H ST, J ST, K ST, L ST, N ST, P ST, Q ST, R ST, S ST, T ST, U ST, V ST, W ST, 3RD ST, 4TH ST, 5TH ST, 6TH ST, 7TH ST, 9TH ST, 10TH ST, 11TH ST, 13TH ST, 14TH ST, 16TH ST, 19TH ST, 21ST ST, 22ND ST, 23RD ST, 24TH ST, 26TH ST, 28TH ST, FRONT ST

Sacramento

But Sacramentans were tenacious, if a little slow to act. Eventually, they built with bricks instead of wood to prevent fire and, in 1863, began raising the streets, sidewalks and buildings by 12 feet to defeat the floods. Natural disaster was prevented, but social and economic decline was not, and it was a slum by the 1950s. In 1969 the city began a $100 million project to restore the area's Gold Rush appearance; today, five million people visit Old Sac each year.

Skip the horse-drawn carriages and self-propelled surries: the best way to explore Old Sac is on foot. Stop by the **Old Sacramento Visitor Center** (*see p291*) for an illustrated map with a self-guided walking tour. The district's 28 acres contain the greatest concentration of historic buildings in California. Perhaps the most significant site is the **BF Hastings Building** (1002 2nd Street), which housed, at one time or another, the BF Hastings Bank, Wells Fargo, the California Supreme Court, the California State Telegraph Company and the Pony Express office.

It was from the Hastings Building that Theodore Judah mapped out the western route of the transcontinental railroad.

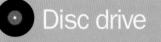

Disc drive

CDs to soundtrack your journey around the Sacramento Valley.

At Folsom Prison Johnny Cash
Recorded 15 miles east of Sacramento.

Gideon Gaye The High Llamas
Beach Boys through a dreamy English filter.

Paradise Circus The Lilac Time
Irresistibly bright, melodious guitar pop.

August The Standard
Dour, sturdy alt-rock from Portland, Oregon.

Nowadays, visitors can learn about the railroad's history and see more than 20 old locomotives and passenger cars at the excellent and informative **California State Railroad Museum** (2nd & I Streets, 1-916 445 6645, www.csrmf.org, $2-$6); for an additional charge, from April to September, the museum offers six-mile, 40-minute train rides along the riverfront.

The **California Military Museum** (1119 2nd Street, 1-916 442 2883, www.militarymuseum.org, closed Mon, $3-$5) sums up California's role in great conflicts with an impressive collection of uniforms, weapons and educational exhibits. Old Sac snaps to attention on the last Sunday of the month, when the Blue Canyon Gang – volunteers who don 1850s dress and stage pioneer-style shootouts – materialise in **Waterfront Park** at the foot of L Street.

Bodies of water are hard to come by in this landlocked, sun-stroked valley, which makes the **Sacramento River** a reassuring sight. A wooden promenade affords views of the river and the golden-yellow Tower Bridge, the middle span of which weighs 2.3 million pounds (a million kilograms) and lifts vertically at one foot per second to allow ships to pass. The **Delta King** (Sacramento River, at K Street) is a restored paddle-wheeler that transported folk between Sacramento and San Francisco and was a haven for drinkers and gamblers during Prohibition. It's now static (*see p291*), but for a closer look at the water, the **Spirit of Sacramento** (110 L Street, 1-916 552 2933, www.spiritofsacramento.com) provides an assortment of cruises, costing $10 to $67.50.

Just south of Old Sacramento is the **Crocker Art Museum** (*see below*); further to the south, you'll find the **Towe Auto Museum** (2200 Front Street, 1-916 442 6802, www.toweauto museum.org, $2-$7), a tribute to California's most depended-on mode of transport.

Crocker Art Museum

216 O Street, at 2nd Street (1-916 264 5423/www. crockerartmuseum.org). **Open** 10am-5pm Tue, Wed, Fri-Sun; 10am-9pm Thur. **Admission** $3-$6; free Sun mornings. **Credit** MC, V.

Housed in the former home of judge EB Crocker, who was so passionate about art that he once bought a cool 700 European paintings in a single two-year period, the museum exhibits early Californian, 17th-century Dutch and Flemish art, plus East Asian ceramics and decorative art, and works by regional contemporaries.

Central California

Old Sacramento. *See p287.*

Downtown & Capitol Mall

Sacramento wasn't always California's state capital. Residents lured legislators here from Benicia in 1854 by promising free use of the courthouse, a refund on moving expenses and land on which to build permanent headquarters. The **Capitol** (1-916 324 0333, www.capitol museum.ca.gov) was completed in 1874, and though a series of renovations stripped the building of its character, work in the '80s restored it to its former glory. Free tours depart hourly 9am-4pm daily; highlights include the opulent Senate and Assembly chambers, designed using the colours from the British Houses of Parliament, and the rather dramatic 12-foot rotunda dome.

The pretty 40-acre **Capitol Gardens** provides a beautiful sanctuary among the city's modest steel and glass skyscrapers. There's a tranquil trout pond and the Camellia Grove, which is where California's official flower blooms in February and March. Particularly striking is the Vietnam Veterans Memorial, a portion of which is engraved with names of the 5,822 Californians who died in the war or are still missing.

California State History Museum

1020 O Street, at 10th Street (1-916 653 7524/www. goldenstatemuseum.org). **Open** 10am-5pm Tue-Sat; noon-5pm Sun. **Admission** $3.50-$5. **Credit** MC, V. The state museum uses both traditional and multi-media exhibits to recount the stories of California's people, land and culture. Artefacts vary from the California State Constitution to surfing magazines.

Midtown

While parts of the city reveal Sacramento's past, Midtown – which is roughly bordered by 15th Street, Alhambra Boulevard, Broadway and E Street – is its here and now: this is where all the action in Sacramento takes place after the politicos go home for the day. But while it really comes alive at night, it also makes for a nice walk during the day. A plethora of cafés, boutiques and shops sit on J Street, while an array of impressive Victorian and art deco homes line the tree-shaded streets throughout. Take a stroll into the **Boulevard Park** neighbourhood (21st Street, between H and F Streets), which contains many distinctive Colonial Revival and Craftsman-style buildings. The 30-room **Governor's Mansion** (1524 H Street, 1-916 323 3047, tours $2-$4) isn't far from here either. It was once home to 12 governors before Nancy Reagan deemed it 'depressing' and consequently packed herself and her hubbie off elsewhere.

Outlying areas

Head outside Downtown and the atmosphere becomes more suburban. However, a few spots merit an extra jaunt. Take Folsom Boulevard east from Alhambra to see the **Fabulous Forties**, Sacramento's most exclusive neighbourhood. And about half a mile east of the Capitol are both **Sutter's Fort** (*see p291* **The original**) and the recently improved **California State Indian Museum** (2618 K Street, 1-916 324 7405), which provides an account of Native American culture.

South of Downtown, 236-acre **William Land Park** (bordered by 13th Avenue, Freeport Boulevard and Sutterville Road, 1-916 277 6060) is the city's most popular outdoor area. Along with picnic areas and playing fields, it contains the **Sacramento Zoo** (1-916 264 5885, www.saczoo.com, $4.50-$10.50), several playgrounds and kids' parks, a nine-hole golf course, an amphitheatre and botanical gardens.

Murder a burger at **Red Rum**. *See p292.*

Where to eat

Food in Old Sac is mostly tourist quality but there are a few standouts. **California Fats** (1015 Front Street, 1-916 441 7966, closed lunch, $$$) serves contemporary Asian food and dim sum in an attractive brick and bamboo space. The **Firehouse** (1112 2nd Street, 1-916 442 4772, closed Sun, $$$$$), located in the oldest firehouse building in California, serves upscale American fare. At **Rio City Café** (1110 Front Street, 1-916 442 8226, $$) the outdoor riverfront deck is the place to enjoy a cocktail with a view.

Most of the city's culinary delights are in Downtown and Midtown. At the high end, **Biba** (2801 Capitol Avenue, 1-916 455 2422, closed Sun, $$$) is a renowned Italian eaterie, while the **Esquire Grill** (1213 K Street, 1-916 448 8900, $$$) offers creative takes on American standards. For lively dining at moderate prices, **Tapa the World** (2115 J Street, 1-916 442 4353, $$$) has nightly guitar music, a great wine list and sangria that won't let you walk straight, and the **Tower Café** (1518 Broadway, 1-916 441 0222, $$) serves an eclectic menu on the lush patio or in a dining room decorated with global artefacts. **Ink** (27 30 N Street, 1-916 456 2800, $$) serves good grub until the wee hours in a tattoo-themed room.

Where to drink

Sacramento is oddly well appointed with brewpubs. Local favourites include **Pyramid Alehouse** (1029 K Street, 1-916 498 9800, www.pyramidbrew.com) and **Rubicon Brewing Co** (2004 Capitol Avenue, 1-916 448 7032); **River City Brewing Co** (545 Downtown Plaza, 1-916 447 2739) gets the nod for its ace burgers. One of the better bars is the **Mercantile Saloon** (1928 L Street, 1-916 447 0792). The city also has three British pubs, among them the **Fox & Goose** (1001 R Street, 1-916 443 8825).

Nightlife

You'll often find hip hop at **Ricci's** (705 J Street, 1-916 442 6741), while other options include the **Rage** (1890 Arden Way, 1-916 929

0232) and **815 L Street** (1-916 443 8155), all of which have regular club nights. **Blue Cue** (1004 28th Street, 1-916 442 7208, closed Sun) is an upscale billiards club/DJ bar, while the popular **Limelight** (1014 Alhambra Boulevard, 1-916 446 2236) is a combination restaurant/bar/meat market with a card room. The city's premier gay club is **Faces** (2000 K Street, 1-916 448 7798), also one of the most popular dance clubs for all sexual persuasions. Along with the **Depot** (2001 K Street, 1-916 441 6823), a loud, modern bar with and a patio, it provides an anchor for the city's tiny gay district, Lavender Heights.

For nightlife listings, check the free weekly *Sacramento News & Review* (www.newsreview. com) or the Friday edition of the *Sacramento Bee* (www.sacbee.com). The latter runs an information line on 1-916 552 5252.

Arts & entertainment

Many of Sacramento's galleries feature work by local artists. Art enthusiasts flock to Midtown once a month for Second Saturday, when galleries stay open late and ply visitors with food, wine and music.

Sacramento has several fine, intimate venues for music. **Harlow's** (2708 J Street, 1-916 441 4693, www.harlows.com) is a '30s-style supper club that offers bands playing anything from rock to salsa almost nightly. **Old Ironsides** (1901 10th Street, 1-916 443 9751, www.theoldironsides.com), the oldest bar in town, draws a good line-up of local and national talent: eclectic Club Lipstick is popular on Tuesdays. The **Fox & Goose** (*see above*) also hosts live music.

Drama-wise, the 178-seat **B Street Theatre** (2711 B Street, 1-916 443 5300, www.bstreet theatre.org) was co-founded by *West Wing* star Timothy Busfield, and produces works by young and emerging writers as well as established playwrights. Popular musicals run all summer at **Wells Fargo Pavilion** (1419 H Street, 1-916 557 1999) and the rest of the year at the **Sacramento Community Center Theater** (1301 L Street, 1-916 557 1999, www.californiamusicaltheatre.com).

Central California

Celluloid trumps live action at two Midtown art-movie houses, both pre-dating World War II: the **Tower Theatre** (16th Street, 1-916 442 4700) and **Crest Theatre** (1013 K Street, 1-916 442 7378, www.thecrest.com). The big sporting draw are the **Sacramento Kings** of the NBA, who play at the **Arco Arena** (1 Sports Parkway, 1-916 928 6900, www.nba.com/kings).

For details of what's on in Sacramento, pick up the free *Sacramento News & Review* (www.newsreview.com) each week.

Where to stay

All the budget chain-hotels are represented, with **Travelodge** (1111 H Street, 1-916 444 8880, $69-$129; *see p54*) and **Best Western Sutter House** (1100 H Street, 1-916 441 1314, $100-$150; *see p54*) the most centrally located of them. However, there are plenty more idiosyncratic options: stay in one of the 44 rooms aboard the **Delta King** (1100 Front Street, 1-800 825 5464, 1-916 444 5464, www.deltaking.com, $139-$350), perhaps, or take a room at the luxurious **Sheraton Grand** (1230 J Street, 1-916 447 1700, www.starwood.com/sheraton, $109-$159), noteworthy for its lobby, the former Public Market Building designed by Hearst Castle architect Julia Morgan. **Amber House** (1315 22nd Street, 1-800 755 6526, 1-916 444 8085, www.amberhouse.com), one of the city's few B&Bs, offers free net access. The **Sacramento CVB** (*see below*) 'Gold Card' scheme gives guests at some hotels discounts for restaurants and attractions.

Resources

Hospital
Sacramento *Sutter Medical Center, 2801 L Street (1-916 454 2222/www.sutterhealth.org).*

Internet
Sacramento *eChannel, 2996 Freeport Boulevard (1-916 447 2290/www.echannelcafe.com).* **Open** 12.30pm-2am Mon-Thur, Sun; 12.30pm-3am Fri, Sat.

Police
Sacramento *Suite 100, 5770 Freeport Boulevard (1-916 433 0800).*

Post office
Sacramento *1618 Alhambra Boulevard (1-916 227 6503).*

Tourist information
Sacramento *Sacramento CVB, 1608 I Street (1-800 292 2334/1-916 808 7777/www.sacramento cvb.org).* **Open** 8am-5pm Mon-Fri.
Sacramento *Old Sacramento Visitor Center, 1004 2nd Street (1-916 442 7644/www.oldsacramento. com).* **Open** 10am-5pm Mon-Fri, Sun; 10am-6pm Sat.

Around Sacramento

The land just outside Sacramento holds little of interest. US 50 east leads to **Folsom**, whose one point of interest is the prison at which Johnny Cash recorded his seminal live album in 1968; further along it is **Placerville** in the Gold Country (*see p304*). Heading south of Sacramento along I-5 or US 99, there's nothing much to see for 50 miles until **Stockton** and the **California Delta** (*see p279*). Taking often-busy I-80 west, meanwhile, will drag you back towards **San Francisco** (*see pp219-259*), but do make time for the small college town a mere 20 minutes west of Downtown Sacramento.

Davis

The University of California's campus dominates the town of **Davis**, just west of Sacramento. This mellow place is perhaps the archetypal Californian college town, liberal, relaxed and altogether agreeable on every level.

It rewards the pedestrian, Davis. Once you're off I-80, explore Downtown on foot: bounded by 1st, 7th, A and G Streets, it's awash with small shops, galleries and restaurants, plus a cinema,

The original

It now looks out of place among the low-slung office buildings and apartments around it, but white-walled **Sutter's Fort** (2701 L Street, 1-916 445 4422, $2-$5) was actually the first man-made structure in Sacramento. A self-contained community of merchants, farmers and craftsmen, the fort was established by John Sutter in 1839. Sutter was a spirited entrepreneur, but he was a lousy businessman and a bit of a pushover, giving immigrants and pioneers food and board – among them the ill-fated Donner Party that nearly perished trying to cross the Sierra Nevada – without charge.

Although James Marshall discovered gold in Coloma while building a mill for Sutter, the Gold Rush ruined him. Sutter's workers deserted him for the mines: en route to the Gold Country, would-be prospectors destroyed the fort, slaughtering his cattle, trampling his crops and stealing his horses. The fort was eventually restored, based on an 1847 map; today, costumed docents lead visitors on a journey to Sacramento's infancy.

Central California

a theatre and the historic **Hattie Webber Museum** (445 C Street, 1-530 758 5637, open Wed & Sat only). Downtown backs on to the campus, highlighted by the **UC Davis Arboretum** (1-530 752 4880) and a number of small museums and galleries (such as the **Design Museum**, 145 Walker Hall, 1-530 752 6223, closed Sat). Davis is a passionately cultured place: witness the $60 million **Mondavi Center**, an immaculate performing arts complex with the budget to book big-name acts (1-866 754 2787, www.mondaviarts.com).

Where to eat

While there are some gems among its galleries and museums, Davis's main attractions are its myriad restaurants. As well as the expected Italian and American eateries, terrific burger joint **Red Rum Burger** (978 Olive Drive, 1-530 756 2142, $) falling into the latter category, there are also small restaurants serving Thai (try **Sophie's Thai Kitchen**, 129 E Street, 1-530 758 4333, $), Japanese (**Jusco**, 228 G Street, 1-530 750 2869, closed Mon, $$), Czech (**Little Prague**, 330 G Street, 1-530 756 1107, $$$) and even Nepalese (**Kathmandu Kitchen**, 234 G Street, 1-530 756 3507, $$). Most of them are excellent value. Downtown's unsubtle bars are less appealing; for a quieter drink, try the **Sudwerks** brewpub east of Downtown (2001 2nd Street, 1-530 756 2739).

Where to stay

There are several decent independent motels located Downtown. The largest is the **Hallmark Inn** (110 F Street, 1-800 753 0035, 1-530 753 3600, www.hallmarkinn.com, $79-$129); the neat **Aggie Inn** (245 1st Street, 1-530 756 0352, $95) is better value. The **Best Western Palm Court** (234 D Street, 1-530 753 7100, $115-$164; *see p54*) offers more amenities at greater expense.

Resources

Hospital
Davis *Sutter Davis Hospital, 2000 Sutter Place (1-530 756 6440/www.sutterdavis.org).*

Internet
Davis *Davis Library, 315 E 14th Street (1-530 757 5593).* **Open** 1-9pm Mon; 10am-9pm Tue-Thur; 10am-5.30pm Fri, Sat; 1-5pm Sun.

Police
Davis *2600 5th Street (1-530 747 5400).*

Post office
Davis *2020 5th Street (1-530 753 0428).*

Tourist information
Davis *Davis CVB, 105 E Street (1-877 713 2847/ 1-530 297 1900/www.davisvisitor.com).* **Open** 8.30am-4.30pm Mon-Fri.

Heading North

The drive north from Sacramento, along either US 99 or I-5, is not a memorable one. Small towns move out of view before you've noticed them; the pancake-flat land offers little scenery. The biggest town on US 99 is **Yuba City**, but the only reason to stop is for gas. **Oroville**, 33 miles north, is nicer yet not much more interesting…

Chico

… But **Chico**, on the other hand, is a thriving, lively community. Beautiful Bidwell Park makes visitors seethe with envy; Chico State University

Rolling on the river

Perhaps nothing can persuade the mildly out-of-shape to get on their bicycles like the promise of a flat ribbon of concrete stretched out along a waterfront. The **Jedediah Smith Memorial Bicycle Trail** (1-916 875 6672) fulfils that promise for 32 miles as it skirts the American River from Old Sacramento to Folsom Lake. The trail isn't entirely flat, but it's pretty close, and there are enough picnic tables, shady trees and river access points to relieve the overexerted.

The trail is accessible from a Downtown connector (C Street, near 19th) or at the Guy West Bridge on the California State University campus, but you're best off starting in Old Sacramento, where rentals are available at Bike Sacramento (1050 Front Street, 1-916 444 0200). After a couple of miles, industrial sights and smells dissipate into more peaceful surroundings. Past Hazel Avenue (mile 23) the crowds really thin, foliage thickens and creatures such as snowy egrets and river otters often come into view.

In the summer, when temperatures can exceed 100°F and clouds are non-existent, explore the trail only in the morning or evening. And, no matter what time of year or day you go, be sure to bring plenty of water.

Little Prague. *See p292.*

infuses the city with intellectual energy; residents still congregate Downtown, as their forebears did a century ago.

Downtown Chico is full of shops, galleries, coffeehouses and restaurants. The free **Chico Museum** (141 Salem Street, 1-530 891 4336, www.chicomuseum.org, closed Mon) features historical photos, portraits and artefacts, plus a re-creation of a Chinese Taoist temple; the **National Yo-Yo Museum** at the Bird in Hand store (320 Broadway, 1-530 893 0545, www. nationalyoyo.org) boasts the 256-pound (16-kilogram 'Big-Yo', the largest working wooden yo-yo in the world. Other attractions include two private houses, both open for tours. The **Stansbury House** (307 W 5th Street, 1-530 895 3848, closed Mon-Fri) is a prime example of Victorian architecture; the three-storey **Bidwell Mansion** (525 The Esplanade, 1-530 895 6144, closed Mon & Tue, $2), built by Chico's founder General John Bidwell, was the first home in California with indoor plumbing.

Chico's **Bidwell Park** (4th Street & Cypress Avenue, 1-530 895 4972), is a geologically diverse natural treasure that extends to the Sierra foothills and contains rugged hiking trails, paved bike paths and swimming holes. Kids love Sycamore Pool, formed by a dammed-up creek, and Caper Acres, a playground with animal-shaped water fountains, sandpits, a castle and jungle gyms. Scenes from *Gone with the Wind* were filmed here.

Where to eat & drink

At the upscale but unpretentious **Red Tavern** (1250 The Esplanade, 1-530 894 3463, closed Sun & lunch Mon-Sat, $$$$) dishes are creatively crafted from local ingredients. **Grilla Bites** (119 W 2nd Street, 1-530 894 2691, closed Sun, $) serves sandwiches, salads and soups, while **Madison Bear Garden** (316 W 2nd Street, 1-530 891 1639, $) is legendary for its Bear Burger.

South of Downtown, Chico's most famous landmark is one of America's most popular microbreweries: the **Sierra Nevada Brewing Company** (1075 E 20th Street, 1-530 893 3520), open daily for tours and drinks. The city also has loads of cosy bars with live music, including scruffy **Duffy's Tavern** (337 Main Street, 1-530 343 7718) and **Stormy's** (132 W 2nd Street, 1-530 891 5065), a mellow spot for blues and jazz.

Arts & entertainment

Chico punches well above its cultural weight. Impromptu galleries crop up everywhere: as adjuncts to cafés and even on the sides of buildings. The **1078 Gallery** (738 W 5th Street, 1-530 343 1973, closed Mon & Sun) is a good showcase for contemporary work, and you can watch regular glassblowing demonstrations at the **Satava Art Glass Studio** (819 Wall Street, 1-530 345 7985, closed Mon & Sun).

The performing arts also impress. The venerable **Blue Room Theatre** (139 W 1st Street, 1-530 895 3749) produces locally written and nationally known scripts; the newly formed **Chico Theatre Company** (166 Eaton Road, 1-530 894 3282) presents classics like *The Goodbye Girl.* The 350-seat **Big Room** at the Sierra Nevada brewery (*see above*) hosts concerts; the **Pageant Theatre** (351 E 6th Street, 1-530 343 0663) is an anti-megaplex with overstuffed couches and independent films.

Where to stay

Charming **Johnson's Country Inn** (3935 Morehead Avenue, 1-530 345 7829, http:// northvalley.net/johnsonsinn, $85-$130) has its own almond orchard, while the **Grateful Bed** (1462 Arcadian Avenue, 1-530 342 2464, $100-$140) is luxurious. Downtown has several value-priced motels, including a **Days Inn** (740 Broadway, 1-530 343 3286, $59; *see p54*).

Red Bluff

The Victorian town of Red Bluff, on the Sacramento River, bills itself as 'the doorway to Mount Lassen'. In truth, the drive to Lassen from Redding, 30 miles north, is rather nicer, but that's not to say the Old West-style Main Street and meticulously restored private residences of Red Bluff aren't worth a look. The **Kelly-Griggs House Museum** (311 Washington Street, 1-530 527 1129, closed Mon-Wed) has a collection of antique furniture and contains a painting by Sarah Brown, daughter of abolitionist John Brown. Two miles outside town, the **William B Ide Adobe State Historic Park** (21659 Adobe Road, 1-530 529

Central California

Sierra Nevada Brewing Co. *See p293.*

8599) honours the only president of the short-lived California Republic, which existed for 25 days between Mexican and American rule.

Just across the Sacramento River and to the south is **Lake Red Bluff Recreation Area** (1000 Sale Lane, 1-530 527 2813), a paradise for boaters, nature lovers and fish fanatics. A paved four-mile, wheelchair-accessible trail presents opportunities for watching the wildlife and enjoying scenic vistas, while TV monitors at the salmon-viewing plaza show live salmon and trout traverse man-made fish ladders.

Where to eat, drink & stay

Red Bluff's best options for food are the **Snack Box** (257 Main Street, 1-530 529 0227, $), serving comfort food for breakfast and lunch; the **Crystal Steak & Seafood Company** (343 S Main Street, 1-530 527 0880, closed lunch, $$), one of the top steakhouses in Northern California; and the English pub-style **Green Barn** (5 Chestnut Avenue, 1-530 527 3161, $$) . Rooms are offered at the simple **Lamplighter Lodge** (210 S Main Street, 1-530 527 1150, www.lamplighterlodge.us, $60-$125), and the more opulent, lushly landscaped **Jeter Victorian Inn** (1107 Jefferson Street, 1-530 527 7574, www.jetervictorianinn.com, $80-$140).

Resources

Hospital
Chico *Enloe Medical Center, 1531 Esplanade (1-530 332 7300/www.enloe.org).*

Internet
Chico *Chico Public Library, 1108 Sherman Avenue (1-530 891 2762).* **Open** *9am-8pm Mon-Thur; 9am-5pm Fri, Sat.*
Red Bluff *Red Bluff Library, 645 Madison Street (1-530 527 0604).* **Open** *2-6pm Mon; 11am-8pm Tue; 2-8pm Wed; 11am-6pm Thur; 2-6pm Fri.*

Police
Chico *1460 Humboldt Road (1-530 895 4900).*
Red Bluff *555 Washington Street (1-530 527 8282).*

Post office
Chico *550 Vallombrosa Avenue (1-530 343 2068).*
Red Bluff *447 Walnut Street (1-530 527 1455).*

Tourist information
Chico *Chico Chamber of Commerce, 300 Salem Street (1-800 852 8570/1-530 891 5556/www. chicochamber.com).* **Open** *9am-5pm Mon-Fri; 10am-3pm Sat.*
Red Bluff *Red Bluff-Tehama County Chamber of Commerce, 100 Main Street (1-800 655 6225/www. redbluffchamberofcommerce.com).* **Open** *9am-5pm Mon-Fri.*

Getting There

By air
Many airlines fly international and domestic flights to **Sacramento International Airport** (1-916 929 5411, www.sacairports.org). From here, you've a choice between a taxi (around $25 to Downtown) or the **Supershuttle Sacramento** ($13 to Downtown; 1-800 258 3826, www.supershuttle.org).

By bus
Greyhound (1-800 229 9424, www.greyhound.com) links Sacramento with, among other cities, San Francisco (2-3hrs, $14 one-way, $23 round-trip) and LA (8½-10hrs, $44 one-way, $82 round-trip). There are also Greyhound stations in both Chico and Red Bluff.

By car
From San Francisco, it's around 90 miles on the eastbound I-80 to Sacramento. From the general Lake Tahoe region, head west on US 50 (if you're at South Lake Tahoe) or I-80 (from Tahoe City and other points north).

By train
There are **Amtrak** (www.amtrak.com) stations in Sacramento (4th & I Streets; *see p288*), Davis (840 2nd Street) and Chico (450 Orange Street). The Coast Starlight heads north to Seattle via Oakland and south to San Diego via Los Angeles; the California Zephyr travels east to Reno. Amtrak's **Capitol Corridor** service (1-800 872 7245) runs more frequent trains daily to Oakland, with connecting onward buses.

The Gold Country

Forget fortune-seekers: these days, it's tourists who are in a rush to get here.

Maybe we'll strike gold...

Regardless of whether or not you spend any time in the Gold Country during your visit to California, spare a thought for a gentleman named James Marshall. Without his eagle eye, it's unlikely not just that this land would have grown into such a charming area: it's also a moot point whether California itself would have evolved in anything like the same way.

It was Marshall who, while building a sawmill in Coloma for John Sutter in January 1848, spotted gold in the water. Try as they did to keep their discovery, and the gold, to themselves, word inevitably got out. Within six months, thousands of miners had come east from San Francisco in the hope of making their fortunes; by 1849, California was overrun by hopeful fortune-seekers from all over the US, who'd spent the winter travelling west. The West had opened up, and the Gold Rush was on.

Those were lively times. Towns cropped up wherever gold was found, and gold was found all over the place, especially in the Sierra Nevada foothills. Some gold needed mining from rock beneath the earth's surface, while some washed up in rivers and streams; still,

if you looked hard enough, you'd find it. There was money to be made, but little was made by the miners. Opportunist entrepreneurs hastily started companies in order to supply the miners with equipment; barkeepers and brothel madams thrived, as miners looked for ways to spend both their evenings and their wages.

It didn't last. Journalist Horace Greeley's 1848 prediction that $1,000 million of gold would show up within four years proved wildly incorrect: in the 11 years between Marshall's first glimpse and the discovery of the Comstock silver lode in Virginia City, Nevada, $600 million of gold was discovered, but the boom was over. Some entrepreneurs remained in business, refining their mining techniques and making a tidy living for a time: the Kennedy Mine in Jackson remained open until 1942, and Empire Mine in Grass Valley only shut its doors in 1956. But other mines vanished as quickly as they had arrived, and the towns that supported them followed suit.

However, these are good times once again in the Gold Country, which essentially stretches the length of Highway 49 (and is named, of

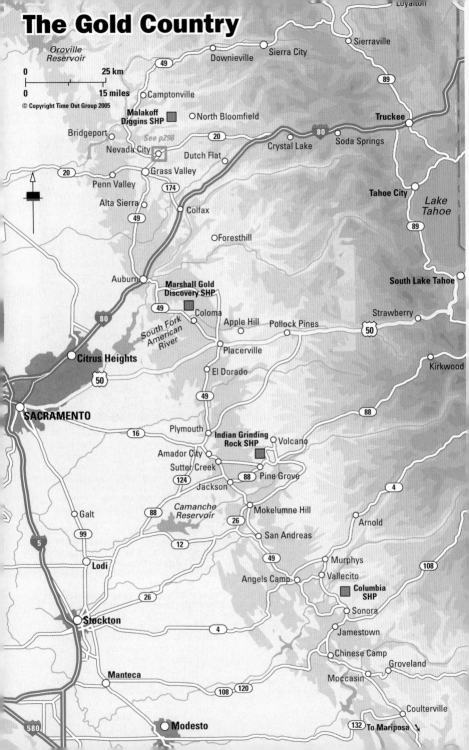

The Gold Country

Oroville
Reservoir

0 ————— 25 km
0 ————— 15 miles

© Copyright Time Out Group 2005

Loyalton

Sierraville

Sierra City

Downieville

49

Camptonville

89

Truckee

80

Malakoff
Diggins SHP

North Bloomfield

Bridgeport

See p298

20

Crystal Lake

Soda Springs

Nevada City

Dutch Flat

20

Grass Valley

174

Penn Valley

Alta Sierra

49

Colfax

Tahoe City

89

Lake
Tahoe

Foresthill

Auburn

Marshall Gold
Discovery SHP

South Lake Tahoe

80

49

Coloma

Strawberry

Apple Hill

Pollock Pines

South Fork
American
River

50

Placerville

Citrus Heights

El Dorado

Kirkwood

50

SACRAMENTO

49

88

16

Plymouth

Indian Grinding
Rock SHP

Volcano

Amador City

Sutter Creek

88

Pine Grove

4

124

Jackson

Galt

88

Camanche
Reservoir

26

Mokelumne Hill

Arnold

99

San Andreas

12

108

Lodi

49

Murphys

Columbia
SHP

Angels Camp

Vallecito

26

Sonora

Stockton

Jamestown

4

Chinese Camp

Groveland

Moccasin

Manteca

108

120

Coulterville

580

Modesto

132

To Mariposa

course, for the pioneering miners of 1849) from the verdant rural towns in the north to drier, plainer settlements such as Coulterville further south. The area has positioned itself as a tourist destination in the last couple of decades, and with great success: it's simple to navigate, relatively affordable and easy on the eye.

And even if some towns do get very crowded in summer, and others wear their heritage a little too tackily, this is still a decidedly pleasant area in which to spend a few days. The relative paucity of accommodation options in the Gold Country (there's hardly a hotel in the entire area with more than 20 rooms; this is real B&B territory, and you'd do well to book in advance) is indicative of the fact that the Gold Country is still a little off the tourist trail. Time your visit outside peak season, and you'll really see the place at its gentle, charming best.

Northern Gold Country

Grass Valley

In June 1850 a man named George McKnight found a little gold in a barely populated area then known as Grassy Valley. However, it wasn't until five months later, when George Roberts found a rich vein of the stuff a mile away, that word began to leak out. A year on, Roberts had been joined by 20,000 hopefuls, drawn by the irresistible whiff of money.

The gold, though, was buried in hard rock, and the prospectors who arrived with such high hopes found they didn't have the skill to mine it. But Roberts's persistence paid off in the end, thanks to help from an unlikely source. The Cornish miners who began to drift into the area two decades after the pair of Georges got lucky brought with them decades of experience mining tin and copper from hard rock, transforming both the mining industry and the town, which, in the late 19th century, was estimated to be as much as 85 per cent Cornish.

The spot where Roberts found gold now forms part of the car park to the 800-acre **Empire Mine State Historic Park** (10791 E Empire Street, 1-530 273 8522, www.parks.ca. gov). Formerly the most successful of the local mines – indeed, it only closed in 1956 – it's now open as a visitor attraction, albeit a slightly unsatisfactory one; the small museum does a nice job, but the mineyard and its equipment are so poorly labelled that you need to take one of the daily tours to get much from the experience. Also here is the handsome Bourn

Cottage, built in 1898 for then-mine owner William Bourn Jr, and some short walking trails (pick up a leaflet at the visitor centre).

The spot where McKnight discovered gold, meanwhile, is in what's now downtown Grass Valley; stop by the **Chamber of Commerce** (*see p302*), housed in the former home of tempestuous entertainer Lola Montez, to pick up a walking tour map. Though the century-old

The Best Gold Country

Things to do
See where it all began at **Marshall Gold Discovery State Historic Park** (*see p303*), try the local wine in **Amador County** (*see p305*) and around **Murphys** (*see p310*)… and, of course, pan for your fortune (*see p307* **Going for gold**).

Places to stay
The area is awash with historic hotels and homey B&Bs. Into the former category fall the **National Hotel** and the **Jamestown Hotel**, both in Jamestown (*see p312*); in the latter are the gorgeous **Red Castle Inn** in Nevada City (*see p299*), Sonora's **Knowles Hill House** (*see p312*) and the **Dunbar House, 1880** in Murphys (*see p310*).

Places to eat
Many of the area's most highly regarded restaurants are in its hotels, among them the **Imperial Hotel** in Amador City (*see p306*). The best stand-alone operations? Try **Citronée** in Nevada City (*see p299*), **Zinfandels** in Sutter Creek and **Poor Red's BBQ** just south of Placerville (*see p306*).

Nightlife
The **Whiskey Flat Saloon** at the St George Hotel in Volcano (*see p308*), the bar at the **National Hotel** in Jackson (*see p308*) and the **Mine Shaft** in Nevada City (*see p299*) are all superbly characterful bars.

Culture
Theatre's the thing: among the amateur groups are the **Volcano Theatre Company** (*see p308*) and Sutter Creek's **Main Street Theatre Works** (*see p306*).

Sports & activities
Unless you're a frog and therefore able to compete at the **Jumping Frog Jubilee** in Angels Camp (*see p310*), your best sporting bet is the rafting and kayaking in the **American River** (*see p303*).

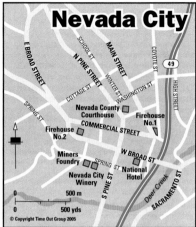

Nevada City

E BROAD STREET
SCHOOL ST
MAIN STREET
COYOTE ST
N PINE STREET
WINTER ST
COTTAGE ST
WASHINGTON ST
HIGH STREET
SPRING ST
49
Nevada County Courthouse
Firehouse No.1
Firehouse No.2
COMMERCIAL STREET
W BROAD ST
Miners Foundry
SPRING ST
National Hotel
Nevada City Winery
S PINE ST
Deer Creek
SACRAMENTO ST

0   500 m
0   500 yds
© Copyright Time Out Group 2005

buildings on Mill and Main Streets now function chiefly as antiques retailers and cutesy gift shops with names such as Confectionately Yours, Grass Valley still feels like the working man's town it was for much of its history. Non-consumer diversions are headed by the **North Star Mining Museum** (Mill Street, at Allison Ranch Road, 1-530 273 4255, closed Oct-Apr); the lower-key **Grass Valley Museum** (410 S Church Street, 1-530 273 5509, closed Sat-Mon) is for completists only. Collectors of amusing road signs may care to make diversions from Grass Valley to the nearby hamlets of **Smartville** and **Rough and Ready**; further west is the small town of **Penn Valley**, home to the intriguing collections of art and antiquities of the **Museum of Ancient and Modern Art** (Wildwood Business Center, 11392 Pleasant Valley Road, 1-530 432 3080, www.mama.org).

Where to eat & drink

The **212 Bistro** at the Holbrooke Hotel (*see below*; $$$), whose menu is studiedly Californian, is the smartest place to eat and probably the best, though **Tofanelli's** (302 W Main Street, 1-530 272 1468, $$–$$$, best approached for its American classics, might argue with that assessment. The **Main Street Café** (215 W Main Street, 1-530 477 6000, $–$$) ought to please those with simpler tastes and skinnier wallets, while Americans after a lump of local flavour (and Brits homesick for Blighty's culinary traditions) should head to one of several shops hawking Cornish pasties – crusty, enclosed pies stuffed chiefly with meat and potatoes. On the Atkins? Don't even think about it.

Where to stay

The historic **Holbrooke Hotel** (212 W Main Street, 1-800 933 7077, 1-530 273 1353, www.holbrooke.com, $75-$125), built in 1851, is keen to play up its past; each of its 28 old-fashioned but perfectly pleasant rooms is named after a famous person who's thought to have slept there, from President Ulysses S Grant to writer Mark Twain. If it's full, there are a handful of motels on the edge of town, including a capacious **Best Western** (11972 Sutton Way, 1-530 273 1393, $85-$110; *see p54*). The Chamber of Commerce (*see p302*) can supply details of the town's half-dozen B&Bs.

Nevada City

Where Grass Valley comes off as a lively, working man's town, or at least as much of one as you're likely to find in this sedate corner of California, Nevada City is a rather sweeter place. Aside from a couple of raffish bars, there's little here to give away its decadent beginnings. The town grew up quickly from its roots as a mining camp; it had become your classic Western Gold Rush town by the 1850s, packed with roistering miners who partied even harder than they worked, and blowsy, good-time gals more than happy to join in the fun.

When the boom turned to bust, the town faded, and even burned to the ground twice. But while such hardships would have (and, in many cases, did) finish other Gold Rush towns, Nevada City held firm, its locals rebuilding the town from scratch and, eventually, from more durable brick and stone. It's these Victorian buildings that make up the bulk of the town's eminently strollable centre, one of the loveliest in the Gold Country and a National Historic Landmark in its own right. A leaflet available at the **Chamber of Commerce** (*see p302*) points out the most notable structures, but the standout buildings are two former fire stations, both dating back to 1861. While **Firehouse No.1** (214 Main Street, 1-530 265 5468, closed Mon-Wed, $1) is now a small museum, **Firehouse No.2** on Broad Street, otherwise populated with low-key shops and restaurants, still functions as a fire station.

The mining connection takes further root at the **Miners Foundry Cultural Center** (325 Spring Street, 1-530 265 5040, www.miners foundry.org, closed Sat & Sun), a granite and stone building from 1859 that now hosts a variety of public and private events and also contains a small museum. Those who've not yet had their fill of history would do well to browse the assorted papers at the **Searls Historical Library** (214 Church Street, 1-530 265 5910,

Central California

open by appointment only), take a tour on the train from the **Nevada County Traction Company** (at the Northern Queen Inn, 402 Railroad Avenue, 1-530 265 0896) or learn about the Gold Rush railroads at the **Nevada County Narrow Gauge Railroad Museum** (5 Kidder Court, 1-530 470 0902, www.ncngrr museum.org, closed Wed & Thur May-Oct, closed Mon, Wed-Fri & Sun Nov-Apr). Other options include the small, science-oriented **Imaginarium** (112 Nevada City Highway, 1-530 478 6400, closed Mon-Fri), trying the local wine at the **Nevada City Winery** (housed in the Miners Foundry garage at 321 Spring Street, 1-530 265 9463, www.ncwinery.com, tasting room open daily, tours Sun), or perhaps catching a play at the 140-year-old **Nevada Theatre** (401 Broad Street, 1-530 265 8587, www.foothilltheatre.org).

However, Nevada City is best approached not for its individual attractions but for its singular ambience. Other towns in the Gold Country might retain (and play up to) more of their tourist-friendly Gold Rush character, but none is quite as delightful as this one.

Where to eat & drink

The plaudits in town are collected first by **Citronée** (320 Broad Street, 1-530 265 5697, closed lunch Sat & all day Sun, $$$–$$$$), an upscale yet approachable spot whose take on Californian cuisine is acknowledged to just edge out the **New Moon Café** (203 York Street, 1-530 265 6399, closed all day Mon and lunch Sat & Sun, $$–$$$). Other entirely worthwhile options include the **Stonehouse** (107 Sacramento Street, 1-530 265 5050, dinner only, $$$), a handsome but informal bar/dining room specialising in American classics, and **Friar Tuck's** (111 N Pine Street, 1-530 265 9093, dinner only, $$$), which has been dishing up steaks, fondues and rather lame music for three decades. Of the town's bars, **Cooper's** (235 Commercial Street, 1-530 265 0116) comes with a dartboard and regular bands; the shambolic, no-nonsense but thoroughly likeable **Mine Shaft** (222 Broad Street, 1-530 265 6310) sticks to the brews.

Where to stay

The **National Hotel** (211 Broad Street, 1-530 265 4551, www.thenationalhotel.com, $79) claims to be the oldest continuously operating hotel west of the Rockies. It looks it, too, and not in a good way; it's a rather saddish place. You're better off at the tidier but rather cutesy **Northern Queen Inn** (400 Railroad Avenue, 1-800 226 3090, 1-530 265 5824,

www.northernqueeninn.com, $85), or at one of the town's numerous B&Bs, especially at the wonderful **Red Castle Inn** (109 Prospect Street, 1-800 761 4766, 1-530 265 5135, www.redcastleinn.com, $120-$170). This Gothic Revival house, completed in 1860, evokes the Victorian era in deliciously authentic fashion over its seven immaculately maintained guestrooms, parlour and hillside gardens. The five-course breakfasts are unparalleled. Other B&B options include **Grandmere's Inn** (449 Broad Street, 1-530 265 4660, www.grand meresinn.com, $172-$208); contact the Chamber of Commerce for a full list. Outdoor types can reserve one of the campsites in **Malakoff Diggins State Historic Park** (sites $10-$15) by calling 1-800 444 7275 or visiting www.reserveamerica.com.

North from Nevada City

Malakoff Diggins State Historic Park (23579 N Bloomfield Road, 1-530 265 2740, www.parks.ca.gov), north-east of Nevada City, was once the largest gold mine on the

Disc drive

CDs to soundtrack your journey around the Gold Country.

***Not the Tremblin' Kind* Laura Cantrell**
A dozen delightful country songs, delivered plainly and without fuss by a singer who, at the time, was the VP of Equity Research at the Bank of America on Wall Street.

Between Here and Gone
Mary Chapin Carpenter
Less catchy than the records that made her famous but every bit as good, *Between Here and Gone* is Carpenter at her most gentle and sympathetic.

***Woodface* Crowded House**
'Weather with You', 'Fall at Your Feet', 'It's Only Natural'… breezy, tender and entirely immaculate guitar-led pop music.

***Aw C'mon* Lambchop**
Perhaps not the best Lambchop album, but certainly their most approachable, soul-tinged country delivered with restraint, tenderness and a wink.

***Autumn* George Winston**
Later records saw Winston descend into lowest-common-denominator new age whimsy, but the pastoral solo piano of *Autumn* still appeals.

Central California

planet, but it didn't last long. When, in 1884, a judge ruled that hydraulic mining was illegal, the mine ceased operation. However, the effects of mining on the landscape still remain, most strikingly in the enormous mine pit itself. The park now contains a small museum and a handful of attractive hikes, of which the nicest is the three-mile Humbug Creek Trail. However, the park's main attraction is the carefully maintained ghost town of North Bloomfield.

North-west of Nevada City, meanwhile, is the small town of **Bridgeport**. Reached via an eight-mile drive west along Newtown Road, Bitney Springs Road and Pleasant Valley Road, it's home to the visitor centre for the peaceful, swimmer-friendly **South Yuba River State Park** (1-530 432 2546, www.parks.ca.gov) and the 229-foot (70-metre) **Bridgeport Covered Bridge**, the longest wooden covered bridge in the world and a real Californian curio.

Named, rather quaintly, for the Gold Rush pioneers of Californian legend, **Highway 49** bisects the Gold Country; the majority of the region's major towns lie on the road. However, the stretch running north and west from Nevada City is Highway 49 – and, for that matter, California driving – at its most beautiful. It's also the start of the Yuba Donner Scenic Byway, a 160-mile loop around Highways 49 and 89, I-80 and Highway 20 (via Truckee and Donner Memorial State Historic Park, for which *see p317*) that adds up to one of the

more attractive drives in the state. A handful of small roads run off 49 into the mountains, most of them impassable without a 4WD vehicle; among them are the Ridge Road that heads east towards **Alleghany**, a town notable for its seclusion and for the tours offered at the **Sixteen to One Mine** (356 Main Street, 1-530 287 3223, www.origsix.com, tours by appointment only, $30-$75). However, if you're short on time, you won't miss much by sticking to the main road.

A few miles north of jolly, secluded **Camptonville**, Highway 49 joins up with the lively North Yuba River and follows its course eastwards through the Tahoe National Forest. There is an assortment of clearly signposted campgrounds en route, at such evocatively named spots as Fiddle Creek, Rocky Rest and Convict Flat (reservations not accepted), but aside from the occasional kayaker, you won't find many signs of life until Downieville.

Downieville to Sierra City

During the Gold Rush, the population of **Downieville** is reported to have topped 5,000, attracted by stories of gold nuggets weighing the better part of 30 pounds (12 kilograms). Your first reaction upon arriving here will be to wonder how they all managed to squish into this picturesque little spot, established by Scottish prospector William Downie in 1849 at

Going underground

It wasn't just gold that was discovered by hopeful prospectors in the 19th century. While hunting for their fortunes in the Gold Country, miners came across several caves, each containing a number of striking natural formations: stalactites and stalagmites, helictites and rimstone dams. The caves were apparently less interesting to their discoverers than the nearby mother lode, but in recent years, they've proved a gold mine of a different sort, and now draw hordes of visitors each year. All the caves in the region are privately owned and operated, and you can't help but wish the National Parks Service was in charge: some of the work converting the caves into accessible visitor attractions has been less than sympathetic. Still, what's done is done, and few visitors seem to mind.

Moaning Cavern (5350 Moaning Cave Road, Vallecito, 1-866 762 2837, www.caverntours.com), named for the

noise made by drops of water falling into a series of holes in the cave, has been welcoming the public since the 1920s. Mark Twain was among those who visited **California Cavern** (9565 Cave City Road, Mountain Ranch, 1-866 762 2837, www.caverntours.com) in the 19th century, though it didn't open properly for tours until 1980; nearby **Mercer Cavern** (1665 Sheep Ranch Road, Murphys, 1-209 728 2101) predates it by several decades. The most recent of the bunch is the showily converted **Black Chasm** just outside Volcano (15701 Pioneer-Volcano Road, 1-866 762 2837, www. caverntours.com), which opened in 2000. Reservations are not required for any of the standard tours. However, Moaning Cavern and California Cavern also operate extended tours lasting up to five hours, for which booking is necessary.

Downieville: even a stopped clock is right twice a day. *See p300.*

the fork of the North Yuba River with what is now called the Downie River. Fewer than 400 people live here these days, in a smattering of pretty but seen-better-days buildings hemmed in by the hills. But while it's rather more sedate than it was 150 years ago at the height of the Gold Rush, life is surely still good for the locals in their thoroughly unpretentious little town, in which sightseeing consists of the **Downieville Museum** (330 Main Street, 1-530 289 3423, closed Oct-mid May) and, cheerily, a set of gallows once used in 1865 to hang a 20-year-old local murderer.

Faced with such charm, near-neighbour **Sierra City** can't compete, but it doesn't do badly under the circumstances. Its Main Street is handsome, and even if you think you've had your fill of mining ephemera, you'll likely find the restored **Kentucky Mine Park** (1-530 277 5446, closed Nov-mid May, and Mon & Tue May-Oct, $1-$5) a charmer; with a museum and stamp mill, it's the best of the mining attractions in the Northern Gold Country.

Where to eat, drink & stay

Downieville is a better bet than Sierra City. Eat at the sweet **Grubstake Saloon** (Main Street, 1-530 289 0289, $$) or the name-says-it-all **Riverview Pizzeria** (Main Street, 1-530 289 3540, $), before adjourning to **St Charles Place** (Commercial Street, 1-530 289 3237) for

a beer. Downieville's accommodation options are chiefly hotel/motel operations, such as the **Riverside Inn** (Commercial Street, 1-888 883 5100, 1-530 289 1000, www.downieville.us, $70-$92.50) and the **Downieville River Inn** (121 River Street, 1-800 696 3308, 1-530 289 3308, www.downievilleriverinn.com, $74-$79), though if you're in a group, consider the three-bed, two-bath **Willoughby's on the River** (171 River Street, 1-800 296 2289, www.willoughbysontheriver.com, $250/night or $1,400/wk).

East of Downieville, tucked into the hillside by the side of the North Yuba River, are a number of secluded cabins. The **Lure Inn** (1-800 671 4084, 1-530 289 3465, www.lureresort.com, $90-$225), just under a mile from Downieville, has several tidy cottages and some basic cabins (no bed linen, electricity or running water); smarter is the **Sierra Shangri-La** (1-530 289 3455, www.sierrashangrila.com, $70-$200), a further mile and a half down the road, which offers eight cabins and three B&B guestrooms in a delightful riverside setting.

While Sierra City does have a number of accommodation options, many are only open for around half the year; falling into that category is the immaculate (if slightly twee) **Holly House** (1-530 862 1123, www.hollyhouse.com, $95-$150) and the more basic **Herrington's Sierra Pines Resort** (1-800 682-9848, 1-530 862 1151, www.herringtonssierrapines.com,

Placer County Courthouse dominates the town of Auburn.

$64-$94). However, one spot that does open all year round is the **High Country Inn** (1-800 862 1530, 1-530 862 1530, www. hicountryinn.com, $95-$150).

Resources

Hospital
Grass Valley *Sierra Nevada Memorial Hospital, 155 Glasson Way (1-530 274 6000/ www.snmh.org).*

Internet
Grass Valley *Flour Garden, 11999 Sutton Way (1-530 272 2043/www.flourgarden.com).* **Open** 6am-6pm daily.

Police
Nevada City *317 Broad Street (1-916 265 2626).*

Post office
Downieville *301 Main Street (1-530 289 3575).*
Nevada City *200 Coyote Street (1-530 265 0263).*

Tourist information
Grass Valley *Grass Valley/Nevada County Chamber of Commerce, 248 Mill Street (1-800 655 4667/1-530 273 4667/www.grassvalleychamber. com).* **Open** 9am-5pm Mon-Fri; 10am-3pm Sat.
Nevada City *Nevada City Chamber of Commerce, 132 Main Street (1-800 655 6569/1-530 265 2692/ www.nevadacitychamber.com).* **Open** 9am-5pm Mon-Fri; 11am-4pm Sat.

Central Gold Country

Auburn

In common with several other towns in Placer County, for which it's the county seat, **Auburn** wears its history with the minimum of charm. Although it's ostensibly a Gold Rush settlement, having sprung up in 1848 when two prospectors struck lucky in the area, it now feels very much like a locals' town for local people, from the minute you exit I-80 (or Highway 49) for the first time and find yourself flummoxed by the atrocious signposting. If the city fathers want people to visit recently spruced-up Downtown, they'd do well to tell them how to get there.

In truth, though, the string of forgettable shops, bars and restaurants that make up Downtown Auburn isn't really worth tracking down. Far better that you should head directly to **Old Town**, a delightful cluster of historic buildings (and a few less interesting modern variants). Pick up a walking tour map from the **Visitor Centre** (*see p309*) and trace the town's history around several blocks. Among the more notable structures are the adorable skinny firehouse (Lincoln Way, at Commercial Street) and the post office mere steps away, the oldest in the state (it opened in 1852).

However, the real eye-catcher is the monumental, hilltop **Placer County Courthouse** (Lincoln Way, at Maple Street), completed at the turn of the last century. It's now home to the **Placer County Museum** (1-530 889 6500, closed Mon), an above-average selection of displays on the area's history. The town's other museums include the **Gold Country Museum** (1273 High Street, 1-530 887 0690, closed Mon), which offers a few illuminating displays but which can be safely bypassed if you've spent time in the mining museums and attractions in Nevada City and Grass Valley, and the **Bernard House Museum** (291 Auburn-Folsom Road, 1-530 888 6891, closed Mon), a restored Victorian house.

If you're heading to (or, indeed, on your way here from) Nevada City and Grass Valley, you've two choices as regards your route. Highway 49 is quicker and prettier, but travelling on I-80 and Highway 174 leads you via **Colfax**, a tidy, tiny railroad town whose founder is commemorated with a handsome statue. The visitor centre, housed in an old railroad car, can provide a walking tour leaflet.

Where to eat & drink

Culinary pickings are slim Downtown, though there is at least a branch of **Z Pie** (799 Lincoln Way, 1-530 888 0520, $); this likeable mini-chain, which also has branches in Placerville and San Luis Obispo, dishes up generous pot pies in its small premises. There's more in Old Town: Mexican restaurant **Tio Pepe** (216 Washington Street, 1-530 888 6445, $) has a nice terrace, **Bootleggers** (210 Washington Street, 1-530 889 2229, closed Mon, $$) churns out good American fare, while the decidedly untouristy **Shanghai** (289 Washington Street, 1-530 823 2613, $$), housed in an original Gold Rush building, has an appealingly straight-shooting bar attached. Pleasant wine bar **Carpe Vino** (1568 Lincoln Way, 1-530 823 0320) provides a more sedate alternative.

Where to stay

Accommodations in Auburn are chiefly chain options. The most notable of the few B&Bs that there are is **Powers Mansion Inn** (164 Cleveland Avenue, 1-530 885 1166, www.vfr.net/~powerinn, $169-$299), which is a Victorian mansion that's been converted into a rather chintzy guesthouse. In Georgetown, about 13 miles east of Auburn, you'll find the **American River Inn** (Main Street, 1-800 245 6566, 1-530 333 4499, www.americanriverinn.com, $85-$115).

Coloma & Marshall Gold Discovery State Historic Park

As you leave Auburn on ever-attractive Highway 49, keep your camera handy. There's little point stopping, as there's nothing to see, but no collection of Gold Country holiday snaps is complete without a shot announcing to your friends and relatives that you made it to the plain and disappointingly unfashionable town of **Cool**.

A little further south sits **Coloma**, a fairly unexciting-looking town seemingly notable only for its watery options: it sits on the South Fork of the American River, and a number of companies offer rafting and kayaking trips along it. Among them are **Arta** (1-800 323 2782, www.arta.org, trips $99-$475), **Whitewater Connection** (1-800 336 7238, www.whitewater connection.com, trips $89-$369) and **Mariah** (1-800 462 7424, www.mariahwe.com, trips $85-$399). Expect to pay around $100 for a day-long rafting expedition. The waters are Class III, and suitable for beginners. However, more experienced rafters may prefer the livelier, less popular Middle Fork; all the abovementioned companies, and others besides, run trips along it from just outside Auburn. Booking is recommended. For information on rafting, kayaking and the river in general, check www.theamericanriver.com.

But while Coloma doesn't look like much, its history is unparalleled. While building a sawmill for German-born agricultural pioneer John Sutter in January 1848, James Marshall spotted specks of what appeared to be gold, an event that led to the epoch-making Gold Rush. The event is commemorated at the charming **Marshall Gold Discovery State Historic Park** (1-530 622 3470, www.parks.ca.gov), popular year-round with parties of Californian schoolchildren for whom the Gold Rush is part of their curriculum. The sweet little museum and reconstructed sawmill (which now runs off electricity) both hold the interest, as does the monument marking Marshall's grave. However, the memory that most kids take away with them is of successfully panning for gold themselves in a number of small troughs.

Where to eat, drink & stay

Eating options in Coloma are limited, but at least the food offered at **Marco's** (1-530 642 2025, closed dinner Mon-Fri and all day Sat & Sun in winter, $) and **Gaston's Beer & BBQ** (1-530 642 0886, $) is cheap, and lines the stomach for an evening at the no-nonsense **Coloma Club** café/bar (1-530 626 6390). Nearby **Sierra Nevada House**, on the corner of Highway 49 and Lotus Road (1-530 626 8096, www.sierra nevadahouse.com, $89-$105), is smarter, and also has nine guestrooms. The well-regarded **Coloma Country Inn** (1-530 622 6919, www.coloma countryinn.com, $110-$135) has a quartet of B&B rooms and a cottage that sleeps up to four.

Placerville

Opinions are divided on exactly how Placerville came to be nicknamed 'Hangtown', but one thing's for certain: it has nothing to do with putting pictures on a gallery wall. A century and a half ago, this was one of the roughest, liveliest and largest towns in this area, having sprung up out of the Coloma discovery of 1848. Today, it's settled down to host a population of around 10,000: it might not sound like much, but it's still enough to make it the biggest town in the Gold Country. This is very much a working town, as evidenced by the string of fast-food eateries near Highway 49.

Placerville's latter-day city fathers would, you feel, love for their town to take on the lucrative respectability of – for example – Nevada City to the north or Sutter Creek to the south. But it's not going to happen any time soon, and nor should it. As befits a town whose most photographed visitor attraction is a shambolic dummy dangling from a noose attached to the upper floor of a bar, Placerville is still nicely ragged around the edges.

Easygoing Main Street is dotted with interesting enterprises, including antiques shops, a second-hand bookstore (the **Bookery**, No.326, 1-530 626 6454), an expansive **Thomas Kinkade** gallery (Kinkade actually grew up here) and **Barefoot Contessa** (No.466, 1-530 621 0122), which deals in '50s-influenced *femme* chic. The El Dorado County Historical Society's **Fountain & Tallman Museum** (No.524, 1-530 626 0773, www.co.el-dorado. ca.us, closed Mon-Thur) has exhibits on the town's history; the nearby **Chamber of Commerce** (*see p309*) maps out a walking tour.

However, to learn more about Placerville, head out of town. **Gold Bug Park** (a mile north of Highway 50 up Bedford Avenue; 2635 Gold Bug Lane, 1-530 642 5207, www.goldbug park.org) offers an illustration of how mining used to work; tours are run for group bookings only. Less hands-on is the **El Dorado County Historical Museum** (104 Placerville Drive, 1-530 621 5865, www.co.el-dorado.ca.us, closed Mon & Tue); it's two miles west of Downtown, at the El Dorado County Fairgrounds.

Where to eat & drink

Placerville's eating and drinking options are all on Main Street. The smartest restaurant in town is **Tomei's** (No.384, 1-530 626 9766, closed Mon, $$–$$$), which dishes up Tuscan-ish nosh in a brick-walled room. **Powell Bros Steamer Co**

The big apple

The area north-east of Placerville and Route 50, centred around the village of Camino, has been an agricultural hotbed since the days of the Gold Rush. However, its own golden age came late in life, and only happened after a failure that threatened the livelihoods of the local residents. Following a blight on already-fading pear orchards in 1964, a group of local farmers got together and began an innovative marketing campaign, promoting apples as the area's main crop and naming the region **Apple Hill**. It worked a treat. Success has bred success: the number of businesses has tripled, while visitor numbers have reached an astonishing half-million a year. Apple Hill is now a tourist attraction in its own right.

From large farms such as **Larsen Apple Barn**, which claims to be the oldest continuously operating apple farm in the area (2461 Larsen Drive, 1-530 644 1415), to smaller roadside stands, countless

companies offer a bewildering variety of home-baked apple-based treats: pies, cakes, pastries, jellies, jams and juices. You can even just buy an apple itself if you prefer. Several wineries dot the area, as do half a dozen Christmas tree farms and the **Jack Russell Brewing Company** (2380 Larsen Road, 1-530 644 4722), which naturally includes an apple-flavoured beer among its products. Other companies add plums, peaches and pears to their lists.

A handful of businesses remain open all year, but the period from late summer until Christmas is when Apple Hill is at its busiest. And busy it certainly is: at weekends, the place is overrun with tourists in search of the perfect pie or the juiciest jelly. Online, www.applehill.com provides details of the area's various retailers and maps of where to find them, along with details on the exact timings of the various fruit harvests (and, thus, when the businesses plan to open).

Hanging around in **Placerville**.

& **Oyster Bar** (No.425, 1-530 626 1091, $$) is another good bet. For something simpler and/or snackier, grab a burger at the **Old Town Grill** (No.444, 1-530 622 2631, lunch only, closed Tue, $) or a smoothie at the tie-dyed **Cozmic Café** (No.594, 1-530 642 8481). Back on Main Street, beer-hounds should brave **Hangman's Tree** (No.305, 1-530 622 3878), or the even scruffier **Liar's Bench** (No.255, 1-530 622 0494).

Where to stay

Though no longer in its original building, the **Cary House Hotel** (300 Main Street, 1-530 622 4271, www.caryhouse.com, $75-$80) has been running since 1857. Reasonable guestrooms are identified by names: those on the second floor are named after wines; those on the fourth after historical figures. There are also a few B&Bs, among them the **Chichester-McKee House** (800 Spring Street, 1-800 831 4008, 1-530 626 1882, www.innercite.com/~inn, $105-$135), and a string of unremarkable, edge-of-town motels for which booking is unlikely to be necessary outside of the main Apple Hill season (*see p304* **The big apple**).

Into Amador County

The drive south from Placerville on Highway 49 is pleasant, but doesn't give its charms away too easily. The towns of **Plymouth**, **Drytown** and **Fiddletown**, the latter east of Highway 49, are blink-and-you-miss-'em kind of places, seemingly with little to entice the visitor to stay for longer than it takes to drive through them. Tiny **Amador City**, a short drive further south, gives off much the same impression.

However, this area is fertile territory for wine-makers, and taking the Shenandoah Road north-east out of Plymouth will lead you in the direction of 20-odd wineries, all of whom welcome visitors for tastings and (more importantly, from their point of view) sales. If you've only time to visit one, head to the **Sobon Estate** (14430 Shenandoah Road, 1-209 245 4455, www.sobonwine.com): founded in 1856, it's also the home of the Shenandoah Valley Museum, which briefly details the history of winemaking in the area. For details of other wineries, contact the **Amador County**

Vintners Association (1-888 655 8614, 1-209 267 2297, www.amadorwine.com) and the **El Dorado Winery Association** (1-800 306 3956, www.eldoradowines.org), or look out for their leaflets in hotels, restaurants and visitor centres.

Where to eat, drink & stay

For the best barbecue in the Gold Country, and perhaps in the whole of California, drive four miles south of Placerville on Highway 49 to El Dorado, and hugely popular locals' hangout **Poor Red's BBQ** (6221 Pleasant Valley Road, 1-530 622 2901, $).

There are many appealing eating and lodging options in **Sutter Creek**, a 15-minute drive south of Plymouth; *see below*. However, Amador City has both under one roof in the shape of the handsome old **Imperial Hotel**, established in 1879 but still going strong (1-209 267 9172, www.imperialamador.com, $100-$140). While the service in the dinner-only restaurant is a little hit-or-miss, the Californian cooking is highly reliable, and the grand old bar's a real winner. Upstairs are six rooms, individually decorated in basic but largely agreeable fashion. Room 5's our favourite.

Sutter Creek

The town of **Sutter Creek** was named for the same John Sutter who was indirectly responsible for starting the Gold Rush (*see p295*). However, Sutter's relationship with the town was vague at best; the area was named for him by a crew of his workers, whom he sent to the area in 1844 to look for lumber. Sutter Creek had become a quartz mining town by the mid 1850s, and a successful one at that. Its deep rock mines – which, like Grass Valley, employed a number of expert miners originally from Cornwall in England – were closed as recently as 1942, since when the town has eked out a sleepy and even cultured existence.

In comparison to the two decent-sized settlements closest to it in either direction, Sutter Creek doesn't feel like a Gold Country town. While both Placerville and Jackson have clung on to their original blue-collar, working-man character, Sutter Creek is a genteel, mannered, even twee place; it's charming, and by God it knows it. Entering town from the north along Highway 49 (which is also known, for a brief stretch, as Hanford Street), the road is dotted with delicate private residences and chocolate-box B&Bs. A few hundred yards south and you'll be on skinny, slow-moving Main Street, a smartly maintained string of buildings that either boast interesting

histories or look like they should. A walking tour leaflet is available from the **Visitor Center** (*see p309*).

Sutter Creek's bona fide visitor attractions are mostly limited to a series of special events, from the deeply silly Great Sutter Creek Duck Race (last Saturday in April) to a blues 'n' booze festival in September. Year-round, the **Knight Foundry** (81 Eureka Street, 1-209 267 0201), set up in 1873 to manufacture mining equipment and now the sole remaining water-powered foundry in the country, offers tours, as does the expensive and over-dramatised **Sutter Gold Mine**, just north of the town on Highway 49 (1-866 762 2837, www.cavern tours.com). The tiny **J Monteverde General Store Museum** (3 Randolph Street), a century-old grocer's shop that's been preserved as a museum, will prove briefly diverting. And if you're here in the evenings, look up the **Main Street Theatre Works** (1-888 243 6789, www.mstw.org), who perform classic plays in summer at a new amphitheatre at the Kennedy Mine in Jackson (*see p308*) or the **Sutter Creek Theatre** (44 Main Street, 1-209 267 1070, www.suttercreektheatre.com). Housed in a former silent movie house, the latter has found a fresh lease of life under new owners, and stages music, theatre and family entertainment.

Where to eat & drink

The cheesy sign outside **Zinfandels** (51 Hanford Street, 1-209 267 5008, dinner only, closed Mon-Wed, $$$$) belies the fact that this is a genuinely top-quality restaurant. Greg West's contemporary Californian menu is highlighted by the fish specials. Its competition in the town comes from **Susan's Place** (15 Eureka Street, 1-209 267 0945, closed Mon-Wed, $$), a restaurant and wine bar whose main appeal is its shaded patio; and the colourful **Daffodils** (53-55 Main Street, 1-209 267 5211, closed Tue, $$–$$$), a good lunch bet. The **Back Roads Coffee House** (74A Main Street, 1-209 267 0440) brews a fine cup o' joe; **Bellotti Bar**, adjacent to Daffodils, ought to be your watering hole of choice.

Where to stay

B&B is a British tradition, so its appropriate that one of the area's nicest such options should be run by an English couple: Roger and Sue Garlick, who've looked after the charming **Grey Gables Inn** since 1994 (161 Hanford Street, 1-800 473 9422, 1-209 267 1039, www.greygables.com, $125-$224). Similarly delightful, albeit slightly posher (and pricier), is the immaculate, low-key **Foxes Inn** (77 Main Street, 1-800 987 3344, 1-209

Central California (sidebar)

Going for gold

If there were any fortunes left to be made from gold in the Gold Country, you'd figure there'd be someone still there making theirs. But though the gold mining industry has long since died out, it is still possible to uncover a few flecks in various locations around the area.

Panning for gold is simple. Take a darkened pan, relatively shallow and about the size of an LP record, and fill it with a few handfuls of gravel and/or sand from the river where you're hoping to find gold. Hold the pan under water and swirl it in a gentle circular motion until a good deal of the sand has ebbed away. Drain some of the water, then put the pan gently back into the water and swirl the pan again, until more of the gravel and sand have disappeared. Gold is heavier than gravel and water, and so by repeating this process, any gold you have collected should eventually collect in the bottom of the pan. No luck? Try, try and try again: you think the Gold Rush prospectors of 1849 gave up after a couple of attempts?

Malakoff Diggins State Historic Park in Nevada County (*see p299*), the **Marshall Gold Discovery State Historic Park** in Coloma (*see p303*), Sutter Creek's **Sutter Gold Mine** (*see p306*), the **Kennedy Gold Mine** in Jackson (*see p308*) and **Columbia State Historic Park** (*see p310*) all allow visitors to pan for gold. But you may even get lucky outside these tourist attractions: the North Fork of the American River in Weimar (eight miles east of Auburn; *see p302*), the Bear River in **Colfax** (*see p303*) and the Briceburg Recreation Area 15 miles east of **Mariposa** (*see p313*) have all been known to yield some of the magical stuff. And in **Jamestown** (*see p312*), Gold Prospecting Adventures (1-800 596 0009, www.goldprospecting.com) offers a variety of supervised gold-panning expeditions.

267 5882, www.foxesinn.com, $155-$215). The town's oldest and largest B&B, however, is the cutesy, old-fashioned **Sutter Creek Inn** (75 Main Street, 1-209 267 5606, www.sutter creekinn.com, $90-$190). Of its 17 rooms, eight have private patios and four have extraordinary beds that hang from the ceiling and gently swing. Keep an eye out for the historic **American Exchange Hotel** (53-55 Main Street, 1-209 267 5211, www.americanexchangehotel.com), scheduled to reopen in early 2005. Any or all of the abovementioned B&Bs are better options than the 52-room **Historian Inn** (271 Hanford Street, 1-209 267 9177, $89.90): guestrooms at the town's only sizeable hotel are mere motel quality at near-hotel prices.

Jackson & around

Sutter Creek too sleepy for you? This might be a little more like it. **Jackson**, set up in 1849 and the seat of Amador County, was once one of the Gold Country's more riotous mining towns, and remained unashamed of its naughty reputation for years. Prostitution was only made illegal here in the 1950s, and stories (probably apocryphal, but who cares?) still abound about the high-stakes poker evenings in the **National Hotel** (*see p308*), a classic Old West landmark. While Sutter Creek's evening pleasures are culinary, Jackson is more of a drinking town. Wallflowers should perhaps steer clear.

Central California

The **Amador County Museum** (225 Church Street, 1-209 223 6386, www.amadorarchives.org, closed Mon & Tue), located in a 150-year-old hilltop mansion north of Main Street, houses a number of intermittently interesting exhibits; the **Kennedy Gold Mine** (1-209 223 9542, www.kennedygoldmine.com, $5-$9), meanwhile, is only open on weekends. Walking tours of the town are conducted by local historian Larry Cenotto every Saturday at 10am, leaving from the Incognito Coffee Shop at 12 Water Street; call 1-209 223 5192 for more information.

While close to 4,000 people live in Jackson, the population of **Volcano**, ten miles east along attractive Highway 88, is barely into three figures. However, this wee hamlet, named by soldiers who naively figured a volcano may have been responsible for the crater in which it sits, is a charming spot with a surprising amount of history: California's first lending library, amateur theatre group and astronomical observatory were established here in the 19th century. None remains, of course, but the **Volcano Theatre Company** (www.volcanotheatre.org) provides a link back to this venerated past, performing in the tiny Cobblestone Theatre and, occasionally, outdoors in its *darling* amphitheatre. Also in town is the ancient but still extant **St George Hotel**, and its attached restaurant (*see below*).

The roads around Volcano, and generally east of Jackson, are prime driving territory: windy, verdant and picnic-friendly, they are also off the beaten track as far as many tourists are concerned. The main draw is **Black Chasm** (*see p300* **Going underground**), but the area also boasts two more attractive sights. North-east of Volcano along Ramshorn Grade is **Daffodil Hill**, a huge (and privately owned) hill blanketed in flowers that's at its most breathtaking from early March to mid April. And south of Volcano in Pine Grove, reached via another pretty series of roads, is **Indian Grinding Rock State Historic Park** (1-209 296 7488, www.parks. ca.gov). The park takes its name from the Native American practice of grating acorns into the marbleised limestone formation to make an edible powder. The on-site Chaw'se Regional Indian Museum adds a little more background.

South and west of Jackson, meanwhile, sit a few unremarkable towns that merit only brief mention. Ten miles along Highway 88 lies **Ione**, a large-ish town notable chiefly for the rebuilt **Ione Hotel** (*see p309*) and the **Preston School of Industry**: completed in 1894 and opened thereafter as California's first reform school, the daunting building has recently found new fame of sorts after former Pavement drummer Spiral Stairs named his new band after it. The Castle, as it's known, is closed to the public. Ten miles south of Jackson on 49 is minuscule

Mokelumne Hill, which offers further lodging options. And a further seven miles down the road is **San Andreas**, in which it's worth stopping only to pick up tourist information in the **Calaveras County Chamber of Commerce** (*see p309*; San Andreas is the county seat) and to have a nose around the above-average **Calaveras County Museum** (30 N Main Street, 1-209 754 4658, www.co.calaveras.ca.us).

Where to eat & drink

Culinary pickings are slim in Jackson itself. **Mel & Faye's Diner** (est 1956), a reasonable roadside eaterie whose stellar local reputation is indicative chiefly of the lack of competition, is now so popular that it was recently forced to relocate to larger premises on Highway 49 (1-209 223 0853, $). A pair of Italian eateries offers a link to the Gold Rush era, when large numbers of Italian immigrants moved to the town; both **Buscaglia's** (1218 Jackson Gate Road, 1-209 223 9992, closed Mon & Tue, $$$) and its near-neighbour **Teresa's** (1235 Jackson Gate Road, 1-209 223 1786, closed Wed & Thur, $$$), which sit a quarter-mile from Downtown, are family-run operations.

However, the smartest dining in the area is at the **St George Hotel** in Volcano (*see below*; $$$). Get there early for a drink at the hotel's bar, the **Whiskey Flat Saloon**: a fabulously atmospheric Old West hangout, it's such a locals' joint that it's usually closed by 10pm. The dim-lit and bawdy saloon bar at Jackson's **National Hotel** (*see below*) is also a locals' affair, but the place only gets livelier as the night gets later, especially on weekends.

Where to stay

The historic **National Hotel** (2 Water Street, 1-209 223 0500, $40-$195) is a shambles these days, but if you're prepared to forego luxury for authentic earthiness, it's worth considering. Of the town's B&Bs, the historic **Court Street Inn** (215 Court Street, 1-800 200 0416, 1-209 223 0416, www.courtstreetinn.com, $125-$190), built in the 1870s, is comfortable but frilly, despite the presence of a few sweet design touches: the Chablis room has a sink made from an old sewing machine case. The grand **Gate House** (1330 Jackson Gate Road, 1-800 841 1072, 1-209 223 3500, www.gatehouseinn.com, $130-$205) is decorated in more tasteful fashion, and has two self-contained cottages that provide a little more privacy than the four rooms in the main house.

But the best lodging in this region sits either side of Jackson. Volcano's **St George Hotel** (1-209 296 4458, www.stgeorgehotel.com, $83-$109) has stood here for over 130 years, but a recent refurbishment has spruced things up hugely. Over in Ione is the lovely **Ione Hotel** (25 W Main Street, 1-209 274 6082, www.ionehotel. com, $70-$80). Originally built in the 1850s, it's been destroyed by fire three times in the last century and a half, but has recently been delightfully rebuilt to something approximating its original specifications. And in Mokelumne Hill is the comfortable, 12-room **Hotel Leger** (1-209 286 1401, www.hotelleger.com, $65-$155).

There's also camping in **Indian Grinding Rock State Historic Park**, either in 23 year-round campsites (reservations not accepted) or – more appealingly – in seven teepee-shaped 'houses' made of cedar and fronted with tree bark. Booking for these U'macha'tam'ma' sites is necessary; call or write to the park (14881 Pine Grove-Volcano Road, Pine Grove, CA 95665).

Resources

Hospital
Placerville *Marshall Medical Center, 293 Marshall Way (1-530 622 1441/www.marshallmedical.org).*

Internet
Auburn *Kinko's, 455 Grass Valley Highway (1-530 887 8800/www.kinkos.com).* **Open** 7am-10pm Mon-Fri; 8am-7pm Sat, Sun.
Placerville *Placerville Library, 345 Fair Lane (1-530 621 5540/www.eldoradolibrary.org).* **Open** 10am-8pm Mon-Wed; 10am-5pm Thur-Sat.

Police
Auburn *1215 Lincoln Way (1-530 823 4237).*
Jackson *33D Broadway (1-209 223 1771).*
Placerville *730 Main Street (1-530 642 5210).*
Sutter Creek *18 Main Street (1-209 267 5646).*

Post office
Auburn *371 Nevada Street (1-530 885 7837).*
Jackson *424 Sutter Street (1-209 223 7720).*
Placerville *3045 Sacramento Street (1-530 622 5174).*
Sutter Creek *3 Gopher Flat Road (1-209 267 0128).*

Tourist information
Auburn *Placer County Visitor Center, 13411 Lincoln Way (1-866 752 2371/1-530 887 2111/ www.visitplacer.com).* **Open** 9am-3pm Mon-Sat; 11am-3pm Sun. When this is closed, visit the less helpful **Auburn Chamber of Commerce** (601 Lincoln Way, 1-530 885 5616, www.auburnchamber.net, 9am-5pm Mon-Fri).
Jackson *Amador County Chamber of Commerce, 125 Peek Street (1-209 223 0350).* **Open** 9am-4pm Mon-Fri.
Placerville *Placerville Chamber of Commerce, 542 Main Street (1-800 457 6279/1-530 621 5885/ www.eldoradocounty.org).* **Open** 9am-5pm Mon-Fri.
Sutter Creek *Sutter Creek Visitor Center, 11A Randolph Street (1-800 400 0305/ www.suttercreek.org).* **Open** call for details.

Columbia State Historic Park. *See p311.*

Southern Gold Country

Angels Camp & Murphys

It's stretching a point to pin it as life imitating art, but **Angels Camp** is one of only a few in the US whose entire tourist industry is based on something that never happened. While drinking in a local saloon one evening in 1865, Samuel Clemens, a resident of nearby Jackass Hill, was told by a bibulous group of miners about a frog famed for his ability to leap huge distances, and a bet that ensued between two local gamblers over whether a second frog could spring higher. Clemens, despite presumably being a little worse for wear himself at the time, managed to keep the bogus yarn in mind; later that year, he published a short story, using his pen-name of Mark Twain, entitled 'The Celebrated Jumping Frog of Calaveras County'.

Fast-forward 64 years. To celebrate the town having its Main Street paved (these old Gold Country towns didn't need much excuse for a party), some bright spark suggested reviving Twain's piece of amusing exaggeration and staging a contest to find the most athletic frog in the region. And so it came to pass that on 20 May 1928, the Pride of San Joaquin, owned by a gent named Louis Fisher, came away triumphant having leapt an impressive three and a half feet from the Main Street pavement.

The **Jumping Frog Jubilee**, as it's now called, has been staged almost every May since then, and is now, by some distance, the main attraction in the town. The event, which attracts 2,000 hopeful amphibians each year, is now part of the Calaveras County Fair, staged each May at the county showgrounds (called, inevitably, Frogtown). The world record, since you ask, is held by Rosie the Ribiter, a frog owned by a Mr Lee Guidici of Santa Clara, which launched itself a scarcely credible 21 feet five and three-quarter inches (6.19 metres) in 1986. The main diversion in Angels Camp other than Frogfest is the impressive **Angels Camp Museum** (735 S Main Street, 1-209 736 2963, www.cityofangels.org), whose fine displays of mining equipment are matched by the wagons and carts housed in their Carriage House.

The little town of **Murphys**, a 20-minute drive east along Highway 4, takes its name from a family of Irish immigrants who arrived in the area in 1844 and immediately set about acquiring all the land they could get their hands on. The Irish heritage is celebrated regularly: check the shamrocks painted on the roads, and if you're in the area in March, look for Murphys Irish Days, wherein more or less everything and everyone turns green for 24 hours. See www.murphysirishdays.org for more details.

But Murphys doesn't need exaggerated blarney to come off as likeable: it's a naturally elegant, bijou little town. Although the Murphy family struck lucky in the late 1840s, taking a reputed $2 million worth of gold from their mines in a mere 12 months, the town plays down its mining history. Indeed, the area's biggest industry these days is wine. The largest winery, by some distance, is the **Ironstone Vineyards** (1894 Six Mile Road, 1-209 728 1251, www.iron stonevineyards.com), a highly ambitious complex that contains a museum and a huge amphitheatre that stages concerts in summer. For details of other local wineries, see www.calaveraswines.org.

Despite the lack of attractions, tourists have been coming in increasing numbers over the last few years. Smart ones pick up a detailed walking tour leaflet and follow it around the town, or even take the free Saturday morning tours along Main Street (meet at 10am in front of the small **Old Timers Museum**, housed in the much-threatened but never-destroyed Peter L Traver building; 1-209 728 1160, closed

Mon-Thur). Even smarter ones spend time at **Calaveras Big Trees State Park** (1-209 795 2234, www.parks.ca.gov), a delightful spot 15 miles east of Murphys notable for its excellent fishing and swimming but named for the immense sequoia redwoods that dominate its landscape; take the North Grove tour to see them up close. However, despite its increased popularity, Murphys and the surrounding area still feel comparatively undiscovered. Get here before it changes.

Where to eat & drink

Restaurants in Angels Camp are functional but not worth a special trip; if you're passing through and fancy a spot of lunch, the **Pickle Barrel** (1225 S Main Street, 1-209 736 4704, lunch only, closed Mon, $) knocks up a decent sandwich. There's better over in Murphys: **Grounds** (402 Main Street, 1-209 728 8663, closed dinner, $$) has long satisfied locals with its American-Italian menu of simple, flavoursome dishes, and has now spawned a sibling in the shape of burger-and-pizza joint **Firewood** (420 Main Street, 1-209 728 3248, $$). **Auberge 1899** (498 Main Street, 1-209 728 1899, dinner only, closed Mon & Tue, $$$$) serves higher-priced French staples.

Where to stay

Murphys offers a variety of lodgings, of which the most venerable is the **Murphys Historic Hotel & Lodge** (457 Main Street, 1-800 532 7684, 1-209 728 3444, www.murphyshotel.com, $50-$100). The hotel makes great play of its history, as well it might: opened in 1856, its guests have included Ulysses Grant and Mark Twain. However, be warned that only nine of its 29 rooms are in the main building; the remainder are forgettable motel-style units adjacent to the hotel itself. Better options include the 14-room **Victoria Inn** (402 Main Street, 1-209 728 8933, www.victoriainn-murphys.com, $95-$310), recently renovated to a very high standard (the octagonal Eucalyptus Hall suite is a particular treat), or the delightful **Dunbar House, 1880** (271 Jones Street, 1-209 728 2897, www.dunbarhouse.com, $175-$260), an exemplary example of how to operate a B&B.

Columbia State Historic Park

Is it a town? Is it a museum? Is it a theme park? **Columbia State Historic Park** (1-209 532 0150, www.parks.ca.gov) can, with varying degrees of accuracy, be tagged as all three, assuming you're a good sport and use your imagination.

Columbia was, for a time, one of the largest Gold Rush towns, and one of the most lucrative: nearly $100 million of gold, around half a billion dollars' worth in today's money, was sourced here in the couple of decades following James Marshall's lucky discovery a little over 80 miles north. 'The Gem of the Southern Mines', they called it, a name that could have come about equally for its buildings as for its gold reserves. When the mining died out in the 1860s, so did Columbia; and that, you'd think, was that.

But while its residents moved on, Columbia, or at least some parts of it, stayed standing. Just after World War II, the Californian authorities bestowed landmark status on the town. The remaining buildings have since been restored and preserved, and the whole site, whose centre is pedestrianised, is now run as one of California's more popular State Historic Parks.

It's a curious place. During the day, large gaggles of schoolkids mill around, entertained (for free) by immaculate costumed actors acting out a series of hokey dialogues, brawls and trials; across the road, a gift shop hawks candies and souvenirs. A museum offers displays about the town's history, but also details its second life. Two hotels stand proudly, but not as mere ornaments. Both are open for business; one has a gourmet-quality restaurant, the other a theatre (the **Sierra Repertory Company**; 1-209 532 3120, www.sierrarep.com). Down the street, a bar fills up on Fridays not with tourists but with locals from nearby Sonora, who down longnecks and listen to a noisy and decidedly un-19th-century bar band.

The fusion of old and new in Columbia is sometimes a little chaotic; the portrayal of the former is also cheesy at times. And yet it all still manages to work very nicely: an afternoon here is an afternoon well spent.

Where to eat, drink & stay

The **City Hotel** (1-800 532 1479, 1-209 532 1479, www.cityhotel.com, $105-$125) and the slightly less impressive **Fallon Hotel** (same details) are both authentic , which is to say that the rooms are handsome, basic and small. If there's no room at the inns, try the **Blue Nile**, a B&B (11250 Pacific Street, 1-209 532 8041, www.blue-nile-inn.com, $105-$135), or the less appealing **Columbia Gem Motel** (22131 Parrotts Ferry Road, 1-866 436 6685, 1-209 532 4508, www.columbiagem.com, $69-$89). Dining-wise, the **City Hotel** also boasts an excellent restaurant ($$$), whose menu of American classics is delivered with skill; the Fallon's only refreshments come at its ice-cream stall. The City Hotel has called its bar **What**

Cheer, and well might you ask; you'll get a more robust welcome up the road at the noisy, beery **St Charles Saloon** (1-209 533 4656).

Sonora

Next to its tourist-drawing neighbour, the town of **Sonora** can't compete. Sensibly, it doesn't even try to. This feels like the most alive, the most current of the Gold Country towns. Evidence of a busy working community is all over the town, from the diners on Washington Street – essentially, the town's Main Street – to the huge superstores just behind it (shielded from tourists' eyes, but there nonetheless).

The town began to grow up in 1848, but this is no standard Gold Rush history. Sonora takes its name from Sonora in Mexico, the original home of its first settlers. The Mexicans were turfed out but the name remained, and the town thrived. However, unlike other Gold Rush towns to the north, Sonora never got around to tapping its potential as a tourist destination. There are attractions north and south of it, not to mention **Yosemite National Park** not far to the east (see p324), and the **Tuolumne County Museum** (158 W Bradford Street, 1-209 532 1317, www.tchistory.org) has some worthwhile Gold Rush memorabilia. But ultimately, Sonora is a town designed chiefly for its residents and rather half-heartedly for its visitors.

Where to eat & drink

Though nowhere has a reputation anything like that of the City Hotel in Columbia, there's a good deal of dining variety in Sonora. The Mediterranean menu served in colourful **One Twenty-Four** (124 N Washington Street, 1-209 533 2145, dinner only, closed Mon & Tue, $$$) is as close as Sonora gets to fine dining. Simpler pleasures can be found at the **Diamondback** (110 S Washington Street, 1-209 532 6661, $), which churns out burgers and other hearty staples; **Old Stan** (177 S Washington Street, 1-209 536 9598, closed Mon & Tue, $$$), where you can munch on hot tapas or something more substantial; and three much-of-a-muchness Mexican joints: **El Jardín** (76 N Washington Street, 1-209 588 0770, $$), **Pablito's** (126 S Washington Street, 1-209 533 1323, $$) and **Alfredo's** (123 S Washington Street, 1-209 532 8332, $$). Bar-wise, try the proudly rough and ready **Iron House Lounge** (97 S Washington Street, 1-209 532 4492), packed on weekends with young and rowdy locals sucking back cheap longnecks and comparing tattoos.

All aboard for **Jamestown**.

Where to stay

You can't miss the **Sonora Days Inn**: built in the late 19th century and housed in a plum corner location (160 S Washington Street, 1-800 580 4667, 1-209 532 2400, www.sonoradays inn.com, $55-$105), its striking Spanish façade can't fail to grab the attention. However, the guestrooms are in need of TLC, and the motel complex that's been built up behind the main building does it no favours. The **Gunn House Hotel** (286 S Washington Street, 1-209 532 3421, www.gunnhousehotel.com, $69-$109), really a motel with bells on, is in better shape, but easily the best place to stay in Sonora is **Knowles Hill House** (253 Knowles Hill Drive, 1-866 536 1146, 1-209 536 1146, www.knowleshillhouse.com, $135-$155). Troy and Eleanor Herriage have decorated their 1920s hilltop home with impeccable taste (no chintz!), and run their four-room B&B in similarly unimpeachable fashion. It's a truly delightful place to spend the night.

Jamestown

The jolly wee town of **Jamestown** was first settled in 1848 by an Oregonian prospector named Benjamin Wood, whose crew of hopeful miners spent a happy few months dragging all the gold they could from a creek that now bears their leader's name. However, the town itself is named for Colonel George James, who turned up the following year, bought everyone present champagne and was soon appointed as the town's chief judge. James, of course, was as bent as a three-dollar bill, and fled town a few years later when the extent of his financial corruption was revealed. The town's mining heyday didn't last much longer than James did, though many do still pan for gold in Woods Creek, and the town's short but decidedly sweet Main Street is evocative of the period, despite the fact that much of it is reconstructed after a series of fires over the last 140 years.

The town got a second lease of life in 1897, with the arrival of the Sierra Railroad, and it's this history that attracts the majority of visitors to Jimtown (as some of the locals call it). Though the town's original railway depot was lost to fire years ago, the 26-acre **Railtown 1897 State Historic Park** (1-209 984 3953, www.railtown1897.org/railtown) still offers an authentic taste of America's Victorian-era rail industry. Clusters of ageing railway equipment sit on tracks and under cover; a few more explanatory displays would be nice, but staff are more than happy to answer any questions that may arise. The park runs steam train rides hourly on weekends (Apr-Oct, $3-$6); at other times, it acts as a popular movie location, with films such as *High Noon* having been shot here.

Where to eat, drink & stay

Jimtown's best restaurants are in the town's hotels, all of them on handsome Main Street. Built in 1859 and run for three decades by natural-born host Stephen Willey, the tidy **National Hotel** (1-800 894 3446, 1-209 984 3446, www.national-hotel.com, $90-$140) is the oldest hotel in town, and comes with an airy bar, a well-regarded restaurant ($$$) and a second-floor balcony that's beautiful in the late afternoon. Down the street, the rebuilt **Jamestown Hotel** (1-800 205 4901, 1-209 984 3902, www.jamestownhotel.com, $85-$175) is marginally larger and marginally fancier, and also comes with an atmospheric bar and a fine-dining restaurant ($$$$; innkeeper Norbert Mede is a former chef). Other options include the Italian staples at **Michelangelo** (1-209 984 4830, dinner only, closed Tue, $$), the Mexican basics at **Smoke Café** (1-209 984 3733, $$) and, for breakfast, the **Mother Lode Café** (1-209 984 3386, closed dinner, $); alternative accommodation can be found at the chintzily decorated **Royal Carriage Inn** (1-209 984 5271, www.royalcarriageinn.com, $75-$150).

Chinese Camp to Mariposa

Heading south of Sonora and Jamestown along Highway 49, signs of life become much rarer. **Chinese Camp**, which was once a sizeable Chinese settlement, is now essentially deserted; **Moccasin** is indeed forgettable, and **Groveland**, a five-minute drive east of it on Highway 120, will detain only those using its handful of hotels as a convenient gateway to Yosemite.

Keep driving, though, and you'll finally reach **Coulterville**. This scratchy little town, named for a couple of adventurous Pennsylvanians who set up a trading post here in 1850 in order to serve the miners working at Maxwells Creek, ceased to thrive over a century ago, but has held firm despite poverty and the inevitable destructive fires. Though few of the town's buildings remain from its 1850s beginnings, the majority of structures do date from the late 19th and early 20th centuries: an adobe general store dating to 1851, a 105-year-old general store now used as a B&B, a former Wells Fargo office now seeing use as the headquarters of the entertainingly inclusive **Northern Mariposa County History Center** (1-209 878 3015, closed Mon & Tue). The entire town is a State Historic Landmark; pick up a walking tour map from the **Visitor Center** (*see below*) and stroll along Main Street, and it's easy to see why.

Edging south along the by-now dipping and curving Highway 49, the scenery is delightful (this is a favourite ride among parties of bikers) and the settlements are few and far between. Finally, a little under 30 treacherous miles south of Coulterville, you'll reach **Mariposa**. On first glance, it's a fairly dreary place whose only immediately apparent selling point to potential visitors is its proximity to Yosemite. But look around a while, and you'll find it's not entirely without its charms. The **Mariposa County Courthouse** is the third oldest continuously operating courthouse in the country, and opens for tours on weekends (1-209 966 3685), while the gold mining exhibits at the tidily curated **Mariposa Museum & History Center** (5119 Jessie Street, 1-209 966 2924, closed Mon-Fri in Jan) shouldn't be overlooked. Two miles south of Mariposa on Highway 49, meanwhile, sits the **California State Mining & Mineral Museum** (1-209 742 7625, http://cal-parks.ca.gov, closed Tue Oct-Apr, $3), whose liveliest exhibit is a bewilderingly immense 13-pound gold nugget discovered in the American River (*see p303*) in 1865.

Where to eat, drink & stay

Groveland's lodgings include the delightful 150-year-old **Groveland Hotel** (1-800 273 3314, 1-209 962 4000, www.groveland.com, $135-$175) and the sweet little **Hotel Charlotte** (1-209 962 6455, www.hotel charlotte.com, $83), while the pride of Coulterville is the **Hotel Jeffery** (1-209 878 3471, www.hoteljefferygold.com, $90-$115), built in 1851 and recently revitalised under new owners. All three places have restaurants. In Mariposa, dining options are limited to a handful of mediocre places on or close by Main Street; stick to something simple from its immense menu, and the **Red Fox** (1-209 966 7900, $$) is probably the best of them. Among the lodgings are the **Mariposa Lodge** (1-800 966 8819, 1-209-966 3607, www.mariposalodge.com, $45-$100) and the **Miners Inn** (1-888 646 2244, 1-209 742 7777, www.yosemite-rooms.com, $60), a pair of motels, and the century-old **Mariposa Hotel-Inn** (1-800 317 3244, $90-$150).

Resources

Hospital
Sonora *Tuolumne General Hospital, 101 Hospital Road (1-209 533 7100/www.tghospital.com).*

Internet
Angels Camp *Angels Camp Library, 185 S Main Street (1-209 736 2198).* **Open** 10am-2pm Tue, Fri, Sat; 10am-5pm Wed, Thur.
Sonora *Tuolumne County Library, 480 Greenley Road (1-209 533 5507).* **Open** 10am-9pm Mon-Wed; 10am-5.30pm Thur-Sat.

Police
Angels Camp *200 Monte Verde (1-209 736 2567).*
Sonora *100 S Green Street (1-209 532 8143).*

Post office
Angels Camp *1216 S Main Street (1-209 736 2220).*
Mariposa *5109 Jessie Street (1-209 966 5798).*
Sonora *781 S Washington Street (1-209 536 2728).*

Tourist information
Angels Camp *Calaveras County Lodging & Visitors Association, 1211 S Main Street (1-209 736 0049/www.calaveras.org).* **Open** 9am-5pm Mon-Fri.
Coulterville *Coulterville Visitor Center, 5007 Main Street (1-209 878 3074).* **Open** 8am-5pm Mon, Wed-Sun.
Mariposa *Mariposa County Visitors Bureau, 5158 Highway 140 (1-209 966 3685/www.homeofyosemite.net).* **Open** 9am-5pm daily.
Sonora *Tuolumne County Visitors Bureau, 542 Stockton Road (1-209 533 4420/www.thegreat unfenced.com).* **Open** 9am-7pm Mon-Fri; 10am-6pm Sat; 10am-5pm Sun.

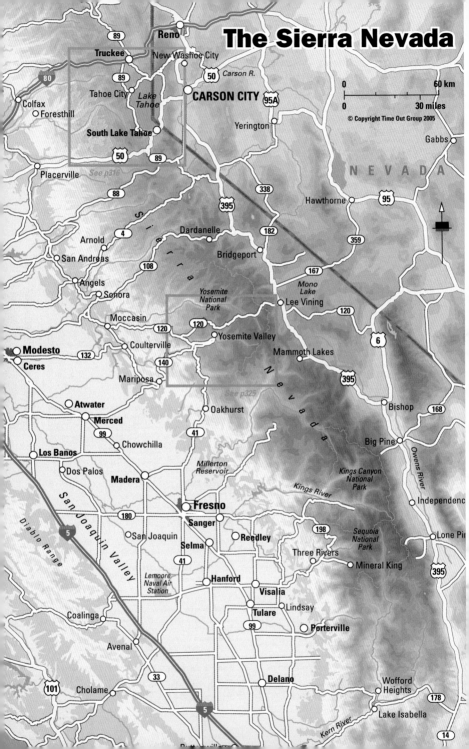

The Sierra Nevada

0 — 60 km
0 — 30 miles
© Copyright Time Out Group 2005

NEVADA

Reno
89
Truckee
New Washoe City
89
Tahoe City
Lake Tahoe
50
Carson R.
80
Colfax
Foresthill
CARSON CITY
95A
South Lake Tahoe
50
89
Yerington
Gabbs
Placerville
See p316
88
Hawthorne
95
338
4
Arnold
Dardanelle
182
395
359
San Andreas
108
Bridgeport
Angels
Sonora
167
Mono Lake
Moccasin
Yosemite National Park
Lee Vining
120
120
120
6
Modesto
132
Coulterville
Yosemite Valley
Mammoth Lakes
Ceres
140
Mariposa
See p325
395
Bishop
168
Atwater
Oakhurst
Big Pine
Merced
99
41
Owens River
Chowchilla
Madera
Millerton Reservoir
Kings Canyon National Park
Los Banos
Independenc
Dos Palos
Kings River
Fresno
180
Sanger
Lone Pin
San Joaquin
198
Sequoia National Park
Selma
Reedley
41
Three Rivers
395
Lemoore Naval Air Station
Hanford
Mineral King
San Joaquin Valley
Visalia
Coalinga
Tulare
Lindsay
Diablo Range
5
99
Porterville
Avenal
33
Wofford Heights
178
Delano
101
Cholame
5
Lake Isabella
Kern River
14

The Sierra Nevada

Ski, hike and climb – or simply gaze on the world's mightiest trees.

The longest and highest single mountain range in the continental United States, the Sierra Nevada spans roughly 400 miles from its southern tip east of Bakersfield to its northern terminus near the Feather River, where it gives way to the Cascade Range. Within its long, skinny expanse – the Sierra range's widest point is a mere 75 miles – lie the highest waterfalls, the biggest trees and the deepest canyon in the country.

The range tends to grow higher as it moves southward: 14,495-foot (4,418-metre) Mount Whitney, the highest peak in the continental US, is found near the Sierra's southern end. The Sierra's crestline and highest summits are all located on the east side, where the mountains' escarpment is the steepest, rising abruptly from the 4,000-foot (1,200-metre) Owens Valley to more than 10,000 feet (3,000 metres) higher at the crest. On the Sierra's west side, the range rises much more gradually, leading from the sea-level Central Valley gently up through rolling foothills and densely forested slopes.

The Sierra Nevada is crossed by several good mountain roads, including the famous 9,945-foot (3,031-metre) Tioga Pass in Yosemite National Park. But don't expect to be able to get anywhere fast: distances are great, and the paved routes are slow and circuitous, winding up, over and around the mighty hills. Yosemite National Park alone is larger than the state of Rhode Island, and speed limits on the park's roads are commonly 45mph or less. Woe to the traveller who tries to get anywhere in a hurry, but considering the wealth of mountain scenery, that's not necessarily a bad thing.

The range includes three major national parks, Yosemite, Kings Canyon and Sequoia, and two national monuments, Giant Sequoia and Devils Postpile. It also includes dramatic Lake Tahoe. With all these national treasures, it's not surprising that parts of the Sierra Nevada are heavily trampled. Adding to the problem is the fact that most of the region is fully accessible only four to five months of the year: the snow-free months last roughly June to October. Hence the name Sierra Nevada, literally a 'snowy range'. Many of the Sierra's high mountain roads are completely closed from 1 November to the end of May, allowing the high country a long winter of blissful rest underneath a blanket of snow.

Unless you're a skier heading for the Sierra's steep slopes in winter, you're left with too brief a window of summer weather to visit this vast mountain playground, with its miles of hiking trails, rivers in which to raft and fish, alpine lakes for swimming, and picture-postcard scenery. The best way to avoid the crowds is to visit at the edges of the summer season: July and August are busiest and best avoided, but June can be spectacular, with most of the rivers, streams and waterfalls running at peak or near-peak flow, and although September and October bring vivid autumn colours, there's an abrupt drop-off in the number of visitors.

Lake Tahoe

The Tahoe region is defined by its 22-mile-long, azure-blue lake. Reaching a maximum depth of 1,636 feet (499 metres), **Lake Tahoe** is the tenth deepest lake in the world and the second deepest in the US. It is blessed with remarkable water clarity, a result of the pure High Sierra streams and snowmelt that drain into it. By any measure, the lake can be counted among the most notable features of the North American landscape. Unfortunately, much of the lake's 72 miles of shoreline – two-thirds of which lie inside California's boundary line, with one-third in Nevada – have been divvied up into highly exclusive parcels of private property.

Shortly after the 1849 Gold Rush, Lake Tahoe became a popular getaway spot for California's newly rich, and luxurious resorts sprang up. When the Comstock Lode was discovered just east of the lake in 1859, the first east-to-west road was built across Tahoe's mountains, roughly along what is now US 50. A massive logging effort began to supply lumber and fuel to the Comstock mines; it's estimated that, between 1860 and 1890, two-thirds of Tahoe's forestland was denuded. Had this rapid development and destruction not occurred, it's likely that Lake Tahoe would have been made a national park. Instead, much of the shore is private and the public lands that do exist are a patchwork of state and federal parkland.

Tahoe remains a major vacation destination, with tourism a billion-dollar industry. More than 200,000 visitors a day pour into the Tahoe basin in peak season, causing frequent traffic jams. For the best experience, avoid summer and winter weekends. Indeed, the lovely autumn off-season of September and October is one of the least crowded and most pleasant times at the lake, when Tahoe's abundant aspen groves put on their annual autumn colour show.

Activities

Besides giving themselves a chance to ogle the world-famous lake, most visitors come to Tahoe in winter to ski or snowboard, and in summer to hike, mountain bike or partake in a variety of water sports: fishing, boating, swimming or simply sunbathing. In every season, travellers come in droves to play the slots at the high-rise casinos on the Nevadan side of the lake, where gambling is legal. Tahoe is one of the few places on earth where you can hike into pristine wilderness, dine at a smart restaurant and then gamble the night away, all in the same period.

If you're here for athletic or recreational purposes, you'll be struck by two geographical features in addition to the huge lake: steep hills and high elevation. There's no way around it: this spectacular High Sierra scenery can only be seen by breathing high mountain air, and lowlanders may take a few days to get acclimatised to the 7,000-foot-plus elevation (more than 2,000 metres).

Tahoe is well suited for outdoor recreation not only because of the scenery but also because it has the necessary infrastructure. There are more than a dozen ski resorts in the Lake Tahoe Basin, including California's largest, **Squaw Valley USA** (*see p319*). Both Squaw and **Kirkwood** (*see p322*) bring in the punters all year round by transforming the ski slopes into mountain-bike runs during summer: bikers pay a daily fee that usually includes a few trips uphill on a gondola.

For those who prefer pavement, Tahoe is laced with paved bike paths: scenic **Truckee River Trail** follows the rushing river waters, while the more utilitarian **West Shore Trail** parallels busy Highway 89 from Tahoe City to Sugar

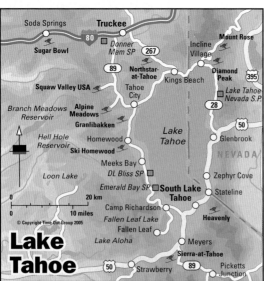

The best Sierra Nevada

Things to do
Visit the **Bodie State Historic Park** ghost town (*see p333*) or the mighty **Thunderbird Lodge** (*see p321*). Stroll among giant sequoia on the **Congress Trail** (*see p341*). Drive up to **Glacier Point** (*see p329*) for unbeatable views.

Places to stay
Kip among longhorn cattle at **Tyson's Canyon Ranch** (*see p322*). Prepare for high country adventures at **White Wolf Lodge** (*see p331*). For the full luxury wallop, **Ahwahnee Hotel** (*see p328*) is the only choice.

Places to eat
For stunning views, try **Mono Inn Restaurant** (*see p334*). **Truckee Diner** (*see p318*) is for the nostalgics, while **Lakefront** (*see p336*) serves outstanding French-Californian nosh.

Nightlife
It's pretty simple: Lake Tahoe's casinos, with historic **Cal-Neva Resort** (*see p319*) the best.

Culture
Apart from a smattering of museums, including **Old Truckee Jail** (*see p317*), you can forget it.

Sports & activities
Winter and summer, you'll have no need to look any further than **Yosemite Valley** (*see p325*). Yet there are plenty of fine alternatives, many of them much less busy. Try the hikes in **Tuolumne Meadows** (*see p330*) or from remote **Mineral King** (*see p342*), climbing **Mount Whitney** (*see p337*), and winter sports at **Sqaw Valley USA** (*see p319*) or **Mammoth Mountain** (*see p336*). Fisherman should start at **Saddlebag Lake** (*see p332*).

Pine Point. Most stretches of the 150-mile **Tahoe Rim Trail** (*see p319*) are open to mountan bikers and, in summer, bike rentals are available at more than a dozen shops.

Since Tahoe is a year-round destination, travellers should plan their visits according to how they want to spend their time. Snow can fall as early as mid October and the spring melt hold off until mid June, but the most dependable time for winter sports is December through March. Summer lasts only three months (mid June to mid September), which is time enough for many thousands of recreationists.

Truckee & around

Frequently overlooked in favour of the cities on the shoreline, **Truckee** is worth a stop for history buffs and railroad enthusiasts. In 1900 the Lake Tahoe Railway was completed between Truckee and Tahoe City, granting tourists a much easier route to the lake.

Truckee is still all about transport. On the busy junction of I-80 and Highway 89, it's a main connecting point for both trains and Greyhound buses. A few highlights are worth a look. The two-storey **Old Truckee Jail Museum** (10142 Jibboom Street, 1-530 582 0893, closed Mon-Fri) showcases the longest operating jail in California, which incarcerated criminals from 1875 to 1964, and the **Sierra Nevada Children's Museum** (11400 Donner Pass Road, 1-530 587 5437, closed Mon & Sun, $3-$7) has educational exhibits suitable for the young ones. Just west of Truckee, at the Castle

Peak exit off I-80, is a year-round celebration of snow sports: the **Western Ski Sport Museum at Boreal Ski Resort** (1-530 426 3666) portrays the history of skiing from the 1850s to today. Old ski movies run continuously in the theatre.

Winter can have a crueller side. Whenever Californians get hungry out on a hiking trip, inevitably somebody cracks a sorry joke about the Donner Party, the ill-fated group of emigrants who in 1846 took what they thought was a shortcut on their way west from Illinois. Caught in a series of early snowstorms at what is now **Donner Lake**, members of the wagon train resorted to cannibalism to survive the

Bare bones in Tahoe. *See p319.*

Central California

premature winter. The tragedy is remembered at the Donner Picnic Area and Emigrant Trail Museum at **Donner Memorial State Park** (off I-80, 1-530 582 7892, www.parks.ca.gov, $1-$3). A museum highlights the mid 1800s emigrant movement with displays including a loaded covered wagon and slides detailing the Donner story. For information, call in at **Truckee Donner Visitor Center** (*see p323*).

Where to eat & drink

There are plenty of dining choices in and around Truckee's gentrified Commercial Row, from the meat loaf and potatoes at the '40s-vintage **Truckee Diner** just across the railtracks (10144 W River Street, 1-530 582 6925, 1-530 582 5235, $) to the Asian-influenced **Dragonfly** (10118 Donner Pass Road, 1-530 587 0557, $$$) and plush and pricey **Moody's Bistro**, beneath the Truckee Hotel (10007 Bridge Street, 1-530 587 8688, $$$$). Breakfast aficionados head for the dozens of omelette varieties at the **Squeeze In** (10060 Donner Pass Road, 1-530 587 9814, closed dinner, $$).

For a night away from the crowds, two restaurants in the Soda Springs area are worth a mention: the **Engadine Café** at Rainbow Lodge (50800 Hampshire Rocks Road, 1-530 426 3661, $$$$) and **Ice Lakes Lodge** at Serene Lakes (111 Soda Springs Road, 1-530 426 7660, www.icelakeslodge. com, $$$). Both have bragging rights for lovely alpine scenery and memorable meals.

Where to stay

The 130-year-old **Truckee Hotel** (10007 Bridge Street, 1-530 587 4444, www.truckee hotel.com, $80-$135), built as a handy stop on the stagecoach route, now sits right by the railroad; cosy, good-value rooms at the other side avoid the noise. An even nicer B&B is the eight-room **Richardson House** (10154 High Street, 1-530 587 5388, www.richardsonhouse. com, $100-$175), high above Truckee's historic district; another excellent option is the **River Street Inn** (10009 E River Street, 1-530 550 9290, www.riverstreetinntruckee.com, $90-$150), a historic B&B that's been renovated to an extremely comfortable and chintz-free standard. (Chaplin stayed here when filming *The Gold Rush*.) Campers can get information on sites from the **Tahoe National Forest Truckee Ranger District** (1-530 587 3558).

North & West Shores

The North and South Shores of Lake Tahoe, although separated by little more than an hour's drive, are culturally a lot further apart. The biggest town on the North Shore, **Tahoe City**, offers plenty of lodgings, shops and restaurants, not to mention the useful **North Lake Tahoe Chamber of Commerce** (*see p323*), but without the cheap glitter of the South Shore's casinos and nightlife. Arguably, Tahoe City's most famous sight is the **Fanny Bridge**, where sightseers lean over the railing to watch

Happy days at the **Truckee Diner**.

migrating trout in the Truckee River. The West Shore is more sedate; which, for many people, is exactly how they want their Sierra break.

Most people head west of Tahoe City to **Squaw Valley USA** (*see p319*), but two museums in town are worth a visit. The **Watson Cabin** (560 N Lake Boulevard, 1-530 583 8717, closed Labor Day-14 June) is the oldest structure in town, built by Tahoe City's first policeman in 1909. Costumed docents are on hand with stories of early 20th-century life. The **Gatekeeper's Cabin Museum** (130 W Lake Boulevard, 1-530 583 1762, closed Wed-Sun 16 June-Apr) depicts Tahoe's late 19th-century reign as queen of California's resort destinations. In those days, before roads were built along the lake shore, travellers criss-crossed the lake by steam ship. Scale models of four such ships are displayed, and the building itself is an authentic hand-carved log cabin. The adjoining **Marion Steinbech Indian Basket Museum**, exhibiting more than 1,000 baskets.

On the far north side of Lake Tahoe, **Kings Beach** is the last town heading east on Highway 28 before Nevada. It's largely unremarkable except for **Kings Beach State Recreation Area** (7360 W Lake Boulevard, 1-530 546 7248), a great place for kids to swim because of the shallow, calm water. Gullible types will enjoy **Tahoe Tessie's Lake Tahoe Monster Museum** (8612 N Lake Boulevard, 1-530 546 8774, closed Oct-May), a souvenir shop that capitalises on rumours that a prehistoric monster, not unlike the infamous creature of Loch Ness, roams the lake.

Just outside Kings Beach, the **Stateline Fire Lookout** (1-916 573 2600) sits smack on the California-Nevada border at an elevation of 7,017 feet (2,139 metres), offering a bird's-eye view of Tahoe's North Shore. After a look around, check out the historic **Cal-Neva Resort** casino (2 Stateline Road, 1-775 832 4000, 1-800 225 6382), once owned by crooner Frank Sinatra. The casino has an Indian Room, containing Washoe Indian artefacts.

Heading south from Tahoe City along the lake's west side, much of the development is replaced by large chunks of public land, particularly three state parks: **Sugar Pine Point**, **DL Bliss** and **Emerald Bay**. Hikers, bikers and cross-country skiers come here to enjoy miles of trails, and campers toast marshmallows under starry skies. History buffs should visit the **Ehrman Mansion at Sugar Pine Point State Park** (7360 W Lake Boulevard, Tahoma, 1-530 525 7982, www.parks.ca.gov, closed Sept-June, $2) to see how the Tahoe rich lived at the start of the 20th century. The curious can take a one-mile walk

downhill to see **Vikingsholm Castle** (1-530 541 3030, closed Sept-June, $3), a Scandinavian-style mansion built on beautiful Emerald Bay in the 1920s. The mansion's owner added a teahouse on Fannette Island, a short distance offshore. It's the only island on Lake Tahoe.

A few of the west shore's hiking trails should not be missed, among them the **Rubicon Trail** (9.0-mile round-trip) at **DL Bliss State Park** (1-530 525 7277, www.parks.ca.gov), which traces the cliffs above Tahoe's crystal-clear waters. Many people hike it one-way (4.5 miles), with a car shuttle arranged at the finish, though few would mind seeing the same scenery from the opposite perspective on their return.

In early summer, take the easy hike from Bayview Campground to **Cascade Falls** (2.0-mile round-trip), which pours a billowing stream of white water into Cascade Lake. Day-hikers who like to swim won't want to miss the **Five Lakes Trail** (4.2-mile round-trip) off Alpine Meadows Road. For something more ambitious, start at one of the **Tahoe Rim Trail** trailheads located on the North Shore (in Tahoe City or at Brockway Summit) and hike a stretch of the 150-mile trail. Information can be obtained from the US Forest Service's **Lake Tahoe Basin Management Unit** (*see p323*).

Squaw Valley USA

Squaw Valley Road (1-530 583 6985/www.squaw. com). **Open** mid Nov-May, June-Oct. **Admission** Day pass $59; $29 seniors, 13-15s; $5 under-13s. **Credit** AmEx, DC, Disc, MC, V.
The 1960 Winter Olympics are a long-vanished memory, but Squaw Valley USA has parlayed the glory of hosting them into its raison d'être. Squaw is most famous for its 4,000 acres of ski runs,

serviced by 31 chairlifts, but the full-service resort offers plenty of summer activities too. A cable car sails 2,000ft (600m) above the ground to the High Camp Bath and Tennis Club, where there's a man-made stone lagoon. An ice-skating rink is open year-round. Stay at the 400-room **Resort at Squaw Creek**, play 18 holes of golf or hike or ride horseback on the hillsides. That said, you might just take a look at this beautiful alpine valley and wonder what it would have been like had the landscape not been scarred for the sake of recreational sports.

Where to eat & drink

Don't miss the chance to have a meal at the historic **River Ranch Lodge** near Alpine Meadows (1-530 583 4264, www.riverranch lodge.com, closed lunch Mon-Fri, $$$$). Diners can choose between sitting indoors or taking a spot on the outside patio by the Truckee River's white water. The menu is classic American: seafood and steak. Other options include the **Bridge Tender Tavern** (65 W Lake Boulevard, 1-530 583 3342, $$). In 2002 it moved across the street from its location next to Fanny Bridge; it still serves delectable burgers, but now has a better river view.

In Tahoma there's the restaurant at charming **Norfolk Woods Inn** (6941 W Lake Boulevard, 1-530 525 5000, www.norfolkwoods.com, $$$) or unassuming little **Stony Ridge Café** (6821 W Lake Boulevard, 1-530 525 0905, closed Tue, dinner, $), with its surprisingly inventive food. Nearby Homewood has *très* European **Swiss Lakewood** (5055 W Lake Boulevard, 1-530 525 5211, closed Mon, lunch, $$$$), where beef Wellington and roast duck are standard issue.

Where to stay

Tahoe City overflows with condo complexes offering vacation lodging, but for something more interesting try the **Mayfield House** (236 Grove Street, 1-530 583 1001, www.may fieldhouse.com, $125-$280), a quality B&B in a remodelled mansion. The 19 river-view rooms at the **River Ranch Lodge** (1-530 583 4264, www.riverranchlodge.com, $70-$165) are hard to come by but worth every penny; the same goes for the **Sunnyside Lodge** (1850 W Lake Boulevard, 1-530 583 7200, www.sunnyside resort.com, $100-$250). More low-key are the 1930s-era cabins at the **Cottage Inn** (1690 W Lake Boulevard, 1-530 581 4073, www.the cottageinn.com, $150-$330), where guests enjoy the use of a private beach on the lake.

On the West Shore, **Tahoma Meadows B&B** (6821 W Lake Boulevard, 1-530 525 1553, www.tahomameadows.com, $95-$245) gets plenty of repeat business for its 14 cabins.

There's also one of Lake Tahoe's most elegant B&Bs: the four-room **Chaney House** (4725 W Lake Boulevard, Homewood, 1-530 525 7333, www.chaneyhouse.com, $155-$245), which was built in the 1920s by Italian stonemasons. But if you must have lakefront lodging, stay at the **Shore House B&B** (7170 N Lake Boulevard, Tahoe Vista, 1-530 546 7270, www.tahoeinn.com, $190-$290), legendary for its gourmet breakfasts.

Campers also have several good choices on the West Shore. All three state parks have campsites you can book in advance: information is available at www.parks.ca.gov, with reservations made at 1-800 444 7275 or www.reserveamerica.com. The **US Forest Service** also runs several excellent West Shore campsites: William Kent, Kaspian and Meeks Bay (1-530 543 2600, www.fs.fed.us/r5/ltbmu).

South Shore

South Lake Tahoe is a city with an identity problem. Straddling the California-Nevada border, the town just doesn't seem to know whether it wants to be a high-rise casino resort or a village of knotty pine cabins.

The most interesting thing in town (not counting the slots) is **South Lake Tahoe Visitor Center** (*see p323*), run by the US Forest Service. You could spend a whole day here attending free lectures and interpretive programmes relating to the Tahoe basin, or heading off on nature walks. The star of the show is the Stream Profile Chamber, an underground structure from which you can see into the depths of Taylor Creek. Through large, glass windows, visitors watch trout and other riparian creatures going about their business. Also useful for information is the **South Lake Tahoe Chamber of Commerce** (*see p323*).

Less than a mile south of the visitor centre is the **Tallac Historic Site** (1-530 544 7383, www.tahoeheritage.org, closed Nov-May), a scenically situated cluster of homesteads and mansions dating back to the late 1800s. Although now mostly destroyed, the Tallac Resort was in 1890 the 'Greatest Casino in America'. The Pope Estate is still intact; tours are offered. Also check out the Washoe Indian exhibits at the Baldwin-McGonagle House.

Summer or winter, you may want to take a ride on the **Heavenly Ski Resort Gondola** (1-775 586 7000, www.skiheavenly.com, $14-$22). The lower terminal for the eight-passenger tram cars is in downtown South Lake Tahoe; the upper end is two or three miles up the mountain. Hike or ski back downhill from the top, or book passage on the *Tahoe Queen* (1-530 541 3364, www.laketahoecruises.com, $9-$28), a monolithic glass-bottomed paddle-wheeler.

A few South Shore trails are a must for every hiker, in particular the **Mount Tallac Trail** (9.0-mile round-trip), with its whopping 3,300 feet (1,000 metres) of elevation gain. The reward, at the summit of 9,736-foot (2,968-metre) Mount Tallac, is a stupendous view of the Lake Tahoe Basin. Another peak worth bagging is 8,895-foot (2,711-metre) **Echo Peak**, accessible via the Glen Alpine trailhead at **Fallen Leaf Lake** (7.4-mile round-trip). If you're looking for a more mellow hike, try the stroll to **Angora Lakes** (3.0-mile round-trip), where a small resort sells lemonade. For trail information, contact the **Lake Tahoe Basin Management Unit** (*see p323*).

Where to eat & drink

Lakefront restaurants on the South Shore are hard to come by, but the **Blue Water Bistro** (3411 Lake Tahoe Boulevard, 1-530 541 0113, closed Sun, $$$) takes up the slack. Here, on a pier built over the water, you can wear your hiking boots without embarrassment as you munch on a hamburger and watch the sun set over the lake. The **Beacon Restaurant** at Camp Richardson Resort (1900 Jameson Beach Road, 1-530 541 0630, $$) has the same kind of beachy atmosphere, plus seating on a deck.

For special occasions, the intimate **Café Fiore** (1169 Ski Run Boulevard, 1-530 541 2908, closed lunch, $$$$) is the spot, with its fabulous Italian cuisine and meagre half-dozen tables. You'll need a reservation. Those on a more modest budget should try the non-trad Mexican food at the **Cantina** (765 Emerald Bay Road, 1-530 544 1233, $$$) and wash it down with one of their celebrated Margaritas.

Where to stay

If you want to gamble without a long commute from your bed, book a stay at **Caesar's Tahoe Resort Casino** (1-775 588 3515, www.caesars. com, $69-$200). Many South Shore lodgings offer free shuttle buses to the casinos: try the **Inn by the Lake** (1-800 877 1466, 1-530 542 0330, www.innbythelake.com, $98-$228) or **Driftwood Lodge** (1-530 541 7400, $40-$160) for good value rooms and easy transport to the tables. Families enjoy the 400-suite **Embassy Suites** (1-530 544 5400, www.embassytahoe. com, $100-$225), with all the amenities of a full-service hotel but no casino.

If you have dollars burning a hole in your pocket, book a stay at one of five rooms or three cabins at the **Black Bear Inn** (1-877 232 7466, 1-530 544 4451, www.tahoeblackbear.com, $240-$295), a luxurious B&B built in the 1990s with an old-style Tahoe look. For the budget-minded,

there's the no-frills **Super 8** (1-530 544 3476, www.super8.com, $55-$65). It isn't easy to get reservations, but **Camp Richardson Resort** (1-800 544 1801, 1-530 541 1801, www.camp richardson.com, $65-$130) is great for a taste of the 'old' Lake Tahoe. Built in the 1920s, the family-style resort has cosy cabins under the pines, plus the Beacon (*see above*). The Pope-Baldwin Bike Path runs by the resort.

Nevadan Tahoe

While most of the Californian side of Lake Tahoe is fully developed private property, the Nevadan side still has abundant shoreline that is managed as parkland and open to the public. A good starting point is the **Tahoe-Douglas Chamber & Visitor Center** (*see p323*), but nature lovers should head for huge **Lake Tahoe-Nevada State Park** (1-775 831 0494, www.state.nv.us/stparks), home to wildly popular **Spooner Lake** and **Sand Harbor**. The former is the starting point for the world-famous Flume Trail, a mountain-biking route that skirts the cliffs high above the eastern edge of Lake Tahoe. The latter is home to white sand beaches and gentle turquoise coves, a favourite spot for sunbathers and photographers.

Just south of Sand Harbor you'll find the **Thunderbird Lodge** (5000 Highway 28, 1-775 832 8750, www.thunderbirdlodge.org, closed Nov-Apr, $10-$25, reservations required), a 16,500-square-foot (1,530-square-metre) stone mansion that's Tahoe's answer to Hearst Castle in San Simeon. The Thunderbird was built in the late 1930s by eccentric multimillionaire George Whittell. Whittell kept lions, tigers and even a small elephant on his property, erected a lighthouse on his 140 acres of lakefront, and built a 600-foot-long (183-metre) underground tunnel to connect his boathouse to the main house. Docents lead one-hour tours around the property, which will leave you with a whole new definition of 'rich'.

If you're curious about the history of mining during California's Gold Rush, don't miss a chance to visit the living ghost town of **Virginia City**. A one-hour drive from the lake, east of US 395 in Nevada, this once-thriving metropolis was the centrepiece of the 1859 Comstock Lode silver strike that served as the main catalyst for the early development of the Lake Tahoe basin. It's all a bit of a tourist trap today, but fascinating nonetheless.

Hikers have a wide selection of trails to choose from on the Nevada side of Tahoe. A favourite is the **Mount Rose Trail** (12.0-mile round-trip). It's a strenuous hike that leads to the summit of 10,776-foot (3,285-metre) Mount Rose, one of the highest peaks in the Lake

Swim in Tahoe

Sure, the water is icy cold. But one look at the azure blue waters of Lake Tahoe and you'll want to dive in anyway. Your best bets are as follows:

North Shore: Speedboat Beach, near the Cal-Neva Casino at Stateline. Large boulders and white sand.

East Shore: Sand Harbor (*see p321*), 2.5 miles south of Incline Village. It's crowded, but has miles of delicate white sand and plenty of picnic areas. Alternatively, drive 2.5 miles south to access a steep trail leading to Secret Cove/Chimney Beach, a string of exquisite coves. You might get an anatomy lesson here: clothing optional is the order of the day.

South Shore: Baldwin Beach, 0.7 miles west of the South Lake Tahoe Visitor Center (*see p323*). Very shallow water along the shore actually makes the temperature reasonable for swimming.

West Shore: DL Bliss State Park (*see p319*), 17 miles south of Tahoe City, is hands-down the lake's loveliest beach.

Travelling south from Lake Tahoe, four mountain passes crossed by state highways connect the Lake Tahoe Basin to the northern region of Yosemite National Park. Each of these – **Echo Pass** (US 50), **Carson Pass** (Highway 88), **Ebbetts Pass** (Highway 4) and **Sonora Pass** (Highway 108) – is a High Sierra destination in its own right.

Most of this land is encompassed in Alpine County, one of the least populated counties in the Sierra but perhaps the most enjoyable to visit. Although many visitors forgo this stretch of the Sierra, opting instead to hightail down US 395 or Highway 49 in a rush to get to Yosemite, those who take the time to meander through here find dense forests, high peaks and dramatic scenery. There isn't much in the way of visitor services, except for a few scattered cabin resorts, because most people come to this region to camp, fish and hike in summer or ski in winter. **Kirkwood Ski Resort** (1-209 258 6000, www.kirkwood.com, lift tickets $13-$62) on Highway 88, about an hour south of South Lake Tahoe, is a great alternative for both downhill and cross-country skiing. In summer, hikers flock to the area between the ski resort and Carson Pass to see one of California's best wildflower shows (July is usually optimal). Two popular trailheads for flower-viewing are at **Carson Pass** and **Woods Lake Campground**. The best source of information on outdoor activities is the **US Forest Service Pacific Ranger District** (1-530 644 2349, www.fs.fed.us/r5/eldorado) and the **Alpine County Chamber of Commerce** (*see p323*).

The blink-and-you'll-miss-it town of **Markleeville**, a few miles south, is famous as the starting point for July's Markleeville Death Ride (www.deathride.com), one of California's premier cycling events. The ride brings even expert riders to their knees with its staggering 16,000 feet (5,000 metres) of elevation change over 129 miles. Even if you'd never think of riding in a bike tour of this magnitude, it's worth coming along just to watch the spectacle. Just outside Markleeville is **Grover Hot Springs State Park** (1-530 694 2248, www.parks.ca.gov), which – in addition to those hot springs – has good hiking and biking trails.

Another popular ski resort is **Bear Valley** (1-209 753 2301, www.bearvalley.com, lift tickets $8-$45), on Highway 4, also home to an annual summer music festival. Just east of Bear Valley is large **Lake Alpine**, a popular spot for camping, fishing and hiking, with a paved bike trail running along its shoreline.

Tahoe area. In the summer wildflower season, don't miss walking a few miles of the **Ophir Creek Trail**, which starts from the Mount Rose Highway some six or seven miles northeast of Incline Village.

Where to stay

Cal-Nevada Lodge (2 Stateline Road, 1-800 225 6382, 1-775 832 4000, $99-$199), which straddles the Nevada border on the North Shore at Crystal Bay, is a typical hotel-casino, except that in addition to comfortable rooms, it also has cabins and chalets for rent. A few miles east at Incline Village, the **Hyatt Lake Tahoe Resort** (Lakeshore Drive, 1-775 831 1111, www.laketahoehyatt.com, $150-$265) has well-appointed rooms and cottages, great service and a first-rate restaurant with a lake view.

The old Gold Rush town of Virginia City has several intriguing lodging options, including the five deluxe guest cottages at **Tyson's Canyon Ranch** (Seven Mile Canyon, 1-775 847 7223, www.nevadaduderanch.com, $95-$165), where a herd of longhorn cattle roam. Nevada's oldest hotel, the 1859 **Gold Hill Hotel** (Highway 342, 1-775 847 0111, www.goldhillhotel.net, $45-$145), still admits guests to its 19 rooms and guesthouses. There's also a saloon and restaurant on the property.

Highway 108 has its own ski destination in **Dodge Ridge** (1-209 965 3474, www.dodge ridge.com, lift tickets $10-$44), which brags of being one of the best places in the state for teaching beginners how to ski. The resort is small and family-oriented. Just below the Dodge Ridge slopes is **Pinecrest Lake**, a well-loved summer vacation destination for families.

Where to eat, drink & stay

Half an hour from Tahoe, **Sorenson's Resort** (14255 Highway 88, 1-800 423 9949, 1-530 694 2203, www.sorensensresort.com, $95-$225) at Hope Valley is a deservedly popular spot. Set on 170 acres, the cabin resort was first developed in the 1920s by Danish sheep-herders. The architecture is mainly Norwegian in style, each of the 30 cabins is unique, and there's an excellent on-site restaurant. In nearby Markleeville, the best bet is the motel-like **Creekside Lodge** (14820 Highway 89, 1-866 802 7335, $69-$89). Unless, that is, you want to fish the Carson River, in which case get one of the cabins at the **Carson River Resort** (12399 Highway 89, 1-877 694 2229, www.carsonriverresort.com, $60-$150).

Further south on Highway 108, you'll find the historic **Strawberry Inn** (1-800 965 3662, 1-209 965 3662, $99-$110). Built in 1939, the inn provides standard motel rooms and a restaurant on the river that's known for its American and California cuisine. The adjacent **Cabins at Strawberry** (1-888 965 0885, 1-209 965 0885, www.strawberrycabins.com, $149-$189) are large, modern structures, well suited for family holidays and group ski trips. Nearby at **Pinecrest Lake Resort** (1-209 965 3411, www.pinecrestlakeresort.com, $125-$220), the Steam Donkey Restaurant offers portions of hearty food big enough to fill a lumberjack.

Resources

Hospital

Tahoe City *Tahoe Forest Hospital, 10121 Pine Avenue (1-530 587 6011/www.tfhd.com).*

Internet

South Lake Tahoe *Avant Garden, 2660 Lake Tahoe Boulevard, Suite 9 (1-530 544 3116/ www.avantgarden101.com).* **Open** 9am-6pm Mon-Wed; 9am-8pm Thur-Sat; 10am-4pm Sun.
Tahoe City *Vicky's Cyber Café, 255 N Lake Boulevard (1-530 581 5312/www.tahoecitycyber cafe.com).* **Open** 8am-6pm Mon-Fri; 9am-6pm Sat.
Truckee *Perkins, 10825 Pioneer Trail (1-530 587 4445/www.perkinsorganicgoodness.com).* **Open** 6am-6pm Mon-Fri; 8am-4pm Sat.

Police

South Lake Tahoe *1352 Johnson Boulevard (1-530 542 6100).*

Post office

South Lake Tahoe *1046 Al Tahoe Boulevard (1-530 544 5867).*
Tahoe City *950 N Lake Boulevard (1-530 583 6563).*
Truckee *10050 Bridge Street (1-530 587 7158).*

Tourist information

Markleeville *Alpine County Chamber of Commerce, Main Street, Markleeville (1-530 694 2475/www.alpinecounty.com).* **Open** 9am-4pm daily.
Nevadan Tahoe *Tahoe-Douglas Chamber & Visitor Center, 195 US 50 (1-775 588 4591/ www.tahoechamber.org).* **Open** 9am-5pm daily.
South Lake Tahoe *South Lake Tahoe Chamber of Commerce, 13066 US 50 (1-530 541 5255/ www.tahoeinfo.com).* **Open** 8.30am-5pm Mon-Sat.
South Lake Tahoe Visitor Center, Highway 89 (1-530 573 2674/www.fs.fed.us/r5/ltbmu/contact). **Open** 8am-4.30pm Sat, Sun.
US Forest Service's Lake Tahoe Basin Management Unit, 35 College Drive (1-530 543 2600/www.fs.fed. us/r5/ltbmu). **Open** 8am-4.30pm Mon-Fri.
Tahoe City *North Lake Tahoe Chamber of Commerce, 245 N Lake Boulevard (1-530 581 6900/www.tahoefun.org).* **Open** 9am-5pm Mon-Fri; 9am-4pm Sat, Sun.
Truckee *Truckee Donner Visitor Center, 10065 Donner Pass Road (1-530 587 2757/www.truckee. com).* **Open** 9am-5.30pm daily.
Virginia City *Virginia City Visitor Center, 86 S C Street (1-775 847 7500/www.virginia city-nv.org).* **Open** 9am-5pm Mon-Fri.

South Lake Tahoe: sun and stars.
See p320.

Central California

Yosemite National Park

With its plunging waterfalls, stark granite, alpine lakes, pristine meadows, giant sequoia trees and raging rivers, **Yosemite National Park** is the undisputed jewel of the Sierra Nevada Mountains, a range that has more than its fair share of breathtaking scenery. It's also, unsurprisingly, one of the country's most popular national parks, playing host to around 3.4 million visitors each year, as many as 20,000 people a day on the busiest summer holidays.

How do you enjoy this natural wonder without being crushed by the crowds? Visit in the off-season, if possible, which means any time besides the summer months of June to September. If you must visit in the high season, try to avoid the perpetually packed, seven-mile-long **Yosemite Valley** and head for some of the lesser-visited areas of the park.

Contrary to popular belief, you don't need reservations to visit (although you should certainly book lodgings in advance if you wish to stay the night). Using public transport to get into the park is difficult, often impossible, but you can drive in at any time, 24 hours a day, 365 days per year. The $20 entrance fee per vehicle is good for seven days; pick up a **National Parks Pass** if you plan to visit other national parks during your visit.

If you want to drive your own car *around* the park, you certainly can: just give yourself plenty of time to get around (and fill up with gas before coming in, as there are no gas stations in the park). Yosemite is massive, with more than 250 miles of roads criss-crossing its 1,200 square miles and 750,000 acres. To see even a respectable chunk, you'll need a few days. Alternatively, once you've arrived, park your car and ride the free shuttle buses around the Valley floor. Or, to avoid the hassles of driving in the Valley and/or steering through the nether regions of the park on circuitous mountain roads, consider taking one of the park's guided tours. In the warm months of the year, these include the two-hour **Valley Floor Tour** (phone the Yosemite Lodge Tour Desk, 1-209 372 1240, $15.50-$20.50), which allows you to view the park from an open-air tram; several other tours take place in enclosed buses. For more on planning, *see p331*.

Activities

When planning a Yosemite trip, don't forget your outdoor gear. The place is a playground for sports ranging from skiing to horseback riding,
from car camping to rock climbing. The vast majority of Yosemite's travellers come to the park to play outside in its mountain landscape.

At the very least, you'll probably go for a hike. With more than 800 miles of paths to walk, visitors can choose from short-and-easy jaunts to world-class destinations such as **Taft Point** and **Vernal Fall**, an exhaustive range of treks to the summits of **Half Dome** or **Clouds Rest**, or a wealth of moderate trails in between the two extremes. For trail suggestions within Yosemite Valley, *see pp326-327*; for southern Yosemite, *see pp329-330*; and for northern Yosemite, *see pp330-331*.

Of course, if you're feeling at all aerobically challenged, you can let Trigger do the walking for you. Three **stables** are located within the park, one in Yosemite Valley (1-209 372 8348, $51-$94), another in Tuolumne Meadows (1-209 372 8427, $51-$94) and yet another in Wawona (1-209 375 6502, $51-$94), all of them closed from autumn to spring (phone for precise dates). Guided rides are offered in a variety of prices and configurations from April to November. Two- and four-hour rides depart daily; all-day rides and pack trips can also be arranged. Don't forget to bring along a carrot or an apple for your trusty steed, since he or she will be doing all the work.

Water lovers will be attracted to the **Merced River**, which bisects the Valley, and **Tuolumne River**, which bisects Tuolumne Meadows. In late summer, the Merced is warm enough for swimming (pick any pool that looks inviting), but in late spring and early summer the best way to experience the river is in an inflatable raft, floating lazily downstream. By no means is this a heart-pumping and pulse-racing river-rafting adventure: 'river meandering' would be a better term, and the half-day activity is mellow enough even for those who can't swim. Inflatable rafts are rented at Curry Village in Yosemite Valley (1-209 372 8319); the put-in point is nearby. Float three miles downstream, then ride a bus back.

You might see people **fishing** in both the Merced and Tuolumne Rivers, but you probably won't see much catching. Yosemite has been hit by a ton of fishing pressure over the years, and the few trout that ply these waters are wary and smart. A better bet is to forget the big rivers and fish some of the lakes of Yosemite's high country, such as **Upper Cathedral Lake**, **Elizabeth Lake** and the **Sunrise Lakes**, which have self-sustaining populations of non-native brook trout. These lakes are all accessible to day-hikers. The Dana Fork and the Lyell Fork of the Tuolumne, accessible by hiking out of Tuolumne Meadows, also provide a good chance of catching trout.

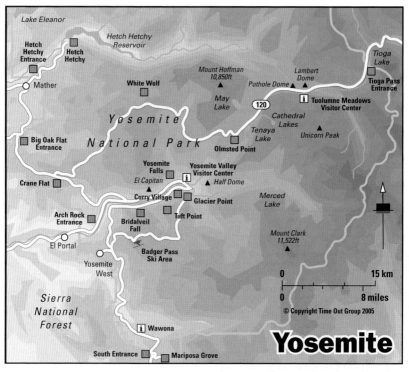

Central California

Yosemite

Show up here any time from, maybe, November to March and you can take advantage of Yosemite's terrific **winter sports**. Practise your figure-of-eights with a head-on view of Half Dome at Curry Village's outdoor ice-skating rink (1-209 372 8341). Rent downhill or cross-country skis, or a snowboard, and carve a few S-turns down the slopes at family-oriented **Badger Pass Ski Area** (1-209 372 1000, www.badgerpass.com, closed early spring-late autumn, lift tickets $11-$31): opened in 1935, it's billed as California's oldest ski resort. It has only five lifts servicing 85 acres of slopes, but there are ample trails for cross-country skiing. Visitors staying in Yosemite Valley can reserve a spot on a bus to Badger Pass and save themselves the hassle of driving in the snow. If you'd rather take part in a winter sport where there's little or no chance of breaking a leg, rent a pair of snowshoes and trudge through the white stuff under the canopy of the giant sequoias, or beyond Mirror Lake into **Tenaya Canyon**. Snowshoes are rented at both Badger Pass Ski Area and the Mountain Shop in Curry Village.

Yosemite Valley

It's estimated that more than half of Yosemite National Park's visitors only see **Yosemite Valley**, even though the Valley makes up less than one per cent of the park. The key to getting the most out of a visit to the 'incomparable Valley', as naturalist John Muir called it, is to show up at the right time of year. To see Yosemite Valley's famous waterfalls at their most impressive, visit in April, May or June; by mid July, the largest falls are a dribble. Ironically, visits to Yosemite Valley peak in July and August, when the waterfalls are diminished and the temperatures are often uncomfortably warm. Avoid these months, with their crowds and traffic jams, if at all possible.

First-time visitors are often surprised by the amount of development in Yosemite Valley, especially in contrast to the more rugged nature of the rest of the park. It is essentially a small city, complete with sewage lines, garbage collection, a dentist's office, a courtroom, a jail, an auto garage and a church. The Valley offers visitors the greatest amount of organised

If you only have one day...

There's an old gag about a Yosemite visitor who goes up to a park ranger and says, 'I'm only visiting the park for one day. How should I spend my time?' The ranger pauses. 'If I only had one day in Yosemite,' he replies, 'I would sit right down and have myself a good cry.' It is indeed a tremendous loss to spend only one day in Yosemite, but if that's the way your holiday is scheduled, you'd better dry your tears and get busy.

First, you'll need to limit your travels to one small portion of the park. For the vast majority of visitors, the portion of choice is **Yosemite Valley**. During busy season, it's smart to park in the Valley as soon as possible after arrival and choose from these transport options:

● Pay for a guided tour on the open-air tram that leaves from Yosemite Lodge.
● Rent a bicycle at Yosemite Lodge or Curry Village and ride the Valley's paved bike paths.
● Design your own tour of the Valley by walking and riding the free shuttle bus.

The option you choose will essentially determine your itinerary.

The open-air tram tours travel all over the Valley and include running commentary from an interpreter. Because you're not in an enclosed bus, you can feel the fresh air and get a much better view than you'd have through your windscreen. Tours last about two hours. By bike, you can easily visit Lower Yosemite Falls and Mirror Lake (park your bike at the trailheads and walk the short distance remaining). You can also tour a large expanse of the Valley, including stops at the visitor centre and at Yosemite Village or Curry Village for supplies. On foot (and by taking short hops on the free Yosemite Valley shuttle bus) you can see most of the Valley's famous sights. However, this requires a little more map-reading and planning than the other options. Whichever option you choose, do make sure you leave enough time in your one Yosemite day to drive to Glacier Point, either in your own car or on the tour bus that leaves from Yosemite Lodge.

To capture the essence of Yosemite, try to squeeze in at least one hike during your stay. A few easy-to-moderate hikes recommended for short-stay visitors are the trails to May Lake and Lembert Dome on **Tioga Pass Road**, and the trails to Sentinel Dome and Taft Point on **Glacier Point Road**. In Yosemite Valley, make sure you take the short walks to **Lower Yosemite Falls** and **Bridalveil Fall**; each of them is less than half a mile. If you have a little more time and don't mind hiking with a crowd, take the spectacular **Mist Trail** to the top of Vernal Fall.

activities, ranging from nature walks to evening slide shows, from ice-skating to photography seminars, from Indian basket-making to rock climbing. To get current information on these activities, pick up a copy of the free Yosemite newspaper, which is handed out at all park entrance stations; it's also available at the **Valley Visitor Center** (located just west of the Village Market) and in most park lodgings.

Besides its waterfalls, Yosemite Valley is best known for its 3,000-foot-high (900-metre) granite walls. The Valley is an undisputed mecca for rock climbers, with Camp 4 the centre of activity, but you don't have to have years of experience to give the sport a try. **Yosemite Mountaineering School & Guide Service** (Curry Village, 1-209 372 8344, $117-$217) conducts beginners' classes from mid April to October. If you'd rather watch the climbers than be one, congratulate yourself on your level-headedness and head to **El Capitan Meadow**, where – with a pair of binoculars – you can watch the slow progress of climbers heading up the grey face of El Capitan. Ever since this massive chunk of granite was first conquered in the 1950s, a succession of bold climbers have inched their way to the top.

Yosemite Valley is laced with 12 miles of smooth, paved bike paths, heavily used by both cyclists and pedestrians. From early spring to late autumn, you can rent a cruiser bike at Yosemite Lodge or Curry Village Recreation Center (1-209 372 1208, 1-209 372 8913, $24.50/day). If you'd rather walk than ride, there are myriad trails: even the laziest visitor can walk the short, wheelchair-accessible pathways to **Lower Yosemite Falls**, **Bridalveil Fall** and **Mirror Lake**, each of them less than a half-mile round-trip.

For those willing to hike a bit further, and do some hill climbing into the bargain, a jaunt on the well-named **Mist Trail** is a memorable experience, particularly in the early season when Vernal and Nevada Falls are gushing. Wearing rain gear is more than just a good idea as you ascend the granite stairsteps alongside Vernal Fall: the spray from the billowing falls can soak you from head to toe. Many hikers just

Tioga Pass Road.

follow the Mist Trail as far as the Vernal Fall footbridge (1.6-mile round-trip); those with more ambition head for the top of Vernal Fall (3.0-mile round-trip, and worth every step); those with energy to burn continue past Vernal Fall to the brink of Nevada Fall (6.5-mile round-trip, with a loop return on the **John Muir Trail**). To access the Mist Trail, park your car at one of the large public parking areas in Yosemite Valley and ride the free shuttle bus to Happy Isles (you can't drive there).

From March to July, the hardiest of hikers start at Camp 4 in Yosemite Valley and make the 7.2-mile round-trip to the top of **Upper Yosemite Fall**, at 2,425 feet (739 metres) the highest waterfall in North America. When the waterfall season is over, a good option for seasoned hikers is the **Four-Mile Trail** (actually 4.8 miles, making a 9.6-mile round-trip), which ascends from Yosemite Valley to Glacier Point. Instead of retracing their steps on Four-Mile, some choose to loop back down from Glacier Point on the **Panorama Trail**, connecting to the Mist or John Muir Trails by

Nevada Fall. This makes a loop trip of about 13 miles, one of the most spectacular treks from Yosemite Valley.

Masochistic types head for the top of **Half Dome** (17.0-mile round-trip) with its punishing 4,800-foot (1,500-metre) elevation gain. The hike is famous for the final ascent of the smoothly rounded dome, on which hikers are aided by steel cables that run 440 feet (130 metres) up nearly vertical granite. You'll need both hands and both feet to attain the summit. Most hikers make it up on adrenaline, but then are rather daunted by the prospect of retracing their steps all the way back down.

Where to eat & drink

The busiest spots in Yosemite Valley are the places that serve food. Indeed, it sometimes appears that people come to this national park just for the chance to eat. Four main areas of the Valley can satisfy your stomach's cravings: Yosemite Lodge, Yosemite Village, Curry Village and the Ahwahnee Hotel.

Mountain Room is the best of the handful of restaurants at Yosemite Lodge. Try to get a table near the windows for a spectacular view of Yosemite Falls. Diners show up wearing everything from high heels to hiking boots. Steaks are popular, but several kinds of grilled fish and chicken are also available. The neighbouring **Food Court** is just a glorified cafeteria, but a good option if you are in a hurry. Next door, the **Garden Terrace** serves all-you-can-eat lunch and dinner buffets.

In Yosemite Village, **Degnan's Deli** is a busy place at lunchtime, with made-to-order sandwiches, salads and soups. **Degnan's Café** serves ice-cream and coffee, while upstairs from both is the **Loft**, a pizza joint that only opens in summer. The **Village Grill**, also closed apart from during the summer, serves burgers and other fast-food items out on a deck.

Curry Village also has a variety of dining options. In the cheap-and-easy category, buy a burrito at the walk-up **Curry Taqueria** window or a pizza at the **Pizza Patio**. Beer is served at the unimaginatively named **Curry Bar** next door. There's also an all-you-can-eat buffet at **Curry Pavilion**, and its adjoining **Coffee Corner** for caffeine addicts.

At the other end of the spectrum, ties and jackets are appropriate attire for dinner at the **Ahwahnee Hotel** ($$$$$); in fact, they're a requirement in all but the hottest months. The Ahwahnee's huge dining room contains dozens of wrought-iron chandeliers and picture windows look out on the Valley. Menu choices change constantly, but certain well-loved items show up frequently, among them salmon Ahwahnee stuffed with Dungeness crab. The Sunday brunches are legendary. Reservations are a must; phone 1-209 372 1489.

Where to stay

Of the seven lodgings available inside the park, four are in Yosemite Valley. Make sure you know what you are getting: they run the gamut from slum-like to extravagant.

Although it might seem a bargain, try to avoid **Housekeeping Camp** ($67), a collection of duplex units that are a strange hybrid of cabin and campsite. Ditto **Curry Village** ($69-$195). Unless you're lucky enough to reserve one of the cosy, wooden cabins (some with private bath), the only lodging is in tent cabins: large tents with wooden floors, beds and electricity. Because the tent cabins are made of canvas and spaced about nine inches apart, a good night's sleep can't be totally guaranteed.

A more civilised choice is the **Yosemite Lodge** ($100-$161), which has all the charm of an average chain motel but is unbeatable for its

central location. The 260 rooms are arranged in several buildings with dreary hallways reminiscent of college dorms, but the rooms themselves are nice. All have private bathrooms.

Those with money to blow should consider a stay at the **Ahwahnee Hotel** ($367-$443), a National Historic Landmark that was built in 1927 of huge timbers and river rock. Some argue that the smallish rooms are overpriced, but the views override any such shortcomings. One side of the hotel faces Glacier Point and Half Dome; the other faces Yosemite Falls. The higher the room, the better the view.

Reservations for in-park lodgings are all made at **Yosemite Reservations** (1-559 252 4848, www.yosemitepark.com). For lodgings from May to September, make reservations six months to a year in advance; if you are unlucky, keep checking back for cancellations. During the rest of the year, it's not difficult to book a room in the Valley, particularly midweek. Rates drop by as much as 30 per cent off-season.

If you're thinking of camping in Yosemite Valley, think again, especially in busy summer season. A Valley campsite is as difficult to reserve as Valley lodgings, maybe more so. Even if you're lucky enough to secure a site, you won't enjoy it: the campsites are packed so tightly, it's like camping in Tent City. For reservations within the park, call 1-301 722 1257 or see http://reservations.nps.gov. But campers are generally better off heading to other regions of the park (*see p331*).

Many visitors opt to stay at lodgings outside the park, sometimes because in-park lodgings are booked, sometimes because of the wider range of options 'outside'. The best bets are on Highway 120, between Groveland and the Big

Yosemite National Park: get up, get on it and get down. *See p324.*

Oak Flat entrance station, and on Highway 140, between Mariposa and the El Portal entrance station. Along Highway 120 choices include the historic **Groveland Hotel** (18767 Main Street, 1-800 273 3314, 1-209 962 4000, www.groveland. com, $135-$175) and, closer to the park, casually elegant **Blackberry Inn** B&B (7567 Hamilton Station Loop, 1-888 867 5001, www.blackberry-inn.com, $120-$150), with beautifully appointed rooms and hearty breakfasts. An intimate choice within only a few miles of the park boundary is a cosy cabin at **Sunset Inn** (33569 Hardin Flat Road, 1-209 962 4360, www.sunsetinnusa.com, $100-$190). Families like **Evergreen Lodge** (33160 Evergreen Road, 1-800 935 6343, 1-209 379 2606, www.evergreenlodge.com, $99-$169), expanded to 50 cabins with a fine restaurant. All these lodgings are not only close to the Valley, but also have easy access to the Gold Rush town of Groveland.

If you choose to stay along the Highway 140 corridor, keep in mind that the temperatures can be very high in summer. Just outside the rather charmless town of **Mariposa**, in the hamlet of Midpines, is a unit of the national KOA (Kampground of America) chain, which rents bare-bones cabins as well as tent and RV sites. Say what you want about an organisation that spells 'cabins' with a K, but the **KOA Yosemite-Mariposa's Kamping Kabins** (6323 Highway 140, 1-209 966 2201, www.koa. com, closed Nov-Mar, $175-$225) are a great deal for families. Within a few miles of the El Portal entrance to Yosemite are two large lodge complexes: **Yosemite View Lodge** (11136 Highway 140, 1-209 379 2681, $85-$120) and **Cedar Lodge** (9966 Highway 140, 1-209 379 2612, $109-$139).

Wawona & Glacier Point

For Native Americans who travelled between the foothills and Yosemite Valley, **Wawona** was the halfway point on their journey. They called it 'Pallachun', meaning 'a good place to stay'. It's also a good place to visit, with fishing and swimming holes in the South Fork of the Merced River, hiking trails, the spectacle of the Mariposa Grove of Giant Sequoias, and the chance to glimpse back in time at the **Pioneer Yosemite History Center** (Forest Drive, off Highway 41, 1-209 372 0200), a collection of buildings stuffed full of Yosemite history.

Not far from Wawona is **Glacier Point**, with a commanding vista that takes in all the major granite landmarks of Yosemite Valley and the surrounding high country. For many Yosemite visitors, this drive-up overlook at 7,214 feet (2,199 metres) is the single most memorable spot in the park. Evening ranger programmes are held frequently; see the Yosemite paper for details.

Only a mile from Glacier Point is the trailhead for two short but spectacular hikes: **Sentinel Dome** and **Taft Point**. Each of these trails is only 1.1 miles one-way and each ends at an unforgettable viewpoint. Several other trails begin along Glacier Point Road, including the easy **McGurk Meadow Trail** (2.0-mile round-trip to an old pioneer cabin and verdant meadow) and the rather more challenging **Ostrander Lake Trail** (12.5-mile round-trip to a granite-bound lake).

Located next to the southern entrance station to Yosemite, the **Mariposa Grove** is the largest of Yosemite's three giant sequoia groves, and is equally visited by serious nature lovers and the video-camera-toting masses. During the summer months, a mandatory free shuttle bus runs from the Wawona Store to the grove. Once you arrive, you can elect to take the **Mariposa Big Trees Tram Tour** (1-209 375 1621, $5.50-$11), a one-hour tour in an open-air tram (spring to autumn, weather permitting). Those willing to hoof it can set off on the easy two-mile loop through the lower grove to see the 2,700-year-old, 100-foot-wide (30-metre) Grizzly Giant and a few other gargantuan sequoia specimens. A longer hike (6.5-mile round-trip) is possible by continuing to the upper grove.

A more strenuous hike in the Wawona area takes you up to the **Chilnualna Falls** (8.2-mile round-trip). This is a great hike to make in the early season, when prolific snowmelt feeds the falls.

Where to eat & drink

The food at the historic **Wawona Hotel Dining Room** (1-209 375 1425, closed Dec-Mar, $$$$) can be relied on to be delicious. And if you have to wait for a table, you'll find the hotel lobby is always hopping with guests making merry. Barbecues are held on the lawn each Saturday in summer.

If you don't mind driving a few miles outside the park, it's worth searching out the **Narrow Gauge Inn** (*see below*; closed lunch, Mon, Tue, Nov-Apr, $$$$), which looks like a cross between a church and a historic hunting lodge. The menu is on the upscale side, with unusual entrées such as fillet of ostrich and venison steak, and the food is outstanding. An added attraction, adjacent to the dining room, is the **Buffalo Bar**, complete with an authentic birch-bark canoe and other old Yosemite memorabilia.

Where to stay

The white-and-green Victorian main building of the **Wawona Hotel** (1-559 252 4848, www.yosemitepark.com, closed Dec-Mar, $113-$170) has a Southern appeal, with a veranda out front and porch chairs on its green lawns. Not far away, at the junction of Highway 41 and Glacier Point Road, is **Yosemite West** (1-559 642 2211, www.yosemitewestreservations.com, $85-$135), an area of private homes within the park boundaries; more than 140 are available for holiday rental. Located in the village of Wawona is the **Redwoods** (1-209 375 6666, www.redwoodsinyosemite.com, $128-$279), another private holding within the park that rents vacation cabins from late spring to early

autumn. Two campsites are found at the park's south end: **Bridalveil** on Glacier Point Road and **Wawona** on Highway 41. Both can be booked by phoning 1-301 722 1257 or visiting http://reservations.nps.gov.

There are also plenty of lodgings just outside the southern park boundary in the town of Fish Camp. Two good choices are the cottage-style **Apple Tree Inn** (1110 Highway 41, 1-888 683 5111, 1-559 683 5111, www.appletreeinn-yosemite.com, $99-$179), located just two miles from Yosemite's southern gate, and the 25-room **Narrow Gauge Inn** (48571 Highway 41, 1-888 6449050, 1-559 683 7720, www.narrowgaugeinn.com, $120-$195). Otherwise, try the **Tenaya Lodge** (1122 Highway 41, 1-888 514 2167, 1-559 683 6555, www.tenayalodge.com, $169-$319), a huge and very well-run 244-room resort.

Tuolumne Meadows, Tioga Pass & Hetch Hetchy

One of the most photographed regions of Yosemite, two-mile-long **Tuolumne Meadows** is a wide, grassy expanse that is bounded by a series of high granite domes and peaks. At 8,600 feet (2,600 metres) in elevation, it's the largest sub-alpine meadow in the entire Sierra Nevada. From its tranquil edges, trails lead in all directions: to the alpine lakes set below the spires of Cathedral and Unicorn Peaks, to a series of roaring waterfalls on the Tuolumne River, and to the summits of lofty granite domes with commanding vistas of the high country.

The region is a natural playground for hikers and backpackers. A deservedly popular trail is the hike to the two **Cathedral Lakes** (7.4-mile round-trip), tucked in below the granite spires of 10,840-foot (3,304-metre) Cathedral Peak. Those seeking shorter, easier treks can head to **Elizabeth Lake** (4.5-mile round-trip, to a granite-bound lake at the base of 10,900-foot/ 13,322-metre Unicorn Peak) or stroll alongside the Tuolumne River on Glen Aulin and Tuolumne Falls (9.0-mile round-trip, with a meagre elevation gain). To feel like a real mountaineer, take on the climb up **Lembert Dome** (2.8-mile round-trip to the granite dome's rounded summit).

The regions on either side of the meadow, following the 39-mile length of Tioga Pass Road from Crane Flat to Tioga Pass, offer more wonders. The drive-to vista at **Olmsted Point** provides an unusual view of Half Dome and a peek into the funnelled granite walls of Tenaya Canyon. Just beyond the overlook, Tenaya Lake sparkles in the sunshine, dazzling first-time visitors with its beauty. Hikers can either set off on the rewarding day-hike to **North Dome**, a granite dome directly across from Half Dome (9.0-mile round-trip) or make the easy, child-friendly jaunt to **May Lake** (2.4-mile round-trip).

Tioga Pass Road reaches the park's eastern boundary at 9,945-foot (3,031-metre) **Tioga Pass**, the highest elevation highway pass through the Sierra Nevada. This is the eastern boundary of Yosemite National Park and the gateway to the Eastern Sierra. Hikers flock to this edge of the park because of the high elevation that can be attained just by driving a car. With trailheads located at nearly 10,000 feet (3,000 metres), hikers have a head-start for such high-elevation destinations as 13,053-foot (3,978-metre) Mount Dana.

Far to the west, and joined to the rest of Yosemite National Park by a 16-mile-long winding road, is **Hetch Hetchy**, the least visited area of the park. Hetch Hetchy Valley was once practically a twin of Yosemite Valley, with the same mixture of high granite walls and free-leaping waterfalls. However, in 1923 it was flooded to create a water supply for the city of San Francisco. This marked the tragic end of a long fight for naturalist John Muir, who had tried in vain to save Hetch Hetchy from the city politicians.

Despite man's best efforts to destroy it, Hetch Hetchy remains beautiful. Visitors can walk along the top of **O'Shaughnessy Dam** and then hike along the shoreline of **Hetch Hetchy Reservoir**, observing the walls of granite above the water line and the waterfalls tumbling into the 360-foot-deep (110-metre) lake. A trail leads to **Wapama Falls** (5.0-mile round-trip), flowing only in spring and early summer. A longer day-hike (or backpacking trip) can be taken to the far end of the reservoir and the **Rancheria Falls**, or to many other worthwhile destinations in this remote region of Yosemite.

Where to eat & drink

There's nothing quite like high mountain air to work up an appetite. Fortunately, the **Tuolumne Meadows Lodge** (1-209 372 8413, closed Oct-May, reservations required, $$$) has as its dining room a big white tent situated right on the river. This is good, fun, communal-style dining; you'll get to know your neighbours at the table. To the west on Tioga Pass Road is **White Wolf Lodge** (1-209 372 8416, closed Oct-May, reservations required, $$$$), with equally good food and a High Sierra setting that can't be beaten, whether you eat inside or out on the deck.

Those looking for takeaway food can stop at the no-nonsense **Tuolumne Meadows Grill** (closed Oct-May, $), next to Tuolumne Meadows Campground, which serves up memorable buckwheat pancakes.

Two miles beyond the park boundary is the historic **Tioga Pass Resort** (1-209 372 4471, www.tiogapassresort.com, $), which has a small lunch-counter-style café. There hearty, delicious sandwiches and big slices of pie are served up with gusto.

Where to stay

Set at the impressive elevation of 8,000 feet (2,400 metres), the wooden and tent cabins at **White Wolf Lodge** ($71-$105) provide ideal accommodation for people who want to explore the trails of the high country. Likewise the tent cabins at **Tuolumne Lodge** ($75). Remember, though, that both lodges are very rustic: location is what it is all about here, not amenities. Both are open from mid June to early September only (1-559 252 4848, www.yosemitepark.com).

The northern region of the park also offers the best camping opportunities in Yosemite. The **Tuolumne Meadows Campground** is well loved because of its location across the road from the trailheads at Tuolumne Meadows. If you don't have reservations, head for one of these four Tioga Pass Road campsites: **White Wolf**, **Yosemite Creek**, **Porcupine Flat** and **Tamarack Flat**. They not only welcome walk-ins, but are also some of the nicest campsites in the park. Two more sites are found in the north-west area of the park, near the Big Oak Flat entrance station: **Crane Flat** and **Hodgdon Meadow**. Reserve sites by phoning 1-301 722 1257 or visit http://reservations.nps.gov to book online; all are open from late spring to early autumn.

Resources

The main visitor centre in the park is in **Yosemite Village**, and should be every visitor's first stop. For up-to-the-minute information on the park, phone **1-209 372 0200** or visit the excellent Yosemite National Park website at **www.nps.gov/yose**. To see a listing of park tours, events and organised activities, check **www.yosemitepark.com**. Park rangers hand out Yosemite maps when you pay your entrance fee and enter the park, but this map is suitable for sightseeing only. If you'd like a detailed map of Yosemite's system of hiking trails, purchase one from **Tom Harrison Maps** (1-800 265 9090, 1-415 456 7940, www.tomharrisonmaps.com).

Central California

The Eastern Sierra

Less visited, but every bit as spectacular as the high country of Yosemite, Sequoia and Kings Canyon National Parks, is the land that lies just east of the parks along the corridor of US 395. Known in generic terms as the Eastern Sierra, this region includes two destination resort towns – **Mammoth Lakes** and **June Lake** – plus a whole host of other attractions: geological oddities, the ghost town of **Bodie**, a cornucopia of high alpine lakes, and the vast, salty sea known as **Mono Lake**.

The Eastern Sierra also includes the trailhead for the epic hike to the summit of **Mount Whitney**, the highest peak in the contiguous United States, and a small but spectacular unit of the National Park system known as **Devils Postpile National Monument**. From Bridgeport to Lone Pine, the Eastern Sierra contains a vast wealth of resources for outdoor recreationists: mountain slopes for skiers and snowboarders; miles and miles of trails for hikers, mountain bikers and equestrians; crystal-clear streams and rivers for anglers; and alpine lakes backed by granite cliffs for photographers.

Activities

On this side of the Sierra Nevada, hikers can access one trailhead after another at the end of almost every road that leads west off US 395. From Bridgeport to Mammoth to Lone Pine, each mountain-bound road is a gateway to the Hoover, John Muir and Ansel Adams wilderness areas and a world of hiking opportunities. There is more day-hiking to be done here than you could accomplish in a year; the pages that follow give trail suggestions near the Eastern Sierra's main towns.

One way to explore the rugged landscape of the Eastern Sierra without working up much of a sweat is to see it from the saddle of a horse. The **Virginia Lakes Pack Outfit** (1-760 937 0326, $45-$90) is located near the end of Virginia Lakes Road, 12 miles north of Lee Vining, and takes riders on day-trips into the Hoover Wilderness. **Frontier Pack Train** (1-760 648 7701, $25-$85) at Silver Lake leads trail rides lasting anywhere from one hour to a full day, following the Rush Creek Trail alongside the gurgling waters of the creek itself. **Mammoth Lakes Pack Outfit** (1-760 934 2434, $35-$110), located in Mammoth Lakes Basin, offers guided horseback rides daily, as well as four- to six-day horseback vacations. Finally, **Convict Lake Pack Station** (1-760 934 3800, $29-$32) at Convict Lake, a few miles

south of Mammoth, leads rides along the lake shore and into John Muir Wilderness. All these companies operate from late spring to early autumn each year.

Some of the best fishing in California is found in the lakes and streams of the Eastern Sierra. Just east of the Yosemite boundary lies **Saddlebag Lake**: at 10,087 feet (3,075 metres), it's the highest Californian lake accessible by car. A resort on its south shore operates a water taxi that transports anglers to the far side of the lake, where they can disembark to hike and fish in the Twenty Lakes Basin. Otherwise you can rent a boat, or fish from Saddlebag's lake shore, for golden, brook and rainbow trout.

North of Lee Vining lies **Lundy Lake**, where brown and rainbow trout are regularly planted by the California Department of Fish and Game. Lundy Lake Resort rents boats with or without motors, but plenty of anglers fish from shore too. A few miles further north on US 395 is Virginia Lake Road and three lakes: **Little Virginia**, **Big Virginia** and **Trumbull**, all planted weekly with rainbow trout. Fly-fishermen head to **Hot Creek** near Mammoth. The creek originates underground, bubbling from a fissure in volcanic rock; it then runs down a narrow gorge, creating an excellent habitat for wild rainbow and brown trout. Fish in excess of 20 inches (that's half a metre) are not unusual. Further downstream is the family-oriented **Hot Creek Geologic Area**, hot springs run by the Forest Service (contact the Mammoth Ranger Station, *see p338*). The springs bubble up from the middle of the river, so bathers pass from hot to cold water with just a single swimming stroke.

Even considering all these summertime activities, the Eastern Sierra's biggest claim to fame is as a winter playground for skiers and snowboarders. Aside from **Mammoth Mountain** (*see p336*), there's a fine cross-country ski resort at **Tamarack Lodge** (1-760 934 2442, www.tamaracklodge.com, day passes $10-$22) on Twin Lakes in the Mammoth Lakes Basin, with around 30 miles of groomed track open to cross-country skiers and snowshoers. **June Mountain** (1-800 626 6684, www.junemountain.com, lift tickets $19-$50) in June Lake is also a respectable ski resort, with 2,500 vertical feet (760 metres) of skiing. Both operate from late autumn to early spring. The **June Lake Ski Resort** caters to families and more casual skiers, although many snowboarders insist that the boarding is better here than at Mammoth. If you'd prefer a non-vertical adventure that's free of charge, strap on a pair of snowshoes or cross-country skis and explore the multitude of winter trails that lace the Eastern Sierra.

Bridgeport

Most of the buildings in tiny **Bridgeport** were
built around 1880, including the picturesque
County Courthouse. But although the town
is pretty enough, three attractions bring visitors
here: a handful of local hot springs, superb
fishing in the nearby Walker River, and the
town's proximity to **Bodie State Historic
Park** (1-760 647 6445, www.parks.ca.gov).

Bodie, located south-east of Bridgeport out in
the middle of nowhere, is the largest unrestored
ghost town in the American West. Gold was
discovered here in 1859 and the town saw its
heyday in the 1870s, when it boasted more
than 30 mines, 65 saloons and dance halls,
three breweries and a population of more than
10,000 people. Like most mining towns, Bodie
eventually suffered a complete decline, but
somehow survived the years intact: the state-
run park is a genuine 1870s gold-mining town,
devoid of the tourist shops and high entrance
fees that are the scourge of many other
Californian ghost towns.

With a careful minimum of assistance
from California State Parks, Bodie's buildings
have withstood the test of time. The town is
maintained in a state of arrested decay: the
powers-that-be don't fix up the structures, but
nor do they let them fall down. Visitors can
walk around the town's dusty streets, peek in
the windows of buildings and imagine what life
was like. A museum is open daily, but there are
no other facilities or food services in the park.
To get to Bodie, turn east on Highway 270 from
US 395 south of Bridgeport. It's 13 miles to the
ghost town and the last few miles are gravel.

Where to eat & drink

Plan to have at least one meal at **Restaurant
1881** (362 Main Street, 1-760 932 1918, closed
lunch, Jan-15 Apr, Mon-Wed 15 Apr-1 Nov,
$$$), which is owned by the family that runs
the Cain House B&B (*see below*). You might not
expect to find sautéed portobello mushrooms
in Bridgeport, but here they are. Down the road,
the **Hays Street Café** (21 Hays Street, 1-760
932 7141, closed dinner, $) is a great stop for
breakfast, with buttermilk biscuits to die for.

Where to stay

For a Western ranch experience, book a
summertime package at **Hunewill Guest
Ranch** (1-760 932 7710, www.hunewillranch.
com, $700-$1,300/5-7 days), a horsey place that
has more than 100 trusty steeds on the property.
Don't forget your cowboy boots. For a fishing
experience, **Twin Lakes Resort** (1-877 407

High country.

6153) on Lower Twin Lake is a fine place to cast
your line, gaze up from the water at the jagged
peaks of the Sawtooth Range and forget your
troubles. The self-catering cottages ($110-$147)
are good value for families. Those more inclined
towards a B&B will rave about the **Cain
House** (340 Main Street, 1-760 932 7040,
www.cainhouse.com, $100-$155), a historic
inn that has been beautifully restored by the
current owners. There are also a few adequate
motels in town, including the **Best Western
Ruby Inn** (333 Main Street, 1-760 932 7241,
$81-$110, www.bestwestern.com).

If you want to visit the ghost town at Bodie
with your kids, there's no better place to stay
than **Virginia Creek Settlement** (1-760
932 7780, www.virginiacrksettlement.com, $58-
$122). Not only is it the closest lodging to Bodie,
but it's also designed to get you in the ghost-
town spirit: the place is like a movie set, with
sleeping cabins bearing clever façades crafted
to look like the buildings of an Old West town.

Lee Vining

Only a few blocks long and wide, **Lee Vining**
is a mere gateway town for travellers heading
to and from Yosemite to the west and sightseers
gawking at the oddness of **Mono Lake**. A
majestic body of water covering 60 square
miles, Mono Lake is three times as salty as
the ocean and 80 times as alkaline: if you have
a swim, it's virtually impossible not to float.
Among its other unique features, Mono Lake
is one of the oldest lakes in America, having
been here for more than 700,000 years.

The most apparent wildlife at Mono Lake
is the thousands of birds. The lake is a major
stopover for migratory species passing over

Central California

the desert lands to the east, but it's also a huge breeding area for Californian gulls: 85 per cent of the gulls the live along the coast are born here. From April to November, visitors can spot thick masses of brine shrimp, on which the birds feed, clustered near the lake surface.

The best introduction to Mono Lake is a walk on the short **Mark Twain Scenic Tufa Trail** at Mono Lake Tufa State Reserve (1-760 647 6331, www.parks.ca.gov). Twain visited the lake in 1863 and described it in his book *Roughing It* as 'one of the strangest freaks of nature to be found in any land'. He was fascinated by the coral-like structures near the edges of the lake. Off-white in colour, these mineral formations (called tufa) are created when underwater springs release water containing calcium from the lake bottom. This water combines with the lake's saline water to form calcium carbonate, the chemical compound that constitutes tufa.

Make time to stop at the **Mono Basin Scenic Area Visitor Center** (*see p338*). The centre is perched on a hill high above Mono Lake, with benches outside that afford a delightful view. To see the lake close-up, you can take one of the canoe tours offered on weekend mornings in summer. No experience is necessary; trips last about an hour. For reservations, call 1-760 647 6595.

Where to eat & drink

The views of Mono Lake from the **Mono Inn Restaurant** (55260 US 395, 1-760 647 6581, closed lunch, Tue, Nov-Apr, $$$$) will blow you away. But the food, which has a California/ Mexican slant, is an even better surprise. In a small gallery, you'll find Ansel Adams prints for sale; the owner is a relative of the great photographer. The only other eaterie in the area that comes close to Mono Inn is **Me and Manuel's**, the restaurant at Tioga Lodge (*see below*). The dining room is a 100-year-old building that has been beautifully refurbished.

At the other end of the dining spectrum, **Bodie Mike's** (1-760 647 6432, closed Oct-Apr, $) in downtown Lee Vining serves big slabs of baby back ribs. The outside deck is always a happening place on summer evenings. There is also the ever-popular **Mono Cone**, a walk-up joint with a burger and shake menu as big as its namesake. No discussion of Lee Vining food would be complete without mentioning the **Tioga Gas Mart** (Highway 120 & US 395, 1-760 647 1088, closed Oct-Apr, $$). It's not often that people look forward to going to a gas station for dinner, but many do it every day. Try the lobster taquitos on a bed of black beans with tomatillo pineapple salsa.

Where to stay

In peak season, it's a very good idea to make reservations in advance: there are many travellers, but little by way of accommodation. The rooms are small at the **Yosemite Gateway Motel** (US 395, 1-800 282 3929, 1-760 647 6467, www.yosemitegatewaymotel.com, $49-$119), but each one has a perfectly framed view of Mono Lake from its windows. The cabins at **Tioga Lodge** (US 395, 1-888 647 6423, 1-760 647 6423, www.tiogalodge.com, $55-$107) also afford a fine lake view, albeit from across the highway. The lodge opened in 2000, but several of its cabins were transported here in the 1880s from Bodie. For something a little less historic, try **El Mono Motel** (51 US 395, 1-760 647 6310, $52-$82), whose unofficial motto is 'We do funky very well'. Considering the low rates, you might expect shabby furnishings, but the rooms are cheerful and fun. The owner operates the adjacent **Latte da Coffee Café**, so you can wander out in your slippers in the morning to get a cappuccino.

For the aspen-lined campsites in Lee Vining Canyon and Lundy Canyon, contact **Mono County Building & Parks Department** (1-760 932 5451, 1-760 932 5252) or **Mono Basin Scenic Area Visitor Center** (*see p338*).

Bridgeport. *See p333.*

June Lake

Some people consider **June Lake** (www.june lake.com) to be a poor cousin of the nearby Mammoth Lakes; others think it's the best-kept outdoor recreation secret of the Sierra Nevada. It all depends on your perspective: sure, June Lake's ski resort (*see p332*) doesn't compare to Mammoth, and it doesn't have a tenth of its lodgings, restaurants and shops, but that's just fine with those who know and love the place.

For starters there are four lakes located on the June Lake Loop (the nickname for Highway 158), all within a 20-minute drive. **June**, **Gull**, **Silver** and **Grant Lakes** have a total of five marinas and a swimming beach, plus outstanding trout fishing. **Reversed Creek**, which runs through this glacial canyon, also offers great fishing.

There's more. There are several good campsites and cabin resorts on hand to provide lodgings, a pack station (1-760 648 7701, $25-$85) is located by Silver Lake for people who want to ride a horse (spring to early autumn), and those willing to walk can choose from a half-dozen trailheads located around the Loop. Good choices include the easy walk to **Parker Lake** (3.8-mile round-trip from the Parker Lake Trailhead) and the more challenging ascent to **Agnew** and **Gem Lakes** (7.0-mile round-trip from the Rush Creek Trailhead at Silver Lake). Hiking information can be obtained at the **Mono Basin Scenic Area Visitor Center** or the **US Forest Service's Mammoth Ranger Station** (for both, *see p338*).

Where to eat & drink

The finest dining establishment in June Lake is the Double Eagle Resort's restaurant, **Eagle's Landing** (Highway 158, 1-760 648 7004, $$$$). Sit indoors and gaze through the floor-to-ceiling windows at Carson Peak and Reversed Creek, or sit on the deck and enjoy the Sierra sun. Dinner entrées include orange-glazed salmon and macadamia-crusted halibut.

The **Carson Peak Inn** (Highway 158, 1-760 648 7575, closed lunch, $$$) opened its doors in 1966. This old-fashioned dinner house serves huge portions: even if you choose 'regular appetite' instead of 'hearty appetite' entrées, you'll have to roll yourself out when it's over.

Where to stay

Most people agree that 110-acre Silver Lake is the prettiest of the four lakes on the June Lake Loop, which is a major reason why **Silver Lake Resort** (Highway 158, 1-760 648 7525, www.silverlakeresort.net, $89-$225) is so

popular. Established in 1916, it's the oldest resort in the Eastern Sierra. The operation includes a general store, cabins, a café, an RV park and boat rentals. The other half-dozen cabin resorts in June Lake are all clean and serviceable, but **Fern Creek Lodge** (4628 Highway 158, 1-800 6219146, 1-760 648 7722, www.ferncreeklodge.com, $65-$238) has more character than the rest: the lodge has been here since 1927, and each of its ten cabins is unique.

If you like the idea of an upscale mountain-cabin resort, **Double Eagle Resort** (5587 Highway 158, 1-760 648 7004, www.double-eagle-resort.com, $259-$319) does it well. The resort's 14 cabins are all tasteful two-bed units with full kitchens and fireplaces. Amenities include microwaves and VCRs; the resort also features a spa and fitness centre, a fly-fishing shop and a full-service salon.

For June Lake campsites, contact the **Mammoth Ranger Station** (*see p338*).

Mammoth Lakes

The town of **Mammoth Lakes** has grown up quickly in the last decade, and Californians are divided on how they feel about it. On one hand, Mammoth is now ultra-convenient: you can buy anything you want, see a first-run movie, dine at a wide selection of restaurants, go to Pilates… basically, do whatever you do in the big city. On the other hand, parts of Mammoth are now hard to distinguish from parts of an LA suburb, except for the looming presence of mountains in the background.

The one area of Mammoth that hasn't changed a bit – mostly because it's owned by the US Forest Service – is the **Mammoth Lakes Basin**, just outside town. This glacially carved canyon features several lakes to which you can drive (Twin, Mary, Mamie, George and Horseshoe) and many more that can be accessed by taking a short, easy hike. There's a cabin resort located on every lake except Horseshoe, and several campsites sprinkled about the basin. Otherwise, there's nothing but great fishing opportunities and hiking trails galore. To get a taste of this magnificent place, hike the trail from George Lake to **Crystal Lake** (3.8-mile round-trip) or the longer **Duck Pass Trail** from Coldwater Campground to a string of lakes: Arrowhead, Skelton, Barney and Duck Lake (10.0-mile round-trip).

Although best known for its first-class ski resort (*see p336*), Mammoth is also entryway to the **Devils Postpile National Monument** (1-760 934 2289, www.nps.gov), a park that features two geological marvels: the Devils Postpile itself, an amazing collection of basalt 'posts' remaining from an ancient lava flow, and 101-foot (31-metre) Rainbow Falls, one of the Sierra's most beautiful waterfalls. Because of the narrow access road that leads into the park, visitors must take a shuttle bus to the ranger station. It is then a short walk to the Devils Postpile, and a bit further to the Rainbow Falls (4.0-mile round-trip). The ranger station is open from mid June to mid October.

Mammoth Mountain

1 Minaret Road (1-800 626 6684/www.mammoth mountain.com). **Open** late autumn-early spring. **Admission** *Lift tickets* $26-$63. **Credit** AmEx, DC, Disc, MC, V.

The slopes at Mammoth Mountain rival those near Tahoe for both size and variety. The ski area has a lot to brag about: 3,500 acres, 3,100 vertical feet (945 metres), and an annual average of 385 inches of snow and 300 days of sunshine. The ski season begins in early November and runs until June or July. The 11,053-foot summit of Mammoth Mountain is accessible on a glass-panelled gondola, and a bundle of chairlifts are always in motion up and down the slopes. In summer, Mammoth Mountain Ski Area turns into Mammoth Mountain Bike Park.

Where to eat & drink

It's easy to assume that a fishing and skiing lodge will serve little besides steaks and burgers, but not so at Tamarack Lodge's dining room. The **Lakefront** (on Twin Lakes in Mammoth Lakes Basin, 1-760 934 2442, closed lunch, reservations required, $$$$) serves outstanding French-Californian cuisine. Try the elk or wild boar medallions. **Convict Lake Resort** (1-760 934 3803, closed lunch, $$$$), just four miles south of Mammoth off US 395, serves up similar dishes at its restaurant. People may come to Convict Lake to fish, hike and get dirty, but everyone cleans up for dinner out of respect for the talented chef.

You might not think of having a seafood dinner in the mountains, but **Ocean Harvest** (248 Old Mammoth Road, 1-760 934 8539, closed lunch, $$$) does a good trade in mahi-mahi and the like. A few doors down, the **Chart House** (106 Old Mammoth Road, 1-760 934 4526, www. chart-house.com, closed lunch, $$$) does what Chart House restaurants do all across the USA: solid, dependable food. **Matsu** (3711 Highway 203, 1-760 934 8277, $$) is a locals' favourite and the best Asian restaurant in town. What kind of Asian? Eclectic, they call it.

Cervino's (3752 Viewpoint Road, 1-760 934 4734, closed lunch, $$$) serves northern Italian food in a casually elegant setting just outside town. But if your favourite kind of Italian food is cheap pizza and pasta, try **Giovanni's** (Minaret Village Mall, Old Mammoth Road, 1-760 934 7563, $) instead.

Where to stay

Something like a small Tahoe in terms of services and amenities, Mammoth Lakes has hundreds of lodging options. Many are bland chain motels, located in town and along the highway: try the **Shilo Inn** (2963 Highway 203, 1-800 222 2244, 1-760 934 4500, www. shiloinns.com, $80-$120). The best Mammoth lodging options are the cabin resorts in the Mammoth Lakes Basin, where you might get a cabin with a view of an alpine lake (or, at least, of piney woods). There are three lakeside resorts that offer similar amenities: **Tamarack Lodge & Resort** (1-800 626 6684, 1-760 934 2442, www.tamaracklodge.com, $84-$185) on Twin Lakes, **Crystal Crag Lodge** (1-760 934 2436, www.crystalcraglodge.com, closed Oct-May, $85-$130) on Lake Mary, and **Wood's Lodge** (1-760 934 2261, closed mid Oct-May, $92-$281) on George Lake. Or you can set up your own tent at one of more than a dozen campsites around Mammoth Lakes, all of them run by the US Forest Service (1-760 924 5500, www.fs.fed.us/r5/inyo).

Bishop

In the Eastern Sierra, Mammoth Lakes is viewed as the glamour destination, with blue-collar **Bishop** seen as its poor cousin. The big event is the annual Mule Days celebration, held

Going up... **Mammoth Mountain**.

every Memorial Day weekend, but this cowboy town also provides important services for people who live anywhere on the Sierra's eastern side, and equally important services for travellers on US 395. The lack of airs and graces doesn't deter large numbers of hikers, anglers, climbers and cross-country skiers, all of whom view Bishop as a destination in its own right.

West Line Street, also known as Highway 168, runs from the centre of town straight up into the mountains to the west. Within a few minutes you can find yourself at an elevation of some 8,000 feet (2,400 metres) in **Bishop Creek Canyon**. There you can plunk a fishing line into South Lake, Sabrina Lake or North Lake; set up your tent at one of dozens of US Forest Service campsites alongside the gurgling waters of Bishop Creek; or set off on any one of many trails that lead into the **John Muir Wilderness**.

Hikers who are looking for a challenge should follow the **Piute Pass Trail** from North Lake Campground to Loch Leven Lake, Piute Lake and spectacular Piute Pass. The scenic pass is six miles away, but the lakes are closer at 2.3 and 3.5 miles out. Alternatively, hike from the Lake Sabrina trailhead to the photogenic **Blue Lake** (6.0-mile round-trip). Each of these hike-in lakes is higher than 10,000 feet (3,000 metres) in elevation. A trailhead near South Lake is the start of a 6.6-mile loop hike to Ruwau, Bull and Chocolate Lakes. From the same starting point, you can also try the shorter out-and-back to Long Lake.

Another interesting sight in the Bishop area is the **Ancient Bristlecone Pine Forest** (1-760 873 2500). Located east of Highway 168 and White Mountain Road, this is where you'll find the oldest living things in the world: ancient bristlecone pines. Among them, the oldest of all is the Methuselah Tree, which has lived for more than 4,000 years. There's a visitor centre and a few short trails that lead into the surrounding forest.

Where to eat & drink

The best-prepared grub you'll find in Bishop Creek Canyon is at **Parchers South Fork Restaurant** (see below). Backpackers coming off the Bishop Pass Trail make a beeline for the place; most have already decided what they'll be ordering ten miles back. Down the road at **Bishop Creek Lodge** (see below), hunting and fishing trophies cover every inch of the dining room's walls, including the lifelike bodies of a

few big trout. There's a limited menu, with hamburgers and sandwiches served all day and steak and chicken entrées for dinner.

In downtown Bishop, there is an abundance of fast food. If you want something a little more interesting, try the excellent California cuisine and good selection of microbrews at **Whiskey Creek** (524 Main Street, 1-760 873 7174, $$). **Amigo's Mexican Restaurant** (285 Main Street, 1-760 872 2189, $) is preferred by those on a budget.

Where to stay

Cardinal Village Resort (1-760 873 4789, www.cardinal villageresort.com, $120-$300) is a destination in itself for historians. Part of an old mining claim, its buildings date back to the late 1890s and are open to guests from mid-spring to mid-autumn. Nearby **Bishop Creek Lodge** (1-760 873 4484, www.bishopcreekresorts.com/bcl, closed Nov-Apr, $90-$250) makes no pretence: it's a fish camp, a base for people heading to South Lake or Sabrina Lake to catch trout all day. Situated at the lofty elevation of 8,300 feet (2,500 metres), the place also attracts hikers who want to traipse the myriad trails of the John Muir Wilderness. Bishop Creek's owners also run **Parchers Resort** (1-760 873 4177, www. bishopcreekresorts.com/parchers, closed Nov-Apr, $80-$170), just down the road. Newer and just a little posher than its sister property, the cabins at Parchers are tucked in between two streams. If you'd rather stay in town, Bishop has dozens of motel chains, many just a few yards off US 395.

Campgrounds are plentiful in the Bishop Creek Canyon, most of them set under a leafy canopy of aspen tree leaves and/or alongside the creek. Get information at the **Bishop Ranger Station** (see p338).

Lone Pine & Independence

If Bishop is a poor cousin of Mammoth Lakes, then the little towns of **Lone Pine** and **Independence** are the poorer cousins of Bishop. There isn't a whole lot here apart from some cheap motels and convenience stores. But this area does have its claims to fame.

Lone Pine, in particular, is well known as the base camp for hikers who wish to tackle 14,495-foot (4,418-metre) **Mount Whitney**, the highest peak in the contiguous United States. Although Whitney is located in **Sequoia National Park** (see p339), the shortest route to its lofty summit begins at

Central California

Whitney Portal in **Inyo National Forest**, just a few miles west of Lone Pine. That said, the phrase 'shortest route' is misleading: the trek from Whitney Portal is still a whopping 22 miles round-trip. While many hikers choose to backpack the route and split the mileage into two or three days, a surprising number of people hike the entire distance in one day. To do so, they spend the night at one of the several campsites near Whitney Portal or in one of many motels in Lone Pine, then get up at 4am to begin the long journey to the summit.

If you want to join the hordes of hikers who can boast of having climbed Whitney, you'll need to plan your journey well in advance. Permits are required for both day-hikes and backpacking trips and can be hard to come by: only a limited number of people are permitted to make the trip each day, and the season is short (generally July to early October). For more information on climbing Mount Whitney, contact the **US Forest Service's Mount Whitney Ranger Station** (*see below*).

If peak-bagging isn't your scene, you might choose instead to tour the **Alabama Hills**, just below Mount Whitney. These rugged, rocky hills have provided a setting for numerous Westerns over the years. Free maps of the area are available around town.

Just north of Lone Pine is the ironically named town of **Independence**. The irony lies in its proximity to **Manzanar Historic Site** (1-760 878 2194, www.nps.gov/manz), a federal parkland commemorating a sad piece of American history. Shortly after the bombing of Pearl Harbor, President Roosevelt signed an order that all people of Japanese ancestry living on the West Coast, even fully fledged American citizens, should be placed in 'relocation' camps. The Manzanar War Relocation Center was the first of them. Although there's not much left besides the remains of a few old buildings, the **Eastern California Museum** (155 Grant Street, 1-760 878 0258, closed Mon, Tue), five miles north in Independence, displays a quite fascinating collection of photographs and works of art from the camp.

Where to eat & drink

After climbing Whitney, you simply have to go to the **Mount Whitney Restaurant** (227 S Main Street, 1-760 876 5751, $$) and order a burger: beef, buffalo, ostrich, veggie or venison.

Where to stay

In summer, almost everyone staying at the **Dow Villa Motel** (310 S Main Street, 1-800 824 9317, 1-760 876 5521, www.dowvillamotel.com,

$82-$115) is climbing Whitney, so you can expect some commotion around 4am. If that's a problem for you, the **Best Western Frontier Motel** (1008 S Main Street, 1-760 876 5571, www.bestwestern.com, $98-$199) is likely to be a little more peaceful. If you'd rather camp out, call the **Mount Whitney Ranger District** (640 S Main Street, 1-760 876 6200, www.fs.fed.us/r5/inyo).

Resources

Hospital

Mammoth Lakes *Mammoth Hospital, 85 Sierra Park Road (1-760 934 3311/ www.mammothhospital.com).*

Internet

Bishop *Kava Coffee House, 206 N Main Street (1-760 872 1010/www.kavacoffeehouse.org).* **Open** 6.30am-7pm Mon-Wed; 6.30am-10pm Thur, Fri; 7am-10pm Sat; 7am-7pm Sun.
Mammoth Lakes *Main Library, 960 Forest Trail (1-760 934 4777/www.monocolibraries.org).* **Open** 10pm-7am Mon-Fri; 9am-5.30pm Sat.

Police

Mammoth Lakes *568 Old Mammoth Road (1-760 934 2011).*

Post office

Bridgeport *29 Kingsley Road (1-760 932 7991).*
Lone Pine *121 E Bush Street (1-760 876 5681).*
Mammoth Lakes *3330 Main Street (1-760 934 2205).*

Tourist information

Bishop *US Forest Service's Bishop Ranger Station, 351 Pacu Lane (1-760 873 2400/www.fs.fed.us/r5/ inyo).* **Open** 8am-4.30pm Mon-Fri.
Bridgeport *US Forest Service's Bridgeport Ranger Station, US 395 (1-760 932 7070/www.fs.fed.us/r4/ htnf).* **Open** 8am-4.30pm Mon-Fri.
Lee Vining *Mono Lake Committee Visitor Center (1-760 647 6595).* **Open** 9am-5pm daily.
Mono Basin Scenic Area Visitor Center, US 395, just north of Lee Vining (1-760 647 3044).
Open 9am-4.30am daily.
Lone Pine *Visitors' Center, US 136 & 395, (1-760 876 6222).* **Open** 8am-5pm daily.
US Forest Service's Mount Whitney Ranger Station, 640 S Main Street (1-760 876 6200/www.fs.fed. us/r5/inyo). **Open** 8am-6pm daily.
Mammoth Lakes *US Forest Service's Mammoth Ranger Station, Highway 203 (1-760 924 5500/www.fs.fed. us/r5/inyo).* **Open** 8am-5pm daily.

Sequoia & Kings Canyon National Parks

On the western slope of the Sierra Nevada, about 75 miles south of Yosemite (*see p324*), lie two less visited but equally spectacular units of the national park system, famous for groves of giant sequoia, soaring mountains, deep canyons, roaring rivers and spectacular hiking trails. Often referred to as 'Yosemite without the masses', **Sequoia** and **Kings Canyon National Parks** offer classic Sierra scenery without the overcrowding that plagues their colleague to the north. The annual number of visitors to Yosemite rose to 3.4 million people in 2003, while less than half that many visited Sequoia and Kings Canyon. Combined.

Managed jointly by the National Park Service since 1943, Kings Canyon and Sequoia demand superlatives. **Mount Whitney**, the highest peak in the contiguous United States, is located in Sequoia (although most people hike to its summit from the east side near Lone Pine, *see p337*). Nor is it alone: several other park peaks rise to more than 14,000 feet (4,200 metres). The largest living tree in the world, the **Sherman Tree** (*see p341*), is to be found in Sequioa's Giant Forest, and there are numerous other record-setting trees in both of the parks.

Adding to the drama of the landscape, three powerful rivers – the **Kings**, **Kern** and **Kaweah** – course through the joint parks. The steep and barren canyons through which these rivers flow are as awe-inspiring as the waters themselves. Carved to a depth of 8,000 feet (2,400 metres) below the summit of neighbouring Spanish Mountain, the canyon of the Kings River is deeper even than the Grand Canyon.

Since December 2000, a new national park unit has been tacked on to the borders of Sequoia and Kings Canyon: **Giant Sequoia National Monument**. Administered by the US Forest Service, not the National Park Service (a distinction largely invisible to visitors), Giant Sequoia National Monument consists of two non-contiguous land areas, one south of Sequoia National Park and the other west of Kings Canyon. Both are intended to increase protection for the last remaining giant sequoia groves in the world. The massive trees, which once ranged across the planet, today grow in only a narrow strip of the Sierra Nevada Mountains, a parcel of land about 40 miles wide and 150 miles long. Only 75 native giant sequoia groves remain; more than half are in Giant Sequoia National Monument.

Visitors can drive into the national parks at any time; the entrance fee per vehicle, good for seven days, is $10. For annual National Park passes and other discounts on admission, contact the National Park Service (*see p403*). For more park information, *see p342*.

Activities

With more than 800 miles of trails from which to choose, hiking is far and away the most popular activity in Kings Canyon and Sequoia. For hiking suggestions within the various park regions, *see pp340-342*. If you'd rather ride than walk, guided hourly, half-day and all-day horseback rides are available between June and September at both **Grant Grove** and **Cedar Grove**; phone 1-559 565 3464 for details, and expect to pay $30-$100.

Fishing is understandably popular in the region, with many rivers and high lakes from which to choose. Rainbow, brook and brown trout are the standard catch, although you might get lucky and haul in a golden trout. Fishing licences and tackle can be purchased at the markets at Lodgepole, Cedar Grove and Grant Grove. Some of the park waters are catch-and-release only; make sure you know the rules before you drop a line.

One of Kings Canyon and Sequoia's more distinctive features is the extensive array of limestone caverns: more than 200 caves are found here. To explore most of them requires advanced caving skills and equipment, but two are open for public guided tours from mid-spring to late autumn. **Crystal Cave** (1-559 565 3759, $5-$10) is located at the end of a winding seven-mile road off the Generals Highway near Giant Forest; tickets must be purchased in advance at Lodgepole or Foothills visitor centres. **Boyden Cavern** (1-559 736 2708, $5-$10) is located right off Highway 180 between Grant Grove and Cedar Grove; you can drive right up and purchase tickets for the next available tour.

There are also plentiful opportunities for winter recreation in the parks. During the ski season (roughly from December to April), snowshoes and cross-country skis can be rented at Grant Grove, Wolverton, Wuksachi Lodge and Montecito Sequoia Resort. Park rangers lead snowshoe walks on most winter weekends, or you can set off on your own. **Montecito Sequoia Resort** (1-800 227 9900, www.montecitosequoia.com) has many groomed tracks.

Central California

Grant Grove

Most visitors get their first glimpse of Kings Canyon and Sequoia at **Grant Grove**, which is located near the Highway 180 entrance to the parks. Here you'll find many essential visitor services (a lodge, a restaurant, a grocery store, a visitor centre, campsites and so on), plus the **General Grant Tree** and several dozen more giant sequoias growing in a large and easily accessible grove. The General Grant holds the distinction of being the third largest tree in the world, and is also known as 'the nation's Christmas tree': a Yuletide celebration has been held under its branches every year since 1926.

Several other short trails begin at Grant Grove, including the quarter-mile **Panoramic Point Trail**, which leads to a 7,250-foot (2,210-metre) ridgetop overlook, best visited in the morning for the clearest visibility. From there, hikers can continue to Park Ridge Fire Lookout for even better views. Visitors staying at Sunset Campground should hike the **Sunset Trail** (5.0-mile round-trip), which leads from the camp downhill to pretty Viola and Ella Falls.

For a longer walk in a giant sequoia grove (and much less people than in Grant Grove), head south on the Generals Highway for about five miles to the Redwood Mountain Grove. Walk a couple of miles down the **Redwood Canyon Trail** for a short out-and-back or, if you have all day, follow the 10.0-mile **Redwood Mountain Loop**.

Where to eat, drink & stay

For dining, try the **Grant Grove Restaurant** (1-559 335 5500, $$): it's basically a large coffee shop, but the food is passable and affordable.

Many of Grant Grove Lodge's rustic cabins look and feel like a throwback to the 1930s; some are only a short step above camping, which may be a good thing or a bad thing, depending on your outlook. If it's the latter, try Grant Grove's newly built **John Muir Lodge** ($109-$149), where each of the 30 rooms has two queen beds and a full private bath. Reserve all Grant Grove lodgings by phone on 1-866 522 6966 or 1-559 335 5500, or online at www.sequoia-kingscanyon.com.

Campers can choose from three sites in the Grant Grove area: **Sunset**, **Crystal Springs** and **Azalea**. For reservations, call 1-800 365 2267 or consult http://reservations.nps.gov.

Cedar Grove

There's undeniable allure about a place called Road's End. That enticing moniker designates the eastern terminus of Highway 180, the Kings Canyon Scenic Byway, with its paved portion coming to an end six miles past **Cedar Grove Village**. If you want to continue through the Sierra from here, you'll have to walk.

Journeying to Cedar Grove and Road's End is half the fun. From the Kings Canyon entrance station near Grant Grove, Highway 180 zigzags east for 31 miles to Cedar Grove, skirting the banks of the roaring Kings River. You'll stop more than a few times to take pictures, especially in early summer, when snowmelt makes the river a tumbling sea of white water. Don't expect much by way of services at Cedar Grove: a few campsites, one lodge and a burger-flipping café put the period to civilisation.

For a mellow introduction to the area, follow **Zumwalt Meadow Trail**, a 1.5-mile self-guided loop that offers views of imposing 8,518-foot (2,596-metre) Grand Sentinel and 8,717-foot (2,657-metre) North Dome, two of Cedar Grove's most impressive chunks of granite. At the edges of fern-filled Zumwalt Meadow lie clear river pools and a fragrant forest of incense cedar and pines. Alternatively, you could take the five-minute stroll to **Roaring River Falls**, a boisterous cascade that funnels through a narrow gorge. Another easily visited cataract, 80-foot (20-metre) **Grizzly Falls**, is found by Highway 180 five miles west of Cedar Grove.

More ambitious hikers head for the **Mist Falls-Paradise Valley Trail** (8.8-mile round-trip), which leads from Road's End to billowing Mist Falls on the South Fork Kings River. The hike has a mere 700 feet (200 metres) of elevation gain, but you must start early in the day to beat the heat. The path tunnels through riverside forest for two miles, then rises on granite slopes to gain grand views of 10,007-foot (3,050-metre) Avalanche Peak and a distinctive granite pinnacle called the Sphinx. Four miles from the trailhead, Kings River fans out over a wide granite ledge and falls 40 feet (12 metres), forming the well-named Mist Falls.

A less visited but no less worthy footpath is the **Hotel Creek Trail**, which climbs two steep miles up to Cedar Grove Overlook. There you'll get to enjoy an inspiring vista of Kings Canyon and all the surrounding peaks. Loop back via the **Lewis Creek Trail** for a round-trip of around eight miles.

Where to eat, drink & stay

The choice of places to eat is minimal around Cedar Grove. The **Cedar Grove Snack Bar** (1-559 335 5500, closed Nov-Apr, $), with counter-service meals and snacks, is a better bet than the less reliable **Kings Canyon Lodge** restaurant (1-559 335 2405, closed Nov-Apr, $$$). Ditto lodgings: your choices are the

Cedar Grove Lodge (1-866 522 6966, 1-559 452 1081, www.sequoia-kingscanyon.com, closed Nov-Apr, $105-$115), an 18-room, motel-style lodge, or the extremely rustic cabins at **Kings Canyon Lodge** (1-559 335 2405, open mid spring-early autumn, $69-$169), 15 miles west of Cedar Grove on Highway 180. Coming to the traveller's rescue are Cedar Grove's four lovely campsites: **Sheep Camp**, **Sentinel**, **Canyon View** and **Moraine** are all near the Kings River, with reservations not required.

Lodgepole & Giant Forest

The central region of Sequoia National Park is where most visitors head, despite the long, winding drive that is necessary to get there from either the Grant Grove Entrance (Highway 180) or the Foothills Entrance (Highway 198). The region's chief attraction is the aptly named **Giant Forest**, home to a number of vast trees including **General Sherman**, the largest living tree in the world. How big? Most people need more than a minute to walk completely around its 103-foot (31-metre) circumference. It is 275 feet tall (84 metres) and still growing: every year it adds enough wood to make another 60-foot-tall (18-metre) tree. The tree is estimated to be around 2,100 years old. Since it's right next to a large parking area, many tourists make a quick stop, snap a few pictures and move on down the road. A better bet is to take a hike on the 2.1-mile **Congress Trail**. It begins by General Sherman and proceeds past a host of other record-holding trees – including the 246-foot-tall (75-metre) Washington Tree (the second largest tree in the world) – until it reaches two dense groupings of sequoias called the Senate and the House. Of the many trails through the park's sequoia groves, the Congress is by far the easiest and most impressive.

Another popular spot, just a few miles south of General Sherman, is **Moro Rock**. This 6,725-foot (2,050-metre) granite dome has a series of ramps and staircases that lead all the way to the top. The view of the Great Western Divide from the summit will knock your socks off, well worth the 20 minutes of huffing and puffing it takes to get there. You ascend nearly 400 stairs along the way.

Nearby Crescent Meadow, which John Muir dubbed 'the gem of the Sierra', is home to **Tharp's Log**, the modest summer abode of Hale Tharp. Tharp was the first white man to enter Giant Forest, building his 'house' inside a fallen, fire-hollowed sequoia. You can look inside and see his rudimentary furnishings.

The **High Sierra Trail**, a popular trans-Sierra route, begins near Crescent Meadow and eventually leads to Mount Whitney, 70 miles

east. Following the trail for a much less demanding three-quarters of a mile will lead you to a lookout known as **Eagle View**, from which you'll stand witness to Moro Rock on your right, Castle Rocks straight ahead, and the dozens of peaks and ridges that make up the Western Divide far across the canyon.

Arguably the best hiking in the parks is found a few miles north of Giant Forest. Campers staying at Dorst Campground shouldn't miss the 4.0-mile round-trip to the giant sequoias that make up Muir Grove. For one of the best views in the park, hike the **Little Baldy Trail**, one mile south of Dorst Campground (3.5-mile round-trip). Many claim that Little Baldy's view of the Silliman Crest, the Great Western Divide, Castle Rocks, Moro Rock, the Kaweah River Canyon and the San Joaquin foothills is the best panorama in the park.

Even small children can manage the 3.6-mile round-trip to **Tokopah Falls**. At 1,200 feet (370 metres), it is the largest waterfall in Sequoia and Kings Canyon. The trail starts at Lodgepole Campground and follows a nearly level path alongside the Kaweah River. For a longer trek, start at the Wolverton trailhead and follow the **Lakes Trail** up and over the Watchtower, a 1,600-foot-high (490-metre) glacially carved granite cliff that offers breathtaking views of the Tokopah Valley below. The trail ends at three gem-like lakes: Heather, Emerald and Pear.

To the south of Giant Forest, in the Foothills region, the elevation drops significantly and the temperature rises accordingly. Here the Paradise Creek Trail leads from Buckeye Flat Campground to a series of tempting swimming holes. A 2.5-mile trail climbs gradually from Potwisha Campground to **Hospital Rock**, which has a display of pictographs on its side. A large, cave-like shelter on the rock's underside was the place where a Native American medicine man healed the sick and injured. Nearby are dozens of grinding holes that were used by Monache Indian women to grind acorns into meal.

In the spring and early summer, the best Foothills area hike is to **Paradise Falls**, starting from Potwisha Campground and totalling around seven miles there and back. This 40-foot (12-metre) waterfall drops along the Marble Fork Kaweah River; wildflowers are here in abundance during April and May.

Where to eat, drink & stay

The Lodgepole/Giant Forest area of Sequoia National Park has the most choices for lodgings and food. The most upscale is the **Wuksachi Village** (1-888 252 5757, 1-599 253 2199, www.visitsequoia.com, $86-$219), a complex that consists of three separate buildings, with 100 newly built guest rooms. The casually elegant 90-seat **restaurant** serves the best food in Sequoia and Kings Canyon and offers stunning views of Mount Silliman.

In Giant Sequoia National Monument, travellers can stay and/or eat at **Montecito Sequoia Resort** (1-800 227 9900, www. montecitosequoia.com), where a three-night package costs $369, or **Stony Creek Lodge** (1-866 522 6966, 1-559 565 3388, www.sequoia-kingscanyon.com, closed Oct-Apr, $125-$135). Montecito Sequoia is run like a High Sierra version of Club Med: there's a heavy emphasis on organised activities, especially for families. Guests choose from motel-style rooms or rustic cabins, and meals are included in the room price for most of the year. Nearby Stony Creek Lodge is smaller and more quaint, with only 11 rooms and a restaurant serving dependable American food. The **Lodgepole Village** area also has a deli and small café.

The more adventurous might want to book a stay at **Bearpaw High Sierra Camp** (1-888 252 5757, 1-559 253 2199, www.visitsequoia. com, $350), a backcountry 'tent hotel', accessible only by taking an 11.5-mile hike. The camp is open from mid June to mid September only and reservations are hugely difficult to come by. To try for a spot, start phoning on 2 January for the following summer.

Five campsites are found in this region of Sequoia National Park: **Lodgepole**, **Dorst**, **Buckeye Flat**, **Potwisha** and **South Fork**. Reservations can be made by phoning 1-800 365 2267 or logging on to http://reservations.nps. gov. Several US Forest Service campsites are located on Giant Sequoia National Monument lands. Contact the **Hume Lake Ranger District** (1-559 338 2251, www.fs.fed.us/ r5/sequoia) for details.

Mineral King

Nobody gets to **Mineral King** by accident. This remote region of southern Sequoia National Park is located at the end of 25 miles of winding road, boasting nearly 700 tight curves and turns. You don't want to make this drive as a day-trip: if you don't plan to stay the night, don't go at all.

After the arduous drive, Mineral King is a hiker's heaven, a glacially carved canyon surrounded by the colourful shale, marble and granite peaks. You'll also find plentiful solitude, wildlife (there are many deer and yellow-bellied marmots here) and wildflowers that last into the late summer. Almost every trail from the valley goes up, usually quite steeply. Hikers looking

for an easy stroll should follow the first mile or two of the **Farewell Gap Trail** along the East Fork Kaweah River. Some people cast a line into the water as they walk, hoping to catch a trout or two. Another mellow hike is **Cold Springs Nature Trail** out of Cold Springs Campground. Like the Farewell Gap Trail, Cold Springs parallels a chattering section of the Kaweah. It also offers fabulous views of Sawtooth Peak, Mineral Peak and Rainbow Mountain.

Those seeking more of a challenge can choose between several trails up to high alpine lakes, including **Eagle Lake** (6.8-mile round-trip), **Mosquito Lakes** (7.4-mile round-trip), **Monarch Lakes** (8.4-mile round-trip) and **Crystal Lake** (10.0-mile round-trip). Each lake is over 10,000 feet (3,000 metres), so expect classic high-country scenery with plenty of stark granite and deep blue water.

Where to eat, drink & stay

Silver City Resort (1-559 561 3223 in summer, 1-805 528 2730 in winter, www.silvercityresort. com, closed Nov-May, $70-$275) is the only commercial enterprise in Mineral King. Its cabins come in a wide range of sizes and configurations, from a tiny one-room shack to large three-bedroom chalets with full kitchens, bathrooms, decks and wood stoves. The small restaurant serves limited meals on most days.

Campers can choose from two car campsites, **Cold Springs** and **Atwell Mill**. Places are first-come, first-served, with no reservations.

Resources

Park rangers hand out Sequoia and Kings Canyon maps when you pay your entrance fee, but you should head to a visitor centre to get full information on current conditions. There are five visitor centres in the parks: **Grant Grove**, **Lodgepole**, **Cedar Grove**, **Mineral King** and **Foothills**. The **Giant Sequoia Museum** is also located in the Giant Forest area. Rangers at any of these locations can help you plan your itinerary.

To get up-to-the-minute information on the parks, phone **1-559 565 3341** or visit the official Kings Canyon and Sequoia website at **www.nps.gov/seki**. To see a full listing of park tours, events and organised activities, check the relevant websites for the park's pair of concessionaires: Delaware North Companies at **www.visitsequoia.com** and Kings Canyon Park Services at **www.sequoia-kingscanyon.com**.

If you'd like a detailed map of hiking trails in the region, **Tom Harrison Maps** (*see p331*) is again the place to go.

Northern California

Features

Northern California

A rugged, weatherbeaten and compelling land.

The main draws in unkempt Northern California are two scantily populated stretches of road, each about 25 miles long, separated by peaceful hills and mountains. Together, the Napa and Sonoma Valleys make up **Wine Country** (*see pp346-362*), the hub of the increasingly esteemed American wine world and also a substantial and lucrative tourist industry in its own right. The several hundred wineries that dot the landscape here all produce wine for commercial consumption across the country (and, in some cases, the world), but the vast majority welcome visitors for tastings and tours of their facilities. And visitors come, in their millions each year.

While the Central Coast boasts breathtaking scenery that's famous the world over, the coast between the Bay Area and the border with Oregon is a different beast: furious, harsh and decidedly untamed. Tiny, quaint

Mendocino (*see pp371-372*) is the closest the **North Coast** (*see pp363-380*) gets to a tourist town. This isn't to say that its coastal comrades are unfriendly, simply that they're plainer, tougher, less buffed up for the benefit of those who pass through; not for nothing has one particularly wild stretch been nicknamed the Lost Coast. The highlights of the drive north are the various affiliated areas that go under the collective banner of **Redwood National and State Parks** (*see pp378-379*).

Inland are the **Northern Mountains** (*see pp381-392*), huge swathes of land officially designated as national forest and, outside of a couple of decent-sized towns, largely free of residents. The driving here is a delight – in road atlases, almost every major highway comes lined with the green dots that denote a scenic route – and the land is dotted with minor but appealing diversions.

Climate

Average daily maximum and minimum temperatures in Northern California.

		Eureka	Lassen NF	Mendocino	Napa	Redding
Jan	max	54°F/12°C	39°F/3°C	56°F/13°C	57°F/14°C	55°F/13°C
	min	41°F/5°C	14°F/–9°C	40°F/4°C	37°F/3°C	36°F/2°C
Feb	max	55°F/12°C	43°F/6°C	57°F/14°C	61°F/16°C	61°F/16°C
	min	43°F/6°C	20°F/–6°C	41°F/4°C	41°F/5°C	38°F/3°C
Mar	max	55°F/12°C	49°F/9°C	58°F/15°C	65°F/18°C	65°F/18°C
	min	43°F/6°C	24°F/–4°C	42°F/6°C	42°F/5°C	43°F/6°C
Apr	max	56°F/13°C	56°F/13°C	59°F/15°C	69°F/21°C	73°F/23°C
	min	45°F/7°C	26°F/–3°C	43°F/6°C	43°F/6°C	48°F/8°C
May	max	58°F/14°C	66°F/18°C	61°F/16°C	74°F/23°C	81°F/27°C
	min	48°F/8°C	33°F/1°C	46°F/8°C	48°F/9°C	53°F/12°C
Jun	max	60°F/15°C	75°F/23°C	63°F/17°C	79°F/26°C	89°F/32°C
	min	51°F/10°C	38°F/3°C	48°F/8°C	52°F/11°C	60°F/16°C
July	max	61°F/16°C	85°F/29°C	64°F/17°C	82°F/28°C	98°F/37°C
	min	52°F/11°C	43°F/6°C	49°F/9°C	54°F/12°C	66°F/18°C
Aug	max	62°F/16°C	84°F/28°C	65°F/18°C	81°F/27°C	97°F/36°C
	min	53°F/11°C	41°F/4°C	50°F/10°C	54°F/12°C	62°F/17°C
Sep	max	63°F/17°C	76°F/24°C	66°F/18°C	82°F/28°C	91°F/33°C
	min	51°F/10°C	35°F/1°C	49°F/9°C	52°F/11°C	57°F/14°C
Oct	max	61°F/16°C	64°F/17°C	63°F/17°C	76°F/25°C	81°F/27°C
	min	49°F/9°C	27°F/–2°C	47°F/8°C	48°F/9°C	50°F/10°C
Nov	max	58°F/14°C	48°F/8°C	60°F/16°C	66°F/19°C	65°F/18°C
	min	45°F/7°C	21°F/–5°C	44°F/7°C	42°F/6°C	40°F/4°C
Dec	max	55°F/12°C	39°F/4°C	56°F/13°C	58°F/14°C	55°F/13°C
	min	42°F/5°C	15°F/–9°C	41°F/4°C	38°F/3°C	35°F/1°C

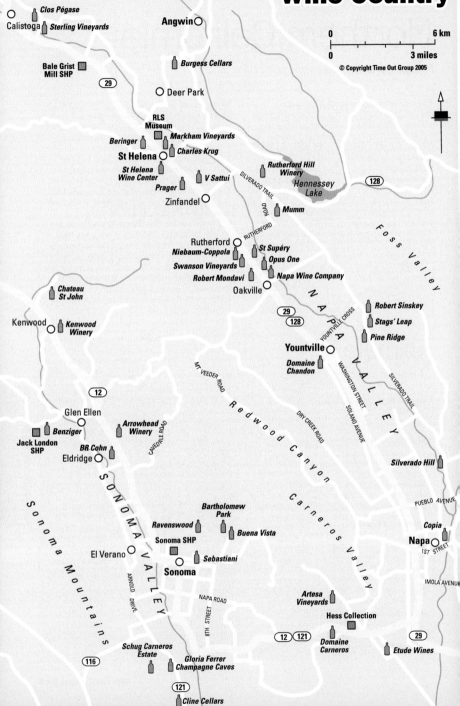

Wine Country

© Copyright Time Out Group 2005

| 0 | 6 km |
| 0 | 3 miles |

Clos Pégase
Calistoga
Sterling Vineyards

Angwin

Burgess Cellars

Bale Grist
Mill SHP

29

Deer Park

RLS
Museum
Markham Vineyards
Beringer
Charles Krug
St Helena
Rutherford Hill
Winery
St Helena
Wine Center
V Sattui
Prager
Hennessey
Lake
Zinfandel
Mumm

SILVERADO TRAIL

128

FOSS VALLEY

Rutherford
RUTHERFORD
Niebaum-Coppola
St Supéry
Swanson Vineyards
Opus One
Robert Mondavi
Napa Wine Company
Oakville

ROAD

Chateau
St John

29
128

Robert Sinskey
Stags' Leap
Pine Ridge

Kenwood
Kenwood
Winery

NAPA VALLEY

YOUNTVILLE CROSS

Yountville
Domaine
Chandon

WASHINGTON STREET

SILVERADO TRAIL

12

Glen Ellen

MT VEEDER ROAD

REDWOOD CANYON

DRY CREEK ROAD

SOLANO AVENUE

Benziger
Arrowhead
Winery
Jack London
SHP
BR Cohn
Eldridge

CANEDALE ROAD

Silverado Hill

PUEBLO AVENUE

Copia
Napa
1ST STREET

SONOMA VALLEY

Bartholomew
Park
Ravenswood
Buena Vista
Sonoma SHP
Sebastiani
Sonoma
El Verano

CARNEROS VALLEY

IMOLA AVENUE

Sonoma Mountains

ARNOLD DRIVE

NAPA ROAD

8TH STREET

Artesa
Vineyards
Hess Collection

Schug Carneros
Estate
Gloria Ferrer
Champagne Caves

12
121

Domaine
Carneros
Etude Wines

29

121

Cline Cellars

116

Wine Country

Raise a glass.

It takes only an hour to drive from San Francisco to Napa and Sonoma Counties, but it really is another world out here. Rolling hills planted with lush rows of tangled vines attest to the region's major industry, but it's the nature of the place that really shocks the system after frantic Frisco. This is not high country, but it's certainly *haute* California.

Agoston Haraszthy de Mokcsa was the first to realise Northern California's viticultural promise. The Hungarian farmer recognised that the region's Mediterranean-type climate and soil, deep but not excessively fertile, were perfect for growing the grapes traditionally used in French Bordeaux and Burgundy wines, and champagne: cabernet sauvignon, pinot noir, chardonnay and sauvignon blanc, among others. Haraszthy planted his 500-acre Buena Vista estate in Sonoma County with vines in the middle of the 19th century; others followed suit. However, it wasn't until a century later that the area really took off as a wine-producing region, after wines from these parts beat classic French wines in a 1976 taste test that's gone down in viticultural history (*see p45*).

Since then, Wine Country has changed hugely. From modest beginnings, the wine industry here has become masterful at marketing itself. It's not just wine they sell so successfully; nor it is all the concomitant balloon rides, black-tie tastings, behind the scenes tours and high-end cultural events. What Wine Country does better than any of the state's other wine-producing regions is sell a lifestyle: idyllic, cultured, romantic and deluxe.

It's a lifestyle to which over five million visitors a year aspire; you won't be alone as you pursue that perfect romantic retreat. Trawling the area can be tiring, as can dodging super stretch limos on the rustic roads. So pace yourself, and plan your visit. Summer can be crowded. Spring, when the hills are verdant and the manicured vineyards are carpeted with mustard flowers, and autumn, when the burnished light and auburn vine leaves lend the place a calming ambience, are far better times.

NAPA AND SONOMA

The difference between the verdant Napa and Sonoma Valleys, separated by a low-lying mountain range, was best expressed by a 1980s

The best Wine Country

Things to do
Your choice isn't just between red, white and rosé: it's between the 400-plus wineries that dot the Napa and Sonoma Valleys. **Robert Mondavi** is a good place for beginners; those with more experience in wine tasting should avoid Highway 29 and stick to the back roads.

Places to stay
As with everything else in Wine Country, accommodation is smart, upscale and expensive. A few standouts: in Napa, there's the super-posh **Meadowood Napa Valley** resort (*see p354*) and the similarly splendid **Auberge du Soleil** (*see p353*); in Sonoma, there's the **Kenwood Inn & Spa** (*see p359*) and the **El Dorado Hotel** (*see p358*).

Places to eat
Hard not to pinpoint the place tagged by *Restaurant* magazine as the best restaurant

in the world: the **French Laundry** in Yountville (*see p351*). There are actually many impressive restaurants in this part of California, though you'll pay for the privilege.

Nightlife
Surprisingly little of note, but the brand-new **DG's** jazz club in Napa (*see p350*) might well be worth a look.

Culture
A handful of wineries boast art collections, among them the **Hess Collection** (*see p350*); the **Di Rosa Preserve** (*see p350*) forgoes the wine and concentrates on the art. For performing arts, there's no finer place than the **Napa Valley Opera House** (*see p348*).

Sports & activities
The climate and the shape of the land make biking a good bet here (*see p359*).

Sonoma Wine Auction invitation that showed folks in black-tie attire being dragged out of a barbecue hoedown, a dig at swanky Napa wine sales. While both valleys retain much of their country charm, Napa is larger, posher, more famous for its wines and hence more popular. It no longer lays sole claim to tarted-up cow towns: Sonoma has its share of chic hotels, restaurants and shops. But no town in either valley is more than a stone's throw from countryside dotted with vines and cows.

Many of the higher-priced wineries are in Napa, but alongside the industry behemoths are smaller, many family-owned. Even in Napa you'll find 'crossroads wineries', off the main route, that don't charge for tastings, a practice now standard at the majority of tasting rooms. While many wineries have on-site picnic areas, it is courtesy to buy a bottle to enjoy with your feast at the gratis table. BYOB is accepted policy at nearly all Napa restaurants: check the corkage fee when making your reservation. It's polite, though, to purchase something from the wine list if you plan on consuming more than one bottle during your meal.

The classic Wine Country route winds through both valleys. Drive up Highway 29 to Calistoga, hitting the towns of Napa, Yountville, Oakville, Rutherford and St Helena on the way. From Calistoga, head west for 12 miles to Fulton, taking Petrified Forest Road to Highway 101, and then take Route 12 south through the Sonoma Valley's major towns and wine areas.

Napa Valley

The 30-mile-long Napa Valley, on the east side of the Mayacamas Mountains, was originally settled by the Wappo Indian tribe several centuries ago. The Gold Rush saw the area's population grow in the 1850s, with Europeans as well as Californians; Prussian immigrant Charles Krug introduced grapes here in 1861.

The valley, bisected by the Napa River, runs from the San Pablo Bay's fertile Carneros region north to Calistoga. There are now 250 commercial vineyards here, along with other, smaller 'custom crush' wineries. Many of the most famous operations are situated on often-busy Highway 29 (aka the St Helena Highway), which runs up the centre of the valley; along the way, towns and villages offer fine dining and shopping opportunities. Boutique wineries are found mostly on the Silverado Trail, a more scenic and less cramped artery to the east, or on the lanes that criss-cross the valley or lead up one of the many hillsides.

One sedate way to tour the valley is aboard the **Wine Train** (1-800 427 4124, 1-707 253 2111, www.winetrain.com). A basic ticket costs $40, though there are more expensive brunch, lunch or dinner excursions ($75-$140). Journeys start from and return to Napa Station (1275 McKinstry Street), heading either to St Helena or Rutherford. The train itself consists of lovingly restored pre-1950s Pullman coaches.

Book lodgings well in advance, especially during summer; if you get stuck, try **Napa Valley Reservations Unlimited** (1-800 251 6272, www.napavalleyreservations.com).

Napa

Napa might once have been a blue-collar town, but the last few years have seen the town grow increasingly tourist-oriented. Most of the changes have centred on historic Downtown, where the national attention paid to the opening of **COPIA** (*see p350*) helped stimulate plenty of investment. The Chamber of Commerce has spent heavily on the new Napa, with a **trolley service** that runs through and near downtown; the restoration of the Gold Rush-era **Opera House** (1000 Main Street, 1-707 226 7372) is also indicative of the renewed civic pride.

The wine industry is also present here, of course. In town, **Vintners Collective** (1245 Main Street, 1-707 255 7150, appointments only Tue) has tastes of around 60 wines from over a dozen boutique wineries that don't have tasting rooms. Other Downtown tasting rooms include **Napa Wine Merchants** (1146 1st Street, 1-707 257 6796), **Back Room Wines** (974 Franklin Street, 1-707 226 1378) and **Wineries of Napa Valley** (1285 Napa Town Center, 1-707 253 9450). All four participate in the Chamber's Wine Tasting Card scheme: a $15 discount card gets you tastings for 10¢ (instead of $2-$10) and free entry to COPIA.

A number of notable wineries sit south-west of the town, along or just off the Carneros Highway towards Sonoma. **Etude Winery** (1250 Cuttings Wharf Road, 1-707 257 5300,

Northern California

Napa. *See p348.*

www.etudewines.com, appointments only), off on the west side of Highway 12/121 down a lovely country road, has forged a reputation for premium pinot noir, as well as cabernet sauvignon and pinot gris. Further along Highway 12/121 is **Domaine Carneros** (1240 Duhig Road, 1-707 257 0101, www.domaine. com), where the pinot you'll be sipping is sparkling: the winery is a satellite of Taittinger Champagne. The views here are spectacular, as they are from the terrace at off-the-beaten-track **Artesa Vineyards & Winery** (1345 Henry Road, 1-707 224 1668, www.artesawinery.com). Up on Mount Veeder, the **Hess Collection** (4411 Redwood Road, 1-707 255 1144, www. hesscollection.com) has, in addition to its wines, a fine selection of contemporary art, including sculptures by Frank Stella.

COPIA: The American Center for Wine, Food & the Arts

500 1st Street (1-800 512 6742/1-707 259 1600/ www.copia.org). **Open** 10am-5pm Mon, Wed-Sun. **Admission** $12.50; $7.50-$10 discounts; free under-6s. **Credit** AmEx, DC, Disc, MC, V.

A vast $50m facility, COPIA puts a new spin on the museum concept in its celebrations of eating, drinking and living well. Art and interactive exhibitions line the walls; cooking and gardening demonstrations crop up in the centre's events calendar, as do concerts and other performances in the outdoor amphitheatre. There are also, of course, daily wine tastings, a well-stocked gift shop and a couple of good eating options: **Julia's Kitchen** (1-707 265 5700), serving gourmet Californian food in elegant surroundings, and the **American Market Café**, which offers lighter fare.

Di Rosa Preserve

5200 Carneros Highway (1-707 226 5991/www. dirosapreserve.org). **Tours** *June-Sept* Mon-Thur, Sat. *Oct-May* Tue-Sat. Booking required. **Admission** $12. **Credit** AmEx, MC, V.

Not quite a museum but not quite a tourist attraction either, the Di Rosa Preserve is most usefully described in plain language: this is a collection of over 2,000 works of art from, for the most part, the Bay Area, all of which have been collected over the last four decades by Rene and Veronica di Rosa. Some pieces hang on the walls; others sit in gardens, by doors and even on the 35-acre lake.

Where to eat & drink

As well as a chic hotel (the **Napa River Inn**; *see p351*), a new jazz club (**DG's**, 530 Main Street, 1-707 253 8474), a pastry shop and a day spa, the restored Napa Mill houses several fine eateries. 'Global comfort food' is no oxymoron at **Celadon** (500 Main Street, 1-707 254 9690, $$$$), with the likes of flash-fried calamari and braised Moroccan lamb on the menu, while chef/owner Greg Cole's popular Napa eaterie **Angèle** (540 Main Street, 1-707 252 8115, $$$$) is a favourite spot for terrace drinks and French country cooking when there's a breeze on the river. The river patio of **Napa General Store** (540 Main Street, 1-707 259 0762, $) is a good place at which to enjoy tasty salads, sandwiches and paper-thin brick-oven pizzas.

Charles Weber livens up the tapas concept with creative Californian touches at upbeat and cosily Mediterranean **Zuzu** (829 Main Street, 1-707 224 8555, $$$$), which has upped the ante on trendy dining. A few blocks from Downtown, **Uva Trattoria** (1040 Clinton Street, 1-707 255 6646, $$$) serves up innovative interpretations of traditional and southern Italian cuisine. Reliable Italian food, albeit with a Californian twist, can be found at **Bistro Don Giovanni** (4110 St Helena Highway, 1-707 224 3300, $$$$), which has a fine patio. The irrepressibly kitsch taste of Kelley Novak, part of the Spottswoode winery clan, flavours her collection of salt and pepper shakers and wind-up toys at **Kelley's No Bad Days Café** (976 Pearl Street, 1-707 258 9666, closed Sun-Tue, $$$). However, the casual yet delicious food is no joke.

Where to stay

Lodgings in Napa run from quaint Queen Anne-style B&Bs to full resorts. The sleek, luxurious **Carneros Inn** (4048 Carneros Highway, 1-707

299 4900, www.thecarnerosinn.com, $295-$595), south-west of Napa, fits into the latter category: its 86 cosy cottages have fireplaces, flat-panel TVs and bathrooms that are almost mini-spas.

Downtown, the upscale feel continues at **Churchill Manor** (458 Brown Street, 1-800 799 7733, 1-707 253 7733, www.churchill manor.com, $155-$275), a B&B housed in a spacious historic mansion; other impressive B&Bs include **Hennessey House** (1727 Main Street, 1-707 226 3774, www.hennessey house.com, $129-$299) and **Beazley House** (try the carriage-house rooms; 1910 1st Street, 1-800 559 1649, 1-707 257 1649, www.beazley house.com, $205-$375). Also Downtown, in the historic Napa Mill, you'll find the deluxe, 66-room **Napa River Inn** (500 Main Street, 1-877 251 8500, 1-707 251 8500, www.napa riverinn.com, $180-$500).

On the north side of the city, near Bistro Don Giovanni (*see p350*), is **La Residence** (4066 Howard Lane, 1-800 253 9203, 1-707 253 0337, www.laresidence.com, $225-$350). The antique-filled main mansion dates back to 1870; other buildings are decorated with a French country feel. Nearby **Oak Knoll Inn** (2200 Oak Knoll Avenue, 1-707 255 2200, www.oakknollinn.com, $285-$450) is one of the valley's most luxurious B&Bs, surrounded by 600 acres (243 hectares) of chardonnay vines. If you've had enough of all things quaint, the **John Muir Inn** (1998 Trower Avenue, 1-800 522 8999, 1-707 257 7220, www.johnmuirnapa.com, $105-$225) is an above-par motel.

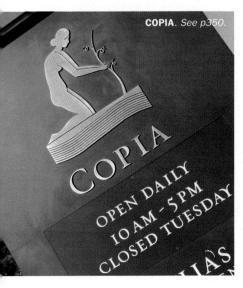

COPIA. See p350.

Yountville

Napa is sometimes categorised, albeit slightly erroneously, as a working man's town. There can be no such illusions held about popular **Yountville**: this is white-collar through and through, as a quick wander along Washington Street will reveal. The road is lined with intimidating shops, upscale restaurants and immaculate lodgings; it's one of those places where if you have to ask how much something costs, you can't afford it. The town is especially delightful in the run-up to Christmas, when it's illuminated in the annual Festival of Lights.

The leading winery within striking distance is **Domaine Chandon** (1 California Drive, 1-707 944 2280, www.chandon.com), which offers an excellent tour ($5) introducing visitors to its stellar Californian interpretation of *méthode champenoise*. The restaurant is a casually elegant setting for lunch. Good local wineries sit on the Silverado Trail: **Pine Ridge** (No.5901, 1-707 575 9777, www.pineridgewinery.com), where you can enjoy (by appointment) barrel to bottle tastings and a cave tour; **Stags' Leap** (No.6150, 1-707 944 1303, www.stagsleap winery.com, appointments only Fri & Sat), still milking the fame bestowed on it by the 1976 Paris tasting (*see p45*); and **Robert Sinskey** (No.6320, 1-707 944 9090, www.robertsinskey. com, appointments only), which produces benchmark pinot noirs and merlots.

Napa Valley Museum

55 Presidents Circle (1-707 944 0500/www.napa valleymuseum.org). **Open** 10am-5pm Mon, Wed-Sun. **Admission** $4.50; $2.50-$3.50 discounts; free under-7s. **Credit** AmEx, MC, V.
Located at the back of Domaine Chandon, the Napa Valley Museum features permanent and changing exhibitions on the art, history and nature of the Napa Valley. Temporary shows have included 'Terra Infirma', responses by 100 local artists to the planet's current condition. California Wine: The Science of Art is a permanent interactive exhibit chronicling the impact of the industry on Northern California.

Where to eat & drink

The **French Laundry** (6640 Washington Street, 1-707 944 2380, $$$$$) was renowned even before Ruth Reichl, then *New York Times* restaurant critic, dubbed it 'the most exciting place to eat in the US' in 1997. But her praise moved the cult of the Laundry into a higher gear. The sublime and often playful food includes such signature items as the 'cornet', a delicate cone of salmon tartare, and a dessert of 'coffee and doughnuts'. Prices are exquisite and you'll have to book two months in advance, but you'll get a world-class meal. Can't afford it?

Northern California

Thomas Keller, lord of the Laundry, also runs urbane **Bouchon** (6534 Washington Street, 1-707 944 8037, $$$$), whose French menu is more moderately priced, and whose adjacent Bouchon Bakery offers beautifully made (and pricey) pastries and breads.

Philippe Jeanty's the other big name here. **Bistro Jeanty** (6510 Washington Street, 1-707 944 0103, $$$$), a casual bistro serving French country dishes such as *daube de boeuf* (beef stew), is his signature restaurant/bar. Newer **Père Jeanty** (6772 Washington Street, 1-707 945 1000, $$$$) has a more Provençal focus, with dishes including the delicious pissaladière, a French-style pizza.

Other restaurants in town include **Piatti** (6480 Washington Street, 1-707 944 2070, $$$), a popular lunch spot serving high-quality Tuscan grilled meats, fish and pastas, and **Hurley's** (6518 Washington Street, 1-707 944 2345, $$$$), an airy Californian restaurant with a wine list to match. **Mustards Grill** (7399 St Helena Highway, 1-707 944 2424, $$$$) lives up to its reputation for deeply flavourful cooking with classics like curry coleslaw with calamari.

Where to stay

Not many budget options here. **Villagio Inn & Spa** (6481 Washington Street, 1-800 351 1133, 1-707 944 8877, www.villagio.com, $310-$575) provides sumptuous, Italianate comfort and style. For nearly three decades, **Napa Valley Lodge** (2230 Madison Street, 1-800 368 2468, 1-707 944 2468, www.napavalleylodge.com, $189-$369) has been offering comfortable hacienda-style accommodation. The five-room **Burgundy House** B&B (6711 Washington Street, 1-707 944 0889, www.burgundyhouse. com, $125-$175) provides congenial European-style lodging at competitive prices; a true push-the-boat-out option, meanwhile, is the thoroughly high-class **Vintage Inn** (6541 Washington Street, 1-800 351 1133, 1-707 944 1112, www.vintageinn.com, $310-$550).

Oakville & Rutherford

The tidy town of **Oakville** is approached by most as the home of the immensely popular **Robert Mondavi Winery** (7801 St Helena Highway, 1-707 226 1335, www.robertmondavi winery.com, reservations recommended), and not without good reason: Mondavi is the man most associated with putting Napa wine on the map. A good bet for first-timers, the winery has tours for every level of expertise and interest.

Other notable wineries include **PlumpJack** (620 Oakville Crossroad, 1-707 945 1220, www. plumpjack.com), which pleases visitors with terrific cabernets and an unstuffy attitude; opulent **Opus One** (7900 St Helena Highway, 1-707 944 9442, www.opusonewinery.com), a joint venture between Mondavi and Baron Philippe de Rothschild; and **Napa Wine Company** (7840 St Helena Highway, 1-707

Up, up and away... Calistoga's **Old Faithful Geyser**. *See p355.*

944 1710), a custom crush facility where boutique vineyard owners make their wines: a dozen labels are available for tasting daily.

Another cluster of wineries draws oenophiles to the nearby town of **Rutherford**, several of them offering attractions for the less bibulously inclined. The lovely setting makes **Mumm** (8445 Silverado Trail, 1-707 967 7700, www.mummcuveenapa.com) a wonderful place to sip sparkling wine, but there are also photos to enjoy, with a permanent collection of work by Ansel Adams and others. At Francis Ford Coppola's **Niebaum-Coppola Winery** (1991 St Helena Way, 1-707 968 1161, www.niebaum-coppola.com), you can see memorabilia from the great man's movies, including an Oscar statuette from one of the *Godfather* films.

The entertaining **St Supéry** (8440 St Helena Highway, 1-707 963 4507, www.stsupery.com) encourages novices, with tastings suitable for first-timers. **Rutherford Hill Winery** (200 Rutherford Hill Road, 1-707 963 1871, www.rutherfordhill.com) has some of the most extensive ageing caves in America. Family-run **Swanson Vineyards** (1271 Manley Lane, 1-707 967 3500, www.swansonvineyards.com, appointments only Wed-Sun) is known for its idiosyncratic 'salon' tastings, meant to recreate the atmosphere of a 19th-century Parisian salon. **Sullivan Vineyards** (1090 Galleron Road, 1-707 963 9646, www.sullivanwine.com, appointments only), known for its terrific cabernets and merlots, is often voted among the best vineyards in the valley for visitors.

Where to eat & drink

Your best eating option in Oakville is the **Oakville Grocery** (7856 St Helena Highway, 1-707 944 8802, $): the original Napa gourmet deli will pack you a hamper with a day's notice. In Rutherford, the **Rutherford Grill** (1180 Rutherford Road, 1-707 963 1792, $$$) wins out with reasonable prices and uncomplicated American fare, such as rotisserie chicken. **La Toque** (1140 Rutherford Road, 1-707 963 9770, $$$$$) is more elegant, Ken Frank preparing innovative food for formal diners. For fiery sauces, fine chorizo and a great deli with super burritos, get to go from **La Luna Market** (1153 Rutherford Road, 1-707 963 3211, $).

Where to stay

The valley's first posh hotel, **Auberge du Soleil** (180 Rutherford Hill Road, 1-800 348 5406, 1-707 963 1211, www.aubergedusoleil.com, $450-$875), has become fancier and fancier over the years. The 'Love Pit' combines rooms in a main building and, dotted over the hills, individual cottages with terraces, as well as a tricked-out spa. The area's other good option is **Rancho Caymus** (1140 Rutherford Road, 1-800 845 1777, 1-707 963 1777, www.ranchocaymus.com, $135-$430), a spiffed-up 26-room hacienda-style inn that boasts La Toque (*see above*) as its on-site restaurant.

St Helena

It's tempting to characterise the upscale restaurants and chic boutiques of **St Helena** as those of just another tarted-up cow town. But the town has real charm and it can be enjoyed in a more modest way than its shiny veneer suggests. Many of the worker bees of the wine industry live here, not just the magnates. It is justly Wine Country's most popular town.

For once, attractions are not solely alcoholic. Those of a cultural bent may enjoy spending part of their day at the **Robert Louis Stevenson Silverado Museum** (*see p354*), before adjourning in the evening to the **White Barn** (2727 Sulphur Springs Avenue, 1-707 963 7002), an authentically low-tech venue (with famously creaky stairs) founded by Nancy Garden 20 years ago and now home to an eclectic selection of performances.

The list of local wineries is led by **Beringer** (2000 Main Street, 1-707 963 7115, www.beringer.com) just north of town. Napa's oldest continuously operating winery, it's still at the top of its class, and offers a range of events from the $5 half-hour tours to the glorious two-hour Saturday picnics ($65). Nearby **Charles Krug Winery** (2800 Main Street, 1-707 967 2200, www.charleskrug.com), founded in 1861, enhances its range of wines with chocolate tastings in summer; next door, **Markham Vineyards** (2812 St Helena Highway North, 1-707 963 5292) exhibits artwork as well as providing good wine in gracious surroundings.

Burgess Cellars (1108 Deer Park Road, 1-707 963 4766, www.burgesscellars.com, appointments only) is a beautiful century-old mountainside winery, with a knock-out view of the valley. The picnic grounds of **V Sattui Winery** (1111 White Lane, 1-707 963 7774, www.vsattui.com) are often overrun, but the gourmet deli makes a visit worthwhile. The **St Helena Wine Center** (1321 Main Street, 1-707 963 1313, www.shwc.com) has a great selection of wines, including cult items. And finally, two relative curios: **Prager** (1281 Lewelling Lane, 1-800 969 7878, 1-707 963 7678, www.pragerport.com), where the speciality is port, and the **Silverado Brewing Company** (3020 Highway 29, 1-707 967 9876, www.silveradobrewingcompany.com), for those more inclined to the grain than the grape.

Greystone Experience

*2555 Main Street (1-707 967 2320/www.greystone-experience.com). **Open** times vary, daily.*
The West Coast branch of the Culinary Institute of America runs numerous courses aimed mainly at professionals, but there are a few week-long 'career changer' wine and food courses. Better, perhaps, to stick with the regular cooking demos (1.30pm and 3.30pm Mon & Fri; 10.30am, 1.30pm and 3.30pm Sat & Sun; $12.50) offered by the pros, or simply to eat in either the Debaun Café, which sells breads and pastries, or the Wine Spectator Greystone Restaurant (1-707 967 1010), which serves excellent Californian cuisine made with local ingredients.

Robert Louis Stevenson Silverado Museum

*1490 Library Lane (1-707 963 3757). **Open** noon-4pm Tue-Sun. **Admission** free. **No credit cards**.*
Robert Louis Stevenson, who honeymooned on Mount St Helena, came over all poetic about Napa's natural splendours – and its wines – in books such as *Silverado Squatters*. The collection here includes a permanent exhibition of artworks with a Napa theme by members of the writer's family, as well as some manuscripts, his wedding ring and marriage licence, and the last words Stevenson ever wrote.

Where to eat & drink

Despite appearances, St Helena has a number of competitively priced eating spots. **Model Bakery** (1357 Main Street, 1-707 963 8192, $) is popular among residents for breakfasts and light lunches; **Ana's Cantina** (1205 Main Street, 1-707 963 4921, $$) is another good lunch spot, morphing into a lively local bar in the evenings. Also on Main is the **Napa Valley Coffee Roasting Company** (No.1400, 1-707 963 4491), smart but kid-friendly **Pizzeria Tra Vigne** (No.1020, 1-707 967 9999, $$) and **Taylor's Refresher** (933 Main Street, 1-707 963 3486, $): a local institution since 1949, its menu offers terrific '50s-style food (hamburgers, thick shakes) next to more contemporary alternatives. There are picnic tables outside.

There are, of course, smarter options. Handsome **Martini House** (1245 Spring Street, 1-707 963 2233, $$$$$) celebrates Napa's bounty with top-quality cooking and, at the downstairs Wine Cellar bar, a huge list of wines. **Terra** (1345 Railroad Avenue, 1-707 963 8931, closed lunch, $$$$$) serves sophisticated European fare with Asian touches in an elegant setting. A few minutes' walk from Downtown, **Tra Vigne** (1050 Charter Oak Avenue, 1-707 963 4444, $$$$$) serves lusty Italian food in a spacious interior or outdoors in the courtyard; there's a shorter, cheaper menu on offer at the adjoining **Cantinetta** (1-707 963 4444, $$). For the **Wine Spectator Greystone Restaurant**, *see above*.

Where to stay

Right in the middle of town, **St Helena Hotel** (1309 Main Street, 1-888 478 4355, 1-707 963 4388, www.hotelsthelena.com, $95-$225) is a renovated, Victorian-era hotel, with a coffee and wine bar. There are a number of other choices along the length of Main Street: the **Vineyard Country Inn** (No.201, 1-707 963 1000, www.vineyardcountryinn.com, $170-$295), whose 21 suites all have wood-burning fireplaces; the luxurious **Inn at Southbridge** (No.1020, 1-800 520 6800, 1-707 967 9400, www.innat southbridge.com, $330-$615); and the delightful **El Bonita Motel** (No.195, 1-800 541 3284, 1-707 963 3216, www.elbonita.com, $89-$289), a mix of art deco and French colonial that's something of a bargain by St Helena standards.

Other, arguably more interesting, options lie further from the town, and none is quite as plush as the **Meadowood Napa Valley** (900 Meadowood Lane, 1-800 458 8080, 1-707 963 3646, www.meadowood.com, $475-$600): made up of 250 acres of sprawling landscaped grounds, it contains a hotel, comfy cottages and lodges, restaurants, and a swanky fitness centre/spa. California's oldest spa (est. 1852), **White Sulphur Springs Inn** (3100 White Sulphur Springs Road, 1-800 593 8873, www. whitesulphursprings.com, $95-$210) provides hotel-style rooms and creekside cottages, as well as a hot tub and sulphur spring and pool.

Calistoga

Calistoga is one of Wine Country's more interesting towns, because it barely relies on the actual wine industry for its tourism. Sure, there are a handful of wineries on the outskirts of Calistoga, the best of them **Clos Pégase** (1060 Dunaweal Lane, 1-707 942 4981, www. clospegase.com) and **Sterling Vineyards** (1111 Dunaweal Lane, 1-707 942 3345, www.sterlingvineyards.com). But Calistoga draws its visitors not with wine but with water.

The geothermal springs of Calistoga have attracted people to the region for the better part of 150 years. Sam Brannan was the first to set up here, opening a spa and resort in 1862 and thereby giving the town its name. Countless others have since followed him here, and the town is now riddled with spas offering a variety of treatments, from dips in mineral pools to baths in volcanic ash thrown up millions of years ago by nearby Mount Konocti. The site of Brannan's original spa is now occupied by the **Indian Springs Resort** (1712 Lincoln Avenue, 1-707 942 4913, www.indiansprings calistoga.com). The charming **Dr Wilkinson's Hot Springs Resort** (1507 Lincoln Avenue,

Testing and tasting at **Clos Pégase** winery. *See p354.*

1-707 942 4102, www.drwilkinson.com) has been open for over 50 years; though 'Doc' himself died in 2004, aged 89, the spa is now run by his two kids. The family-friendly **Calistoga Spa** (1006 Washington Street, 1-707 942 6269, www.calistogaspa.com) and the **Golden Haven Spa** (1713 Lake Street, 1-707 942 6793, www.goldenhaven.com) also offer a variety of treatments; for a list of other spas, check with the Chamber of Commerce (1-707 942 6333/www.calistogafun.com).

Calistoga's other main attraction is also water-related. The **Old Faithful Geyser** on the edge of town (1299 Tubbs Lane, 1-707 942 6463, www.oldfaithfulgeyser.com) is one of only three geysers on earth that blasts out water and steam at regular intervals – every half-hour or thereabouts (times do vary, so call to check) – to heights of anywhere from 60 to 100 feet (18 to 30 metres) in the air. It's an extraordinary sight and certainly worth the detour.

Where to eat & drink

Calistoga's restaurants are concentrated on Lincoln Avenue. **All Seasons Café & Wine Shop** (No.1400, 1-707 942 9111, $$$$) pairs fine wines with pleasant Californian food; sturdier American classics dominate at **Brannan's** (No.1374, 1-707 942 2233, $$$$) and the great **Flatiron Grill** (No.1440, 1-707 942 1220, $$$). Bucking the Lincoln Avenue trend, **Wappo** (1226 Washington Street, 1-707 942 4712, closed

Tue, $$$) dishes up everything from New York steaks to Thai curries in a calming setting. Those in search of a little more action might prefer bar/restaurant **Hydro** (1403 Lincoln Avenue, 1-707 942 9777, $$$), or the friendly, approachable brewpub beneath the **Calistoga Inn** (*see below*); both have live music at various times of the week.

Where to stay

A great many of Calistoga's accommodation options are tied to its spas. All four resorts listed above offer lodgings, as do the **Mount View Hotel** (1457 Lincoln Avenue, 1-800 816 6877, 1-707 942 6877, www.mountviewhotel. com, $150-$325) and many of the town's other spas. Call or check online for details of the spas' various packages of spa treatments and hotel accommodation; you can usually save money. The town also has a number of smart B&Bs, including the **Brannan Cottage Inn** (109 Wappo Avenue, 1-707 942 4200, www.brannan cottageinn.com, $135-$175), the only surviving guesthouse of the 25 built by Sam Brannan in 1862, and the **Cottage Grove Inn** (1711 Lincoln Avenue, 1-800 799 2284, 1-707 942 8400, www.cottagegrove.com, $215-$325), where accommodation is provided in a number of small cottages. However, your money is likely to go a little bit further at the plainer **Calistoga Inn** (1250 Lincoln Avenue, 1-707 942 4101, www.calistogainn.com, $75-$125).

Northern California

Dr Wilkinson's Hot Springs Resort. *See p355.*

Resources

Hospital
Napa *Queen of the Valley Hospital, 1000 Trancas Street (1-707 252 4411/www.thequeen.org).*

Internet
Napa *i-café, 1652 Jefferson Street (1-707 254 3600).* **Open** 8am-8pm Mon-Fri; 9am-5pm Sat, Sun.

Police
Calistoga *1235 Washington Street (1-707 942 2810).*
Napa *1539 1st Street (1-707 257 9223).*
St Helena *1480 Main Street (1-707 967 2850).*

Post office
Calistoga *1013 Washington Street (1-707 942 6661).*
Napa *1625 Trancas Street (1-707 255 0190).*
St Helena *1461 Main Street (1-707 963 2668).*
Yountville *6514 Washington Street (1-707 944 2123).*

Tourist information
Calistoga *Calistoga Chamber of Commerce, Suite 9, 1458 Lincoln Avenue (1-707 942 6333/www. calistogafun.com).* **Open** 10am-5pm Mon-Fri; 10am-4pm Sat; 11am-3pm Sun.
Napa *Napa Valley Conference & Visitor Center, 1310 Napa Town Center (1-707 226 7459/www. napavalley.com).* **Open** 9am-5pm daily.
St Helena *St Helena Chamber of Commerce, 1010 Main Street (1-800 799 6456/www.sthelena.com).* **Open** 10am-5pm Mon-Fri; 11am-3pm Sat.
Yountville *Yountville Chamber of Commerce, 6516 Yount Street (1-707 944 0904/www.yountville.com).* **Open** 10am-3pm daily.

Sonoma Valley

The Sonoma Valley is home to about 200 wineries. However, the main attraction of a Sonoma tour is the valley itself, where working farms and rustic barns dot the countryside. The county's topography is diverse, from beaches to redwood forests and rolling hills. It's also agriculturally rich, and towns such as Glen Ellen and Sebastopol are brimming with farms full of fruits, veg and livestock.

Sonoma County's quaint, family-owned wineries are more secluded than many of their Napa neighbours, giving visitors the sensation of having escaped from the real world. The **Sonoma County Wineries Association** (1-800 939 7666, 1-707 586 3795, www.sonoma wine.com), located near US 101 in Rohnert Park, organises winery tours and daily tastings.

Sonoma

Although its central plaza is now ringed by restaurants, bookshops, a cinema (the delightful 70-year-old **Sebastiani Theatre**, 476 1st Street East, 1-707 996 2020) and food shops, the town of **Sonoma** retains the feel of old California. The town was founded in 1823 as the **Mission San Francisco Solano** (*see p358*), today part of the loose affiliation of historic sites known as **Sonoma State Historic Park** (*see p357* **State perks**). The town hall and Bear Flag Monument, marking the site where the Californian Bear Flag first flew, bear further witness to history: for the 25 days of the riotous Bear Flag Revolt in 1846, this was the capital of the independent Republic of California. It's still rewarding to have a wander Downtown: pick up a leaflet from the visitor centre (*see p362*). Kids, though, may prefer it if you headed a mile outside Downtown to **Sonoma Train Town** (20264 Broadway, 1-707 938 3912, www.traintown.com, closed Mon-Thur Sept-May, $3.75), which keeps young 'uns entertained with a miniature steam train, a petting zoo and even waterfalls.

Sonoma's history is intertwined with that of the Californian wine industry, which began here (*see p347*) at what is now the **Historic Buena Vista Winery** (18000 Old Winery Road, 1-800 926 1266, www.buenavistawinery.com). Of the nearly 40 wineries in the valley, several are near the main plaza. **Bartholomew Park Winery** (1000 Vineyard Lane, 1-707 935 9511, www.bartholomewparkwinery.com) is great for picnics, with grounds that nestle beautifully atop a small overlook; it also holds a museum of photos, soil samples and other viticulturabilia.

State perks

Wine Country boasts a number of beautiful and intriguing places to get out in the open air that will redden the nose only by excess sun or the coldness of the wind. Some have attractions historical, but all of them offer beauties natural.

NAPA VALLEY

Three miles north of St Helena on Highway 29, **Bale Grist Mill State Historic Park** (1-707 942 4575, www.parks.ca.gov, closed Mon-Fri) is the site of a water-powered mill that dates back to 1846. Once the centre of Napa Valley's social activity, it was here that settlers gathered to gossip and exchange news while their corn and wheat were ground into meal or flour. The mill was in use as late as the early 1900s.

Bothe-Napa State Park (1-707 942 4575, www.parks.ca.gov) is located between St Helena and Calistoga west of Highway 29, and offers camping, picnicking and swimming, plus hiking among redwood, tanoak, huge firs and madrone. Many species of animal have been seen here, among them bobcats, deer, raccoons and coyotes. There's also a Native American Garden and the 19th-century Pioneer Cemetery.

The **Land Trust of Napa County** (1-707 252 3270, www.napalandtrust.org) organises naturalist walks all over the area. Some are open to the public, but others are for members only; check before you make plans.

In 1880 the famous author honeymooned in what is now **Robert Louis Stevenson State Park** (1-707 942 4575, www.parks.ca.gov). Located on Highway 20 north of Calistoga, the park now offers plenty of good hiking through canyons by turns forested or covered in chaparral. If a slope faces north, you'll mainly find evergreens; if it faces south, thorn bushes and shrubs. Mount St Helena offers

expansive views of the countryside; the site where Stevenson's cabin once stood has been clearly marked.

SONOMA VALLEY

Among the historic buildings in **Sonoma State Historic Park** (363 3rd Street West, 1-707 938 9559) are the most northerly mission in California (*see p358*), the town hall and General Mariano Guadalupe Vallejo's ornate Victorian home, Lachryma Montis (1-707 938 9559, $2). Vallejo was in charge of the colonisation of what was at that time Mexico's northern border, and spent a few weeks imprisoned by the Bear Flag revolutionaries as a result.

Best known for the remains of the eponymous writer's Wolf House, a 1911 Spanish-style structure that burned down weeks before its owner was due to move in, **Jack London State Historic Park** (2400 London Ranch Road, Glen Ellen, 1-707 938 5216) commands acres of beautiful flora, with a mixed forest where oaks, madrones, California buckeye, Douglas fir and coastal redwoods perfectly complement ferns and manzanita. London's ashes are, by his request, under a boulder that was left over from the building of the house; more prosaic Londonabilia (sunhat, typewriter) is now displayed in the House of Happy Walls.

The adobe buildings that give **Petaluma Adobe State Historic Park** (3325 Adobe Road, 1-707 762 4871, www.parks.ca.gov, $2) its name are the remains of General Vallejo's huge ranch. Within there are period furniture and other artefacts, and the site has good picnicking spots.

For details on other parks in the region, contact **Sonoma County Regional Parks** (2300 County Center Drive, Suite 120A, 1-707 565 2041, www.sonoma-county.org).

Northern California

Sebastiani Vineyards (389 4th Street East, 1-707 938 5532, www.sebastiani.com) may not be the most charming of wineries, but it does give another perspective on the ubiquitous family. Less than a mile from the plaza, **Ravenswood Winery** (18701 Gehricke Road, 1-707 933 2332, www.ravenswood-wine.com) is known for its zinfandels, its friendly tasting room and its weekend barbecues. **Cline Cellars** (24737 Highway 121, 1-707 940 4000, www.clinecellars.com) makes Rhône-style wines and zinfandel, all poured in a 19th-century farmhouse.

The Carneros area includes southern Sonoma as well as Napa; wineries take advantage of the cooler climate to produce excellent pinot noir grapes and sparkling wines. The **Gloria Ferrer Champagne Caves** (23555 Highway 121, 1-707 996 7256, www.gloriaferrer.com) is worth a visit to witness the intricacies of the centuries-old process of making sparkling wine. The **Viansa Winery** (25200 Arnold Road, 1-707 935 4700, www.viansa.com), a Tuscan-style winery on a knoll run by Sam and Vicki Sebastiani, also sells Italian food and has a two-bedroom cottage available to rent. The **Schug Carneros Estate Winery** (602 Bonneau Road, 1-707 939 9363, www.schugwinery.com) specialises in Burgundy-style pinot noir and chardonnay; it also runs, by appointment, tours of the underground cave.

Mission San Francisco Solano

363 3rd Street West (1-707 938 9560). **Open** 10am-5pm daily. **Admission** $2; free under-17s. **No credit cards.**
Founded in 1823 as the last and northernmost of the Franciscan missions, Sonoma's whitewashed adobe mission served as a Mexican outpost in the 17th century, but is now on the edge of the city's plaza. Missionaries planted the region's first vines here (to make wine for Mass). Now restored, the humbly atmospheric mission houses a museum of 19th-century watercolours by Chris Jorgenson. There's a farmers' market here in summer.

Sonoma Valley Museum of Art

551 Broadway (1-707-939 7862/www.svma.org). Open 11am-5pm Wed-Sun. **Admission** $5; free under-17s.
Newly renovated, the Museum of Art features a variety of rotating exhibitions, both international and local. It also shows collectors' hoards and presents exhibits on aspects of cultural history, such as Dia de los Muertos (the Mexican Day of the Dead).

Where to eat & drink

Carlo Cavallo does a bang-on job at **Sonoma-Meritâge** (165 W Napa Street, 1-707 938 9430, closed Tue, $$$$), his diverse menu focusing on southern French and northern Italian cuisine but using fresh, seasonal Californian ingredients,

usually featuring a variation on Dungeness crab. The five-course tasting menus are great value. **Café la Haye** (140 E Napa Street, 1-707 935 5994, $$$$) serves straightforward food, focusing on local organic produce; it's a favourite with more sophisticated Sonoma diners. For a spicy change of pace, try **Maya** (110 E Napa Street, 1-707 935 3500, $$$), a casual spot serving great Mexican fare and, at the lively bar, endless types of tequila.

For food that tastes authentically French (even if the spelling goes astray), drop in to postage stamp-sized **La Poste** (599 Broadway, 1-707 939 3663, closed Mon & Tue, $$$$). Right off the square, it turns out excellent bistro fare, including 'steak frittes' (*sic*) and cassoulet. Another French-themed bistro, where foie gras is a speciality, is the nearby **Sonoma Saveurs** (487 1st Street West, 1-707 996 7007, closed Mon, $$$$), housed in a historic adobe building that was completed in 1845 by General Vallejo's son-in-law. On the square is **Cucina Viansa** (400 1st Street East, 1-707 935 5656, $$$), where you'll find all things Italian (wine bar, gelato counter, espresso bar, deli, restaurant). Picnickers should get supplies from **Artisan Bakers** (750 W Napa Street, 1-707 939 1765) and **Vella Cheese Company** (315 2nd Street East, 1-707 938 3232, closed Sun).

Where to stay

Two good options on Sonoma Plaza are the **Sonoma Hotel** (1-800 468 6016, 1-707 996 2996, www.sonomahotel.com, $110-$245) and the comfy **El Dorado Inn** (1-707 996 3030, www.hoteleldorado.com, $135-$190), above Piatti's restaurant. To spoil yourself, the **Ledson Hotel** (480 1st Street East, 1-707 996 9779, www.ledsonhotel.com, $350-$395) has six ultra-deluxe rooms at prices to match. Also near the plaza are the **Victorian Garden Inn** (316 E Napa Street, 1-800 543 5339, 1-707 996 5339, www.victoriangardeninn.com, $139-$259), a lovely B&B with nicely appointed rooms and gardens. The **Fairmont Sonoma Mission Inn & Spa** (18140 Highway 12, 1-866 540 4499, 1-707 938 9000, www.fairmont.com/sonoma, $239-$749) is on a very different scale: roughly 40,000 square feet (3,720 square metres), to put a figure on it. Built in 1927, Wine Country's original resort is ensconced within distinctive pink walls and features its own source of healing thermal mineral water and an 18-hole golf course.

Glen Ellen & Kenwood

The small town of **Glen Ellen** was once the home of Jack London, adventurer, farmer, autodidact and one of the most prolific authors of his day. London's book *The Valley of the Moon* was set partly in the Sonoma Valley (the Native American word *sonoma* means 'many moons'); in **Jack London Historic State Park** (*see p357* State perks) are the charred remains of Wolf House, the author's huge home.

The pick of the area's viticulture can be found at the **Arrowood Vineyards & Winery** (14347 Sonoma Highway, 1-707 935 2600, www.arrowoodvineyards.com), nearby **BR Cohn Winery** (15000 Sonoma Highway, 1-707 938 4064, www.brcohn.com) and the **Benziger Family Winery** (1883 London Ranch Road, 1-707 935 4046, www.benziger. com). The latter makes its wines using biodynamic farming methods, a holistic form of organic agriculture devised in the 1920s by Rudolf Steiner, and also runs daily tram tours of the estate. Fans of the olive will want to check out the **Olive Press** (Suite 15, 14301 Arnold Drive, 1-707 939 8900, www.theolive press.com), a state-of-the-art organic olive-processing mill with a tasting centre.

To many, nearby **Kenwood** is synonymous simply with the **Kenwood Winery** (9592 Sonoma Highway, 1-707 833 5891, www. kenwoodvineyards.com), a friendly Sonoma winery known for wine made from grapes grown on Jack London's former ranch (novelist Haruki Murakami drinks a bottle from here on his birthday each year). The original barn, now the tasting room and shop, dates from before Prohibition. Also renowned is **Chateau St Jean** (8555 Sonoma Highway, 1-707 833 4134, www.chateaustjean.com), beautifully situated at the base of Sugarloaf State Park.

Where to eat

The theme is obvious at the **Fig Café** (13690 Arnold Drive, Glen Ellen, 1-707 938 2130, closed lunch, $$$); among the delights are fig, goat's cheese and pecan salad. In Kenwood, the 17-year-old **Kenwood Restaurant & Bar** (9900 Sonoma Highway/Highway 12, 1-707 833 6326, $$$$) turns out commendable California fare; casual, affordable **Café Citti** (9049 Sonoma Highway, 1-707 833 2690, $$) produces pastas and other Italian dishes.

Where to stay

Consistently rated the top Wine Country resort, the historic **Kenwood Inn & Spa** (10400 Sonoma Highway, 1-800 353 6966, 1-707 833 1293, www.kenwoodinn.com, $375-$700) has

Beating the bottle

When one winery starts to blend into the next and you realise that every bottling line looks the same, it's time to get off the spittoon circuit and remember that Wine Country was, and is, a natural paradise. Indeed, the landscape can often be enjoyed without even getting out of your car, but more active sorts will not be satisfied with that brand of leisurely sightseeing. For them, a plenitude of biking, hiking, fishing, golfing and water sports options await.

If you're bored of the car, but still fancy some open country, you can even treat yourself to a **hot air balloon ride**, which has become strangely popular here. They're not cheap (expect to pay $200 upwards), but then few things in Wine Country are. And anyway, you do at least get a good service: many companies will pick you up from your hotel, and some will even give you a champagne brunch afterwards. Be sure to book in advance; details of tours offered by Above the West Ballooning (1-800 627 2759), Adventures Aloft (1-800 944 4408) and Balloon Aviation (1-800 367 6272) can be found at www.napavalleyaloft.com.

There's plenty of terrific **biking** in Wine Country, with long flat stretches, gentle hills and steady inclines ensuring you don't have to be an off-road champ to explore the many country roads. Parks with extensive bike trails include Napa's **John F Kennedy Park** (Napa, 1-707 257 9529) and in Sonoma, **Eagle Regional Park** (Sebastopol, 1-707 527 2041) and **Spring Lake County Park** (Santa Rosa, 1-707 539 8092). If you've not brought your own bike, rent a machine from St Helena Cyclery (1153 Main Street, St Helena, 1-707 963 7736), Getaway Bikes (1117 Lincoln Avenue, Calistoga, 1-707 942 0332) or Bicycle Trax (796 Soscol Avenue, Napa, 1-707 258 8729). Expect to pay around $7-$8 per hour or $25-$30 a day.

The Napa River feeds into the San Pablo Bay and thence the ocean, which means you can sail to China from here. But if you're taking things one adventure at a time, **kayaking** rentals are available. Mako Marine (1-707 251 5600) and Napa River Adventures (1-707 224 9080) both rent kayaks for around $50 a day; the latter also runs riverboat cruises.

just enjoyed a major renovation; the reopened property has Italianate courtyards, a French-style spa and a guests-only bistro on the premises. In Glen Ellen, the **Gaige House Inn** (13540 Arnold Drive, 1-800 935 0237, 1-707 935 0237, www.gaige.com, $150-$375) is just about serene enough to justify the high prices. Sit by the pool, where a creek gurgles in the sunshine and time simply stops. **Jack London Lodge** (13740 Arnold Drive, 1-707 938 8510, www.jack londonlodge.com, $70-$160) is a straightahead motel that offers easy access to the Jack London State Park (*see p357* **State perks**).

Santa Rosa

Its population is twice that of the city of Napa, but Santa Rosa still manages to retain the same kind of low-key appeal as its southerly neighbour. Historic Railroad Square is the city's busy downtown area, with the usual array of shops and restaurants, but the real visitor attraction is the park on the corner of Santa Rosa and Sonoma Avenues: **Luther Burbank Home & Gardens** (*see below*). The North Bay's premier arts centre, the **Luther Burbank Center for the Arts** (50 Mark West Springs Road, 1-707 546 3600, www.lbc.net, closed Mon & Tue, $2), is also here and houses the region's only museum dedicated solely to modern art. More off-beat attractions include **Safari West** (*see p361*) and the **Charles M Schulz Museum** (*see below*).

The area around Santa Rosa boasts several fine vineyards. **Kendall-Jackson Wine Center & Garden** (5007 Fulton Road, 1-707 571 7500, www.kj.com) is just outside the city in Fulton and has a state-of-the-art tasting room and education centre. **Hanna Winery & Vineyards** (5345 Occidental Road, 1-707 575 3371, www.hannawinery.com) makes quality Alexander Valley and Russian River Valley zinfandel, cabernet and merlot, as well as a variety of whites, while **Matanzas Creek Winery** (6097 Bennett Valley Road, 1-800 590 6464, www.matanzascreek.com) has stunning fields of lavender as well as vineyards.

Charles M Schulz Museum

2301 Hardies Lane (1-707 579 4452/www.schulz museum.org). **Open** noon-5pm Mon, Wed-Fri; 10am-5pm Sat, Sun. **Admission** $8; $5 discounts; free under-3s. **Credit** AmEx, MC, V.
This museum commemorates the life and work of the cartoonist who created Snoopy, Charlie Brown and the whole *Peanuts* gang, bringing his creations to life with fun, interactive exhibits. Displays include a rotating exhibit of more than 100 original *Peanuts* strips and a stunning 17ft by 22ft (5.2m by 6.7m) tiled wall depicting Charlie Brown attempting to kick a football held by Lucy.

Luther Burbank Home & Gardens

Santa Rosa Avenue, at Sonoma Avenue (1-707 524 5445/www.lutherburbank.org). **Open** *Apr-Oct* 10am-4pm Tue-Sun. **Admission** $4; $3 discounts; free under-12s. **No credit cards**.

Life is vine and dandy in **Sonoma**. *See p356.*

America's most renowned horticulturist, Burbank developed more than 800 new varieties of plants during his life; his former house and grounds are now a national historical landmark. Docent tours (booking not necessary) and themed gardens explain and demonstrate this botanical pioneer's work.

Safari West

3115 Porter Creek Road (1-707 579 2551/www. safariwest.com). **Tours** *Spring-autumn* 9am, 1pm, 4pm daily. *Winter* 10am, 2pm daily. **Admission** $59; $28 discounts. **Credit** AmEx, MC, V.
Safari West is a different way to slice Sonoma: African-style. Guides lead you on safaris, lasting up to three hours, among such exotic creatures as giraffes, zebras, wildebeest, impalas and lemurs on the 450-acre ranch. It also has wonderfully idiosyncratic lodgings (*see below*).

Sonoma County Museum

425 7th Street (1-707 579 1500/www.sonoma countymuseum.com). **Open** 11am-4pm Wed-Sun. **Admission** $5; $2 discounts; free under-12s. **Credit** AmEx, MC, V.
Housed in a restored 1910 post office, this museum explores the history of Sonoma County with changing exhibitions of art and historical artefacts. You'll also find a fine collection of works by Christo and Jeanne-Claude, including original drawings alongside collages, photographs and small sculptures.

Where to eat & drink

Willie's Wine Bar (404 Old Redwood Highway, 1-707 526 3096, closed Tue, $$) does great small plates and serves good wine by the glass, while hip and inexpensive **Tex Wasabi's** (515 4th Street, 1-707 544 8399, $$$) is a popular combination of barbecue style and Japanese sushi. Tuscan-influenced **Caffè Portofino** (535 4th Street, 1-707 523 1171, closed Sun, $$$) has an extensive list of Sonoma wines by the glass, and late dinner hours.

Where to stay

Vintners Inn (4350 Barnes Road, 1-707 575 7350, www.vintnersinn.com, $210-$395) is a 44-room boutique hotel, a prime place to stay for some proper Wine Country relaxation. Chef/author **John Ash**, one of the pioneers of fresh California cuisine, has his eponymous eaterie on the premises (1-707 527 7687, $$$$$).
Taking pride of place on Railroad Square for nearly a century, **Hotel La Rose** (308 Wilson Street, 1-800 527 6738, 1-707 579 3200, www. hotellarose.com, $109-$264) is a hospitable B&B. The **Gables** (4257 Petaluma Hill Road, 1-800 422 5376, 1-707 585 7777, www.thegables inn.com, $105-$195) is a lovely old Victorian Gothic inn, on several secluded acres. If you fancy a resort hotel, try the large, affordable

FountainGrove Inn (101 FountainGrove Parkway, 1-800 222 6101, 1-707 578 6101, www. fountaingroveinn.com, $109-$249). Meanwhile, the lodgings at **Safari West** (*see above*; $225-$300) are in unique safari tents. There's also a cottage available, but the tent option is hardly slumming it, with proper beds plus verandas that provide commanding views.

Healdsburg

It's hard to believe **Healdsburg** used to be a bohemian enclave for Left Coast Californian artists like Richard Diebenkorn. Today it's a high-priced, highfalutin boutique town where Bay Area boomers come to drop some serious cash. Find a spot around the fountain in the main plaza and you can watch the opposite ends of the spectrum in motion: middle-aged white guys in luxury SUVs rubbing up against Mexican day labourers waiting for their next job. While most of Sonoma County's farm towns have eschewed makeover into luxury spa destinations, Healdsburg wears its affluence with confidence. Only here can you take a vineyard tour on a horse-drawn carriage; **Flying Horse Carriage Company** (1-707 849 8989) can provide the ponies, albeit at a hefty price. Gourmet food stores, artisan bakeries and sleek restaurants bring in consumers in herds, but the **Healdsburg Museum** (221 Matheson Street, 1-707 431 3325), with Pomo Indian baskets and other cultural artefacts, is pretty good.
The Villa Fiore hospitality centre at the **Ferrari-Carano Winery** (8761 Dry Creek Road, 1-707 433 6700, www.ferraricarano.com) sits like royalty on a throne, offering one of the valley's most spectacular vistas. **Seghesio Family Vineyards** (14730 Grove Street, 1-707 433 3579, www.seghesio.com) is known for its Italian-varietal reds: Venom, from a vineyard on Rattlesnake Hill, packs a wallop of bright cherry fruit. Visit on a Friday afternoon and patriarch Ed Seghesio will regale you with tales of his 77 years as a winemaker. Famous for their sauvignon blanc (marked 'Fumé Blanc' and easily recognised by the sailboat label), **Dry Creek Vineyard** (3777 Lambert Bridge Road, 1-707 433 1000, www.drycreekvineyard. com) is the other notable winery in the area.
Just north of Healdsburg, in the Alexander Valley area up towards Geyserville, are several other good wineries: **Murphy-Goode Estate** (4001 Highway 128, 1-707 431 7644, www. murphygoodewinery.com), **Geyser Peak** (22281 Chianti Road, 1-707 857 9400, www. geyserpeakwinery.com) and **Chateau Souverain** (400 Souverain Road, 1-888 809 4637, www.chateausouverain.com).

Northern California

Where to eat & drink

There are two steadfastly popular options on Center Street in Healdsburg, **Ravenous** (No.420, 1-707 431 1302, closed Mon & lunch Tue-Sun, $$$$) and **Zin** (No.344, 1-707 473 0946, $$$$), with the latter's applewood-smoked pork chop with andouille sausage and corn bread stuffing a real favourite. Healdsburg Avenue is home to the excellent **Manzanita** (No.336, 1-707 433 8111, closed Mon & lunch Tue-Sun, $$$$) and **Willi's Seafood & Raw Bar** (No.402, 1-707 433 9191, $$$). The fabulous Hotel Healdsburg (*see below*) is home to award-winning chef Charlie Palmer's **Dry Creek Kitchen** (No.317, 1-707 431 0330, $$$$$), whose changing menus are based on fresh seasonal ingredients. **Felix & Louie's** (106 Matheson Street, 1-707 433 6966, $$$) is a lively and cavernous hipster hangout serving quality pastas at reasonable prices. There're Thai and Chinese joints near the plaza, which provide a welcome respite from the Cal-cuisine spotlight. The town is also well appointed with places to find quality picnic fodder: try the gourmet **Oakville Grocery** (124 Matheson Street, 1-707 433 3200) and **Bruno's Marketplace** (102 Healdsburg Avenue, 1-707 431 1781), which combines an Italian deli with a great range of organic produce and other speciality foods that should satisfy the needs of even the pickiest picnicker.

Out of town, the sandwiches at **Dry Creek General Store** (3495 Dry Creek Road, 1-707 433 4171, $) are basic, but there's atmosphere at the wine-tasting bar in the back. The **Jimtown Store** (6706 Highway 128, 1-707 433 1212, $$) in Alexander Valley is a Sonoma fixture. Try one of its innovative salads or spreads (the fig and olive combination is particularly delicious) and you'll know why.

Where to stay

A number of decent motels off the freeway will serve as a good base if you don't want to blow your entire wad on accommodation, but for high-flyers, the **Hotel Healdsburg** (25 Matheson Street, 1-800 889 7188, 1-707 431 2800, www.hotelhealdsburg.com, $245-$795) is pure luxury. Can't afford a room? Book a treatment at the hotel's day spa and lounge by the pool in VIP-training. Gimmicky **Duchamp Hotel** (421 Foss Street, 1-800 431 9341, 1-707 431 1300, www.duchamphotel.com, $295-$375), named after conceptual artist Marcel Duchamp, has artist-themed cottages (Man Ray, Miró, etc) set in what feels like an unfinished industrial park. Light on hospitality for the money, it does at least serve a smashing breakfast.

Hospital

Sonoma Valley *Sonoma Valley Hospital, 347 Andrieux Street (1-707 935 5000).*

Internet

Santa Rosa *Starry Net Café, 630B 3rd Street (1-707 568 5035).* **Open** 8.30am-10pm Mon-Thur; 8.30am-11pm Fri; 10am-11pm Sat; 2-9pm Sun.
Sonoma *Adobe Net Café, Suite 100, 135 W Napa Street (1-707 935 0390).* **Open** 7am-7.30pm Mon-Thur; 7am-8.20pm Fri, Sat; 1-5pm Sun.

Police

Sonoma *175 1st Street West (1-707 996 3602).*
Healdsburg *238 Center Street (1-707 431 3377).*
Santa Rosa *2796 Ventura Avenue (1-707 543 3600).*

Post office

Glen Ellen *13720 Arnold Drive (1-707 996 9233).*
Healdsburg *404 Center Street (1-707 433 2267).*
Santa Rosa *730 2nd Street (1-707 528 8783).*
Sonoma *617 Broadway (1-707 996 9311).*

Tourist information

Sonoma *Sonoma Valley Visitors Bureau, 453 1st Street East (1-707 996 1090/www.sonomavalley. com).* **Open** 9am-5pm daily.
Healdsburg *Healdsburg Chamber of Commerce & Visitors Bureau, 217 Healdsburg Avenue (1-707 433 6935/www.healdsburg.org).* **Open** 9am-5pm Mon-Fri; 9am-3pm Sat; 10am-4pm Sun.
Santa Rosa *Santa Rosa CVB/California Welcome Center, 9 4th Street (1-707 577 8674/www.visitsanta rosa.com).* **Open** 9am-5pm Mon-Thur; 9am-6pm Fri; 9am-5pm Sat; 10am-5pm Sun.

Getting there

By boat

You can get a ferry from San Francisco to Vallejo, with **Blue & Gold Fleet** ($9.50 one way, $15 day pass, 1-415 773 1188, www.blueandgoldfleet.com), from where hourly buses run to Napa (Napa Valley Transit, 1-800 696 6443, $1.50) each weekday; weeekend service is sparser.

By bus

Although the distances between attractions make a car the easiest way to do Wine Country, there are buses from San Francisco. **Golden Gate Transit** (1-707 541 2000, $7.25) operates commuter routes to Santa Rosa and Sonoma; **Greyhound** (1-800 231 2222, www.greyhound.com, $14-$15) runs mid-afternoon services to Sonoma and Napa.

By car

Wine Country is an hour by car from San Francisco over the Golden Gate along US 101. Turn east at Ignacio to Highway 37 and take Highway 121 north. From here, Highway 12 takes you along the Sonoma Valley and Highway 29 heads through Napa Valley.

The North Coast

Lumbering train towns and limber country villages.

Back in the 1500s, Spanish conquistadors dropped anchor along much of the North Coast, claiming vast chunks of land. Open season was declared, despite the fact that Native Americans had lived peacefully in the region for centuries. Still, it was the discovery of gold at the end of the 1840s that jump-started the whole region. When boomtown San Francisco became the Paris of the Wild West, it was the North Coast that happily supplied her lumber and food. After the Gold Rush, the region's rowdy lumber towns practically melted away, but the 1960s saw a steady trickle of artists, back-to-landers and dropouts moving in. Where the bohos go, tourists eventually follow.

Northern California wears its Wild West counterculture roots like a badge of honour, yet the reality is that the area has been picked over and gentrified. Escalating real-estate prices and the arrival of sophisticated bon viveurs turned the region's rugged quality into ultra-expensive, primped-up inns and spas that survive on the patronage of well-heeled baby boomers, the only group who can afford to regularly eat and dine here. Between **Bodega Bay** and **Fort Bragg** you're as likely to spot Big Foot as score a bed for under $100 a night.

Despite skyrocketing prices, the natural beauty of coastal **Sonoma** and **Mendocino Counties** is still accessible and, of course, as exhilarating as ever it was. Forget about the warm sun and silky sands of Southern California: here it's all about rough and inhospitable sea, walks along driftwood beaches, fog shrouding the rocky coastline and hundreds of miles of isolated hiking. There's also fantastic seafood to catch and eat, migrating grey whales in season, and paddling and sunbathing along the many river estuaries.

Further inland, there are the relaxed and unspoilt resort villages of the **Russian River**. Bohemians, bikers and, more recently, burned-out city workers have kept the 16,000-strong population diverse. Book a few days in the friendly, laid-back resorts of **Guerneville** and **Monte Rio**, along the banks of the river, or simply wander between the small offbeat towns – **Freestone**, say, or **Graton** – along some of the best scenic backroads in California. Should the 100 or so wineries become a bore, there are also breweries and distilleries, apple orchards and world-class organic horticulture of all varieties, as well as little pockets of railway history in Victorian towns like **Occidental** and **Duncans Mills**.

Even visitors looking for that California of toothsome communes and bohemian retreats will find what they're after on the North Coast. They'll just have to stay on the highway as far as the **Lost Coast** and **Humboldt County** to find the authentic experience and genuine value for money they were looking for.

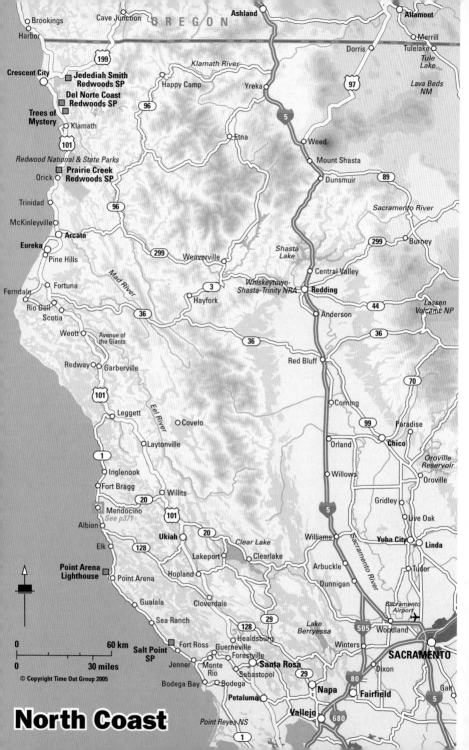

North Coast

The Sonoma Coast

Bodega Bay & Jenner

A blanket of cool, shifting fog will most likely greet your arrival in **Bodega Bay**. It's the only commercial port between San Francisco and Fort Bragg (see *p372*) and, though tourists come in steady numbers, the place remains a no-frills, blue-collar fishing town. Most of the action is by the harbour, where a number of wharf restaurants and delis serve whatever was freshly caught ('fresh' meaning flash-frozen at sea: fleets venture 30 or 40 miles out for days at a time). If you have the stomach, deep-sea fishing excursions are available: **Wil's Fishing Adventures** (1580 East Shore Road, 1-707 875 2323, $15) offer bay and harbour tours. Bodega and its southerly neighbour Tomales Bay (see *p264*) are famous for their oyster beds, and as a breeding ground for Great Whites.

Just north of town, left on Westshore Road, is a fine spot for whale-watching and coastline views. You can also visit the 15-storey hole dug decades earlier to house a nuclear reactor. The plan was scuppered when alarmed locals pointed out to the electricity company that they were building on top of the San Andreas Fault. Today it's a pleasant spot for local wildlife.

You can hire surf gear, bikes and kayaks at the **Bodega Bay Surf Shack** (1400 Highway 1, 1-707 875 3944); it offers surf lessons too. **Sonoma Coast Visitor Center** (see *p367*) can indicate the best places for tide pooling, surfing and nature trails, as well as locations immortalised in Hitchcock's The Birds, shot here in the early 1960s.

A brief excursion inland brings you into the town of **Bodega**, another draw for Hitchcock fans. Most mooch around taking photos or take a tour of the **Potter Schoolhouse** (1-707 876 3257), now a private residence. Visits are by reservation only and contingent on the current owner's inclination to open her gates; there are tours at 2pm from Thursday to Sunday. Worth a browse on Bodega's main street is **Seagull Antiques Gifts & Collectibles** (17191 Bodega Highway, 1-707 876 3229, closed Mon-Fri). Among old copper pans, ageing furs and the plaintive gaze of elkhead trophies, you may still find a well-preserved 1979 copy of *Playboy*. Next door is the psychedelic **Northern Lights** surf shop (1-707 876 3032).

Heading out of Bodega Bay on Highway 1 takes you through 17 miles of state parks and beaches. Pick up a free *Sonoma Coast Guide* at the Sonoma Coast Visitor Center (see *p367*) for maps and beach reviews. **Salmon Creek**

Beach is always popular with hikers and surfers; otherwise, turn off at **Shell Beach** to watch crabs, starfish and other critters in the tide pools, or to start a hike on the **Kortum Trail**. During summer, roadside stands selling smoked salmon snacks sit along the highway.

The first town north of Bodega Bay is **Jenner**. Most people stop here to watch the comical slumber of 300-plus harbour seals. Outstripping Jenner's population by two to one, the seals noisily mate and raise their pups on the rocky outcrops at the mouth of the Russian River. Pull off the road at Goat Rock for a good vantage point. If you want to head inland to the little towns and resorts of the Russian River (see *p367*), take Highway 116 east before Jenner.

Further north on Highway 1 is **Fort Ross**. Finished by the Russians in 1812, the fort once marked the furthest extent of the Russian empire. Alaskan fur-trappers settled here to hunt sea otter, but by 1841 the otters were gone and the Russians sold up to famed gold

The best North Coast

Things to do
For the most part, you make your own entertainment (see below **Sports & activities**), but there are three travel-related doozies: cruise the **Avenue of the Giants** (see *p375*), ride the **Skunk Train** (see *p372*), and **drive through a tree** (see *p380* **Tree-ring circus**).

Places to stay
Camp in **Redwood National & State Parks** (see *p379*), or hole up at one of the many cute spots in **Mendocino** (see *p372*).

Places to eat
There's great organic food at **Pangaea** in Gualala (see *p370*), and fabulous seafood at Trindad's **Seascape** (see *p376*).

Nightlife
The best brewpub is in **Fort Bragg** (see *p373*), and **Arcata** (see *p376*) has some lively bars. There's also a gay scene in **Guerneville** (see *p368*).

Culture
Nothing worth a special detour.

Sports & activities
Plenty to do here: fishing in **Bodega Bay** (see *p364*), boating on the **Russian River** (see *p366*) and hiking in **Redwood National & State Parks** (see *p378*).

Northern California

Disc drive

CDs to soundtrack your journey around the North Coast.

Disintegration The Cure
As epic and widescreen as Robert Smith and pals ever got.

Rabbit Songs Hem
Immaculate pastoral Americana: piano, mandolin and pedal steel; Sally Ellyson's crystalline voice and Dan Messé's rich, heartbreaking songs.

Lost in the Lonesome Pines Jim Lauderdale with Ralph Stanley and the Clinch Mountain Boys
Old school bluegrass at its best.

Wonderful Rainbow Lightning Bolt
Amps to 11! A terrifying piledriver of an album, all the more surprising for it having been made by two men called Brian.

Saint Mary of the Woods James McMurtry
His dad's Larry, author of *Lonesome Dove*, but McMurtry's a fine storyteller in his own right. The Americana of *Saint Mary* is dark and rousing, and occasionally, as on 'Chocktaw Bingo', both at once.

Live in Tokyo Brad Mehldau
Thoughtful, touching solo piano work from the New Yorker. Includes 19-minute version of Radiohead's 'Paranoid Android'.

discoverer John Sutter. The place now attracts half a million visitors a year, but only one original building remains inside the stockade walls; the rest are just reconstructions. Still, any disappointment is offset by the spectacular headland setting and 3,000 acres of surrounding parkland. **Fort Ross State Historic Park** visitor centre (*see p367*) has details on the enlightened Russians and Native Americans who once lived harmoniously here.

Less than ten miles north of Fort Ross are the 6,000 acres of **Salt Point State Park** (1-707 847 3221, 1-707 865 2391). It's popular with divers hunting for prized abalone, the giant succulent shellfish that inhabits these parts, but landlubbers head up to the highest point of the park to see the 100-year-old pygmy forest. Neighbouring **Kruse Rhododendron State Reserve** is worth a visit in spring, when the 30-foot (nine-metre) hot-pink rhododendrons that it protects put on a splashy show.

Cruise past sleepy **Sea Ranch** unless you're looking for an expensive, long-stay vacation home or itching for a round of golf. The multi-million-dollar homes, many of them weekend retreats for wealthy Bay Area folk, are part of a living-lightly-on-the-land movement that flowered in the '60s and '70s. As such, they're recognised for their environmentally sensitive planning and architecture: what some see as weather-bleached beauties, others may regard as drab, uninspired boxes. By way of contrast, check out the pure folly of the **Sea Ranch Chapel**, which would look right at home in the middle of Tolkien's Shire.

Where to eat & drink

The **Tides Wharf & Restaurant** (800 Highway 1, 1-707 875 3652, $$) has wall-to-wall views of the bay and seafood, soups and New York steak on the menu. **Lucas Wharf Restaurant & Bar** (595 Highway 1, 1-707 875 3522, $$$) offers much the same, but you can also order fish and chips for half the price from the Lucas deli window next door, sit on benches outside and mix with white-bearded fishermen. A favourite among locals is the **Sandpiper Dockside Café & Restaurant** (1410 Bay Flat Road, 1-707 875 2278, $), a no-frills formica café that hasn't changed much since the '60s; more upscale and relatively new is the tiny **Seaweed Café** (1580 E Shore Drive, 1-707 875 2700, closed Mon-Wed & lunch Thur-Sun, $$$$), squeezed into the Blue Whale Building just off Highway 1, run by a French lady who serves up tasty French-style roasts. The **Duck Club** restaurant (in the Bodega Bay Lodge, *see below*; $$$$) is known far and wide for its California-French cuisine, but the sumptuous oceanfront dining comes at a price.

In Bodega, try the **Casino** (17150 Bodega Highway, 1-707 876 3185) for beer, oysters and pool. In Jenner, the Victorian-furnished wine bar at the **Mystic Isle Café** (10400 Highway 1, 1-707 865 2233, closed Tue, $$) is great to slump into; the co-owner, a former opera singer, livens up the weekend's entertainment.

Where to stay

Bodega Bay Lodge & Spa (103 Highway 1, 1-800 368 2468, 1-707 875 3525, www.woodside hotels.com/bodega, $225-$500) has big, bold views of the ocean. The **Inn at the Tides** (800 Highway 1, 1-707 875 2751, www.innatthetides. com, from $150) is more upscale; the **Bodega Harbor Inn** (1345 Bodega Avenue, 1-707 875 3594, www.bodegaharborinn.com, $65-$285) is cheaper. Jenner is dominated by **Jenner Inn & Cottages** (10400 Highway 1, 1-707 865 2377, www.jennerinn.com, $98-$218), a spread comprising 20 separate buildings.

Northern California

There's nowhere to stay along the first stretch of Highway 1 out of Bodega Bay, but there are two excellent campsites: the popular and sheltered **Bodega Dunes** in Bodega Bay and, further north, **Wright's Beach** (for both, call 1-707 875 3483). You can also camp at the **Reef Campground** (1-707 847 3286), a mile south of Fort Ross.

Resources

Internet
Bodega Bay *Business Services Unlimited, 1400 Highway 1 (1-707 875 2183/www.bodegabaycopy. com).* **Open** 9am-6pm Mon-Fri; 10am-2pm Sat.

Post office
Bodega Bay *537 Smith Brothers Road (1-707 875 3529).*
Jenner *10439 Highway 1 (1-707 865-2822).*

Tourist information
Bodega Bay *Sonoma Coast Visitor Center, 850 Highway 1 (1-707 875 3866/www.bodegabay.com).* **Open** 10am-6pm Mon-Thur; 10am-8pm Fri, Sat; 10am-7pm Sun.
Jenner *Fort Ross State Historic Park, 19005 Highway 1 (1-707 847 3286/1-707 865 2391).* **Open** 10am-4.30pm daily.
Salt Point State Park, 25050 Highway 1 (1-707 847 3221/1-707 865 2391/www.parks.ca.gov). **Open** *Summer* 10am-3pm daily.
Salmon Creek *Salmon Creek Ranger Station, 3095 Highway 1 (1-707 875 2603).* **Open** hrs vary; call ahead.

Russian River

Sebastopol

Sebastopol is a crunchy, progressive farm town, and a good example of what Sonoma County is all about: hippie moms behind the wheels of their bumper-stickered Subarus make comfortable bedfellows with farm workers in pick-ups. The town's mainstay is the famous Gravenstein apple – you can smell 'em in the air – and apple sauce was first canned here. The town centre has a couple of thriving and heavily trafficked commercial streets: **Main Street** is an 'aromatherapy row', with smart boutiques selling herbal elixirs, books about witchcraft and yoga, and racks of pastel-coloured women's clothes made from hemp.

Where to eat, drink & stay

Along with the new boutiques, a number of lush new eateries have popped up in recent years. **K&L Bistro** (119 S Main Street, 1-707 823 6614, closed Mon & Sun, $$$$), for example,

serves fresh Cal-cuisine in a contemporary setting. The handmade ice-cream at **Screamin' Mimi's** (6902 Sebastopol Avenue, 1-707 823 5902) has made it a local institution, but some of the flavours are way out in left field; ask for free samples. For a formica-top fry-up, **Pine Cone** (162 N Main Street, 1-707 823 1375, closed dinner, $) is the town's best diner; for a room, the **Sebastopol Inn** (6751 Sebastopol Avenue, 1-800 653 1082, 1-707 829 2500, www.sebastopol inn.com, $148-$178), a large, pink Victorian set behind the old railway station, is a better option than the chains on the outskirts of town.

From Sebastopol

Highway 116, aka the Gravenstein Highway, takes you north out of Sebastopol towards **Forestville**. This stretch of road has a good reputation for its antiques stores, but also boasts **Kozlowski Farms** (5566 Gravenstein Highway, 1-707 887 1587). It's just before Forestville: look for a hand-painted sign on your left. The farm is famous for own-made jams, chutneys, fruit pies and other delicious locally grown and freshly baked produce.

A little off the grid (take Graton Road off Highway 116 between Guerneville and Sebastopol), **Graton** is another creative enclave. As well as a fascinating Native American history (*see p368* **The earliest settlers**), the town has eye-catching art at **Graton Gallery** (9048 Graton Road, 1-707 829 8912). Keep west on Graton Road and you'll find the pretty town of **Occidental**, tailor-made for visitors looking to spend a couple of hours in Quaintville, 1875. Besides the white-painted Victorians on the slopes of the Russian River Valley, the town is given over to gift shops and galleries, where you'll find your grandmother the perfect present.

Three miles south of Occidental along the fittingly named Bohemian Highway is the little village of **Freestone**, home to no more than 50 folks. The **Wildflour Organic Bakery** (140 Bohemian Highway, 1-707 874 2938, closed Tue-Thur) serves sticky buns the size of dinner plates, but for a more unusual kind of pampering you'll have to walk across the street to **Osmosis** (209 Bohemian Highway, 1-707 823 8231). Spa lovers come here from all over California to 'ferment' in fragrant wooden tubs filled with fine-ground cedar ($75-$80). This is the only cedar enzyme bath spa outside Japan.

Where to eat, drink & stay

On the way to Forestville, stop by **Stella's Café** (4550 Gravenstein Highway, 1-707 823 6637, closed Tue, $$$). Built with remnants from San Francisco's 1939 International

The earliest settlers

The Spanish may have regarded the land they claimed here as empty, but it had in fact been populated for around 12,000 years by the time they parked their johnny-come-lately boats. It says much that, by 1920, the Bureau of Indian Affairs felt the need to purchase only 14 acres of land in order to house what remained of the region's main tribes: the Coastal Miwok and Southern Pomo Indians. Thus the Graton Rancheria was established.

Situated outside **Graton** (*see p367*), this tract of land was such steep terrain that it was difficult to build homes: by the 1950s, no reservation had taken hold. The government grabbed its opportunity: it sold off the land and, in 1958, took away Indian sovereignty. Tribal leaders took their case to Washington, DC in 2000; a decade later, President Clinton restored federal status and sovereignty to the Graton Rancheria Indians, a true triumph.

Exposition, it's famous for its fresh-off-the-tree apple pie. In Graton, the **Underwood Bar & Bistro** (9113 Graton Road, 1-707 823 7023, closed Mon, $$$) gets busy at weekends with a crowd just about stylish enough to match the decor. The dining patio out back has the added attraction of a sunken bocce ball court. **Willow Wood Market & Café** (9020 Graton Road, 1-707 823 0233, $$$), on the opposite side of the street, isn't as creative with the decorations, but the cuisine, especially desserts, is satisfying.

Grab a drink at kitsch **Negri's Restaurant & Bar** on Main Street (1-707 823 5301) if you stop in Occidental. The food isn't much to write home about, but this 1960s joint lures the Buick-driving old-timers in just for the nostalgia kick. Otherwise, give the **Union Hotel** (No.3703, 1-707 874 3555, $$), across the way, a try: it no longer provides accommodation, but it does have a café and bakery, pizza parlour and Italian-style dining room. For somewhere to stay, Freestone's **Green Apple Inn** (520 Bohemian Highway, 1-707 874 2526, $89-$99) is a plain but pleasant B&B down the road from Osmosis (*see p367*).

Guerneville

Back in its '30s and '40s heyday, **Guerneville** had a vintage Vegas-by-the-River kind of atmosphere; people travelled up from the city by train to see big-band headliners like Benny Goodman. After the railways disappeared, bikers and hippies drifted in, but by the '60s San Francisco's gay community had made it their summer camp: **Fifes Guest Ranch** (*see p369*) became the first openly gay resort in the country. The late '90s evisceration of the tech sector encouraged many part-timers to get out of the rat race and move here. About 50 per cent of businesses are gay- or lesbian-owned, but Guerneville is a well-integrated mix of straights, gays and families whose old-world charm remains intact to a remarkable degree.

Guerneville's premier attraction is paddling about on the Russian River, either in one of the ubiquitous yellow canoes or floating on an inner tube. The nearer to the ocean you paddle, the more likely you are to be escorted by sea otters diving under your boat. Call ahead to reserve a canoe ($50) from **Burkes** (8600 River Road, 1-707 887 1222, http://burkescanoetrips.com) in Forestville. A shuttle service picks you up at the downriver end of the trip and returns you to your car. In the centre of Guerneville, **Johnson's Beach** (1-707 869 2022) has always been a great place to swim, sunbathe and relax, and also rents out canoes and kayaks.

For two easy excursions just minutes from town, visit the **Korbel Champagne Cellars** (13250 River Road, 1-707 824 7000) and **Armstrong Woods State Reserve** (1700 Armstrong Woods Road, 1-707 869 2015, www.parks.sonoma.net). The latter is an atmospheric primeval redwood grove that was set aside by nature-loving (or guilt-ridden) lumber boss James Armstrong in the 1880s. The 310-foot-tall (90 metre) Parson Jones Tree, only minutes inside the park, will stop you in your tracks. Pick up a self-guided trail map at the visitors' centre. There's also a pack station (1-707 887 2939, closed winter & summer, $60) about a mile in, which offers horse treks through the tranquil 800-acre wood in spring and autumn.

Korbel, meanwhile, offers free champagne tastings in faux-chateau surrounds. The cellars also produce several reds, most of them pretty poor, but it's a nice enough spot to order a bottle of fizz, sit on the deck and get a buzz going before touring the cellars. For serious tipplers, Russian River is best known for its pinot noir, as the climate's a little cooler than Napa Valley. If you carry on past Korbel along River Road, there are 70-odd wineries from which to choose; hire a bicycle or ask about wine tours at the resort if you don't want to take home a DUI as a souvenir.

Where to eat & drink

There's a bit of everything on Guerneville's long, wide Main Street. Outposts like the **Bull Pen** sports bar (14246 1st Street, 1-707 869 3377) and **Club Fab** cabaret (16135 Main Street, 1-707 869 5708) still put on a flamboyant show, but they attract less of the cruisey crowd these days: nesters have come here, leaving their wilder days back in San Francisco. **Pasta Boys Deli** (16337 Main Street, 1-707 869 1665, $), **Coffee Bazaar** (14045 Armstrong Woods Road, 1-707 869 9706, $) and **Sparks** (16248 Main Street, 1-707 869 8206, closed dinner Mon-Thur, $$), a great vegan restaurant, all do busy trade. The **Stumptown Brewery** (15704 River Road, 1-707 869 0705), a shabby-looking microbrewery, attracts a straighter crowd; watch out for the 'Hippies use the side door' greeting as you walk in, then glug a pint of Rat Bastard.

Where to stay

The pink Mission Revival mansion housing the **Applewood Inn** (13555 Highway 116, 1-800 555 8509, 1-707 869 9093, www.applewoodinn.com, closed lunch, $$$$, $185-$345) lays on the area's gourmet dining and deluxe lodgings. The restaurant's lemony, fire-lit decor is a little self-conscious. The **Creekside Inn & Resort** (16180 Neeley Road, 1-707 869 3623, www.creeksideinn.com, $90-$175) offers the best breakfast in town, served only to guests staying in the inn rooms. Comfortable, well-equipped, self-catering cottages of various sizes surround the main house.

Fern Grove Cottages (16650 Highway 116, 1-707 869 8105, www.ferngrove.com, $79-$129) is another favourite. Most of the cottages have retained their classic 1920s charm, complete with wood-burning fireplaces. The famous **Fifes Guest Ranch** (16467 Highway 116, 1-707 869 0656, www.fifes.com), celebrating its centenary in 2005, has a rambling summer camp feel thanks to its setting in 15 acres of meadow. Accommodation here ranges from the rustic (camp for $25-$100) to the minimalist modern ($65-$290). Volleyballs and cocktails are served at the poolside bar.

There's lots of good camping here: the **Schoolhouse Canyon Campground** (12600 River Road, 1-707 869 2311) is popular and overlooks the Korbel winery.

Around Guerneville

The most visible attraction in Guerneville's sister resort of **Monte Rio** is the eccentric-looking movie house. The **Rio Theater** (20396 Bohemian Highway, 1-707 865 0913) has been showing movies inside a portable World War II supply hangar since 1950; there are plastic seats and a roll-up screen (accounted for by the town's vulnerability to flooding in winter), while a large section of Cristo's *Running Fence* hangs from the auditorium ceiling.

Monte Rio is also on the map for hosting the cult-like gatherings of the **Bohemian Grove**. A cross between the Davos World Economic Forum and Burning Man, the Bohemian Grove is an elite gathering of CEOs, presidents and GOP cheerleaders who come to play boy scouts in the redwoods each summer. According to the probably apocryphal reports, guests light a huge bonfire on the final night and hold satanic sacrifices on the banks of the river. The *San Francisco Chronicle* reported that George Bush Snr and Donald Rumsfeld checked in to the Hill Billies camp at the 2004 get-together. Lesser mortals can try swimming, kayaking, canoeing and cycling to pass the time.

A short drive along Highway 116 to **Duncans Mills**, west of Guerneville, will get you into an agreeably sunny valley setting. In the late 1800s Black Bart stopped often for a drink here after a day robbing the Wells Fargo stagecoach. A few restored cabooses and the charming old **Depot Museum** (1-707 865 1424), on Highway 116 at Moscow Road, are about all that's left of the town's glory days feeding lumber and vacationers on to the North Pacific Coast Railway. But the place has enough charm left to make roaming through the remaining handful of restored historic buildings, galleries and restaurants a pleasure.

Where eat, drink & stay

If you're thirsty in Monte Rio, have a drink at the **Pink Elephant** (9895 Main Street, 1-707 865 0500); when you're hungry, have a healthy big breakfast at the **Wonderland Café** (20391 Highway 116, 1-707 865 9705, closed dinner, $). For classy dining and lodgings, try the **Village Inn** (20822 River Boulevard, 1-800 303 2303, 1-707 865 2304, www.villageinn-ca.com, closed lunch, $$$$, $85-$195). The views over the river from the dining room and cocktail decks are a boon. The **Rio Villa Beach Resort** (20292 Highway 116, 1-707 865 1143, $100-$170) rents several quaint – some overly quaint – riverside apartments, with access to a private beach.

The **Blue Heron Restaurant** (253 Steelhead Boulevard, 1-707 865 9135, closed Mon, $$) in Duncans Mills is a locals' hangout; satisfying portions of seafood, burgers and microbrews are served to the accompaniment of live music sessions. For a blast from the past, book a night at the **Superintendent's House** (24951 Highway 116, 1-707 865 1572, from $85).

Located up on the hill, it was the company house of the Duncans Mills Lumber Corporation, but now has a few well-preserved B&B rooms.

Resources

Hospital
Sebastopol Palm Drive Hospital, 501 Petaluma Avenue (1-707 823 8511/www.palmdrivehospital.com).

Internet
Guerneville Coffee Bazaar, 14045 Armstrong Woods Road (1-707 869 9706). **Open** 6am-9pm daily.

Police
Sebastopol 6850 Laguna Parkway (1-707 829 4400).

Post office
Guerneville 14060 Mill Street (1-707 869 2167). **Occidental** 3805 Bohemian Highway (1-707 874 3606). **Sebastopol** 290 S Main Street (1-707 823 2729).

Tourist information
Russian River Russian River Chamber of Commerce & Visitor Center, 16209 1st Street (1-707 869 9000). **Open** 10am-5pm daily.

Mendocino County

Gualala

The wide estuary of the **Gualala River** (pronounced 'Wah-LA-la'), which forms the natural border between Sonoma and Mendocino Counties, anchors the busy, faintly attractive town of **Gualala**. As on the Russian River (see p367) to the south, you can rent canoes and paddle inland here. Alternatively, find a spot on one of the sandy river beaches for a sunbathe and a splash: the water temperature won't stop your heart like a dip in the ocean will. **Adventure Rents** (1-707 884 4386), behind the Century 21 real-estate office in the Cantamare Center, rents canoes and kayaks ($25-$50 for two hours). The town itself is little more than a convenient place to pick up supplies and fill up the tank, but behind the dreary façades lurks a thriving arts community: it's symbolised by the **Gualala Arts Center** (46501 Gualala Road, 1-707 884 1138), which showcases local talent and hosts **Art in the Redwoods** each August.

Where to eat, drink & stay

The creative use of organic ingredients and ethnic recipes at **Pangaea** (39165 S Highway 1, 1-707 884 9669, closed Mon, Tue & lunch Wed-Fri, $$$$) gets a consistent thumbs-up from the spoiled palates of Bay Area foodies.

The **Gualala Hotel** (39300 S Highway 1, 1-888 481 5151, 1-707 884 3441, www.gualala hotel.com, $45-$120) is the town's main historic building. Built for $6,000 as the 19th century became the 20th, it was owned by Italian ranchers for five decades. The mustard-yellow façade evokes the opulence of a bygone era, but the rooms look like they were furnished from a thrift store. North of Gualala, the unusual **St**

Whale-watching

The California grey whale makes an exhausting 13,000-mile journey between Mexico and Alaska each season to mate in the warm waters of Baja California. The whales journey for three months in each direction and several months languishing in warm lagoons, fattening up their calves for the cold journey north. Mothers and calves like to stay close to shore, and display a clockwork-regular pattern of coming up for air, spouting like a geyser and gracefully submerging again: usually for three minutes, though they can stay under for as many as 15.

Every year orcas circle certain whales for attack, particularly vulnerable calves; despite the efforts of their mothers, a number of youngsters are lost each season. Yet this is nothing in comparison to the damage that was wrought by human beings: the grey whale was hunted to virtual extinction in the late 1800s. Fortunately, the population has recovered remarkably well since the whales received full protection from the International Whaling Commission in 1947; in 1994 the California grey whale was removed from the federal list of endangered species.

It's now easy to watch the whales in action as they cruise along. If you're here from January to early May, you should be able to catch the annual spectacle from coastal vantage points such as **Mendocino** (see p371) or **Point Reyes** (see p264). Better still, go out on a whale-watching boat tour: **Oceanic Society Expeditions** (1-800 326 7491, 1-415 474 3385, www.oceanic-society. org, $60-$63) runs great trips from San Francisco, with a naturalist always on board ready to answer your questions.

Orres (1-707 884 3303, www.storres.com, $90-$260) is inspired. It's also impossible to miss, with its heavy timber construction, ornate onion domes and towering stained-glass windows. The lovely domed dining room complements the fine food, with the same creative chef having been at the hotel for more than 25 years. The rooms are expensive but impressive.

Point Arena & Mendocino

Point Arena is on the books as California's smallest incorporated city. The one-block main street is home to an assortment of brightly painted art deco storefronts (some boarded up), a lone saloon (whimsically closed much of the time) and a restored art deco theatre that stages ornery old blues shouters as well as classic plays. There's free fishing off the rebuilt public pier on the south side of town at **Point Arena Cove**, an old whaling station. The cove attracts scores of surfers and divers, the latter coming to explore a wreck from the '40s.

A couple of miles north, at the tip of a truly stunning peninsula, is the historic **Point Arena Lighthouse**. The original was destroyed in the 1906 earthquake but soon rebuilt; this is a treacherous stretch of coastline. Whale-watchers, bird fanciers and lighthouse buffs all gather to climb the 145 steps, for which efforts they are rewarded with eye-popping views at the top: some claim to have seen Hawaii from here.

North of Point Arena, the scenery changes from dense woodland to the rolling hills of dairy country, with abandoned farm buildings, weather-worn red barns and grazing livestock completing the bucolic scene. Look out for signs to the **Ross Ranch** (1-707 877 1834) at Mile Marker 24, which offers equestrians and romantics two-hour beach rides ($60); call ahead to book. The five miles of dunes and lagoons are a favourite for those seeking seclusion and those who welcome rough surf and chilly (50°F!) water. By the time you reach **Elk**, you'll be green around the gills: the route winds up steep grades, sometimes at speeds of only 20mph. Yet this former lumber town is worth the haul for the setting: like many of its coastal cousins, it sits high on ocean bluffs and coves, overlooking staggering rock formations.

But of the many cute Victorian coastal towns scattered along the North Coast, all of which may be blurring into each other by this point, **Mendocino** is the cutest. Weekend wedding

parties and the kind of straight-laced older folk that like their beds plump and waistlines plumper keep the place afloat. The town started serendipitously: in 1852 speculator William Kasten survived a shipwreck here, took a look around and liked what he saw, particularly the lucrative redwood timber. A thriving lumber town appeared almost overnight.

Mendocino hasn't changed much since then, with many early New England-style buildings still claiming prime spots on the flat, grassy headlands overlooking the Pacific. Its small grid of wide streets, walkable in a half-hour, has been designated a **State Preservation District**, but is better known to anyone with a TV as the setting for *Murder She Wrote*: **Blair House** (45110 Little Lake Street, 1-707 937 1800, www.blairhouse.com, $100-$210), a B&B, served as protagonist Jessica Fletcher's home. If you're interested in the area's history and the Pomo Indians who once thrived here, visit the **Ford House Museum & Visitor Center** (735 Main Street, 1-707 937 5397) and the **Kelley House Museum** (45007 Albion Street, 1-707 937 5791, closed Wed). Most people prefer ambling along a Main Street lined with gift stores, chi-chi boutiques, art galleries and cafés, and the splendid **Mendocino Hotel** (*see p372*).

Where to eat, drink & stay

Point Arena Cove has a couple of dining options and one great place to stay: the **Coast Guard Historical Inn** (695 Arena Cove, 1-707 882 2442, www.coastguardhouse.com, $125-$245). Rooms and cottages are beautifully decorated in masculine American Arts and Crafts style. Wallet willing, book in at the white-gabled 1850s **Little River Inn** (1-707 937 5942, www.littleriverinn.com, $110-$325), so cute that its toll-free number is 1-800 INN LOVE. The Inn practically *is* the town, with golf course, tennis courts, day spa, cooking classes, a restaurant and a bar with panoramic views.

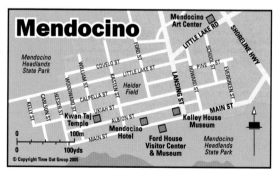

Northern California

MacCallum House.

Artist Kendrick Petty has been putting his eclectic stamp on Elk's **Greenwood Pier Inn** (5928 S Highway 1, 1-800 807 3423, 1-707 877 9997, www.greenwoodpierinn.com, $130-$300) for 36 years; the result is a clifftop Victorian compound that's part *Alice in Wonderland* and part Balinese temple, home to large stone Buddhas, copper dragons and a whole sculptured miscellany lining the pathways. Skip the café, but enjoy the terraced oceanfront decks. Hospitality in Elk is best sought at **Bridget Dolan's Pub & Dinner House** (1-707 877 3422, $$), a friendly Irish pub that's mercifully free of the clichéd decor. Behind the pub are a number of private cottages, part of **Griffin House** (5910 S Highway 1, 1-707 877 3422, $118-$218) and named after colourful characters of Elk; many have decks and ocean views. There's good food, some vegan, at **Queenie's Roadhouse Café** (6061 S Highway 1, 1-707 877 3285, closed dinner & Tue, Wed, $).

Mendocino's Main Street is home to the grand **Mendocino Hotel** (No.45080, 1-707 937 0511, www.mendocinohotel.com, $95-$295) and to **Dick's Place** (No.45080, 1-707 937 5643), the town's only old-time bar. Standout lodgings are all over town, fully restored Victorian ladies with matching cottages set among English rose gardens trimmed by white picket fences. Miss Marple would have loved it. **MacCallum House** (45020 Albion Street, 1-800 609 0492, 1-707 937 0289, www.maccallumhouse.com, $135-$375), owned by friends who jacked in their city careers to return home and become innkeepers, is decorated with flair.

Mendocino also boasts a number of excellent places to eat. The best is **Café Beaujolais** (961 Ukiah Street, 1-707 937 5614, closed lunch,

late Nov-Jan, $$$$$), a loveable operation that serves immaculate French-influenced cuisine in a century-old farmhouse. Also at the high end, **955 Ukiah Street** (1-707 937 1955, www.955restaurant.com, closed lunch & Mon, Tue, $$$$) impresses with its slightly Mediterranean take on California cuisine; **Ravens**, at the Stanford Inn (Highway 1 & Comptche Ukiah Road, 1-707 937 5615, $$$) dishes up smashing veggie fare. For breakfast and lunch, the **Bay View Café** (45040 Main Street, 1-707 937 4197, $$) serves decent food that nonetheless takes second place to the stunning views from the second-floor windows.

Three miles north of Mendocino, the small hippie town of Caspar is home to the **Caspar Inn** (14957 Caspar Road, 1-707 964 5565, www.casparinn.com). A steady roster of DJs spin funk, ska and hip hop to an appreciative mixed crowd. If sleep deprivation isn't an issue for you, some of the area's only cheap beds are upstairs: rooms with shared bath cost $60.

Fort Bragg

If you've had your fill of Victorian ephemera, boutique accommodation and questionable art, **Fort Bragg** is a blue-collar breath of fresh air. Originally a military outpost, then a lumber and fishing centre, it's now the region's reliable workhorse. Tourism has taken off in the last few years, with travellers cottoning on to hotels and restaurants that are cheaper than most places on the North Coast. Visitors are best off sticking to the historic old town along Main, Franklin and Laurel Streets.

The **Guest House Museum** (343 N Main Street, 1-707 961 2840, closed winter), built entirely of redwood, was the home of Charles Russell Johnson, founder of the Union Lumber Company. The museum has a fine collection of old photos, showing off the town's heritage and colourful barons. In a Victorian storefront across the street is the **Triangle Tattoo & Museum** (356B N Main Street, 1-707 964 8814), where curators Mr G and Chinchilla create beautiful designs using everything from traditional Maori and Native American patterns to Holocaust tattoos and post-9/11 stars and stripes.

The locally beloved **Skunk Train**, out of service for many years, is again taking visitors on a narrated journey into the past from the Laurel Street station and ticket office (No.100, 1-800 866 1690, www.skunktrain.com). For three and a half hours, this vintage train chugs along the scenic Noyo River, on an old logging route through tunnels, across some 30 bridges, and (hopefully from early 2005) into the town of Willits 40 miles inland. You can travel one-way, take a round-trip or sample shorter journeys via North Spur. Book the 9.30am ride on Tuesday, Wednesday, Thursday or Saturday for the steam ($45), rather than diesel ($35), engine.

Willits itself is in an area where you'll find some of the region's ugliest tract-housing. The only real attraction, unless you're a dairy farmer, is Seabiscuit lore. California's most famous little racehorse lived near the town at the **Ridgewood Ranch** (1-707 459 5382), along with his flamboyant owner Charles Howard (Jeff Bridges in the movie). Call ahead to ask about tours, available by reservation only.

Where to eat & drink

The **North Coast Brewing Company** (444 N Main Street, 1-707 964 3400, closed Mon & Tue) comes with an excellent reputation. There's tasting in the taproom across the street, and free tours of the brewery. There's a good local breakfast place at the back of the **Company Store** (301 N Main Street, 1-707 964 4974), next to the Skunk Train Depot. Above the Company Store is **Mendo Bistro** ($$$), an unfussy dining room with award-winning crab cakes.

Eggheads (326 N Main Street, 1-707 964 5005, closed dinner, $) is a narrow diner café serving large breakfasts, waffles, burgers and salads. There's usually a queue at weekends. **Café Prima** (124 E Laurel Street, 1-707 964 0563, $$) skips California and heads straight for Africa, the Middle East and Central America.

Where to stay

Motels (some with ocean views, others stuck between supermarkets and malls) line the main highway north and south of Fort Bragg. None is more curious than the **Grey Whale Inn** (615 N Main Street, 1-800 382 7244, 1-707 964 0640, www.greywhaleinn.com, $99-$192.50), a former World War II hospital with wheelchair ramps instead of stairs on the upper floors. The historic **Old Coast Hotel** (1-707 961 4488, $85-$205) is centrally located on N Franklin and lives up to its name, at least on the outside. Restored in recent years, the rooms are unpretentious, if a little floral. If you have room for one more B&B, the **Avalon House** (561 Stewart Street, 1-707 964 5555, www.theavalonhouse.com, $85-$155) is a stylish late 19th/early 20th-century Arts and Crafts country home with lovely gardens, although the colour-themed guestrooms might be a little cutesy for some. The **Coast Motel** (18661 Highway 1, 1-707 964 2852, $39-$109) is clean and comfortable, and one of the most reasonably priced motels in the area.

Hopland & Ukiah

Inland, on US 101 heading north from Healdsburg (*see p361*), **Hopland** has a long tradition of hop-growing. Indeed, it was home to the state's first microbrewery: the Mendocino Brewing Company, which is now the **Hopland Brewery** (13351 US 101 S, 1-707 744 1361,

Ineffably charming **Mendocino**. *See p371.*

Northern California

closed Tue & Wed). Thirty years ago, beer lovers came to Hopland to escape their diet of Bud and Coors; today the place is a shadow of its former self, no longer brewing on the premises. If you're more interested in hand-distilled brandies and grappas than pinots and petite sirahs, the **Jepson** distillery (10400 US 101 S, 1-800 516 7342, $7), just north of Hopland, and the more prestigious **Germain-Robin** (3001 S State Street, 1-707 462 0314, closed Sat & Sun), outside Ukiah, have reeled in accolades from around the world.

Hopland is also the turn-off (east on Highway 175) to Lake County and the rustic resort area of **Clearlake**. This series of connecting freshwater lakes, the largest in California, is mostly populated with local families taking their annual bass-fishing holiday (at least, that's what Dad's up to). For a more exciting and scenically spectacular (if man-made) lake vacation take a trip up to the Northern Mountains and Shasta Lake (*see p381*).

Further up US 101, is what Healdsburg used to be: **Ukiah**, a quiet agricultural town. A visit to the **Grace Hudson Museum & the Sun House** (431 S Main Street, 1-707 467 2836, www.gracehudsonmuseum.org, closed Mon & Tue), the latter the artist's Craftsman bungalow, is a neat diversion for anthropologists.

Resources

Hospital

Fort Bragg *Mendocino Coast District Hospital, 700 River Drive (1-707 961 1234/www.mcdh.org).*

Internet

Gualala *Copy Plus, 39225 S Highway 1 (1-707 884 4448).* **Open** 9am-5pm Mon-Thur; 9am-6pm Fri.
Fort Bragg *Seal of Approval, 260 Main Street (1-707 964 7099).* **Open** 9am-5pm Mon, Wed-Fri; 10am-6pm Sat.

Police

Fort Bragg *250 Cypress Street (1-707 961 2800).*
Willits *125 E Commercial Street 150 (1-707 459 6122).*
Ukiah *300 Seminary Avenue (1-707 463 6242).*

Post office

Fort Bragg *203 N Franklin Street (1-707 964 2302).*
Mendocino *10500 Ford Street (1-707 937 5282).*
Point Arena *264 Main Street (1-707 882 2515).*
Ukiah *224 N Oak Street (1-707 462 8814).*

Tourist information

Fort Bragg *Fort Bragg-Mendocino Coast Chamber of Commerce, 333 N Main Street (1-800 726 2780/ 1-707 961 6300/www.mendocinocoast.com).* **Open** 9am-5pm Mon-Fri; 9am-3pm Sat.
Mendocino *Mendocino State Parks, PO Box 440 (1-707 937 5804/www.parks.ca.gov).* **Open** 8am-4pm Mon-Fri.

The Lost Coast & Beyond

The Lost Coast

You've made it this far? Congratulations. You've reached the wildest part of California. If you have the time and determination to navigate the steep, twisting roads that penetrate this unyielding no-man's land, or if you're just a masochist after that especially gruelling hike, the Lost Coast won't disappoint.

The beginning of this northerly adventure starts as the coast-hugging PCH has to take a sharp right. Heading towards **Leggett** (it's gimmicky, but you'll get a kick out of driving through its giant redwood; *see p380* **Tree-ring circus**), then cross the **Eel River** (parched and sluggish in summer, a snaking swell during winter) to where Highway 1 meets US 101. West of 101 – and barely reachable on secondary or dirt roads in winter – are 90 miles of seismically wounded coastline, guarded by 60,000 acres of **King Range National Conservation Area** and **Sinkyone Wilderness State Park**. Unstable near-vertical cliffs and palisades made it impossible to force the coastal highway on through here; that the area endures the highest rainfall in the state of California didn't help. A helicopter is handy to have around here.

Find the town of **Redway**, just east of Garberville on US 101, and take the Briceland-Thorne Road for a slow winding excursion into the King Range to Shelter Cove. A second access route into the northern part of the wilderness starts in **Weott**, at the southern end of the scenic drive known as the **Avenue of the Giants** (*see p375*). Follow Mattole Road towards the tiny town of **Honeydew**.

Shelter Cove is the main launching pad for punishing multi-day hikes, dirt-road excursions and gentler coastal strolls. Settled on practically the only benign slope in the area, it contains a handful of amenities, including a restaurant and coffee shop, a campsite, a general store and four places to stay (*see p375*). **Black Sands Beach** at Shelter Cove isn't, as its name might suggest, sandy, but it is covered with flat black stones that make the sound of its crashing waves a delight. From here, pick up the **Lost Coast Trail** north past the old Punta Gorda Lighthouse and on to the mouth of the Mattole River, or head south through the tough ravines of the **Sinkyone Wilderness**. For trail maps, conditions, unexpected wildlife encounters and other information, stop by the **Bureau of Land Management** (*see p378*).

Where to stay

Try **Inn of the Lost Coast** (205 Wave Drive, 1-707 986 7521, www.innofthelostcoast.com, $95-$105), recently taken over by new owners, or pitch up at **Shelter Cove RV & Camp** (412 Machi Road, 1-707 986 7474, $19-$30).

Humboldt County

About 200 miles north of San Francisco you enter the alpine wonderland of **Humboldt County**, home of the redwoods, the last surviving Pacific Lumber town and some of the best home-grown weed in California.

One of the county's highlights is the **Avenue of the Giants** (www.aveofthegiants.com), a 31-mile portion of old US 101 between Pepperwood and Phillipsville that pays homage to the mighty redwoods that grow only in this region. The drive, which runs parallel to US 101 south of **Weott**, takes you through one of the last remaining virgin redwood groves: some of these trees are more than 2,000 years old and, as much as you strain skyward, you just can't see the treetops. Signs along the way invite you to visit the Chimney Tree, the Shrine Drive-Thru Tree, the Eternal Treehouse and other individual giants, but the real high comes from the sensation of *drivus uninterruptus* as you proceed through **Humboldt Redwood State Park**. Imagining a seed the size of a tomato growing into a 35-storey skyscraper gives you some idea of why the *Sequoia sempervirens* stirs up such a sense of wonder and humility.

South of the park on US 101 is the peculiar hippie enclave of **Garberville**, 65 miles south of Eureka and rumoured to be the epicentre of the California dope industry. By the looks of some of the locals, pot and hemp production are thriving. Recommended excursions from Garberville are to **Benbow**, two miles south, and delightful **Fortuna**, about 15 miles south of Eureka.

Staying with the county's lumber heritage, spare a few hours to tour **Scotia**, the last town owned by the Pacific Lumber Company. Take the Scotia exit from US 101, about 20 miles south of Eureka. It's hard to miss from the highway: 'Pacific Lumber' is etched on huge hangar-size buildings that back on to the river. The visitor centre is on Main Street, near the Fisheries building. Take the self-guided tour (weekdays only) and you can watch a massive modern-day lumber plant in action. The tour literature goes to great lengths to paint today's forestry as a friend of tree huggers; without this emphasis on responsible logging and sustainability, you might feel like an animal rights activist trapped in a research lab. There's

a museum and the grand '20s-era **Scotia Inn** (100 Main Street, 1-707 764 5683, www.scotia inn.com, $100-$275), well worth poking around.

Take the Fernbridge/Ferndale exit off US 101 (south of Eureka) and you'll find yourself in a flat river valley filled with barns, farmhouses and grazing cattle, with a ridge of pine-covered mountains in the background. Here resides **Ferndale**, referred to as 'the North Coast's Living Museum'. A well-preserved Victorian town, it's been declared a state historical landmark but still provides a home for dairy farmers, loggers and artists. The main drag is lined with soda fountains, butcher shops and saloons; the **Ferndale Museum** (515 Shaw Avenue, 1-707 786 4466, closed Mon & Tue) is small, but worth a quick look to fill in the gaps.

Where to eat & drink

There's no fancy dining in Garberville, but you can pick up organic bagels and Mexican-to-go, burgers, shakes and smoothies, plus a decent cup of Joe, all along the main street.

There's more to excite the palate in Ferndale. For a hearty American breakfast or lunch, go to **Papa Joe's** on Main Street: old wood floors, a long counter and shelves lined with vintage food products combine for a lovely ambience. Stop by the **Candy Stick Fountain & Grill** (361 Main Street, 1-707 786 9373) if you want to sit down at a formica counter for a banana split. **Curly's Bar & Grill** (400 Ocean Avenue, 1-707 786 9696, $$), in the Victorian Inn, serves standard California fare, pastas and fish dishes, and has an inviting old wooden bar. The restaurant and saloon at the **Hotel Ivanhoe** (*see p375*; closed lunch, $$$), set in a building reminiscent of the Gold Rush, serves pastas, scampi and steaks. Tie up your horse out front, kick off your spurs and start with a slug of bourbon.

Where to stay

There are a handful of Alpine-inspired lodgings on the main Redwood Drive in Garberville. **Lone Pine Motel** (No.912, 1-707 923 3520, $60-$100) and the **Sherwood Forest Motel** (No.814, 1-707 923 2721, www.sherwoodforest motel.com, $60-$100) have the most character and, important in the searing heat of summer, pools. There's also **Richardson Grove Campground & RV Park** (750 US 101, 1-707 247 3380, $15-$22), if you don't mind a little Christianity with your camping.

Ferndale's **Hotel Ivanhoe** (315 Main Street, 1-707 786 9000, www.hotel-ivanhoe.com, $95-$145) was built in 1870, burned down a couple of times and reopened recently. The Western-style rooms were refurbished by the current

Northern California

owners after watching too much John Wayne; still, all have roomy showers, queen beds and sturdy Victorian furnishings. Just around the corner, the **Fern Motel** (332 Ocean Avenue, 1-707 786 5000, $65-$85) is a cheaper alternative: it's a modern, rather out-of-place grey motel.

Eureka

Eureka, like Fort Bragg, is a working-class city proud of its industrial heritage, with huge logging trucks still rumbling through town. On first impression, it's not an attractive city, with grimey chainstores, motels, used car lots and belching millworks blotting the horizon. But it's better than that. The section around 2nd and 3rd Streets, between C and M Street, is awash with grand Victorians, boutiques, antiques stores, galleries, hotels and waterfront cafés.

Pick up a brochure at the town's visitor centre (*see p378*) and take a self-guided tour of some of the old lumber mansions. The best of the bunch is the pink and spectacular **Carson Mansion** (143 M Street), now a private members' club for the Ancient Order of Inghamars. Judging by the number of signs hammered into the lawns, trespassing would be ill-advised, but a gawp at the outside explains its status as one of the most photographed Victorians in California. The renovated former Carnegie Library building at 7th and F Streets is now home to the **Humboldt Cultural Center** (422 1st Street, 1-707 826 3226), and the city's history is recounted at the **Clarke Memorial Museum** (240 E Street, 1-707 443 1947, closed Mon & Sun), which has a large collection of Native American baskets. The city also regularly plays host to classic car rallies.

Overlooking Humboldt Bay on the south side of Eureka (off US 101) is what's left of the old **Fort of Humboldt**. Established in 1853, the fort played broker between warring displaced Native Americans and the white settlers who swarmed here during the Gold Rush. It was abandoned in 1870 and most of the original buildings are long gone, but during the summer you can tour the reconstructed hospital and surgeon's quarters. To get a closer look, take a tour on the *Madaket*, the oldest operating passenger ship on the coast. It's operated by the **Humboldt Bay Maritime Museum** (423 1st Street, 1-707 445 1910, closed Mon & Sun) on 1st Street, just across from the Waterfront Café, and you hop aboard at the foot of C Street.

Where to eat

On F Street, **Mazzotti's** (No.305, 1-707 445 1912, $$) comes recommended by locals for its lively atmosphere and big portions, while

Kyoto (No.320, 1-707 443 7777, $$$) serves excellent and creative Japanese dishes. For a special night out, residents head to **Avalon** (3rd & G Streets, 1-707 445 0500, closed lunch & Mon, Tue, $$$). **Bless My Soul** (29 5th Street, 1-707 443 1090, closed lunch & Sun, $$) serves well-priced fried catfish and creole dishes. For a big steak, sink into a leather booth at the **Rib Room** (518 7th Street, 1-707 442 6441) inside the Eureka Inn, a Tudor-style behemoth that was built in the '20s but is now relegated to a part of town overrun with used car lots. Winston Churchill and Robert Kennedy stayed here in its pomp. Call ahead to check it's open; in late 2004 it was undergoing refurbishment.

In the Henderson Center, **Fresh Freeze Drive-In** (Harris & F Street, 1-707 442 6967) is a local institution, a classic '50s drive-in serving large sundaes and fabulous shakes.

Where to stay

Lodgings in Eureka fall into two categories: chain motels and historic hotels or the erstwhile mansions of lumber barons. The latter were built around the late 1800s, and do a pretty authentic job of transporting you back to a more glamorous time. The **Eagle House Victorian Inn** (139 2nd Street, 1-707 444 3344, $75-$125) has a rather musty feel when you enter but has a ballroom and massive, gracious

Grub's up

Follow the road out of Eureka towards Arcata, then take a left after the Samoa bridge, and you'll reach the fabulous **Samoa Cookhouse** (445 W Washington Street, 1-707 442 1659), the last authentic lumberjack cookhouse in the West. During the halcyon days of the lumber industry, cookhouses were common, and an essential complement to a lumberjack's long hours of labour. If the food wasn't up to scratch, workers would switch mills in search of better. This cookhouse dates back to 1885; there's a small museum at the end of the dining hall when you've finished gorging. The food is served at long tables with checked tablecloths in typical Italian family style, and the courses come fast and often: soup, salad, big hunks of bread, a main of roast meat with gravy and veggies, and apple pie and coffee to finish. All this for under 15 bucks, with seconds available free of charge.

Avenue of the Giants. See p375.

waterfront rooms. **Abigail's Elegant Victorian Mansion Historic Inn** (1406 C Street, 1-707 444-3144, $115-$326) also rents out several tastefully restored Victorian houses (around $500). The **Carter House Inn** (301 L Street, 1-707 444 8062, $125-$300) and **Cornelius Daly Inn** (1125 H Street, 1-707 445 3638, $90-$210) are also great. If these break the bank, every chain motel you can think of lines the south side of the city.

Arcata & Trinidad

It's a scruffy and somewhat vague little town, **Arcata**, which is just the way its locals like it. Author Bret Harte lived here during the 19th century, but the dominant influence today is **Humboldt State University**, a liberal-minded college whose raggedy student population lives up to every stereotype you'd dare throw at them. The town's centred around **Arcata Plaza** (at 9th & G Streets): despite the presence of some fine old buildings, the square's main memorable feature is the incongruous presence of several palm trees.

On and around the plaza are clustered a number of student-friendly stores, cafés and bars; there's usually a student or five hanging around here, distractedly counting the days until the next **Kinetic Sculpture Race** (*see p57*). Though both **Redwood Park** and **Arcata Community Forest** are attractive places for either a picnic or a hike, and **Arcata Marsh** draws plenty of ornithologists (Arcata Marsh Interpretive Center, 600 S G Street, 1-707 826 2359), Arcata is better approached in the evening, at least if you like a drink.

The titchy town of **Trinidad**, a dozen or so miles up the coast from Arcata, is a rather different kettle of fishermen. Aside from the popular fishing trips that depart from the

harbour, the town's other main attraction is Humboldt State University's **Telonicher Marine Laboratory** (570 Ewing Street, 1-707 826 3671), an academic set-up that nonetheless has an aquarium that's open to the public. A half-dozen miles north from Trinidad is **Patrick Point State Park** (1-707 677 3570, campsite reservations 1-800 444 7275), which offers interesting insights into the Yurok Indians who originally settled this area; further north is coastal **Humboldt Lagoons State Park** (1-707 488 2041). Both parks have campsites and a handful of trails; for more information, consult www.parks.ca.gov.

Where to eat & drink

The best place to eat in the area, and not only because it's open all day, is the **Seascape** (1-707 677 3762, $-$$$): located by the pier in Trinidad, it serves terrific breakfasts first thing in the morning and fabulous seafood at night. Also in Trinidad – or, rather, just outside it – is the highly regarded **Larrupin** (1658 Patrick's Point Drive, 1-707 677 0230, closed lunch & Tue, Wed, $$$$), which serves sophisticated dinners in a smart but hardly formal room.

In Arcata, impressive Italian food is on the menu at **Abruzzi** (in Jacoby's Storehouse, 780 7th Street, 1-707 826 2345, closed lunch, $$$$); **Folie Douce** (1551 G Street, 1-707 822 1042, closed lunch & Mon, $-$$$) is more adventurous, with a menu that surfs the very edges of California cuisine. The **Pacific Rim Noodle House** (1021 I Street, 1-707 826 7604, $), meanwhile, serves decent and cheap noodle dishes, perfect for lining your stomach before settling into a cocktail or seven at the **Alibi** (which also serves above-par food; 744 9th Street, 1-707 822 3731) or one of the other, earthier bars near Arcata Plaza.

Northern California

Where to stay

Connoisseurs of chain motels have a wide choice in Arcata; among the familiar names here are **Best Western** (4827 Valley West Boulevard, 1-800 528 1234, 1-707 826 0313, $59-$159), **Comfort Inn** (4701 Valley West Boulevard, 1-800 228 5150, 1-707 826 2827, $69-$149) and **Super 8** (4887 Valley West Boulevard, 1-707 822 8888, $59-$85). For more on all, *see p54*. There are, though, some worthy independent operations, most obviously the clean, comfortable **Hotel Arcata** (708 9th Street, 1-800 344 1221, 1-707 826 0217, www.hotelarcata.com, $79-$150), with its lovely street sign and clawfoot tubs. Trinidad has a number of small inns and B&Bs: among them are the **Lost Whale Inn** (3452 Patrick's Point Drive, 1-800 677 7859, 1-707 677 3615, www.lostwhaleinn.com, $170-$230), five of whose eight rooms have ocean views, and the Cape Cod-style two-room **Trinidad Bay B&B** (560 Edwards Street, 1-707 677 0840, www.trinidadbaybnb.com, $170-$195), with its collection of antique clocks.

Resources

Hospital
Eureka *St Joseph Hospital, 3700 Dolbeer Drive (1-707 445 8121/www.stjosepheureka.org).*

Internet
Eureka *Kinko's, 2021 5th Street, Suite C (1-707 445 3334).* **Open** 6am-midnight Mon-Thur; 6am-9pm Fri; 9am-9pm Sat, Sun.

Police
Arcata *736 F Street (1-707 822 2428).*
Eureka *604 C Street (1-707 441 4060).*
Fortuna *621 11th Street (1-707 725 7550).*

Post office
Arcata *799 H Street (1-707 822 3370).*
Eureka *337 W Clark Street (1-707 442 1768).*
Garberville *368 Sprowl Creek Road (1-707 923 2652).*

Tourist information
Eureka *Eureka-Humboldt County CVB, 1034 2nd Street (1-707 443 5097/www.redwoodvisitor.org).* **Open** 9am-5pm Mon-Fri.
A free travel planner is available via the website.
Eureka *Main Street Information Bureau, 123 F Street 6 (1-707 442 9054).* **Open** 9am-4pm Mon-Fri.
Ferndale *Ferndale Chamber of Commerce, PO Box 325 (1-707 786 4477/www.victorianferndale.org/ chamber).* **Open** hours vary; call ahead.
Garberville *Garberville-Redway Chamber of Commerce, 784 Redwood Drive (1-800 923 2613/ 1-707 923 2613/www.garberville.org).* **Open** 8am-4pm daily.
Shelter Cove *Bureau of Land Management, 768 Shelter Cove Road (1-707 986 5400/www.ca.blm.gov).*

North to Oregon

Redwood National & State Parks

North of Arcata and Trinidad, signs of life grow sparser; the only settlements to speak of on the route to Crescent City are **Orick** and **Klamath**, whose combined population is less than 2,000. Good job, then, that there's plenty of natural scenery to draw the attention. The redwoods you've already passed are mere warm-ups to what lies up here. This forest, once threatened by the all-powerful lumber companies but now safeguarded for future generations, falls under four banners: **Redwood National Park**, **Prairie Creek Redwoods State Park**, **Del Norte Redwoods State Park** and **Jedediah Smith Redwoods State Park**. However, while each has its own ranger station, the quartet is essentially managed as one long string of forest (there's a four-in-one visitor centre in Crescent City), and best approached as such by the visitor.

There are trails galore in and around the four parks, some lengthy but many simple and accessible. The most popular trail in the area is the brief, mile-plus trek to **Lady Bird Johnson Grove** in Redwood National Park, a striking collection of trees dedicated to the nature-loving wife of President Lyndon B Johnson. Not far behind it in the popularity stakes is the mile-long **Fern Canyon Loop** in Prairie Creek Redwoods State Park (a ten-mile drive from Orick via raggedy Davison Road), highlighted by an unexpected waterfall; hiking boots are recommended, as you'll have to get across the gentle Home Creek in order to get there and back. If you're at Fern Canyon, stop at **Gold Bluffs Beach**, a lengthy stretch of largely deserted sand with several small but surprising waterfalls. Also in Prairie Redwoods State Park is **Elk Prairie**, the best place in the area to take a peek at the local elk population.

All four parks contain short hikes. But there are also a number of fine drives for the really lazy traveller, offering excellent scenery from the driver's seat. The best is **Howland Hill Road** in Jedediah Smith Redwoods State Park (accessible via Elk Valley Road south of Crescent City), which winds around six miles through an old-growth redwood forest; at the end of it, there's access to a number of small trails, among them the tiny **Stout Grove Trail** to the enormous Stout Tree.

However, the most impressive scenery is offered on longer trails. Sections of the 30-mile **Coastal Trail**, which runs all the way north to

Crescent City, are spectacular; ask park rangers for instruction on a stretch of it suitable for your time and energy levels, but try and fit in the impressive Klamath Overlook close to the town of Klamath. A real gem is the **Redwood Creek Trail** (16-mile round-trip, accessible from just outside Orick), popular with local birdlife – herons, ducks, eagles – as well as humans. The trail takes in **Tall Trees Grove**, whose name rather understates the fact that the trees found here are not just tall but eye-bogglingly immense: one 360-foot (110-metre) monster is believed to be among the world's tallest. (The grove is also accessible via a more manageable three-mile round-trip trail for which you'll need a permit, available from the visitor centre, just outside Orick.)

For details of other hikes in this area, and there are far too many to detail in any depth here, visit one of the visitor centres. The rangers are more than happy to offer advice on which trails you should take, whether to take in particularly impressive scenery or simply to avoid the crowds during summer; the area never gets Yosemite-busy, by any means, but some trails are considerably less popular, and thus more joyously solitudinous, than others.

Where to eat, drink & stay

There are few eating or lodging options between Trinidad and Crescent City, and those that do exist are fairly ordinary. Your best best is **Rolf's Park Café** (1-707 488 3841, closed dinner, Tue, Oct-Apr, $), just north of Orick, a thoroughly agreeable operation run by a garrulous German gentleman; specialities of the house include elk and wild boar, though the breakfasts are also terrific. Rolf also runs a motel, just next door to the café.

However, a good number of people take advantage of the parks' campgrounds. **Redwood National Park** contains only a handful of basic campgrounds; most head, instead, for the more developed sites in the three state parks (note that the facility in Del Norte is open only during summer). Fees are $20 a night in summer, when reservations are recommended (1-800 444 7275) and $15 the rest of the year; the exception is the small facility at Gold Bluffs Beach ($15/$14).

Crescent City

The **Crescent City** economy depends on three separate money-makers, all of which have helped shape the town's character. The first, and most traditional, is the fishing industry; **Ocean World** (304 US 101, 1-707 464 3522, $4.95-$7.95), an agreeable if slightly pathetic

Redwood National Park.

aquarium, and the 150-year-old **Battery Point Lighthouse** (1-707 464 3089, closed Mon & Tue), the oldest still-extant lighthouse on the West Coast and now open for tours, nod to this after a fashion, but a more accurate representation of it comes from the assorted salty gents who gather nightly at a pair of Downtown bars. The second is tourism: the town is scattered with motels that provide lodgings for coastal vacationers looking to break their journey. And the third? Pelican Bay maximum security prison. Ho-hum.

Where to eat, drink & stay

Eating options here are nothing about which to get excited. Still, if you're hungry and stuck here, **China Hut** (928 9th Street, 1-707 464 4921, $) does what you might expect. Accommodation is no more of a thrill, almost exclusively motels. Chains include a **Travelodge** (353 L Street, 1-800 578 7878, 1-707 464 6124, $65-$159) and a nicer **Best Western** (655 US 101 South, 1-800 557 3396, 1-707 464 9771, $79-$175; *see p54*); among the independents are the **Curly Redwood Lodge** (701 US 101 South, 1-707 464 2137, www.curlyredwoodlodge.com, $43-$86).

Resources

Hospital
Crescent City *Sutter Coast Hospital, 800 E Washington Boulevard (1-707 464 8511/ www.suttercoast.org).*

Tree-ring circus

Not all the trees on the North Coast are subject to state control. Long before the preservation movement took off, securing the future of Redwood National Park and its three related state parks, a handful of cunning entrepreneurs moved in, brandishing chainsaws and gaudy signs, and hijacked some of the monsters for their own curious motives. The result is a series of archetypal roadside attractions that enchant and appal in roughly equal measure.

The most popular is the **Trees of Mystery** in Klamath (1-800 638 3389, www.treesof mystery.net, $5-$12), a not especially mysterious collection of trees and trails that takes second billing to a disturbing 49-foot (15-metre) wooden statue of logger Paul Bunyan and a smaller but no less eerie figure christened Babe the Blue Ox by its owners. Kids and kitsch-hunters love it; nature-loving adults are usually less impressed.

Other entrepreneurs resorted to rather more basic manipulation of the land for their fortunes, with the result that there are no fewer than three trees in the area that have had their bases hollowed out wide enough to allow cars to pass right through them: the **Tour-Thru Tree**, just off US 101 along Highway 169 south of Klamath; the **Shrine Drive-Thru Tree** at Myers Flat; and the original **Chandelier Drive-Thru Tree** in Leggett (*pictured*), still the most popular of the bunch. All provide amusement for about as long as it takes the passenger to hop out, the driver to manoeuvre the car carefully into the gap and the requisite snapshot to be taken. Admission fees run $2-$3.

But the best of all the curiosities is **Confusion Hill** in Piercy (1-707 925 6456, www.confusionhill.com, $5-$7): open since 1949, it's a classic of the post-war roadside genre. The attractions include a cutesy train that runs half-hour rides through the forest, a

cabin carved into the shape of a shoe and a monstrous 40-foot (12-metre) totem pole, but the real peach is the Gravity House, a masterful piece of visual deception: the floors and walls of the house slope the 'wrong' way, leading to a decidedly queasy experience. When last we visited, we encountered a fiftysomething couple who'd stopped here out of sentiment: one of them had been taken here as a child decades earlier. It was, she said, no different today.

Police

Crescent City *686 G Street (1-707 464 2133).*

Post office

Crescent City *751 2nd Street (1-707 464 2151).*

Tourist information

Crescent City *Redwood National & State Parks: Crescent City Information Center, 1111 2nd Street (1-707 464 6101 ext 5064/www.nps.gov/redw).* **Open** *9am-5pm daily.*

Hiouchi *Jedediah Smith Redwoods State Park Visitor Center, US 101 (1-707 464 6101 ext 5113/www.nps.gov/redw).* **Open** *mid-May-mid Sept 9am-5pm daily.*

Orick *Redwood National & State Parks: Thomas H Kuchel Visitor Center, US 101 (1-707 464 6101 ext 5265).* **Open** *9am-5pm daily.*

Prairie Creek Redwoods State Park *Prairie Creek Redwoods State Park Visitor Center, Newton B Drury Scenic Parkway, off US 101 (1-707 464 6101 ext 5300).* **Open** *Mar-Oct 9am-5pm daily. Nov-Feb 10am-4pm daily.*

The Northern Mountains

On a trail with the lonesome pines.

Carving up **Shasta Lake**.

For seasoned travellers, mooching around the northern backcountry is all about empty roads and fresh mountain rivers that feed into dozens of placid lakes. It's about listening to the buzz inside your head because it's so darn peaceful outside. For squeamish urbanites, it's more like a trip to *Deliverance* territory, the perfect place to dump a body or get dragged off by a wacko religious cult. Either way it's easy to forget you're in a state whose population is 35 million, since so few of them seem to have made it here. Reason enough, perhaps, for you to show up.

Spread around **Redding**, there's a volcanic wilderness the size of Ohio. **Shasta Lake** and **Shasta Mountain** draw the most visitors in summer and winter, but **Trinity Lake** and **Mount Lassen** east are just as impressive. Most of the mapped towns amount to nothing once you arrive, but **Weaverville, Lewiston, McCloud** and **Dunsmuir**, with rich mining and railroad histories, all make an impression. And the astonishing geological structures of the **Lava Beds National Monument** make the long journey into the furthest northern reaches of California an enticing prospect.

Shasta Lake & Trinity Alps

Despite recent efforts to turn **Redding** into a destination rather than a drive-through on the way to Mount Shasta and the lakes, there's little reason to stop in this commercial city at the top of the Central Valley. Don't let the northern latitude fool you: it's a blazing hot hellhole in summer, and old-fashioned Downtown looks like it's on life support. The town's tourist attraction is **Turtle Bay Exploration Park** (*see p384*), which offers some canopied relief from the concrete sprawl.

It is, however, the lake to the north that draws visitors here. Completed in 1945, Shasta Dam was built to harness the Sacramento, Pit and McCloud rivers; the aftermath is a stunning recreational lake. Surrounded by postcard snow-capped mountains and pine forests, **Shasta Lake** has 365 miles of shoreline, making it the largest lake in California. It's also warm, in contrast to its frigid rivals.

Revellers arrive by the SUV-load in summer, carrying booze, food, sunscreen and CDs on to houseboats for several days of partying. Over

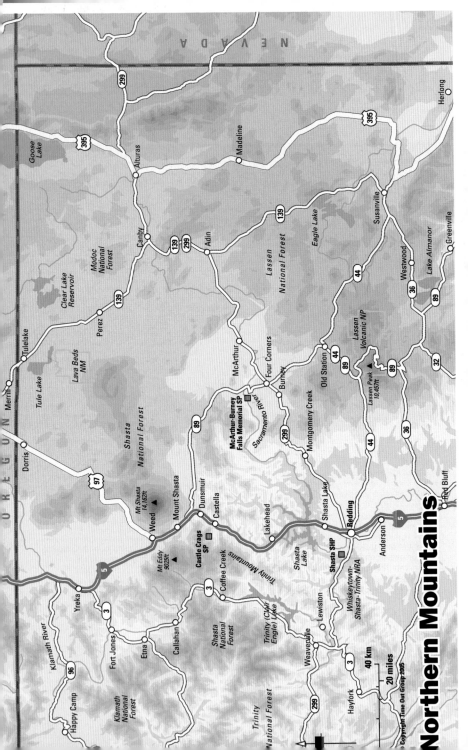

Northern Mountains

Northern Mountains

The best

Things to do

Marvel at **Shasta Dam** (see 381); explore **Weaverville**'s Chinese history (see p384); or see the birds in **Klamath Wildlife Refuges** (see p391).

Places to stay

McCloud Historic Hotel (see p389) is the luxury option; **Lewiston Hotel** (see p385) has the atmosphere without giving you the fiscal pain. Camp out beside **Hat Creek** (see p390).

Places to eat

Shasta Sunset Dinner Train (see p387) offers fine vistas and the power of steam, while **Jack's Grill** (see p385) offers a proper steak.

Nightlife

You best bet? Heft a pickaxe into the **Diggin's** (see p385).

Culture

Do reverence at the **Living Memorial Sculpture Garden** (see p387).

Sports & activities

Hire a fast boat on **Shasta Lake** (see p381). Make like a Martian in **Lassen Volcanic National Park** (see p389). Go spelunking in **Lava Beds National Monument** (see p391). Ski in winter and bike in summer at **Mount Shasta Ski Park** (see p386). Take a serious hike in **Trinity Alps Wilderness** (see p384).

the years, the houseboats have morphed into ridiculous parodies of royal cruise liners, now providing staterooms, surround-sound stereos, satellite TVs, hot tubs, water slides and the like. Imagine: we once thought soaking up the sun and cooling off in the lake, then finding an inlet to light a campfire and watch shooting stars was entertainment enough. There are always some liquored-up louts screaming around on obnoxious jet-skis, but the lake's big enough for you to be able to chug to a quieter spot.

No one has driven across the **Shasta Dam** since 9/11, when it was barricaded off for obvious reasons. Those fascinated by large public works (many of them built during the Great Depression) or simply awed by the scale of this concrete theatre (the face alone covers 32 acres) can take a highly enjoyable educational journey inside its tunnels and hydraulics. Free tours leave several times daily from the visitor centre across the lawns from the dam; contact Shasta Dam Tour Information on 1-530 275 4463. Be prepared for an 'Are you a terrorist?' security grilling and a long list of what you may not take inside.

Formed around 250 million years ago, the crystalline cathedral chambers of **Lake Shasta Caverns** underscore the dramatic geology and history of the area. Tickets, available from the Gift Shop (20359 Shasta Caverns Road, 1-530 238 2341, www.lake shastacaverns.com), cost $18 and the tours take in a scenic ride across the lake.

The 'ruins' along Highway 299, about 12 miles west of Redding, are the ghost of Shasta City, once a thriving Gold Rush town. Now designated **Shasta State Historic Park**,

it's hardly the Parthenon; for some, it's nothing more than a bunch of red-brick shells. There's some mining memorabilia in the 1861 **County Courthouse** (1-530 243 8194, closed Mon & Tue, $2), one of a handful of buildings that have been restored along the highway. When you see **Whiskeytown** on the map, it conjures up images of brawling lawlessness. But there's no town here, just a fishing lake and a somewhat dilapidated post office-cum-general store. Bear this in mind when you see the turn-off.

The tiny town of **Lewiston**, on the southern borders of the wilderness, is a whiff of the Wild West on the banks of the Trinity River. It's near impossible to find unless you're touring the back roads with particular rigour (for directions, see p392) and, measured in amenities, it's more of an afternoon browse than a major stopover. You could lose yourself for a few hours in the antiques store (look for the vintage gas pumps out front), packed to the rafters with Victoriana, vulgarities and rifles, as well as an old saloon bar pocked with bullet holes. Only Calamity Jane is missing. Lewiston is also a sweet spot for fly-fishing, kayaking and hiking; there's also some decent rafting in the winter.

More than a third of Trinity County's residents live in **Weaverville**, the county seat. You could easily dismiss it as another nicely preserved historic Victorian town, sitting in a wide basin at the foot of the Trinity Alps. But it's by far the most interesting town in the region – and not at all easy to get to, over a steep mountain pass on Highway 299 West. The woody aroma from a mountain of water-cooled lumber halfway through town is the first clue that this is the region's economic centre.

Northern California

Chinese prospectors were among the earliest settlers after the Gold Rush, building California's first Taoist temple at **Joss House** (Main Street, at Oregon, 1-530 623 5284, closed Mon & Tue, $2). There are hourly tours from 10am to 4pm, but it is still a place of worship. For more clues to Weaverville's gold mining past, visit the **Jake Jackson Memorial Museum** (1-530 623 5211, www.tcoek12.org/~museum), with its well fleshed-out indoor and outdoor exhibits including the town's old jail cell in the basement. Also on Main Street, you'll find California's longest-operating drugstore and many of the old verandah-front stores, far from being stuffed with tourist drivel or recipients of Disneyland-style makeovers, remain regular commercial businesses.

Some 20 miles north of Weaverville lies the boating and fishing haven of **Trinity Lake**. As at Shasta, you can rent houseboats, water skis and patio boats from a handful of lakeside marinas (for details of where to stay, *see p385*). Alternatively, continue up Highway 3, past the pretty village of Coffee Creek, and you'll be rewarded with some of the best white-water runs in the area. Nearby **Scott Mountain** attracts cross-country skiers in the winter months. With some of the largest peaks in the Trinity Wilderness reaching 9,000 feet or more (nearly 3,000 metres), hiking and skiing around these parts aren't for the faint-hearted.

Perhaps 50 miles north-west of Redding on Highway 299, you enter the **Trinity Alps Wilderness**. The state's second largest protected wilderness, it consists of half a million acres of rivers, canyons, mountain ranges, national forests and lakes. Hikers and campers are unlikely to find a more remote area of California, particularly in the western parts.

Head to Weaverville to plan your activities, and take note: every year the rescue services issue a warning to take a compass and a good map with you, as many of the dirt roads and forest trails are not even marked. Visit the **Trinity Country Chamber of Commerce** (*see p392*) to scope things out. You can also take a peek at what inspires local talent at the nearby **Highland Arts Center** (503 Main Street, 1-530 623 5111, closed Sun Jan-Apr).

Turtle Bay Exploration Park

840 Auditorium Drive, at Highway 44 (1-800 887 8532/1-530 243 8850/www.turtlebay.org). Exit 1 west off Highway 44. **Open** *June-Oct* 9am-5pm daily. *Nov-May* 9am-5pm Tue-Sun. **Admission** $11 adults; $6-$9 discounts; free under-4s. **Credit** AmEx, Disc, MC, V.

Turtle Bay opened on the banks of the Sacramento River in 2004. Along with hands-on educational exhibits in the museum, the $64-million park contains the McConnell Arboretum and Botanical Gardens (due for completion in 2005). Celebrated architect Santiago Calatrava, creator of the Olympic Stadium in Athens, designed the park's Sundial Bridge. Lit up at night, it's just about worth the money.

Where to eat & drink

Redding regularly touts its 200 restaurants, but finding one open on a Sunday is next to impossible. **Buz's Crab Seafood Restaurant**

Whiskeytown: no town, so bring your own whiskey. *See p383.*

(2159 East Street, 1-530 243 2120, $) is a local favourite that serves fish specials, trucked in fresh from the coast each morning, at simple Formica tables in vinyl booths. Downtown **Jack's Grill** (1743 California Street, 1-530 241 9705, http://jacksgrillredding.com, closed Sun, $$) is classic '40s inside and out, and known for its 16oz New York steak. For a drink, stop by the **Post Office Saloon & Restaurant** (1636 Market Street, 1-530 246 2190).

The **Lewiston Hotel** (*see below*) has a roomy bar with pool table and horseshoe pits; if you're staying in town, you can get a good steak in the hotel restaurant (1-530 778 3823, $$). And Lewiston's two hotels both have great decks out back for drinks overlooking Trinity River.

Fortunately for this under-populated area, Weaverville boasts several fine taverns and eateries. **La Grange Café** (226 Main Street, 1-530 623 5325, $$$) is a comfortably airy bar and bistro, with butt-numbing bar booths and more salubrious seating in the restaurant. The ribs and soups are highly recommended. If you've ever wanted to swagger through swinging saloon doors, here's your chance: the **Diggin's** (106 Main Street, 1-530 623 3423), next door to La Grange, is a lovely bar filled with locals, nostalgia buffs and, behind the bar, brews from Alaska and the Pacific Northwest. The **Red Dragon** (401 S Main Street, 1-530 623 3000, closed Sat & Sun, $) is a comfortable dinner option, with traditional lanterns casting red hues rather than the fluorescent white of most Chinese restaurants. Across the street from the temple, it's located in a superb old building that was one of the West's earliest brewhouses. **Trinideli** (201 Trinity Lake Boulevard, 1-530 623 5856, closed Sun, $) is a stucco-fronted cottage converted into the friendliest deli in town: order an egg and bacon croissant and park yourself at a table outside.

Where to stay

Most of Redding's accommodation is spread between the various off-ramps along I-5. On Twin View Boulevard are both a **Ramada** (No.1286, 1-530 246 2222, $74-$139) and a **Motel 6** (No.1250, 1-530 246 4470, $48-$56; for both, *see p54*); the more seasoned **Stardust Motel** (1200 Pine Street, 1-530 241 6121, $42) and **Thunderbird Lodge** (1350 Pine Street, 1-530 243 5422, $42-$55) fill out a row of weary cast-offs Downtown. Fancier hotels and prices can be found on Hilltop Drive.

There are more than 400 houseboats to rent around the lake, but you'll have to plan ahead: many are reserved weeks in advance. Check out **www.shastalake.com** for a list. Along with houseboats, you can rent every other imaginable

Disc drive

CDs to soundtrack your journey around the Northern Mountains.

***Music for Zen Meditation* Tony Scott**
Jazz clarinet meets Japanese shakuhachi and koto. Get spiritual under Mount Shasta.

***Velvet Undergound* Velvet Underground**
'Thought of you as my mountain top…'
Lou Reed quietly finds his folk.

***Shleep* Robert Wyatt**
Dreaminess from the prog drummer most likely to be mistaken for a gold miner.

floating device by the day or hour. At **Shasta Marina Resort** (18390 O'Brien Inlet Road, Lakehead, 1-530 238 2284, 1-800 959 3359), houseboat rentals for three nights range from $870 (mid-season, sleeping six) up to a deluxe $2,100 (mid-season, sleeping up to 16). If terra firma is more your style, resorts rent out small cabins along the shore. The full-service marina at **Silverthorn Resort** (1-530 275 1571, 1-800 332 3044) has a restaurant and pub, a grocery store and a pro-sport shop. It offers studios and one- or two-bed cabins from $105 a night.

Stop by the city of **Shasta Lake** to save money on basic camping or boating supplies. Resembling a giant trailer park, the city sprouted in the late 1930s when thousands of workers arrived looking for jobs building the dam. There are several RV parks, campgrounds and motels for day-trippers who want to be able to reach the southern shores of the lake. For more information, contact **Shasta Lake Chamber of Commerce** (*see p392*).

A number of comfortable motels line the stretch of Highway 299 that leads into Weaverville's historic downtown, many filled with lumber workers during the week. **Motel Trinity** (1112 Main Street, 1-530 623 2129, from $55), strung year-round with lights, has comfy, spotless, pine-panelled rooms with kitchenettes, and a decent-sized pool out back. The two-storey Victorian **49er Motel** (718 Main Street, 1-530 623 4937, $55-$65) suffered a routine makeover in recent years, but the grounds and pool make up for any lack of character within.

Indulging its past, Lewiston has the unique **Lewiston Hotel** (Deadwood Road, 1-800 286 4441, 1-530 778 3414, www.lewistonhotel.net, $55-$65), an old stagecoach stop. Authentically furnished rooms upstairs give you every reason to believe you're loitering around the late 1800s, particularly on a trip along the landing to the shared bath. The **Old Lewiston Inn** (1-530 778 3414, www.theoldlewistoninn.com, $100) is a primmer affair, laying on the modern luxuries and losing personality in the process. Still, it does serve a breakfast of champions.

If you're heading to Trinity Lake for a few days, **Wyntoon Resort** (1-800 715 3337, 1-530 266 3337, www.wyntoonresort. com) offers a range of campsites and RV hookups (from $25), as well as cabins and cottages (from $75). There's a pleasant pool and clubhouse set among the firs, and a full arsenal of boats and other water toys to rent.

Mount Shasta & around

Teddy Roosevelt, the first environmentally minded US president, saw the beauty and value of this wilderness in far-northern California and in 1907 set aside more than two million acres for protection. This vast area today is known as the **Shasta-Trinity National Forest**.

The volcanic snow cone of **Mount Shasta** dominates the horizon: at 14,162 feet, it's the second-highest volcano in the United States after Mount Rainier. The alpine outpost of **Mount Shasta City**, a straight ten miles from the foot of the mountain, is the jumping-off point for all the mountain's summer and winter attractions. Germans may feel at home among the pine woods, shingle storefronts and Alpine lodgings here, but it's a pretty humdrum supply hub with the usual cluster of fed-up teenagers looking like they drew the short straw.

The most popular trailhead to the summit begins at the ranger's station at **Bunny Flat**. You'll need to sign the ranger's register and pick up a (free) climbing permit to enter the wilderness area. You can also continue along the paved road up to the 8,000 feet marker, thereby enjoying the tundra-like terrain above the treeline without even getting out the car. June and July are the best months to climb the mountain, which the absurdly fit or foolish complete in about 14 straight hours. If you don't want altitude sickness and a thoroughly miserable slog, camp overnight and take a couple of days over your adventure. There are plenty of outfitters back in town to supply the obligatory crampons and axes for navigating the ice fields at the top. For a full climbing FAQ and more on the two main camp areas, go to **www.mtshastachamber.com** and click on the 'Recreation' link. You can also pick up all the maps and info you need at the **Mount Shasta CVB** (*see p392*).

The mountain is revered among the Native Americans who first settled here and attracts plenty of modern-day pilgrims. The **Mount Shasta Ski Park** (1-530 926 8610, www.skipark.com) keeps the chairlifts running year-round, ferrying adrenaline-starved mountain bikers around all summer, then skiers and snowboarders as soon as the snows arrive: which they do, like clockwork, to the tune of 300 inches (770 centimetres) a year. There's even floodlit skiing at night.

The town of **Weed** (some visit just for the T-shirt), in the middle of Siskiyou County and 50 miles from the Oregon state line, is another useful base for exploring the wilderness around Mount Shasta, particularly for excursions to nearby **Lake Shastina**. The town sits on the edge of the enormous Klamath Basin and rewards arrivals with fabulous panoramic views of the Lower Cascades, an awesome setting for a round of golf. There's plenty of charm in Weed's historic Downtown and

Castle Crags

The 6,500-foot (1,670-metre) granite monoliths that give **Castle Crags State Park** its name actually sit just outside the 4,350-acre park, but preside over the landscape like a giant oracle, inspiring hikers, campers and passing rubberneckers who can see them from I-5. In 1855, before their ill-fated defiance of the US Army in what is now **Lava Beds National Monument** (*see p391*), Modoc Indians took on miners here, armed only with bows and arrows, in what is believed to have been the last engagement in which Native Americans used only traditional weapons. The consequences for the Modoc warriors were no less savage for being predictable.

The area was mined for chromium as late as the 1950s, but is now tucked under the protective wing of the 1984 California Wilderness Act. There are 28 miles of trails through open meadows and forest terrain for hikers, but the flaky rock surface makes the crags themselves too dangerous for climbers. The fast-flowing and frigid **Sacramento River** also runs through the park for a couple of miles. This natural abundance in a (relatively speaking) compact space makes Castle Crags one of the best parks in the area to pitch a tent for a few days and take to wandering.

There are multiple camping options in the park, including environmental sites – even a mineral springs for your morning ablutions. For details, call 1-530 235 2684 or check online at www.parks.ca.gov.

Rollin', rollin', rollin'...
Mount Shasta. *See p386.*

considerable energy has been ploughed into creating a sense of 19th-century life at the **Historic Lumber Town Museum** (303 Gilman Street, 1-530 938 0550, closed Oct-May).

Take Highway 97 north-east from Weed for about 12 miles and you'll come across a landscape of alien sculptures. The **Living Memorial Sculpture Garden** (Highway 97, www.livingmemorialsculpturegarden.org) is artist and Vietnam vet Dennis Smith's personal contemplation of war. Ten metal warriors stand eerily on the altiplano, with brilliant-white Mount Shasta providing the perfect backdrop.

When you consider you can fit the entire population of Siskiyou County into a baseball park and yet the county envelops an area five times the size of Rhode Island, you get some sense of the remoteness here. Around 2,000 of Siskiyou's residents live in the attractive river-canyon backwater of **Dunsmuir**, south of Weed. Unlike many old railroad towns that have been consigned to living-museum status, this one's very much alive, at least in terms of its trains. The deliciously nostalgic sound of train horns echo around town as the Pacific Union comes through. The town's other main attractions run along a couple of streets: the artists' studios, cafés and gift shops have taken

up residence in some of the handsome old red-brick railroad buildings along Sacramento Avenue; just about everything else is up above on Dunsmuir Avenue, the town's main drag.

According to notices posted about town and the scores of drinking fountains, the town has 'the best water on Earth'. All of it is diverted from the nearby (highly attractive) **Mossbrae Falls** and comes out agreeably pre-chilled on a hot day. There's really nothing much to do in Dunsmuir except hang out in laid-back cafés or watch the freight trains go by, tempting you to hop on like a latter-day Huck Finn. And the inactivity is precisely Dunsmuir's appeal.

The abundance of old railway lines and fine mountain scenery inspired someone to their eureka moment: putting the two together, they created the **Shasta Sunset Dinner Train**, which runs from the wooden railroad station in **McCloud**. McCloud waterfalls and Lake McCloud are other easy excursions.

Shasta Sunset Dinner Train

Main Street (1-530 964 2142/www.shastasunset. com). **Tickets** $82.48. **Credit** AmEx, Disc, MC, V. Lush vintage cars pull out of McCloud at 6pm most evenings to take diners on a three-hour journey through the foothills of Mount Shasta. A few hours

Dunsmuir. *See p387.*

idling through Douglas fir and ponderosa pines might seem interminable to some, but an elegant four-course meal with wine quell the urge to jump off and the generally older crowd have a jolly good time. If the profusion of food and scenery doesn't sedate you, Norah Jones recycled above your booth surely will. Head for the open-air carriage for a great photo of Mount Shasta, and rest assured that no retail opportunity has been sacrificed in the preparation of your journey: a travelling gift store brings up the rear.

Where to eat & drink

Everything you'll need is along the main Shasta Boulevard. **Nebiolini's Vet's Club** (406 N Mount Shasta Boulevard, 1-530 926 3565), with walls paying homage to Marilyn Monroe, is the best-looking (and oldest) watering hole in town. **Coffee Connection** (408 N Mount Shasta Boulevard, 1-530 926 2622) next door attracts more people, but live Christian folk music under lights that could land a 747 might frighten off casual passers-by. A local pointed to the **Gold Room** (903 S Mount Shasta Boulevard, 1-530 926 4125) as a swinging night-time joint, which proved fanciful: our Friday evening there was spent hunched at a widescreen TV.

For breakfast, head to the busy **Black Bear Diner** (401 W Lake Street, 1-530 926 4669, $). The outside could have been built by Barney Rubble and the bear-themed tourist schlock within quickly palls, but it reels in the crowds with comforting breakfasts and steakhouse dinners. **Lalo's Mexican & American**

Restaurant (520 N Mount Shasta Boulevard, 1-530 926 5123, $$) serves Mexican dinners, steaks and some vegetarian plates, while the Age of Aquarius is alive and well at the **Berryvale Grocery** (305 S Mount Shasta Boulevard, 1-530 926 1576, $), with chimes, crystals and tofu burgers all palpable signs of Mount Shasta's spiritual allure. (The grill here closes at weekends.)

If you've made it to Weed, you won't go wrong with the $7.99 all-you-can-eat buffet lunch at the **Hungry Moose Restaurant** (86 N Weed Boulevard, 1-530 938 4060). The **Hi-Lo Café** (*see p389*) is another popular travellers' hangout, with breakfast served all day.

In Dunsmuir, the **Cornerstone Bakery & Cafe** (5759 Dunsmuir Avenue, 1-530 235 4677) serves a very good Mediterranean salad, chowders and own-made pastries. The **Brown Trout** (5841 Sacramento Avenue, 1-530 235 0754), along the railway, is a great spot for a coffee and some retail action. The airy adjoining gallery has more of a creative bent for gifts and jewellery than most emporiums in town; listen for the sound of a stream running underneath the floorboards. In a single-storey Victorian just around the corner, **Cafe Maddalena** (5801 Sacramento Avenue, 1-530 235 2725, closed lunch, Mon-Wed, Jan-mid Mar, $$$) has an excellent reputation for dinner. If there's any nightlife, it's the deco-fronted **Blue Sky Room** (5855 Dunsmuir Avenue, 1-530 235 4770), the bar adjacent to the dining room of Sengthong's Thai restaurant, where jazz and blues bands play at weekends.

Where to stay

Accommodation in Shasta City is plentiful and typically comes in the form of a motel fashioned into an alpine lodge. The family-run **Finlandia Motel** (1612 S Mount Shasta Boulevard, 1-530 926 5596, $43-$100) has the most personality, plus spacious rooms and a Finnish sauna. The cavernous **Tree House Motor Inn** (111 Morgan Way, 1-530 926 3101, $94-$104) has generic but spotless rooms with balconies (some with Shasta views), and a heated indoor pool. There's also an RV park (hookups $27-$29) and KOA **campsite** (900 N Mount Shasta Boulevard, 1-530 926 4029) on the outskirts of town.

Those seeking some self-reflection should head for the peaceful **ShasTao Hermitage** (3609 N Old Stage Road, 1-530 926 4154, www.shastao.com, $125). This yoga and Zen retreat has a couple of spiritually defined lodgings and an impressive stack of Eastern and Western philosophy to brood over. One of the ShasTao's owners is an accomplished dressage instructor, so there's Zen of a different kind to be had outside, watching the beautiful Arabians put through their lateral paces. Call ahead to ask about retreat packages.

Apparently, there's no place too remote for a national motel chain to roll out the welcome mat. On the outskirts of Weed you'll find both a **Comfort Inn** (1844 Shastina Drive, 1-530 938 1982, $70-$80) and a **Motel 6** (466 N Weed Boulevard, 1-530 938 4101, $70-$80; for both, *see p54*). The **Hi-Lo Motel & RV Park** (79 S Weed Boulevard, 1-530 938 2731, from $50) offers more rustic rooms, some of them with views of Mount Shasta.

For a spa encounter without monogrammed towels and music piped in from the Tibetan Top 10, try the alpine simplicity of **Stewart Mineral Springs Resort** (4617 Stewart Springs Road, 1-530 938 2222), four miles west of Weed. Spend a night in a teepee (from $24) or a full-service house ($325) and your day hopping from steaming bath to ice-cold creek.

For another unique experience, book into the **Railroad Park Resort** (100 Railroad Park Road, exit off I-5, 1-530 235 4440, $70-$90), just outside Dunsmuir. Here you'll sleep inside colourful converted antique railway cars with dramatic canyon views up to the granite towers of Castle Crags (*see p386* **Castle Crags**) and dine in a restored dining car. For swimmers, there's a pool or the creek. RV hookups and tent pitches are also available. In Dunsmuir there's a row of neon-flickering motels and rental cabins at the south end of Dunsmuir Avenue; some are more spruced up than others, but all are set among the trees with easy access to the Sacramento River. **Cave Springs Motel** (4727 Dunsmuir Avenue, 1-530 235 2721, www.cave springs.com, $39-$68) is a cheerful option.

A fine way to round off a trip aboard the Shasta Dinner Train is a night at the exquisite **McCloud Historic Hotel** (408 Main Street, 1-530 964 2822, www.mccloudhotel.com, $100-$235), which is across the street from the equally historic rail station. The hotel has the feel of a comfortable hunting lodge and the decadent suites upstairs are enormous.

Lassen National Forest

Situated to the east of Redding, **Lassen National Forest** isn't so much a forest as a massive and diverse wilderness. At the top of California, it covers close to 2,000 square miles, including at least part of seven counties: Lassen itself, Butte, Modoc, Plumas, Shasta, Siskiyou and Tehama. If that's not mind-boggling enough, three sizeable geological forces collide here: the Cascades range to the north, the Sierra Nevada to the south, and the Great Basin desert to the east.

The jewel at the centre of this wilderness is the **Lassen Volcanic National Park** ($10). For volcanologists, arriving here is like successfully landing on Mars: all four types of the world's volcanoes are present. Declared a national monument in 1916 after several years of volcanic fireworks had smothered and recast the landscape, this thermal wonderland is best enjoyed by car. Take the scenic (the only) route through the park, sweeping around three sides of Mount Lassen and enjoying what Mother Earth's cauldron has discharged: a brilliant spectacle of painted dunes, silent lakes, glacial canyons, sulphur vents and flowering meadows. There are eight camping areas, the largest at **Manzanita Lake** near the north-west entrance to the park, and 150 miles of marked trails, including 17 miles of the famous **Pacific Crest Trail** (the West Coast's answer to the Appalachian Trail), which cherry-picks its way between Mexico and Canada.

Lassen's 400,000 annual day-trippers barely stray from the designated points of interest and vistas along the drive. But campers and hikers who stay within the park bounds are rewarded with the opportunity to explore the vast lava plateau from **Summit Lake**, on the eastern side of the park, which is only accessible by foot; snowshoeing and cross-country skiing in winter mean the park can offer year-round activity. The elevation increases from around 5,000 feet (1,500 metres) to a maximum of 10,457 feet (3,187 metres) at Mount Lassen Peak, with different elevations giving the area a rich diversity of climate and habitat. Like many of its neighbours along the Pacific Ring of Fire, **Mount Lassen** has been bubbling back to life in recent months, so check in advance whether ascents of the final denuded slopes are possible.

The park's headquarters are in the town of **Mineral** (*see p392*), nine miles outside the southern park boundary. Pick up maps and free permits (if you plan overnight backcountry hiking) from here or the **Loomis Museum** (39489 Highway 44, 1-530 595 4444 ext 5180, closed Sept-mid May, Mon-Thur mid May-June), near Manzanita Lake, which contains Atsugewi Indian baskets and geological displays, as well as photos taken by the eponymous BF Loomis of the 1914-15 eruption. You can get supplies at the **Manzanita Lake Camper Store** (1-530 335 7557, closed Oct-May). A new visitors' centre is due to open at the south-west entrance by 2006.

The area around **Lassen Forest** is pure dreamland for outdoor adventurers, but it's just as good from the front seat of a car. The **Lassen Scenic Byway**, designed to create a visual banquet of scenery, loops four different highways around the forest. After cruising through the Volcanic Park, follow Highway 36 south-east into Plumas County and take the byway around beautiful **Lake Almanor**. Keep east on 36 and you'll come to the historic city of **Susanville**. This Lassen County hub was part of Nevada until Californian surveyors arrived in the 1860s and claimed it as their own. After spending a day shooting at one other, the Californians declared victory over the Nevadans and took the town as their spoils. In a subtle twist, Susanville's fastest growing employer today is the California State Prison service. **Eagle Lake**, the second largest natural lake in California, is close enough to the city to be visited as a day-trip. The lake is so alkaline that only one species of trout is able to survive there.

If you're heading back to McCloud (*see p387*) on Highway 89, you can fill up with gas at **Old Station**, which also has a couple of supply stores and cafés. And definitely stop at **Hat Creek** for a wander along a truly sparkling, clean, trout-filled creek. As hot as it gets during summer, this water will freeze your kneecaps off within 30 seconds. Otherwise, there's no reason to stop along this flat and monotonous stretch of pine forest. Turn west on to Highway 299, though, and you'll reach **Burney**, the only substantial stop between Shasta and the Volcanic Park. It's the sort of depressing, low-rent strip best seen at 80mph, but the handful of motels, stores and restaurants make it a useful full-service base for exploring the park. Nearby **Burney Falls** are striking, and the short loop trail to the base of the waterfalls should only take you half an hour. **Britton Lake** has launches for boating and fishing, but the residue washing up around the rim doesn't exactly invite you in for a dip.

Where to eat, drink & stay

In Mineral, nine miles from the park's south-west entrance, the **Lassen Mineral Lodge Resort** (1-530 595 4422, www.minerallodge.com, $72-$85) has motel rooms, campsites and RV hookups. In the park itself there's one place that serves food: the snack bar at **Lassen Chalet** (1-530 595 3376, closed Oct-May, $), which is just inside the south-west entrance. Those who wish to stay in the park have a choice of eight **campsites** – all of them first-come, first-served. You can apply for a wilderness permit if you wish to camp outside the designated areas; call 1-530 595 4444 ext 5134 for more information.

Hat Creek has a number of pleasant waterside camping and picnic areas, but Burney is the option for those whose tastes don't run to nights under the stars. The **Green Gables Motel** (37385 Main Street, 1-530 335 2264, www.greengablesmotel.com, $49-$85) shines out – rooms have televisions with (hallelujah) HBO – and there's **Burney Bowl** (37424 Main Street, 1-530 335 2294) if you're stuck for something to do in the evening. Many residents head for the **Hungry Moose** (37453 Main Street, 1-530 335 5152, $) for supper. There's wireless 'net access and doughnuts at trim, red-and-white **Coffee Station** (37371 Main Street).

About 12 miles west of Burney on Highway 299 is the remote town of Fall River Mills, which is a popular golfing spot (there's an 18-hole championship course) in a scenic river valley. Most visitors check into majestic **Fall River Hotel** (24860 Main Street, 1-530 336 5550, www.fallriverhotel.com, $65-$75): at night the

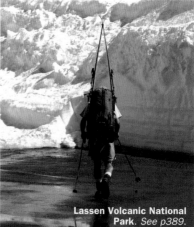

Lassen Volcanic National Park. *See p389.*

hotel's big old-fashioned neon sign is the only beacon around besides the moon. The solitary setting is a little Norman Bates, but once inside you'll find a lively crowd of ranchers, hunters, fishermen and golfers in the down-to-earth bar ordering up the T-bone dinner. Rooms are large and packed with antiques.

Yreka & Lava Beds National Monument

Yreka is another Gold Rush town, its main attraction the **Yreka Western Railroad** (*see below*). There's gold to be ogled in the 19th-century **Siskiyou County Courthouse** (311 4th Street, 1-530 842 8340) and neatly combined displays on Native American and settler history at the **Siskiyou County Museum** (910 S Main Street, 1-530 842 3836, closed Mon, Sun, $2). Nonetheless, for most visitors Yreka is just an access point and refuelling stop for Klamath National Forest. And, to answer most people's first question last, you pronounce it as it was once spelled: Wyreka ('Why-reeker'), a Native American name for Mount Shasta.

Largely lying to the west of Yreka, **Klamath National Forest** is a huge area. The Klamath, Salmon and Scott Rivers all flow through it, providing opportunities for serious white-water rafting, as well as more leisurely outdoor pursuits such as fishing and canoeing. Contact the **Klamath National Forest Supervisor's Office** (1312 Fairlane Road, 1-530 842 6131, closed Sat, Sun) for information. There are plans to open an interpretive centre, but no date had been set as we went to press.

Head into the extreme north-eastern corner of California and you'll find most people are pleasantly surprised to bump into a tourist. A shame, since there are several treats out here. Off Highway 139, **Lava Beds National Monument** (1-530 667 2282 ext 230, www.nps.gov/labe) is a wonderfully weird volanic landscape, an exhilarating case-study for geologists and a bleak fantasyland for everyone else. As well as the more than 20 lava tubes that are open to members of the public who enjoy spelunking, there's Mushpot Cave – lit and signposted – for the less intrepid. Bring tough-soled shoes (the lava is razor-sharp), but you can pick up torches, protective hats and maps at the visitors' centre; they also supply a good guide to origin and meaning of the vast, ancient petroglyphs in the north-eastern corner of the park. Of historical interest is **Captain Jack's Stronghold**, which is in the northerly section. This was where Kentipoos – known as Captain Jack – led Modoc resistance to resettlement by the US government in the early 1870s.

Kentipoos and some 50 Modoc warriors holed up in this natural fortress through a bitter winter, repulsing perhaps ten times their number of US soldiers. The starving Indians were eventually put to flight, and Kentipoos betrayed and hanged.

Another wonderful volcanic creation is **Medicine Lake**, 14 miles to the south in **Modoc National Forest**. Once a volcanic crater, the lake has big slips of glassy, black obsidian. Geologists will enjoy the self-guided geology drive, details of which can be obtained from the McCloud ranger station (1-530 964 2184) on Highway 89. To the east are the **Warner Mountains**, which attract winter sports fans with **Cedar Pass Snow Resort** (1-530 233 3323, http://cedarpasssnowpark.com, closed Mon-Fri & May-Nov) and backpackers in summer with some of California's best wilderness hiking. With so few tourists about, you'll get all the solitude you can handle. The only real city is **Alturas**, which isn't much to speak of but does have the usual shops and motels. The city is home to **Modoc County Museum** (600 S Main Street, 1-530 233 2944, closed Mon, Sun) and, more importantly, to the **Modoc National Forest Supervisor's Headquarters** (*see p392*).

While you're out here, spend some time in the **Modoc National Wildlife Refuge** (1-530 233 3572) or **Klamath Wildlife Refuges**, both impressive natural habitats, albeit under threat from modern agriculture. Ornithologists would do particularly well to visit in autumn: Klamath Basin is in the middle of the Pacific Flyway, which means some 250 species of bird pass through. In the winter this is also the best place south of Alaska for bald eagles. The **Klamath Basin National Wildlife Refuges Visitor Center** on Tule Lake (*see p392*) is a good source of information.

Yreka Western Railroad

300 E Miner Street, at Center Street (1-530 842 4146/1-800 973 5277/www.yrekawesternrr.com). **Open** *Departures* 11am daily. **Tickets** $14; $7 children. **Credit** AmEx, Disc, MC, V.

As far as tourists are concerned, the 'railroad' is a single, black, steam-powered Baldwin engine, dating back to 1915 and pulling a mixture of open-top and enclosed cars at a sedentary 10mph. After a series of financial disasters (not least a tunnel fire) the railroad had to suspend operations until spring 2005. Call ahead or check online for news. If the train is running, try to book a place in the caboose or engine car.

Where to eat, drink & stay

For healthy eating in Yreka, there's a range of good vegetarian dishes, at **Nature's Kitchen** (412 S Main Street, 1-530 842 1136, closed Sun, $), **Grandma's House** (123 E Center, 1-530 842 5300, $) does good breakfasts and lunches, and there are a couple of excellent Chinese restaurants: **China Dragon** (520 S Main Street, 1-530 842 3444, $) and **Ming's** (210 W Miner, 1-530 842 3888, $). The **Rex Club** (111 S Main Street, 1-530 842 2659) is the watering hole with the most local advocates.

Yreka's motels are concentrated on Main Street: **Best Western Miner's Inn** (No.122, 1-530 842 4355, 1-800 528 1234, $88) and the **Klamath Motor Lodge** (No.1111, 1-530 842 2751, $59) are both reliable. There are many camping options, with **Waiiaka Trailer Haven** (240 Sharps Road, 1-530 842 4500) the nearest to town. Outdoorsy types would be better off sampling one of the 26 campsites in Klamath National Forest; details are available from the **Klamath National Forest Supervisor's Office** (*see p391*).

Resources

Hospital
Weaverville *Trinity Hospital, 410 N Taylor Street (1-530 623 5541).*

Internet
Weaverville *Main Library, 211 Main Street (1-530 623 1373).* **Open** 1-6pm Mon-Thur.

Police
Mount Shasta *303 N Mount Shasta Boulevard (1-530 926 7539).*
Weaverville *101 Memorial Drive (1-916 623 3740).*

Post office
Dunsmuir *5530 Dunsmuir Avenue (1-530 235 0338).*
Mount Shasta *300 N Mount Shasta Boulevard (1-530 926 1343).*
Weaverville *204 S Miner Street (1-530 623 3740).*

Tourist information
Alturas *Modoc National Forest Supervisor's Headquarters, 800 W 12th Street (1-530 233 5811).* **Open** 7.30am-4.30pm Mon-Fri.
Lassen Volcanic Park *Headquarters, SR-36 East, Mineral (1-530 595 4444/www.nps.gov/lavo).* **Open** *Sept-June* 8.30am-4.30pm Mon-Fri. *July-Oct* 8.30am-4.30pm daily.
Mount Shasta *Mount Shasta CVB, 300 Pine Street (1-530 926 4865/www.visitredding. mtshastachamber.com).* **Open** 10am-4pm daily.
Redding *Redding CVB, 777 Auditorium Drive (1-530 225 4100/1-800 874 7562/www.visitredding. org).* **Open** 8.30am-6pm Mon-Fri; 10am-5pm Sat.
Shasta Lake *Shasta Lake Chamber of Commerce, 1650 Stanton Drive (1-530 275 7497/www.shasta lakechamber.org).* **Open** 7am-4pm Mon-Fri.
Tule Lake *Klamath Basin National Wildlife Refuges Visitor Center, 4009 Hill Road (1-530 667 2231).* **Open** 8am-4.30pm Mon-Fri; 10am-4pm Sat, Sun.

Weaverville *Trinity County Chamber of Commerce, 211 Trinity Lakes Boulevard (1-800 487 4648/1-530 623 6101/www.trinity county.com).* **Open** 9.30am-5pm Mon-Fri.
Yreka *Yreka Chamber of Commerce, 117 W Miner Street (1-530 842 1649/www.yrekachamber.com).* **Open** 9am-5pm Mon-Fri.

Getting there

By air
There are daily flights between **Redding Municipal Airport** (6751 Woodrum Circle, 1-530 224 4321) and San Francisco.

By bus
There are Greyhound stops (1-800 231 2222, www. greyhound.com) in **Dunsmuir** (5814 Dunsmuir Avenue) and on N Mount Shasta Boulevard in **Mount Shasta City,** as well as ticket offices in **Weed** (628 S Weed Boulevard, 1-530 938 4454, 1-800 231 2222), **Yreka** (115 Miner Street, 1-530 842 3145) and **Redding** (1321 Butte Street, 1-530 241 2070).

By car
I-5 will take you from near Sacramento to **Redding**. Keep north for **Shasta Lake, Dunsmuir, Mount Shasta** and **Yreka**; take Highway 299 west for **Shasta** and **Weaverville**, or east for **Burney**; and Highway 44 east for **Lassen National Volcanic Park**.

By train
There are **Amtrak** (1-800 872 7245, www.amtrak.com) stations in Redding (1620 Yuba Street) and Dunsmuir (5750 Sacramento Avenue), but they are unmanned. You'll need to reserve tickets in advance, by phone or online. From here a daily train heads north to Seattle or south to Los Angeles.

Getting around

By bus
Local buses are operated by **RABA** (1-530 241 2877) from its depot on Redding's California Street. **Greyhound** (1-530 938 4454) runs buses between Dunsmuir, McCloud, Mount Shasta, Weed and Yreka.

By car
On the I-5, **Shasta Caverns** are around 15 miles north of Redding (take the O'Brien/Shasta Caverns Road exit). The entrance to **Mount Shasta Ski Park** is 10 miles east of I-5, on Highway 89; **Burney** is also on 89, a short detour west of the intersection with Highway 299. To visit **Mount Shasta**, take Lake Street out of Mount Shasta City and follow the Everitt Memorial Highway for about 14 miles to the Bunny Flat ranger's station. To get to **Lewiston**, look for the scenic loop road heading east off Highway 3 (north of Weaverville). There are three routes to **Lassen Volcanic National Park**: Highway 44 from Redding, Highway 32 from Chico or (best if the weather is rough) Highway 36 from Red Bluff.

Directory

Directory

Getting Around

California's major population centres are linked by efficient bus and airline networks, and there are a handful of Amtrak routes, but if your trip involves anything more than a couple of urban stops, the most practical – and often the only – way to travel around the state is by car. And practical, of course, is only half the story: driving is a quintessential part of the California experience, so much so that we've devoted a chapter to it. *See pp27-32.*

By air

California has more than 30 passenger airports, six of them major international gateways. This means that not only is there easy air access to the major cities but few wilderness areas are more than a couple of hours' drive from an airport car rental lot. All the major US airlines serve San Francisco, Sacramento, Los Angeles and San Diego. British Airways and Virgin Atlantic fly direct to Los Angeles and San Francisco, and Air Canada goes to both those destinations plus Burbank, San Jose and Santa Ana/Orange County. Regional US airlines tend to fly to at least one airport in major urban areas; one based in the West, such as AlaskaAir, Allegiant, Frontier and Sun Country, serve several.

There isn't a particularly extensive network of internal routes within California outside the major hubs, especially if you want to fly direct. Airlines offering the best choice are American Airlines/American Eagle, Southwest, United Airlines/

United Express and US Airways. None of these offers any form of network pass.

Note that Reno/Tahoe International Airport might be the best entry point if you're travelling in or from the north.

Los Angeles International Airport (LAX)

1-310 646 5252/www.lawa.org.
LAX is situated on LA's Westside. Most flights from Europe arrive at the Tom Bradley International Terminal; Virgin Atlantic, based at Terminal 2, are the main exception. The easiest way to get into LA is by cab, which'll cost $20-$50 depending on your ultimate destination.

San Francisco International Airport (SFO)

1-650 821 8211/www.flysfo.com.
SFO is 14 miles south of San Francisco, near US 101. A new BART train station opened in SFO's international terminal in 2003, so it's now possible to get into Downtown San Francisco in half an hour.

San Diego International Airport (SAN)

1-619 400 2400/www.san.org.
San Diego was once the air capital of the west, and its airport, Lindbergh Field, has an august history and a location right near Downtown.

Major airlines

Air Canada *1-888 247 2262/ www.aircanada.com.*
Alaska Air *1-800 252 7522/ www.alaskaair.com.*
Allegiant Air *1-800 432 3810/ www.allegiantair.com.*
America West *1-800 235 9292/ www.americawest.com.*
American Airlines/American Eagle *1-800 433 7300/ www.aa.com.*
British Airways *1-800 247 9297/ www.britishairways.com.*
Continental Airlines *domestic 1-800 523 3273/international 1-800 231 0856/www.continental.com.*
Delta *domestic 1-800 221 1212/ international 1-800 241 4141/ www.delta.com.*

Frontier Airlines *1-800 432 1359/ www.frontierairlines.com.*
Northwest *domestic 1-800 225 2525/international 1-800 447 4747/ www.nwa.com.*
SkyWest *1-800 453 9417/ www.skywest.com*
Southwest Airlines *1-800 435 9792/www.southwest.com.*
Sun Country Airlines *1-800 359 6786/www.suncountry.com.*
United Airlines/United Express *domestic 1-800 864 8331/ international 1-800 538 2929/ www.united.com.*
US Airways *domestic 1-800 428 4322/international 1-800 622 1015/ www.usairways.com.*
Virgin Atlantic *1-800 862 8621/ www.virgin-atlantic.com.*

By bicycle

California offers some glorious opportunities for recreational and sport cycling (*see p33*) but the dominance of the automobile, long distances and tough terrain mean that as a whole the state is far from ideal cycle-touring country, and your bike will be an encumbrance if you aim to take in the state's major highlights. However, if you're interested in a locally based touring holiday, there are plenty of opportunities in the Sierras and coastal ranges and their foothills, particularly around the Bay Area and the Gold Country, accessible through trains that permit bicycle carriage (*see p395*).

By bus

Greyhound (1-800 229 9424, www.greyhound.com) runs regular and generally frequent bus (coach) services along virtually all California's freeways – but seldom beyond. The service is reliable and functional, not luxurious.

Several smaller metropolitan areas run their own shuttle buses to LAX and SFO; check airport websites for details.

Green Tortoise's hippie-esque sleeper-bus adventures come in somewhere between tour and transport, a good value way for non-drivers to defy the lack of public transport. California itineraries include Northern California ($299 plus food, six days) and Death Valley ($159 plus food, three days). Get details from 1-800 867 8647, 1-415 956 7500 or www.greentortoise.com.

By rail

In California **Amtrak** (1-800 872 7245, www.amtrak.com) runs seven passenger services, on lines heading north–south with three spurs running east. California's **internal routes**, the Capital Corridor, San Joaquins and Pacific Surfliner, run multiple services daily, generally sticking to the timetable. Using these, you can travel the south coast between Paso Robles and San Diego or explore the Bay Area cities.

Four of these services are **long distance**, extending deep into the vastness of the continent; they are not spiffy commuter runs but pieces of living (sometimes only barely) history that survive more due to freight than passenger traffic. A driver turning up late for a shift in Tallahassee can cause a train to arrive into Los Angeles several hours late – three days on. Long-distance services are neither fast (12 hours from Oakland to Los Angeles), frequent (daily at best) nor conveniently timed, and can be staggeringly unreliable. It's best to view travel on these trains as a diversion rather than a method of transport.

But what a diversion. A long-distance train trip is a magnificent, even glamorous experience. The views and the

engineering are superb, and so are many of the facilities, with glass-roofed observation cars and full-service diners the norm. If you don't get a sleeper, the prices can be astonishingly low (and ten per cent less booked online).

Amtrak's 'Thruway' bus services connect trains with major destinations near – and sometimes not so near – stations. This makes it possible to reach, for example, Yosemite or Las Vegas (largely) by train.

The **California Rail Pass** buys free travel for up to seven days over a 21-day period for $159 (adults) or $80 (2-15s). It is valid only on internal routes. International visitors (not from the US or Canada) can buy a Western-area **USA Rail Pass** for 15 days from $210 off-peak, which is valid on all routes.

California Zephyr (daily, long-distance). The Zephyr runs east from Emeryville, on the Berkeley side of San Francisco's Bay Bridge, to Sacramento and then on to Chicago, with the last California stop at Truckee, 5.5hrs later (followed by Reno, Nevada). It's a beautiful cliff-clinging cross-Sierra ride scheduled for daytime in both directions.

Capitol Corridor (8-12 services daily, internal). Efficient commuter transit in the Bay Area: San Jose, Emeryville, Oakland, Sacramento, Auburn and intermediate stops. A good gateway to the Gold Country. Bikes can be carried.

Coast Starlight (daily, long-distance). The north–south route for the West Coast, running from Seattle to LA. Its California stretch goes through Redding and Chico in the north, then Sacramento and Emeryville/Oakland before running south along or near the Pacific Coast. The Pacific Surfliner (*see below*) covers some of the same ground.

Pacific Surfliner (up to 12 services daily, internal). Efficient modern commuter travel down the Western Seaboard, from Paso Robles to San Diego via LA, with some useful stops (San Luis Obispo, Santa Barbara, Anaheim). Services are faster and more frequent south of LA, from which you can reach San Diego in 2.5-3hrs. Panoramic windows give great views, business class has video monitors and laptop powerpoints, and the buffet serves local wines and microbrews. Bicycles carried.

San Joaquins (6 daily, internal). Runs from Oakland/Emeryville

over the Sierras, with a spur to Sacramento, and then down the Central Valley to Bakersfield, with stops at Merced, where there are three daily Thruway connections to Yosemite, and Fresno, for Sequoia and Kings Canyon National Parks.

Southwest Chief (daily, long-distance). The LA–Chicago route goes east through the desert, with stops at Barstow and Needles and a Thruway connection to Las Vegas. You can change on to the Grand Canyon steam railway in Williams, about 150 miles into Arizona.

Sunset Limited (3 times a week, long-distance). The great southern route, ending in Florida. The stretch through California runs south-east from LA in the late evening, stopping at Palm Springs at around 1am.

By road

See p29 **Renting a car**.

Maps

You pays your money and takes your choice with California highway maps, available at gas stations and bookshops. If you're a member of the American Automobile Association (or the British AA), you just takes your choice – maps are free to members, and include some good city plans.

Your bog-standard fold-out state map or US road atlas will be good enough for most driving needs. If you want more detail, Benchmark Maps' *California Road & Recreation Atlas* marks and lists park and leisure facilities and includes larger-scale landscape maps.

For hiking or off-road driving, use USGS topo map sheets or downloads (buy from www.usgs.gov) or dedicated outdoor maps such as National Geographic's *Trails Illustrated* (www.trailsillustrated.com).

For complete satellite maps of the state, go to http://terra server-usa.com, or to http://mapserver.maptech.com/homepage/index.cfm for free viewing of USGS topographical maps. Aerial coastline maps are at www.californiacoastline.org.

There's much more
to Air New Zealand
than New Zealand.

0500 555 747   **www.airnewzealand.co.uk**

Start your holiday on a high with a stopover in California. We fly from the UK to Los Angeles, with a new route between San Francisco and Auckland, allowing you to take time out to experience the best of the Golden State on your way to New Zealand. Our blockbuster 64kgs total baggage allowance per person will be a huge hit, as will the amount of legroom you can stretch out and enjoy. Oh, did we mention our award-winning gourmet food and wines all served in true Kiwi style? Dreaming about it is one thing. Being there is everything. Visit our website now or give us a call and make California part of your New Zealand experience.

Bringing New Zealand closer.

AIR NEW ZEALAND

A STAR ALLIANCE MEMBER

Resources A-Z

Addresses

Written addresses in California follow the standard US format. Any room and/or suite number usually appears after the street address, followed on the next line by city name and zip code.

Age restrictions

Alcohol (buying and drinking) 21
Driving 16
Sex (heterosexual and homosexual) 18
Smoking 18

Attitude & etiquette

California is famously casual, but if you're doing business, particularly in LA, make it an expensive, stylish casual; if you're here to go out on the town, make it a dressed-up casual – or even a full-on dressed up. Where the climate is warm, beige, cream, black, taupe, olive, grey and pale peach are the 'power' colours, whereas Hawaiian shirts or any sign of gold or white will peg you as a tourist, though sober shorts are OK. Pay attention to social pleasantries.

Children

Offering manifold diversions at all points on the scale from mindless to educational, every kind of outdoor fun known to man and a concentration of commercial attractions rivalled only in Florida, California is a failsafe children's destination. Automotive culture is an egalitarian one, with roadside rest and food stops fully family-equipped and friendly. Laws that mandate wheelchair access to public facilities are also good for buggies, as are the short, level (often interpretive) trails at state/national parks, which also run lots of kids' activities, as well as the Junior Ranger Programme. Rented cars can be equipped with child seats (ask when you book).

California is so stuffed with surefire child-pleasers that it's hard to pick out the best. Disneyland (*see p119*) is an obvious winner, as are San Diego's SeaWorld (*p76*) and the Monterey Bay Aquarium (*p216*). The big cities have plenty of the usual zoos, observatories and children's museums, and family-friendly tourist areas like LA's Santa Monica Pier and Fisherman's Wharf in San Francisco. Children, like adults, will get a kick out of California icons like San Francisco's cable cars and the Hollywood sign. And never underestimate the power of nature: America's tallest trees, hottest desert and biggest whales will also appeal.

For more detail on the best places to take the children, see www.travelforkids.com.

Couriers/shippers

The major companies below can send everything from an overnight parcel to a non-urgent shipment, nationally and worldwide, and pick up from most locations. Note that standard post offices (*see p401*) are reliable and offer good value for delivery of packages and priority mail.

DHL *1-800 225 5345/www.dhlusa. com*. **Open** usually 8am-8pm Mon-Fri. **Credit** AmEx, Disc, MC, V.
Federal Express *1-800 463 3339/ www.fedex.com*. **Open** 9am-6pm Mon-Sat. **Credit** AmEx, DC, Disc, MC, V.
UPS *1-800 742 5877/www.ups.com*. **Open** 24hrs daily. **Credit** AmEx, MC, V.

Consumer

California Attorney General's Office Public Inquiry Unit *1-800 952 5225/http://caag.state.ca. us/consumers*. **Open** 24hrs daily. Reviews consumer complaints. Call to make a complaint about consumer law enforcement or any other agency.
Department of Consumer Affairs *1-800 952 5210/deaf callers 1-916 322 1700/www.dca.ca.gov*. Investigates complaints and gives info for over 40 state agencies.

Consulates

For a complete list, consult the Yellow Pages, or phone directory assistance (411).

Australia *Los Angeles 1-310 229 4800/San Francisco 1-415 536 1970/www.austemb.org*.

Travel advice

For up-to-date information on travelling to a specific country – including the latest news on safety and security, health issues, local laws and customs – contact your home country government's department of foreign affairs. Most have websites packed with useful advice for would-be travellers.

For vital information for travellers to the US, *see also p399* **Passport regulations**.

Australia
www.smartraveller.gov.au
Canada
www.voyage.gc.ca
New Zealand
www.mft.govt.nz/travel

Republic of Ireland
http://foreignaffairs.gov.ie
UK
www.fco.gov.uk/travel
USA
www.state.gov/travel

Canada *Los Angeles 1-213 346
2700/San Francisco 1-415 834
3180/www.canadianembassy.org.*
New Zealand *Los Angeles 1-310
207 1605/San Francisco 1-415 399
1255/www.nzemb.org.*
Republic of Ireland
*San Francisco 1-415 392
4214/www.irelandemb.org.*
United Kingdom *Los Angeles
1-310 481 0031/visas 1-310 481
2900/San Francisco 1-415 617
1300/www.britainusa.com.*

Customs

International travellers go
through US Customs directly
after Immigration. Give the
official the filled-in white form
you were given on the plane.

Foreign visitors can import
the following duty-free: 200
cigarettes or 50 cigars (not
Cuban; over-18s) or 2kg of
smoking tobacco; one litre of
wine or spirits (over-21s); and
up to $100 in gifts ($800 for
returning Americans).

In California you must
declare and possibly forfeit
plants or foodstuffs. Check **US
Customs** online (www.cbp.
gov/xp/cgov/travel) for details.

UK Customs & Excise
allows returning travellers to
bring in £145 worth of gifts
and goods and an unlimited
amount of your own money.

Disabled travellers

California's strict building
codes have ensured equal
disabled access to all city
facilities, businesses, parking
lots, restaurants, hotels and
other public places. Some older
buildings present problems,
but many of these have been
retrofitted. Public transport –
long-distance trains aside –
is designed to be accessible.

Rental car companies all
have adapted vehicles, but
require three days' notice; a
week is better. State and
national parks work hard to
ensure wheelchair access to at
least some of the highlights,
along with accommodation
and campsites, and to provide

an experience of value for
people with visual and hearing
impairments; details are on the
individual websites.

Good general travel info and
contacts are available online
at www.spinlife.com/zine or
www.mossresourcenet.org.
California Relay Service *TTD to
voice 1-800 735 2929/voice to TTD
1-800 735 2922.* Relays phone calls
between TTD and voice callers. The
service is available 24hrs daily.
**Society for the Advancement
of Travel for the Handicapped**
*1-212 447 7284/fax 1-212 725
8253/www.sath.org.* Offers advice
and referrals for disabled travellers
planning trips to all parts of the US.

Electricity

The United States uses a
110-120V, 60-cycle AC voltage.
Most foreign appliances except
dual-voltage flat-pin shavers
will require an adaptor. Note
that most US DVDs, videos
and TVs use a different
frequency from European ones.

Emergencies

911

Call 911 statewide from landlines,
public phones and cell phones for
all genuine emergencies, including
coast guard and mountain rescue
(your call is re-routed as required).

Poison Information
Center

1-800 876 4766.

Gay & lesbian

In Southern California, no
eyebrows will be raised at
same-sex couples in urban
areas – LA and San Francisco
are two of the world's most
gay-friendly cities – and you'd
be unlucky to get any attitude
in the boondocks. In Northern
California, you might find
isolated incidents of bigotry.

The Southern California *Gay
& Lesbian Community Yellow
Pages* lists almost every gay
business; find it at www.gay
communitydirectory.com and
at gay and lesbian bookshops

(the iconic A Different Light,
www.adlbooks.com, has San
Francisco and LA branches).

Health & medical

US residents with health
insurance should check that it
covers travel away from home,
for both emergency and non-
emergency treatment. Most
policies do, but some HMO
coverage particularly is limited.
Take insurance cards with you.

Non-US residents should take
out comprehensive medical
insurance before they travel,
and check it pays up front.
Emergency rooms are obliged
to treat genuine emergencies,
but will do whatever they can
to make you pay.

Ensure your cover includes
any activities you are planning.
Some dangerous sports may be
excluded, with 'dangerous' a
matter of opinion about which
the insurance company is
always right. If you're in any
doubt, check. Take details
of your policy and contact
numbers with you, also leaving
them with someone at home:
check with your insurers before
you agree to any payments.

A few clinics provide basic
health care to those Americans
who can't afford adequate
insurance. They may agree to
treat foreigners. If your medical
problem is not an emergency
and you have no insurance, try
to get an appointment at these.

Haight-Ashbury
Free Clinic

*558 Clayton Street, at Haight Street,
Haight-Ashbury, San Francisco
(1-415 487 5632/www.hafci.org/
medical). Bus 6, 7, 33, 37, 43, 66,
71.* **Open** 1-9pm Mon; 9am-9pm Tue-
Thur; 1-5pm Fri; 24hr answerphone.
Free primary health care. Speciality
clinics include podiatry, paediatry,
chiropractics and HIV testing. You
will need to make an appointment.

LA Free Clinic

*8405 Beverly Boulevard, at N
Orlando Avenue, West Hollywood
(1-323 653 1990/www.lafreeclinic.
org). I-10, exit La Cienega Boulevard
north.* **Open** 9am-5pm Mon-Fri.

Directory

Free medical and dental care. There are other locations at 6043 Hollywood Boulevard and 5205 Melrose Avenue.

Abortion & contraception

Condoms are widely available in drugstores and supermarkets across California. Check the packaging for FDA approval. If you're taking oral contraception, be sure to bring adequate supplies. If you fly in and there's a significant time difference, it's usually better to take an extra pill rather than one less; check with your doctor. The morning after pill is not available over the counter in the US but can be obtained with a prescription, for which you should approach a doctor or clinic. For specialist family planning clinics – where you can be sure of advice and treatment without a hidden agenda – contact Planned Parenthood on 1-800 230 7526 or at www.planned parenthood.org.

If you are considering an abortion, our advice is to wait until you return to your support structures back home. If this is problematic, Planned Parenthood can again offer advice.

AIDS & HIV

AIDS/HIV hasn't gone away in California. Be sure to follow safe sex practices.

AIDS Healthcare Foundation Clinic (AHF)
www.aidshealth.org
Specialist HIV/AIDS medical provider, offering quality care regardless of ability to pay, with 12 California locations.

CDC National STD & AIDS Hotline
1-800 342 2437. **Open** 24hrs daily. Advice, information and referrals.

California AIDS Foundation Hotline
1-800 367 2437/www.aidshotline. org. **Open** 9am-5pm Mon, Wed-Fri; 9am-9pm Tue.
Offers up-to-date information on HIV and advice on safe sex. The website lists 1,000 organisations providing HIV, AIDS and STD services.

Dentists

Your insurers may require you visit a particular dentist. If you have to find one yourself, ask at your hotel or check at www.cda.org.

Doctors

Again, the first people to contact are your insurers, and the second the staff at your hotel. You can also use the Yellow Pages, or look up the county medical association in the White Pages. To check a doctor's record and credentials, visitwww. medbd.ca.gov or call 1-916 263 2382.

Hospitals

Hospitals are listed at the end of each area section. Otherwise, check the Yellow Pages or at your hotel.

Helplines

Most addiction crisis and suicide prevention helplines are run locally: look under the organisation's name in the White Pages.
Child Abuse Hotline
1-800 422 4453.
National Domestic Violence Hotline
1-800 799 7233.
National Rape, Abuse & Incest National Network
1-800 656 4673.

ID

Always carry an official picture ID on your person. You'll need it to buy or drink alcohol (even if you look well over 21) and, in security-sensitive times, failing to be ready with the documents is unwise. UK residents are recommended to get the credit-card style photo driving licence so they don't have to use their passport as ID. If you're travelling near the Mexican border, be prepared to stop at checkpoints and keep your passport handy.

Insurance

Non-nationals should arrange comprehensive baggage, trip-cancellation and medical insurance before they leave. US citizens should consider doing the same. Read the small print: consequences of security scares, including cancelled flights, may not be covered.

Internet access

If you're travelling with a laptop, contact your ISP or cable company before leaving

Passport regulations

As part of the programme to tighten border security, the United States now requires visitors travelling under the Visa Waiver Program (VWP) to present a machine-readable passport in order to be admitted to the country. VWP countries include the UK, Australia and New Zealand. Machine-readable passports contain either a magnetic strip or barcode. The standard-issue EC/EU maroon passport is machine readable. Each traveller, including all children, need their own passport, which must be valid for at least a further six months.

Passports issued to VWP travellers on or after October 26 2005 must contain biometric data; for the US's purposes, index finger prints and a digital photo. Prior to that date, officials will be 'enrolling' VWP travellers at borders, by taking fingerprint scans and a photo. Whether the countries concerned can sort out the admin and technology required to issue biometric passports, and the US to read them, by this date is still subject to question: one deadline extension has already been necessary.

Before you travel, visit www.travel.state.gov/visa and click on 'temporary visas' to check the current situation.

Directory

home to ask about access numbers and roaming tariffs. AOL (US) offers a telephone-based audio email service to subscribers at an extra charge. If you have a wireless card and the relevant account (the dominant supplier is iPass, www.ipass.com), you can log on at Starbucks and many Kinko's; for more wi-fi access points, see www.wififreespot. com/ca.html. Most hotels have connections, ranging from ISDN lines to wireless to a compatible phone jack; some have web TV, though this can be frustrating to use. Brits whose ISP can't offer service in California should consider www.net2roam.com, which offers worldwide access on a pay-as-you-go basis.

Internet access points are listed throughout this guide. For more options, ask at the tourist office (which may have a terminal you can use).

Legal help

If you are arrested and held in custody, call your insurer's emergency number or contact your consulate (*see p397*) for advice and assistance.

Money

The US dollar ($) is divided into 100 cents (¢). Coin denominations run from the copper penny (1¢) to the silver nickel (5¢), dime (10¢), quarter (25¢) and less-common half-dollar (50¢). There are also two $1 coins: the silver Susan B Anthony and the gold Sacagawea. Notes or 'bills' are all the same green colour and size; they come in denominations of $1, $5, $10, $20, $50 and $100. The $20 and $50 have recently been redesigned with features that make them hard to forge, including, for the first time, some subtle colours other than green and black. Old-style bills remain legal currency.

ATMs

ATMs are the most convenient way for visitors to top up their funds. Either use your credit card and PIN to withdraw money (interest will be charged) or avail yourself of such networks as Cirrus and Plus, which allow you to withdraw money direct from your account (again using your PIN) from any machine with the right symbol. Non-US visitors don't have to pay the advertised charge, but their own bank will levy a fee.

Follow the usual safety procedures when using an ATM: check the slot for interference, be discreet about your PIN and stick to brightly lit, populated locations.

ATMs are widespread; find your gas and find your cash. But don't count on there being one just around the corner if you're travelling in out-of-the-way areas: take a cash reserve or some travellers' cheques.

Banks

Banks are usually open from 10am to 4.30pm Monday to Thursday, until 6pm on Friday, and from 10am to 2pm on Saturday. They are closed on Sunday. Most major banks can raise cash on a credit card. They also offer competitive currency exchange rates, along with international banking services and travellers' cheques.

Bank of America *1-800 944 0404/ www.bankofamerica.com.*
Citibank *1-800 285 3000/ www.citibank.com.*
Wells Fargo *1-800 869 3557/ www.wellsfargo.com.*

Costs

Never take a hotel, car rental or attraction price as gospel. Enquire whether your AAA/AARP/frequent flyer/hotel chain membership card or anything else you can think of gains you a discount and always ask for the best rate. Look out for coupon books at gas stations: they might save you 20 bucks and are a useful way of seeing what's around. Online, try www.destinationcoupons.com.

Credit & debit cards

Don't think of coming to California without at least one major credit card, not only for purchases but for security on cars, rooms, ski rental and so on. **MasterCard** and **Visa** are accepted almost universally; **AmEx** is also prominent.

If your debit card has the chip technology to work with a countertop PIN machine, it should work in the US. A small number of retailers allow

you to get 'cashback' with a PIN debit card payment: Target and Wal-Mart are probably the best known.

For lost/stolen credit cards, call the numbers below. Get the loss report number for ATM/debit cards from your bank in advance.

American Express *1-800 992 3404/travellers' cheques 1-800 221 7282/www.americanexpress.com.*
Diners Club *1-800 234 6377/ www.dinersclub.com.*
Discover *1-800 347 2683/ www.discovercard.com.*
MasterCard *1-800 622 7747/ www.mastercard.com.*
Visa *1-800 847 2911/www.visa.com.*

Emergency funds

If you need money wired to you, **Western Union** (1-800 325 6000, www.westernunion.com) can receive funds from anywhere, at commission rates of around 10%. AmEx offices (*see below*) also offer this facility.

Tax

Sales tax – added to most purchases on top of the marked price – varies from 7.25% to 8.75% in California. Hotel tax runs from 6% to 14% (in LA and San Francisco), which can put a sting in the tail of your bill.

Travellers' cheques

Travellers' cheques are less common these days, but remain useful as a way of carrying a large cash sum that's replaceable in case of loss or robbery. Dollar-denomination travellers' cheques are accepted pretty much everywhere, and you can often keep the change in cash. You may need to show ID. Travellers' cheques can be purchased from banks and currency exchange offices.

The loss report numbers are 1-800 221 7282 (AmEx), 1-800 223 7373 (MC) and 1-800 732 1322 (V). Travelex's website, www.cashmy cheques.com, gives copious listings of banks and currency exhange offices. AmEx offices are listed on http://travel.americanexpress.com.

American Express Travel Services

Los Angeles *327 N Beverly Drive, between Brighton & Dayton Ways, Beverly Hills (1-310 274 8277/ http://travel.americanexpress.com). I-10, exit Robertson Boulevard north.* **Open** *10am-6pm Mon-Fri; 10am-3pm Sat.*
San Francisco *455 Market Street, at 1st Street, Financial District (1-415 536 2600/www.american express.com/travel). BART*

Montgomery or Embarcadero/Muni Metro F, J, K, L, M, N/bus 2, 5, 6, 7, 9, 21, 31, 38, 66, 71. **Open** 9am-5.30pm Mon-Fri; 10am-2pm Sat.

Natural hazards

California suffers periodical earthquakes. If you're unlucky enough to be caught in one, do exactly what you're told. Local authorities have well-rehearsed contingency plans. The prosaic truth is that you are far more likely to suffer from sunburn, so wear a hat, sunblock and sunglasses.

Outdoor enthusiasts face an alarming range of hazards, but the reality is that there are very few casualties and you won't be among them if you take the right precautions.

Bears & lions

The Sierras are the natural habitat of the black bear. Bears naturally avoid humans, but they have come to associate them with food – and they have an acute sense of smell. Keep all food in a car boot, food storage locker (in picnic areas and campsites) or bear canister (in the back country). If you encounter a bear in a developed area, shout and wave at it to scare it away; in the wilderness, keep your distance, do nothing to engage it and it will avoid you.

California has 4-6,000 mountain lions (aka pumas, panthers and cougars), but it is unlikely you'll encounter one on a non-desert hike. If you do, stay where you are, gather the party together and, as a last resort, throw sticks and stones.

Critters & crawlers

In the desert, especially clambering over rock, look where you put your hands and feet to avoid disturbing snakes and scorpions. And wear long trousers, tight at the ankle. If you are bitten, forget the folk remedies and seek medical help immediately. Rattlesnakes are California's only poisonous snakes. They're big enough to spot quite easily: the few fatalities that do occur are usually because the human approached the animal, not the other way round.

Only a couple of the many scorpion species found in California are venomous, and those are a risk only to the young and frail.

Dehydration

Never rely on being able to find water during a hike. In the desert, carry four litres per person per day as the absolutely barest minimum. It seems an improbable amount, but it's necessary.

Disease

Always filter or treat water taken from outdoor sources to eliminate the risk of giardiasis.

Lyme disease is present in California, but not widespread. Still, if you find a tick on your body, prise it off from the snout and wait to see if flu-like symptoms, usually preceded by a rash radiating from the bite site, develop. Treatment is by antibiotics.

On hikes in mountain, canyon and coastal areas, look out for poison oak, a common shrub with oak-like green leaves that redden in autumn. It can cause severe skin irritation. Learn to recognise the plant at park visitors' centres or www.enature.com.

Newspapers & magazines

The left-of-centre *Los Angeles Times* (www.latimes.com) is the state's paper of record. Its coverage of local and worldwide events is extensive, sometimes excellent – in April 2004 the paper scooped an impressive five Pulitzer Prizes. The Sunday 'Calendar' section of the *Times* covers the arts, with one section on Hollywood films and locally produced TV, the other on architecture, art and the performing arts.

Complaining about the *San Francisco Chronicle* (or 'the Comical', as locals call it) has become a Bay Area cliché. Good columnists make it an entertaining Sunday read, but it lacks the punch and vigour of a big-city newspaper. Do pick it up, though, for the Sunday 'Datebook', known as the 'pink' (after the pink paper on which it's printed), a tabloid entertainment and arts supplement, complete with listings and reviews.

Though the venerable monthly magazine *Los Angeles* fashions itself as *Vanity Fair* and the *New Yorker* rolled into one, it's lighter and shallower than either. *San Francisco Magazine*, on the other hand, is an increasingly lively, glossy monthly, covering everything from local politics and policy issues to the Bay Area's fine restaurant scene.

Most Californian cities of any size have an alternative weekly magazine, available free from dispensers and in many venues throughout town. These are the best reference for listings of what's on locally.

Opening times

Government offices open at 8am or 9am, but for most businesses, banks included, it's generally 10am. Offices stay open until around 4.30-5pm, shops until 7-8pm – though this varies hugely throughout the state. Some banks and post offices open on Saturday morning; most shops open on Sundays, though they tend to close early. In the cities, many shops, boutiques and museums have a day or two when they are open until 8pm or 9pm, and many stay open on Sunday from noon until 5pm or later.

Postal services

US mailboxes are red, white and blue, with the bald eagle logo on the front and side. There is usually a timetable of collections and list of restrictions inside the lid. Due to fears of terrorism, post exceeding a certain weight must be taken to a post-office counter. For couriers, *see p397.*

Post offices are usually open 9am to 5pm, but often have last collections at 6pm. Many are open on Saturdays from 9am to 1pm. There are often stamp vending machines and scales in the lobby, open out of hours. For general information and locations, check the phone book, dial 1-800 275 8777 or consult www.usps.com.

Poste restante

If you need to receive mail but don't know what your address will be, have it sent to: General Delivery,

Directory

[your name], plus the address, zip code included, of the post office from which you'd like to collect it (to find locations, *see p401*).

Safety

Other than through bad luck, you are unlikely to encounter crime anywhere outside the big cities, and even those – or at least, the parts of them that you'd naturally visit – aren't at the top of the US crime hit parade. Unlikely as it may sound, LA – the place that invented the terms 'car-jacking' and 'drive-by shooting' – is actually a safer place for visitors than, say, Florida. A few areas where you should be careful after dark include parts of Silver Lake, Hollywood, Koreatown, Compton, Echo Park, Highland Parks, Downtown and Venice. In San Francisco, only a few areas warrant caution during daylight hours and are of particular concern at night. These include the Tenderloin, north and east of Civic Center; SoMa, near the Mission/6th Street corner; Mission Street, between 13th and 22nd Streets; and Hunter's Point near 3Com Park. Golden Gate Park should be avoided at night.

It still makes sense to be cautious in the cities: don't fumble with your wallet or a map in public; always plan where you're going and walk with brisk confidence, preferably not on your own at night. As a motorist, avoid coming off the freeway in unfamiliar areas, never cut anyone off in traffic or yell epithets at other drivers, never drive too slowly or too quickly, and always take a map with you. Keep your car doors locked while driving; avoid parking in questionable areas (when in doubt, use valet parking); always lock your car.

When you're on the road, don't pick up hitchhikers and have a mobile phone with you in case of breakdown.

Smoking

California was the first state in the US to ban smoking in all enclosed public areas. This includes not only obvious places such as shops, restaurants, cinemas and other public buildings, but also waiting areas, ticket lines, elevators, public toilets and also some 35,000 bars and casinos across the state. Most hotels also prohibit smoking, except in designated rooms. Smoking has been banned on some beaches, including Los Angeles County beaches and Malibu, and some other public recreation areas; city-run outdoor spaces in San Francisco, including parks, may be following suit.

In warmer areas, restaurants and bars have terraces where smoking may be allowed, and street ashtrays are often found close to the doors of bars. Bars entirely owned by their staff may also allow smoking.

Telephones

The local *Pacific Bell Yellow Pages' Customer Guide* is a valuable resource that gives essential emergency numbers, instructions on how to use public phones and information on call rates. Phone books are also a source of useful local information and maps.

Dialling & codes

Collect calls (reversing the charges) *0.*
Local enquiries *411.*
National enquiries *1 + [area code] + 555 1212 (if you don't know the area code, dial 0 for the operator).*
International calls *011 + [country code] + [area code] + [number].*
International country codes *UK 44; New Zealand 64; Australia 61; Germany 49; Japan 81.*
Police, fire or medical emergencies *911.*

Free codes

1-800, 1-866, 1-877, 1-888.

Making a call

Direct dial calls

If you're calling a number with the same area code as the phone from which you're calling, dial the (seven-digit) number without the area code. If you're calling a different area code, dial **1 + three-digit area code + seven-digit number.**

International calls

Dial **011** followed by the country code (UK **44**; New Zealand **64**; Australia **61**; Germany **49**; Japan **81** – see the telephone book for others). If you need operator assistance with international calls, dial **00**.

Public & hotel phones

On a hotel phone, you may have to dial **0** or **9** before dialling the number. Check rates before you call: at more expensive hotels particularly, using a phonecard, credit card or payphone will work out cheaper, especially on long-distance or international calls (though you'll be charged a flat rate, usually a dollar, even for free calls). Smaller hotels and motels may not allow you to call long-distance unless you call collect or use a credit card (or leave your card at the desk).

Public payphones are plentiful. Operator and directory calls are free. Local calls cost 35¢, with the cost increasing with the distance (a recorded voice will tell you to feed in more quarters). Make sure you have plenty of change as pay phones only take coins. It's nigh on impossible to make international calls using cash at a coin-op payphone, but card-op ones are on the increase. Otherwise, use your MasterCard credit card with **AT&T** (1-800 225 5288) or **MCI** (1-800 950 5555), or buy a phonecard – which gives you a fixed amount of time anywhere in the US, less internationally – from stores such as Rite-Aid, Sav-On and Walgreen.

Mobile/cellular phones

Whereas in Europe mobile (cellular) phones work on the GSM network at either 900 or 1800mHz, the US does not have a standard mobile phone network that covers the whole country, which means that visitors from other parts of the US will have to check with their service provider that they can use their phone in California. The state does offer access to the GSM network at 1900mHz, so European visitors – with tri-band handsets that work in the US – should contact their service provider before they leave. Also check the price of calls: rates will be hefty and you will probably be charged for receiving as well as making calls. So buy a local SIM card for your own phone, rent a phone for the duration of your stay, or simply buy one with prepaid time on it.

TripTel

Los Angeles *Tom Bradley International Terminal, LAX (1-310 645 3500/www.triptel.com).* **Open** 7am-10pm daily. **Credit** AmEx, DC, Disc, MC, V.
San Francisco *1525 Van Ness Avenue, at Pine Street, Pacific Heights (1-877 874 7835/www. triptel.com). Bus 47, 49.* **Open** 8am-6pm Mon-Fri; 9am-5pm Sat. **Credit** AmEx, DC, Disc, MC, V. Cell phone rental from $3 a day, plus from 95¢ a minute for incoming and outgoing calls anywhere in the USA.

Time & dates

California operates on **Pacific Standard Time**, eight hours behind GMT (London), three hours behind Eastern Standard Time (New York), two hours behind Central Time (Chicago) and one hour behind Mountain Time (Denver). Clocks go forward by an hour on the last Sunday in April, and back on the last Sunday in October.

Tourist information

California Tourism

http://gocalif.ca.gov.
California Tourism offers good information and accommodation search facilities. You can order a brochure via the site or by phoning 1-800 462 2543. California Tourism splits the state into 11 regions, each with its own California Welcome Center, as listed below. These Welcome Centers are accessed online at www.cwc.com.
Anderson *1699 Highway 273 (1-530 365 1180).*
Arcata *1635 Heindon Road (1-707 822 3619).*
Auburn *13411 Lincoln Way (1-530 887 2111).*
Barstow *2796 Tanger Way, Suite 106 (1-760 253 4782).*
Los Angeles *Beverly Center, 8500 Beverly Boulevard, Suite 150 (1-310 854 7616).*
Merced *710 West 16th Street, Suite A (1-209 384 2791).*
Oceanside *928 North Coast Highway (1-760 721 1101).*

San Francisco *Pier 39, Building P, Suite 214B (1-415 956 3493).*
Santa Ana *Westfield Shoppingtown Mainplace, 2800 N Main Street, Suite 112 (1-714 667 0400).*
Santa Rosa *9 4th Street (1-800 404 7673).*
Yucca Valley
56711 Twentynine Palms Highway (1-760 365 5464).

California State Parks

www.cal-parks.gov.
State parks and all their facilities listed in a searchable database.

National Park Service

www.nps.com.
The NPS site offers a wealth of planning information for each park.

USDA Forest Service

www.fs.fed.us
Forestry Service's online HQ, packed with information and references.

Visas

Under the visa waiver scheme, citizens of the UK, Australia, New Zealand, Japan and most west European countries do not need a visa for stays in the US of less than 90 days (business or pleasure) if they have a passport valid for six months and a return (or open standby) ticket and an appropriate passport; *see p399.* Canadians and Mexicans do not normally need visas but must have legal proof of residency. All other travellers need visas. Full information can be obtained from a US embassy or consulate. The US embassy is on at www.usembassy.org.uk/

Your airline will give you two forms: one for immigration and one for customs (*see p398*). When you land, expect the customs/immigration process to take about an hour. Treat officials with respect, and be sure to have every detail in order. There have been reports of disproportionate reactions to minor transgressions. If you think that you have been treated badly, report it on 1-877 227 5511.

US Embassy Visa Information
(UK only) *Information 09055 444 546 (£1.30/min).* **Open** 8am-8pm Mon-Fri; 10am-4pm Sat.

When to go

California is an area of great climatic variation and extremes. It's entirely possible to travel from the blazing heat of 100°F to sub-zero temperatures in an afternoon. As a very general rule, summers are warm and most precipitation occurs in winter. Temperatures rise and humidity falls as you travel south. However, extremes of terrain complicate this picture. Snow lingers all summer on the mountaintops, and desert nights can be extrememly cool. Winds render a hot day unpleasant, coastal fog can keep out the heat of the sun until midday, particularly in summer, and smog settles over cities and, increasingly, wilderness areas too.

In spring, the desert and alpine meadows bloom and the temperature is generally pleasant, but the snow melts slowly, leaving parts of the Sierras inaccessible (the Tioga Pass through Yosemite closes Nov-June). Summer is gorgeous in the Sierras, but almost unbearable in the deserts, particularly Death Valley. Autumn is generally pleasant but with a scorched, smoggy post-summer note.

The most detailed forecasts and reports, including flood and fire warnings, are at http://cdec.water.ca.gov/ weather.html. For 24-hour smog and air-quality checks in the southern state, contact **South Coast Air Quality Management District** (1-800 288 7664, www.aqmd.gov).

Public holidays

New Year's Day (1 Jan); Martin Luther King Jr Day (3rd Mon in Jan); President's Day (3rd Mon in Feb); Memorial Day (last Mon in May); Independence Day (4 July); Labor Day (1st Mon in Sept); Columbus Day (2nd Mon in Oct); Election Day (1st Tue in Nov); Veterans' Day (11 Nov); Thanksgiving Day (4th Thur in Nov); Christmas Day (25 Dec).

Directory

Further Reference

Fiction & poetry

Charles Bukowski *Hollywood*
The legendarily drunk poet's musings on making a movie in Tinseltown.
Raymond Chandler
The Big Sleep; Farewell, My Lovely; The Long Goodbye
Philip Marlowe in the classic hard-boiled detective novels.
James Ellroy
The Black Dahlia, The Big Nowhere, LA Confidential, White Jazz
Ellroy's LA Quartet is a masterpiece of contemporary noir; the black and compelling *My Dark Places* recounts his search for his mother's killer.
Steven Gilbar (ed)
California Shorts
Short stories. About California.
Allen Ginsberg
Howl and Other Poems
The rants that caused all the fuss back in the Beat 1950s.
James Dalessandro *1906 A Novel*
A fictional, though grippingly researched, account of San Francisco's year of earthquake and fire.
James Gardner *Fat City*
Bleak but beautifully told tale of boxers in smalltown Stockton.
Glen David Gold
Carter Beats the Devil
A sleight-of-hand comedy thriller set in 1920s San Francisco.
Sue Grafton *A is for Alibi*, et cetera
Kinsey Millhone, the unconformist protagonist of the alphabetically ordered crime series, lives in a thinly disguised Santa Barbara.
Dashiell Hammett
The Maltese Falcon
One of the world's best detective novels, sest in a dark and dangerous San Francisco.
Helen Hunt Jackson *Ramona*
A flawed novel but a fascinating historical document, *Ramona* is Hunt Jackson's retelling of the plight of Native Americans in early California.
Jack Kerouac *Big Sur*
Kerouac finds spiritual solace on the Central Coast. See also: *On the Road, The Subterraneans, Desolation Angels* and *The Dharma Bums*.
Jack London
The Valley of the Moon
Set in the Sonoma Valley.
Armistead Maupin
The *Tales of the City* series of happy hippy families are the classics but all Maupin's work is readable and insightful.
Walter Mosely
The *Easy Rawlins Mystery* series
The heir apparent to Marlowe, Easy Rawlins is an African-American PI in post-war LA. See also: *Always Outnumbered, Always Outgunned.*

Anne Packer
Mendocino and Other Stories
Sensitive short-story imaginings.
Thomas Pynchon *Vineland*
Drug goings-on on northern California, both thriller and polemic.
Budd Schulberg
What Makes Sammy Run?
Furious attack on the studio system by one of its employees.
Wallace Stegner *Angle of Repose*
Pulitzer-winning novel from one of the West's greatest chroniclers, about a historian who retires to his ancestral home in Grass Valley.
John Steinbeck
Cannery Row, The Grapes of Wrath
The Great Californian Novels.
Amy Tan *The Joy Luck Club; The Bonesetter's Daugher*
Three generations worth of San Fran's Chinese immigrants' experience.
Newton Thornburg
To Die in California
1970s classic, half-noir, half lyric, in which an Illinois farmer exposes the state's immoralities in a quest for the truth about his son's death.
Bruce Wagner *I'm Losing You; I'll Let You Go; Still Holding*
Biting Hollywood satire.
Nathaniel West
The Day of the Locust
Classic, apocalyptic raspberry blown at the movie industry.

Non fiction

Kenneth Anger *Hollywood Babylon*
The dark side of Tinseltown.
Mark Arax & Rick Wartzman
King of California: JG Boswell and the Making of a Secret American Empire
Fascinating, award-winning and little told tale of agricultural politics in the Central Valley.
Reyner Banham *Los Angeles: The Architecture of Four Ecologies*
Architectural history and paean to life in the fast lanes.
Walton Bean *California: An Interpretive History*
Anecdotal account of California's shady past.
Peter Belsito & Bob Davis
Hardcore California: A History of Punk & New Wave
What it says on the tin.
Leon Bing *Do or Die*
History of LA gang culture.
Po Bronson
The Nudist on the Late Shift
Unblinking treatise on the Silicon Valley scene.
Louise Amelia Knapp Smith Clappe *The Shirley Letters from the California Mines*
A doctor's wife writes from the mining camps of the early 1950s.

Jacqueline Cogdell DjeDje & Ted Gioia *West Coast Jazz: Modern Jazz in California, 1945-1960*
More musical history.
Jacqueline Cogdell DjeDje & Eddie S Meadows (eds)
California Soul: Music of African-Americans in the West
A collection of interesting essays.
James Conaway
The Far Side of Eden
Powerplays and skulduggery behind the Napa Valley idyll.
William Crondon, ed *John Muir – Nature Writings: The Story of My Boyhood and Youth; My First Summer in the Sierra; Stickeen; The Mountains of California; Essays*
An anthology of the naturalist/activist's key texts.
Victor Curtis Hanson
Mexifornia: A State of Becoming
Part history, part political analysis, part memoir.
Mike Davis *City of Quartz; Ecology of Fear; Magical Urbanism: Latinos Reinvent the US City*
Exhilarating Marxist critique of LA's city 'planning'; more apocalyptic LA-bashing, this time focusing on LA's precarious ecology; Davis's view of Latino influence on modern cities.
Andres Duany, Elizabeth Plater-Zyberk, Jeff Speck *Suburban Nation: The Rise of Sprawl and the Decline of the American Dream*
Damning indictment of the kind of urban growth that has beset LA.
Jim Heiman
California Crazy and Beyond
A gorgeous illustrated book on California roadside curiosities.
Kristian Lawson et al
California Babylon: A Guide to Sites of Scandal, Mayhem and Celluloid in the Golden State
Michael Lewis *Moneyball*
How coach Billy Beane and the Oakland A's turned the received wisdoms of baseball on their head.
Frank McLynn
Wagons West: the Epic Story of America's Overland Trails
This one stands out from the multitude of pioneer literature for its clarity, thoroughness and readability.
Marc Reisner *Cadillac Desert; A Dangerous State*
The role of water in California's history and future; a projection of apocalypse founded on shifting tectonics and hairtrigger irrigation.
Eric Schlosser *Reefer Madness*
One section deals with labour expoitation in the California strawberry fields.
Randy Shilts
And The Band Played On
Still the most important account of the AIDS epidemic in San Francisco.

Rebecca Solnit *River of Shadows: Eadweard Muybridge and the Technological Wild West*
A California photographer takes a pciture of a horse and 'the world we now live in' is born. Superb.
Kevin Starr *Coast of Dreams: California on the Edge*
Kevin Starr is the definitive state historian. This is the seventh instalment of his chronicle, updating the Golden State to the age of Arnie.
WA Swanburg *Citizen Hearst*
An entirely unsycophantic biography of the the legendary press baron and creator of Hearst Castle.
John Winokur
War Between the State
That's California, and the war is civil, between the north and south.
Tom Wolfe *The Electric Kool-Aid Acid Test; The Pump House Gang*
Alternative lifestyles in trippy, hippy 1960s California.

Publishers

For academic titles, though often not dustily so, view the catalogues of the **University of California Press** (www.ucpress.edu) and **Stanford University Press** (www.sup.org). Good starting points for outdoor explorations are **Falcon** guides (www.globepequot.com), **Foghorn Outdoors** (www.foghorn.com), the **Sierra Club** (www.sierraclub.org) and Bay Area specialist **Wilderness Press** (www.wildernesspress.com). **Audubon** (www.audubon.org) publishes the definitive field guides to North American flora and fauna.

Specialist guides

Peter Alden *National Audubon Society Regional Guide to California*
Not just flora and fauna but regions, astronomy, geology and climate, too. Essential.
Jim Cassady & Fryar Calhoun
California Whitewater
Describes the most popular rivers for whitewater rafting.
John Coale
Canoeing the California Highlands
A surveys of the most scenic mountain lakes in the state.
Ann Dwyer
Easy Waters of California
An exhaustive survey of waterways without whitewater. Available from www.californiakayakacademy.com.
Lynne Foster
Adventuring in the California Desert
All-encompassing guide covering everything from hiking and camping to nature identification.
Marjorie Gersh-Young *Hot Springs & Hot Pools of the Southwest*
The definitive resource on California's hot springs.

Lars Holbek & Chuck Stanley *The Best Whitewater in California*
Guide to 180 whitewater rivers and creeks primarily for expert kayakers, including coastal rivers.
Shaw Kobre & Bob Fagan
Golf California Universitee
Indispensibly comprehensive guide to courses all over California.
Martha Perantoni *Ski & Snowboard California's Sierra Nevada*
The best printed guide to the slopes of Northern California.
Tom Stienstra & Ann Marie Brown *California Hiking*
What it says: an outstanding guide to over 1,000 hikes all over the state. Other books in the excellent Foghorn Outdoors series include *California Camping* and *California Fishing*, both by Stienstra; *250 Great Hikes in California's National Parks* and *Northern California Biking* by Brown; and Parke Puterbaugh & Alan Bisbort's *California Beaches*.

Movies

American Graffiti (1973)
George Lucas's Modesto childhood, enthusiastically revisited.
Boogie Nights (1997)
The 1970s and '80s San Fernando Valley porn industry uncovered in all its amateurish, sleazy glory.
Boyz N the Hood (1991)
Can a right-thinking father stop his son falling prey to the culture of gang violence in South Central LA?
Big Wednesday (1978)
John Milius's coming-of-age surf movie, set against the background of the Vietnam war.
Bullitt (1968)
The Steve McQueen film with the all-time greatest San Fran car chase.
The California Trilogy (2000-2002)
Astounding documentary work by James Benning, making stark, unnarrated frames of the California the tourist board doesn't show you.
Chinatown (1974)
Roman Polanski's dark portrait of corruption – political and moral – in the boom time of 1940s LA.
Crumb (1994)
Impressive biopic about the San Francisco cartoonist.
Double Indemnity (1944)
Billy Wilder's sexy, sweaty, classic film noir, adapted from a novel by James M Cain, with dialogue by Raymond Chandler.
Easy Rider (1969)
The doomed psychedelic travelogue kicks off in LA and heads for desert.
East of Eden (1955)
James Dean, John Steinbeck and northern California locations.
El Norte (1983)
Life as part of the LA underbelly of illegal immigrants searching for a better life in the north.

Falling Down (1992)
Michael Douglas turns vigilante terrorist in a hellish LA of traffic, gangs and overpriced corner shops.
The Gold Rush (1925)
Chaplin's comedy classic includes the unforgettable shoe-eating scene.
Heat (1995)
Michael Mann's sprawling crime drama captures the steely glamour of modern LA. See also *Collateral* (2004).
The Long Goodbye (1973)
Robert Altman's homage to Chandler, with Elliott Gould playing Philip Marlowe as a shambling slob.
Mulholland Dr. (2001)
David Lynch's compelling modern *noir*. His 1996 film *Lost Highway* also focuses on LA.
Play Misty for Me (1971)
Clint spins some sounds in Carmel.
Singin' in the Rain (1952)
The best movie ever made about Hollywood?

Websites

For websites detailing what's on when in major cities, see the following pages: **Las Vegas** *p193*; **Los Angeles** *p139*; **San Diego** *p82*; **San Francisco** *p251*.

www.beerpage.com
All about California beers.
www.californiaauthors.com
A survey of local writers.
www.cgcw.com
The Connoisseurs' Guide to California Wines, online.
http://creekin.net
A guide to whitewater rafting and kayaking in California.
http://dir.yahoo.com/Regional/ U_S__States/California/
California-specific search engine.
www.desertusa.com
All about the deserts.
http://gorp.away.com
Fine resource for information on US national parks.
www.mapquest.com
Directions.
www.norcalmovies.com
http://socal.southwestmovies. com
Movie locations in California.
www.parks.ca.gov
Official guide to state parks.
www.nps.gov
National parks of the US. Indispensable.
www.reserveamerica.com
Campsite reservations.
www.roadsideamerica.com
A countrywide guide to roadside attractions and curiosities.
www.sierraclub.org
Wilderness advocates; offers full information on local events (talks, guided walks, etc).
www.visitcalifornia.com
The California Travel & Tourism Commission's official site.

Directory

Index

Pages numbers in **bold** indicate section(s) giving key information on a topic; *italics* indicate photographs. There are sub-indexes within the main index for Las Vegas, Los Angeles & Orange County, San Diego and San Francisco.

Advertisers' Index

Please refer to the relevant sections for full details.